THE PAINTER'S TOUCH

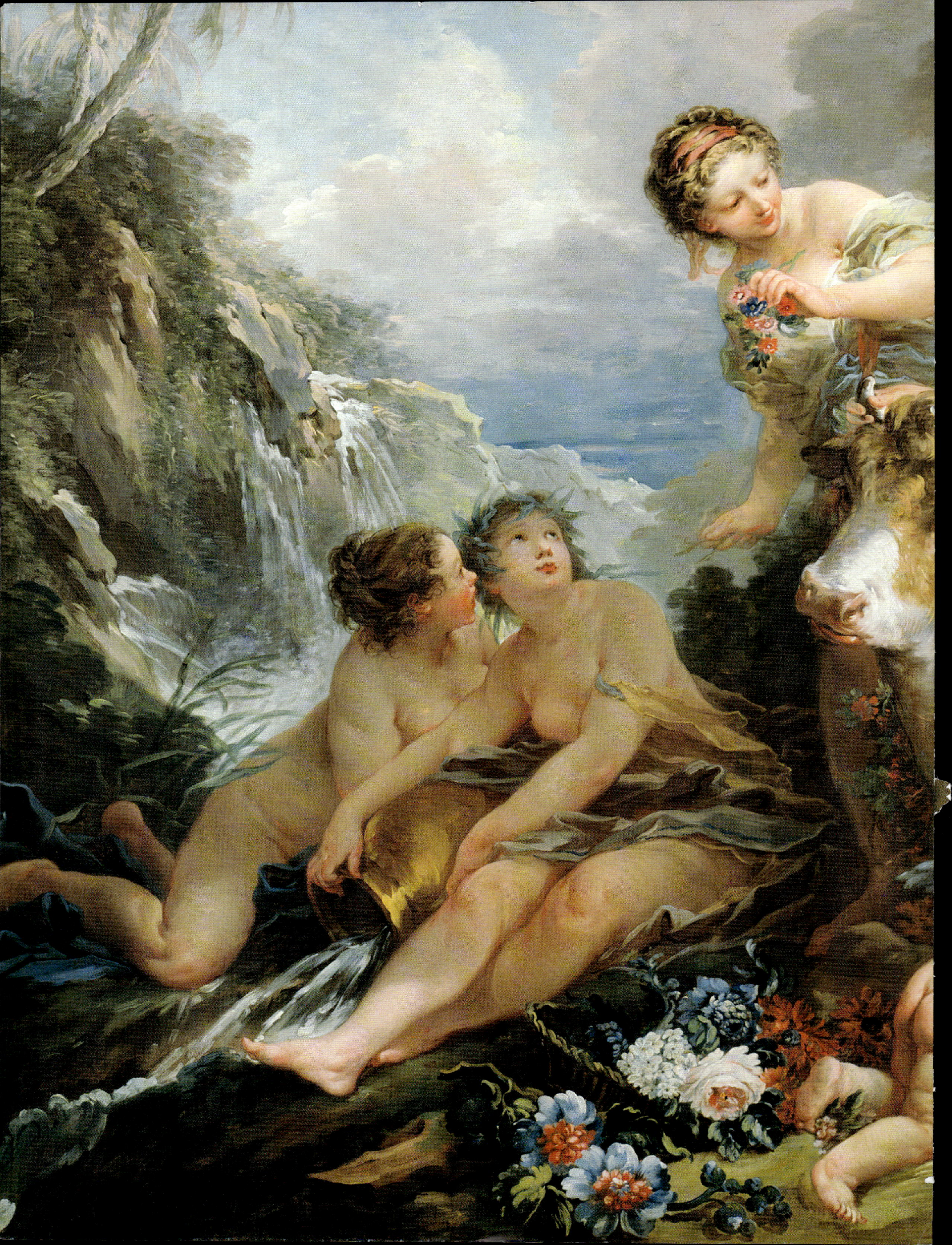

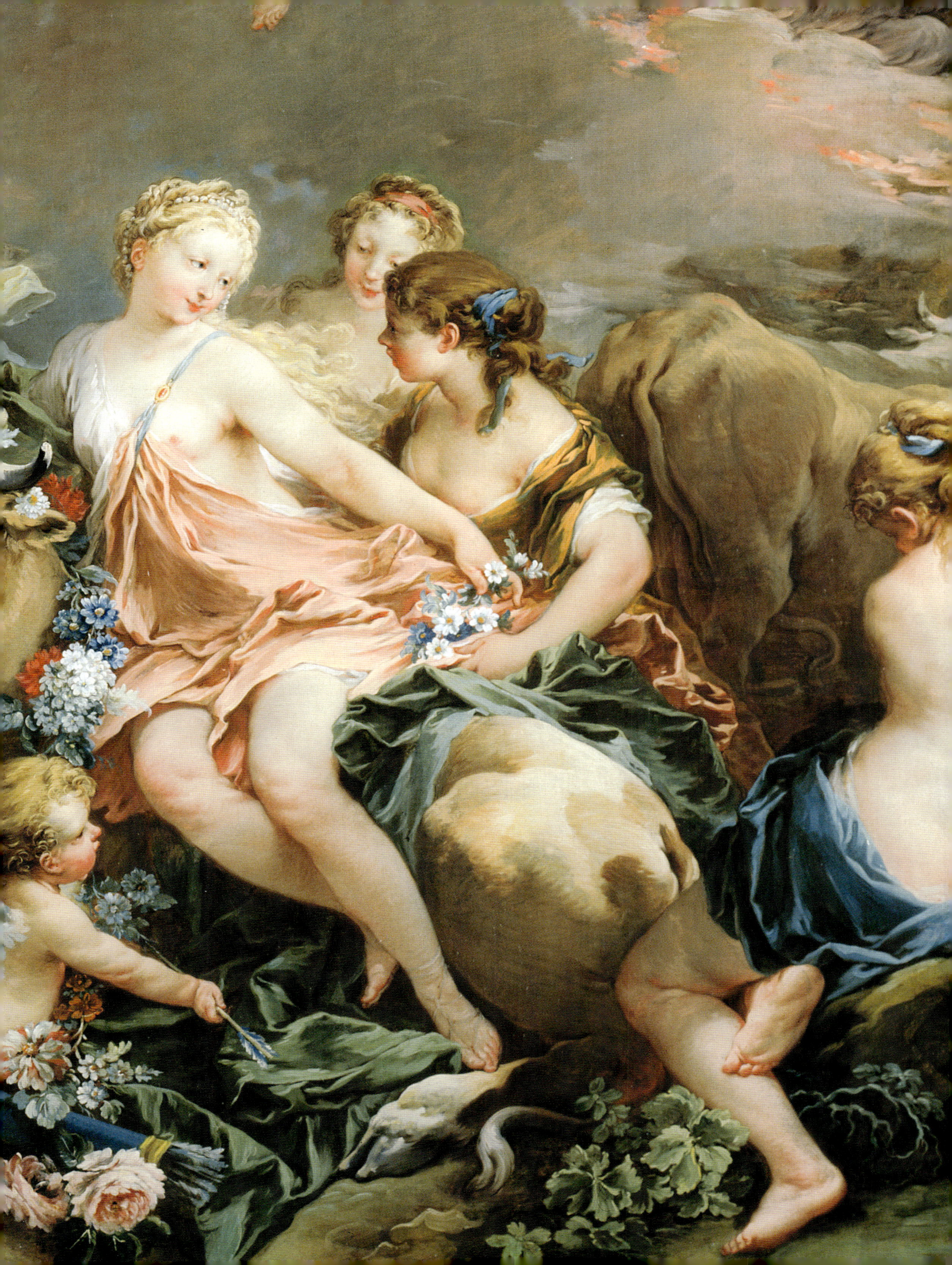

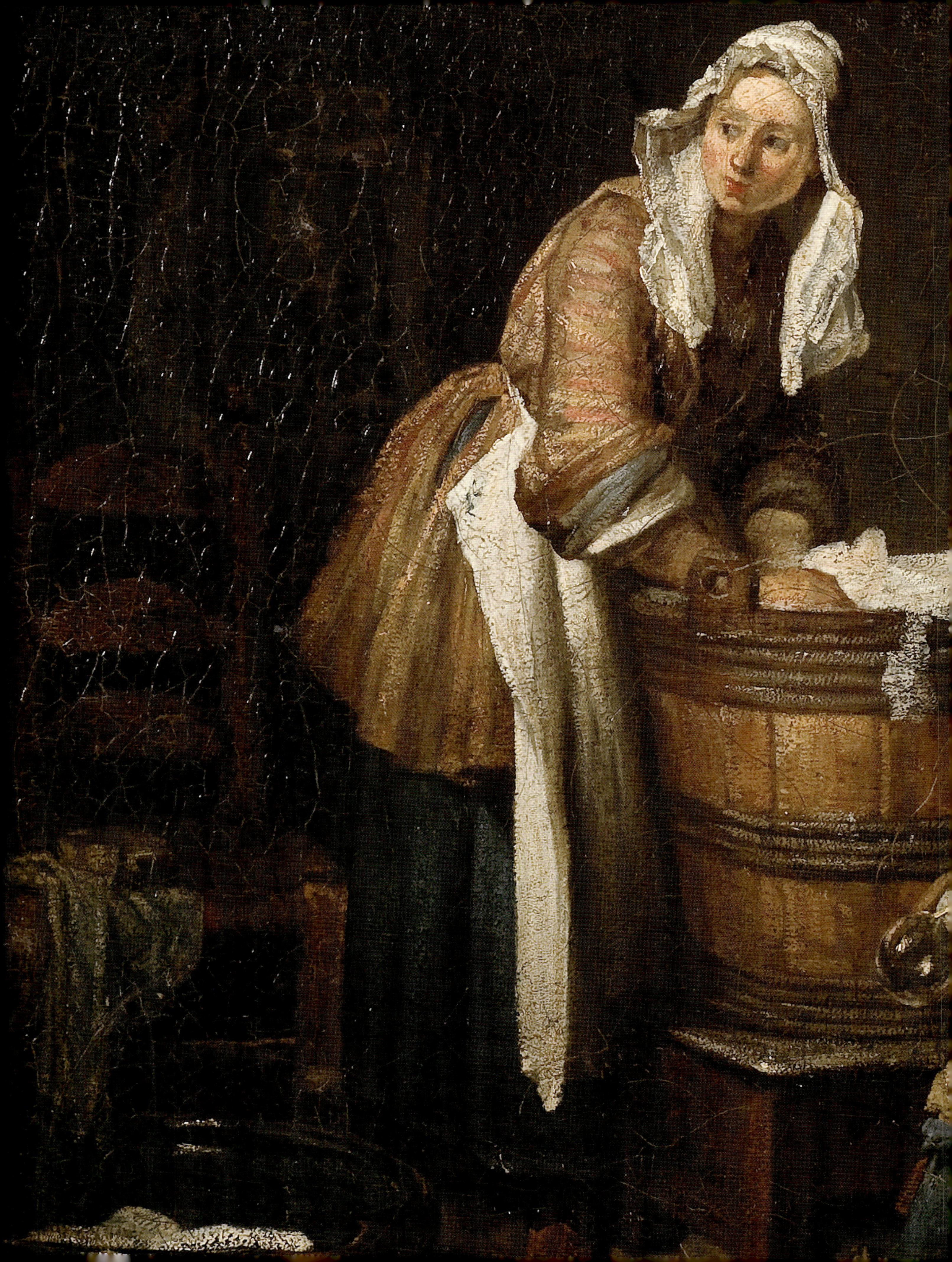

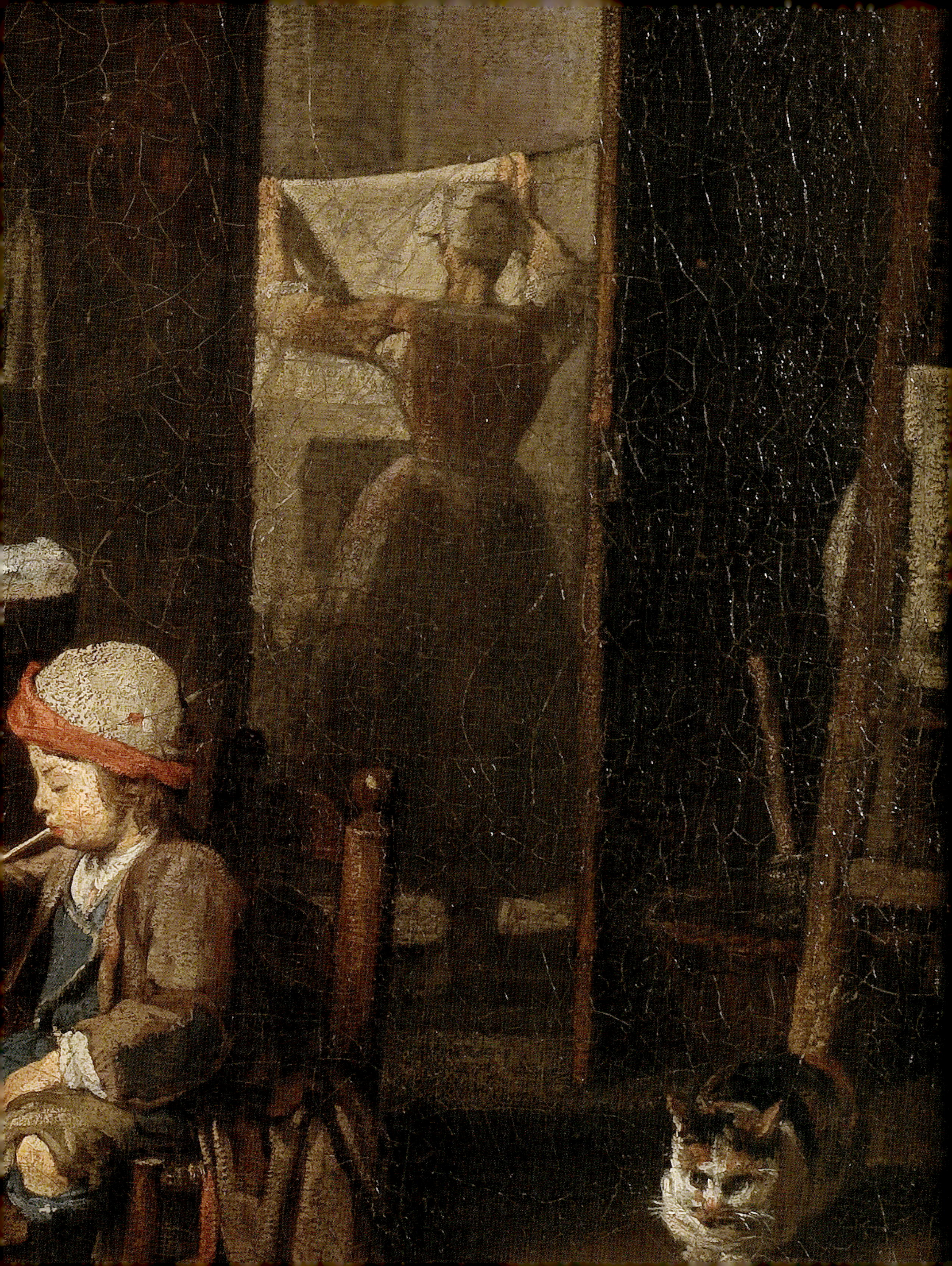

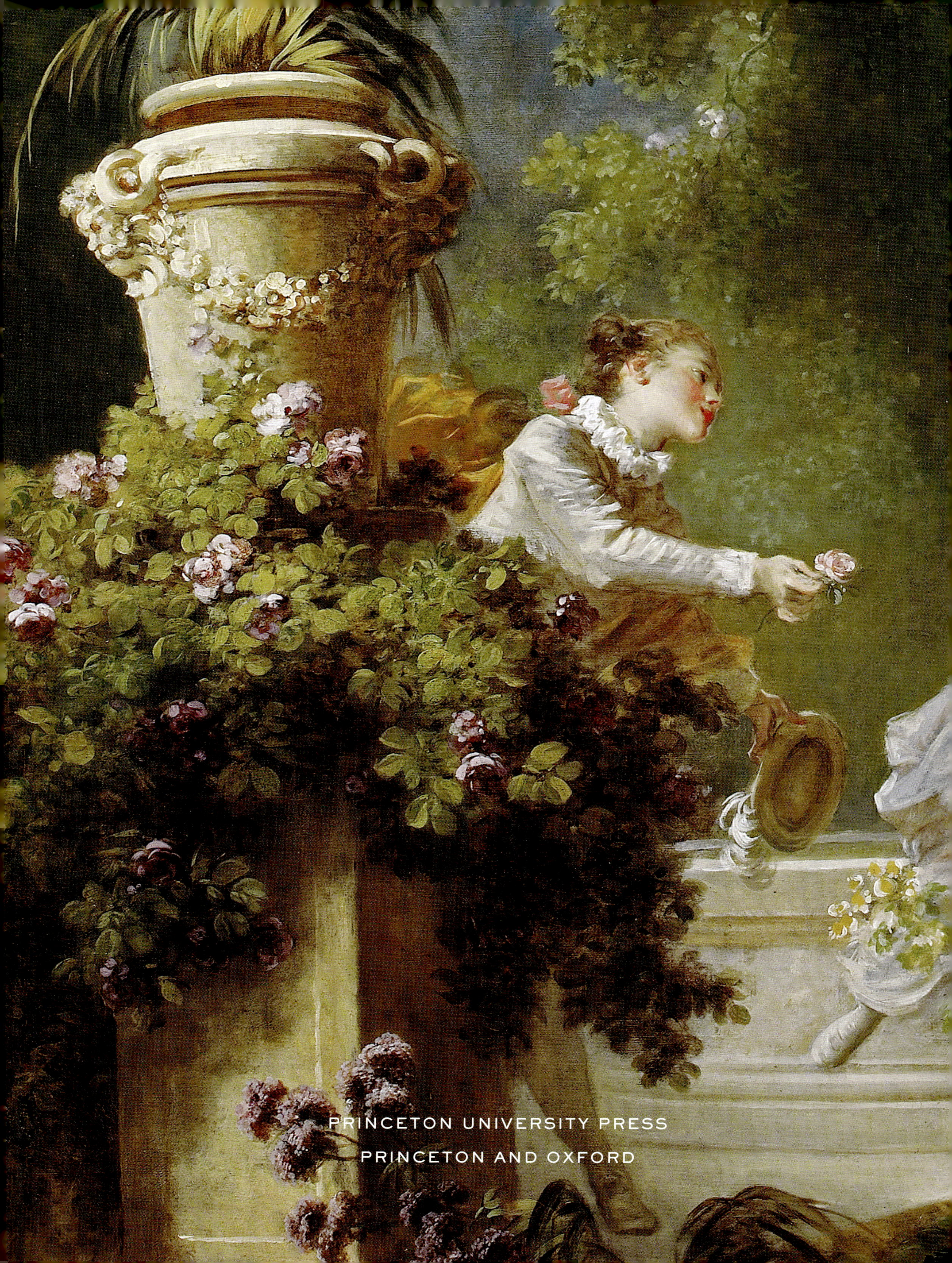

PRINCETON UNIVERSITY PRESS
PRINCETON AND OXFORD

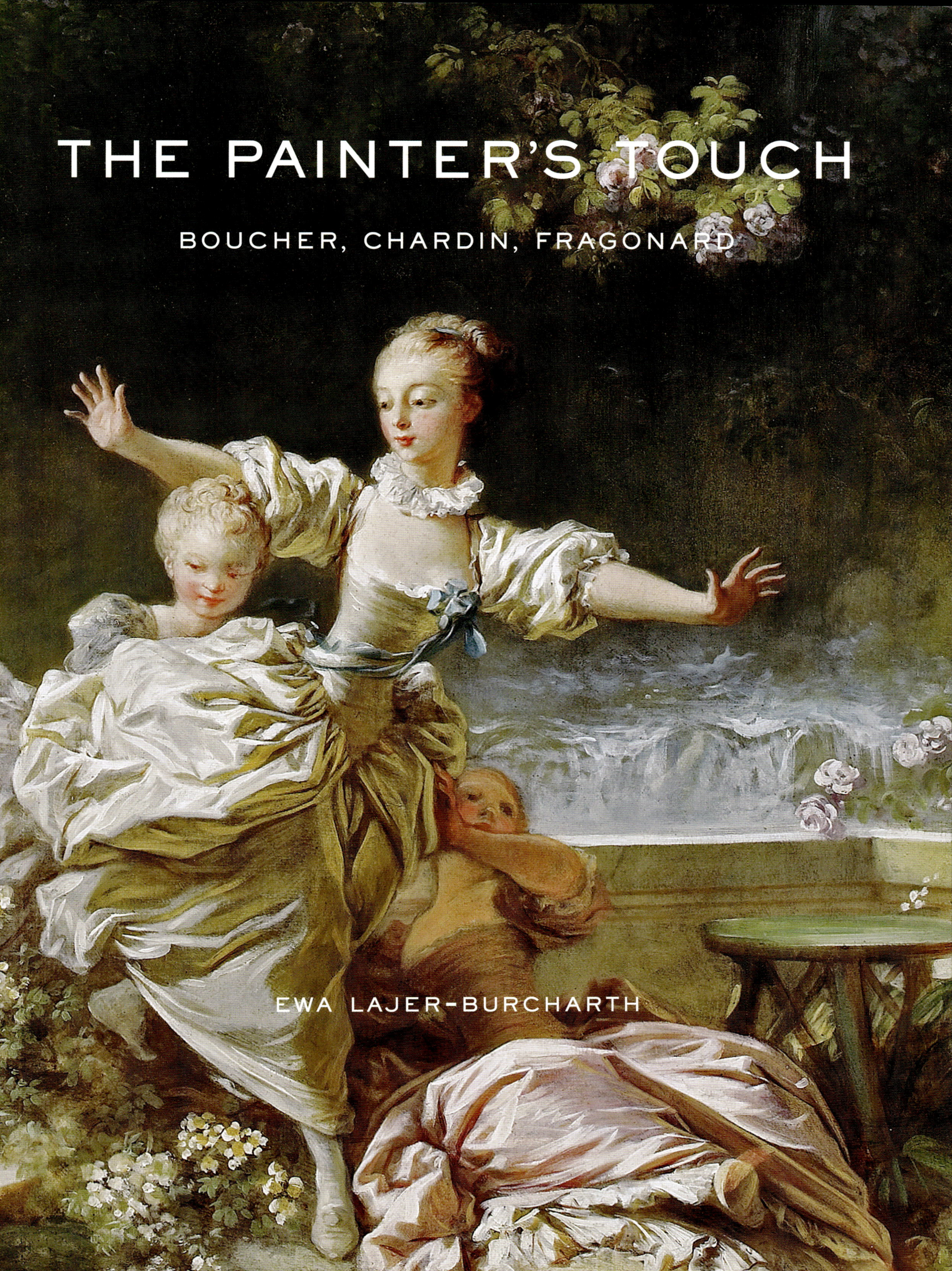
THE PAINTER'S TOUCH
BOUCHER, CHARDIN, FRAGONARD
EWA LAJER-BURCHARTH

Published by Princeton University Press, 41 William Street, Princeton, New Jersey 08540

In the United Kingdom: Princeton University Press, 99 Banbury Road, Oxford, OX2 6JX
press.princeton.edu

Cover art:
Detail from Jean-Siméon Chardin, *The Ray*, 1725–26. Oil on canvas. Musée du Louvre, Paris, © RMN-Grand Palais / Art Resource, NY, photo: Stéphane Maréchalle

Front matter illustrations: pp. ii–iii, detail of fig. 1.34; pp. iv–v, detail of fig. 2.44; pp. vi–vii, detail of fig. 3.60; p. x, detail of fig 2.78

Chapter opening illustrations: p. 2, detail of fig. 3.47; p. 8, detail of fig. 1.48; p. 86, detail of fig. 2.82; p. 176, detail of fig. 3.5; p. 237, detail of fig. 3.74

First paperback printing, 2022
Paper ISBN: 978-0-691-23831-9
Cloth ISBN: 978-0-691-17012-1

Library of Congress has cataloged the cloth edition as follows:

Names: Lajer-Burcharth, Ewa, author.
Title: The painter's touch: Boucher, Chardin, Fragonard / Ewa Lajer-Burcharth.
Description: Princeton : Princeton University Press, 2017. | Includes bibliographical references and index.
Identifiers: LCCN 2016056803 | ISBN 9780691170121 (hardback : alk. paper)
Subjects: LCSH: Painting, French—18th century. | Boucher, François, 1703–1770—Criticism and interpretation. | Chardin, Jean Baptiste Siméon, 1699–1779—Criticism and interpretation. | Fragonard, Jean-Honoré, 1732–1806—Criticism and interpretation.
Classification: LCC ND546 .L35 2017 | DDC 759.4—dc23 LC record available at https://lccn.loc.gov/2016056803

British Library Cataloging-in-Publication Data is available

Publication of this book has been aided by Anne and Jim Rothenberg Fund for Humanities Research at Harvard University

Designed by Diane Gottardi, Pennington, NJ

This book has been composed by Amy Storm in Minion Pro, Adobe Caslon Pro, and Sackers Gothic

Printed in China

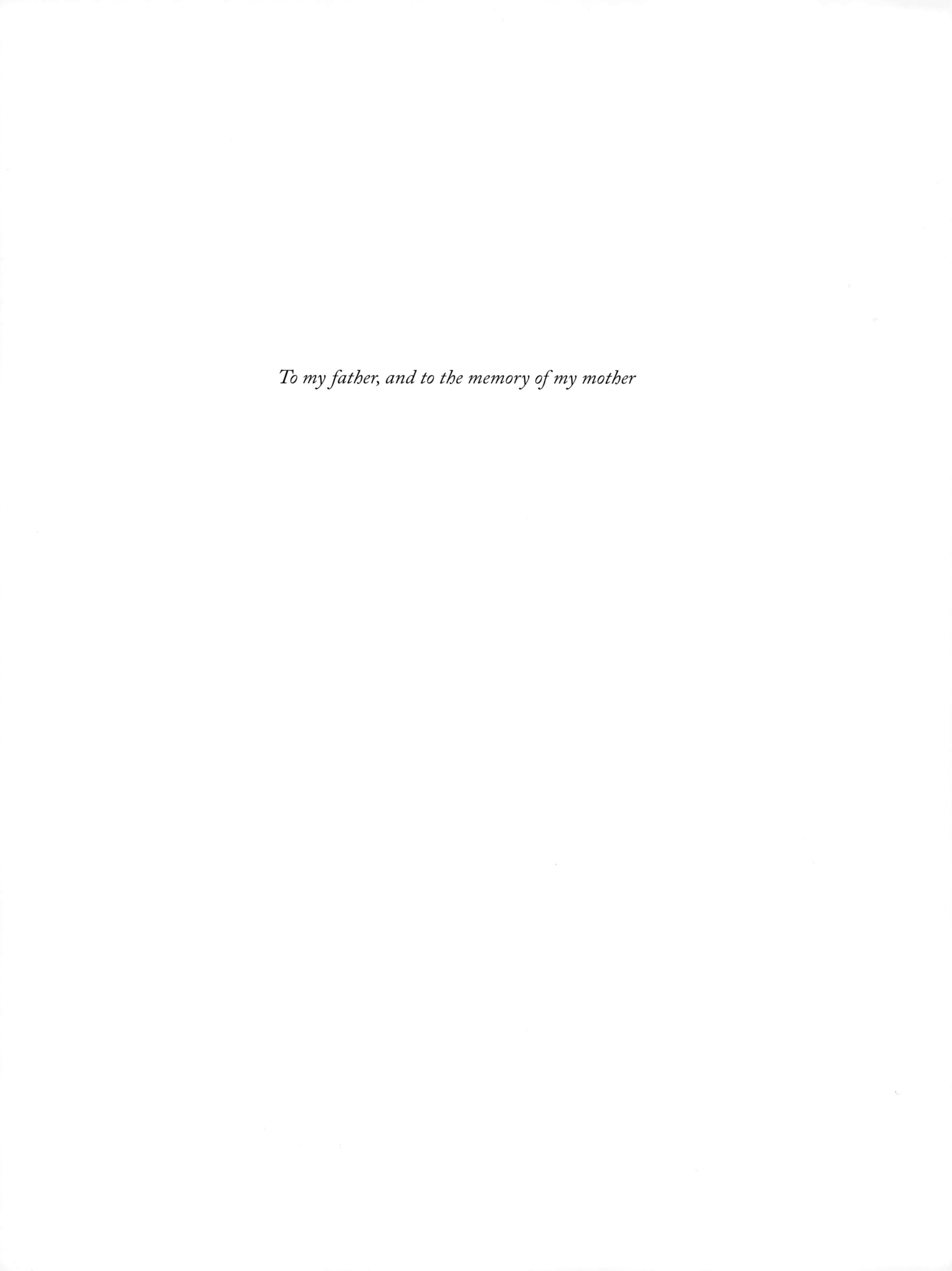

To my father, and to the memory of my mother

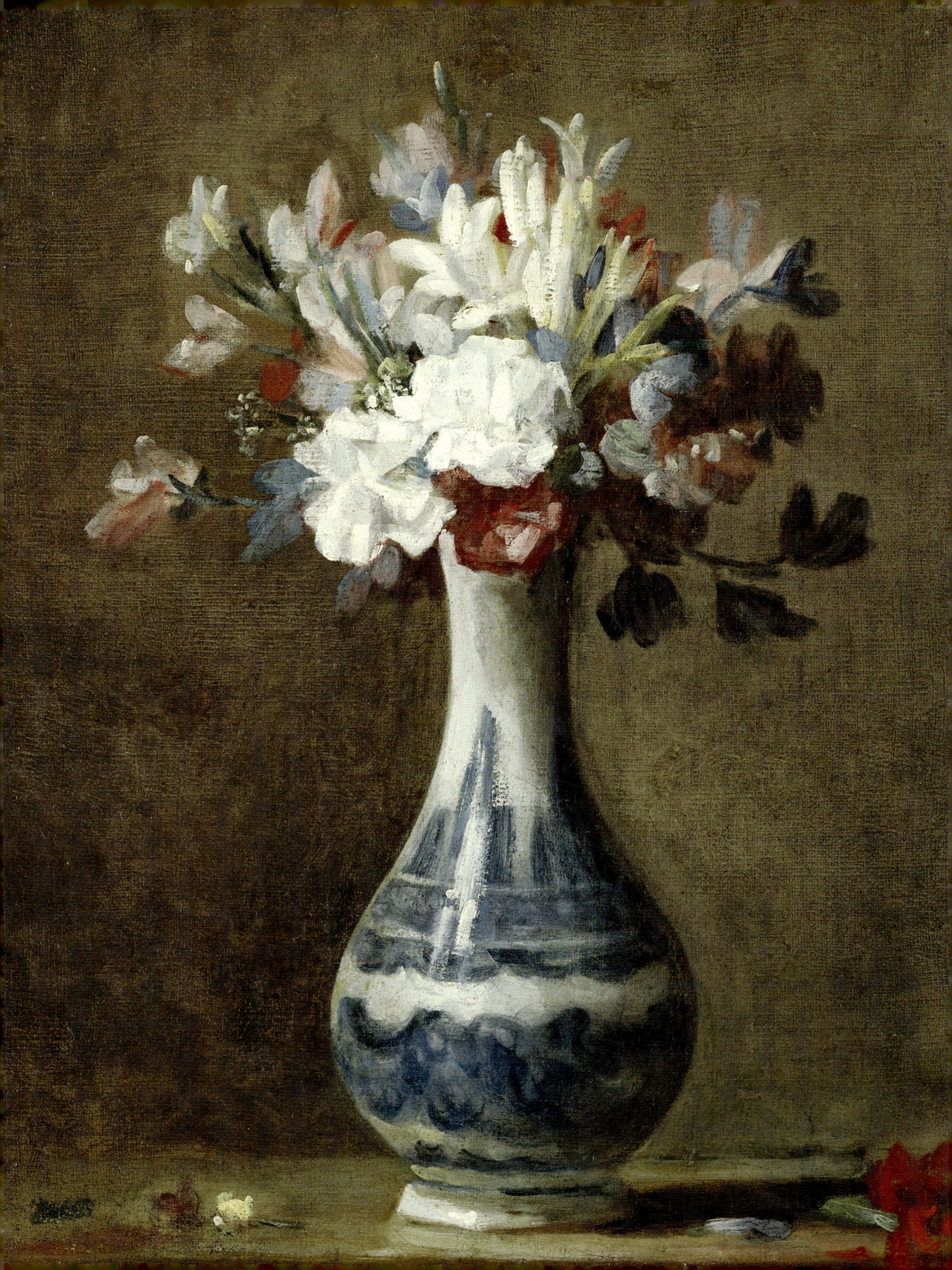

Contents

Acknowledgments xii

Introduction 3

Chapter 1: Boucher's Tact 8

- Materiality and Personality 9
- Touch and Tact 13
- The Commercial Imagination 22
- Personal Mythologies 33
- The Promiscuous Self 47
- The Artist as Consumer 73
- Pompadour's Painter 80

Chapter 2: Chardin's Craft 86

- Deep Materiality 87
- The Object (Inside/Out) 95
- The Blind Touch 111
- Underneath the Visible 123
- The Subject 139
- The Return to the Object 155
- The Painter 165

Chapter 3: Fragonard's Seduction 176

- Eros and Individuality 177
- The Unseen 186
- Being and Becoming 191
- Pictorial Seduction 199
- The Erotic Mother 203
- The Artist's Pleasure 208
- The Painter's Touch 212
- Love and Life 223
- Ars Erotica 236

Notes 238

Bibliography 271

Index 287

Image Credits 297

Acknowledgments

I have many individuals and institutions to thank for their help and support in the long period of this book's gestation. First and foremost, I thank my friends and colleagues for the exchanges and conversations that inspired and sustained me over the years. Yve-Alain Bois, Giuliana Bruno, Margaret Carroll, Briony Fer, Tamar Garb, Isabelle Graw, Stephen Greenblatt, Anne Higonnet, Molly Nesbit, and Beate Söntgen have contributed to my thinking and have been important to me in key ways. The unexpected loss of Svetlana Boym, a close friend and interlocutor since my earliest days at Harvard, was a source of great grief for me. I am deeply indebted to Linda Nochlin, who has been the most wonderful and treasured friend and steadfast supporter of my work. I am grateful to my fellow *dix-huitièmistes*—Colin Bailey, Mimi Hellman, Melissa Hyde, Mark Ledbury, Erika Naginski, Satish Padiyar, Katie Scott, Kristel Smentek, and the late Mary Sheriff whose disappearance at the time when this book goes to press is especially painful—for many fruitful exchanges that I enjoyed and profited from over the years. I am most obliged and deeply thankful to those friends and colleagues who have read parts of or the entire manuscript at different stages: Lucia Allais, Caroline Jones, Ruth Mack, and Sophia Roosth (the members of my Radcliffe Institute writing group); Erika Naginski and Kristel Smentek (participants in another writing group); John Goodman; Anne Higonnet; Meredith Martin; David Pullins; and Joseph Koerner. Their feedback, ideas, and encouragement were invaluable to me.

Dialogue with other scholars, colleagues, and friends at different stages of elaboration of this project, among them Norman Bryson, Michel Chaouli, Thomas Crow, Susan Dackerman, Patrice Higonnet, Lynn Hunt, David Joselit, Stephen Melville, Helen Molesworth, Mignon Nixon, Eyal Peretz, Todd Porterfield, Susan Siegfried, Perrin Stein, Dror Wahrman, Eunice Williams, and Stefan Wolohojian, proved most important. Many colleagues in Paris generously shared their knowledge and offered all kinds of advice and support in the past as well as more recently: Philippe Bordes, Emmanuel Bouju, Susanna Caviglia-Brunel, Marie-Anne Dupuy-Vachey, Charlotte Guichard, Étienne Jollet, Anne Lafont, Christian Michel, Régis Michel, and Marie-Catherine Sahut. I will miss my conversations with René Démoris whose loss for the history of eighteenth-century art and theory is irreparable.

In the Department of History of Art and Architecture at Harvard, I have profited from a continuous dialogue and teaching experiences with my colleagues, among them Benjamin Buchloh, Maria Gough, Jeffrey Hamburger, Robin Kelsey, Joseph Koerner, Carrie Lambert-Beatty, Yukio Lippit, Gülru Necipoğlu, Alina Payne, Jennifer Roberts, David Roxburgh, Eugene Wang, and

Henri Zerner. Deanna Dalrymple, the department's administrator, has been, as always, supportive in myriad ways. I owe a special thanks to Neil Levine, my former colleague in the department and a dear friend, for his help in pushing this book off my desk in the direction of the publisher. I have continued a rewarding conversation with another former colleague and friend, Irene Winter. At Harvard, intellectual exchanges with Homi K. Bhabha, Robert Darnton, Sylvaine Guyot, Patrice Higonnet, Christie McDonald, Erika Naginski, Antoine Picon, Alison Simmons, Diana Sorensen, Susan Suleiman, and Krzysztof Wodiczko have been invaluable.

I profited from the kindness and generosity of many people in the museum and art world who answered my queries and helped in my quest for illustrations, among them Colin Bailey, at the Morgan Library and Museum; Joseph Baillo, at the Wildenstein Gallery; Xavier Salomon, at the Frick Collection, New York; Margaret Morgan Grasselli, at the National Gallery in Washington; Eva Lena Karlsson and Martin Olin, at the Nationalmuseum in Stockholm; Daniel Birnbaum, at the Moderna Museet; Pierre Rosenberg, of the Académie Française; Marie-Catherine Sahut and Guillaume Faroult, at the Louvre; Christophe Léribault, at the Musée du Petit Palais, Paris; Katherine Baetjer and Perrin Stein, at the Metropolitan Museum; Édouard Kopp, Elizabeth Rudy, and Miriam Stewart, at the Harvard Art Museums; and Alan Wintermute, at Christie's. Many thanks also to Jean-Pierre Cuzin, Alastair Laing, and Florian Rodari.

My research and writing were supported by fellowships from the Wissenschaftskolleg in Berlin and the Radcliffe Institute of Advanced Study. I am deeply grateful to these institutions, and to their respective leaders, Luca Giuliani and Liz Cohen, for their support and for the opportunity of rich and productive exchanges with the intellectual communities they provided. Special thanks go to Judith Vichniac who made many things possible at the Radcliffe Institute. A Harvard College Professorship funded part of my leave, enabling me to write. I have also greatly benefited from invitations to guest lectures and conferences where I presented and discussed parts of this material. The conferences included: "Genre Painting in Eighteenth-Century France," at the Center for Advanced Study in Visual Arts, National Gallery of Art, Washington, DC (2003); "Everything but the Truth: Boucher Reconsidered," at the Getty Research Center, Los Angeles (2003); "The Lure of Object," at the Clark Art Institute, Williamston, MA (2004); "Dialogues in Art History," at the Center for Advanced Study in the Visual Arts, National Gallery, Washington, DC (2005); "Boucher and the Enlightenment," at the Wallace Collection, London (2005); "Art History Workshop," at the Center of Eighteenth-Century Studies, Indiana University (2007); "The Mellon Seminar," at the Getty Research Institute, Los Angeles (2007); "Violences du rococo," at Sorbonne 3, Paris, and Nanterre (2009); "Le Siècle Français: The French-Polish Artistic Relations in the Modern Era," at the National Museum and the Institute of History of Art, Warsaw University (2009); "Inside and Outside the French Eighteenth Century," at the University of California at San Diego (2009); and "The Distinguished Scholar Session for Rosalind Krauss," at the CAA Annual Meeting, Los Angeles (2012). I thank the individuals who extended invitations to these events: the late Philip Conisbee; Melissa Hyde and Mark Ledbury; Stephen Melville; Elizabeth Cropper and Therese O'Malley; Jo Hedley; Dror Wahrman; Ann Bermingham and Mary Sheriff; Jacques Berchtold and Chrisophe Martin; Andrzej Pieńkoś and Agnieszka Rosales-Rodriguez; Norman Bryson; and Yve-Alain Bois. Lectures at many institutions in the United States and in Europe—among them Southwestern College, Georgetown, Texas; Bryn Mawr

College and Philadelphia Museum of Art in Philadelphia; Dartmouth College; University of Concordia, Montreal University, and McGill University, Montreal; Princeton University; Wissenschaftskolleg in Berlin; Institute for Critical Theory, Zürich University; Ruhr Universität, Bochum; Universität Duisburg-Essen; Städelschule, Frankfurt; Columbia University; and the Mahindra Humanities Center, Harvard University—and the responses and feedback I received on these occasions were immensely helpful. I am grateful for these invitations to Lisa Saltzman and David Cast, the late Angela Rosenthal, Johanne Lamoureux and Todd Porterfield, Eileen Reeves, Yve-Alain Bois and Christopher Heuer, Julia Gelshorn and Philip Ursprung, Beate Söntgen, Johannes F. Lehmann, Isabelle Graw, Seth McCormick, The Bettman Lecture Student Committee at Columbia University, and Homi K. Bhabha.

Dialogue with the students in the seminars I taught at Harvard was crucial for the development of my thinking on the material presented in the book. For conversation, inspiration, research assistance, and other support, in the present and in the past, I give special thanks to Cabelle Ahn, Frédérique Baumgartner, Gokçan Demirkazik, Catherine Girard, Sarah Grandin, Ashley Hannebrink, Adela Kim, Issa Lampe, Leora Maltz-Leca, Meredith Martin, the late Chris Meyer, Andrei Pop, David Pullins, Gabriella della Rosa, Elizabeth Rudy, Sasha Wachtel, Aaron Wile, and Oliver Wunsch.

Friends who have been part of my wonderful intellectual community in Cambridge contributed to this project in more ways than they know: Jim Ackerman and Jill Slossburg-Akerman, Alide Cagidemetrio, Amanda Claybough, Homa Farjadi, Melissa Franklin, Mohsen Mostafavi, Martin Puchner, Werner Sollors, Ramie Targoff, and, an *escapée* to New York, Marina van Zuylen. For keeping my intellectual connection to Poland—via eighteenth- and nineteenth-century French art — alive, special thanks go to my faithful and dear friends, Iwona Danielewicz and Katarzyna Zabrocka-Muthesius.

I am grateful to Michelle Komie, my excellent editor at Princeton University Press, for her commitment and support for my project. I also thank Ben Pokross, Hannah Zuckerman, Steven Sears, and Mark Bellis who provided assistance with the project at the press. I greatly appreciated Dawn Hall's exemplary work as copyeditor. Diane Gottardi beautifully designed the book. The publication of the book was supported by grants from Harvard University: the History of Art and Architecture Department publication subvention; Anne and Jim Rothenberg Fund for Humanities Research; and Faculty of Arts and Sciences Tenured Publication Fund. Enormous thanks are due to Ashley Hannebrink who provided vital assistance in preparing the manuscript for publication, and to Cabelle Ahn and Sarah Grandin who stepped in to help at crucial moments. The book would have never arrived on the publisher's desk without their aid.

Last but not least, I am indebted to those who are closest to me. My Danish family, Bente, Jacob, and Thomas Burcharth, and the late Max Burcharth, whom I miss very much, sustained me in many wonderful ways over the years. My husband Martin and my daughter Zofia provide me daily with love, laughter, and pleasure, the meaning of which is beyond words. I dedicate this book to my father, Andrzej Lajer, who so eagerly awaited and rejoiced in its completion, and to my mother, Barbara Lajer; her loss was shattering, but her love and enthusiasm live in me.

THE PAINTER'S TOUCH

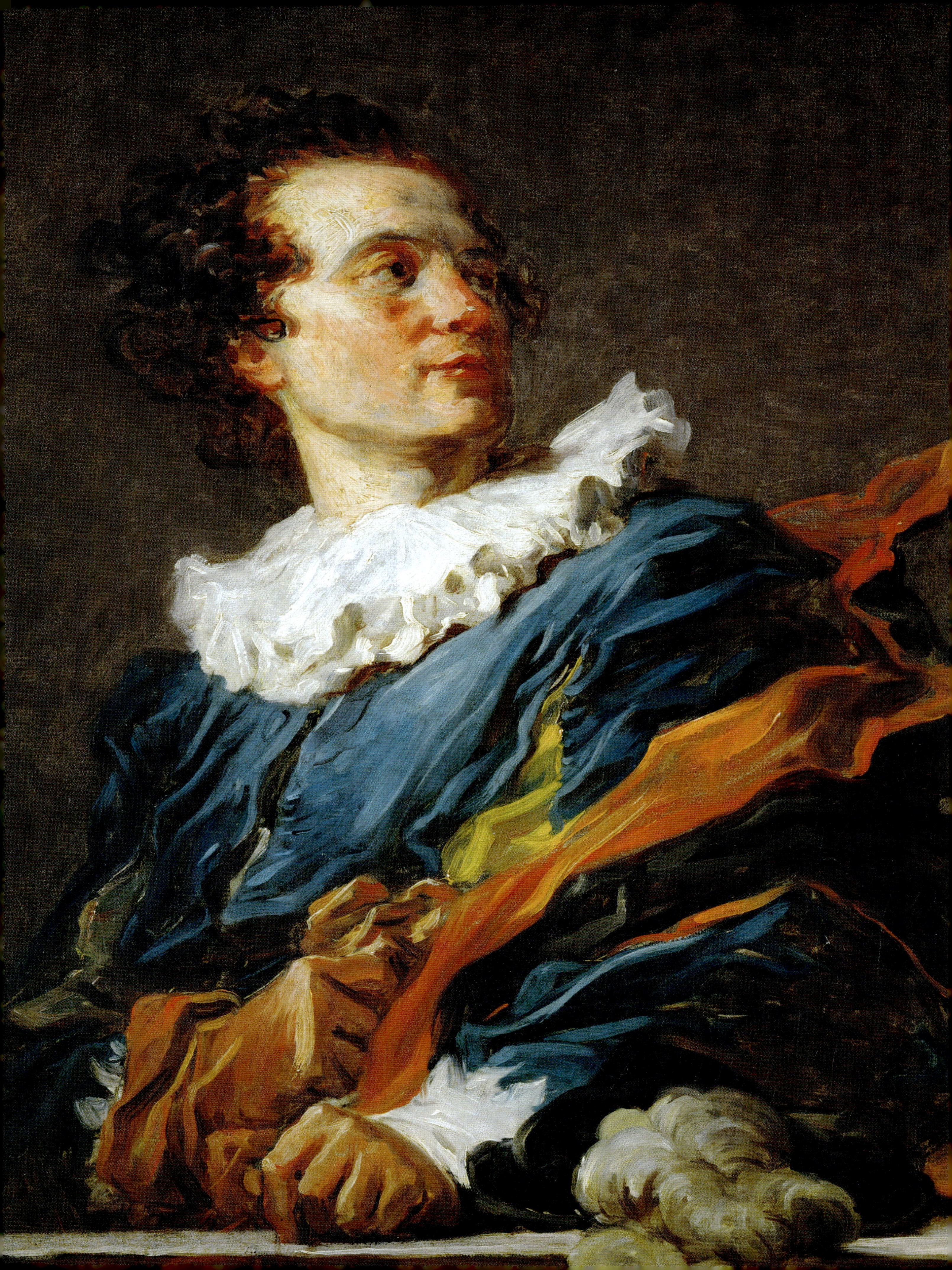

Introduction

This book offers a reassessment of three major French eighteenth-century painters, François Boucher (1703–1770), Jean Siméon Chardin (1699–1779), and Jean-Honoré Fragonard (1732–1806). Recognized as important already in their time, these artists were "rediscovered" in the second half of the nineteenth century by the brothers Goncourt who championed their individual pictorial styles as the epitome of eighteenth-century art.[1] Since then the three painters have entered the art historical canon. No survey of eighteenth-century art can be written without including a discussion of Boucher, Chardin, and Fragonard. Yet the position they occupy in the art historical narrative of the early modern period is odd, at once very prominent and underdefined. This is largely due to the fact that the models of analysis that served to construct this narrative do not easily accommodate these artists' work. Neither stylistic, nor semiotic, nor sociocultural criteria that have been used to situate these painters in the accounts of the artistic culture of their time have rendered justice to their individuated modes of practice and their importance as such.[2]

The Painter's Touch argues that the concern with individuality and artistic self-individuation is at the very core of Boucher's, Chardin's, and Fragonard's respective practices. This does not imply, however, a return to the celebratory approach of the Goncourts. Individuality is considered not as a "natural" effect of artistic talent but as a self-aware pursuit manifest in specific pictorial strategies and modes of operation. One of the central arguments of the book is that these artists recognized and self-consciously embraced the material and technical aspects of making as a means of self-definition, though each of them did so for different reasons and in different ways. It is precisely the material level of their productions that this book brings to the fore. Moreover, it seeks to recover the connections between these artists' differently individuated pursuits and the cultural notion of individuality that constituted one of the central preoccupations of the Enlightenment.

The book's title encapsulates its conceptual and material focus as well as its method. To place Boucher, Chardin, and Fragonard under the auspices of "The Painter's Touch" is to emphasize this strategic embrace of materiality as the crucial link between their diverse aesthetic projects. In the eighteenth-century commentaries on art, touch was commonly associated with artistic personality and pictorial self-awareness.[3] Boucher's "mellifluous" handling, Chardin's chromatic "magic," and Fragonard's "lively" touch were seen by their contemporaries as the distinguishing feature of their art.[4] The discussion here, however, does not simply extol these artists' outstanding pictorial skills but rather illuminates the import and implications of their investment in the mode of making and its relevance to self-conception. Touch is both an empirical fact and a metaphor for a key aspect of their practice, their particular modes of working, and their individualized approaches to artistic process. I discuss the operations of surface in Boucher's practice, the "deep materiality" of Chardin's paintings, and the performance of the unruly body in Fragonard's work as self-conscious strategies embraced by these artists in order to distinguish their art and themselves.

It was through their highly individuated approach to process and handling that these painters negotiated their position in the artistic culture of their time. On this level, touch, in its various modalities, describes the mode of operation developed by each artist to navigate the cultural domain. The book shifts attention away from the official artistic institutions that have traditionally been considered as the defining context of eighteenth-century pictorial practice to the aspects of production that were not institutionally confined. For although all three painters were members of the Academy and profited from their institutional affiliation (for example, by gaining access to the Salon exhibitions), it was their investment in the domains and issues considered extraneous or irrelevant to the academic notion of art—the market, the medium, and the body—that shaped their aesthetic ambition and directed their professional pursuits.

The significance of Boucher's output thus becomes clearest when we consider it in relation to the emergent culture of consumption within which the painter self-consciously inscribed his entire practice. In chapter 1, I suggest that, rather than the quintessential rococo painter defined by elite patronage, Boucher must be recognized as, above all, a highly successful commercial artist whose work was governed by a particular quality of touch, his *tact*, a term referring to an at once professional and personal (commercial and subjective) openness to the demand of the other.

Chardin's case, discussed in chapter 2, is a story of a specialist in minor genres who, by the sheer "magic" of execution comes to be considered the quintessential painter of his time. I suggest that his touch—and the character of his art—have much to do with the artisanal context of the guild to which the painter initially belonged and the domestic context, it too steeped in the artisanal ethos of labor (the painter's father was a cabinetmaker), in which he operated through much of his career. By both drawing on and striving to separate himself from artisanal modes of production, Chardin developed his particular *craft*: a highly personal, affective, and interiorized approach to the pictorial medium.

In Fragonard's erotic oeuvre, discussed in chapter 3, it is the body embraced as both a subject of representation and its key instrument manifest in the material structure and texture of the work that constitutes the defining impulse of pictorial practice. To reconstruct what I take to be a coherent aesthetic project in Fragonard's output, it is not enough to establish analogies between the style and iconography of his paintings and the thematics of love in the literature of this period, as has been done persuasively in current scholarship.[5] It is, rather, a matter of discerning a deeper, at once conceptual and material connection between the painter's process and the new materialist understanding of corporeality and sexuality. It is within this discursive framework that the distinct contours of Fragonard's aesthetics of eros—and the logic of its *seduction*—become visible.

My choice of touch as a concept epitomizing artistic process was motivated by its pertinence to these painters' modes of working but also by a desire to address a more general question of the painter's experience. At the time when these artists worked in France, experience gained unprecedented authority due to the influence of British empiricism, John Locke in particular; as Michael Baxandall observed, whether or not eighteenth-century French painters actually read Locke is not even relevant—the culture was Lockean.[6] Yet if the importance of empiricism for eighteenth-century pictorial practice has been widely recognized, notably in the accounts of the viewer's experience, it has not been brought to bear on the painters' own experience of their processes of making.[7] Can touch reveal to a historically distant observer something of the effects of this experience? What does the act of painting *do* to, or for, the painter? What are the implications of the particular habits of hand and mind? At stake in this inquiry is not simply the phenomenology of making but its formative aesthetic and subjective effects.

These questions are all the more important given the new conceptualization of touch that emerged in this historical period. In French sensationist philosophy, touch was established as the paramount cognitive faculty and a key instrument of subjective formation. As Étienne Bonnot de Condillac argued in his *Treatise on the Sensations* (1756), building on the insights of Locke, it is only through touch that we come to realize the boundaries of our own bodies and recognize ourselves as ourselves.[8] These ideas may be brought to bear on the painters' tactile involvement with their own work in order better to gauge its effects and significance. For example, I suggest that Boucher developed his "tact" through his prolonged aesthetic and kinesthetic engagement with Watteau's art: the activity of reproducing Watteau's oeuvre by etching it, as the young Boucher did for five formative years in his career. For Chardin, who worked unassisted, it was the intimate, both material and mental experience of his own paintings that transformed the painter and his practice. There was an interconnection between the thematics of touch in his paintings and his own exercise of it on the canvas. In Fragonard's case, it was not only the painter's hand but also his performative use of his entire body in the making of his works, and the way in which this corporeal engagement testified to his enlivened conception of the canvas (or other supports) that are noteworthy for this study.

The notion of touch invites such "activated" conception of the work of art. As it was conceived in the eighteenth century, touch was the only sense that was based in duality and required reciprocity: it takes two to touch (two surfaces, two objects, or two selves).[9] This recognition allows us to perceive the relation between the painter as a subject of the creative process, and the painting as its object, in different terms. For just as the painter touches his painting, so, it may be imagined, does the painting touch him. The fundamentally reciprocal dimension of touch encourages us to consider the painting itself as the agent of the process, and to explore how this interactive object *behaves* rather than merely what it looks like—an approach that is especially relevant for Fragonard's internally animated work but also, if for different reasons, for Chardin's. This shift of attention from the function of painting as an image to its material dimension as an object does not merely provide a fuller account of the work but leads to some surprising discoveries.

Rephrasing the act of painting as an encounter—at once physical and imaginary—with the canvas reveals a more complex rapport of the artist to the object of creation. Focusing on how the painter as a subject *materializes* in the work of Boucher, Chardin, and Fragonard as, in a sense, a function of the object (of painting), rather than the other way around, this tactile analysis proposes a different model of artistic subjectivity. It provides a different view of the creative process than the traditional account that puts the painter in charge as its initiator and its master. It also allows for the recognition of the complex role of gender in both the process and its results.

Woman occupies a privileged place in the practice of Boucher, Chardin, and Fragonard. Venuses and Dianas preside over Boucher's mythological paintings, and it is the notable absence of men that distinguishes his domestic genre paintings from those of his contemporaries, notably Jean-François de Troy's. In Chardin as well, the entire realm of domesticity is defined exclusively through female figures—the laundresses, kitchen maids, servants, mothers, and *bourgeoises*. As Ella Snoep-Reitsma has noted, "the remarkable thing about Chardin's compositions is that they are virtually devoid of men."[10] In Fragonard's paintings, although couples abound, the woman's body is invested with particular importance as the locus and carrier of eros. But if the role of the female figure is central in these works, it is also complex and ambivalent. Thus, while in a number of Fragonard's depictions of female nudes, woman is staged as object of desire, she is also defined as its subject (for example, in such seduction scenes as the *Happy Lovers* [see fig. 3.6] or *The Stolen Shift* [see fig. 3.8], where the woman's eager complicity in the act, or the palpable physiological manifestation of her own arousal, are made evident). In Boucher's and Chardin's genre scenes, woman represents a new ideal of the self linked to, respectively, commodity consumption and domestic pleasures.

Iconographically prominent, woman is important also in the ways her body *informs* these painters' respective productions, in its latent function, at once significant and ambiguous. Thus, in Boucher the female body acts as a sign for, or a signature of the artist, insofar as it both represents and obfuscates him. In his mythological paintings, the female nude epitomizes the status of the painting as an object of sensual pleasure, a luxury commodity, but it also represents a certain mirage of the self under its spell. The woman's body is mobilized in Boucher to articulate the new aesthetics of objecthood—painting as a precious possession—*and* the subjectivity associated with it. In Chardin, the female figure performs no less ambiguous functions; for example, in his genre paintings, women are depicted with attention and respect as the main, often solitary, subject of these representations, and yet are also, oddly, devoid of subjectivity, a bodily presence inscribed by mental absence. In Fragonard, what matters is not only what the painter depicts but also what remains invisible and yet defines the logic of his paintings, the latent maternal body as a generative font of representation.

In sum, the relation of the (male) painting subject to the painted object (and by extension to painting *as* an object) escapes the predictable hierarchy that governs the traditional visual constructions of gender. More complex patterns of relatedness, reciprocity, and reliance emerge if we consider the material, rather than only visual, register of these works. This approach complicates the definition of the male painter's individuality; his artistic and subjective autonomy is shown to be predicated not on self-sufficiency but on dependence on femininity.

The Painter's Touch does not, though, only address the role of painting in the formation of artistic identity. It is also a book about the people and worlds that the artists fleshed out in representation. The book's tactile focus, on this level, speaks to its deep concern with the new importance material life acquired in the eighteenth century as was depicted in multiple ways in the works discussed here. Whether it is in the mythological realm of gods' lives (as in Boucher), or in the realm of everyday life (depicted by both Chardin and Boucher), the works under discussion reveal the new social and cultural relevance of the material aspects of individual and collective existence. While Boucher and Chardin attend to the individuating dimension of material possessions and to the pleasures and profits of engagement with things, Fragonard's work testifies to the ways in which the materialist conception of body and nature reconfigured men's and women's relation to themselves and to each other. Casting a close and slow look at these paintings, the book explores, on the one hand, the preoccupation of the painters with their art and identity, and, on the other, the concerns of the people inhabiting the depicted worlds with their lives and their selves. The book suggests that the thematics of individuality in the work of these three painters is inseparable from the distinct aesthetic, formal, and technical aspects of these representations. It is not only the "what" but also the "how" of his painting that established Boucher as the visual mythologist of the self in the era of consumption, Chardin as the painter of interiors and interiority, and Fragonard as the promoter of modern eros.

This point brings us to the larger question of meaning. The choice of touch as both a structuring concept and dominant metaphor in this book emphasizes the material, as opposed to only visual register of paintings as a site of signification. In this regard, *The Painter's Touch* partakes in the broader methodological shift toward materiality in art history and in the humanities at large. In this book, however, attention to materiality has particular reasons and goals. There is, to begin with, a strong historical reason that warrants such methodological focus: the surge of materialism in the eighteenth century. Materialism was, arguably, the most provocative, radical mode of thinking that fundamentally challenged traditional approaches to knowledge. In the period under consideration, it did not amount to a coherent body of doctrine, but rather made itself manifest in diverse approaches linked by the refusal of metaphysics and a focus on matter.[11] By the mid-eighteenth century, matter became a widely debated epistemological and ontological paradigm, a model of knowing the world and a structure of being. From this new materialist perspective, the world appeared as a matrix of differences within which a human being amounted to nothing else but a particular combination of molecules. The principle behind a reimagined universe ceased to be God or any other metaphysical agency, but was instead a logic of material organization, the grasping of which hinged on the distinction between different kinds of materialities. A passage from the French materialist synthesis offered in Paul Thiry d'Holbach's *Système de la Nature* (1770) epitomizes this understanding of the world:

> *From the stone formed in the entrails of earth by an innermost combination of analogous and similar molecules that came together, to the sun, this vast reservoir of inflamed particles that lit the firmament; from the numbed oyster to the active and thinking man, we see an uninterrupted progression, a perpetual chain of combinations and movements from which beings result that do not differ from one another but in the variety of their elementary substances, and the combinations and proportions of these substances, from which originate infinitely varied modes of being and acting.*[12]

Specific connections between different strands of eighteenth-century materialism and painting are proposed and discussed in detail in the individual chapters of this book. Here I only want to articulate a more general assumption that has informed my discussion—namely, that the emergence and dissemination of the materialist outlook contributed to what one may call the "materialization" of eighteenth-century vision. The language of description referring not to the image but to the morphology of the world became available, contributing to the recasting of the "period eye" in palpably material and embodied terms.[13] Pronouncements such as d'Holbach's—his is a late example of established materialist habits of description—opened up the natural realm to cultural interpretation based in the diverse "combinations and proportions" of material elements. Conversely, the material realm of culture—including painting—was opened up to a morphological kind of analysis to identify the "infinitely varied" modes not of being and acting but of *meaning*.[14] It is thus for particular historical reasons that eighteenth-century paintings may be considered as molecular formations organized by brushstrokes, a field of haptic and not only optic experience, a tactile morphology of marks and traces.[15]

At the core of *The Painter's Touch* is the question of how the distinct logic of making discernible in the works of these artists—the operations of surface in Boucher, the deep materiality of Chardin, the dynamic morphological structure in Fragonard—can be seen to produce the *effect* of a person, including the painter's own. One of the book's arguments is that the experience of different material realms explored by these painters—the commercial realm, the realm of painting as a medium, the physical domain of the body—had an impact on the conception of the self not only in its social but also psychic functioning. While the term "psychic" was not yet established in eighteenth-century vocabularies in the sense that it is now, there was an epistemic space of psyche avant la lettre.[16] Materialism was crucial for defining the contours of this space insofar as it put into question the existence of the soul. Whether one followed a brand of materialism that posited a material soul or another that denied the soul's existence altogether, conceiving the body as a particular organization of matter meant confronting the idea of an agency that was irreducible to the body and that governed its operations.[17] It is the relation between this epistemic space and the painting of self that this book explores.

The special interest of *The Painter's Touch* lies in articulating the nature of painting's contribution *qua* painting to the Enlightenment discourse on individuality. This period has been recognized as the very moment of the cultural, philosophical, scientific, and political invention of individuality.[18] Whether manifest in the philosophical attempts to theorize personal identity, the adoption of the first-person narrative as a predominant literary form, the emergence of the cultural concern with privacy, or, later in the century, the legal and political conceptualization of human rights, the individual person was a key concern of French eighteenth-century culture. Individuality has also been the subject of rich scholarship that has considered different aspects of the eighteenth-century origins of the modern self, its modernity having to do with its new status as a problem of representation.[19] What has been largely absent from these diverse archaeologies of the modern self, however, is a sustained consideration of the domain of visual arts and material culture.[20] If *The Painter's Touch* situates paintings in this larger interdisciplinary context, it asks, specifically, *how* painting as a historically distinctive medium contributed to it in vital ways. This is another motivation behind the privileged place materiality holds here. The premise of the book is that paintings are a source of meanings not produced elsewhere. Capable of conveying ideas and formulating arguments, though not in words, paintings generate their own form of discourse. This does not, to be sure, imply a disregard for texts or historical contexts. On the contrary, specific circumstances and ideas are considered carefully in this book, and new contexts are proposed for the interpretation of painting. The point is, however, to recover the specific contribution of painting to the historical and discursive texture of its time.[21] While the relevant discourses of the moment—whether a debate on luxury, the sensationist understanding of subjectivity, the Buffonian conception of nature, or theories of sexual reproduction—are key for *locating* the argument of the paintings, it is what paintings actually "say" in brushstrokes, impasto, texture, and thickness of paint, how they work with, but also *exceed* or *counter* these discourses that concerns me. This is the aim of the close material analyses I conduct in these pages.

Ultimately, my hope is that in recasting our understanding of Boucher, Chardin, and Fragonard, the book will also alter our sense of the place and role of painting in the nascent culture of modernity. The emergence of modern artistic culture in the eighteenth century has been linked to the radical change in the conditions, modes, and function of the experience of art. Whether we think of the new public realms of the Salon exhibitions and the new public discourse, art criticism, which they generated, or of the new private spaces and practices of appreciation and assessment of art (collecting, connoisseurship, and the institutions and discourses of art trade), the encounter with an art object entered the very core of social—individual and collective—experience.[22] The present study seeks both to contribute to and complicate the existing account of the origins of modern aesthetic experience by engaging with the initial encounter—of the painter with the canvas—that brings the work of art into existence. What the book reconstructs are the non-verbal forms of a dialogue that defines this encounter and that materializes in and through touch.

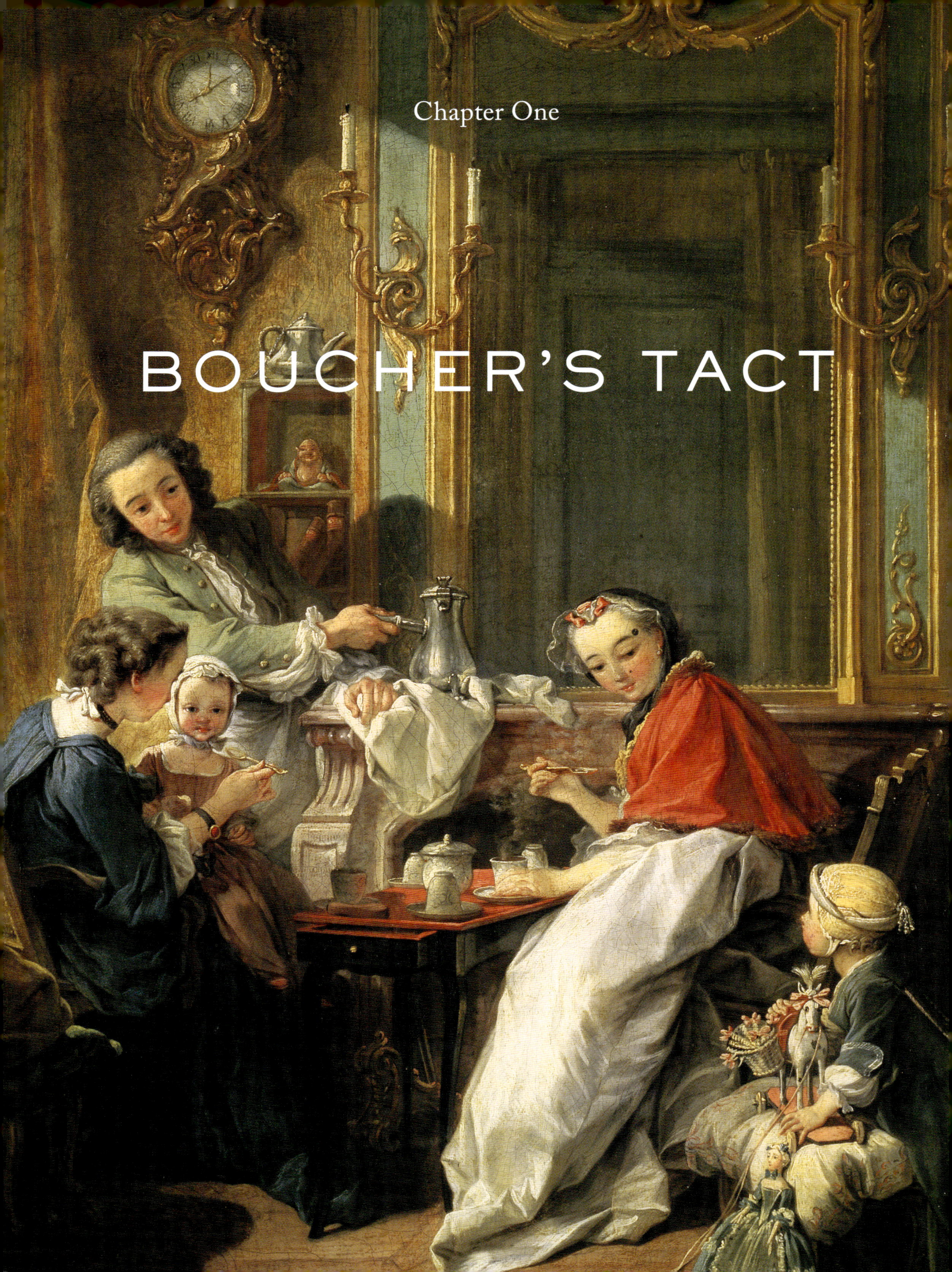

Chapter One

BOUCHER'S TACT

MATERIALITY AND PERSONALITY

*Boucher has a handling (*un faire*) so much his own that, if one gives him even a small detail to execute on a piece of canvas, one instantly recognizes it as his.*

—DIDEROT

Clad in gray velvet, white lace, and a powdered wig with curls rolling down his back, his manicured nails highlighted to emphasize his well-groomed appearance, Gustaf Lundberg's *François Boucher* epitomizes the eighteenth-century image of an accomplished artist (fig. 1.1).[1] Painted in 1741 as Lundberg's reception piece to the Royal Academy in Paris, Boucher's likeness rehearses the Titianesque formula of a gentleman's portrait—familiar to French artists, as Philippe de Champaigne's portrait by his nephew, Jean-Baptiste, attests (fig. 1.2)—to convey the dignity of Boucher's professional status. The portrait inscribes itself within a tradition of artistic representation that had originated in the late seventeenth century with Charles Le Brun, the first director of the Academy, who, in 1683, had himself painted by Nicolas de Largillière in sumptuous attire to signal not only his wealth and status but also the idea of distance between artistic creation and manual labor (fig. 1.3). This conceptual dissociation was at the core of the Academy's mission, as Le Brun saw it, and thus also at the core of the academic artist's self-image.[2] Although clearly smaller in its scale and ambition, Lundberg's likeness, painted as it was expressly for the Academy's eyes, similarly suggested an artist operating at a distance from the material bases of his work. The work itself does not even appear in this image.

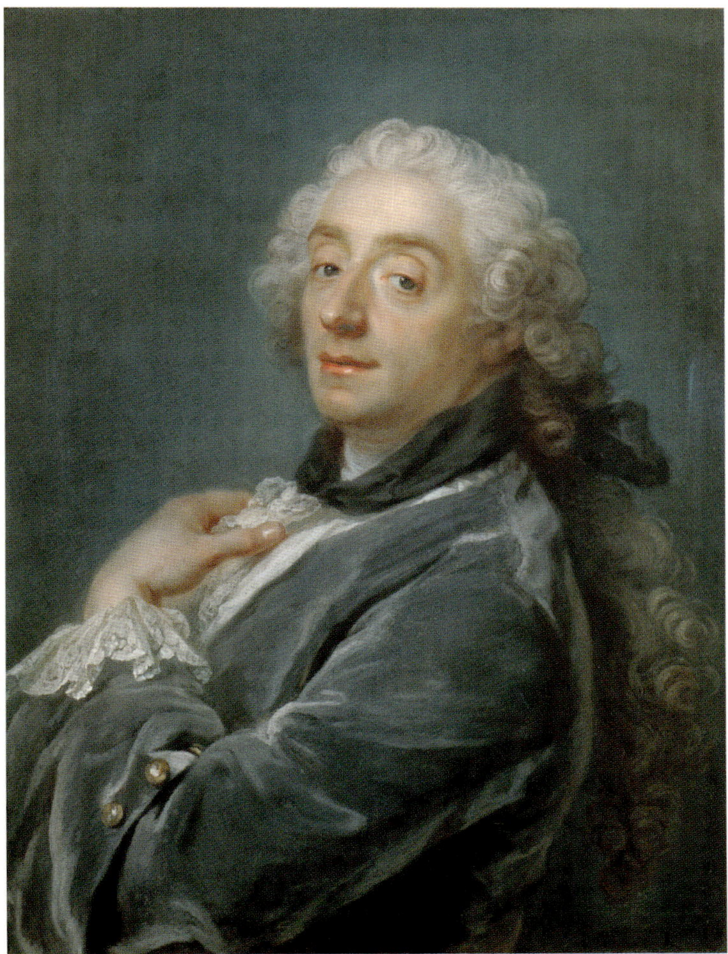

1.1.
Gustaf Lundberg,
François Boucher, 1741.
Pastel on blue paper.
Musée du Louvre, Paris.

Boucher was indeed a prominent member and eventually even director of the Academy. He was also, like Le Brun, a court artist, gaining, if only late in life, the title of the First Painter to the King.[3] Moreover, in art history, Boucher has come to epitomize a style, rococo, associated with the social elites of the Ancien Régime. His elegant pose and laced attire in Lundberg's portrait, and the pastel brio of its delivery, evoke this association. Yet none of Boucher's official functions could be said to have determined the character and importance of his output. Nor does rococo as a stylistic category describe the most salient aspect of his artistic enterprise. Extending from ambitious depictions of history and mythology to designs for porcelain cups and snuff boxes, Boucher's aesthetic project is most striking in the sheer vastness of its scope and material diversity of its manifestations. By his own estimate he produced about ten thousand drawings and more than a thousand paintings, including oil sketches, without mention of his different design projects.[4]

The exceptional productiveness of the painter has often been mentioned by his commentators, not without an occasionally deprecating comment about the ostensible facility of his brush.[5] His inventiveness, too, was already noted by his contemporaries, one of whom declared outright that Boucher was "the most ingenious artist of our century."[6] Yet the notions of productivity and ingenuity do not allow us fully to grasp the significance of Boucher's versatile art. What we need to consider are Boucher's modes of making and operation as an individual artist that made possible the unusual abundance and

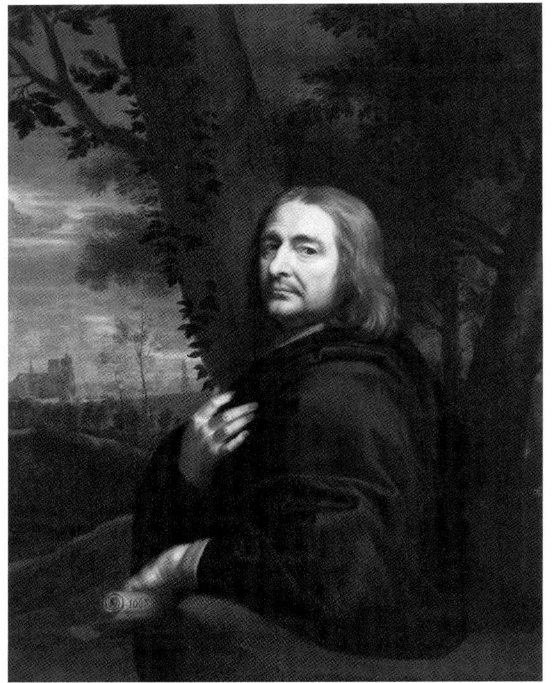

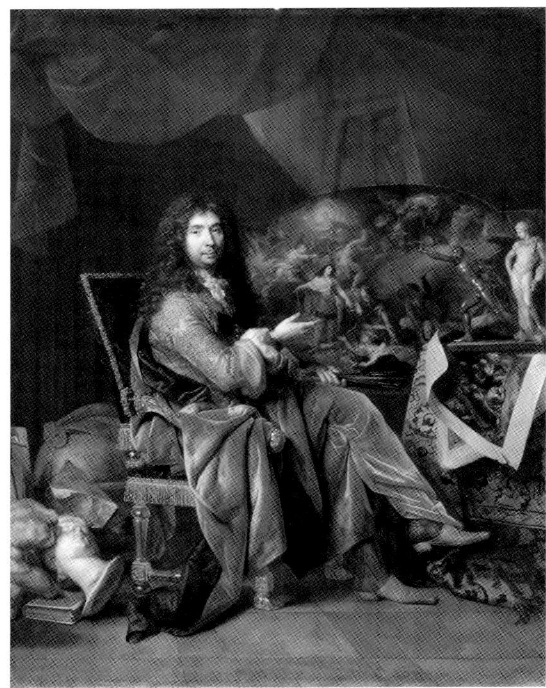

1.2.
Jean-Baptiste de Champaigne, *Portrait of Philippe de Champaigne*, 1668. Oil on canvas. Musée du Louvre, Paris.

1.3.
Nicolas de Largillière, *Charles Le Brun*, 1683. Oil on canvas. Musée du Louvre, Paris.

spread of his productions. Without rejecting existing institutional structures and traditional patronage, Boucher devised his own ways of artistic functioning, matched by his particular technical skills, which enabled him to extend his trace beyond the narrow precincts of "art," onto the material world at large. It is in the expansiveness of his practice that the novelty and interest of Boucher's approach resides, an approach that signals a new—and in a key sense modern—kind of artistic self-awareness grounded in the very materiality of the work, an approach through which Boucher was, in a sense, able to materialize himself.

Diderot once observed that Boucher's style of execution was so much his own that it was instantly and unmistakably recognizable even in a fragment of a painting.[7] This observation evoked a tradition of appreciating pictorial handicraft as the mark of the artist that went back at least to the seventeenth century, notably to Roger de Piles.[8] In Diderot's time, it was revived and given new emphasis by several writers, notably Charles-Nicolas Cochin, who saw *le faire* specifically as a vehicle of artistic personality. Using the term in its technical as well as stylistic sense, Cochin formulated in his writings an extensive apology for the material effects of a work of art.[9] Diderot, on the other hand, was ambivalent about the individuating potential of le faire. Although he appreciated a skillful rendering—an appreciation he developed only gradually by writing the Salon reviews, having started out as a *litterateur* with no experience in artistic or technical matters—the effect of painting was for him overdetermined by what it depicted and the ideas it evoked. Thus while praising Boucher's exceptional painterly skills, such as imagination, facility, even magic of execution, Diderot saw the artist's talent marred by the lack of the quality he most highly esteemed, namely, truth.[10] For the critic, the fact that Boucher was recognizable in every bit of his painting could only be a dubious asset.

Diderot's assessment of Boucher cast a long shadow over art history's approach to the painter's work. It would not be an exaggeration to state that despite the frank partiality of the critic's views and the relatively limited reach of his writings originally addressed to an elite and foreign audience, Diderot's account became the art-historical "truth" of Boucher's work.[11] As a consequence, the subsequent discussions of his practice were not simply negative but limited to a concern with "what" rather than "how" he painted.[12] Having inherited Diderot's approach to eighteenth-century art understood as, largely, a moral rather than material practice, we have lost a sense of why, in the eyes of some of his contemporaries, Boucher could appear as "no longer a painter, but Painting itself."[13]

Diderot's hold on the art-historical understanding of the artist has, however, begun to loosen in recent years. In the wake of several important exhibitions of Boucher's work—beginning with the large monographic show organized in 1986, followed by others, smaller in scope, in the early 2000s—and the new research on the various aspects of his practice, a different kind of Boucher has begun to emerge.[14] We now have a fuller picture of his relation to the artistic, cultural, and social contexts of his time and a more thoroughly documented record of his engagements in different domains of cultural production. Moreover, we have been presented with the idea of Boucher as an essentially modern artist. Contradicting the long-standing historiographic tradition of understanding his work as a negative foil of artistic modernity—an example against which novel and ambitious aesthetic practice defined itself in eighteenth-century France, and the opposite to what, later, modernism came to stand for—several scholars have explored the thoroughly modern aspects of the artist's activities, such as his involvement in innovative forms of theater and music, his relation to his patrons, especially Madame de Pompadour, his appropriative practice of exoticism, and his embrace of reproductive technologies.[15]

My discussion in this chapter seeks to expand and recast the definition of Boucher's modernity by focusing on the question of individuality. I am interested in the ways in which Boucher's practice posed the problem of the individual, in a multiple sense: as a figure in his work, as the work's addressee, and as the artist himself insofar as he can be seen to have manifested himself—the key question being how—in his productions. It was something of a cliché during the artist's lifetime that Boucher's work reflected his personality. This association revolved around the idea of sensual pleasure that Boucher's paintings were seen to produce and that tended to be identified as the painter's own. "Born sensitive, likeable and voluptuous, he almost always saw himself drawn toward the Graces whose painter he was generally recognized to be," stated Antoine Bret, expressing a widely shared opinion, in his obituary of the artist.[16] The notion of the Graces evoked here had both aesthetic and social connotations; it referred to the female figure as a representation of a certain aesthetic ideal—that of grace—but also to specific kinds of women—actresses, dancers—associated with sensual or, more directly, sexual pleasure.[17] The sexual pleasure connection was explicit in Jean-François Marmontel's statement that Boucher, whom he knew from gatherings at the salon of Madame Geoffrin, "did not see the Graces in a good place; he painted Venuses and the Virgin after the nymphs of the coulisses, and both his language and his pictures bore the stamp of his models' manners and the tone of his studio."[18] Whether dismissive or sympathetic, these commentaries were underwritten by a reductive collapse of Boucher's iconography onto his (presumed) biography.

What I am concerned with is the possibility of discerning a different kind of relation between the work and its maker, one that is irreducible to iconography or biography. The central problem posed by Boucher's practice has to do, in my view, with its remarkable visual or morphological consistency and its resulting recognizability, not only, as Diderot saw it, in painting, but also across different mediums. The question is how this remarkably consistent visual language may be seen to speak of—or for—its producer, Boucher. What did it mean to say that, as Diderot asserted, his faire so evidently "belonged" to him? What relation between the artist and his work can be discerned in his so unfailingly identifiable manner? At stake in this consideration is, first of all, a better understanding of how Boucher's painting and his work at large functioned as a material practice and how this practice could be seen, on the level I would call morphological, as Boucher's "own."

Such reconsideration of Boucher's output raises a broader question of artistic identity and the means by which it was asserted and maintained in the early modern period. In one powerful model of analysis, the eighteenth century has been seen as the originary moment of artistic modernity; marking the advent of the public sphere, it shaped the formation of the public persona of the artist.[19] Associated with the discourse and institutions of the Enlightenment, such as the Academy and the Salon, this view of modernity has marginalized Boucher. Although the artist exhibited his work at the Salon, he did not fully embrace its principle of publicness, which manifested itself in the emergence of art criticism as the voice of the public opinion. His attitude is evident in the image with which Boucher entered the struggle to define the mission of contemporary painting but that could also be taken to represent how he understood his own pictorial practice. In a frontispiece that he designed for abbé Le Blanc's pamphlet published in 1747 in response to La Font de Saint-Yenne's criticism of the state of pictorial production in France, Boucher depicted an allegory of Painting besieged by Jealousy, Ignorance, and Drunkenness (fig. 1.4).[20] A version of Melancholia, a gagged woman, inactive, dejected, and seated by her canvas, personifies Painting, while the mocking horde of harpies and asses that surround her represent the critics as incompetent intruders into the domain of art.

The image sought to boost Le Blanc's arguments in defense of the artists attacked by La Font for their lack of attention to broader societal and national interests.[21] As Thomas Crow has observed, the frontispiece not only positioned Boucher as a vehement opponent of the new conditions shaping artistic practice since the late 1730s, that is, the regular official public art exhibitions and the institution of the critic as the aesthetic arbiter that these exhibitions brought about; his frontispiece also aligned Painting with what it did not visualize, its hidden agenda, namely, the lucrative promise of the market endangered by the emergence of critical discourse.[22] The point is that the critics were recognized as a potentially disturbing factor not only for artistic creativity and aesthetic autonomy but also for the financial well-being of the artists, and that Boucher was instrumental in articulating and publicizing this view.

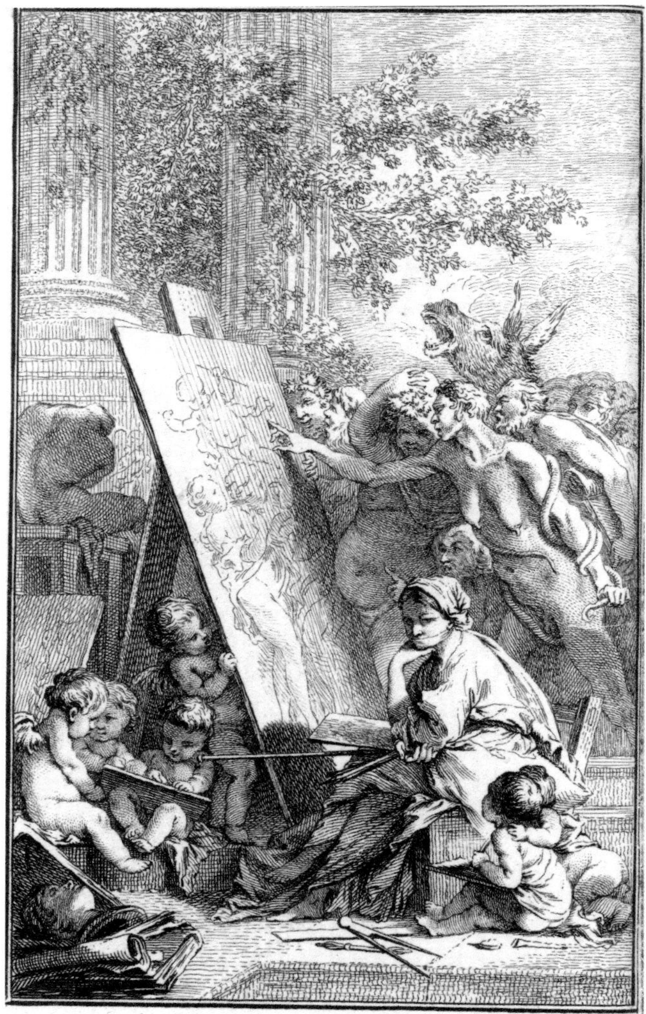

In this analysis, the market appears as a regressive factor, a pull of anti-modernity that delays the beneficial modernizing effects of the public sphere. Yet the market may also be seen differently, as the basic condition of another, commercial modernity, and, in this sense, an important factor in artistic production in Boucher's time.[23] Much recent scholarship has been devoted to the reassessment of the commercial sites of production, reception, and dissemination of art. We now have a better sense of the role of art dealers, auctions, and accompanying publications in which a new modern language of attribution and appreciation of art was formulated in eighteenth-century artistic culture.[24] These new commercial establishments were not simply responsible for the economic well-being of artists, nor was the art market as such merely the site where financial fortunes of artists were made. Linked to collectors and *amateurs*, these new institutions and the discourse they generated contributed to the social life of art, if in a circumscribed sense, by shaping the private—individual or collective—modes of its experience.[25] The commercial sphere has been acknowledged as one of the key components of early modern artistic culture.

Boucher's practice inscribes itself in this commercial context—and in the broader realm of commercial modernity—more deeply than has been realized.[26] That the artist pursued various commercial projects, such as designs for luxury goods or for the print trade, has been well established. What is less clear is how these activities should be situated in relation to his practice at large. Already during his lifetime, the artist was criticized for his commercial pursuits. In modern literature, the responsiveness of his practice to the demands of the market has also been recorded largely, if not exclusively, in terms of financial gain.[27] Scholars have noted how successful and prosperous the artist became as a result of his commercial savvy.[28] We know for a fact that Boucher left a considerable fortune after his death, amounting to about 150,000 *livres*, more than half of which was obtained from the sale of his collection of art and curiosities.[29]

Boucher's financial success is important—it is essential to have the exact sense of his wealth—but the commitment of his practice to the commercial context cannot be assessed in purely economic terms; it had other aesthetic and symbolic implications. As many social and cultural historians have argued, the growing importance of the commercial sphere in the eighteenth century had an impact not only on the life and material comfort of society but also on how society, and individuals, including artists, came to understand and imagine themselves.[30] Coming to terms with the market was not solely a

1.4.
Jacque Philippe Le Bas after François Boucher, *Painting Mocked by Envy, Stupidity, and Drunkenness*, frontispiece to [abbé Le Blanc], Lettre sur l'exposition des *Ouvrages de Peinture, Sculpture, &c. de l'Année)*, 1747. Houghton Library, Harvard University.

financial but also an aesthetic opportunity—and challenge—for the artists to reconceptualize their practices and to reimagine themselves. Boucher took this opportunity, and challenge, seriously. As Katie Scott has demonstrated, his creative involvement in the print trade was crucial for securing the artist's reputation, exemplifying the key role of the market in the formation of artistic identity.[31] I consider, more broadly, how the market informed the artist's work in different mediums and how his multifarious practices, underpinned as they were by an economic self-awareness, contributed to the formation of Boucher's artistic personality.

I am proposing that Boucher was a commercial artist in a particular, modern sense of the term, that is, someone whose entire output manifests, in different ways, an interpretive engagement with the market recognized as a defining condition of social, cultural, and artistic functioning. Boucher's work was, in other words, a product of what I call a *commercial imagination* to account for the aesthetically creative mode in which the artist made sense of the economic conditions of his practice, but also to evoke these conditions' own partly imaginary status. For the market in Boucher's time was not only an empirical reality but also a cultural construct.[32] How the artist understood and processed its existence had to do not only with what it actually was and how it operated, but also with how it was imagined and—intensely—discussed in his time. The commercial imagination designates a particular kind of artistic responsiveness to the economic conditions discernible in Boucher's works, a receptive mode of aesthetic functioning that, while mobilizing the faculty of imagination, produced specific material effects.

This brings us back to Lundberg's portrait. Although the portrait shuns the conception of the artist's material engagement in pictorial production, it does allude to the importance of touch. Boucher's manicured hand fondling his jabot, notwithstanding the distilled elegance of this gesture suggesting a distance from manual labor, points nonetheless to the importance of the hand as such, and through it, to what I call Boucher's *tact*.

TOUCH AND TACT

Il n'a pas les doigts engourdis
Ce peintre qui dans son nom porte
Le marchand qui les vendredis
Ferme sa boutique et sa porte.

—Ch. F. Panard

The appreciation of Boucher's outstanding pictorial skills was often expressed in terms of praise for his touch, which his contemporaries judged to have been invariably easy, light, elegant, and refined.[33] Symptomatic of an increasing attention to the material aspects of painting, these were common enough terms for artistic excellence at the time. Lightness of touch, a quality that was expressly promoted by the renowned *amateur*, comte de Caylus, under the term of "la légèreté d'outil," referred to the capacity of the painter to convey effortlessness of execution. The refined touch implied a knowing approach to technique, one that was both animated and self-aware.[34] These expressions trickled down to the level of less specialized and deliberately coarse commentary exemplified by a quatrain about Boucher in a collection of verses on prominent artists published in 1744 by a minor poet and playwright, Ch. F. Panard. Playing on the literal meaning of Boucher's name in French, Panard praised the painter's skill by contrasting it with the brutal touch of a butcher. Although recognized for his exceptional manual dexterity, Boucher was not the only artist whose touch was then appreciated. Chardin, as we shall see in the next chapter, was just as renowned for his magic of execution—it was in fact his faire, rather than Boucher's, that Cochin, for one, most consistently championed.[35] What distinguished Boucher as an artist was, rather, a certain quality of touch that I will call tact.

The two notions, touch and tact, were not unrelated. In the eighteenth century the term "tact" was prevalently used in reference to the sense of touch ("le sentiment du toucher"), which is how the 1708 edition of Antoine Furetière's *Dictionnaire Universel* succinctly defined it.[36] It is precisely under "tact" that one could find the main entry on touch in Diderot and d'Alembert's *Encyclopèdie*, its very length reflecting the importance of this faculty in the materialist discussion of the body and the self.[37] As the entry's author, Chevalier Louis de Jaucourt, specifies, tact refers not only to the sensory capacity of the whole body, but specifically to the inside surface of one's fingers, "the true organ of touch."[38] (This is, we may note, precisely what Lundberg's portrait evokes in representing the painter's fingers grasping the lace of his jabot.)

At the same time, "tact" was used also in another, figurative sense in the seventeenth and eighteenth centuries. We find its briefest definition in the 1762 edition of the *Dictionnaire de L'Académie Française*: "To have tact that is keen, reliable, which is to say to judge keenly, reliably in the matter of taste."[39] In this definition, tact amounted to a capacity for discernment that had moral, social, and aesthetic connotations. In his *Système de la Nature*, Baron d'Holbach spoke of the "moral tact" as a capacity for distinguishing between good and reprehensible acts, a capacity that, as he argued, was acquired, though it might seem innate.[40] In a social context "tact" was often used to describe an ability to intuit or foresee.[41] This is the meaning that informed the word's common modern usage as referring to polite or pleasing behavior.[42] As such, the notion of tact was caught up with a certain bodily skill, describing a mode of existence in the social arena that was fortuitous, appreciated by others, and also beneficial for the one who was tactful. Finally, in aesthetic terms, "tact" was often used as an equivalent to "taste," something that may be developed through practice rather than learned from rules, or a matter of intuition rather than learning. Diderot referred to it on many occasions, for example, when he scolded Baudouin, a genre painter and Boucher's son-in-law, in his *Salon of 1767* for his lack of it.[43]

Drawing on aspects of its eighteenth-century usage, I suggest a simultaneously broader and more specific notion of tact as an adaptive aesthetic conduct, a method (a tactic) of artistic accommodation to the demands of the other. In late seventeenth- and early eighteenth-century manuals of *honnêteté*, the capacity to be accommodating vis-à-vis the needs and wishes of others was considered to be the most essential asset of a gentleman. As the renowned writer on honnêteté, Chevalier de Méré put it: "In order to become and be known as an *honnête homme*, the most important factor, in my view, is to discern in all things the best means of pleasing others, and to be able to put them into practice."[44] "Anyone who knows how to be accommodating can confidently hope to be pleasing," agreed an author of another manual, Nicolas Faret.[45] In order to acquire the skill of complaisance one had to master the art of decoding hidden messages and undeclared desires, that is, to develop an almost magical capacity "to get inside" the other.[46] "One has to pay attention to everything that happens in the hearts and the minds of the people one entertains," explained Méré, "and to grow accustomed to divining their feelings and thoughts from almost imperceptible signs. This ability, which is dark and difficult for those who are not practiced in it, gradually becomes clearer and in the end easy."[47] The acquisition of such skill is like learning a foreign language, which one can master through love and study. But it is also comparable to sorcery, "for it instructs us in divination, which is how we discover a great many things that otherwise we would never know and that could serve us very well. . . . It requires that we penetrate people's unspoken thoughts and, very often, their most closely guarded secrets."[48] Key for the acquisition of this magic skill were two strategies. The first was *souplesse* (suppleness, or adaptive flexibility of manner), for "the persona . . . of an *honnête homme* . . . must transform itself as the occasion warrants."[49] The second, *insinuation*, was also of strategic importance according to many writers concerned with the ideal of honnêteté.[50] In Méré's understanding, it amounted to the capacity to "work subtly beneath the surface of the other," a term with physical and psychological resonances.[51]

These behavioral terms aptly describe the *technical process* that proved crucial for Boucher's artistic formation. I am referring to his engagement, at the very outset of his career, in the reproduction of the work of Antoine Watteau. Boucher won the Prix de Rome in 1723, at the age of twenty, but due to exceptional circumstances he was not able to go to Italy to complete a course of study at the French Academy in Rome until later.[52] Instead, he continued to work in Paris in the printing trade, where he had been engaged before, chiefly in the workshop of the printmaker Jean-François Cars. Having come into contact (possibly through Cars) with Jean de Jullienne, the patron, friend, and great admirer of Antoine Watteau, Boucher was engaged in the project of reproducing the oeuvre of Watteau, who died in 1721.[53] Other artists were also hired for the project, but Boucher emerged as its leading contributor, executing roughly 119 out of 350 etchings after Watteau's drawings for the *Figures des différents caractères de paysage et d'études dessinées d'après nature par Antoine Watteau*, which came out in two volumes in 1726 and 1728.[54] He also produced a significant num-

1.5.
Antoine Watteau,
Italian Troupe, ca. 1715.
Red, black, and white chalk, gray ink, on paper. Kupferstichkabinett, Staatliche Museen, Berlin.

1.6.
François Boucher after Antoine Watteau,
Italian Troupe, ca. 1726.
Etching, first state. Musée du Louvre, Paris, Rothschild Collection.

ber of etchings after Watteau's paintings and decorative work subsequently published in the two volumes of *L'Oeuvre gravé d'Antoine Watteau*.[55] Because of the scope and range of his contribution to it, the *Recueil Jullienne* (as all the volumes came to be called) constituted the main arena for the development of Boucher's tact.

Jullienne recognized the high quality of Boucher's work from the start, assigning him not only a great number of plates in the *Figures de différents caractères* but also some of the more prestigious ones intended for full-page reproduction.[56] He was asked to reproduce full and half figures, both male and female, in elaborate costumes, among them all the Persian ones; the figures of actors and popular entertainers; all the landscapes, of which there were twelve; portraits; and group scenes. Moreover, it would be fair to say that Boucher was, to an extent, not only the *re*-producer but also the *producer* of Watteau's work. According to the painter Jean-Bernard Restout, Boucher copied autograph drawings by Watteau that were not in Jullienne's collection, which implies that the younger artist's re-creations of Watteau's work served as models for him and other artists participating in Jullienne's reproductive enterprise.[57] No doubt in recognition of the quality of his contribution, Boucher was also asked to execute the frontispieces for the two volumes of the *Figures*: a portrait of Watteau based on Boucher's drawing after the artist's self-portrait and an allegorical composition titled *The Graces at the Tomb of Watteau*, etched by Boucher after his own design.[58]

For *L'Oeuvre gravé*, Boucher executed twenty-one etchings after Watteau's paintings, arabesques, and panel decorations, roughly one-twelfth of the total.[59] His somewhat smaller contribution to the second phase of Jullienne's project was no doubt due to Boucher's departure for Italy in the spring of 1728.[60] Before he left, though, the artist produced five significant prints that were advertised in the *Mercure de France* in December 1727 and offered for sale separately, before their inclusion in the *Receuil*.[61] Among them was the *Italian Troupe* notable not only for its high quality of execution but also for the fusion of Boucher's trace with Watteau's, particularly identifiable today in that Watteau's original drawing of it has been preserved (figs. 1.5 and 1.6).[62] The drawing, now in Berlin, was most probably made by Watteau

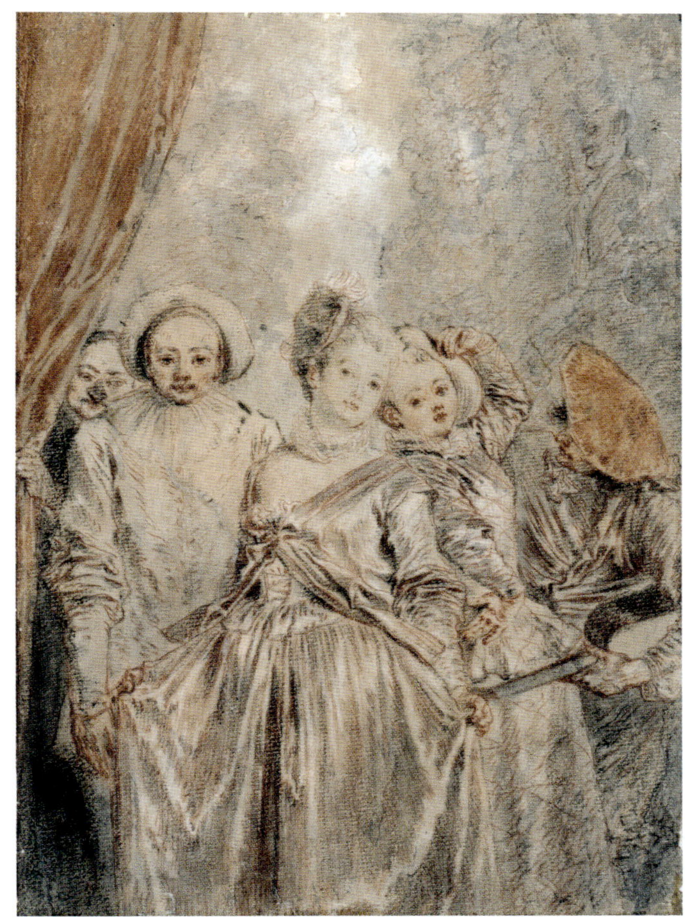

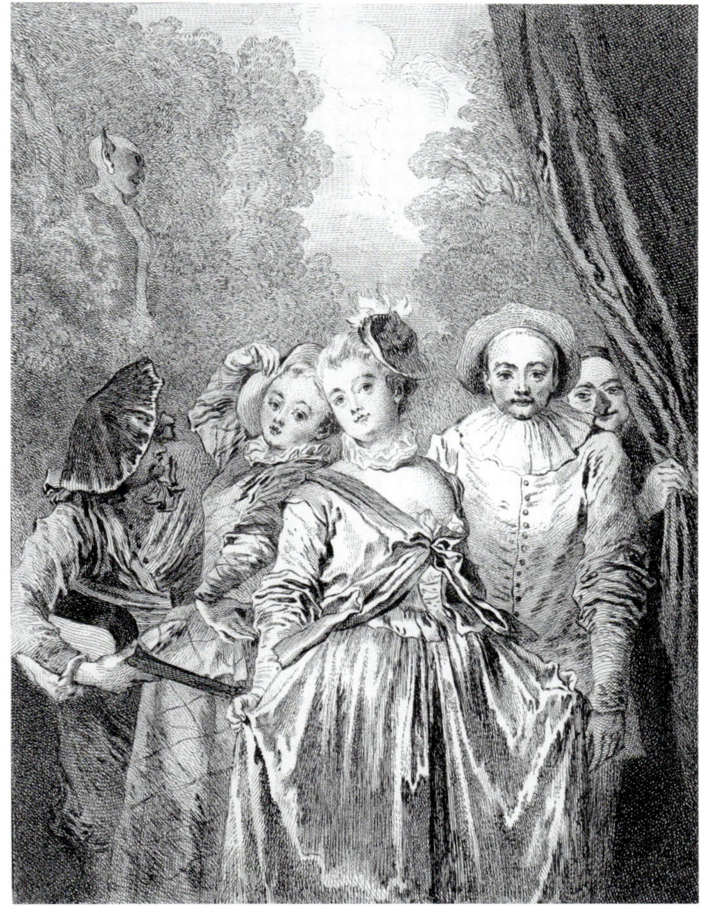

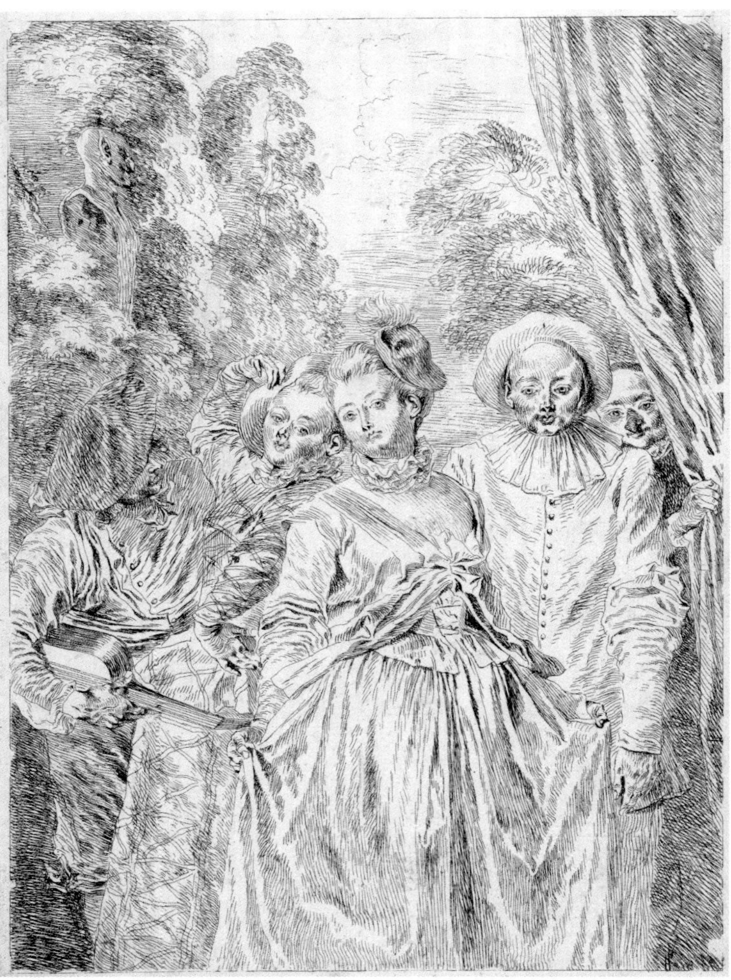

1.7.
Antoine Watteau,
Italian Troupe, ca. 1715–16.
Etching. Bibliothèque nationale de France, Paris.

after his own painting to serve as a *modello* for his etching (fig. 1.7).[63] Boucher used Watteau's original, but before he proceeded to etch it, he apparently retouched the sheet, which had been slightly damaged by incisions Watteau had made in order to transfer his work onto the copperplate. (Note in figure 1.5 the changes made in the areas around the mouth and eyes of the actors.) Moreover, the fidelity with which Boucher reproduced every aspect of the original drawing and the exact correspondence between the size of his etching and Watteau's own suggest that he too transferred the design directly onto the plate by reincising the contours.[64] In effect, we witness Boucher's double insertion of himself into another artist's trace, which was first retouched by the younger artist on the original sheet and then retraced on the plate. The *Italian Troupe* thus exemplifies the degree to which Boucher's hand became vital for the visual articulation of Watteau's oeuvre.

Watteau's hand, on the other hand, gained paramount importance in the process of Boucher's own artistic self-definition. The duration of his close engagement in the project is significant. Between 1722–23 and 1727 he was intimately involved with Watteau's work, handling it daily, and, given the number and quality of the sheets he produced, and the pay of 24 livres per day he received (a reasonable income), he was unlikely to have been doing much else.[65] For roughly five years, Boucher's artistic activity consisted, literally, of "working subtly beneath the surface of the other," the process of etching used by him encouraging such peculiar morphological intimacy.[66] One aspect of etching that distinguished it from other reproductive techniques was its subtly dialogical quality: the way in which it required the artist to *insinuate* himself into another artist's trace while allowing him a considerable freedom regarding the precise mode of re-creation. As described by Cochin (in his influential eighteenth-century reedition of Abraham Bosse's treatise), etching involved transferring the original design onto a varnish-coated plate, usually by first rubbing the reverse side of the drawing to be reproduced with a sanguine stick or pencil until its outlines became visible. That side was

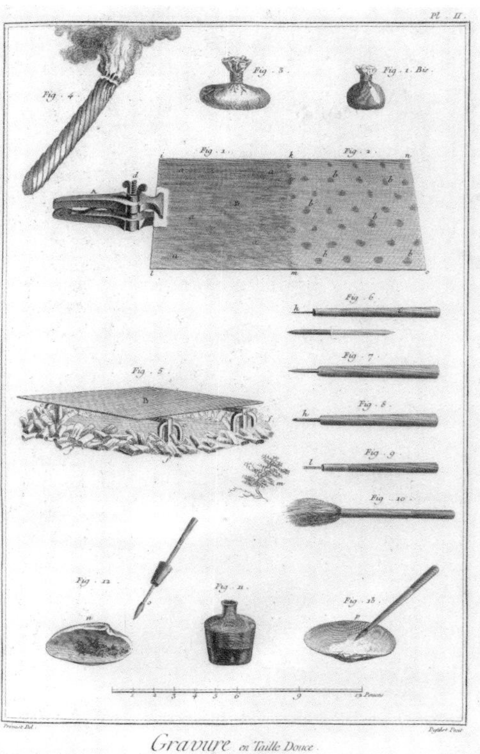

1.8.
Plate II of the entry "Gravure en taille douce," in *L'Encyclopédie, ou Dictionnaire raisonné des sciences, des arts et des métiers*, 1767. Houghton Library, Harvard University.

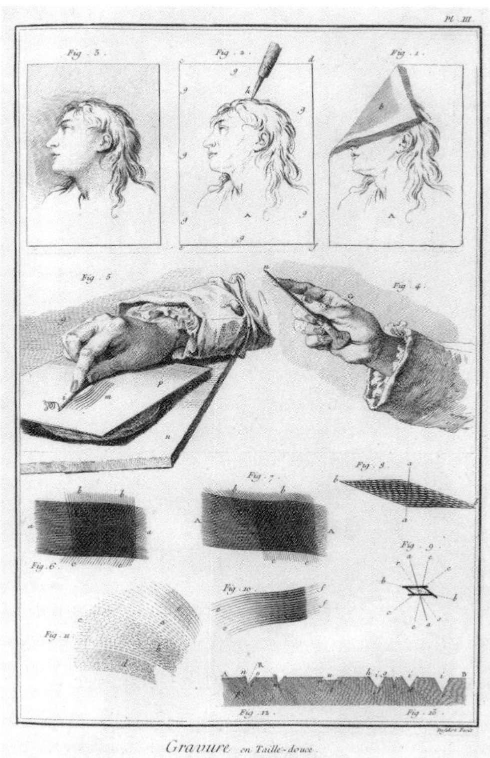

1.9.
Plate III, "Gravure en taille douce," in *L'Encyclopédie, ou Dictionnaire raisonné des sciences, des arts et des métiers*, 1767. Houghton Library, Harvard University.

then applied to the varnished plate and retraced with a blunted needle.[67] The resulting outlines had to be fixed to prevent accidental effacement. This was done by heating up the plate. (The tools used in this process, from etching needles to torch and furnace, are represented on Plate II illustrating the entry on etching in the *Encyclopédie* [fig. 1.8].[68]) As a result of the heat, the greasy sanguine particles melted slightly and fused with the varnish, producing shadowy outlines—phantoms of the original traces—into which one inserted the etching needle, piercing through the layer of varnish and thereby effectively getting *under the skin of the trace*. (This aspect of the procedure is shown in three stages in the upper part of Plate III, fig. 1.9.) Once the design was etched, the plate was submerged in azotic acid (*l'eau-forte*, the French term for the whole procedure), which bit the areas exposed by the needle.

The intense and prolonged exposure to Watteau's art installed a host of motifs, figures, gestures, and poses in the artist's mind, providing him with a visual repertory from which he drew throughout his career.[69] Yet Watteau's effect also worked on a deeper, morphological level, manifesting itself in Boucher's approach to the process of making. First, through repeated limning of someone else's trace, Boucher acquired a certain bodily routine, a *habit of hand*.[70] It allowed him to interiorize not only a stock of images but also another artist's touch. (Remember that tact was then understood to be an acquired quality, not an innate one.) This was not simply a matter of learning to mimic Watteau; it also fostered the development of a new flexibility, mobility, and adaptability in Boucher's own manner through the exercise of his predecessor's touch. Describing Boucher's efficacy and skill in acquitting himself of his task, Pierre-Jean Mariette noted that "his light and lively touch seems to have been made for this job."[71] Indeed, careful examination of Boucher's sheets reveals ample evidence of the deftness of the still young and relatively inexperienced artist with the etching needle. A comparison of Boucher's full-page etching of the *Bust of a Woman under the Hood of Her Mantle* with Watteau's original drawing of it (figs. 1.10 and 1.11) reveals the subtlety of the younger artist's treatment.[72] With great delicacy Boucher translated Watteau's masterful handling of light on the woman's skin into a skein of traces wrapped around her face, including dark spots that in the hands of a less accomplished etcher could easily have become inarticulate blotches.

Moreover, Boucher's repeated reproduction of Watteau's artistic trace amounted to an exercise in aesthetic complaisance, a training in morphological accommodation. Reproductive etching is a particularly suitable medium for this kind of training. Despite the relative freedom of movement it affords the etcher's hand, this mode of reproduction is not as free as drawing on paper.[73] A hand moving a needle through a varnished surface encounters resistance. Moreover, one has to pay close attention to prevent losing track of the original trace. Whether one was following the sanguine stick's contours previously transferred onto the plate and fused with the varnish or, according to another method of image transfer, connecting the dots one had made at the strategic points of the original design (such as those we find in Watteau's drawing of the *Italian Troupe*), the etcher obviously had to proceed at a pace slower than that afforded a draftsman. It is this slight deceleration of touch necessitated by the etching process that, given the extent and scale of Boucher's assignment, must have enhanced the dexterity of his hand and helped develop an unusual receptiveness of his line.[74]

One can speculate that this receptiveness had not only kinesthetic and aesthetic dimensions but a subjective one as well.[75] It may be assumed to have induced a particular kind of artistic self-reflexivity, a recognition of the embeddedness of one's own trace in that of an other, and thus of the trace's always dialogical nature. Reproductive etching renders this aspect the more salient in that the reenactment of another artist's trace is literal—a reproduction. Routinely performed, this act of reproduction may be likened to a psychic operation wherein the etcher's mark is inscribed by a memory-trace, a latent

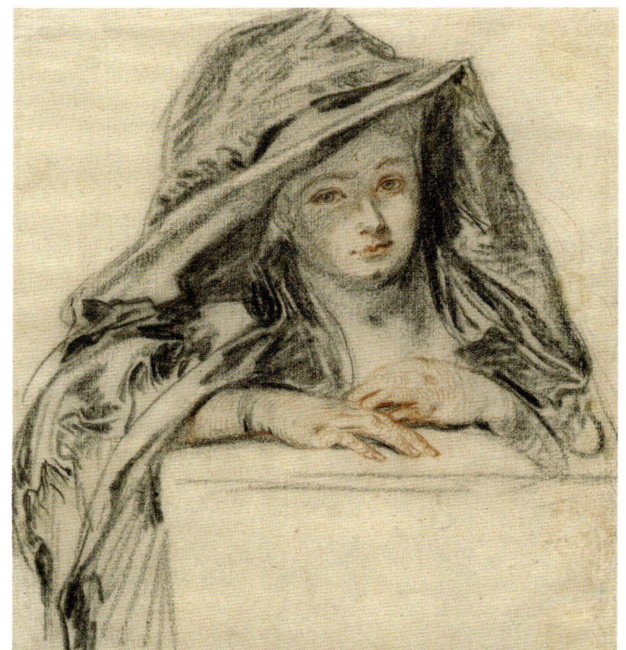

1.10.
Antoine Watteau, *Bust of a Woman under the Hood of Her Mantle*, ca. 1719. Red and black chalk on paper. The Clark, Williamstown, Massachusetts.

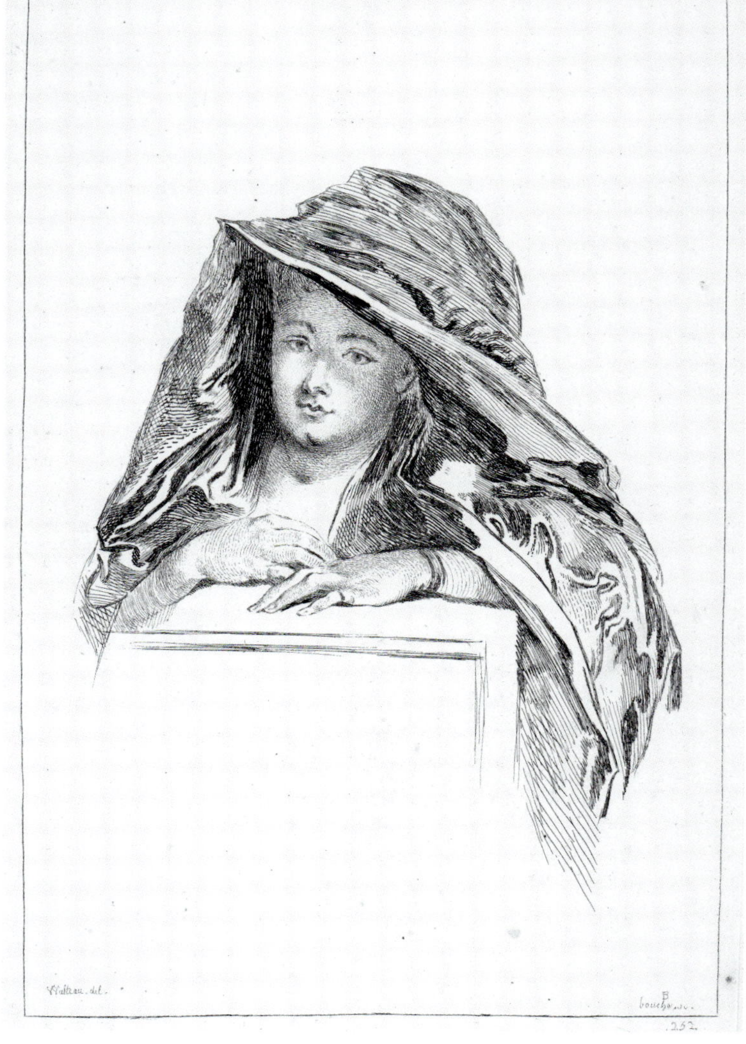

1.11.
François Boucher after Antoine Watteau, *Bust of a Woman under the Hood of Her Mantle*, etching. Musée du Louvre, Paris.

souvenir of another artist.[76] My argument is that the young Boucher's prolonged performance of the quasi-mechanical task of transposition of Watteau's work created the ground for both an aesthetic and psychic transfer: it generated an internal mechanism of self-articulation based in the reciprocation of traces, and made the artist aware of it. In other words, Boucher's discovery of his touch through the process of reproduction of another artist's touch led him to develop an imaginary model of self-identity that was inscribed by alterity.[77] On this level, Boucher's tact is not only the capacity to skillfully—tactfully—transpose someone else's touch, but also an ability to anticipate and recognize an otherness *within one's own*, thus implying a certain measure of distance from it. Prompted by the reproductive process to think of himself as a system of graphic relations, Boucher acquired a capacity for self-abstraction.

This technically grounded self-discovery was related to a lesson of a more general nature that Boucher learned by working on Watteau: a lesson in reproduction as the means of constructing an artistic oeuvre and, through it, of establishing oneself as an author. Jullienne's endeavor not only addressed itself to discerning amateurs and artists; it had a more specific purpose that crystallized in the course of the publication, namely, the construction of a body of work that would stand in for Watteau.[78] Unlike the similar reproductive project of the eminent art collector Pierre Crozat that focused on the artists from the past, the *Receuil Jullienne* was devoted to a single contemporary French artist.[79] It was in order to represent this artist as a modern master, and to convey the specific nature of his achievement as a draftsman, that Jullienne, himself an artist *manqué*, undertook his reproductive project.[80]

Jullienne's preface to the first volume of the *Figures* suggests as much. Explaining his unconventional decision to publish Watteau's drawing studies—a kind of work that was not widely considered to be of interest at the time—Jullienne made the point that these drawings were radically different from the productions of other artists.[81] This novelty had to do with Watteau's idiosyncratic method of working in which detached figure studies, rather than studies of the whole composition, had a preeminent role in constructing an image.[82] Unmoored from their context, Watteau's figures illustrated, in Jullienne's mind, the quintessence of his style and also stood in a special relation to the artist himself. The preface implied that although the drawings illustrated different characters, their style and function pointed to one artistic personality—that of Watteau.

Julliene's publication was a symptom of the larger process of cultural invention of the "author" in this period.[83] Although it was not legally recognized in France until the end of the eighteenth century, the "author" emerged as an increasingly important category in the field of artistic and cultural production.[84] Commercial initiatives such as Jullienne's—and later those of the dealer Edmé Gersaint, who introduced a catalogue raisonné of the artist's oeuvre—performed a key role in this process.[85] At once artistic and commercial, these venues were the very site of elaboration of the new meaning of the artist as the function of his/her work, and, as such, they were the catalysts in the broader process of the cultural invention of authorial personality.

It is precisely as an author that Watteau appears in the frontispiece to the first volume of the *Figures de différents caractères* (fig. 1.12). Etched by Boucher after Watteau's self-portrait, now lost, the frontispiece represents the artist in half figure, holding a *porte-crayon* in one hand and a portfolio of his drawings in the other. As such, Watteau's image performs a demonstrative function—*Ecce auctor!*—but also, implicitly, raises the question of authorship as a matter of the relation between the artist and his work (the portfolio), or between the artist's body, draped in fur-lined coat, and its traces (the porte-crayon). What highlights and complicates this question is the presence of another author—Boucher—who has insinuated himself into this representation through a savvy game of proper names. Thus, underneath the etched image, we find a standard, that is, doubled inscription referring to the division of labor on the print: "Watteau pinxit" on the left, "Boucher sculpsit" on the right. Boucher, however, repeats this pair of signatures *within* the image, placing one on each side of the cover of the portfolio held by Watteau, and thus creating the ambivalent impression that the works contained in the portfolio are of joint authorship.[86]

The quartet of signatures graphically conveys Boucher's eagerness to mark his contribution to Watteau's oeuvre but also his self-consciousness about his own authorial status acquired during this reproductive exercise. The internal repetition of proper names moves the author from the frame into the image itself, that is, from the discursive (legal or commercial) margin of the work—a position of someone who holds the copyright privilege to it—to the position of someone recognizable within the work itself, in its very morphology.[87] Directly involved in the manual fabrication of the image, the author, Boucher suggests, is someone who may therefore be conceived as its *material effect*. Taken together, the signatures represent a specific historical moment in the development of the cultural meaning of the author, a moment in which, besides the notion of authorship as a legal and commercial mechanism (copyright), a sense of the author as a morphological function of his or her work, that is, as an effect of his/her bodily trace, began to emerge.

The very fact that Boucher chose the form of signature to hint at his authorship is telling. At the time when he scribbled his name on the frontispiece, the signature was in the process of acquiring its modern function as an autograph of a person, a unique bodily trace. Although this process has been long in the making—its origins in France, as Beatrice Fraenkel has demonstrated, reached back to the sixteenth century—it was only in the early eighteenth century that the written form of a proper name turned into a fully personalized sign, a mark of an individual.[88] Yet in order to function as a reliable proof of identity, the newly valued signature also entailed a constraint on individuality: one had to always sign in the same way. It was precisely the visual consistency of its written form, its reproducibility, that turned the proper name into a *sign* of individual identity. A product of one's own individual mode of writing, the signature had to acquire legibility, grace, and elegance through training. Writing manuals flourished. The *Encyclopédie* published a separate entry on *écriture* understood as a fine style of mark-making, with a series of plates illustrating the different aspects necessary for achieving it: the proper position to be assumed by the writer, the suitable desk and seat, the appropriate writing implements, as well as the right manner of holding the pen.[89] Illustrations were also provided for the preparatory exercises recommended for the hand to gain a certain kinesthetic fluency (fig. 1.13), for training in writing capital letters, and for developing smooth cursive connections. The adoption of a signature as the preeminent mode of self-identification, and the new emphasis on proper writing style, inaugurated a new understanding of identity based on the idea of the consistency of the self capable of generating reproducible signs through the mastery of its body and hand.[90]

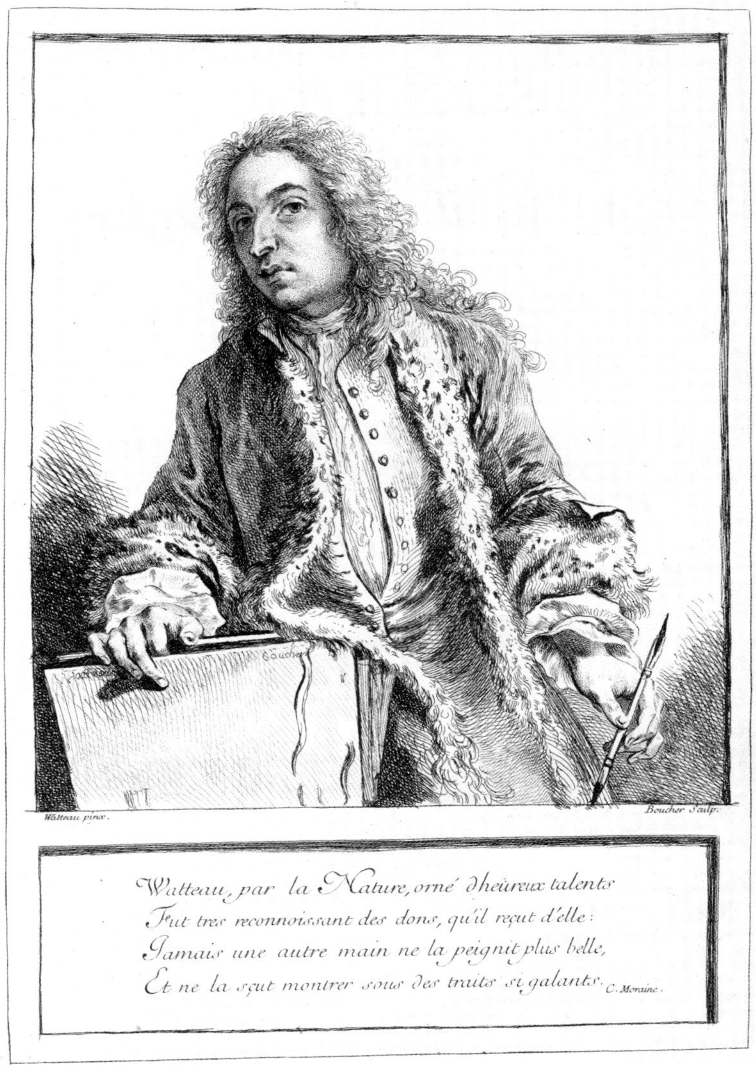

1.12.
François Boucher after Antoine Watteau, *Portrait of Antoine Watteau*, ca. 1735. Frontispiece to *Figures de différents caractères*, vol. 1. Etching. National Gallery of Art, Washington, Widener Collection.

It is exactly such an attempt at self-consistency through the mastery of the hand that we witness in Boucher's tremulous signature scratched inside the frontispiece. Its uncertain, provisional form, as if the hand were still rehearsing a movement about to become a manual routine of the signing self, suggests the young artist's trial to *assume* his trace as the means of self-identification.[91] But the signature's strategic placement on another artist's oeuvre points also to his intuitive recognition of the work itself as a site of identity: a product of the artist's trace that was, in and of itself, understood as a signature, that is, a reproducible sign of a unique, embodied self always already embedded in the trace of another artist. The placement of the signature suggests an understanding of the work, the oeuvre, not as self-same, but as a field of the other, a site of alterity within which the artist must negotiate his place. Thus Boucher's doubling of

1.13.
Exercices Préparatoires, Plate VIII of the entry "Écriture," in *L'Encyclopédie, ou Dictionnaire raisonné des sciences, des arts et des métiers*, 1763. Houghton Library, Harvard University.

signatures on the Watteau "self-portrait" not only challenged (if playfully) Watteau's exclusive rights to the image, it challenged, too, the idea of a single person as the *origin* of the work. It suggested that the field of representation consisted of endlessly reproducible traces without origins and gestured toward recognition of the author as the effect of this understanding of the trace.

Thus, if the *Figures des différents caractères* established Watteau as an author, it also helped Boucher to develop his own distinct sense of authority. The publication also suggests, however, a major difference in the self-understanding of the two artists. Watteau, who never signed his works, defined himself as an artist through the trope of the mask, the perception of identity as a masquerade being repeatedly thematized in his work.[92] For this reason, his elusive art, and the artist himself, have often been associated with the social and cultural ideals of honnêteté.[93] Boucher's success in reproducing Watteau's work, and the souplesse with which he did it, may well be seen as a feat of politesse befitting an artist-gentleman. Yet it is evident that Boucher's tact in this matter amounted to something radically different. His success in the project of reproduction had to do with Boucher's capacity for (self-)abstraction, a capacity to which his whole practice testifies, if in different ways. The suppleness of his fingers—praised, if through inversion, in Panard's quatrain—was predicated on a partial renunciation of identity, a recognition of the image as a field already inscribed by the trace of an other that Boucher declared himself ever ready to assume. The reproduction of Watteau enabled him to develop a sense of his own trace as an authorial sign of a particular kind, forever receptive, always accommodating, a line harboring the memory of another line, a touch inscribed by an other. This is, in sum, how Boucher acquired his tact.

My point is that the artistic importance of the Watteau project for Boucher must be measured not in terms of "influence"—though there is much of it discernible in Boucher's oeuvre—nor in terms of "identification" with the work or with its author, but in terms of its deep morphological impact. The experience of someone else's work allowed the artist to interiorize not only a stock of images but also another artist's touch and, through it, to develop a distinct sense of his own. Moreover, the lesson of Watteau—the lesson of souplesse and of the benefits of reproduction—also prodded Boucher to

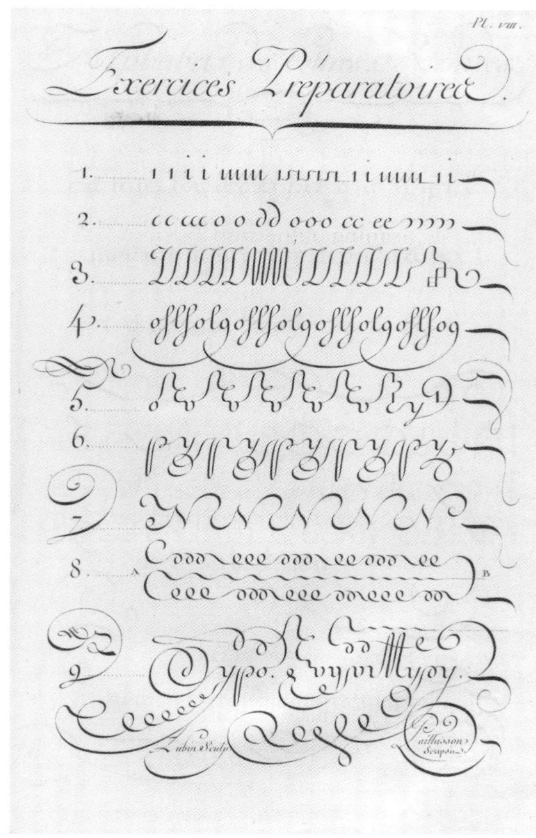

embrace a mode of operation that was different from the one customarily adopted by ambitious artists pursuing an academic career. This was a mode motivated by a concern with self-reproduction in the realm wherein Boucher imagined his place as an artist, not in the narrow precincts of art, but in the wider world of material goods produced by globalized commerce.

THE COMMERCIAL IMAGINATION

For long now this painter has been called a painter of fans.

—Grimm

It has often, and justly, been emphasized how productive, and hard working, Boucher was and how diverse his activities were.[94] He was reported to have worked "more than twelve hours a day from the moment in his childhood when he first picked up pencils until the very end of his life,"[95] and his versatility was both admired and decried by his contemporaries. Thus, in his otherwise effusive obituary of Boucher, Restout spoke in mildly reproachful tones about the artist spreading himself too thinly by taking up the type of assignments—painted overdoors, carriage panels, even the design of the then-fashionable cut-out marionettes—that were not worthy of his talent (fig. 1.14).[96] While Restout blamed the frivolous taste of the time for the unwelcome expansion of Boucher's practice, he also indicated that, aside from financial needs, it was a result of the artist's "too complaisant imagination."[97]

Restout's comment raises the thorny issue of the commercial dimension of Boucher's practice. Part of a wider trend to disregard or condemn this aspect of the artist's work by his contemporaries—a view epitomized by Friedrich Melchior, baron von Grimm's sarcastic dismissal of Boucher as the painter of fans—Restout's remark implies that involvement in commercial design was deemed incompatible with artistic ambition. Such a view was symptomatic of a more general anxiety about the rising importance of the market as a factor in cultural and artistic production at the time, an anxiety that had to do, on the one hand, with ailing official patronage for the arts, and, on the other, the dramatically increased commercial opportunities for circulating visual forms linked to the rising prominence of professional art dealers and the new developments in technologies of reproduction. Because Boucher was one of the most prominent painters of his time *and* one of the most commercially visible artists, he attracted more negative attention than any other artist, becoming a "classic" example of artistic decadence, even for some of his admirers.[98] Thus, in his obituary of the painter, Bret echoed Restout's mildly reproaching argument about Boucher's commercial expansion, though he linked it more directly to the lack of proper patronage of painting, a condition that, in his view, led to the degradation of the arts in general.[99]

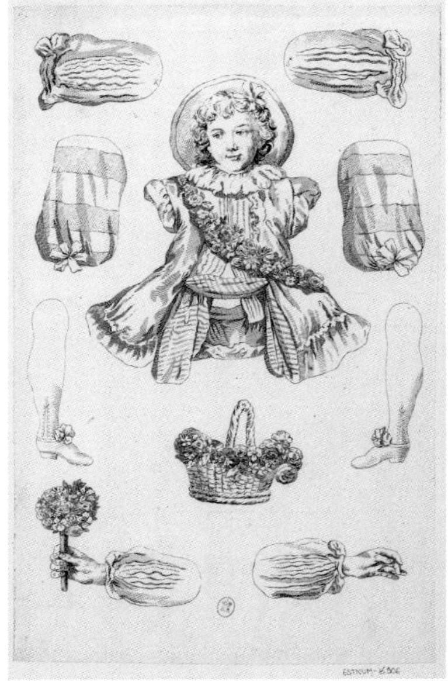

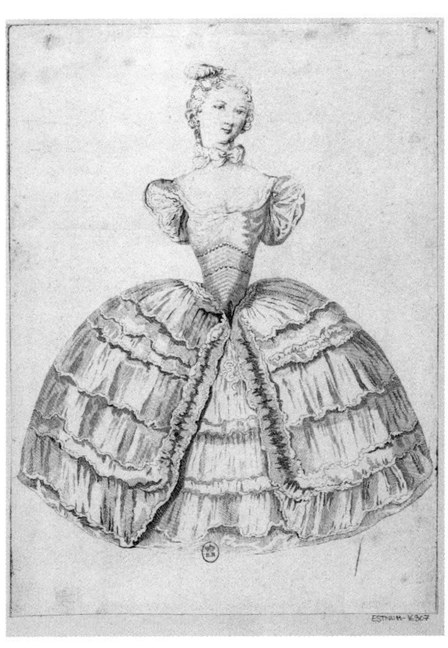

1.14.
François Boucher, designs for cut-out marionettes. Bibliothèque national de France, Paris.

This historical view has long lingered in modern accounts of the painter's work wherein commercial projects, notwithstanding the increased scholarly attention they now receive, tend to be considered as peripheral to his pictorial enterprise.[100] Thus, for example, although our sense of how extensive Boucher's involvement in commercial design was has considerably grown, this knowledge has hardly inflected our understanding of his aesthetic project at large or his artistic identity.[101] Yet even the most cursory view of Boucher's entire output challenges the belief that openly commercially motivated work occupied a marginal position in his output. Throughout his career, Boucher was willing to engage his representational skills, both drawing and painting, in the creation of all kinds of material objects, the amount and diversity of which was in itself uncommon, and he maintained vital connections with the milieu of *ornemanistes* throughout his life.[102] It is not by chance that, in the trade card of the printmaker and dealer Gabriel Huquier, a frequent collaborator of Boucher in diverse publishing venues, his name was ranked not among the painters—Le Brun, Watteau, Van Loo, whose modest quarto volumes were tucked in on the lowest shelf—but among the major decorators of the period, Meissonier, Oppenord, and Lajoüe, represented by the prominently displayed octavos (fig. 1.15).[103]

Whether or not Boucher could indeed be called a *décorateur*, the sheer number of his decorative designs invites us to reassess the relation between these projects and Boucher's practice at large.[104] The fact that the artist persisted in his commitment to the domain of commercial production despite his successful and financially rewarding career as a painter gives us all the more reason to do so. Boucher was not, *pace* Grimm, just a painter of fans, but this epithet raises a question of how to think about the artist's extensive and persistent engagement in the design of commodities and how to understand the role of this engagement in his career and in the development of his self-conception as an artist.

Boucher's entire enterprise could be said to have been *permeated* by the market: it defined his approach to art making as such and its effects were discernable throughout his diverse productions. Moreover, it seems to me that, behind Boucher's artistic expansion and diversification, there was a logic irreducible to the financial gain derived from it. Through commercial repetition, reproduction,

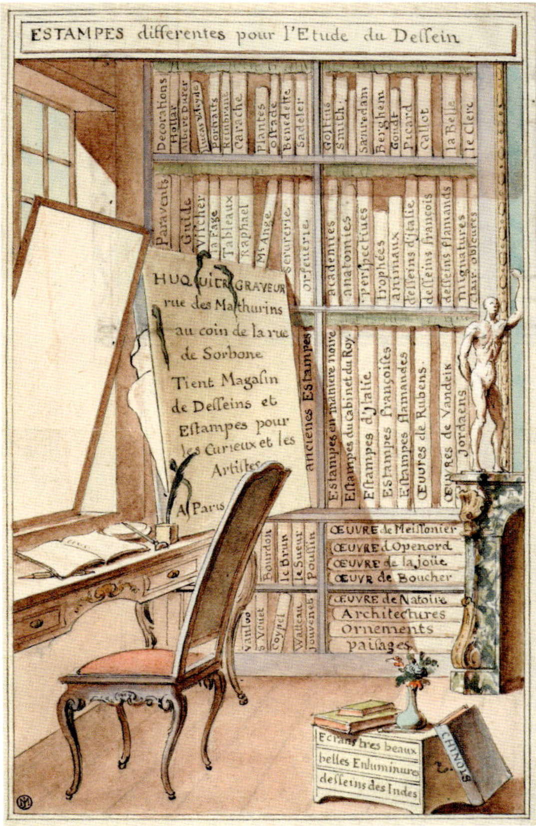

1.15.
Gabriel Huquier, *Project for a Trade Card*, 1749. Pen and brown ink, black chalk, brown wash, and watercolor, with white highlights. École nationale supérieure des beaux-arts, Paris.

and circulation of his work, Boucher enlarged the definition of what constitutes an artist's oeuvre and positioned himself as an artist within a domain exceeding the academically defined category of "art" (without, however, abandoning the latter). In this sense, he brought the lessons gained from his commercial engagement with Watteau's work to another level. Under the rubric of Boucher's name a whole new material realm of goods (not only images) came into being, an effect that, far from being a refraction of Boucher's practice, was inherent in its very aims. It was indicative of the artist's ambition to situate his work, and himself, within the new realm of commercial modernity.

Commerce was in Boucher's times an important sector of human activity but it was also, increasingly, a context that absorbed the entire society, profoundly redefining the modes in which it functioned and imagined itself. One indication of the role of commerce in shaping the collective self-imagination was the double meaning of the term in its eighteenth-century usage: "commerce" referred to buying, selling, and exchanging goods, but also, metaphorically, to social intercourse of all kinds. The stock phrase "*le doux commerce*" which was used at the time to convey both the benefits of trade and a mode of social interaction illustrates the connection between the two meanings.[105] The question is how the increased importance of the commercial model of social functioning affected the way in which artists imagined themselves and their role in society.

Restout's evocation of Boucher's "complaisant imagination" as a factor in the commercial spread of his practice gives us a hint of an answer to this question insofar as it may be taken to suggest the artist's recognition of the market as the condition of artistic existence and functioning. "My taste is to please," Boucher was once reported to have said.[106] While we should not, of course, take such statements at their face value, the phrase indicates not only the artist's willingness to oblige his patrons, but also his readiness to anticipate and respond, as an artist, to a more abstract commercial demand. I am calling this ability a "commercial imagination" in order to emphasize the way in which the market shaped Boucher's practice as an economic and aesthetic principle, to recover, that is, how his tact operated on the commercial register.

Boucher's ability to identify and feed the market for his work, and even for the by-products of his working process, has been recognized and studied by modern scholars. Drawing has been seen as the chief domain in which Boucher exercised this awareness. As it has been established, from the 1730s, Boucher developed an approach to drawing as an autonomous and marketable form of art.[107] This is how one may define the numerous "presentation drawings" produced by Boucher himself after his own work and destined expressly for sale, some of them already framed. The highly finished pastel drawing of the *Boy Holding a Parsnip* (1738) that, rather than being drawn from life (as were Watteau's motifs of this kind), was based on Boucher's own earlier painting of a *Kitchen Maid and a Young Boy*, is one example of the artist's self-pastiching practice(figs. 1.16 and 1.17).[108] A drawing of the *Naiads with a Triton*, based on the figures appearing in the lower right foreground of his tapestry cartoon for the *Rising of the Sun*, is most likely an illustration of a related strategy used by Boucher, namely, his "recycling" of already existing preparatory studies as presentation drawings (fig. 1.18). Fully conscious of the market for such by-products of the working process, the artist would often take a drawing he had originally made as a study and embellish it by adding highlights and other details in order to sell it.[109]

Boucher's habit of reelaborating his own work was related to the increasing vogue for collecting autonomous drawings witnessed in France from the 1740s on.[110] Boucher was an important figure in this phenomenon. He set the trend for exhibiting drawings as independent works of art at the Salon and, among the draftsmen feeding private collections, he was probably the most prolific.[111] The *Naiads with a Triton* belonged to the renowned drawing collection assembled by Barthélemy-Augustin Blondel d'Azincourt, who reputedly owned five hundred sheets by Boucher, and whose wife, Catherine-Charlotte-Edmée de la Haye des Fosses, was also an avid collector of drawings.[112]

This new status of the drawing as a collector's item also entailed an aesthetic adjustment, namely, a change in execution and drawing style. From the 1730s, Boucher began adapting his style to enhance the display quality, or what Beverly Schreiber Jacoby has aptly termed the "wall power" of his drawings.[113] The legibility of forms became the most important objective. To obtain it, Boucher reduced the number of figures, enlarged their size in relation to ground, and used fewer accessories. A red chalk drawing of a *Reclining Nude* whose body has been turned into an elegant arabesque stretching diagonally across the sheet of paper is one early example of this new display-oriented style (fig. 1.19). A later *Reclining Nude*, once in the collection of Catherine the Great, illustrates the development of this style toward even greater figural autonomy and more manifestly bold handling (fig. 1.20).[114] Made expressly to be sold, such drawings were often already framed—or prefabricated as "collector's items"—in the artist's studio. For this purpose, Boucher employed one of the

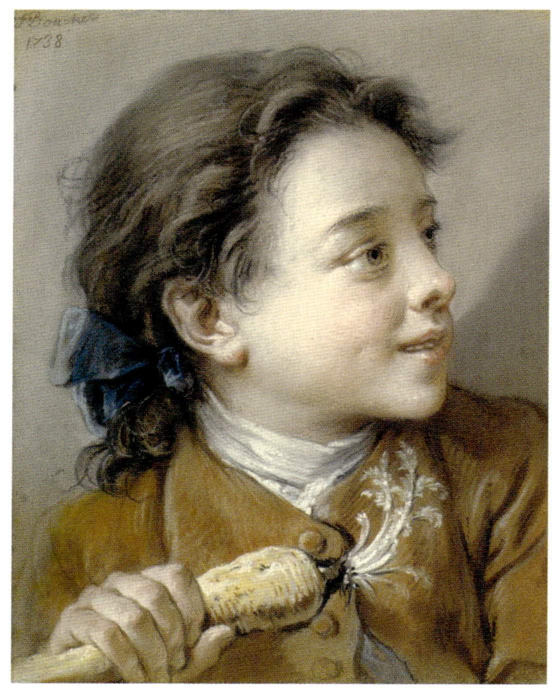

1.16.
François Boucher, *Boy Holding a Parsnip*, 1738. Pastel on buff laid paper. Art Institute of Chicago, Helen Regenstein Collection.

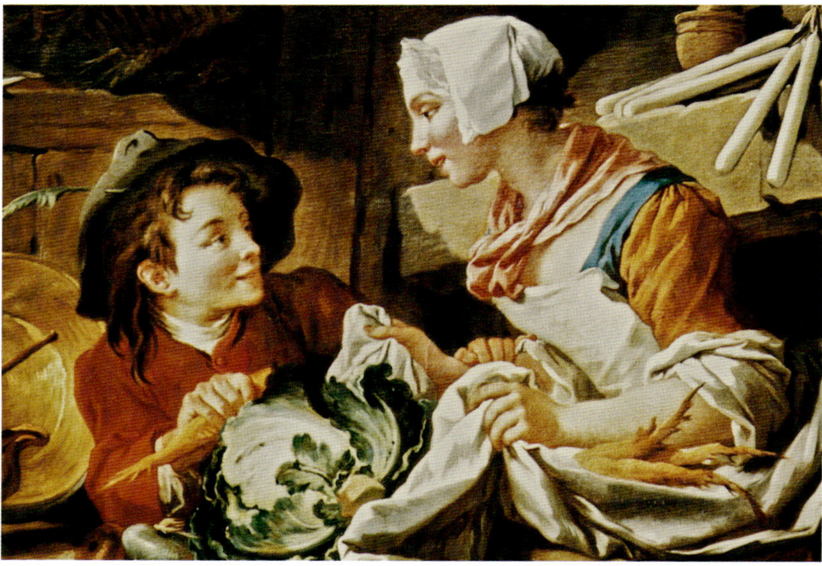

1.17.
François Boucher, *Kitchen Maid and a Young Boy*, 1735. Oil on Canvas. Private Collection.

1.18.
François Boucher, *Naiads with a Triton*, ca. 1750–53. Red chalk, red chalk wash, highlights in white chalk, black chalk, and stumping. Musée du Louvre, Paris.

1.19.
François Boucher, *Reclining Nude*, late 1730s. Red and white chalk on light tan antique laid paper, partial framing lines in black chalk and black ink, laid down. Harvard Art Museums/Fogg Museum, Cambridge, Massachusetts, bequest of Meta and Paul J. Sachs.

1.20.
François Boucher, *Reclining Nude*, 1763. Black, red, and white chalk on tan laid paper. Museum of Fine Arts, Boston, gift of Robert Treat Paine, 2nd.

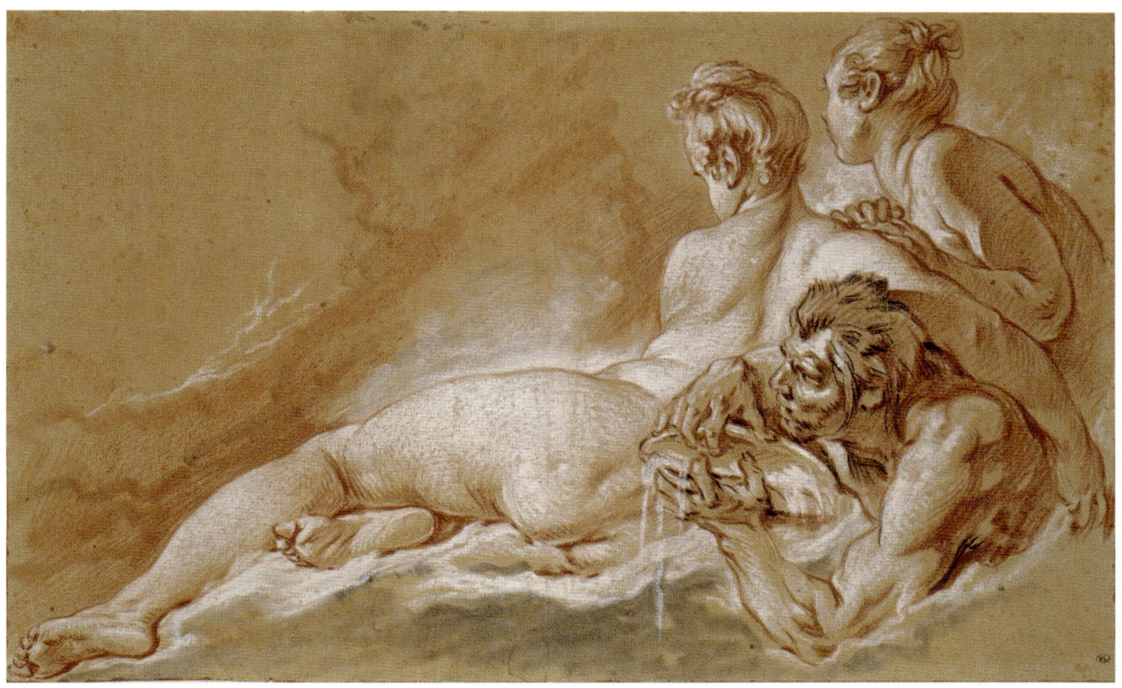

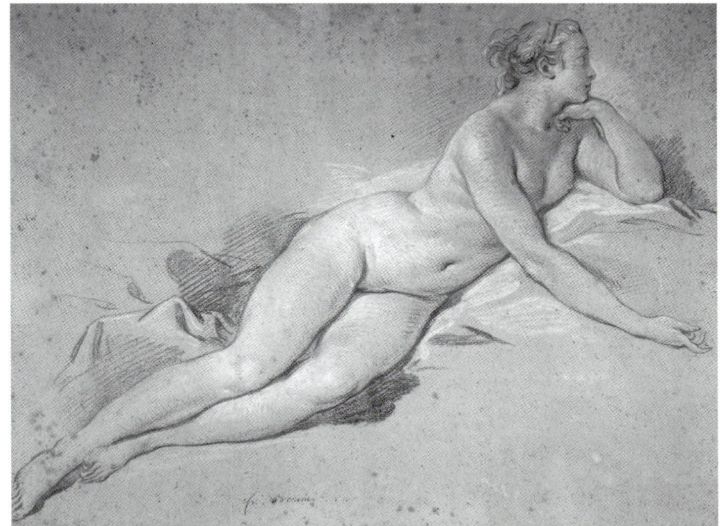

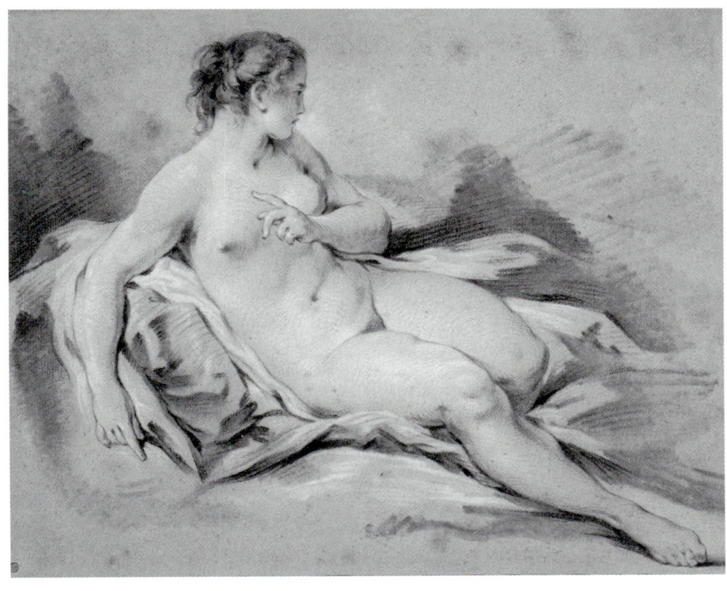

most sought after frame makers of the period, Jean-Baptiste Glomy, whose distinct mounts, with their gold fillets and green tinted borders, enhanced the jewel-like quality of the drawing, signaling the shift in its status from a record of creative process to a decorative object.[115]

By creating drawings for the market, Boucher also generated a demand for these objects, putting pressure on his own production. This is what Bret, among others, hinted at in his obituary of the artist when he mentioned the collectors besieging Boucher's studio in search of works they had seen in other *amateurs*' holdings as the main factor behind the artist's prolific output: the number of Boucher's drawings circulating on the market increased to more than ten thousand.[116] (By contrast, Watteau's entire drawing output has been estimated to comprise only between two to four thousand drawings.[117]) Some drawings, like the *Naiads with a Triton*, were quite elaborate, others less so, being done quickly in an effort to meet the growing appetites of the collectors. One of Boucher's students, Johann Christian von Mannlich, who was in his studio from 1765 to 1768, described the artist occupied with drawing every morning while he took hot chocolate in his *cabinet*. "He could never make enough of these works for the *amateurs* and the dealers who would pay him two *louis* for a piece."[118]

The pressure of demand manifested itself also in the artist's studio practice. As Mannlich, again, reported, the artist routinely asked his students to copy his own drawings that he would then merely retouch—and thus authorize—before selling them as his own.[119] The Hertford House *Triton*, based on the figure in the lower left of the *Rising of the Sun*, that, in its broad treatment simulates rather than achieves modeling of the body, is one example of such studio practice.[120] This approach generated problems, as the note Boucher felt obliged to publish in the *Mercure de France* of May 1755 indicates. In it, Boucher disowned a series of prints produced by his frequent collaborator, the engraver Charles Duflos, and circulating on the market. Purportedly based on Boucher's original drawings, the prints were denounced by the painter as based instead on the second-rate work by his "least advanced pupils, without the participation of the author of these paintings," and he added that he "can neither recognize nor acknowledge his work in such unfaithful copies."[121] The affair speaks to the risks involved in running the studio the way Boucher did. Notwithstanding these problems, Boucher was evidently willing to "share" his trace, an attitude that left his work vulnerable to a potential confusion between the original and a copy. Boucher's embrace of reproductive print for the purpose of disseminating his work was, as Scott has asserted, a clear indication that the artist recognized its potential as a career- and reputation-building tool.[122] Scott and others have documented Boucher's sustained reliance on professional printers, with whom, notwithstanding the episode with Duflos, he collaborated throughout his career. From the 1750s, he entrusted his drawings to Gilles Demarteau, who specialized in crayon-manner engraving, a technique exceptionally well suited for the reproduction of drawings in that it allowed for the imitation of both the color and the texture of the crayon trace, which etching could not provide.[123] Offering a simulation of drawing, it was also relatively inexpensive.[124] Together with two other new techniques, the fully colored engraving, and engraving in pastel manner, mastered by another enterprising print maker, Louis-Marin Bonnet, the crayon manner engraving allowed for the circulation of the facsimile reproduction of the artist's work to a wider market.[125] While both Demarteau and Bonnet practically built their careers as printers on Boucher—the principal provider of the kind of imagery that, as Kristel Smentek has demonstrated, enabled their business to flourish—they, in turn, helped his work acquire a broader commercial appeal and reach a higher degree of recognizability. This entailed some alteration of the artist's original designs. Demarteau modified Boucher's drawings to create more auton-

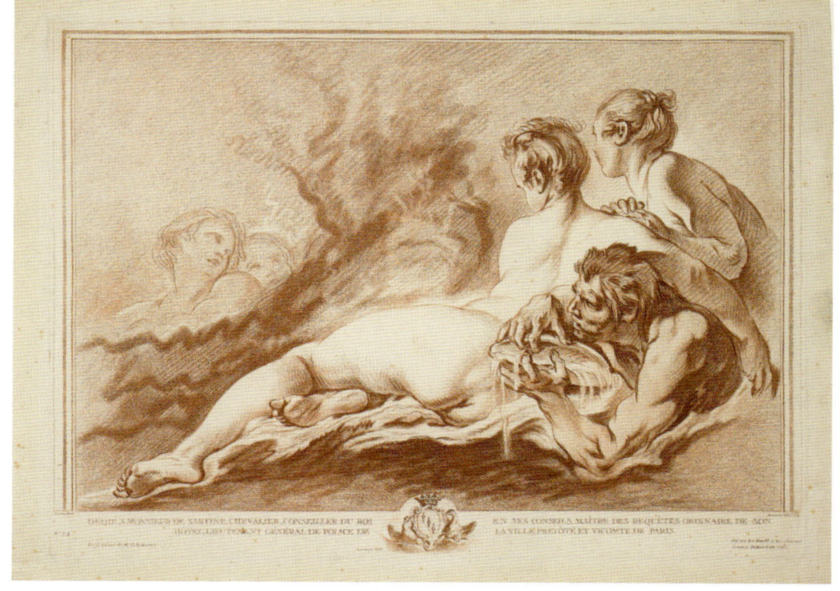

1.21.
Gilles Demarteau after François Boucher, *Naiads with a Triton*, ca. 1761–62. Crayon manner engraving. Musée du Louvre, Paris, Rothschild Collection.

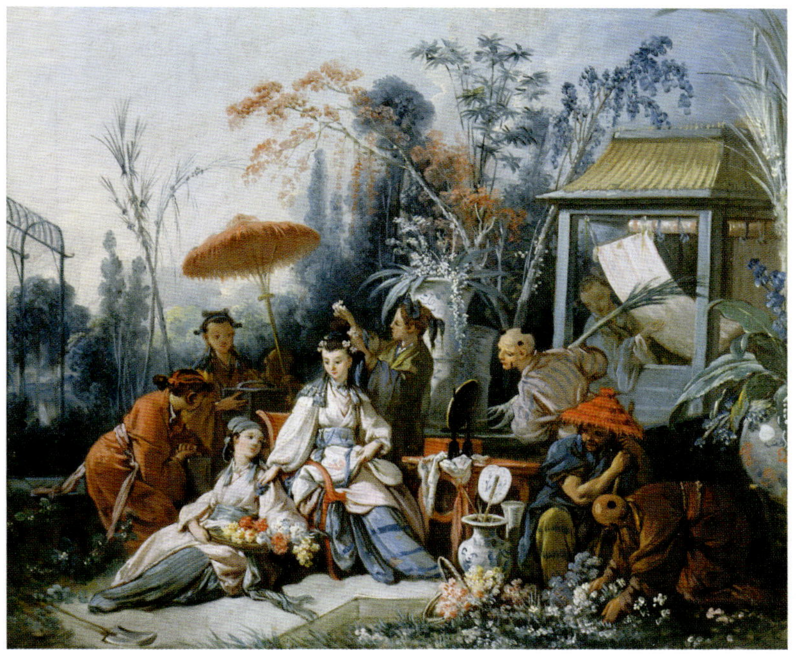

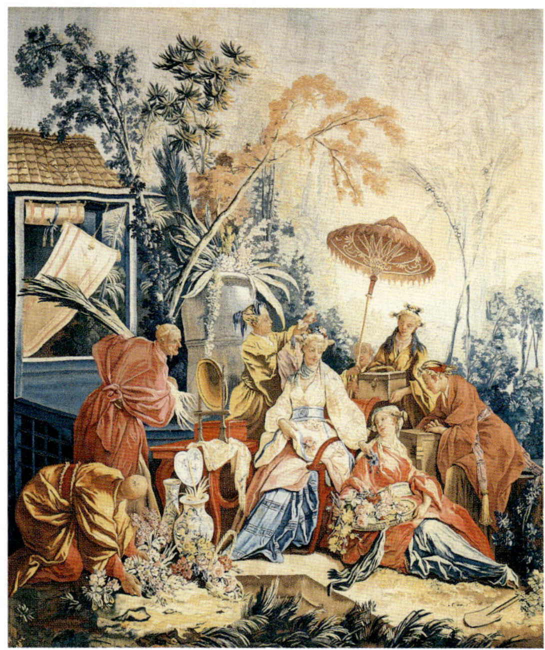

1.22.
François Boucher,
The Chinese Garden,
design for Beauvais tapestry manufactory. 1742.
Musée des Beaux-Arts et d'Archéologie, Besançon.

1.23.
The Chinese Garden,
Beauvais tapestry after design by François Boucher. 1743–53.
Palazzo Reale, Turin.

omous compositions suitable for the print market: he added two figures looming in the background and altered the shading in his widely reproduced print of the *Naiads with a Triton* (fig. 1.21; see fig. 1.18).[126] Similarly, Bonnet, advertising his pastel simulation of Boucher's *Flora*, suggested that it was, in a sense, an improvement on the original.[127] That Boucher entrusted his work to these printers and accepted their revisions indicates he was not only well aware of the advantages of reproduction as the means of propagating his work but also open to the contribution of others to the formation of what was widely received as his style and oeuvre.[128]

The point about Boucher's self-marketing strategies may be extended to incorporate not only the artist's expressly self-reproductive practice in drawing and prints but also other kinds of artistic activities of a more or less openly commercial nature, and the different mediums he embraced, that allowed him to circulate his touch in the much broader domain of things. The very beginnings of Boucher's career were commercial. His first employment, by Jean-François Cars, was for the design of thesis prints and book illustrations, and his second most significant early employment was the work he did for Jullienne.[129] Long after Boucher had made a name for himself as an academic painter, however, he continued employing his pen and brush in diverse commercial projects. Although other artists too engaged in commercial design, the scope and extent of Boucher's activities were unusual.

He produced designs for the tapestry manufacture at Beauvais, where his complex, multifigured compositions on mythological, exotic, and pastoral subjects defined the artistic profile of the establishment between 1734 and 1755 (figs. 1.22 and 1.23).[130] He also worked for the Gobelins manufactory of which he became the artistic director (*surinspecteur sur les ouvrages*) in 1755, a position that gave him the opportunity to exert aesthetic influence over, if not to dominate, the entirety of French tapestry production for roughly thirty years.[131] Boucher's involvement in porcelain design was equally important in quality and scope. His models were vital for the development of the French porcelain manufactories at Vincennes and Sèvres, and his aesthetic influence has been judged all pervasive.[132] The multiple purposes of Boucher's designs are illustrated by his *Little Gardener*, which served as the model for a biscuit sculpture of *Le Jeune Suppliant* and for painted decoration on a tea service.[133] Boucher's name became synonymous with a certain aesthetic that defined French porcelain in the late eighteenth century, a phenomenon epitomized by the commercial term "*goût Boucher*" used in the eighteenth-century sales catalogs of the Sèvres products.[134]

Theater design was another domain to which Boucher contributed significantly, designing for the Opéra, with which he was involved repeatedly—from 1737 to 1739; 1744 to 1748; and again from 1761 to 1766, when he became the Opéra's artistic director—and for the popular venues, the Opéra comique

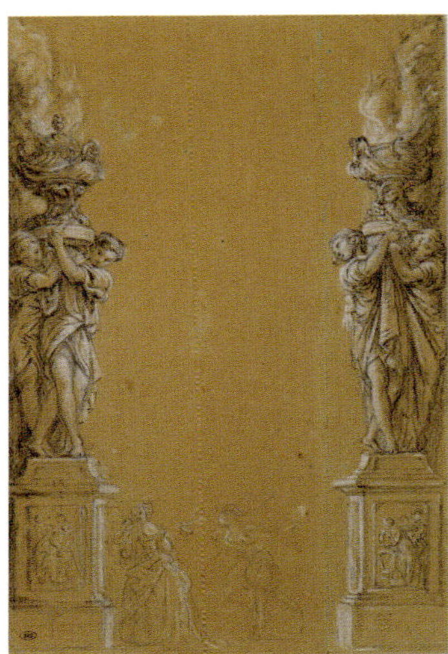

and the Théâtre de la Foire, with which he was involved on at least three documented occasions between 1743 and 1754.[135] A design preserved at the Musée d'Art et d'Histoire in Narbonne illustrates the initial stages of this type of work (fig. 1.24).[136] Last but not least were designs for diverse decorative objects and ornaments published in compendia, many of them by Huquier. Such were the two volumes of the *Recueil de Fontaines*, projects for fountains based on drawings commissioned from Boucher and published in 1736 and 1738 by Huquier.[137] There were designs for screens (fig. 1.25); for cartouches (fig. 1.26); for vases; for decorative clocks; and for fans, such as the elaborate design for a fan leaf with a mythological scene, *Bacchus and Ariadne*, now at the National Gallery of Canada (see fig. 1.29).[138] A number of designs for funeral monuments indicate Boucher ventured into this domain as well.[139] Finally, there are a number of miscellaneous decorative designs, published individually or in series, such as the *Suite de Cinq Sens* and *Suite de Quatre Elements*, which he had executed for Huquier, and *Les Delices de l'Enfance*, published by Audran in 1742.[140]

The scope and ambition of Boucher's designing endeavors clearly indicate that the artist systematically and self-consciously employed his talent in the design of desirable things, seeking to position himself as an artist in the emergent culture of consumption. The term refers to both the economic condition tied to the increased circulation of luxury and consumer goods in eighteenth-century France and the concomitant shift in the ways in which French society functioned and conceived itself. It describes a moment in which the entire society, not only elites, came increasingly to depend on material possessions and when the idea of possession itself became a key factor in social and cultural self-definition, collective and individual, social and psychological.

Paris was the center of an explosion in luxury consumption. The luxury trades had thrived in the capital city since the sixteenth century due to the growing affluence of its inhabitants, the dense concentration of artists and artisans, and its abundant labor force. But it was in the eighteenth century that the market for luxury came to prevail in the city's economy, generating new modes of consumption and new desires for consumer goods.[141] The luxury trades that flourished in Paris and its environs at the time—weaving, porcelain manufacture, gold- and silversmithing, clock making, bookbinding, and the manufactures of objects for interior decoration or intimate use, such as screens and fans—were precisely those for which Boucher provided his designs.

As many scholars have recognized, the proliferation of available goods irreversibly altered the relation between people and objects, generating the new habits—and the new ethics—of conspicuous consumption, including the consumption of art.[142] New buying patterns emerged that signaled the taste for novelty and luxury spreading within a wider social spectrum. That the society as a whole experienced a consumer revolution was not lost on contemporary commentators. Voltaire in his eulogy on luxury

1.24. LEFT
François Boucher, *Design for Theater Animated by Figures*, ca. 1760. Black and white chalk. Musée d'Art et d'Histoire, Narbonne.

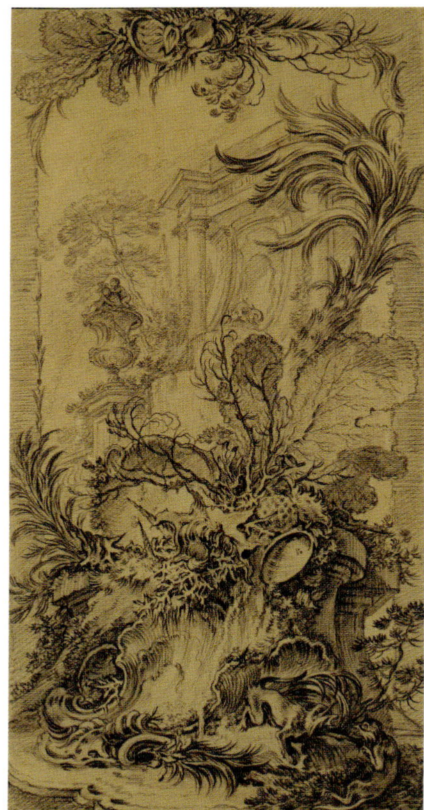

1.25. BELOW LEFT
François Boucher, *Rocaille*, design for *Nouveaux Morceaux pour des paravants*, published in 1737. Black chalk on brown paper. École nationale supérieure des beaux-arts, Paris.

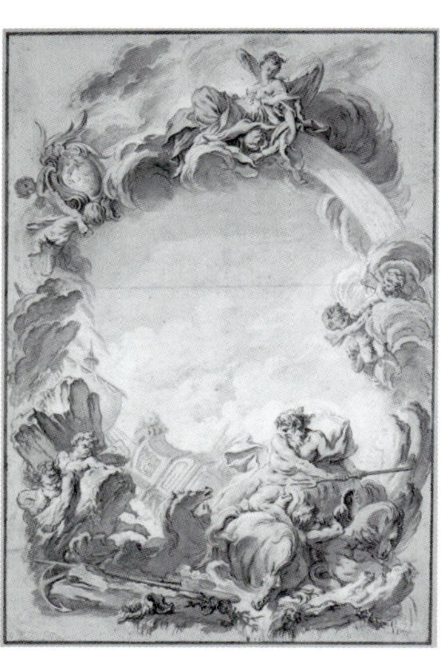

1.26. BELOW RIGHT
François Boucher, *Neptune's Chariot*, ca. 1735–36, design for *Livre de cartouches Inventés par François Boucher, Peintre du Roi.* Albertina, Vienna.

1.27.
The Grape Eaters, Vincennes porcelain manufactory, likely after design by François Boucher, 1752. Biscuit porcelain. Musée nationale de Céramique, Sèvres.

1.28.
François Boucher, *Autumn Pastoral*, 1749. Oil on canvas. The Wallace Collection, London.

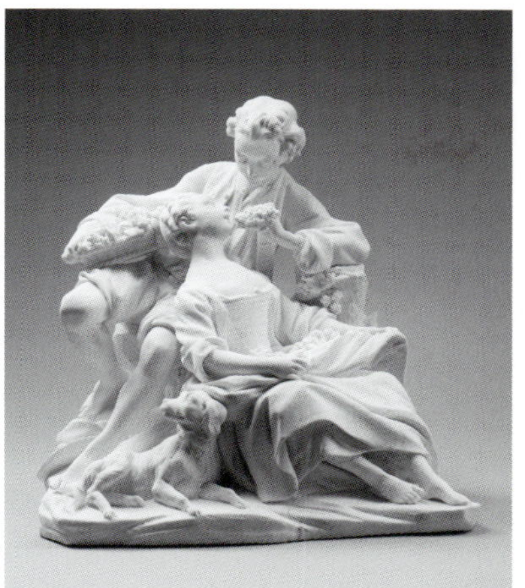

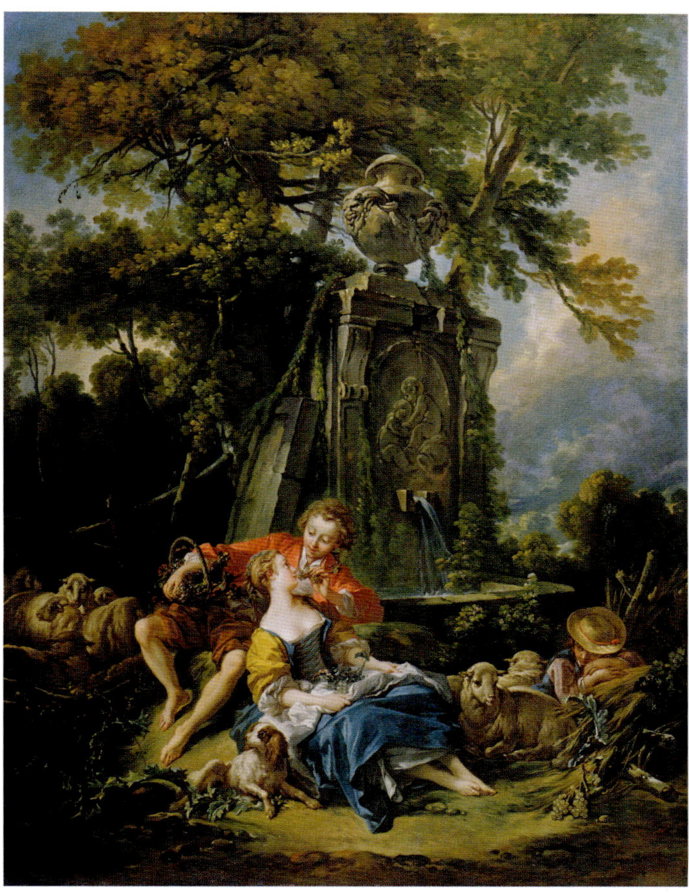

written in 1736, observed: "Thus one sees in England and in France, by hundred channels circulating abundance. The taste of Luxury enters all (social) ranks."[143]

The proliferation and circulation of objects inevitably changed ways of living but also the symbolic meaning of the usage of things.[144] The appearance of *populuxe* and semiluxury items and the circulation of secondhand luxuries not only blurred the distinction between ordinary and luxury consumption but also contributed to the confusion of social signs that produced, in turn, a gradual erosion of social distinctions.[145] The spread of consumption marked the advent of what Daniel Roche has called the "culture of appearances," referring not only to the new mode of dressing as a representation of a new system of values but also to the emphasis on display and performance as a pervasive social phenomenon. The theatricalization of society and of the individual rooted in the practices of consumption was one of the key issues in contemporary critiques of commercial modernity.[146]

Another key aspect of the culture of consumption was the increasing commercialization of culture itself. To an unprecedented degree, culture in the eighteenth century began to appear as something to be had for money, and its forms, venues, and the media through which it was disseminated spoke of its commodified status with increasing clarity and eloquence.[147] The way in which rococo as a new elite style of interior decoration was transformed through print reproduction into a widely disseminated commodity is a key example of this process.[148] If rococo was indeed a "modern taste," it was because of its immersion in the marketplace, a quality recognized by its promoters and critics alike.[149]

Boucher was the major contributor to the new world of goods, his designs being used for both ends of the consumption spectrum: for high-class, expensive luxury products, such as tapestries and snuff boxes, and for such semiluxuries as fans.[150] What is most important, his commercial endeavors were inseparable from his artistic practice at large. There are many examples of the interconnections between Boucher's painting and commercial designs. As the *Grape Eaters* biscuit statuette of 1752 based on a design—most likely Boucher's own—focused on the central group in his *Autumn Pastoral* (1749) indicates, the artist had no qualms about adapting motifs from his large-scale paintings for decorative purposes (figs. 1.27 and 1.28).[151] Nor did he shy away from "recycling" his high-end designs for smaller and more affordable objects; for example, he reused the composition of *Bacchus and Ariadne* from his tapestry cartoon for the Beauvais series of the *Loves of the Gods* in his design for a leaf fan (figs. 1.29 and 1.30).[152] Nothing, though, better illustrates Boucher's self-consciousness about these interconnections than his *Chinese Gallant* (fig. 1.31), a painting *en camaïeu bleu* that simulates a commercial object, a porcelain tile. Epitomizing the deliberate elision of the distinction between "high" and "low," the work flaunts the contrast between its considerable size—a format of the large cabinet picture or a mid-size history painting—and its technique of the small-size ornamental tiles, between its elaborate frame normally used for paintings and the purely decorative use-object it contains. Putting both genre painting and the decorative object in quotation marks, this work conveys an idea of repetition and the interchangeability of designs within different—and reversible—modes of practice, a kind of cross-fertilization that challenged the sense of discrete material and cultural status of the products of Boucher's hand. As such, it indicates that, beyond the models made expressly for manufacture, the artist conceived of none of his work as exempt from reproduction and dissemination in other mediums. Boucher's repeated reuse and recirculation of motifs within his own output signals his embrace of novelty and variety, the key qualities of commercial wares, as the paramount principles of his own production. What this circulation of motifs also indicates is the self-consciousness of the artist

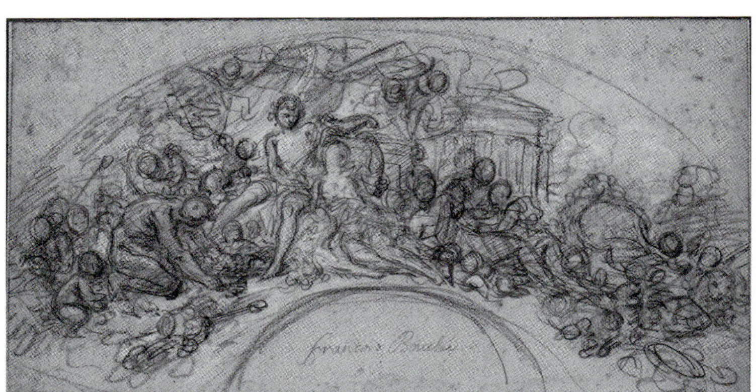

1.29.
François Boucher, *Bacchus and Ariadne*, design for a fan, ca. 1749. Red, white, and black chalk on laid paper. National Gallery of Canada, Ottawa.

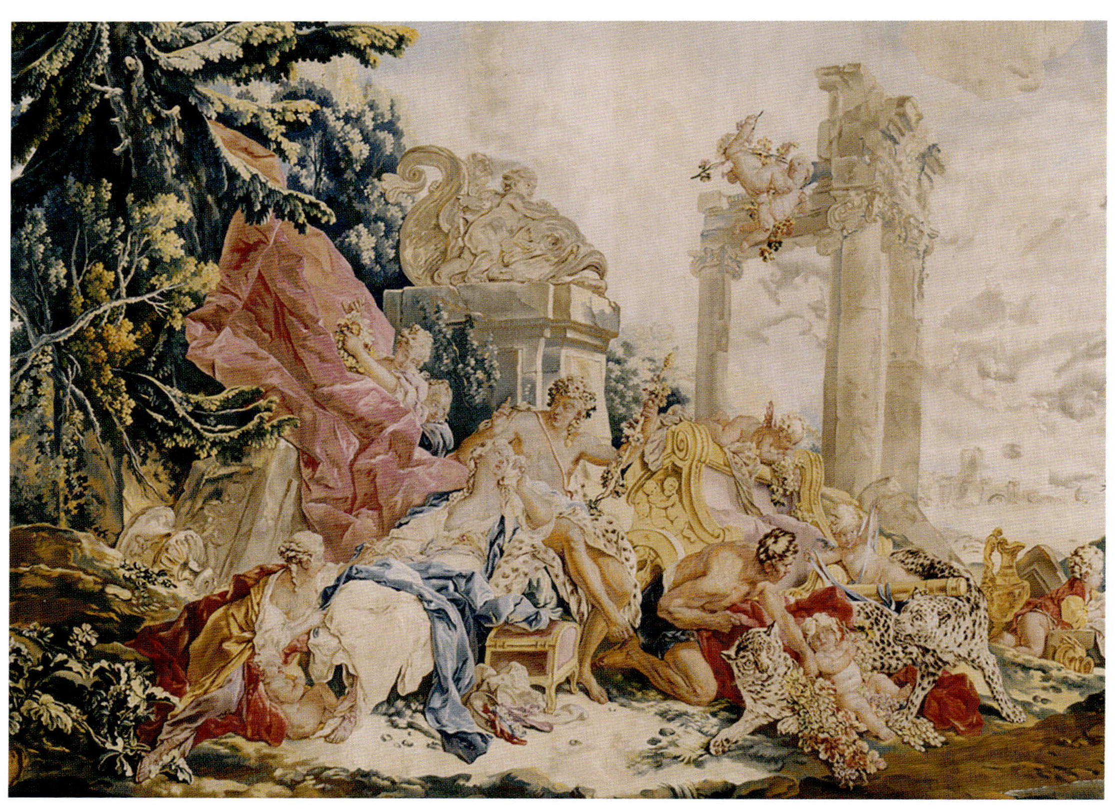

1.30.
Bacchus and Ariadne, Bacchus Transformed into Grapes, from the *Loves of the Gods* series, Beauvais tapestry, woven after a cartoon by François Boucher, 1748–70. Wool and silk, linen interface, and cotton lining. The J. Paul Getty Museum, Los Angeles.

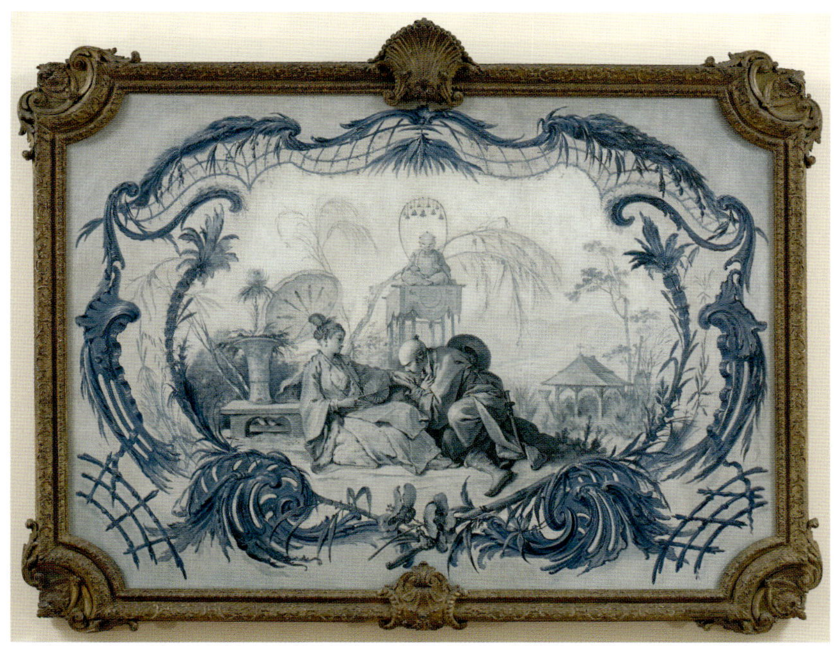

1.31.
François Boucher, *Chinese Gallant*, ca. 1742. Oil on canvas. The David Collection, Copenhagen.

as their producer, a fact made conspicuous in the *Chinese Gallant*. Through their mobility within his practice, these motifs established a network of interconnections across different forms and media, a web spun by the same hand and pointing to the intermedial persona of the author.

Boucher's contribution to the dissemination of the *goût rocaille* has frequently been acknowledged, but it has not been recognized that he self-consciously strove to construct *himself* as a *goût* or a style.[153] Yet it seems to me that Boucher's frenetic productivity was motivated by a desire to reproduce the artist himself, to paraphrase Bret, "in a thousand different forms."[154] Spreading his forms and motifs across several domains at once, Boucher's design practice was an instrument of commercial self-reproduction. It entailed, though, reproducing oneself in a specific way, as a system of traces recognizable across a wide spectrum of things, an abstraction identifiable with a specific individual—a visual style that came to function like a signature. Diderot referred only to Boucher's pictorial practice when he observed that the painter's style of execution was so much his own that it was unmistakably recognizable even in a fragment of a painting. However, this is, effectively, a description of the effect that made Boucher identifiable not only in paintings and drawings but also in the wider domain of objects. From his hand emerged a blueprint for an entire material realm of luxury and semiluxury commodities—and a consistent aesthetic of the thing as a delightful possession—bearing his stamp. It is thus that Boucher himself came to function as a style—the "goût Boucher," as the advertisements for Sèvres porcelain put it—and that his entire commercial production could be understood as his oeuvre, a kind of authorial manufacture.[155]

This is, let us note, different from saying Boucher's practice amounted to a kind of exquisite craftsmanship, a view epitomized by Georges Brunel's observation that "Boucher made pictures like a cabinetmaker makes furniture."[156] What differentiated the artist was precisely this expansive authorial ambition that pointed toward a new kind of commercially grounded aesthetic individualism, a self-consciousness about style as a form of representation of an individual, if in a specific, abstracted sense. Boucher's mobility across different materials and mediums and his reliance on the reproducibility of his forms, emphasized by Scott, distinguished him from a traditionally understood artisan working, as did a cabinetmaker, in a single medium.[157]

If Boucher's artistic imagination was, as Restout claimed, "complaisant," it was because it was commercial, in a specific sense. It implied the artist's capacity to imagine his work—and to conceive of himself as an artist—on an arena broader than the sphere of either pictorial or artisanal production, in a realm of circulation and exchange of the new kind of desirable objects that redefined the contours of social and individual experience. Such capacity entailed a very different mode of artistic operation from that determined either by the structures of traditional patronage or by official artistic institutions, such as the Academy. It called for a recognition of one's place as an artist in a shifting, unpredictable field of expectations defined by an other—the consumer—a category far less specific than an individual patron, or the state, and less articulated or knowable than the Salon public. The commercial artist had to be able to imagine the consumer his or her product was likely to attract, and, to some degree at least, foresee the subjective level at which this product would be received, and which it would have to solicit—the level of desire and fantasy. In other words, the work itself had to anticipate the subjective taste—the desire and fantasy—of this "other."

This is what Boucher's design practice makes evident, what it represents besides and beyond the immediate use-function of his individual designs. What we see repeatedly manifest in the very structure of his projects is the artist's willingness to draw *for an other*, to provide outlines for someone else's work, as Watteau once provided for him, or for something else—a tapestry, a vase—to materialize within these outlines. This inclination to *share* the visual field with an other amounts, though, not only to the literal sense of preparing the ground for another artist or craftsman, be it a printmaker or a porcelain painter, to execute, reproduce, or fill in his design, but also to an ability—at once aesthetic and subjective—to anticipate the imaginary addressee of his products. The empty frames, such as those Boucher designed for the *Livre des Cartouches* published by Huquier, the frontispieces awaiting inscription, may in their very form be taken as a representation—an allegory—of this ability (see fig. 1.26). They announce themselves structurally as a field of expectation for someone or something that will use, complete, and/or give sense to it. Behind many of Boucher's projects, such as those for fountains and screens, there was no specific patron or specific occasion for which these forms were intended but rather an abstract idea of demand for such forms, or their potential marketability. Such designs may be taken as illustrations of a more general principle of accommodation that links Boucher's multifarious productions and is built in the very structure of his work, part and parcel of its morphology and its function.

Boucher's designs testify to a certain model of sociability associated not only with the culture of consumption but also to the form of subjectivity that went with it. "Drawing for an other" is not unlike "dressing for an other" and analogous manifestations of the investment in display characteristic of the culture of appearances.[158] Repeatedly setting the stage for its invisible consumer, Boucher's work represents a form of consumer subjectivity that is rooted in the performance, a self that operates in, and depends on, the social theater of another person's opinion or gaze. This capacity for solicitation and accommodation of an other, in multiple senses of the term, constitutes the general principle that linked Boucher's multifarious production. Thus, far from constituting the margins, however lucrative, of his artistic practice, design offered Boucher an arena on which to exercise his most significant talent, namely, his tact. Tact must be recognized, therefore, as at once a commercial and a subjective strategy, one that served to accommodate others—clients, consumers, the market—but also Boucher himself. It was a matter of complaisance understood not as a gratuitous act of politesse but as a vital strategy for professional and personal functioning. As an artist, Boucher himself is that modern subject, who, as Rousseau was to put it, "knows how to live in others," who thrives in the others' gaze or trace—that of his engravers, publishers, collectors, but also the consumers of the objects shaped by his designs.

There was, however, a double edge to Boucher's brilliant exercise of tact in his design projects, his works' capacity to anticipate and accommodate the other being ambivalently accommodating of himself. Some projects speak to it more eloquently than others. Boucher's designs for cartouches and frontispieces, with yawning voids at their center, may also be seen as indirect self-representations of their producer: not as an enigma (the master trope of Watteau's oeuvre) but as an abstraction, which verges on disappearance. The costs of representing and disseminating oneself through such forms become most evident in Boucher's *Group of Children around a Drapery*, a drawing for the frontispiece to the volume of his own designs as engraved by Pierre Aveline, where the name "Boucher" appears like a ghost, barely inscribed in the empty field of the cartouche (fig. 1.32).[159] Its faint appearance suggests the cartouche as the *phantomic* image of Boucher—his invisibility as a mercurial subject of his productions.

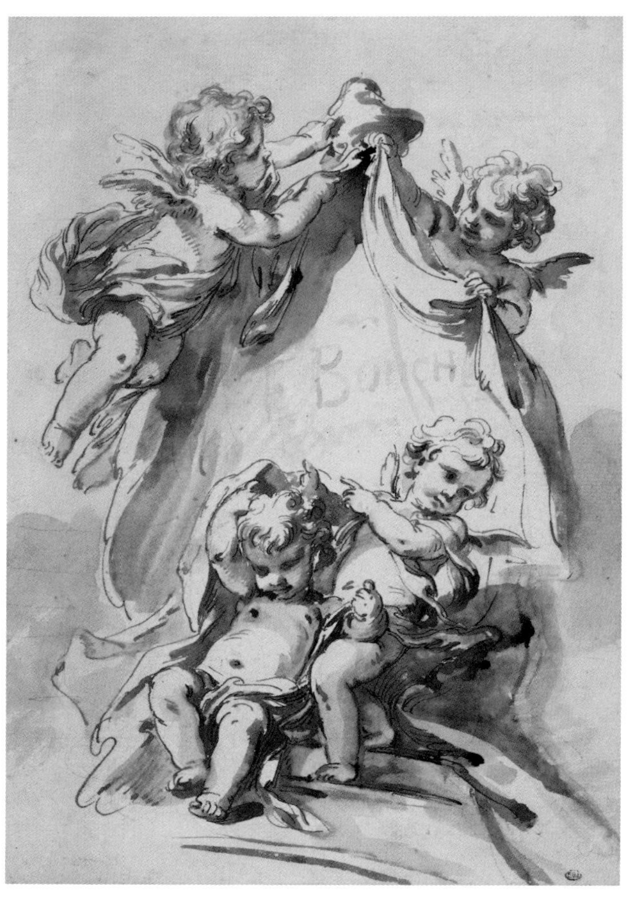

1.32.
François Boucher, *Group of Children around a Drapery*, design for frontispiece to the *Premier Livre de Groupes d'Enfants*, ca. 1735–40. Pen and brown ink, brown wash, over black chalk. École nationale supérieure des beaux-arts, Paris.

PERSONAL MYTHOLOGIES

But if luxury is to become personal, materialistic luxury, it must be predicated on an awakened sensuousness.

—WERNER SOMBART, Luxury and Capitalism

How an artist could employ his skills in designs for an increasingly commercialized society is evident. But how was one to *paint* in the era of consumption? A series of large-scale mythological paintings produced by Boucher for the Parisian lawyer François Derbais offers an instructive answer. Executed between 1732 and 1734 for the billiard room of Derbais's *hôtel particulier* on rue Poissonnière, these paintings illustrate the boldness with which Boucher sought to situate himself as an aspiring artist in the commercial culture of modernity.[160] Much indicates that Boucher used this commission, which he may have instigated, as a shortcut to the public arena after he returned from Italy, when, awaiting admission to the Academy as a full member, he was eager to make himself known.[161] Mariette reported that Boucher's desire for recognition was so strong that he would have painted these canvases for nothing.[162] Another commentator, Papillon de la Ferté, asserted that "these ingenious compositions attracted a throng of admirers, who publicized the talents of the young artist."[163] Whether, as some scholars have suggested, the painter wished to attract the attention of other potential private patrons, or, alternatively, to seek state commissions from the tapestry manufactories, the Derbais paintings signal that Boucher was able to recognize, perhaps even create, a career-launching opportunity for himself, rather than simply counting on institutional protection (a lesson he may have learned from winning the Prix de Rome without actually getting the travel funds stipulated by the prize).[164] Moreover, they suggest his recognition of the commercial potential for his art, which, far from causing a deterioration in quality imputed later by some of his critics amounted to a significant aesthetic innovation.[165]

Not much is known about François Derbais, except that he was the son of a sculptor, Jérôme Derbais, from whom he had inherited a small fortune, that he was a lawyer—an *avocat au Parlement*—and that he owned a collection of paintings.[166] Because of his relative anonymity, and because, as the contemporary sources indicate, Derbais most likely did not commission the paintings but rather accepted Boucher's offer, one may well think of him as a consumer of art rather than a patron, that is, a surrogate for the idea of individual commercial demand rather than someone actively engaged in defining the program of the commission. It is also relevant that due to the expansion of commerce in luxury goods and the social spread of consumption, the *hôtel particulier* had lost its status as a strictly aristocratic building type, and townhouses such as Derbais's were becoming consumer's abodes par excellence.[167] They were being perceived, above all, as representations of an individual (*un particulier*), whose identity was articulated through consumption. The Poissonnière district (le Faubourg Poissonnière) where Derbais's hôtel was situated, was one of the new areas of the city where the building of such dwellings began to flourish in the first decades of the eighteenth century and continued to the century's end.[168]

The shift in perception of the building left its mark on its form, as the representation of social distinction became less important than the expression of the owner's individuality. Interior planning became more particularized, evidencing a greater variety and greater specialization of rooms.[169] Emphasis on comfort, privacy, and the individualization of space, even spatial idiosyncrasy, became most important as the building increasingly strived for the architectural definition of its owner as a person. Although we do not possess adequate information about Derbais's dwelling to have a clear idea of its appearance, the very mention of the "billiard room" in his posthumous inventory indicates a functional division of rooms typical of modern individuated dwellings.[170]

The painting and decoration of such rooms were crucial for their functional definition, thus turning the hôtel particulier into a new field of commercial opportunity and competition for both artisans and artists. The stakes were high, in part because of the promise of high profits such a decorating assignment provided. As the historian Michael Stürmer has pointed out, by the 1780s, when the boom for luxurious townhouses in Paris peaked, the cost of interior decoration amounted to as much as 75 percent of the building budget.[171] But the cultural stakes were also considerable, raising the question of aesthetic survival of the painters who, it was felt, were being pushed out of the domain of interior decoration by skilled artisans. It was feared that the new

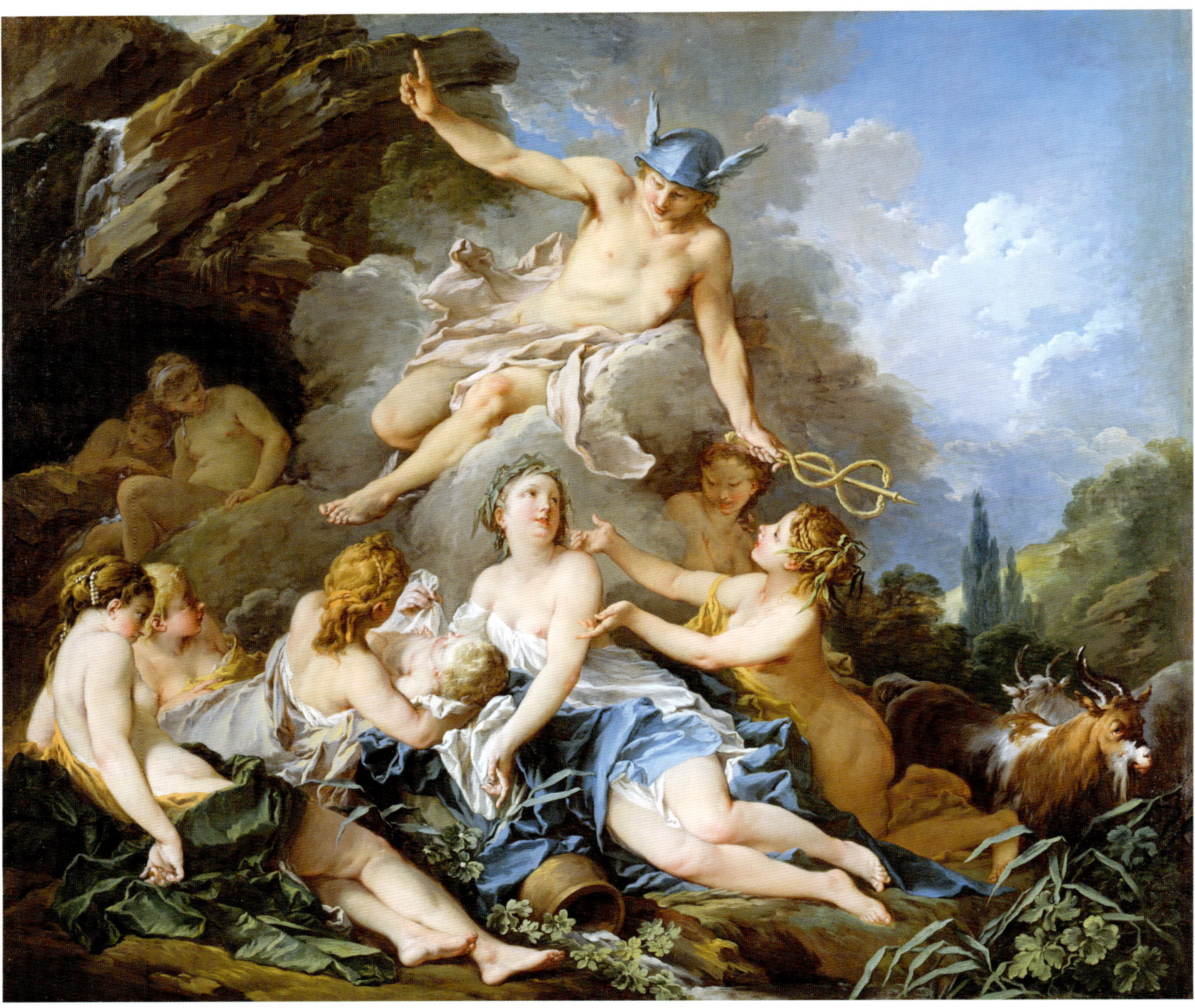

1.33.
François Boucher, *Mercury Confiding Bacchus to the Nymphs*, 1732–33. Oil on canvas. The Wallace Collection, London.

decorative schemes designed by leading architects, such as Germain Boffrand and Ange-Jacques Gabriel, left no place for painting.[172] By the mid-eighteenth century the complaint about painting having been replaced by the non-representational aspects of interior decoration was a common trope of the anti-rococo reaction.[173]

The building boom, like the more general dissemination of luxury goods, also generated a considerable amount of anxiety about aesthetic taste. The figure of the new Croesus indulging in a building folly in Voltaire's *Temple of Taste*, written at about the time when Boucher painted his pictures for Derbais, exemplified this worry.[174] Linked to the shift in the cultural and social status of the hôtel as the dwelling of an elite consumer was not only fear about the possible loss of space in which painters could exercise their art but also the emerging concern about the potential loss of its aesthetic quality. An opportunity to decorate the interior of an hôtel particulier thus posed a challenge for a painter in more ways than one.

In choosing Derbais's abode as the arena of his pictorial debut, Boucher must have recognized the commercial opportunity as well as aesthetic challenge it offered him as a painter, a challenge that amounted to a redefinition of decorative painting as a genre. It is reasonable to assume that in offering his services to Derbais, Boucher was not only eager to make himself known but was also determined to carve out a space for his art in the new domain of luxury consumption of which the hôtel particulier was a prime site.

The decorative set Boucher produced for Derbais consisted of five large canvases representing mytho-

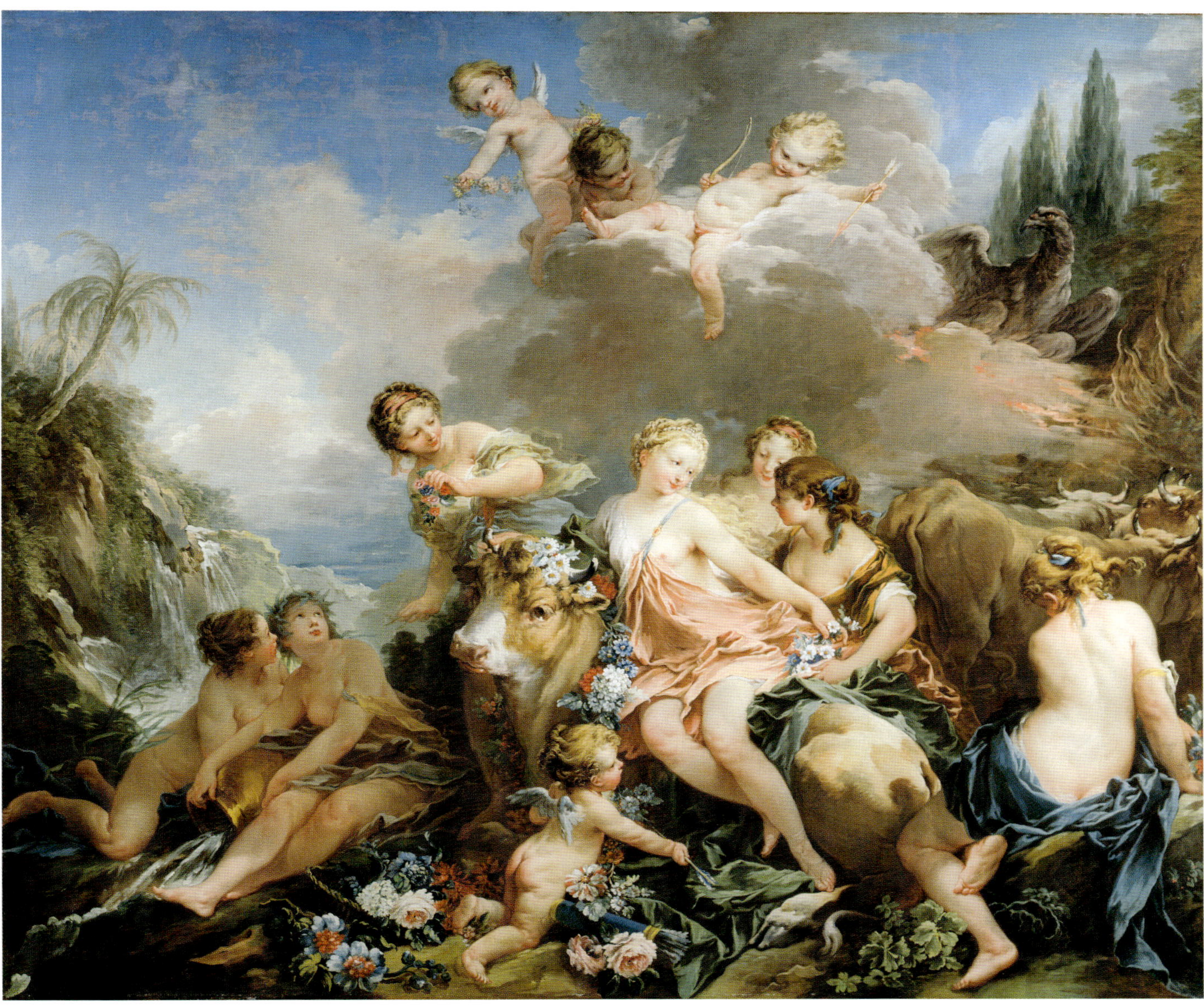

1.34.
François Boucher, *The Rape of Europa*, 1733–34. Oil on canvas. The Wallace Collection, London.

logical subjects: a large painting of *The Birth of Venus* (ca. 1731); a pair consisting of *Mercury Confiding Bacchus to the Nymphs* (fig. 1.33) and *The Rape of Europa* (fig. 1.34), presumably done in 1732–33 and 1733–34, respectively; and a set of vertical pendants, *Venus Requesting Arms from Vulcan* (1732) and *Aurora and Cephalus* (1733) (figs. 1.35 and 1.36). He also painted an overdoor with putti (*Amours*) for the billiard room and four overdoors for the stairway of the house with images of children engaged in activities representing the four seasons.[175] The size of the mythological paintings was important—it was the first time Boucher produced canvases of such large format—as was the scale of the project.[176] Moreover, the vertical pendants were the first works signed and dated by Boucher. This is significant, indicating not only the importance the young artist evidently attached to these canvases but also his rising self-consciousness about himself as an author, that is, as someone engaged in the production of an identifiable, chronologically ordered oeuvre.

Reinventing the language of large-scale decorative mythologies, Boucher's canvases for Derbais were most notable in their effort to redefine the effect of a decorative painting as a desirable material object. The vertical pendants, *Venus Requesting Arms from Vulcan* and *Aurora and Cephalus*, accomplished this task most persuasively. The multifigural depictions of the *Birth of Venus*, the *Rape of Europa*, and the *Mercury Confiding Bacchus*, though seemingly more ambitious, were in some respects more conventional.[177] The very choice of subject matter in the vertical pendants—mythical scenes of female seduction based on Virgil's *Aeneid* and Ovid's *Metamor-*

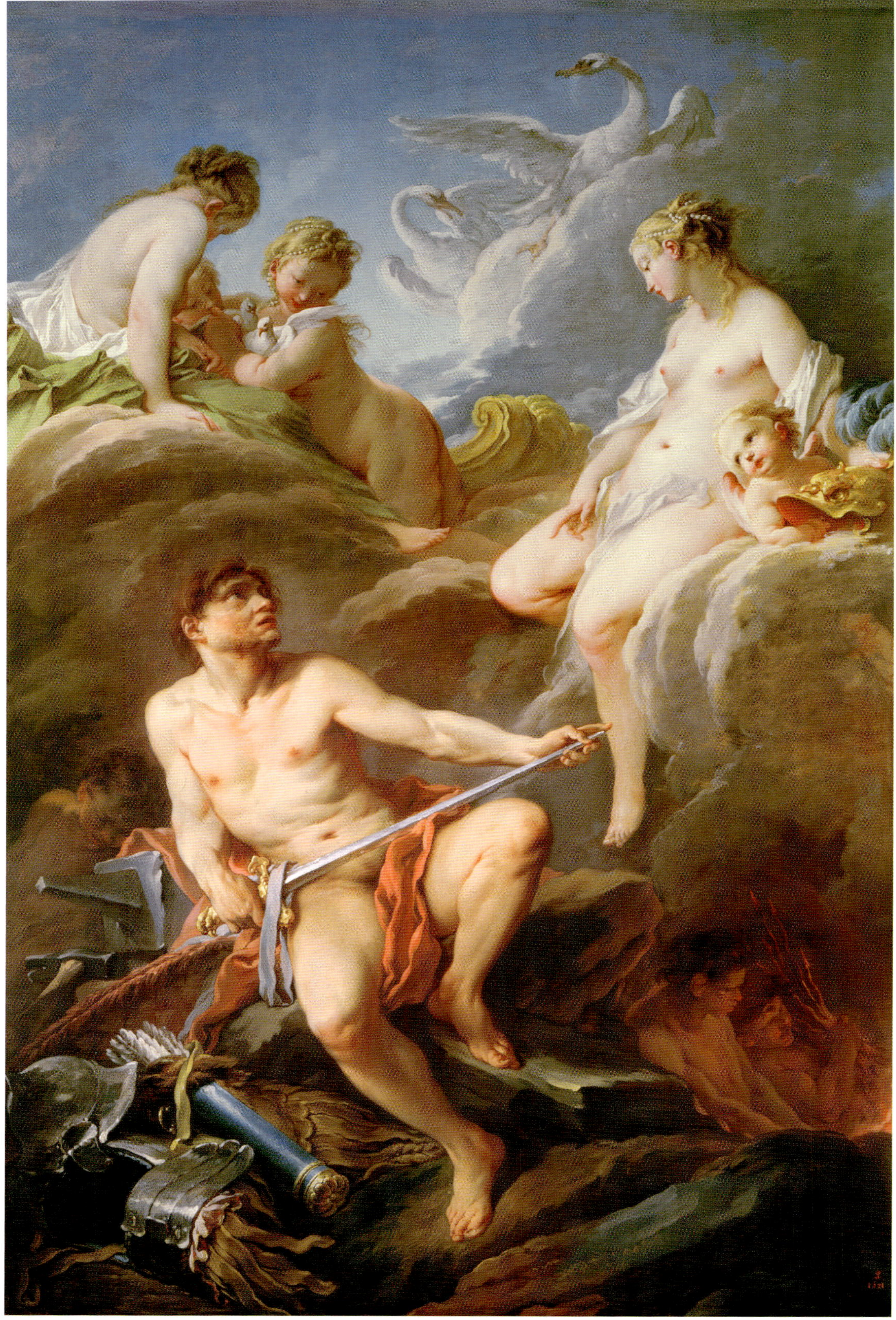

1.35.
François Boucher, *Venus Requesting Arms from Vulcan*, 1732. Oil on canvas. Musée du Louvre, Paris.

1.36.
François Boucher, *Aurora and Cephalus*, 1733. Oil on canvas. Musée des Beaux-Arts, Nancy.

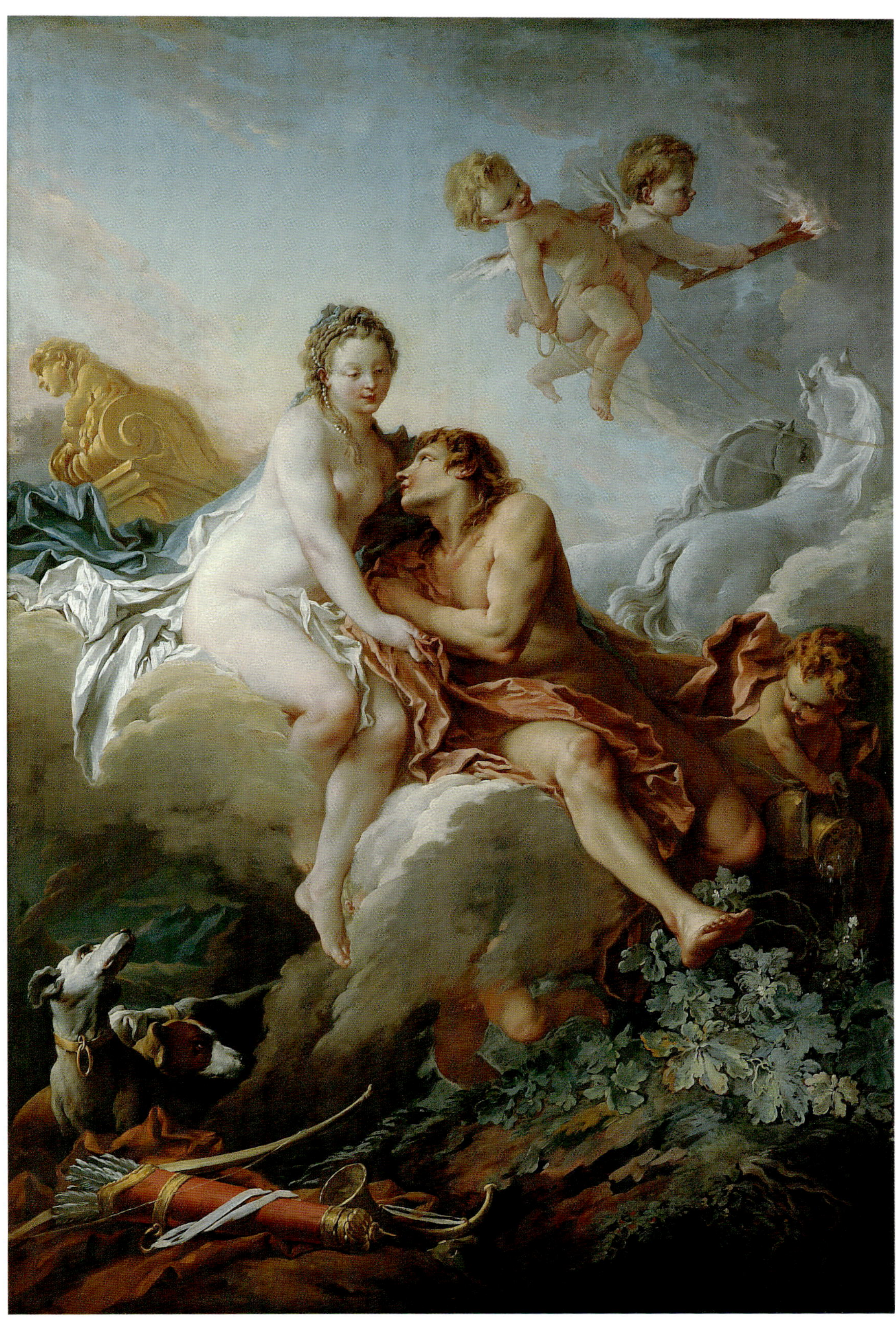

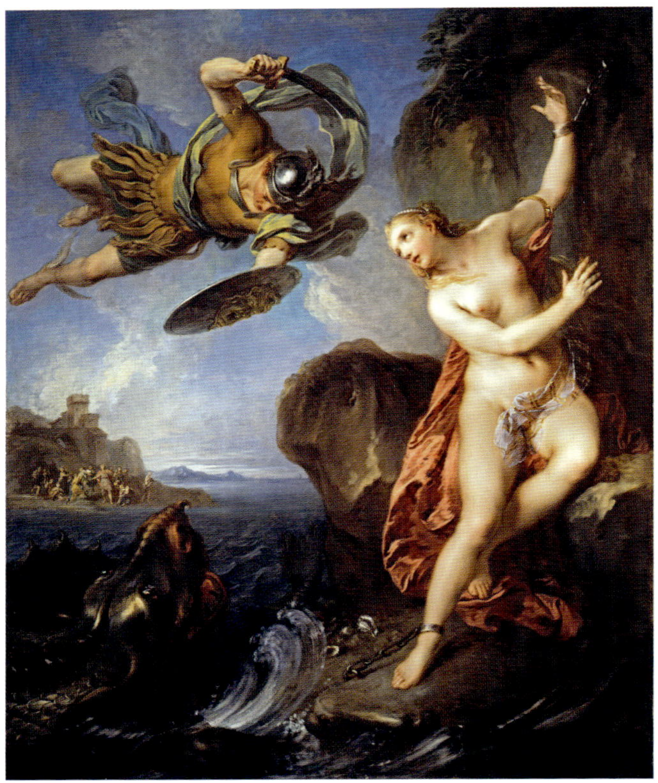

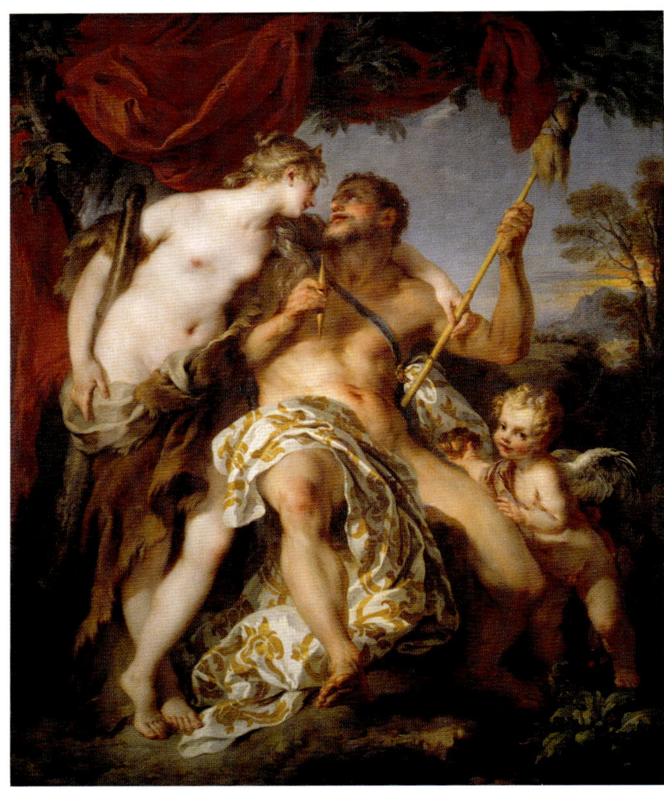

1.37.
François Lemoyne, *Perseus and Andromeda*, 1723.
Oil on canvas. The Wallace Collection, London.

1.38.
François Lemoyne,
Hercules and Omphale, 1724.
Oil on canvas.
Musée du Louvre, Paris.

phoses—indicated the erotic intent of these paintings.[178] The Ovidian source was also used by Boucher's teacher, François Lemoyne, in the comparable pendants of *Perseus and Andromeda* and *Hercules and Omphale* executed in the early 1720s for the financier François Berger (figs. 1.37 and 1.38). Shown at the Salon of 1725, these ambitious and much admired private commissions may have inspired Boucher, especially by their sensuous rendering of the female nude.[179] Yet Boucher's overall approach to the amorous subjects is markedly different from his teacher's, and, one may add, from other contemporary artists' depictions of similar themes.

The difference is apparent, first of all, in Boucher's treatment of the body and in the way he defines its role within the space of representation.[180] If in Lemoyne the figures were firmly anchored by their narrative function, in Boucher, they are primarily the agents of display. They do not perform any significant action but are shown engaged in amorous interaction, their poses and gestures emphasizing their corporeal reciprocity, which is, one may note, only loosely related to the textual source. Cephalus is shown readily responding to Aurora's charm, whereas, according to Ovid, the young hunter, enamored with another woman, was far more ambivalent about the goddess's advances.[181]

Nudity is the single most defining feature of these figures. Although the painter includes some of their requisite attributes—such as Vulcan's forge tucked in under the cloud beneath the figure of Venus, or the watering can that refers to the dew associated with Aurora as the personification of Dawn—iconographic specificity is not his major concern.[182] Nor is he interested in a reliable spatial definition of the locale that Lemoyne, in the Berger pendants, felt obliged to provide. His protagonists appear in a quasi-abstract setting, filled with an amorphous substance and cluttered with disparate fragments and few attendant figures. No logic governs this shallow and overcrowded space, wherein bodies and things float in defiance of gravity. Their artful disarray has, of course, been carefully composed—in each canvas, the prominent diagonal alignment of the main figures is counterbalanced by the opposite, more latent diagonal arrangement of their attendants, attributes, and assorted fragments—but this composition is quite arbitrary, in the sense that it does not correspond to any narrative development nor establish a clear hierarchy of meaning among the elements of the painting.

In their lack of narrative emphasis and their carefully staged disorder, these compositions resemble decorative designs more than history paintings. This impression is enhanced by their elongated form, a format similar to the shape of an ornamented screen panel, such as Boucher's own design, *Rocaille*, produced at roughly the same time (see fig. 1.25). The compositional resemblance of *Venus and Vulcan* to *Rocaille* is especially close, with Venus's pose echoing the arabesque shape of the palm rising above the cluster of natural and man-made collectibles. This comparison brings forth the function of the body in Derbais's pendants as just one of many beautiful objects put on display, a collectible natural formation—like the shells and corals in *Rocaille*—making the decorative purpose of these canvases the more evident. (One may note that the somewhat obvious pyramidal composition of both the *Birth of Venus* and *Mercury Confiding Bacchus* testify to a similarly display-oriented and decorative rather than narrative purpose.) What distinguishes the paintings from the ornamental designs is, though, the manifestly erotic quality of display underscored by the nudity of the main figures. As was the custom in the practice of history painting, Boucher did careful studies for these figures from the model, some of which have survived (fig. 1.39).[183] They give us a sense of his careful choice of poses and gestures, a development of body language that will become typical of his mythological repertory. And yet, notwithstanding these rehearsals, the major signifying task of these large-scale nude figures seems to be not narration or expression but the transmission of an erotic charge. With margins cropped and attendant figures pushed to the side, the protagonists' bodies seem pulled close to the painting's surface, an effect enhancing their erotic appeal.

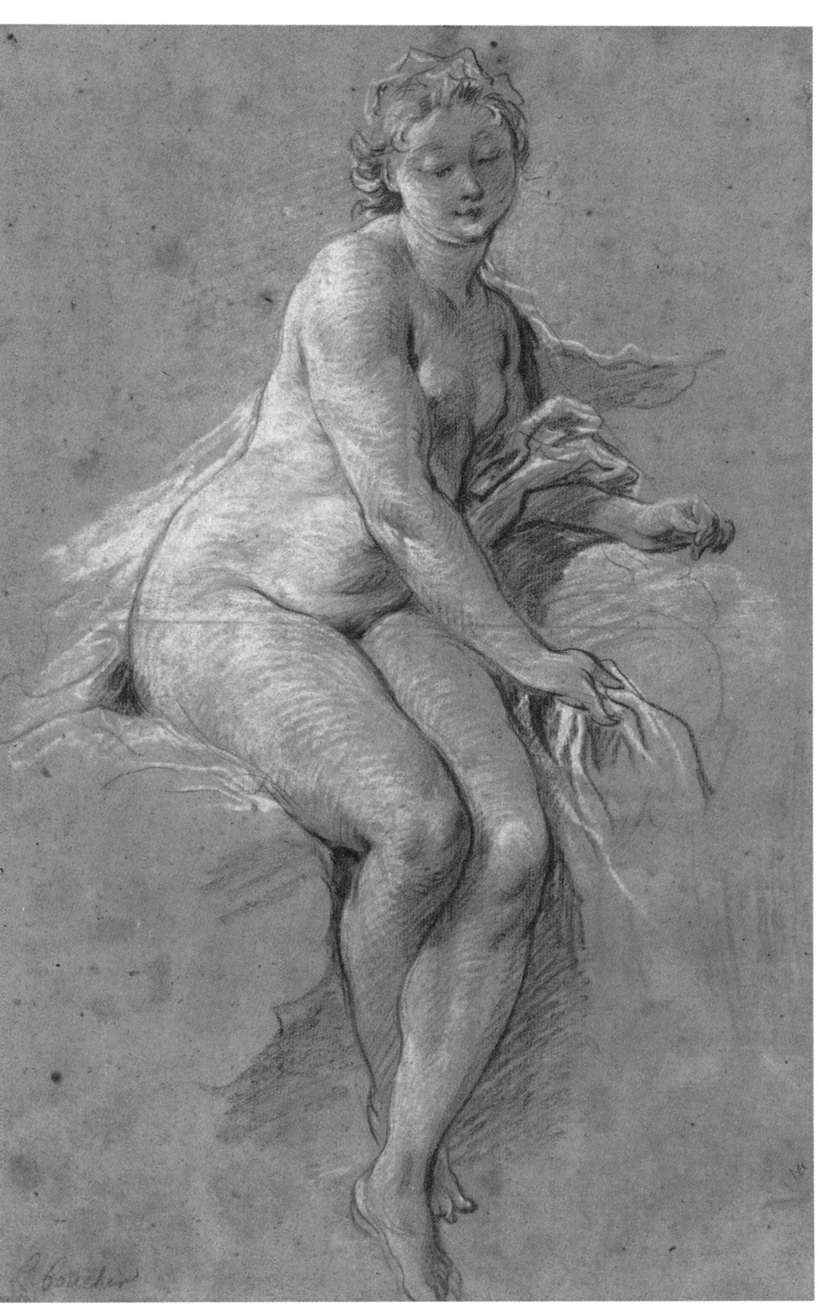

1.39.
François Boucher, *Aurora*, ca. 1733. Red and white chalk on brown laid paper, with later framing line in brown ink. National Gallery, Washington, DC, gift of Gertrude Laughlin Chandler.

It is the woman's body that Boucher clearly privileges in its erotic mission. Both Venus and Aurora are placed in the limelight, hovering above their partners whose admiring gazes relay the desiring look of the spectator. From the airborne cloud on which she is seated, the woman presides over, and speaks for, the space of eros that these canvases flesh out. (This is also true of the other three mythological paintings wherein the woman's body functions as a sensual focus of the composition even when this is not warranted by the iconography. Thus, in *Mercury Confiding Bacchus*, the nymph below Mercury is staged so prominently as to be easily taken for the main protagonist of this scene.[184])

This is, though, an eros of a specific kind. Scholars have noted the "brazen sensuality" of Boucher's vertical pendants.[185] Yet let us note that while erotically suggestive, the interaction between the figures is by no means explicit. There is no smooching, no avid grabbing of bodily parts, as in *Hercules and Omphale* painted by Boucher in the same period (1731–34) for a different purpose (fig. 1.40). In *Venus and Vulcan*, the sexual encounter, evoked by Vulcan's not-so-subtle sword and the piece of fabric that flows promisingly out of Venus's genital "source," seems suspended, or deferred, their nude bodies appearing somehow inert, focused on self-display rather than action. In *Aurora and Cephalus*, the goddess's body languidly slides down onto her lover's, her pose marking the diagonal descent of the entire composition, a tumultuous cascade of bodies and things tumbling down across the canvas. Not only does Boucher depart from the standard iconography in rendering Cephalus reciprocating, rather than resisting, Aurora's love, he also, in a sense, deactivates Aurora by turning her from an agent of seduction into a passive token of a pictorial commotion in which both she and her lover seem to have been caught. It is precisely this interpretation of the female body as the face of a movement of the entire pictorial surface that I want to emphasize—the effect conveyed most visibly by the positioning of the female figures but also by the manner of rendering their soft and snowy flesh as a palpable but exceptionally smooth surface on which the viewer's eye may glide unobstructedly—the opposite of, say, the late Rembrandt's barnacled flesh that traps or saps the gaze.

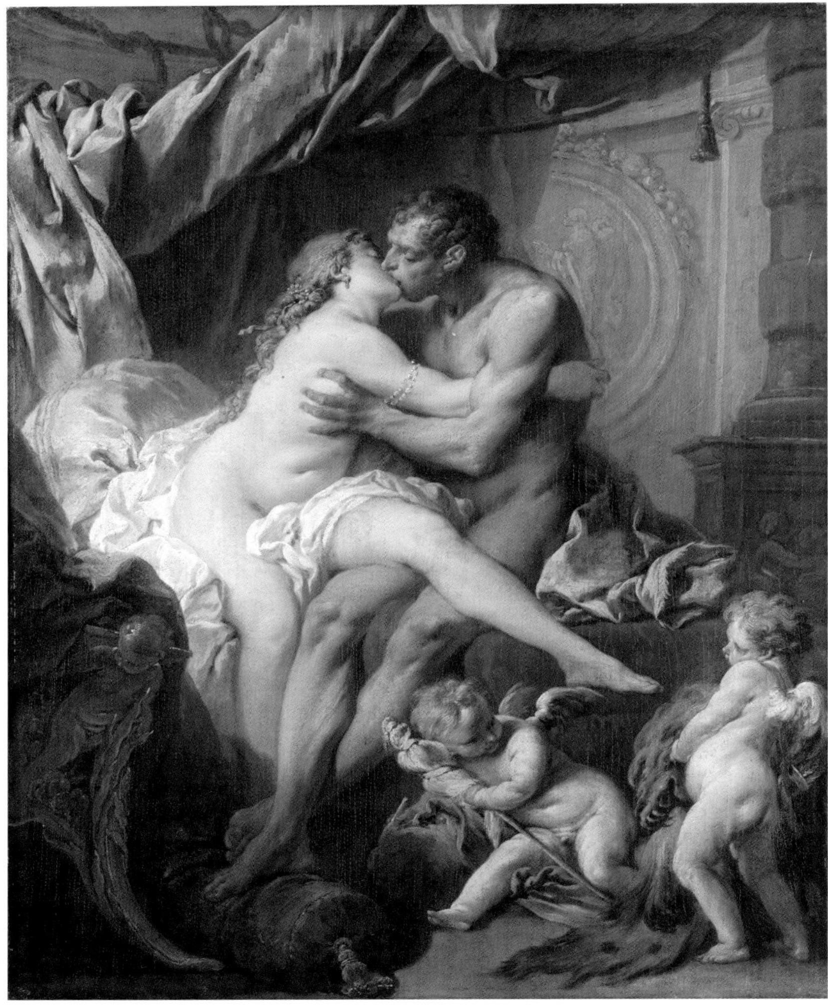

The erotic function of the woman in these pendants is to define the *painting itself* as a token of desire, a material object that carries an explicit promise of sensuous gratification likened by the mode of execution to the appeal of female flesh. The corporeal dominance of women in the two paintings must be seen in terms of this strategic function. So too must be their underplayed iconographic specificity and the generic quality of their bodies that repeat almost the exact same body type, not only in the pendants but in the other three canvases painted for Derbais as well. (This "cloning" effect may have been responsible for confusion about the subject of *Aurora and Cephalus*, which, at the moment of its sale later in the century, was taken to represent *Venus and Adonis*.[186]) The identity of the women in both pendants, and of the female protagonists in the three other canvases, is aligned—or confused—with Venus (they share the same bodily type—a small head with blond hair decorated with pearls, smallish breasts, and plump thighs—a type Boucher was to modify later, aiming at a greater robustness and firmness of the flesh in an effort to enhance its sensual appeal). This alignment is all the more significant if we realize that Venus was not only a figure of sensual pleasure but was also used to represent other forms of eros. For example, in the seventeenth-century depictions of the *kunstkammer*, Venus often figured as an allegory of the desire to own and amass rare objects.[187]

It is precisely the association between erotic and other forms of possession that Boucher conveys in these paintings by his suggestive treatment of objects, notably the attributes of male figures in each scene. Placed prominently in the lower left corner of each pendant, the armor forged by Vulcan and Cephalus's hunting tools vie for the viewer's attention almost like a third protagonist in each scene. (This impression is particularly strong in the pieces of armor at Vulcan's feet, which seem strangely alive, as if they were inhabited by some invisible warrior.) With their palpable textures and vivid colors—as in Cephalus's red leather quiver with its golden trimmings and blue satin strap—they appear like collectibles sold at the time by the *marchands merciers*; the compressed and cluttered space of these paintings may indeed resemble a shop window display. (That Mercury, who featured prominently in the *Birth of Bacchus*, was not only the messenger of gods but also the patron of merchants may also be of relevance to the commercial appeal of this set of paintings.) Yet in their overstaged mode of presentation, they appear not only as luxury objects but also as tokens of desire involved somehow in the erotic scenarios represented here. Note, moreover, that though they belong to men, these attributes are compositionally aligned with women,

1.40.
François Boucher, *Hercules and Omphale*, ca. 1731–34. Oil on canvas. The Pushkin State Museum of Fine Arts, Moscow.

the armor appearing at the end of the diagonal originating in Venus; Cephalus's gear having been placed directly under Aurora's body.

This eroticized rendition of things brings to mind Werner Sombart's dictum, contained in his book on *Luxury and Capitalism*, that "if luxury is to become personal, materialistic luxury, it must be predicated on an awakened sensuousness."[188] Linking consumption to sensual pleasure, this statement summarizes the main argument of Sombart's early twentieth-century theory of capitalist development in which he proposed that human psychology played a significant, if not more important role as the economic factor. For Sombart, luxury—the demand for it, its production, and its effects—was at the origins of capitalism, rather than the other way around, the pursuit of sensory pleasure through the experience of material objects was a major motive for economic development. Although flawed in many ways, Sombart's analysis remains intriguing because of his insistence on the psychological and erotic determination of economic process.[189]

Sombart's discussion of luxury helps us to recognize that Boucher formulates in these paintings an aesthetic of seduction of a particular kind. What he paints is neither the love of the gods nor human sexuality per se but the love of things, the sensual appeal of luxury. The brilliance of execution displayed in these canvases reinforces their effect. Their saturated colors and bold handling, which Boucher's contemporaries recognized as uncommon at the time, were clearly meant to advertise the young and yet relatively unknown painter's chromatic skills.[190] But this technical brio aimed also at turning the paintings themselves into enticing objects. This is what the extraordinarily sensuous treatment of their surface was all about. It transformed the pendants into material rather than merely visual forms of seduction. Not only the viewer's sight but also the viewer's touch was being courted, a desire to possess, not only to look, thus stimulated. At stake in this sensuous solicitation was not only a new visual idiom but also a suggestion of the new status of painting as an element of interior decor. Transforming the pendants into appealing objects, Boucher diminished the distance separating his paintings from other luxury commodities that furnished Derbais's fashionably appointed house, including, as his inventory attests, a substantial number of overmantel mirrors that La Font de Saint-Yenne would soon denounce as the single most pernicious element of contemporary interior decor, at once a threat to ambitious painting and a metaphor of its deplorable fate in commercialized society.[191] Mannlich's later reference to Boucher's paintings as "furniture" (*tableaux comme meubles*) also comes to mind here.[192] To phrase it differently, Boucher's approach signaled not only a change in the signifying economy of the painted image—what Norman Bryson has aptly called the eroticization of the plane of signifiers—but also its entry into the domain of economy tout court.[193]

The space of the erotic encounter between gods announced itself to be a site of the viewer's encounter with a seductive material thing—a commodity. The role of the female figure was to make this seduction explicit; she was a cipher of the desire that underlies the consumerist immersion in the sphere of inanimate things that these paintings render so animatedly, such as the "inhabited" armor at Vulcan's feet. Through the female figure, in other words, Boucher disclosed—and exploited—the erotic nature of human attraction to material possessions. And thus he also engaged with the subjective register of consumption.

Subjectivity is at issue in Derbais's pendants on two interrelated levels. One has to do with these paintings' mode of address, another with the pattern of human interaction in them that may be seen to represent a certain model of selfhood. In their thematic emphasis on eros and their exceptionally sensuous handling of paint, the pendants addressed themselves explicitly to an individual subject understood as a function of the senses and linked, above all, to sensual pleasure. Unlike Poussin, who, a century earlier, used the Ovidian theme of Aurora and Cephalus to represent the moral dilemma of desire—his Aurora is shown filled with love and desperate to retain Cephalus, who remains, nonetheless, determined in his refusal (fig. 1. 41)—Boucher is not concerned with the moral drama of wanting but with the want itself understood as the experience of the senses bound to a surface. No deep affect or tension is shown. Boucher's figures, as one commentator put it, bear "peu d'expression."[194] It is the lustful experience of flesh and of the painting as a lustful surface (lust *as* the experience of surface) that interested this painter. The "showiness" of execution—vigorous handling, animated brushstrokes, a "mellifluous touch" (*pinceau moëlleux*), and vivid, even garish colors—drove this point home.[195]

Ancient myth was, moreover, represented by Boucher as a terrain of private fantasy based on the experiences of the senses. The subjects, though based on specific literary sources, did not require erudition to be grasped and appreciated. Boucher offered idiosyncratic interpretations that emphasized and encouraged a play of imagination linked to the interaction between the main figures in each pendant.[196] The erotic encounter has been distilled into abstracted imagos of carnal reciprocity between two individuals—Venus and Vulcan, Aurora and Cephalus—who, with their attributes downplayed, make their identification as specific deities or as protagonists of particular stories optional. Because of the way in which these figures were rendered, their amorous reciprocity, though referring to the libidinal nature of their relations, also helped establish an eroticized relation of the viewer to the canvas, turning it into a terrain of self-projection. In other words, the sensualized relation between the figures stood in for the viewing subject's relation to an erotically charged *illusion of itself* conveyed by these canvases. Their function was, in this sense, not unlike that of the plethora of overmantle mirrors decorating Derbais's interiors: they were the carriers of a certain kind of self-image. What was at stake in these mythological fantasies was not only a new decorative idiom but also a model of subjectivity associated with the emergent culture of appearances: a self caught up with a mirage of itself, a subject as an effect of a sensuous surface.

To understand better this vision of subjectivity we must turn briefly to the work of Boucher's contemporary, Pierre Carlet de Marivaux. For in Marivaux's writings we find a parallel creative investigation of the relation between appearance and selfhood in the era of early consumption. Thus, in his two novels, *Le Paysan Parvenu* and *La Vie de Marianne*, Marivaux describes not only the vicissitudes of his protagonists—the social ascent of a simple country boy and of a young orphaned woman of uncertain social origins, respectively—but also dwells on these characters' psychological development as their social status changes and they become immersed in luxury goods, especially clothing. In both novels, the key moment of the character's transformation has to do with his or her acquisition of a new sartorial persona that marks the protagonist's social elevation and also leads to his or her acquisition of a theatricalized sense of self. It is this concept of the *imaginary self* sustained by appearances that Marivaux's novels explore.[197]

Published around the time Boucher was painting for Derbais, 1734–35, *Le Paysan Parvenu* describes how its protagonist, Jacob, the upstart peasant of the title, became the "man of the world," Monsieur de la Vallée.[198] What Marivaux reveals is the complex psychological transformation of his hero that accompanies his social rising, especially the way in which the protagonist mobilizes his original persona of the simple country boy to internally negotiate his new social identity. Jacob does not simply become Monsieur de la Vallée but acquires a sense of himself as a compound being, one in whom *two* identities, or two subjective positions, coexist. For example, it is, as the hero puts it, only from the perspective of "the little peasant" that being the worldly man appears so sweet to him. Describing his acquisition of new fashionable clothes, Marivaux's protagonist comments: "What, now, slippers and a dressing gown for Jacob! For it was in considering myself as Jacob that I was so deliciously astonished to see myself in that dress; it was from Jacob that Monsieur de la Vallée borrowed all his joy. This moment was so sweet because of the little peasant."[199]

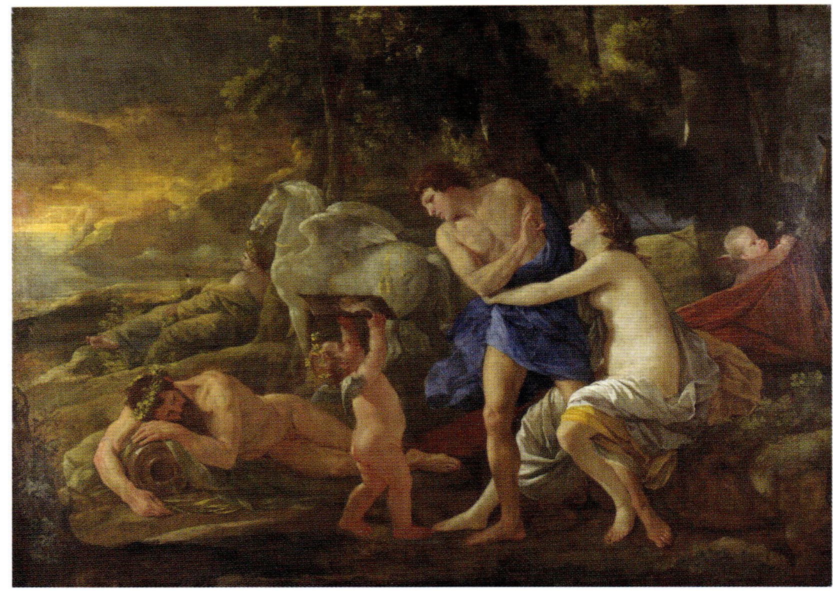

Second, Jacob reveals how this internally split sense of self is linked to the external spectacle of appearance. This is evident in his description of an encounter with a woman he liked, as he put it, "not because of her," but because of her rank, "very lofty in comparison with mine." It is, though, his perception of the visual appearance of rank that matters the most: "I saw a woman of condition with *a certain style* which seemed to include servants and equipage, and who found me attractive, who allowed me to kiss her hand but did not wish people to know it; in a word, *who raised us, my pride and me*, from their original worthlessness; for before this moment

1.41.
Nicolas Poussin, *Cephalus and Aurora*, ca. 1630. National Gallery, London. G. J. Cholmondely Bequest, 1831.

had I valued myself as anything? Had I felt what self-love is?"[200]

The attentions of this stylish female apparition are crucial for the hero's sense of his self-worth, *her* love key for the development of *his* self-love. The feminine spectacle of a "lofty rank" is, in a sense, a mirage of Jacob himself. It is important to note that the duality implied by his vision—the woman not as she is but as she *appears* to him from his own lowly position—is reflected by the internal doubling evoked by Jacob when he speaks of "my pride *and* me." (Pride—*mon orgeuil* in the original—must be understood in a positive sense, close to personal dignity, or pride in oneself.[201]) The emergence of the hero's inner sense of self-worth, his newly complex subjectivity, is shown to depend on the charming spectacle of benevolent femininity.

There is, in my view, a connection between Jacob's vision of a woman and Boucher's feminine apparitions, which is to say that the latter, like the former, function not only as depictions of a specific person, or, in Boucher's case, deities, but as an *internal fantasy* on which the male self envisioned in these paintings depends. Shown "hanging" on their seductresses' alluring gaze, Vulcan and Cephalus may be understood as visual equivalents of Marivaux's Jacob in that they represent subjects taken in by the spectacle of the female body that is also a version of themselves. The emphatic reciprocity between the figures could be seen to represent the very structure of subjectivity evoked by Marivaux: a model of the self based on being both spectator and spectacle for someone else's gaze.

The Boucher/Marivaux analogy is important for our appreciation of the role of women in the Derbais paintings. It becomes clear that though the woman is staged as the privileged, erotically charged *object* of the look—for both the male figures within the painting and the viewer—she is also defined as a *subject*, not only of her own desiring gaze anchored in the male figures but also by being the central element of a certain vision of subjectivity. In other words, Boucher's woman embodies the attraction of commodity—something like an impressive equipage or a beautiful dress that produces, in Marivaux's words, a certain *style* of appearance—and also the mirage of the self under its spell. What Marivaux's writing helps us discern in Boucher's paintings is the image of the self split within itself, a vision of a compound identity of which the two aspects are represented by the male and the female figures.

This model of subjectivity has much to do with how the economic sphere and the market itself were perceived at the time, this perception being, as historians of the period have pointed out, itself a kind of fantasy, or a mirage.[202] The consumer-directed economy was in this period in France still in its early stages of development, and this development was, moreover, markedly uneven.[203] The economy was not entirely driven by the consumer demand, but it was *imagined* to be so. Emerging from Marivaux's novels and Boucher's paintings is, accordingly, a conception of the self that corresponds to this imaginary perception. Both recognize the self as, essentially, a *fiction* that the spread of commodities helped produce and sustain. Such a view is predicated on the recognition of commodities as instruments mediating the subject's relation to the world rather than separating it from it (or from itself), commodities, that is, as forms of representation that help the self develop an image of itself, contributing to the emergence of its imaginary function.[204]

In this way, Boucher's pendants are *personal mythologies*: they represent a certain myth of the self in the early stages of commercial modernity, a subject imagined outside the confines of Christian ethics, driven by self-interest and pleasure—like Marivaux's Jacob who, in his own words, wrote his memoirs "not only to instruct others but to amuse myself"—a subject given to illusions, and capable of deceit, in a word, the kind of self heralded by the proponents of commercial modernity, beginning with Bernard Mandeville and the French propagators of his ideas, notably Voltaire, and one that Rousseau was soon to denounce as aligned with seeming rather than being.[205] Boucher appropriates mythology for the construction of a certain modern mirage: a pictorial illusion of the world of desirable things and of the self inhabiting this world, a subject locked into an image.

The paintings also provide a mythic vision of the individual who inhabited the new Parisian hôtels, including the inhabitant of the hôtel Derbais, Derbais himself, as a kind of mirage. This is to say that they represent the notion of fantasy that shaped both the new architectural interior for which these spectacular canvases were painted, but also resonate with the forms through which the design of such spaces was disseminated at the time. This was the notion of fantasy that was prominent at the time in the commercial domain of decoration illustrated by publications such as Pierre-Quentin Chedel's *Livre des Fantaisies, Cartouches, Ornements*, published in 1738.[206] In such books, fantastic forms of frames, cartouches, fountains, and whole gardens of imaginary delights proliferated. Their function was to offer ideas for interior design, but they also embraced personal fantasy in another sense, as publications aiming at individual clients, circulating in relatively affordable print editions that could be bought by professionals seeking ideas for interior decor and also by the larger, amateur audience, as tools for home entertainment and definition of identity.[207]

Boucher himself was, as we have seen, an active contributor to this new decorative imaginary. The canvases executed for Derbais marked his effort to reinvent painting as the key component of this domain of fantasy that was both commercially grounded and operating on a personal register of the consumer's pleasure. With this gesture, placing painting squarely in the service of the inhabitants of the new hôtels, Boucher reached for a broader constituency than the traditional aristocratic clientele of decorative painting. He sided, to put it crudely, with those who could pay for the fantasies to be fleshed out in their houses conceived as the representations of themselves. And what he offered these consumers was neither mere decoration nor a mere mirror reflection, but the visual means of imagining themselves, the stuff from which these individuals could construct their own myths. Boucher's painting presented this new audience with the image of the effect of the new world of objects on the conception of individual identity.

At the same time, these two paintings may also be seen to represent Boucher. With Derbais's commission, Boucher made a bid for an artistic identity, and the fact that these were his first signed and dated works confirms their importance as self-representations. This self-definition—a bold declaration of his artistic self-worth—hinged, like Jacob's, on the spectacle of the woman. But if the woman is a figure of Boucher, it is in a specific sense, as a stand-in for his work, his sign, aligned with, and equivalent to, his signature. It is not that Boucher identifies with femininity. Rather, what we witness in his works is a sort of dis-identification, the assumption of an image—specifically, the image of the female body under which Boucher places his signature in each pendant—as the product of his hand that stands for him but also, in a sense, obscures him.[208] His highly stylized image of the woman's body—its generic quality; its alignment with the painting's surface—functions not unlike the artist's signature, that is, as the stylized index of his body: both say "it is me" only insofar as I am not in it, as a consistent and reproducible sign that stands for me in my absence.

In this sense, the female figure is a *mirage* of the artist. Boucher's entire practice is marked by a kind of subjective evacuation that has to do with his development of a consistent "signature" style based on a generic vision of femininity. First inaugurated in Derbais's paintings, this "feminine" vision, and Boucher's stylistic consistency of which it became a mark—enough to think of the parade of Venuses in his art—was inseparable from the artist's own consistent but abstracted sense of identity.[209] As one modern commentator has observed, referring to women in Boucher's painting in general: "there is *no one* there."[210] It is this eclipse of the artist as a subject of his painting that the motif of the putto in *Aurora and Cephalus* hovering, almost entirely obfuscated by the cloud, directly above the artist's signature suggestively conveys—the image of the artist as a producer of illusions that both reproduce and obliterate him (fig. 1.42).[211]

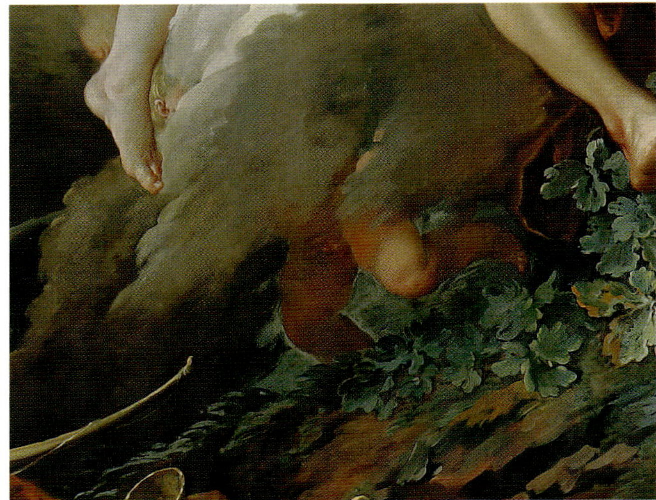

1.42. ABOVE
François Boucher, *Aurora and Cephalus*, detail of fig. 1.36.

1.43. OPPOSITE TOP
François Boucher, *Venus Requesting Arms from Vulcan*, detail of fig. 1.35.

1.44. OPPOSITE MIDDLE
François Boucher, *Leda and the Swan*, 1742. Oil on canvas. The Resnick Collection, Los Angeles.

1.45. OPPOSITE BOTTOM
François Boucher, *Dark-Haired Odalisque*, 1745. Oil on canvas. Musée du Louvre, Paris.

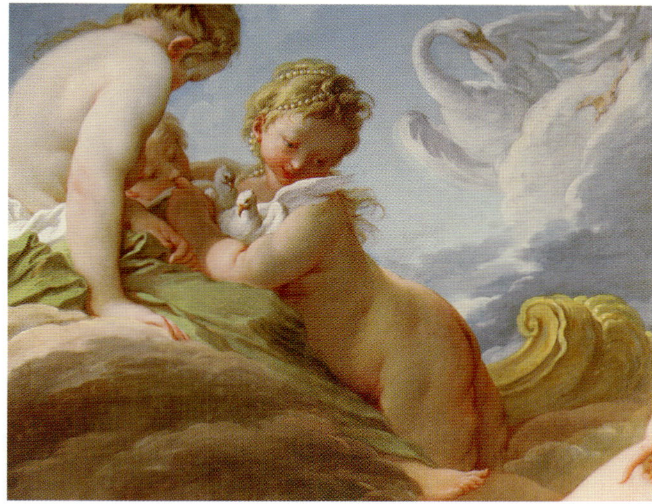

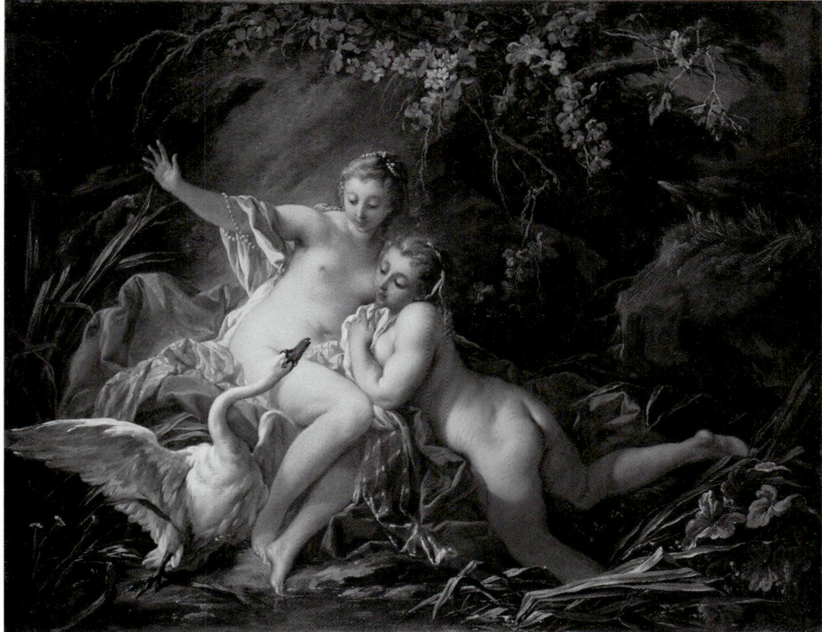

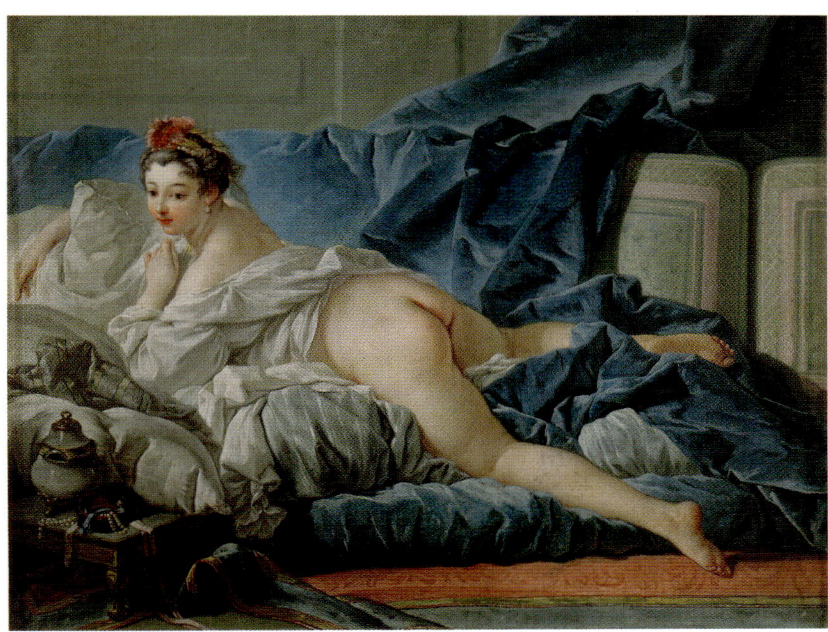

The Derbais pendants were Boucher's signature pieces in more than one way. Together with the rest of the group, they initiated his career as a painter. They secured recognition for his uncommon pictorial skills. But, as I have been arguing, they also performed a specific cultural function: they launched Boucher as the visual mythologist of the consuming self, a new kind of personality emerging in France in the early eighteenth century, linked to the flow of commodities and to the new lifestyle enabled and defined by them. The paintings inaugurated Boucher's investment in the female body as the key element of this new, personal form of mythology, and as the signature aspect of his practice. Not only did the female body assume the central position as the privileged locus of aesthetic invention, it also came to represent his practice as nothing else did, epitomizing the status of his work as an accommodating object for the new subject.

The effect of the pendants on Boucher's work is epitomized by the extended life of one particular figure in *Venus and Vulcan*, the nymphet reclining on a cloud with her behind exposed, in his productions (fig. 1.43). Evidently the painter recognized he had hit on a vein of gold with the young woman's pose: he repeated it in numerous paintings and drawings, from the *Leda and the Swan* (fig. 1.44), to the *Dark-Haired Odalisque* (fig. 1.45), to the Munich *Girl on the Sofa*, also known as the *Blonde Odalisque* (fig. 1.46).[212] Among his female creations, this one was most like his signature, something recognizably his own. By the mid-1750s, "Boucher" as a market product was identified with the female body featured in these paintings.

A pastel study of a woman's foot, now at the Musée Carnavalet, epitomizes the at once commercial and psychic economy of the transformation of a woman into a sign for the artist (fig. 1.47). Rather than a preparatory drawing, this is most likely a reprise of the motif from the Munich painting, *Girl on the Sofa*, made for commercial purposes. It has been suggested that Boucher followed the demand of the connoisseurs eager to possess a bit of his oeuvre, a fragment of something the artist had already done.[213] As such, *Study of a Foot* is an example of the artist's willing self-commodification. What the corporeal fragmentation in this work also makes patently evident is the artist's willing self-fetishization. This breaking apart—not only of a woman's body but also of the artist's own work—epitomizes the sexual logic behind the transformation of his art into a luxury commodity.

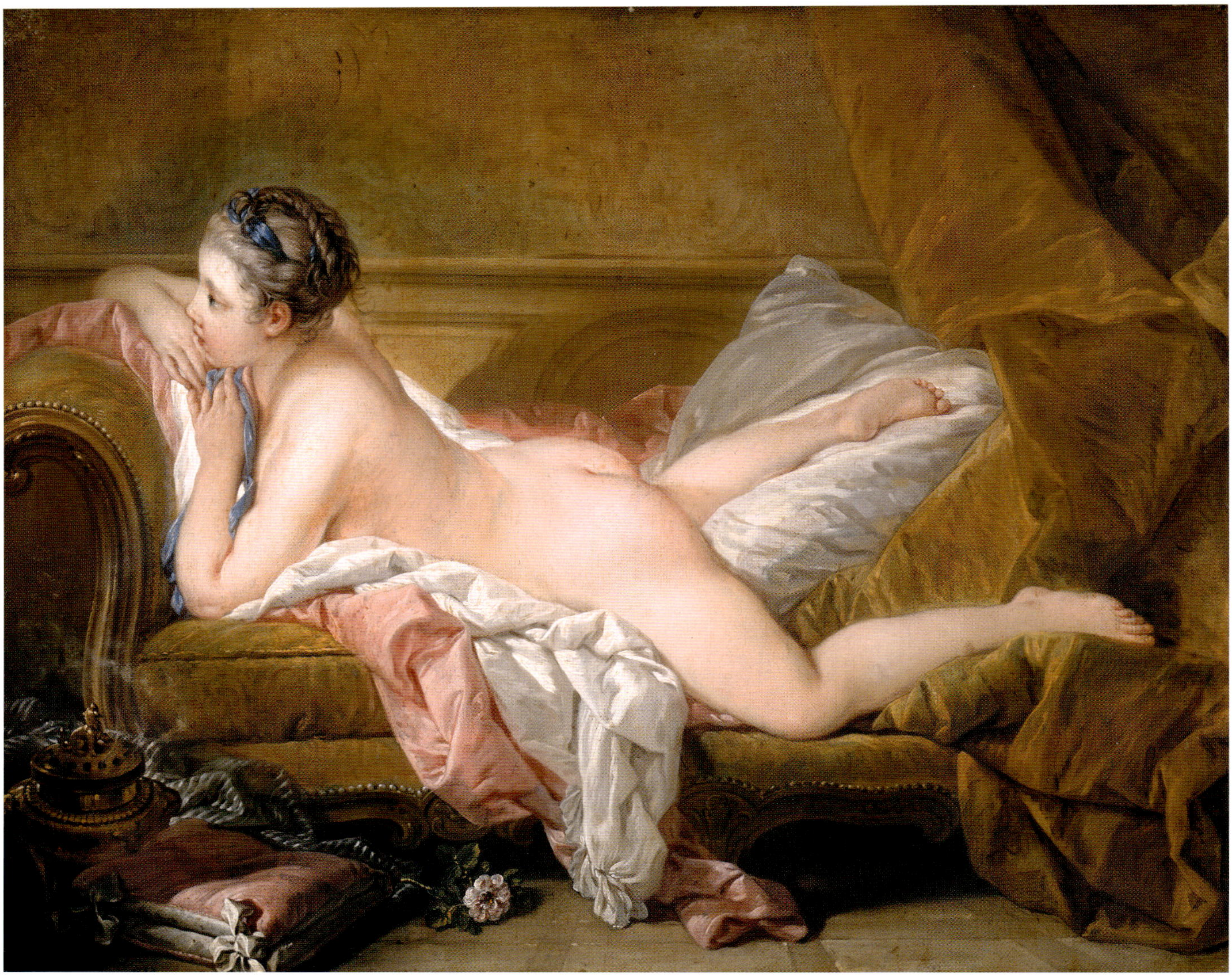

Staging both a slice of his vision and his conspicuous faire (the showy rendition of the woman's foot with its pink toes, of the bluish white pillow on which it rests, and of the swath of golden yellow fabric framing it), this image is perhaps the most succinct statement about how Boucher came to understand his practice in the wake of Derbais's commission.

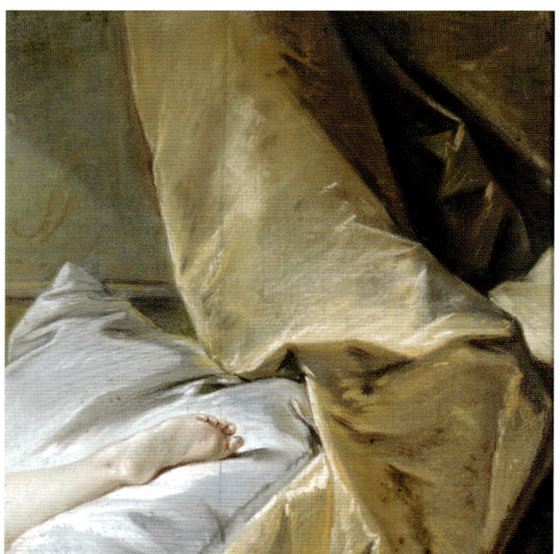

1.46.
François Boucher, *Girl on the Sofa*, also known as the *Blonde Odalisque*, 1752. Oil on canvas. Alte Pinakothek, Munich.

1.47.
François Boucher, *Study of a Foot*, 1751. Pastel on paper. Musée Carnavalet, Paris.

THE PROMISCUOUS SELF

I was so moved by the pleasure of imagining what [my appearance] would bring about that I was almost breathless.

—MARIVAUX, La Vie de Marianne

The immersion of Boucher's painting in the burgeoning culture of consumption, so successfully inaugurated by his decorative series for Derbais's hôtel, came also to inform his brief but significant foray into genre painting in the early 1740s.[214] Boucher launched himself into the production of highly finished smaller-scale paintings that provide compelling testimony to the rising importance of consumer goods within the social realm and within Boucher's own aesthetic project. Although some of them were commissioned by specific individuals, taken as a group, these works, which included *Le Déjeuner*, or *The Breakfast* (fig. 1.48); *La Toilette*, or *A Lady Fastening Her Garter* (see fig. 1.56); *A Lady on a Day Bed* (see fig. 1.66); and *La Marchande de modes*, or *The Milliner* (see fig. 1.57), nonetheless signaled the broader ambition, at once aesthetic and commercial, motivating Boucher's practice at that time. In taking them on, the painter not only responded to the demands of the specific patrons but, more speculatively, also sought to position himself in an art market that was dominated by Dutch and Flemish cabinet pictures.[215] He may have wanted to prove his skills in executing the kind of small-scale images, known then as the "*sujets galants et agréables*," that were a specialty of his older colleague Jean-François de Troy and that were much in demand at the time, their marketability enhanced by the promise of an extended life through the medium of reproductive prints.[216] Yet it is also evident that the aesthetic import of these canvases cannot be fully accounted for by Boucher's mimicry of Dutch genre or his commercial rivalry with another French painter.

The significance of these images resides, in my view, in how they depict contemporary practices of consumption and reveal the growing importance of commodity in everyday life and in the cultural imagination, especially in imagining the self. It is not only that Boucher displays in these paintings a whole array of luxury goods: from sumptuous decorative objects, such as a wall clock, or a porcelain vase mounted in gilt bronze, to inexpensive trinkets, such as a Chinese figurine, or a fan. It is that he makes evident the transformation of these diverse luxurious goods into personal possessions, objects of individual relevance, comfort, and pleasure. It is the very birth of commodity in the most basic early sense of the word as, literally, an *accommodating object*, that we witness in these depictions of daily life. They demonstrate how all kinds of meaningless or unnecessary things—luxurious, in the sense of superfluous, goods—acquire meaningful existence as vehicles of convenience, personal pleasure, and sensory gratification.[217] Depicting different aspects of daily life—mostly, but not only, that of the elites—these works suggest that the proliferation of goods changed patterns of social behavior but also helped shape an emergent sense of individual identity. Briefly put, they envision how commodities were *interiorized*, that is, how they were being incorporated into the physical space of an architectural interior, altering its contours and function as an arena of private life, but also how they began to recast the subjective ideal of interiority understood as inner space.

In all of the works in question Boucher engages the format of so-called *tableau de modes*, mastered by Jean-François de Troy in the 1720s and '30s, a type of painting that records the daily rituals of fashionable society, predominantly of women.[218] Boucher's exercises in this subgenre, however, are marked by a subtle shift in emphasis from the idea of fashionable sociability toward a greater prominence of the fashionable *thing* at the core of human interaction. It is, in other words, not only the relations between people but also the effects of the depicted subjects' engagement with the objects, and its consequences, that we are given to appreciate in these canvases.

There were both economic and discursive factors behind the rising concern with the effect of things on people, epitomized by the debate on luxury, when Boucher was painting his cabinet pictures, in themselves a type of luxury object. The very meaning of luxury was destabilized by the unprecedented spread of commodities. When in his *Lettre sur le Luxe* published anonymously in 1745, the writer and savant André François Deslandes remarked that luxury amounted to no more than "some bagatelles transformed into things of importance," his assertion signaled a degree of uncertainty about the meaning of the term he was trying to define.[219] Diderot summed up this sense of semantic ambiguity when he wrote

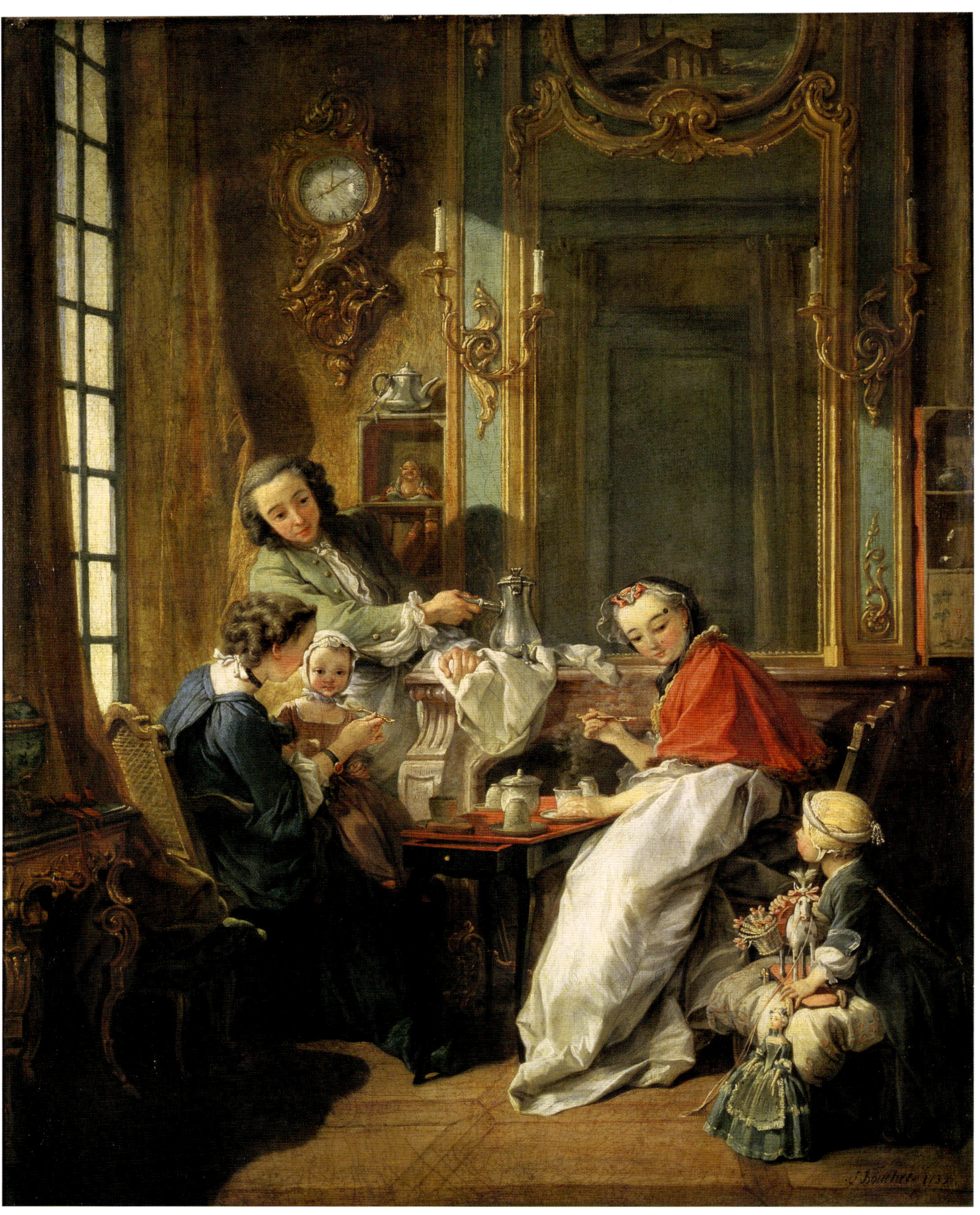

1.48.
François Boucher, *Le Déjeuner*, or *The Breakfast*, 1739. Oil on canvas. Musée du Louvre, Paris.

in the *Encyclopédie*: "We say, without any of us being mistaken, of an infinity of objects of all sorts, *that they are luxuries*, but what is this *luxury* that we attribute so infallibly to so many objects?"[220] The vexing question of meaning emerged with particular force in considerations regarding the social and individual effects of luxury consumption.

Although luxury was an established topic of discussion and critique in France since at least the seventeenth century, notably by classical republicans and Christian moralists, the luxury debate was rekindled in the early eighteenth century by the advent of what Thorstein Veblen later termed the culture of "conspicuous consumption."[221] Another factor contributing to the renewed concern with luxury was the engagement of French intellectuals, among them Voltaire, with the ideas of Bernard Mandeville, the provocative British defender of luxury. Mandeville's *Fable of the Bees*, first published in England in 1714 and appearing in multiple revised editions throughout the century (notably in 1723 and 1728), was debated on both sides of the Channel even before it was translated into French in 1740.[222] Mandeville recognized that commerce brought about dramatic shifts in human behavior and self-conception in two key respects: increased dependence on things and reliance on the opinion of others. But these behavioral symptoms were determined not by external circumstances but by the inherent qualities of human personality. Self-interest was, in Mandeville's view, the prime motive of human action, and he considered the concomitant notions of desire and pleasure as the motors not only of individual functioning but also of economic and social development. Recognizing private vice as a source of common good, Mandeville understood the modern economy to be founded upon the satisfaction of desire, a correlation he found most promising insofar as "the wants of Man are innumerable."[223]

In the mid-1730s, Voltaire and the economic theorist Jean-François Melon popularized the British thinker's ideas in France.[224] In his *Man of the World*, published in 1736, and *The Defense of the Man of the World*, which followed in 1737, Voltaire proposed what may be termed a Mandevillian revision of honnêteté, that is, a recasting of the elite ideal of politeness and polish in commercialized terms, as grounded in material possessions. Thus Voltaire's worldly man unabashedly declares:

J'aime le luxe, et même la mollesse,
Tous les plaisirs, les Arts de toute espèce,
La propreté, le goût, les ornemens:
Toute honnête homme a de tels sentimens.[225]

Voltaire's boldly epicurean conception of the self corresponded to Mandeville's recognition of self-interest and desire as primary stimulants of human actions, as did his pleasure-driven subject's manifest lack of concern for the moral implications of his inclinations.[226] If the honnête homme of Meré and other seventeenth-century social theorists of politeness based their distinction on the moral esteem of others, Voltaire's *mondain* relies in his self-definition on his material possessions as the source of both pleasure and self-image—in the eyes of others and his own. The "man of the world" vaunts his predilection for luxury in all its material manifestations, from coffee, wine, and spices to art, precious objects, and elegantly decorated dwellings. He is, in other words, essentially a consumer. Yet as Voltaire provocatively insists, it is precisely as such that this exemplary individual is a benefit for society; his appetite for luxury is not only a stimulant of commerce, economic growth, and national prosperity but also a contribution to cultural and artistic development—Voltaire places special emphasis on the benefits of consumption for the development of the arts—and, more generally, to civilizational progress. Ultimately, like superfluity itself—for Voltaire "a very necessary thing"—the worldly man is presented as socially and culturally indispensable to modern society.[227]

The new subjective ideal sketched out in *Le Mondain* proved, however, to be highly controversial; the response revived the older moralist tradition, represented by Montaigne and La Rochefoucauld, that was critical of individuals driven by *amour-propre* and excessive love of refinement and pleasure.[228] The most influential critical view of luxury consumption was offered at midcentury by Jean-Jacques Rousseau. Formulated in his *Discourse on the Arts and Sciences* (1750) and developed most forcefully and influentially in the *Discourse on the Origins of Inequality among Men* (1755), Rousseau's critique raised the issue of the profound subjective losses entailed by commercial modernity in general, and by the spread of consumption of superfluous goods in particular.[229] In Rousseau's view, consumption of unnecessary goods turned man into a socialized, artificial individual, a self defined by vanity and self-love, and by the rituals of display and performance that transformed all intersubjective relations, such as friendship, and the self itself, into mere appearances.[230] A person was reduced to an actor, a manipulator of masks: "it was necessary to appear to be other than what one in fact was. To be and to seem to be became two altogether different things and from this distinction came conspicuous ostentation, deceptive cunning and all the vices that follow from them."[231] Rousseau contrasted the self-reliant "savage" who "lives within himself" with the modern sociable individual who is "always outside of himself, knows how to live only in the opinion of others" from whose judgment alone he draws the sentiment of his own existence.[232] The gist of Rousseau's insight was that possessions are not only morally exhausting—a condition recognized and cynically embraced by Mandeville—but that they may eventually be dispossessing, causing a kind of subjective evacuation.[233]

Painted before Rousseau's strongly worded condemnation of luxury took hold of the public imagination, Boucher's images appear as visual endorsements of, if not apologies for, luxury consumption. Upon closer scrutiny, however, these images of life with luxury reveal more complex questions lurking behind the notion of consumption. As they document the ascendancy of the thing in social life and in the cultural imagination, they also speak, indirectly, about how the circulation of commercial goods altered the nature of human relations and the relation of human beings to themselves.

Le Déjeuner, painted in 1739, is the earliest example of Boucher's engagement with the theme of life under the spell of the commodity. A small gathering of people—two women, two children, and a servant—is shown nestled in a corner of a room, taking their small repast.[234] They are most likely drinking coffee, which became a highly fashionable beverage among Parisians in the 1730s and '40s.[235] Its pleasures were vaunted by, among others, Voltaire who, in his *Defense of the Worldly Man*, linked its popularity to the international expansion of trade, and, more ambivalently, by Johann Sebastian Bach who wrote a *Coffee Cantata* denouncing the addiction to it in 1732.[236] It was often fed to children, as other images from the period—including Jean-Etienne Liotard's portrait of his sister and niece at breakfast (1754)—indicate.[237] Most notable in Boucher's painting is the way in which this basic act of consumption is shown to produce a sense of intimacy, establishing the connection between the members of the group and defining their relation to the interior. The women and children have taken over this part of the room and made it their own: a portable lacquer table, one of those exotic furnishing items rendered fashionable by the boutiques of the marchands merciers, was pulled up by the fireplace for the occasion, and they gathered around it to perform their improvised ritual. They appear entirely natural, their intimacy unforced, yet this effect of naturalness has been carefully, if imperceptibly, orchestrated. Note, for example, how the demand for the desirable drink travels diagonally across the canvas, establishing the link between the figures: from the little girl leaning against her chair and looking up, to the woman in the scarlet tippet who turns her head toward the girl as if in response to her request, to the butler, leaning forward, ready to serve. Another concatenation is created by the internal echoes between the servant's hand reaching for the *cafetière*, the hand of the woman feeding the child on her lap, and again, in the reversed gesture of the woman in the red cape bringing a spoon to her mouth. These visual rhymes produce a sense of inner circulation and exchange, the bond of consumption that ties the group together. The coffee pot held by the butler has been placed, as if strategically, at the very center of the painting, equidistant from its four sides, confirming its latent importance. Its bottom-heavy, bulbous shape, typical of cafetières, engages in a subtle formal dialogue with the swirl of the rococo sconce above it and, through the white cloth spilling over the top of the mantelpiece, with the porcelain sugar pot and the cup below, creating a sense of morphological consistency of the image. A fashionable commodity—coffee—is established as an invisible yet key aspect of this painting, the act of its consumption securing the internal coherence of the depicted scene.

This is quite different from what de Troy represented some eight years earlier in his *Reading at the Salon* (fig. 1.49).[238] Here, too, we witness an intimate gathering of people in a fashionably decorated interior, with some of its elements quite similar to those that appear in Boucher's canvas, such as the large overmantle mirror flanked by rococo sconces and even the silver teapot much like Boucher's cafétière, standing, alone, on the mantelpiece. This solitary item, however, remains unused. De Troy's group is absorbed in a *lecture*, an act of leisure rather than consumption. A book, not a beverage, is at the center of the picture. This mode of passing time is, moreover, most sumptuously staged, defining this activity as a socially specific enactment of class. Attired with

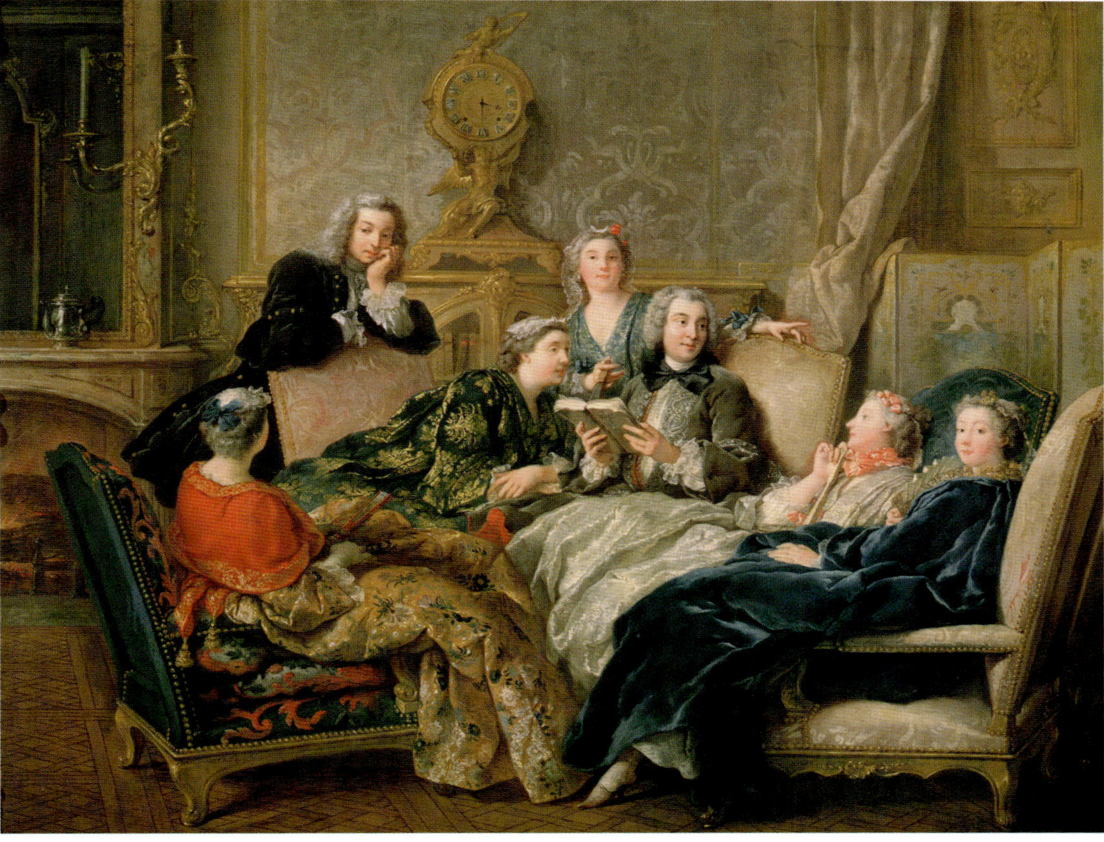

1.49.
Jean François de Troy, *Reading at the Salon*, 1731. Oil on canvas. Houghton Hall, Norfolk, collection of the Marchioness of Cholmondeley.

elegance and at conspicuous expense, de Troy's individuals succumb to a momentary distraction but also show themselves ever ready for another one. A woman in a teal velvet robe turns away from the group to cast a half-inviting, half-querying glance at us, as if asking "Who are *you*? Do you belong with us?"

The gist of de Troy's project is to convey the idea of leisure as the sublime privilege of aristocracy, the very mark of social distinction. In Boucher's painting, on the other hand, the emphasis has shifted from social privilege to personal pleasure. To begin with, his is not an image of elite sociability as much as a representation of elite *private life*. Luxury is not a token of social entitlement as much as a source of personal well-being and bodily comfort. Although the figures in the *Déjeuner* are elegantly dressed, it is not opulence but informality and convenience that their attire, a version of morning wear, or the *déshabillé*, conveys. Moreover, material things perform a different function than in de Troy's canvas. Every person in Boucher's painting is shown holding an object that in some way is involved in the act of providing pleasure, for oneself, or for others—a spoon, a cup, a coffee pot. The commodity, Boucher's image says, is a kind of thing that is literally—bodily, personally—accommodating.

The act of consumption produces a new kind of connectedness between people, an intimacy that cuts across generations, linking adults to children, and also traverses the social boundary between masters and servants. The servant—whose presence is the more conspicuous in comparison to de Troy's exclusively upper-class assembly—is shown to be an integral part of this gathering. The ease with which Boucher's individuals occupy their space, their embeddedness in it, is also remarkable. The sense of comfort extends from furniture to the surroundings that Boucher's protagonists made visibly their own. Their elegantly appointed room is "personalized" by a plethora of knickknacks inserted within its decorative scheme. How exactly an elite interior should be decorated was being codified at the very time when Boucher employed his brushes in representation of the new ideals of domesticity. New models of interior design were being disseminated in print, contributing to the commercialization and relative democratization of the new decorative taste (the *goût moderne*). The key propagator of architectural design and the author of a new typology of elite interior spaces, Jean-François Blondel, who published his first book, *De la Distribution des Maisons de Plaisance* just two years before Boucher painted his *Breakfast*, would have certainly approved of Boucher's interior.[239] Yet Boucher's representation of elite space includes what the architectural design books did not, the traces of personal use that act like a handwritten gloss on the main "text" of this interior. What else are the two small *étagères* suspended on each side of the overmantle mirror for than to display, in addition to books, a silver pot, a small, probably clay magot, and other assorted trinkets, which, together with the lacquered table and the étagères themselves, are the telltale signs that the inhabitants of this room have done their shopping at the marchands merciers?[240] There are, to be sure, also more obviously luxurious objects, such as the porcelain *pot-pourri* mounted in bronze that stands atop a rococo console, or the large, elaborately decorated clock hanging on the wall, both clearly indicating the inhabitants' wealth and taste. But it is above all the display of the inexpensive and superfluous items—these "bagatelles" metamorphosed into things of importance, as Deslandes described them[241]—that give this room its distinct character. The small format of Boucher's painting, half the size of de Troy's, brings it closer to those bagatelles decorating the room than to the more luxurious items in it, thus defining the painting itself as a personal possession.[242]

It is the importance of commodity in the multiple senses of the term—as a commercial article, an object of pleasure, and an attribute of private space—that Boucher's painting brings to the fore. The focus on consumption, rather than leisure per se, as the defining aspect of elite life, and, as a consequence of it, a new ideal of intimacy that is not class based but derives from access to commodities and to the pleasures they provide, are the two key, novel aspects in Boucher's painting.

The Breakfast speaks of a historical phenomenon existing on a wider scale. Studied by historians, eighteenth-century Parisian household inventories from the 1730s and 1740s on revealed an overwhelming presence of all kinds of personal possessions, not only in elite dwellings but in less affluent ones as well.[243] Evidently luxury, in its different forms, was being discovered by the Parisian population at large, and this discovery produced a significant change in the mode of living across different social strata, contributing to the invention of privacy in the spatial and, more broadly, cultural sense of the word. The interior came to be understood and lived as an intimate space defined by the presence of an array of personal items in it, the objects of taste, vehicles of sensory gratification.[244]

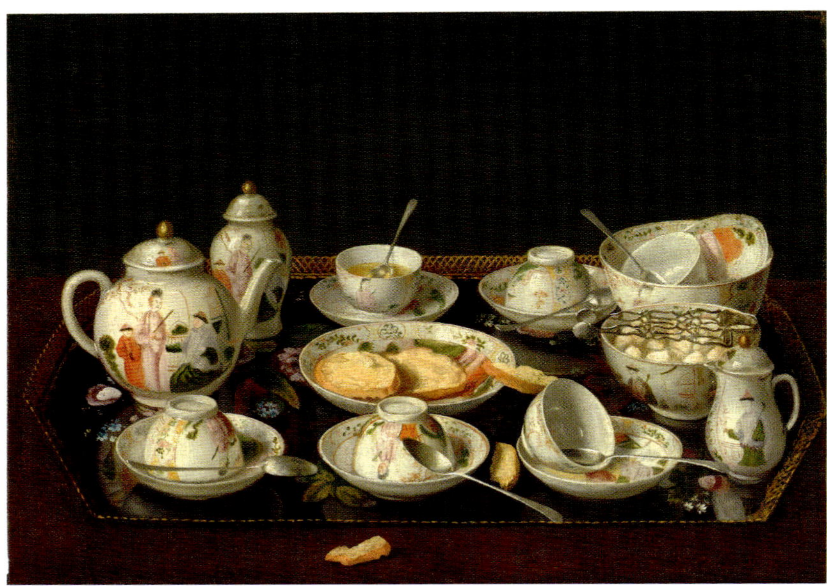

1.50.
Jean-Étienne Liotard, *Still Life: Tea Set*, ca. 1781–83. Oil on canvas mounted on board. The J. Paul Getty Museum, Los Angeles.

The fine tea set, depicted in one of Jean-Étienne Liotard's late still lifes, attests to the newly widespread, personal engagement with one of the era's quintessential, increasingly available commodities, Chinese porcelain (fig. 1.50).[245] Someone has just enjoyed a teatime snack and left the accessories of this light repast on a tray: the empty teacup overturned by a spoon; the leftover tea visible in another; sugar lumps ready to be served with the silver tongs poised on the rim of the bowl; and the remnants of bread on the plate, speak eloquently of pleasures taken. These manifest traces of use are not symbols of *vanitas*, as in the Dutch seventeenth-century precedents for such depictions, but signifiers of *commoditas*, indexes of consumer's enjoyment.

Le Déjeuner also registers this new appreciation of small possessions—the porcelain coffee service standing on the red lacquered table among them. Clearly, they are featured not as proofs of affluence but as personal accessories of daily gratifications. Even the children in Boucher's painting are shown to have already tasted the pleasures of consumption. While the younger child is being fed the fashionable drink by a spoon, the older one leans against her stool in eager anticipation. Although still young enough to have her head protected against bumps with a special scarf tied around her bonnet, the girl displays her many toys with a consumerist panache akin to that of the adults. Clutching her hobby horse like a precious possession, her doll, a miniature effigy of a fashionable lady leaning against her stool, the little girl is an image of a child in the era of consumption, a symptom of the growing dependence on commodities that encompassed all ages.

If Boucher represents not the members of a social elite but, more specifically, consumers, his painting suggests what being a consumer amounted to at that time, the *relation to the object* this role implied. This relation is interesting, especially from our perspective of late, postindustrial capitalism that associates commodity with the subjective effects of alienation and reification. None of these could be detected in Boucher's representation. On the contrary, there is, as we have noted, a sense of connectedness between people and things, a sense of being enlivened and gratified by consumption that his painting exudes, just as, in Liotard's still life, the objects appear enlivened by the pleasure taken in them.

It is not only that they inhabit their space with ease, fit comfortably into their chairs, enjoy their things. It is their sweet *complicity* with their possessions, what Marivaux defined as "la douce sympathie" between people and things, that Boucher makes visible. Marivaux used the term to describe the experiences of his novel's heroine, Marianne, upon her arrival in Paris, which, as Peter Brooks has argued, marked Marianne's symbolic entry into the world.[246] As she put it: "There was a *sweet sympathy* between my imagination and the objects that I was seeing, and I was guessing that one could derive from this multitude of different things endless gratifications (*agréments*) that I did not yet know, in sum, it seemed to me that pleasures lived in the midst of all this."[247]

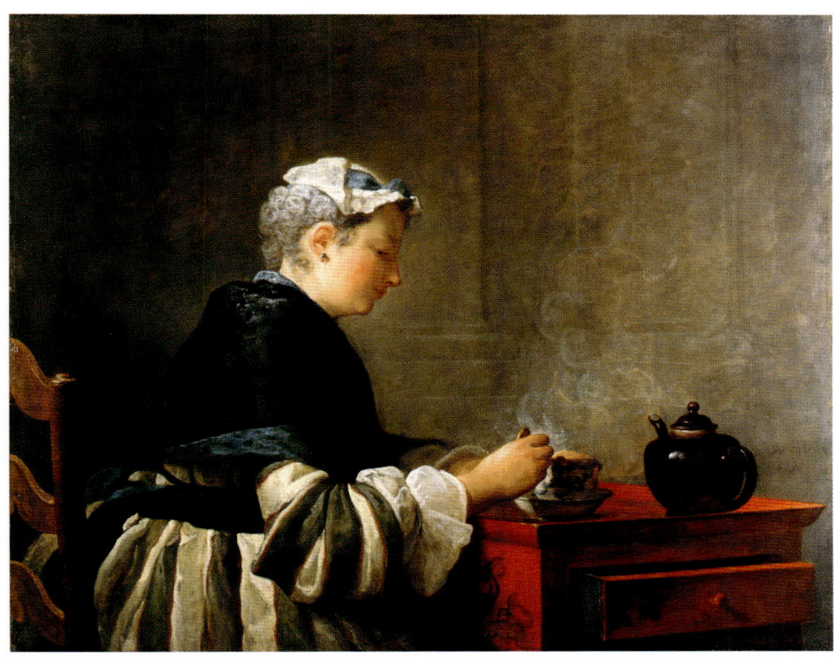

1.51.
Jean-Siméon Chardin, *Lady Taking Her Tea*, 1735. Oil on canvas. The Hunterian Museum and Art Gallery, University of Glasgow.

The rewarding relation of Boucher's figures to their objects can be described in similar terms. Like the children with their toys, the adults in his painting are shown to cherish their objects. The woman in the scarlet cape gently holds her coffee cup in one hand while slowly raising the spoon to her mouth with the other, the warm steam rising from the cup registering not only the temperature of her drink but also her connection to the object that contains it. The point is that it is not only pleasure but also a sense of subjective liaison—sympathy—with an object that we are given to see. Making evident the attachment of the depicted figures to their small possessions, underscoring the care and grace with which they handle their objects, and materializing the privileged link between the body and the thing, the painter shows how small luxury possessions, such as a coffee cup, were, in a sense, *interiorized.* We may say that the woman is shown not only sipping her coffee but also "ingesting" the effect of commodity, that is, acquiring the habit of accommodation provided by consumable goods.

Boucher, let us note, is not the only painter who represents this kind of intimacy with things at the time. We find similar depictions of consumption as a personal ritual in Chardin's *Lady Taking Her Tea*, painted in 1735 though exhibited at the Salon four years later, or in Liotard's slightly later pastel of *The Servant with Hot Chocolate.*[248] Like *Déjeuner*, these images testify to the new kind of attention brought to the small luxuries of daily life and to consumption as an act of focused attention, a source of intense personal satisfaction, chiefly women's. Chardin's lady—likely a portrait of the painter's first wife, Marguerite Saintard—is shown in an act of quasi-communion with her cup of tea (fig. 1.51).[249] The steam rising up from it fills the room with a palpable aromatic promise of the reward in which the woman seems enveloped, oblivious to the surrounding world. The painting extols the small but absorbing pleasures of everyday life—a cup of tea is all that is needed—and the new sense of intimacy with its instruments. The particular interest of Chardin's painting for this discussion lies, though, in the way the painter anchors this idea of sensory reward in a specific object, the porcelain cup, probably an import, as one of those cherished personal belongings that could be found in the after-death inventories from this period—such as that of Marguerite Saintard's herself.[250] In other words, it is not only the new philosophy of the perceiving body discussed by Michael Baxandall in his analysis of this painting but also the new economy of bodily pleasures that is at stake in this image.[251]

In his *La Chocolatière*, Liotard, too, creates an impression of an almost eucharistic connection to the object of consumption (fig. 1.52). Although he stages the hot-chocolate-bearing servant like a quasi-saint, she is clearly an agent of corporeal rather than spiritual satisfactions. Posed against a white background, with floor boards as the only indication of the room, this figure appears as austere and monumental as the Evangelists from the wings of the Northern Renaissance altarpieces.[252] Her hieratic pose bestows gravity onto her mundane task of serving a refreshment. Let us recall that hot chocolate was, like coffee, a newly fashionable beverage at the time, both in public establishments, such as coffee houses, wherein both beverages could be consumed, and in private houses.[253] Liotard is the visual ethnographer of this new private habit, registering in the smallest of details all of its accessories: the porcelain cup with thick dark-brown crust of hot chocolate rising to the brim, a transparent container within which the cup is held for protection from the heat generated by its content, and the glass of water for quenching thirst after consumption of this rich concoction. Combined with the maid's hieratic immobility and her intense concentration on her task, the careful rendition of these objects conveys how important such daily pleasures have become and how important became also the instruments—and purveyors—of these pleasures.

Despite their differences, both paintings represent an altogether new kind of relation to the object made possible by the new conditions of circulation and exchange of consumer goods. Relaying the sense of importance of simply feeling content, of the fleeting quotidian *bonheur* anchored in new kinds of small, superfluous yet significant goods, these depictions indicate the effect of consumption on bodily but also subjective existence.

The Breakfast makes evident how the new mode of experiencing objects—their status as commodities—bears upon the structures of both individual and collective life. Here we witness not a solitary communion with commodity but the immersion of the entire household in the practice of consumption. The interior is not, as it was in the paintings by Chardin and Liotard, a barren theater of the subject's intimate encounter with its objects, but a richly appointed space within which different members of the household coexist. Boucher's inclusion of the servant in his tableau of consumption is particularly telling.[254] The only man in this scene of familial intimacy, the butler appears as a substitute for the paternal figures in the seventeenth-century Northern representations of family life Boucher clearly drew upon. One example, which the artist may have known at least through an engraving, is Flemish painter Isaac Koedyck's *Weaver's Shop*. The figure of a woman feeding a baby on her lap is strikingly similar to one of Boucher's protagonists, as is the father-weaver shown leaning over his loom in the background (fig. 1.53).[255] Yet if this model underwrites Boucher's scene of domestic life, his is not a traditional image of a family. For the defining power of kinship or marriage has been supplanted by the apparently more important bonds of consumption that the figure of the servant facilitates. Like the housemaid featured in

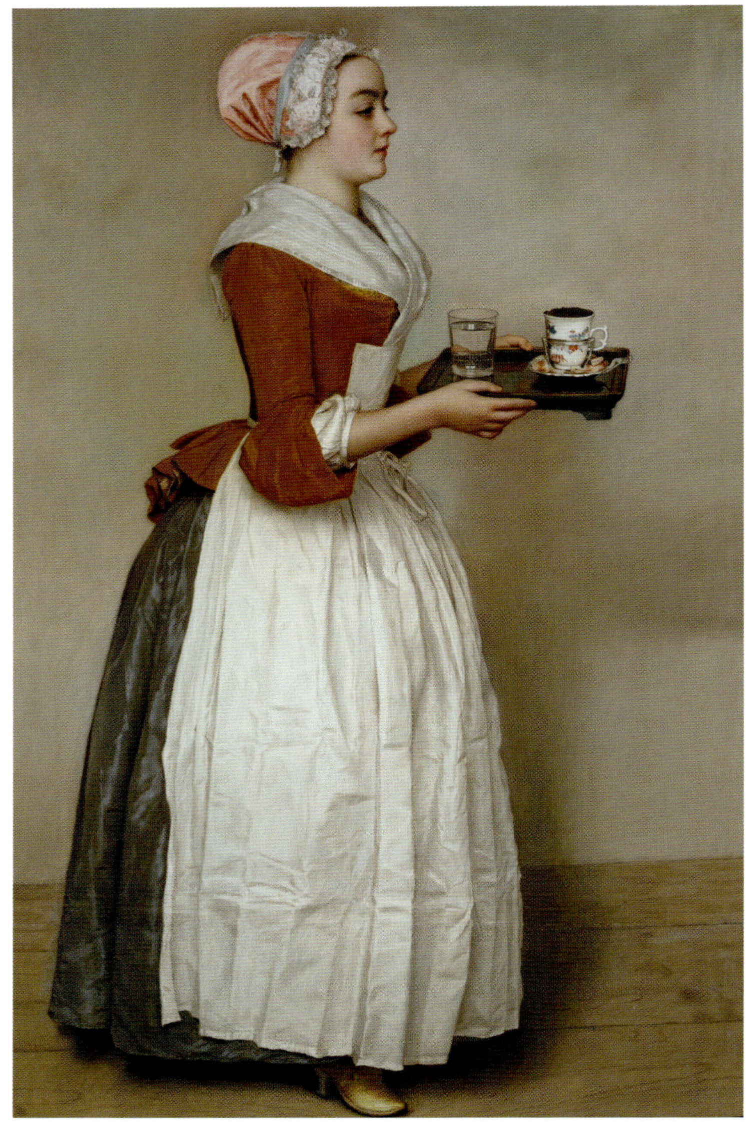

1.52.
Jean-Étienne Liotard, *La Chocolatière* (or *The Servant with Hot Chocolate*), ca. 1744–45. Pastel on parchment. Gemäldegalerie Alte Meister, Dresden.

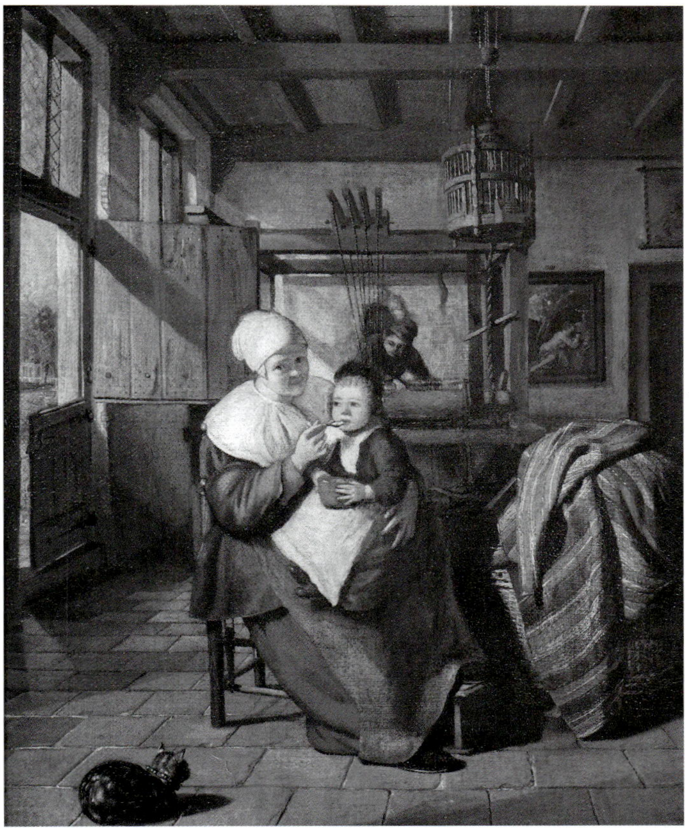

1.53.
Isaac Koedyck, *Weaver's Shop*. Musée des Beaux-Arts, Lille.

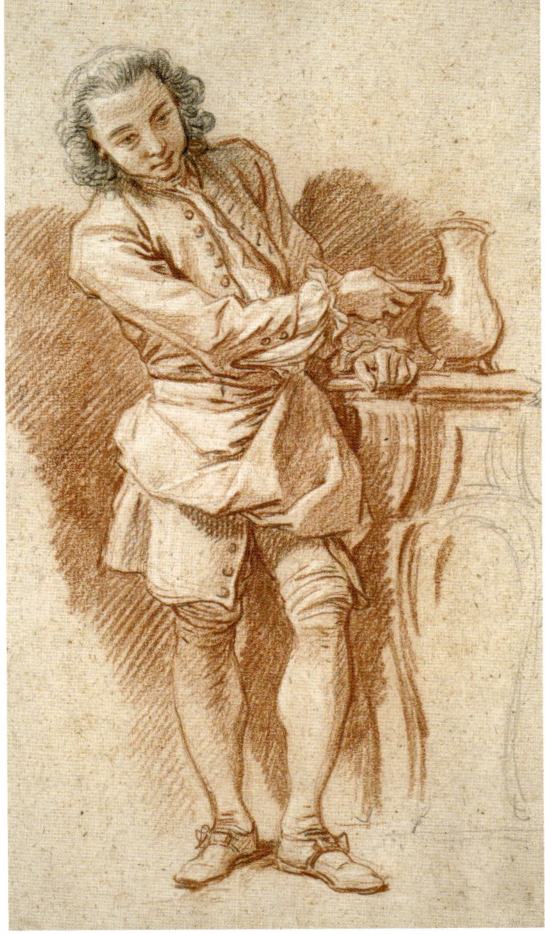

1.54.
François Boucher, *Study of a Valet with Coffee Pot*, ca. 1739. Red chalk, with black chalk, and touches of graphite, heightened with white chalk, on buff laid paper. Art Institute of Chicago, Helen Regenstein Collection.

Liotard's pastel, Boucher's butler is a symptom of the new social and cultural role of the servants. In the world newly permeated by desirable and acquirable things, servants became agents of accommodation and providers of their employers' personal comforts and pleasures, that is, the elite households' conduits of consumption.[256]

Rather than an embodiment of the paternal function, as was the father hovering in the background in Koedyck's image, Boucher's figure is the mediator between people and their objects, and the way he is painted emphasizes this.[257] He is not simply someone who serves what others need but the go-between, a figure straddling both the world of people and the world of things. On the one hand, he appears to be inseparable from the scene. His leaning pose, his physical proximity to the group, his hand grasping the handle of the cafetière, which is echoed in the gestures of others, inscribe him firmly within their intimate circle. Notwithstanding his attendant's mien, he may indeed be taken as one of them. (Marivaux's *Paysan Parvenu* as a story of a butler who married his mistress comes to mind.) But, he is also, more intriguingly, painted as if he were an integral part of their physical surroundings. Inserted in the shallow space between the window and the mantelpiece, his body appears as if it were sprouting directly from the wall, part and parcel of the interior decoration.[258] His legs are not visible—though in a preparatory sheet Boucher drew him in full figure (fig. 1.54)—and the left side of his torso seems to have been "eaten away" by the curtain, as a result of which he seems to be attached, like the étagère behind him, to the wall. Like the small magot behind him, he appears to be both a person and a thing.[259]

The butler's hybrid status raises the issue of social and personal identity in Boucher's representation of domestic life. How, we may ask, does personal accommodation affect the persons thus shown being accommodated? How did the new ideal of personal comfort based in the consumption of goods shape the way people understood themselves *as persons*?

This is not, to be sure, a question that Boucher's painting addresses directly. His figures are all endowed with generic physiognomies that do not convey a strong sense of subjective presence or distinct personality. They may well be seen to illustrate what has been described by cultural historians as "the generic or typological nature of eighteenth-century characterization."[260] Yet Boucher's painting also hints at a more developed sense of individuality, though through means other than facial expression or body language. It imparts that there is a relation between the newly accommodating interior and the emergence of the new cultural ideal of interiority, that the personalization of space results in the emergent sense of the person *as a space*.

The way in which the trope of exteriority subtly reinscribes this view of the interior may be taken as one such indirect commentary on selfhood as a space formed by the habits of consumption. For, self-absorbed and self-sufficient as it may seem at first, this enclave of privacy opens itself up toward us, letting us in, as if inadvertently, to what is going on. The butler leans forward, the woman in the red mantle turns around to attend to her child's demand, and we feel admitted into their closed circle, privy to their ritual. Although neither of them looks directly at us, they seem to know they are being looked at—the child seated on the woman's lap gives them away by looking at us directly, if with a somewhat vacant, unseeing stare. The exterior is what this interior space separates itself from, and yet also what it includes or opens up to, at once oblivious and cognizant of the outside world.

This is not, however, a matter of "absorption" understood by Michael Fried as a trope manifesting the concern with pictorial autonomy in eighteenth-century painting.[261] What is going on here has to do less with how one constructs a compelling visual fiction focused on a human subject than with how this subject envisions itself in the visible world. *The Breakfast* depicts how human capacity to imagine oneself was transformed by the advent of a realm of things that allowed for an engrossing material existence increasingly cut off from any principles of transcendence.[262] This transformation implied a fundamental change in the relation between the visible world and the seeing subject: focused upon its own realm, the subject could begin, so to speak, to see itself *from within itself*. The "world's gaze" became the internalized principle that defined not only social but also internal functioning of this new kind of person.[263]

Nothing conveys this effect of internalized exteriority more eloquently in the painting than the motif of the mirror. The reflection it provides—the multiplied rectangles of the opposite wall that suggest a door to another room, or a closet, framed by a curtain drawn to the sides—conveys a sense of space that exists beyond the represented room but remains inaccessible, invisible. The door is shut. It leads to nowhere. The existence of something beyond can be inferred but it cannot be located (fig. 1.55). Differing from the doors in seventeenth-century Dutch genre painting that rarely fail to open onto another, adjacent space, or onto the outside (Pieter de Hooch's interiors come to mind), Boucher's aperture is at once suggested and closed off by an endless replication of flat surfaces.[264] The point is not that the mirror indicates the existence of another pocket of interiority that cannot be seen, but rather that it *installs* this other space within the space of the room we are seeing. The reflection produces, moreover, a sense of depth that is defined emphatically, through the replication of flat frames, as a surface. In curious contrast to the richly appointed room that we are given to see, this other interior seems barren, barely articulated, and conspicuously unadorned—like the settings in the paintings of Chardin and Liotard we have looked at before. Serving as the immediate backdrop of the woman in a red mantle who is turned away from it and toward her child, the mirror reflec-

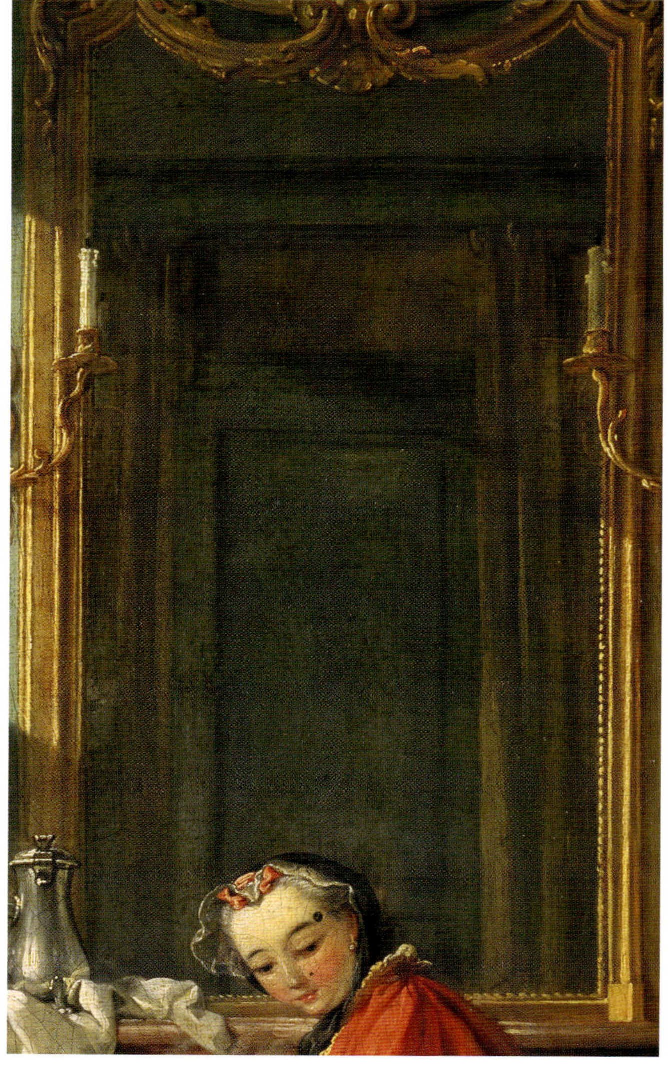

1.55.
François Boucher, *Le Déjeuner*, or *The Breakfast*, detail of fig. 1.48.

tion suggests itself as a figure of *her* interiority, that is, as a space different from her outward existence in this one. One can say that the mirror "returns" the interior to her as an image of her own internal space. Moreover, it defines it as a peculiar kind of space, a personal depth that is only a surface and that remains inaccessible to her, or of which she seems unaware.

What we have is not the traditional motif of the mirror as the device of vanity or narcissistic self-confirmation. It is not a surface of self-reflection, one in which one may recognize—or misrecognize—oneself (the mirror reflects no one), nor a reassuring echo of the full riches of this dwelling space. Rather, it is a kind of abstracted illusion—a *sign* of space—aligned, moreover, with another form of illusion, the painting above it. A figure of an internalized exteriority, the mirror hints at what the immersion in the field of objects that define the realm of the visible in the era of consumption *does* to the inner life of the subject. It reveals a kind of outwardness emerging within the self. This is not to say that the painting suggests a reduction of the once-deep and fully fleshed self to a mere appearance. It would be tempting to construct such an argument, following the now familiar association, first suggested by Rousseau, of commodity with reification, consumption with alienation.[265] Rather, the opposite may be argued: that the emphasis on exterior *creates* a sense of interior. The barren, abstract space reflected in the mirror stands for a key aspect of the subject of consumption, envisioning its self-abstracting alignment with visual representation that is at once constraining and enabling. It represents the self that exists for others, for show—a self that Rousseau was to denounce later as aligned with "seeming" rather than "being"—but also one that becomes visible and intelligible—to others and to oneself.[266]

It is thus that this entirely convincing representation of the *douceur de la vie* within the fashionably appointed interior, an image of the safely, sweetly interiorized life, subtly registers the ambivalent effect of this life linked to the concomitant subjective *exte*riorization. As if unbeknownst to itself, the painting intimates that the investment in personal possessions, the subjective liaison with the objects, results in the transformation of one's own self into a quasi-decorative object of the world's gaze. The figure of the butler epitomizes this; he is both a three-dimensional person and a decorative item, not unlike the exotic trinkets on the étagère. All the figures in this painting are, in fact, shown to be animated in a way that closely resembles the internal animation of the interior decor. Their bodies are shown leaning, turning, or twisting gently, like the sconces, the frame of the clock, the legs of the console, the trimmings on the wall, with the flow of their clothes underscoring this analogy, as does the inexpressive, unindividuated quality of their faces. They seem to be all tropes.[267] Yet at the same time, the painting points out that such emphasis on the exterior produces an emergent sense of interiority, a spatial recognition of oneself as a being with a discrete "inside," such as the one the mirror "installed" to the woman in the red tippet, a realm that, though invisible to her, is her own.

Despite its small format and its status as "mere" genre, Boucher's *Breakfast* takes on some of the major questions haunting the emergent "culture of appearances": consumption's subjective effects. Do commodities allow for individuation or, on the contrary, standardization of the self? Is the reliance on objects a basis of subjective autonomy or reifying dependence? Although Boucher cannot be seen to deliver a firm judgment on these matters—this is not, after all, his role—his painting does make some important suggestions. If it registers the transformation of the self into surface in the nascent culture of consumption, it also sketches out an emergent self-consciousness about oneself as a divided entity. This is a subjectivity marked by the split between the (signifying) exterior and the (signified) interior, that is, by the structure of the sign that enables the self to represent itself—to others and to itself—but also one that installs the element of the invisible, the unknowable (the unconscious) within the self. It is in this sense that Boucher may be said to paint a recognition of life in the new interior as generative of inner life.

—·—

That consumption transforms both the physical interior and the cultural notions of interiority is also evident in two cabinet pictures that Boucher produced for his Swedish patrons, *La Toilette* and *La Marchande de modes*. Both paintings focus on a specific aspect of consumption, namely, fashion. Painted in 1742 for Count Carl Gustaf Tessin, a Swedish envoy to Paris, *La Toilette*, also known as the *Lady Fastening a Garter*, depicts a young woman who is dressing, assisted by her servant (fig. 1.56). The woman's social rank is uncertain: she is about to don a laced cap called a *commode* that married women wore at home at the time, but her uninhibited pose indicates that she may well be a courtesan.[268] *La Marchande de modes*

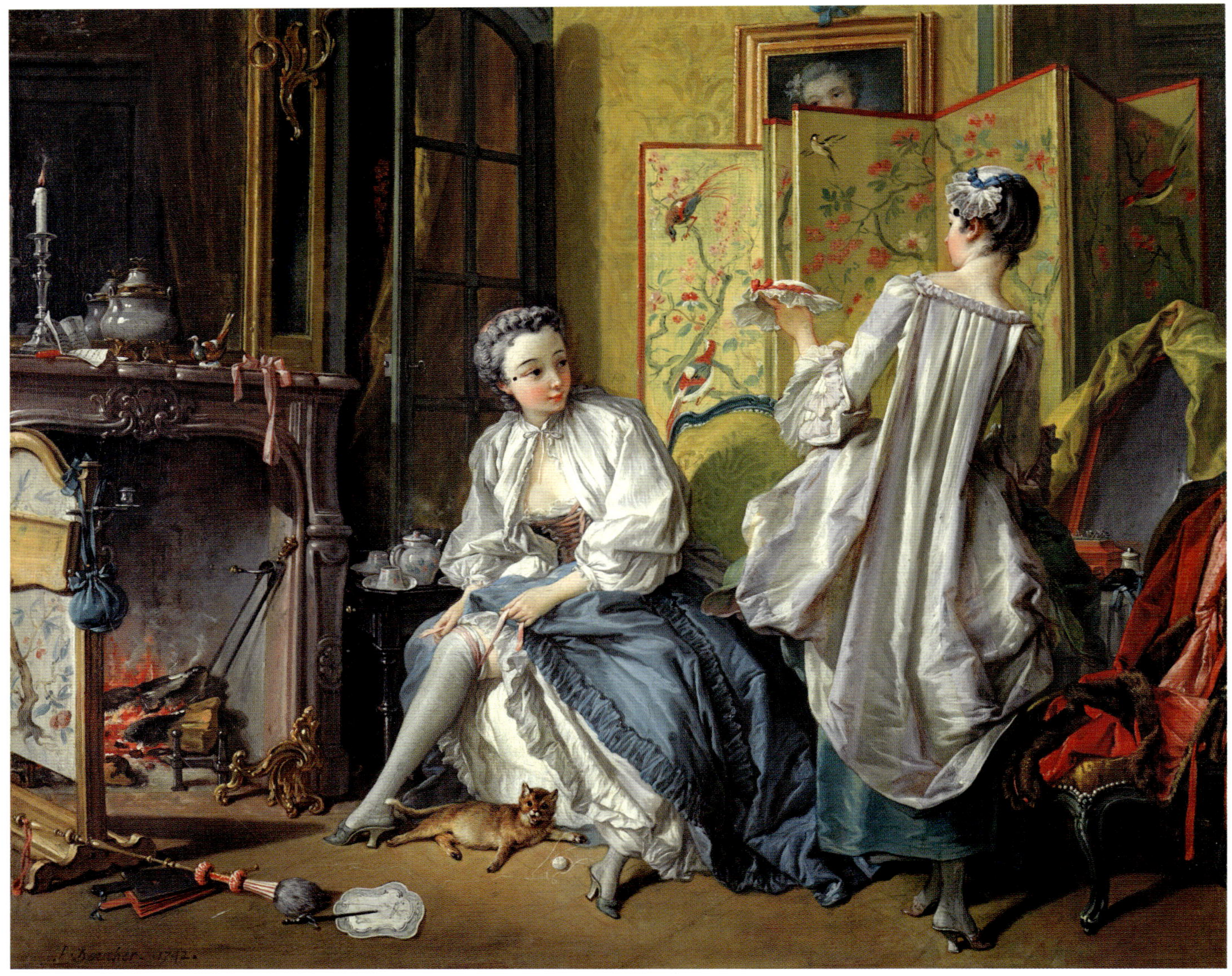

(*The Milliner*), painted in 1746, was part of a larger commission orchestrated by Tessin for Crown Princess Louisa Ulrika of Sweden (fig. 1.57). Also known as *Morning*, it was to be the first of a series of paintings—never completed by Boucher—representing different activities performed at four times of day.[269] Here, the morning toilette of a young lady has been interrupted by a visit from a *modiste* offering her wares. The paintings differ in tone, with *La Toilette*, commissioned by Tessin, being more frivolous than the perfectly decorous toilette scene painted for the Swedish princess. What they share, though, is an approach to fashion as both a social phenomenon and a cultural symptom of an ongoing change in the relation between representation and identity. This change is manifest in Boucher's own approach to representation, specifically, his treatment of the tableau de modes as a particular type of image.

As a pictorial subgenre, the tableau de modes was in and of itself a visual symptom of the burgeoning consumer culture wherein fashion acquired a newly prominent status. This was due to a combination of factors, including the global expansion of trade, the wider availability of textiles, especially cotton, and dyes, and the development of new modes of manufacture that allowed for the production of cheaper versions of luxuries, that is, *populuxe* or *semiluxe* items.[270] The silk stockings that the woman in *La Toilette* is putting on exemplify the populuxe articles that signaled the wider social spread of fashion. No longer limited to court elites, fashion was commercialized, affecting the functioning of society at large. Whereas in earlier times clothing was either made to measure for the rich or, in case of the poor, sewn by the wearers themselves, in the early eighteenth century we witness the emergence of new commer-

1.56. ABOVE
François Boucher, *La Toilette*, or *A Lady Fastening Her Garter*, 1742. Oil on canvas. Museo Thyssen-Bornemisza, Madrid.

1.57. OPPOSITE
François Boucher, *La Marchande de modes*, or *The Milliner*, 1746. Oil on canvas. Nationalmuseum, Stockholm.

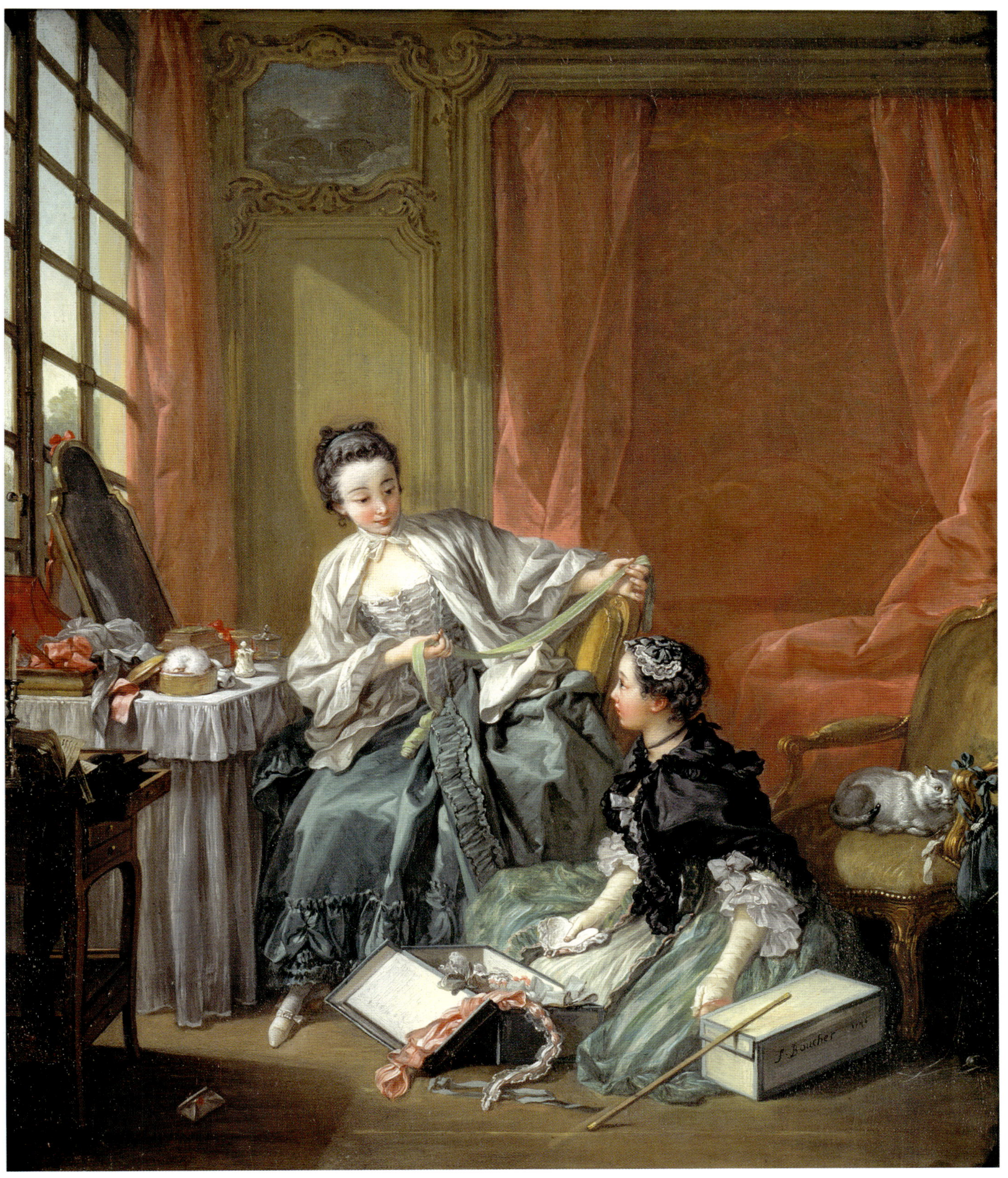

cial establishments producing ready-to-wear clothing, such as the one depicted in Antoine Raspal's painting of 1760 where cheaper versions of elite dresses in printed cotton are shown hanging on the wall behind the seamstresses (fig. 1.58), and of the retailers, mostly female, known as the *marchandes de mode*, such as the one featured in Boucher's painting for Louisa Ulrika.[271] Fashion ceased to be a discrete, socially circumscribed phenomenon, and became, in its diverse forms, an aspect of social life at large, permeating different social strata and generating a new corporeal semiosis.[272]

Boucher's two paintings engage with this new significance of fashion. In both paintings the concern for appearance is shown to have permeated the rituals of women's everyday life and—albeit in a less direct mode—to have affected their social and personal identity. Fashion, however, also inflects Boucher's approach to a genre scene, resulting not only in a new interpretation of the toilette theme but also in a novel mode of representation. Briefly put, his emphasis shifts from anecdote to description, from narration to enumeration.[273] What results, in both paintings, is an image of an interior rich in material detail yet marked by an uncertainty of meaning.

It is, again, in comparison to earlier depictions of such scenes that Boucher's distinct approach becomes salient. The iconography of a woman's toilette was most often used in the eighteenth century to represent a situation ripe with erotic allusion. Such was, for example, Nicolas Lancret's *Morning*, one of a series of paintings titled *The Four Times of Day* (an assignment similar to one of Boucher's Swedish commissions), shown at the Salon of 1739.[274] In Lancret's canvas, the woman's morning ritual has been interrupted by a visit from an abbé who is shown transfixed by his hostess's intimate charms, which she "inadvertently" reveals to him while serving tea. Another example that may have directly inspired Boucher, Jean-François de Troy's *The Garter* of 1724, is too, a visual anecdote of seduction in which a woman fends off a man offering to help tie her garter (fig. 1.59).

Boucher's most obvious difference from these two examples is that he forgoes the courting implications of the toilette theme. In both paintings he subtracts the male figure from the scene and brings to the fore the interaction between women. But it is an interaction of a peculiar kind: nothing happens. Objects are passed in silence from one woman to another: the servant hands a lace bonnet to her mistress, a lady admiringly inspects a ribbon received from her milliner. The fashionable accessory, in a sense, replaces the customary man of the toilette scenes. What Boucher depicts is not social intercourse but an encounter with commodity. The narrative ties between figures are substituted by the effect of circulation and exchange of fashionable items between the servant and her mistress, by the marchande to her client. This transmission suspends the traditional temporality of a genre scene: one has the impression that the bonnet is just one among many things that will be continuously passed on—the red fur-trimmed cape lying on the armchair ready to be worn indicates as much—just as the dress trimmings will endlessly emerge from the milliner's boxes for her client's inspection.

It is this flow of things that defines the roles of women in these paintings as supplier and receiver of commodities and that engages their bodies in a kind of uneventful, quasi-mechanical reciprocity, a version, we may note, of the figural reciprocity of the mythological figures in Derbais's paintings. But this reciprocity is commercially defined: it speaks of shopping, not courting. The women's gestures are rudimentary, their faces expressionless. No comments are exchanged, nor are messages communicated. The fashionable accessory—the laced cap, the velvet ribbon—is the crux of their interchange, and *it* is where eros resides.

It is the desirability of the material object—the attraction of commodity—that these toilette scenes stage. One may of course argue that *La Toilette* is

1.58. BELOW
Antoine Raspal, *Seamstress's Workshop in Arles*, 1760. Oil on canvas. Musée Réattu, Arles.

1.59. OPPOSITE
Jean-François de Troy, *The Garter*, 1724. Oil on canvas. Williams College Museum of Art, Williamstown, Massachusetts. Gift of C. A. Wimpfheimer, Class of 1949.

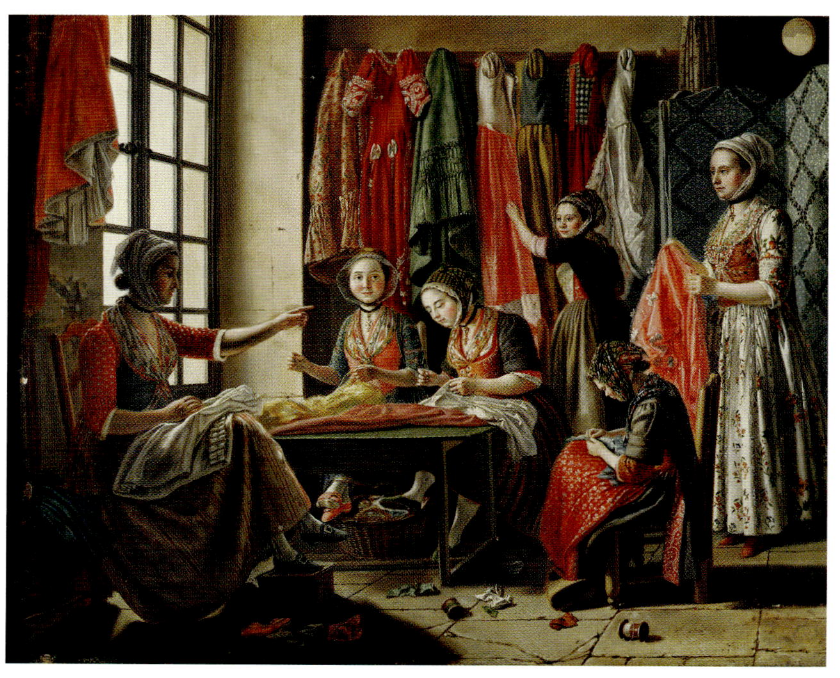

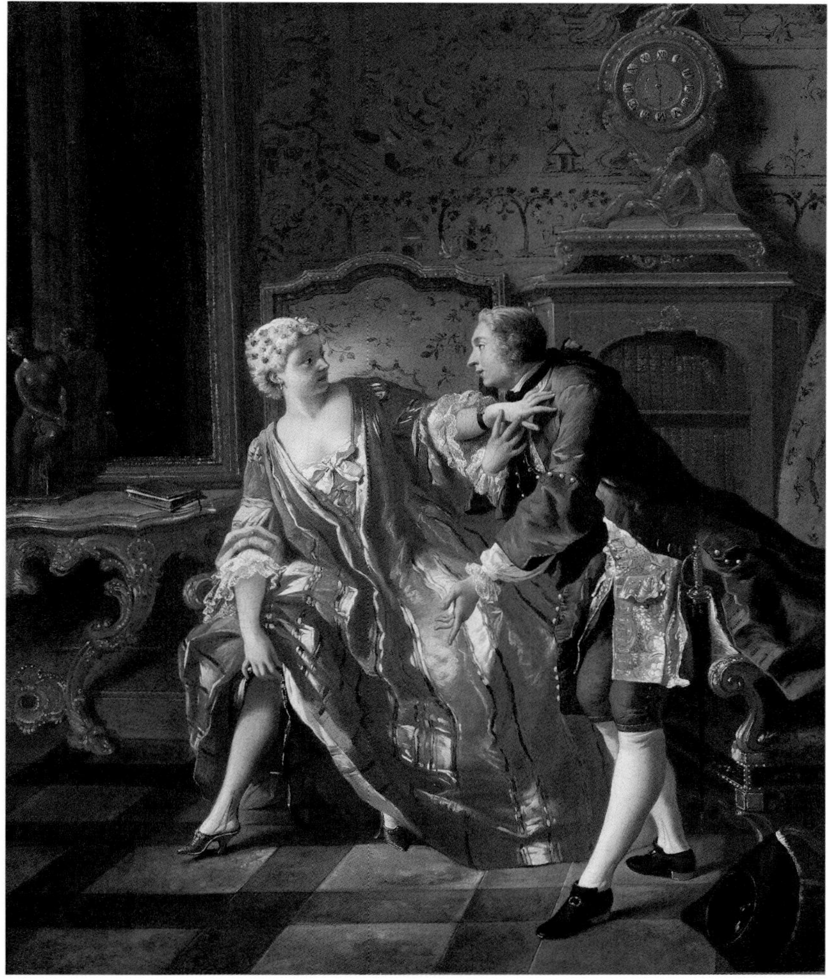

interpersonal, and predictably gendered, dynamic between woman and man, or, between the figure in the painting and her imaginary viewer. It invites us to consider, before anything else, the personal gratification the depicted woman *herself* obtains from her bodily accessories, the pleasure of donning a commodity. What Boucher paints is the personal—and personalizing—dimension of fashion having to do with the sensory gratification provided by the thing. The glint of flesh next to the garter the woman ties around her stocking suggests just that. If it is an erotic tease, it evokes an eros that has less to do with courting, and male-female relations, as in de Troy, than with a budding human attraction to things.

And it is things, as much as bodies, that *La Toilette* "shows off." The sheer number of objects scattered about this small room and the very mode of their presentation—pell-mell, without hierarchy or order—is remarkable. The additive, discontinuous fashion in which they are represented—like a "laundry list" of luxurious and semiluxurious possessions, from an ornamental screen, to a China set, all kinds of decorative trinkets, a fan, and plethora of other items lying on the floor—renders this interior unkempt and confusing. Although not as crammed, the interior space of *The Milliner* also features a plethora of small possessions. The lady's toilette accessories teem on her table, and other personal belongings spill from the drawers of the small adjacent table, just as the milliner' s wares are drawn out of her box and strewn on the floor.

This quasi-enumerative mode of representation creates an impression—especially strong in *La Toilette*—of the painting as an elaborately disordered still life, rather than a genre scene. The attention given to the external details of women's attire contributes to the sense of mild confusion between objects and beings. Boucher's inclusive brush does not miss any aspect of his protagonists' appearance: the slightly powdered hairdo called "the sheep's head" (*tête de mouton*) sported by the lady tying her garter, and the prominent black *mouche* (a beauty spot) on her face; the peignoir to protect her dress from hair powder during its application; the elegant high-heel slippers both she and her servants wear, her servant's shiny *robe volante retroussée*.[276] In *The Milliner*, Boucher details the green satin morning robe decorated with *falbalas*, and the peignoir of the lady; her pale peach satin slipper with a buckle and bow showing from underneath the rim of her dress; the white gloves with cut-off fingers worn by

still an essentially "male fantasy about how women behave in the absence of men,"[275] and that, as such, it is addressed to an invisible male viewer. The pose of the woman tying her garter is undeniably revealing and even sexually provocative. Yet such a reading—locating eros in the woman's body understood as the object of male pleasure—does not allow for the full appreciation of the investment in the fashionable item itself as the libidinal object in Boucher's painting. The erotic subtext in this picture has less to do with interpersonal relations than with the relation of persons to things. This is what defines the main protagonist—the fashionable woman—in these scenes. Accessories are shown to be key in the production of her seductive appearance, and this production is what these paintings are "about," *La Toilette* most explicitly in that it lets us in on the very process of dressing the body.

Sombart's insight, evoked in the earlier section of this chapter, is also of relevance for it draws our attention to the sensory satisfaction derived from commodity as imaginable on a level different from the

the milliner, and so on. Through such details the women's bodies appear inscribed within a continuum of things, rather than a network of human relation, such as those envisioned in Lancret's and de Troy's tableaux de modes.

This emphasis on sheer description raises the fundamental issue of meaning in these interior scenes—both how and what they signify. The disarray of objects in *La Toilette* has often been read emblematically, *à la* seventeenth-century Dutch paintings, as signs that possess a hidden moral meaning, here having to do with the sexual promiscuity of the woman.[277] The motif of the cat playing with the ball of yarn on the floor, almost directly under the woman's petticoat, seems a rather obvious sexual reference, as does the steaming pot of tea next to her, or the open fireplace with a log burning inside. The general disorder of things in this interior would stand for a moral disorder, constituting an indirect commentary on the conduct of its inhabitant.

Yet Boucher's insistently descriptive and disordered presentation of objects may well be seen as canceling out their potentially emblematic eloquence. Such an assortment of fashionable bagatelles—most of which are recognizable as specific imports in the latest *chinoiserie* taste[278]—amounts not to a network of symbolic allusions but to a mere collection of things, the materialization of commodities as such. Their random appearance cramming the interior resembles the commercial space from which some of these objects came, such as the imagined Chinese merchant's outlet of exportable exotica depicted by an unknown artist (fig. 1.60).[279] This is not to say that the objects in Boucher's painting have *no meaning* but that their meaning is linked to the effect of metonymy rather than metaphor: generated by the relation of contiguity, rather than depth, it glides on the paintings' surface. Their random accumulation points to their contingency as signifiers of fashion, their status as at once desirable and superfluous things with an uncertain and unstable significance dependent on the current fad. It is precisely this quintessential aspect of luxury, its superfluity, that Boucher makes obvious. If these provisionally assembled things—the porcelain bird, the teapot, the fan, the garter—speak, it is in a language different from their Dutch precedents in that it lacks moral coherence or, for that matter, *any* signifying consistency. The mobile, metonymic structure of the painting matches their thematics of commercial exchange but also underscores the nature of this commercially induced desire, its logic based in continuous substi-

1.60.
Interior of a Chinese Shop (fan leaf), Holland, ca. 1680–1700. Gouache on paper, mounted on wooden panel. Victoria and Albert Museum, London.

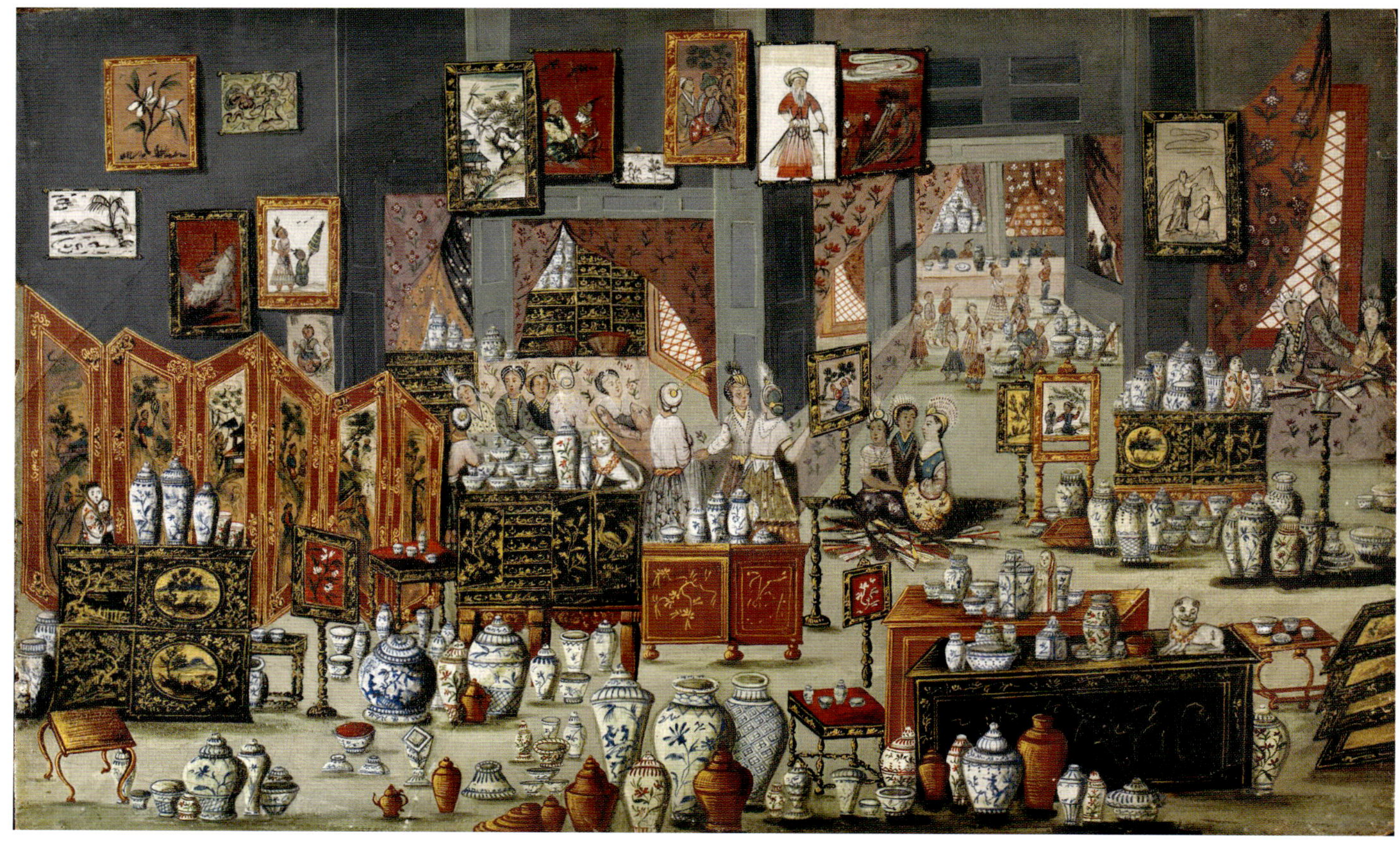

tution—a metonymic drift—of one thing for another, with no loss or lack involved.[280] And what this provisional, libidinally invested mode of presentation helps convey is the quality of life under their spell, a mode of existence governed by the principles of randomness, change, and sensual pleasure.

At the time Boucher was painting, the effect of fashion on everyday life was a favored subject of social commentary. Many contemporary observers derided or deplored fashionable consumption as the mindless pursuit of novelty and change. Béat-Louis Muralt, a Swiss traveler visiting Paris in the 1720s, exemplifies a typical reaction of dismay at the pace with which fashion produced changes in the mode of dressing in the capital. Even servants, he observed with mild alarm, were required to be stylish and could be dismissed simply on the grounds of not following the latest fad.[281] Writing in the mid-1750s, Deslandes paints a similar picture of French society in the grip of fashion: "To change the style of their clothing or of their furniture every six months seem nothing but a light distraction. . . . Being outmoded is a terrible embarrassment: a failure of taste, of invention."[282]

If *La Toilette* represents this mode of fashionable living, it does not impart a sense of indignation about it. Boucher's women clearly belong to the elegant society (*le beau monde*) defined, in Deslandes's words, by taste "for the frivolous, the apparent, for a certain external decoration."[283] But Boucher restrains from opinionating; he describes. Even if one can discern an occasional residual metaphor within his essentially descriptive mode of representation—such as a cat playing under the woman's skirts, a motif imported from Northern genre painting—there is no consistent moral program in this painting. Boucher's image signifies *promiscuously*, inconsistently, equivocally, and is therefore as disorienting or confusing as the interior it represents. This ambivalent mode of signification signals what these paintings are "about": not traditional morality but the new ethics of consumption. Their subjects are the pleasures of shopping and of fashionable possessions and the mode in which these pleasures redefine human comportment and the meaning of life in the era of consumption, which is to say of life *with* and *in* things. In this regard, they tell us something more specific than what Voltaire, for one, had to say about the matter. Suggesting a degree of abstraction, of instability by the very mode in which they construct their meaning, these paintings formulate a new language of things that is both legible and unreliable.

This uncertainty or inconsistency of meaning manifests itself also in the definition of the individuals in these paintings—their relationships and their identity. If we saw the social identity of the woman tying her garter as dubious, we are no more certain about the identity of her attendant. Sartorially, she does not seem to differ much from her mistress (fig. 1.61). Wearing a robe volante, also known as a *robe negligée*, tucked into the pockets of her petticoat for comfort, silk stockings, high-heel mules, and a laced cap of her own, this figure is as stylish, and as aware of it, as the main protagonist of this scene. She may well be, as some commentators have suggested, a modiste rather than a maid.[284] (We may note that, in Boucher's preparatory drawing, this figure is drawn in a shorter version of the robe volante typically worn by maidservants and, more generally, lower-class women, though the elaborate ruffles on her sleeves, more typical of elite dress, are still confusing as indicators of her *état* [fig. 1.62].[285]) A similar effect can be discerned in *The Milliner* where the modiste, in her striped satin robe and flounced sleeves, a black satin mantle, a lace cap, and gloves, is no less modishly clad than her client. It is only the position she occupies on the floor, at the foot of the lady that indicates her subaltern status.

Using dress to blur as much as define his figures' social rank, Boucher registers changes occasioned in French society by fashion and the rise of populuxe goods. In the early decades of the eighteenth century the strict distinctions and hierarchies of usage governed by sumptuary laws began to disappear, resulting in a new confused and confusing semiology of clothing.[286] The resulting confusion of social signs was commented upon with increasing frequency throughout the eighteenth century. Thus the Marquis de Mirabeau complained in 1756 about paying profuse compliments to a man wearing a coat of black silk drugget and a well-powdered wig who turned out to be "his saddler's head assistant."[287] Another contemporary commentator reporting on the changes wrought by fashion in the everyday life of the provincial town of Montpellier found it profoundly revolting that "a chambermaid [was] as artfully decked out as her mistress."[288] Games of imitation and role reversals between masters and servants rendered possible by fashion developments were the subjects of plays written by Marivaux in the 1720s and '30s, such as *L'Isle de la Raison* and *L'Isle des Esclaves*.[289] As Daniel Roche has observed, changes in the uses of clothing scrambled the marks of social

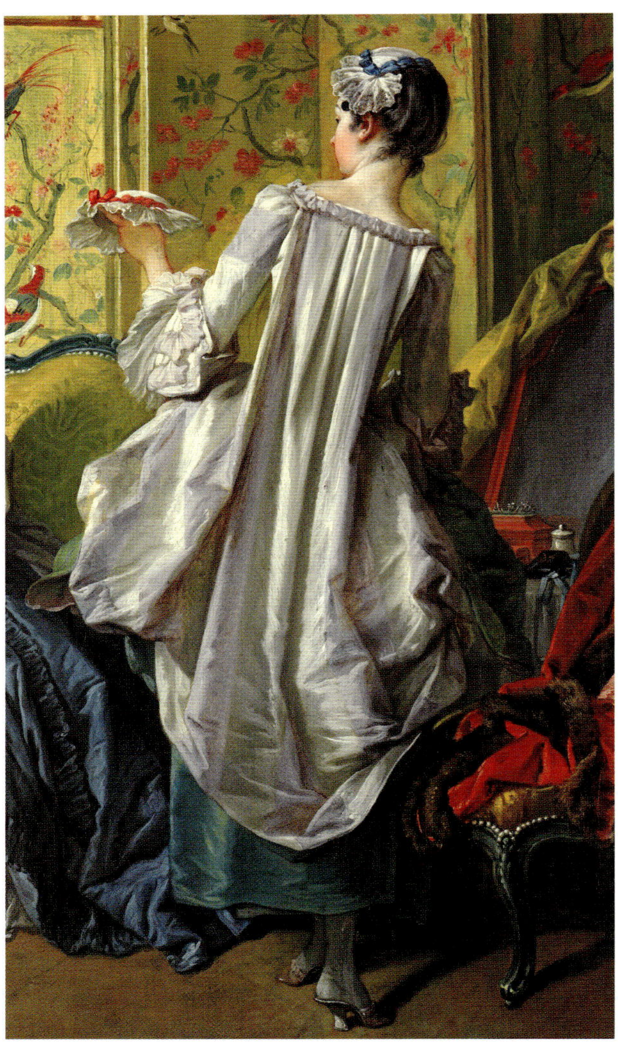

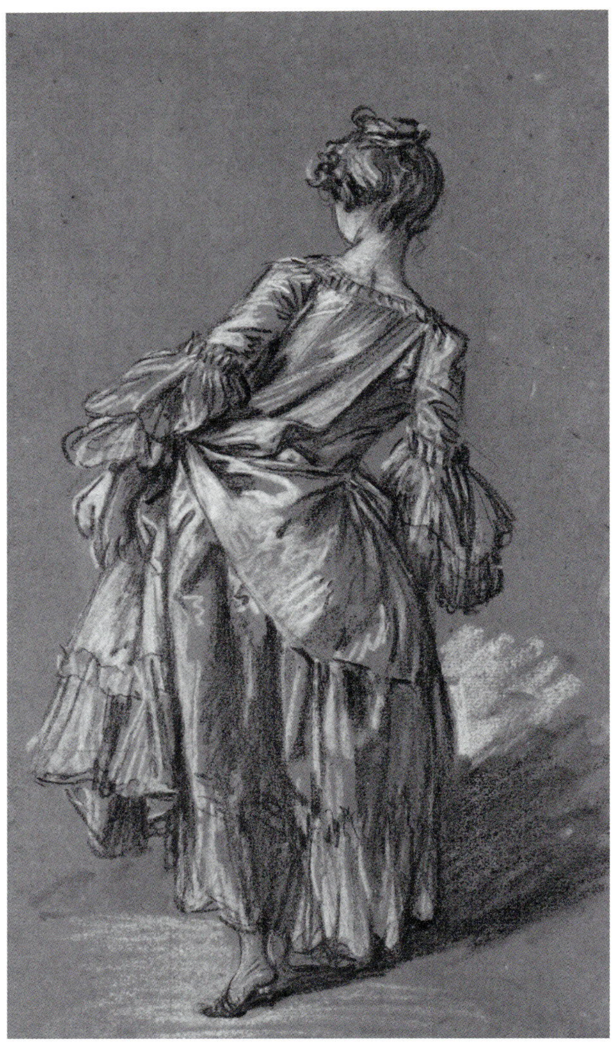

1.61.
François Boucher, *La Toilette*, or *A Lady Fastening Her Garter*, detail of fig. 1.56.

1.62.
François Boucher, *Standing Woman Seen from Behind*, ca. 1742. Black, red, and white chalk, with stumping, on gray brown paper. Fondation Custodia, Frits Lugt Collection, Paris.

rank and, to an extent, also the ranks themselves. "Valets and masters, maidservants and mistresses were confused in the urban theater as they had long been in theatrical convention."[290]

In his theaters of domesticity, Boucher stages a similar kind of confusion. Fashion in his paintings is shown as a source of these women's identity but also as the very factor that destabilizes it. Elaborately clad, both mistresses and their attendants are linked by the mimicry that the historian Sarah Maza speaks of in her analysis of the relations between masters and servants in eighteenth-century France.[291] Boucher's paintings, however, blur not only social but also subjective boundaries. They speak of the elusive or inconsistent nature of personal identity in the era of consumption. The attendant handing a bonnet to the "lady" points to this new kind of subjective instability. With her backward stance and her head shown in *profil perdu*, she is a direct descendant of the pictorial universe of Watteau and, as such, yet another proof of the importance of the Watteau's work for Boucher's own (fig. 1.63). But the way in which Boucher uses this figure signals a subtle but significant transformation of his predecessor's figural language: from a fashionable person in Watteau, the woman has morphed in Boucher's work into a *cipher* of fashion itself. How a *femme de chambre* performing her functions as a personal body servant to her mistress could look is illustrated by Boucher's drawing of a similar, if far less ambiguous scene, now in Stockholm (fig. 1.64).[292] By comparison with the solicitous maid tying her mistress's corset in the Stockholm sheet, the pose of our figure seems indeed more fitting to a marchande de modes than a servant not only in how she holds the bonnet but also in the way she presents *herself*. Her entire body is shaped by what appears to be a deliberate act of sartorial demonstration, and her face shown in profil perdu contributes to the impression that her figure has taken on the role of human physiognomy—of fashion. We are dealing with a different kind of elusiveness than Watteau's. Rather than being reticent, our servant/modiste seems to thrive on self-exposure: she is the embodiment of promiscuous self-display. And as such, Boucher's figure represents something broader than herself: she evokes a new mode of social behavior and the new mode of subjective existence it entailed.

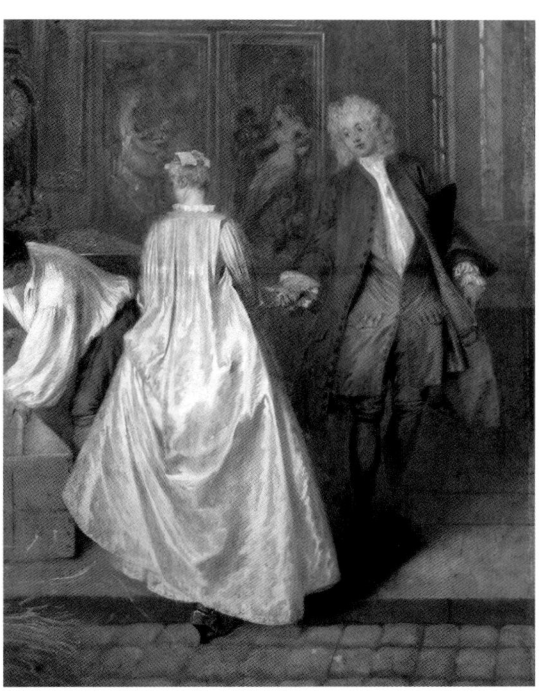

1.63.
Antoine Watteau, *Gersaint's Shopsign*, 1721, detail. Oil on canvas. Schloss Charlottenburg, Berlin.

Marivaux's *La Vie de Marianne* offered one of the most perceptive contemporary accounts of the kind of promiscuity that became a mode of social comportment rather than a specific character trait. The novel, which appeared in installments between 1731 and 1742, was on everyone's lips and may well have been read by Boucher. In one of the most striking passages, Marivaux describes the social debut of his heroine, who, having found employment and modest income, arrives at church for Sunday mass dressed for the occasion: "The seat I have chosen put me in the midst of people. . . . What a feast! It was the first time that I was going to relish the merit of my smart figure. I was so moved by the pleasure of imagining what it [my appearance] would bring about that I was almost breathless. For I was sure of my success, and my vanity saw in advance all the looks that would fall on me."[293]

This act of self-display provides Marianne with a sense of previously unknown gratification. It also produces in her an enhanced self-awareness linked to being a spectacle that she herself produces and controls. Having become self-conscious about operating under the gaze of others, she calculates all her movements and gestures to produce the best possible effect. For example, she feels compelled to repeatedly adjust her headdress (*coiffe*) so that her "naked hand could thus be shown, a gesture that entailed also the exposure of almost half of my well-rounded

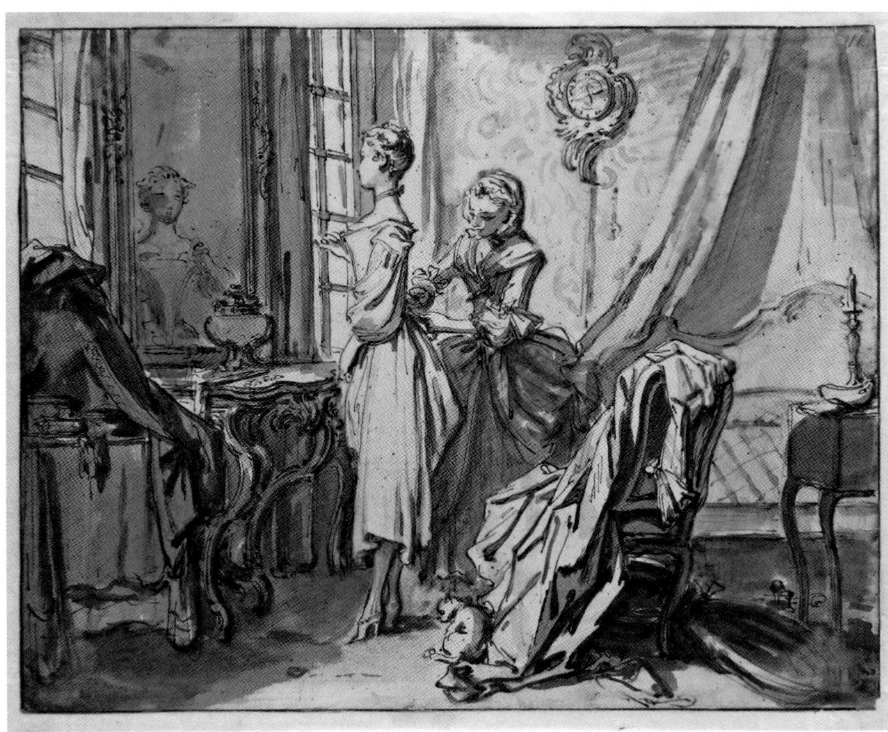

1.64.
François Boucher, *Lady and Maid*, ca. 1742–45. Pen with brown ink and bister wash, over indications of black chalk. Royal Academy, Stockholm.

arm."[294] The ideal of cutting a good figure is shown to have affected not only one's mode of dressing but also one's body language.[295] Down to the smallest gesture, Marianne's comportment is permeated by the imperative of *visual promiscuity*, that is, by a readiness to receive a randomized glance of no one in particular, a glance as such. Acutely aware of existing in the visual field of the other, Marianne represents a new idea of the self as a function of what I have called the world's gaze, which becomes the defining condition of her social but also her subjective existence. (She imagines herself in relation to the pleasure she produces in others.) This kind of promiscuous receptiveness to the look of others is shown, moreover, to be part of a broad social phenomenon in which different social strata, both men and women, partake. Describing the people gathered in the church, she observes: "I saw them leaning down, or propping themselves up, then straightening up, passing smiles and greetings left and right, less by politeness or social duty than in order to variegate their poses, to appear nice or important, and show themselves from different sides."[296]

It is precisely the self-conscious performance of the body (and self) that we witness in the figure of Boucher's servant. Turned away from us so as to better display her sartorial accomplishments, she is visibly caught in a calculated effort—note the slight strain in her neck—to show herself to her best advantage. She conveys the idea that her performance is not addressed to anyone in particular—neither us nor anyone else in this picture—but to the idea of the look itself that she has internalized and that shapes the mode of her appearance and her understanding of herself. Showing off in front of no one, in a thoroughly private space, this femme de chambre is an embodied proof of how the world's gaze, as the look *from within* oneself, came to define people's relation to themselves, both their self-esteem (Marianne's amour-propre) and their self-image. This is what her promiscuous persona, at once conspicuous and undetermined, is about.

As such, this figure leads us back to her mistress, helping us to perceive that *her* promiscuity is not (or not only) a matter of sexual conduct, but a symptom of something broader, a new kind of self-understanding based on appearances that emerges in the culture of consumption in its early stages. To be promiscuous, as Marivaux's Marianne demonstrates, means to be dependent not only on the looks of others but also on what these looks mediate, that is, the very principle of social visibility ("the world's gaze"), a principle through which one's own sense of oneself is produced and reinforced. In Boucher, this principle is mediated primarily by things that are not only prominent but also endowed with their own look. Such is notably, in *La Toilette*, the pair of eyes casting a glance at the scene from the portrait hanging on the wall, the rest of the face to which they belong being cropped by the folding screen.

That screen, an architectural element of clothing, is the most prominent and perhaps the most eloquent signifier of the worldly look in the sense I am suggesting.[297] Staged against it, Boucher's figures are simultaneously set off from the rest of their interior and pushed forward to view. Thus, paradoxically, while procuring privacy for the lady's intimate ritual, the folding screen also *exposes* her and her attendant. As such, it serves an important function: it underscores the provisional and promiscuous nature of identity defined through appearances but also its new imaginary dimension. The screen suggests an internal division within the self, making evident the existence of an extra space behind the foreground theater of appearances, a room from within which the self may cast a look at itself (as does the portrait) and imagine itself. This decorative object may be seen to formulate an argument similar to that of the mirror in the *Breakfast*, namely, that the nascent culture of consumption inaugurates a self that is volatile, surface-bound, an effect of illusion but also ultimately irreducible to these qualities—a self that exceeds itself.

The Milliner shares in this logic of promiscuity—the logic of the subject in the era of consumption—manifest in the body language of its protagonists, for example, in the way the lady's body "opens" up to view as she unravels the ribbon, her gesture defining not only what she does but *how she is* in the world, her movements and gestures, even in the privacy of her bedroom, permeated by the notion of self-display. Accordingly, the bedroom itself is defined as a locus of display. Although the space opens up to an alcove bed, a site of potentially gallant associations, it is not gallantry as much as promiscuity—in the sense that I am proposing—that is at stake here, a point made clear by comparison to de Troy's *Lady Attaching a Bow to a Gentleman's Sword* (1734), which depicts a similar situation (fig. 1.65).[298] Boucher not only supplants the courting scene with a basic ritual of consumption, dispensing with the male character and moving the milliner herself from a position on the

1.65.
After Jean François de Troy, *Lady Attaching a Bow to a Gentleman's Sword*. Oil on canvas. The Nelson-Atkins Museum of Art, Kansas City, Missouri. Purchase: William Rockhill Nelson Trust

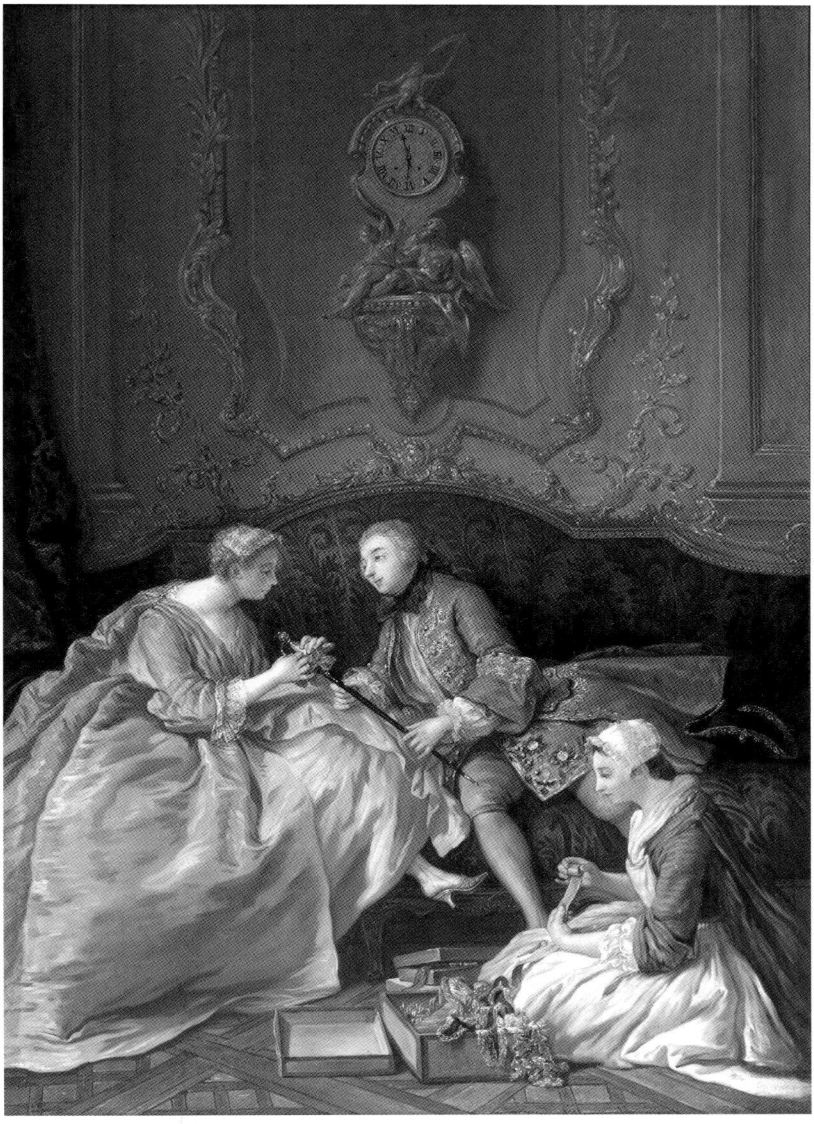

narrative margin in de Troy's painting, to the center of the scene, as the interlocutor of her client. He also stages the scene against an alcove bed that functions similarly to the mirror in the *Breakfast* or the screen and the door left ajar but leading to nowhere in *La Toilette*, that is, as a motif of an inaccessible yet insistent interiority. If the bed's curtains are dramatically animated, they are so for the singularly undramatic purpose of staging an empty bed, an interior expanse of salmon pink wherein absolutely nothing happens, and not much can be seen.[299] This background theater of color serves only to make the more visible the promiscuous display in the foreground, drawing our attention to the animated speech of clothing and accessories that define this woman's pleasure of the day. In and of itself it is a figure of different promiscuity: it is not the stage of an erotic act, but rather a mere attribute of a promiscuous self defined by appearances—not a place but a *sign* of a new kind of person.

—·—

The idea that new habits of consumption, and the new mode of living associated with them, engendered a new model of subjectivity—the promiscuous self—is conveyed most suggestively by *The Lady on a Day Bed* (fig. 1.66). As with the *Breakfast*, the originating circumstances of this work are unknown. Painted in 1743, it was long believed to be a portrait of Boucher's young wife, Marie-Jeanne Buzeau. But there is no evidence to warrant this identification, nor is there any indication that the painting is a portrait rather than a genre scene.[300] The uncertainty about what type of image this is, and the elusive nature of the woman's identity—is she a sitter or a model? a specific person or a generic personage?—are, in my view, at the very heart of the problem this painting formulates: the problem of who, and how, one *is* in the era of goods.

Rather than representing a specific individual, Boucher offers us a visual *fiction* of a private person analogous to those constructed by his contemporary, Marivaux. Boucher's lady cannot be defined by her social position; her identity is as unclear to us as were Marianne's origins to her contemporaries and even to herself. Orphaned as an infant in a carriage accident that stripped her parents of all identifiable marks of their social standing, Marivaux's heroine enters the world as an unknown and remains a socially enigmatic figure throughout the novel.[301] Boucher too imagines a person in quest of identity, but one more specifically mediated by material possessions. *The Lady on a Day Bed* is an image of a self that exists in, and identifies itself through, the realm of things. The painting insists upon this formative relation of the self to objects, revealing it to be at the very core of the subjective fiction it offers to view.

Reclining on a day bed, the young woman of fashion, dressed in a white taffeta *robe à la française*, embodies the newly persuasive idea of modern domestic comfort within accommodating interior space. The type of small room in which she is shown—a cabinet or a *boudoir*—exemplifies the increased architectural concern with the idea of commodity understood as convenience, a concern that resulted in the new functional division of space and a new approach to scale.[302] Cochin was only half joking when he remarked that "from now on, the higher the person's station in life, the smaller [her] apartment will be."[303]

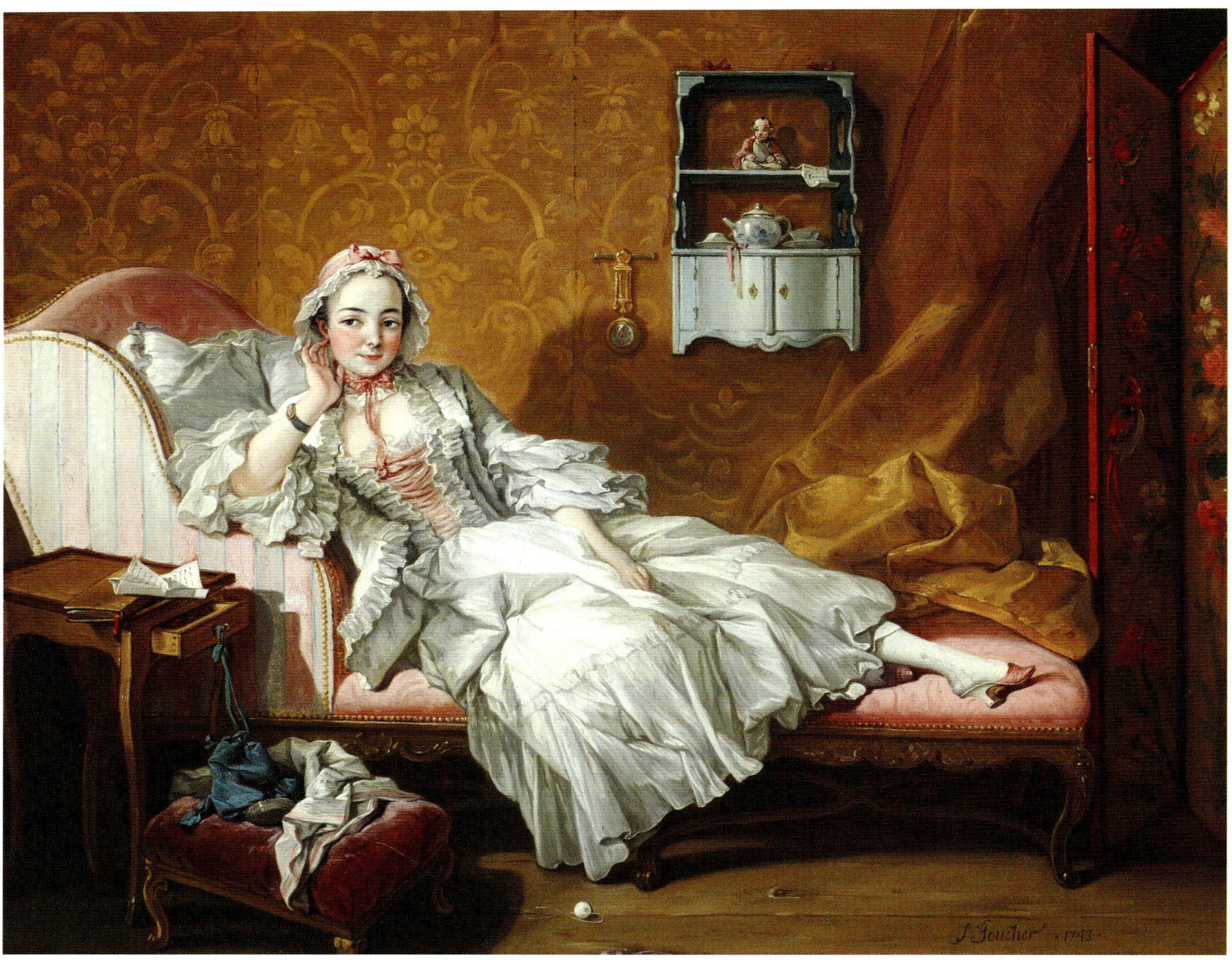

It is above all the way in which the young woman occupies this space, making it her own, that conveys a sense of ease. Sheltered and anchored by her things—fashionable furnishings and knickknacks typical of the stock of the marchands merciers—the woman embodies the notion of a self that is at once accommodated by her surroundings and at ease with itself: contained and content.

Yet this image of interiorized existence is traversed by an undercurrent of exteriority, that is, by something that signals both the depicted person's and the painting's acute awareness of the outside world. There can be no doubt that however domesticated and gratified, this woman is also on show, and she knows it. This is what distinguishes her from Watteau's introspective *Woman Reclining on a Daybed*, a drawing Boucher may have seen when he worked for Jullienne (fig. 1.67).[304] The folding screen pushed to the side accentuates the deliberateness of her self-display and the swag of drapery pulled up to reveal a sliver of something hidden—a door or a closet?—reinforces this impression. The image as a whole seems simultaneously intimate and indiscrete; we are granted access to something that is usually inaccessible and yet has staged itself carefully for us to look at.

Like Marivaux's Marianne, Boucher's lady is well aware of the social temptation to show off oneself: looking askance, she strikes a pose shaped by an eager anticipation, if not solicitation, of *le monde*'s gaze. But, unlike Marianne, she is not in a public space but in the privacy of her room, with no one else visible. She seems to be performing for herself, as did the "overproduced" servant in *La Toilette*, which is what distinguishes her from the run-of-the-mill coquette. Her promiscuity is not simply flirtatious—that is, a social game—but cuts deeper: it suggests the subjective dependence on the gaze of others—the world's gaze—and is a sign of her investment in external appearance as a

1.66. OPPOSITE
François Boucher, *A Lady on a Day Bed*, 1743. Oil on canvas. The Frick Collection, New York.

1.67. RIGHT
Antoine Watteau, *Woman Reclining on a Daybed*, 1718. Fondation Custodia, Frits Lugt Collection, Paris.

1.68. BELOW RIGHT
Joos van Cleve, *Saint Jerome in His Study*, 1521. Oil on panel. Harvard Art Museums/Fogg Museum, Cambridge, Massachusetts. Gift of Howland Warren, Dr. Richard P. Warren, and Mrs. Grayson M. P. Murphy.

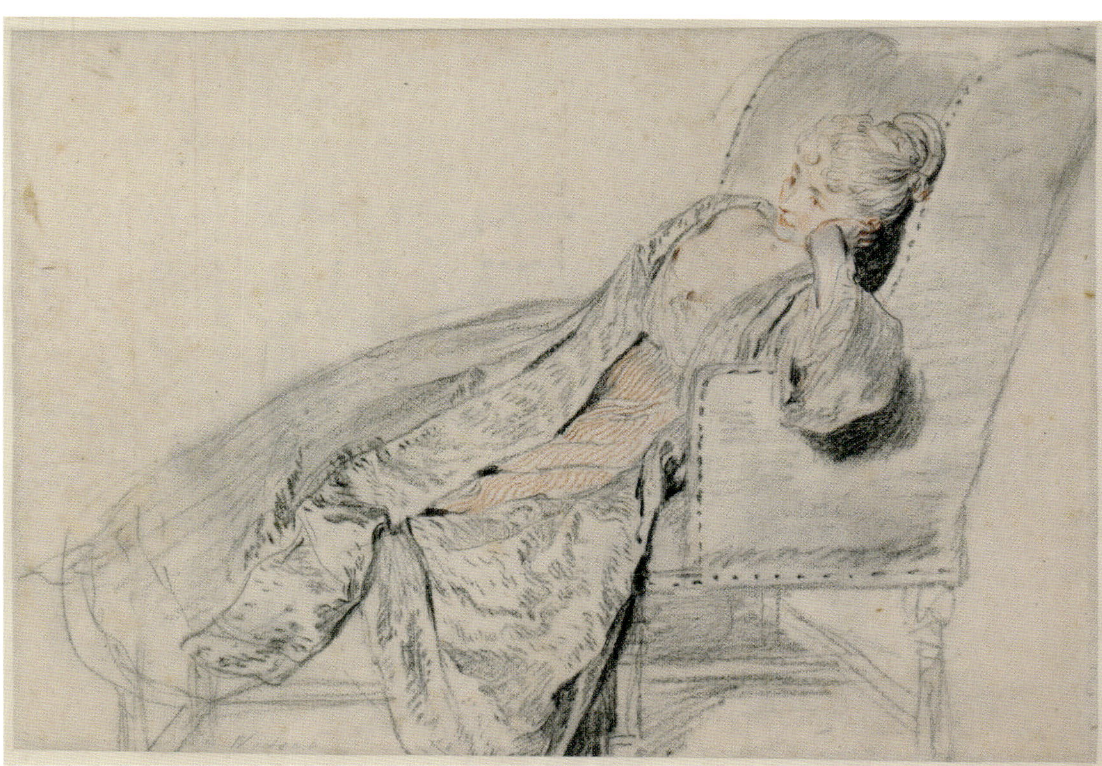

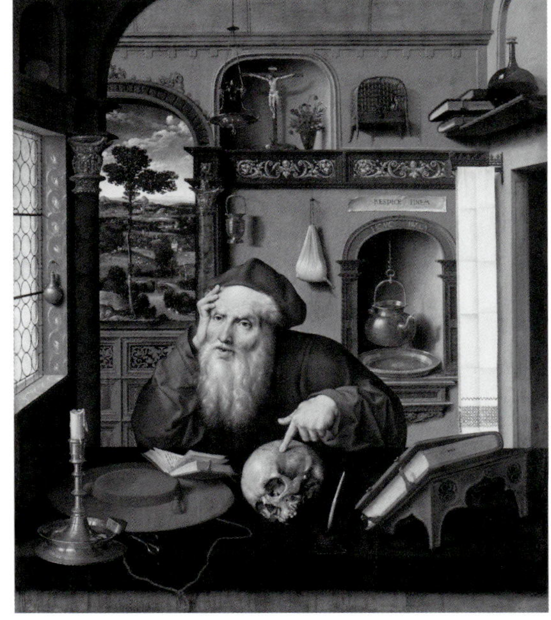

privileged interface of the subject with that gaze. In this sense the woman embodies the self as an appearance even to herself. Exposure, or self-exposure, is shown to be at the heart of interior existence, in both the physical and the psychic senses of the word.

If the lady's promiscuity is part and parcel of her definition as a private person, privacy is here, paradoxically, predicated on the assumption of a kind of internal publicness, on the existence of others whose regard is crucial not only for how one is for the outside world but also for how one imagines oneself. It is this notion of private space as a location in which *one relates to oneself* that Boucher's interior conveys. Note that the boudoir, as a room type, was a descendant of those earlier spaces of retreat and solitude—the monk's or hermit's cell, or, later, the learned person's cabinet (the *studiolo* of the Italian Renaissance)—in which one sought to develop self-awareness or self-understanding either through meditation on one's relation to God or through study. Resonances of these earlier religious and contemplative spaces linger in this lady's room: in its small size, relatively sparse furnishings, and in the residual meaning of things, such as the étagère on the wall echoing the simple shelves in a hermit's cell where a Bible or a book of prayers and perhaps a skull would be placed, as in Joos van Cleve's *Saint Jerome in His Study* (fig. 1.68). Boucher clearly reworks this earlier model of devotional or contemplative space to arrive at an image of a space of a thoroughly secular self-experience. (Let us recall that the etymology of *boudoir* derives from the French *bouder*: to sulk, indicating the connection between a type of space and the idea of subjective functioning, of being in a certain mood.[305]) Objects of consumption have replaced attributes of devotion and learning. Crucifix and books gave way to a porcelain tea set and a Chinese magot. What these objects mediate is not one's relation to divine authority, or to the body of knowledge, but one's relation to oneself, beginning with one's own body.

This mode of self-experience revolves around pleasure, and objects are its most evident source. It is not only that this woman obviously relies on her belongings for comfort; it is that she depends on them in a more fundamental sense, for being herself. This is conveyed by the rendering of her body as if *inscribed* by her objects, her recumbent position—she is unfolding on her bed like her screen—mimicking the arrangement of her furniture, the shapes, colors, and textures of which reinforce this connection: the daybed with its pink and off-white striped upholstery echoing her dress's color scheme; the little table by her side extended by an upholstered puff on which the soft shapes of the assorted objects—the blue purse, and the white *fichu* bordered in pink (again, a chromatic echo of the woman's dress)—are laid out not unlike her own body on the daybed. Together with the folding screen and the swath of the somewhat gratuitously raised drapery, these objects produce the effect of a promiscuous outward pull—the drawer of the little table left open, the ball of yarn rolling on the floor, and so on—that may well be seen as hints at this woman's sexual availability. In this spirit, the Frick painting has been compared to Boucher's far more sexually explicit *Dark-Haired Odalisque*, painted around the same time, spread on a blue sofa with her exposed bottom in the air (see fig. 1.45).[306] Yet such a comparison obscures the important differences between these two works, preventing us from understanding the different kind of eros that is at stake in the Frick painting.

Unlike the *Dark-Haired Odalisque* or, for that matter, its later blond version, the *Girl on a Sofa* (see fig. 1.46), the erotic dimension of *The Lady on a Day Bed* has to do with the woman's relation to herself that this painting constructs. It is the woman's own pleasure in her body that we are invited to contemplate. Her hand suggestively plunged into the folds of her dress, between her thighs, hints at an autoerotic caress. The meaning of such gestures was well established both in the libertine fiction of the period that abounded with descriptions of solitary women seeking erotic gratification in their own bodies, and in visual representation, exemplified by Boucher's son-in-law, Pierre-Antoine Baudouin's images, *The Reading* (ca. 1765) (fig. 1.69) and *The Midday Heat* (the latter popularized by Emanuel de Ghendt's engraving). In Baudouin's works, the woman's autoerotic act is induced by reading a novel.[307] The implicit autoeroticism of Boucher's figure is, on the other hand, grounded not in reading but in her experience of her own space, her objects and accessories, including her dress, and in her relation to herself that these objects mediate. Most importantly, Boucher's autoeroticism is not as narrowly sexual as Baudouin's. To put it bluntly, it is not onanism but narcissism that we are dealing with. Hers is a gesture of the narcissistic recognition of one's own body as a potentially gratifying surface of one's self.

Narcissism is not merely a form of self-love, but a mechanism of subjective formation, an instrument for developing a self-identity. Insofar as it describes the subject's early relation to the object, this mechanism must have acquired particular resonance in the burgeoning era of consumption, as an unprecedented flow of goods became available to a wide sector of society, simultaneously increasing the opportunity for individual sensory gratification and exerting pressure on the individual psyche. Evident in contemporary commentaries on consumption, the repeated encounter with commodity raised the question of the individual relation to the object and, therefore, to oneself, affecting, that is, the way in which one imagined oneself as an entity performing this repeated relational act. Narcissism is precisely the term for comprehending this internal process. In it, the self identifies itself with the desirable object, which is to say, assumes the object as an *image* of itself, so as to become like it—desirable first and foremost to itself. Freud describes the gist of this process in a memorable phrase wherein the Ego addresses itself to the Id: "Look you can love me too—I am so like the object."[308] On the level of psychic experience, the attraction to commodities may be described as a loving investment in the object that functions as a kind of internalized mirror of the self, an auxiliary self within the self, rewardingly reciprocating.[309]

What we see in the Frick painting is a subject in a perfectly reciprocal relation to its object(s). The woman's self-awareness, and self-pleasure, are insepara-

1.69. BELOW
Pierre-Antoine Baudouin, *The Reading*, ca. 1765. Gouache. Musée des Arts Decoratifs, Paris.

1.70. RIGHT
François Boucher, *A Lady on a Day Bed*, detail of fig. 1.66.

ble from her rapport with her things, her furnishings, and other decorative items that "inhabit" her, as much as she inhabits her room—they have been internalized by her. It is her psychological investment in her objects that also channels the world's gaze, and she is aware of it. Nothing signals her self-awareness more tellingly than her at once discrete and conspicuous gesture of touching her cheek (fig. 1.70). It is as if she were literally pushing forward her brightly lit, powdered, and rouged facial put-on, her finger touching right at its edge, creating almost an impression that this mask of a face could easily come unhinged if she pushed any harder. Brought to the fore, her "mask" underscores the message the whole figure is engaged in formulating—"Look at me!"—and that conveys her interiorized dependence on others, her desire to be seen, as the very condition of subjective existence. Yet the gesture of the woman also signifies her recognition of the face/mask as the screen

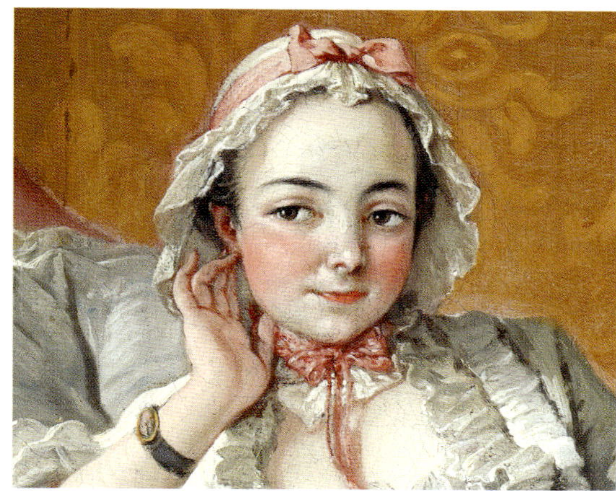

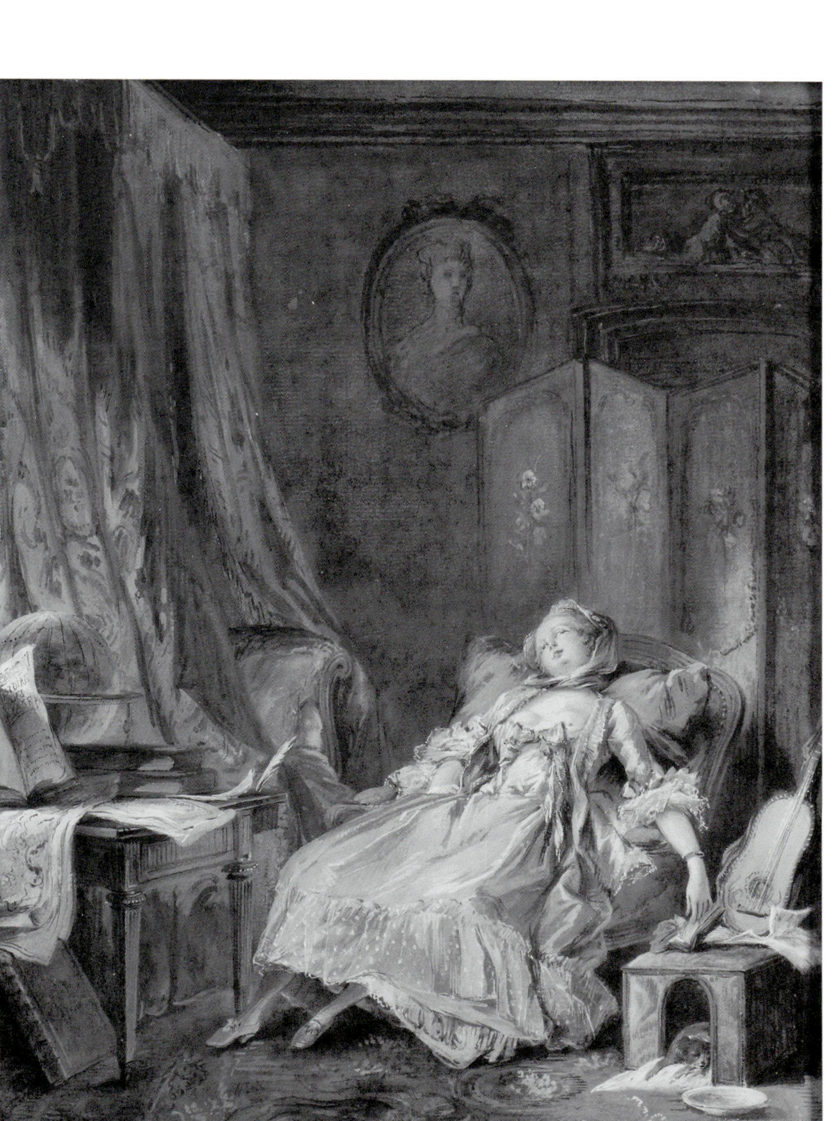

for the gaze, hinting at her capacity to play with it. It says: "I *know* I am being looked at." As such, it encapsulates this painting's particular relation to self-representation that I call modern.

The modernity of the canvas resides in the way in which Boucher's figure *displaces* the question of authenticity as the defining feature of the subject. In this regard, the painting situates itself in a cultural moment of transition between early moralist discourse that championed the authentic self and later eighteenth-century critique of inauthenticity as a side effect of modern times. The perspicacity of Boucher's position can be better appreciated if we compare it to an early eighteenth-century print by Nicolas Guérard, *Mascarade Universelle*, a critique of appearances that featured the mask as a trope of inauthenticity (fig. 1.71).[310] Boucher's work undoes the assumptions that operate in Guérad's image: the self is shown by Boucher to have accepted the mask as a form of self-representation. Falsity is not at issue. The mask does not usurp the putative authentic self but allows it to represent itself to its advantage. If there is a suggestion of something else existing beyond the mask—as the woman's gesture of "unhinging" it implies—it is not construed as better or more authentic than what we are given to see. In fact, there is no direct information about the subject's invisible interiority: it may be there, but it remains inaccessible, just as there is something, we are led to believe, that exists behind the decorative screen pushed to the side and that we can glimpse through the lifted curtain—some *other* space, another interior. All we can say is that this woman's "inner" space amounts to a distance from the mask signaled by her gesture.

Rather than a hindrance for the authentic self, the mask is shown in Boucher as necessary and salutary, something that makes the self intelligible—to others and to itself. In that, Boucher anticipates the later definition of the person in the *Encyclopédie*: "It is said that the word 'person, persona' is derived from *personando*, the action of playing a personage, of imitating or counterfeiting, and it is claimed that its first meaning was that of a mask."[311] What Boucher visualizes is, more specifically, a mask that has already been *internalized* by the subject and has become part and parcel of its subjective functioning. Comfortable in her interior, but also comfortable with herself, Boucher's woman represents the idea of autonomous interior existence, in a physical and psychic sense, predicated on the recognition of being a visible surface for others. With her gesture, combined with her amused expression, she communicates, moreover, her awareness of the gratifying potential of play with the mask.

The painting underscores the deeply rewarding dimension of this new sense of subjective autonomy, making vivid the connection between the pleasure one takes in fashionable objects and the pleasure one takes in oneself. As such, it represents the emergence of a socioeconomically grounded narcissism understood not as a trait of character but as the formative mechanism of the early modern self. As Boucher sees it, the identification of this early subject of consumption with its objects results not in reification but in a discovery of her own desirability, of being a lovable object, for herself as well as for others. It allows her to develop a libidinal relation to her own body, as is suggested by her pose and her gestures.

Thus *The Lady on a Day Bed* provides a paradigmatic image of the self defined by appearances, the dressed-up interiority that we saw suggested in different ways in the group of paintings discussed above. It represents a model of subjectivity that emerged in the culture of consumption: a self transformed into a sign, visually consistent but semantically unstable. Let us note that, while representing women as consumers, Boucher's paintings inflect the then common association of femininity and commodity by constructing women as figures of the new *subject* of the era of consumption. They also invite us to draw different conclusions from those often made about women as figures of corruption in eighteenth-century culture and in the modern interpretations of Boucher's work.[312]

How, we may ask, do these canvases define their maker, Boucher? What fiction of the artistic self do they help construct? The most obvious sign of the artist's presence in these paintings is his signature,

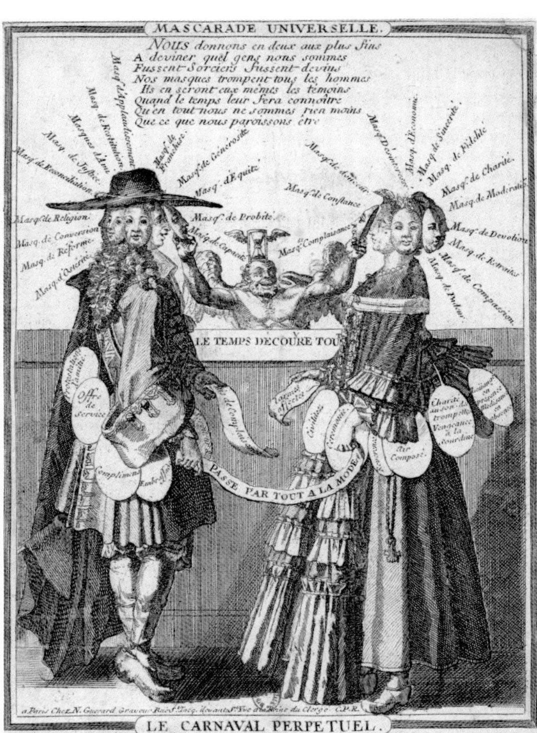

1.71. LEFT
Nicolas Guérard, *Mascarade universelle*, early 1700. Engraving. Bibliothèque nationale de France, Paris.

1.72. OPPOSITE TOP
François Boucher, *A Lady on a Day Bed*, detail of fig. 1.66.

1.73. OPPOSITE BOTTOM
François Boucher, *La Marchande de modes*, or *The Milliner*, detail of fig. 1.57.

the placement of which is as deliberate as it is visible, especially in *The Milliner* and *The Lady on a Day Bed*. In the Frick painting, Boucher's signature appears twice: on the bottom right of the painting, where we may well expect it (*f. Boucher, 1743*), and, less predictably, scribbled on the scrap of paper lying on the étagère's shelf next to the Chinese figurine, as if the artist wished to spell out where he belongs in this image of consumption (fig. 1.72). In *The Milliner*, the signature and the date are placed on the milliner's box (*f. Boucher 1746*) (fig. 1.73). In both cases, the placement of the signature signals the artist's alignment with trade, and with the commodity itself.[313]

The paintings situate Boucher as an author in the domain of consumption, as a producer of paintings that in themselves function like commodities, the understanding of the term *commodité* being broad enough at the time to encompass such understanding.[314] One of their primary goals was, no doubt, to establish Boucher as a producer of smaller-scale paintings with an explicitly commercial purpose for which he himself set the price: 600 livres, specifically when "there was finish."[315] This venture proved only partly successful, and he abandoned it at the end of the 1740s, either, as it has been suggested, because of the price, which may have been set too high, or because these meticulously finished paint-

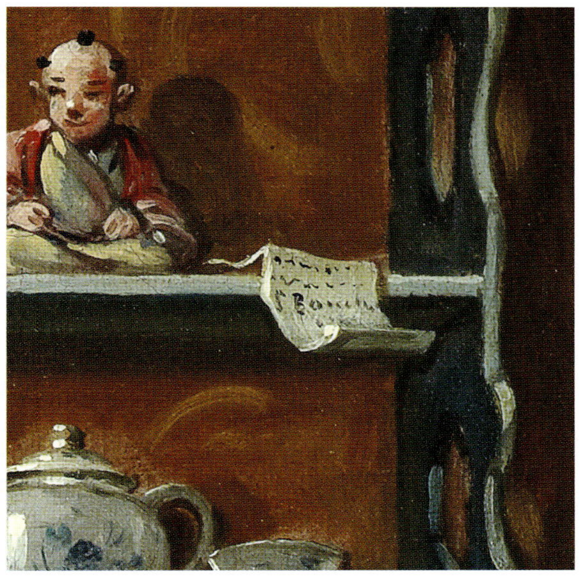

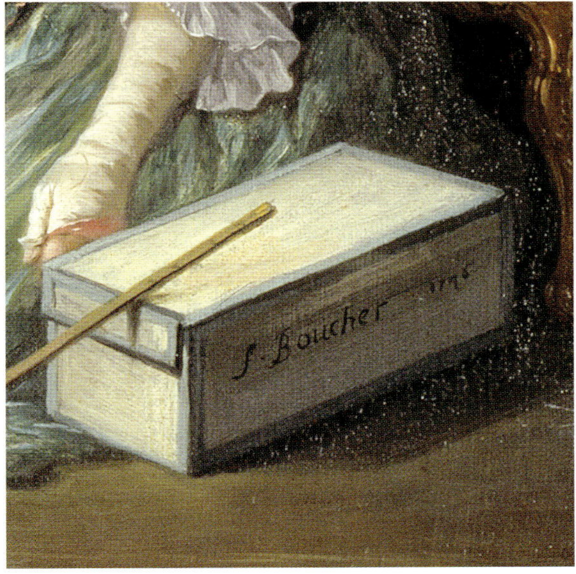

ings proved too labor intensive and too strenuous for the painter's sight, compared to more lucrative types of assignments, such as the overdoors.[316] (I would be inclined to believe that the patronage of Pompadour dating from the late 1740s on was, as Boucher himself indicated, the major reason for his abandoning of genre.[317]) Nonetheless, the importance of these paintings is undeniable, both as representations of the self and as commentaries on artistic identity in the era of consumption: in their very deployment of the painter's signature, they signal the emergence of the artist-author as a promiscuous persona bound to the visual performance of his/her proper name, an author both defined by, and abstracted from, his own oeuvre.

THE ARTIST AS CONSUMER

He most ardently desired everything that pleased him and . . . rarely renounced his wish to possess what gratified him.

—Pierre Rémy

Just as Boucher's work and authorial persona were immersed in, and defined by, commodity culture, so was the artist's private person.[318] The most obvious manifestation of this was Boucher's collecting habit. It was well known among his contemporaries that the artist was an avid collector of natural history specimens and other curiosities as well as art. His cabinet, which he began forming in the late 1730s and that contained a rich collection of shells, corals, polyps, rare minerals, precious stones, fossils, insects, and stuffed animals, among others, was frequently mentioned by contemporary visitors.[319] It was also repeatedly described in the eighteenth-century shell collectors' guide books and compendia of conchology, such as Antoine-Joseph Dezallier d'Argenville's treatise on the natural history of shells, which stated that, amid all things collected by Boucher, "shells especially attracted attention, whether it was because of the rarity of the specimens, or because of their size, or else because of the shine and variety of their colors, combined with their excellent state of preservation. The choice of minerals in it was the most precious, and so were the sea fans and corals; the most noticeable among the latter was a red articulated coral, more than two feet tall."[320]

We also know that Boucher was an avid shopper for *objets de goût*, works of art, antique gems, and medals, which, like the shells and the minerals, could be found at the boutiques of the marchands merciers and at public auctions. In 1737–38 he acquired exotic and decorative objects from Gersaint, among others; at the sale of the La Roque collection organized by Gersaint in 1745, in addition to a large amount of shells, he bought antique Chinese and Japanese lacquered furniture. It was, then, at about the time he was working on his pictures of life in the era of luxury consumption, that the artist himself became an eager consumer of luxuries. Many of Boucher's new purchases appeared as the accessories of the fashionable ladies featured in these paintings.[321] It was

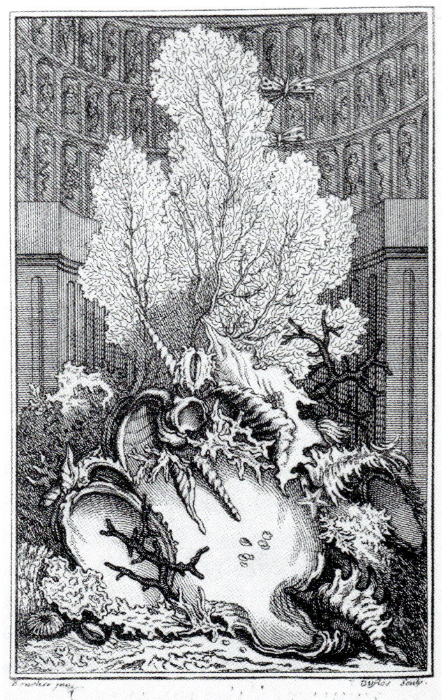

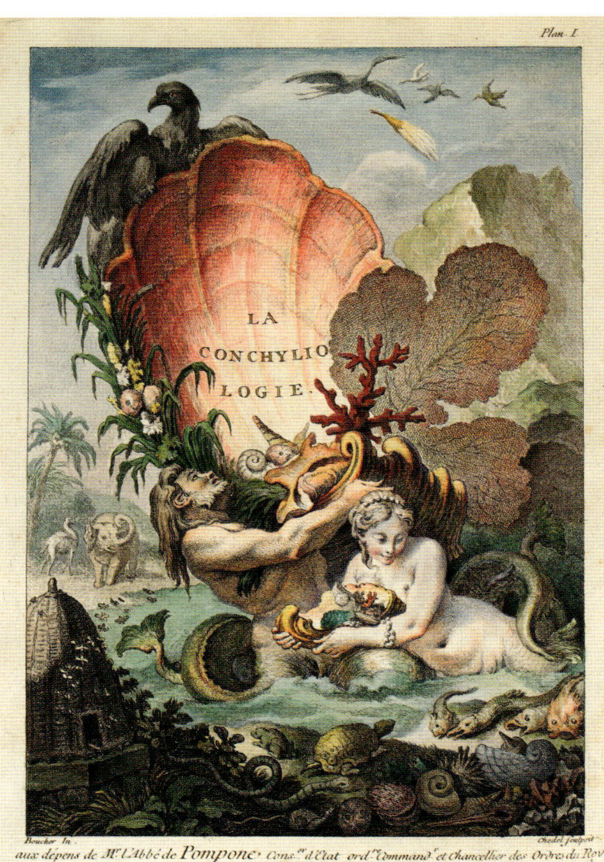

1.74.
Claude-Augustine Duflos II after François Boucher, frontispiece to Edme-François Gersaint, *Catalogue raisonné de coquilles et autres curiosités naturelles*, 1736. Courtesy of Fine Arts Library, Harvard University.

1.75.
Pierre-Quentin Chedel after Boucher, frontispiece to Dezallier d'Argenville, *L'Histoire naturelle, éclaircie dans une de ses parties principales, la conchyliologie*, [1742] 1757, American Museum of Natural History Library, New York.

also in this period that he began to form his collection of art. In 1741 he purchased a considerable number of old master drawings at the sale of Pierre Crozat's renowned collection. He was also present at some of the most significant art sales of the period, including Jullienne's, organized in 1767 by the prominent art dealer Pierre Rémy.[322] Boucher's collection grew to include paintings, drawings, and sculptures by several major Italian, Northern, and French masters, Chinese and Indian works of art, and works by his contemporaries.[323] It was so considerable that the posthumous sale of his estate, organized in February 1771 by Rémy, was an event attended by *le tout Paris*. All the major figures in the Parisian art trade, the well-known collectors, as well as the artists were in attendance.[324]

Collecting was not unusual among accomplished artists; even high-class artisans in the seventeenth and the eighteenth centuries and quite a few of Boucher's contemporaries (including his younger colleague Anne Vallayer-Coster) shared his passion for shells.[325] Collecting practice gained in scope and importance in this period, not only among the elites but also among those of humbler descent.[326] Natural specimens, scientific instruments, and exotic objects could be found in most reasonably well-to-do households in the eighteenth century. Drawings too were highly appreciated collectibles, and several artists, notably Jean-Baptiste Oudry, were known for their significant holdings.[327] Growing interest in the new science of nature (*histoire naturelle*), in the physical sciences, and a new understanding of art and creativity fueled this spread of collecting in the eighteenth century. What most allowed it to flourish, however, were commercial developments: the increased importation of luxury goods from Asia and the West Indies, the new role of the marchands merciers as the principal distributors of these exotic goods and objects of art, and the concomitant development of consumer appetites for material possessions ungoverned by need.[328]

Boucher was directly involved in the commercial promotion of curiosities by designing frontispieces for the publications accompanying their sales, such as Gersaint's catalogue raisonné of shells published in 1736 (fig. 1.74), and for manuals for shell collectors, such as Dezallier d'Argenville's *History of Conchology*, first published in 1742 (fig. 1.75). The artist's own collection was the result of the newly flourishing commerce in curiosities to which he contributed. What can it tell us about the artist?

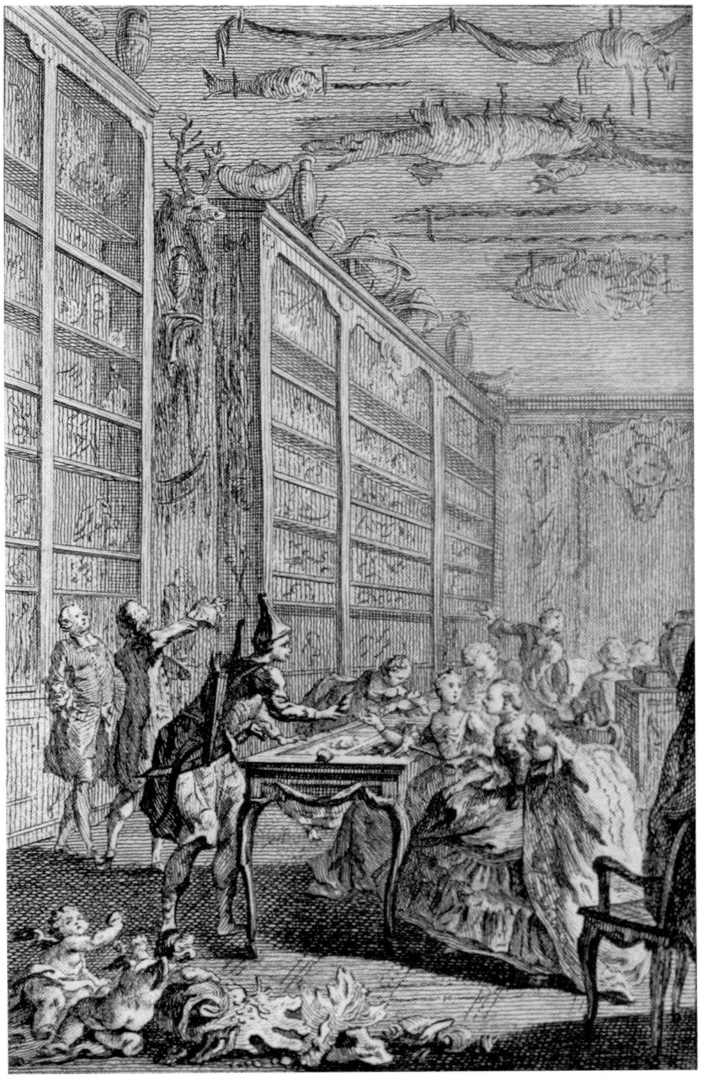

1.76.
Augustin de Saint-Aubin after Gabriel de Saint-Aubin, frontispiece to Pierre Rémy, *Catalogue raisonné, d'une collection considérable de coquilles rares et choisies du Cabinet de M. L*** [Marquis de Bonac]*, 1757. Bibliothèque nationale de France, Paris.

The salient aspect of Boucher's collection was not only the high value and quality of its contents—archival sources suggest that the artist spent most of his money on it—but its careful and artful arrangement.[329] His shells, rocks, and corals were presented like art in cases designed specifically for this purpose, their remarkably aesthetic presentation described in collectors' guides of the period. The 1767 edition of Dezallier d'Argenville's guide book noted the distinctly decorative display of Boucher's holdings: "This ingenious painter placed his shells on glass-covered tables; they present to the eyes of the viewer an enameled parterre that seems to rival nature. On the left, upon entering, one finds a glazed display case richly filled by sea fans, minerals, precious stones etc. which are of great beauty."[330] Listed among Boucher's possessions in his posthumous sale catalog, the "sixteen tables of different size with glazed cases for the display of shells" and the "shell cabinet veneered in violet wood by Oeben, with bronze mounts by Philippe Caffieri" confirm the sense of elegance and sophistication conveyed by the guide book's description and give us a sense of its considerable size.[331]

This elaborate presentation situated Boucher's collection within the new culture of display of natural history exemplified by several elite collections formed at the time. Luxurious furnishings made specifically for the display of specimens were part and parcel of that culture. A still extant pair of *coquilliers* (ca. 1720–30) that was part of the scientific cabinet of a prominent early eighteenth-century collector, Louis-Léon Pajot, comte d'Ons-en-Bray, installed at his country house at Bercy, near Paris, gives us a sense of the one owned by Boucher. Made of mahogany, each of them had eighteen drawers in marquetry and gilt bronze for the display of shells.[332] Illustrated catalogs of the renowned collections, such as that of a Dutch luxury merchant, Levinus Vincent, offer views of how shells were displayed in elaborate parterre arrangements in the drawers of shell cabinets.[333]

The use of such furnishings was symptomatic of a broader concern with the aesthetic dimension of display that characterized the eighteenth-century culture of curiosity. While the sixteenth- and seventeenth-century Kunst- and Wunderkammern emphasized the unusual, shocking, or unique aspects of objects, the eighteenth-century curious gaze focused above all on the beauty and the visual pleasure provided by the object.[334] These were also the qualities emphasized by the mode of display of collections of the *curieux*. Gabriel de Saint-Aubin's midcentury rendition of Marquis de Bonnac's cabinet of natural history, featuring visitors poring over the tables with glazed-over cases for the display of rocks and shells, such as those mentioned in Boucher's sale catalog, conveys the sense of priority given to the visual aspects of collecting in this period (fig. 1.76).[335] As Bettina Dietz and Thomas Nutz have argued, the distinctly aesthetic code that governed French *curiosité* of the eighteenth century trained collectors and viewers to look for specific qualities in the objects that would convey aesthetic beauty and visual pleasure.[336] The most renowned collection of curiosities in the first half of the eighteenth century, the "mechanical and physical cabinet" of Joseph Bonnier de la Mosson, the treasurer of the États du Languedoc, colonel of the regiment of Dragons-Dauphins, and an amateur scientist, epitomizes these new aesthetic principles of display.[337] We have a good sense of how this stunning cabinet, installed in Bonnier's house on

Paris's rue Saint-Dominique, looked from the drawings of Jean-Baptiste Courtonne executed between 1739 and 1740, possibly with an intention that they be engraved.[338] Recording in minute detail the elaborately decorated cabinets in which Bonnier's specimens were stored, Courtonne's sheets visualize the elegance and the architectural and decorative ambition that went into the creation of Bonnier's cabinet (fig. 1.77). The specimens, though carefully researched by the owner, were not arranged in a scientific or taxonomic manner but orchestrated so as to produce formal effects based on their shape and the color.

Bonnier's collection and the eighteenth-century practice of curiosity at large have been analyzed in sociocultural terms, as a means of positioning the collector in society. A cabinet such as Bonnier's amounted to an elitist performance of style that was part of a broader social spectacle aimed at production of prestige.[339] Yet one could also note that in its elaborate mode of presentation, with its extravagant furnishing and its idiosyncratic juxtaposition of decorative elements, Bonnier's collection exceeded the goal of producing social prestige, pointing to the uniqueness and eccentricity of its owner as an individual, to his particular taste as a tool of not only social but also personal distinction.[340] It is this moment of self-individuation through taste that one must consider in thinking about eighteenth-century curiosity collections, including Boucher's.

Although certainly more modest than Bonnier's cabinet—which the artist certainly knew of, if not saw in situ, having designed the frontispiece for its sales catalog—Boucher's collection exemplified the predominant concern with the aesthetics of display.[341] From contemporary testimonies we know that, like Bonnier's, Boucher's collection was vastly heterogeneous and that it lacked any organizational principle other than that of decorative coherence. This was confirmed by many visitors, including a Polish traveler in Paris, Count Michał Mniszek, who observed that Boucher had "an immense magazine of curiosities of art and nature, arranged solely for the look, without any order, a sheer multitude of rare and well preserved pieces."[342] As Pierre Rémy's commentary on Boucher's mode of collecting, contained in his preface to the sale catalog, indicates, visual pleasure—the collector's own—was the paramount factor in the formation and display of his holdings: "all that which could please the eye became for [Boucher] an object worth searching for and he would not want anything else. Rarity without pleasure had no attraction whatever for him; thus, he did not make any effort to construct ordered or systematic collections [*collections suivies*]; in each category of objects he chose nothing other than that which could please, either by the form or the color."[343] According to Rémy, the collection itself was a result of an essentially aesthetic pursuit of beautiful things, and it was beauty more than rarity, appearance more than knowledge, that interested Boucher. He appears to be a typical eighteenth-century curieux, his collection organized according to an aesthetic code rather than hermeneutics of wonder, his personal gratification recognized as the prime motive behind the formation and display of his holdings.[344]

As Rémy made clear, however, Boucher's taste for pleasure was a quality honed through consumption. It is the consumer indulging his desire for objects that Rémy describes as he tries to "naturalize" it: "This taste for everything agreeable that nature bestowed on Monsieur Boucher caused him ardently to desire all that which pleased him and to rarely renounce his wish to possess what gratified him."[345] What made this unbridled pursuit possible was the development of the commercial market for curiosities, their enhanced circulation, and their new status as commodities, that is, not only objects that may be had for money but also tokens of personal pleasure. It is precisely this dimension of the rare object as a commodity that, more than anything else, accounts for the heterogeneity of visually orchestrated collections, such as Boucher's own. Mingling high art (old

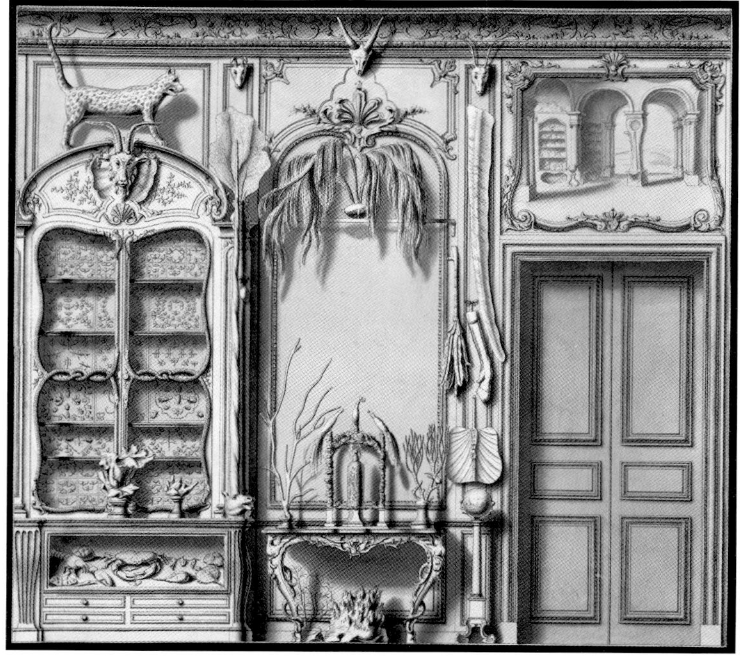

1.77.
Jean-Baptiste Courtonne, *Second Natural History Cabinet of Bonnier de la Mosson*, ca. 1739. Pen and ink drawing. Institut national d'histoire de l'art, Jacques Doucet Collection, Paris.

master's drawings and paintings by the renowned Italian, Flemish, and French artists) with Chinese figurines, Boucher was the kind of collector whom the eighteenth-century critics of curiosité objected to: a consumer motivated solely by the "desire to possess" (*envie de posseder*).[346]

It is the image of Boucher as an avid consumer taking intense pleasure in the object that we find in Mannlich's souvenir of his teacher. Mannlich vividly describes the aged Boucher's almost infantile joy at opening a case of minerals sent to him as a gift by another collector. The artist admired every piece with tears in his eyes, but then retained only very few of these items, putting the others aside for bartering.[347] The account makes clear Boucher's understanding of the collectibles not only as precious possessions—he was known, as Mannlich recalls, to have paid as much as 600 livres each for some of his shells, a price he asked, we remember, for a carefully executed genre picture of his own—but as cherished objects, tokens of, one might say, "douce sympathie." But it makes equally manifest the status of the collectible as the object of exchange. The difference from the traditional collector was subtle but important; it stemmed from the way in which the growing market for natural curiosities infused them with a new meaning and value, at once calculable and precarious, definable and enigmatic. The shells Boucher collected were for him, in other words, not only valuable, they also shone with the mysterious light of commodity, with the magical quality objects have in a child's eyes.[348] Mannlich marvels at the seemingly incompatible aspects of Boucher's approach to the object: his deeply emotional engagement combined with a calculating, almost cynical view of it as an item of commercial exchange. These are the aspects that define the attitude of a collector as a consumer in the early stages of commercial modernity.

The most important implication of the new status of curiosities as commodities was, though, that they could function as signs—for and of the collector. As tokens of his pleasure, the collectibles represented Boucher himself, as a person, and as an artist. The connection between his mode of collecting and his profession was noted by his contemporaries. Thus Bret linked the aesthetics of Boucher's collection to his being an artist endowed with chromatic discernment.[349] Rémy too suggested the aesthetic pleasure manifest in Boucher's arrangement of his collection had to do with the aesthetic competence of the painter, with his "picturesque and graceful taste" (*goût pittoresque et plein de graces*) that "very few people could claim."[350] Moreover, Rémy linked Boucher's good taste to his agreeable social persona: refined and witty, pleasing and accommodating.[351] Taste is understood as a professional as well as personal attribute; it defines Boucher as an artist (someone devoted to pleasure and grace) and as a particular person (agreeable and accommodating).

My argument is that Boucher quite self-consciously used the collection as a form of professional self-representation that helped convey the visual and aesthetic consistency of his persona as an artist. Not exactly a shop sign, it was an image—an aesthetic spectacle—of an artist operating under the aegis of the sign. The aesthetic consistency between the things Boucher collected and the art he made is represented in the 1742 frontispiece the artist designed (and Pierre-Quentin Chedel engraved) for Dezallier's guide book for amateur shell collectors (see fig. 1.75): shells, sea fans, and corals are intertwined with aquatic creatures from the painter's mythological repertory. What emerges from the embrace of a triton and a sea nymph is, this time, not a Venus but another fantasy: a concoction of sea marvels (corals, conches, and madrepores) as a creation of a curieux-consumer's imagination. As always (for example, as in his earlier frontispiece to Gersaint's *Catalogue raisonné des coquilles*), Boucher renders his shells not with emphasis on accuracy but with an imaginative panache, as stylish abstractions assembled into a decorative arrangement—a still life—their slightly distorted or adjusted forms representing a consumer fantasy of natural forms as collectibles, which is to say, objects that circulate on the market. They are drawn, accordingly, from the perspective of a consumer, their distortions and embellishments (like the embellishments of the actual shells that were offered in sale at the time only after they were cleaned and polished to acquire a desirable veneer), represent what a natural history specimen amounts to when it becomes an object of curiosité.[352] The sea marvels in this frontispiece are no less fantastic than the sea creatures that populated Boucher's paintings, both set in an exotic landscape the disjunct elements of which signify "natural history" as a domain of a collecting amateur, an aesthetic spectacle. As such, the commercially induced fantasy space of this frontispiece—for Dezallier's publication was part and parcel of the new culture of acquisition of curiosities—is also an indirect representation of Boucher's cabinet of curiosities: a dream of the artist as a consumer.

The artist's recognition of his holdings as a form of self-representation is confirmed not only by the care he took in arranging their display but also by the prominent place—at once private and public—he accorded the collection within his house, which itself manifested a considerable concern with decoration and display. Boucher's new lodgings and studio at the Louvre, obtained in 1752 after the death of the King's First Painter, Charles-Antoine Coypel, testify to the aesthetic ambition of the painter about his interior's appearance (fig. 1.78).[353] The rooms at the Louvre were not only ampler and more prestigious than the spaces in which he lived before but also allowed the artist to have his studio under the same roof as his living quarters. This was a significant change from his previous situation—until then, his life and work had been conducted in separate spaces and different parts of the city—and the artist clearly saw the new lodgings as a representational opportunity.[354] Before moving in, he insisted on having the apartment renovated and entirely refurnished. Even if the authorities initially refused to provide him with the relatively modest sum of 758 livres he requested for this purpose, the artist went ahead with the renovation, ultimately spending as much as 9,000 livres on it out of his own pocket.[355] (The sum equaled nine times Boucher's yearly pension from the king in these years.[356])

The Louvre dwelling, where Boucher lived with his family for about twenty years, became a repository of exquisite things, the elegant and luxurious abode of a man of distinction. Its decor was impressive enough to have been praised by no less an expert than Jean-François Blondel in the final volume of his *Architecture Françoise* published in 1756.[357] To suit his needs, which included the display of his collection of art and curiosities to its full advantage, the artist changed the internal division of space. As a result, according to the plans preserved in the National Archives (fig. 1.79), the artist's cabinet was situated immediately adjacent to a spacious room housing his studio (the *grand atelier*), a significant fact in view of my argument about the role of Boucher's collection as a form of professional self-representation. His spacious living quarters, containing a room for the servant on an entresol, were next to the studio.[358] As this layout indicates, the artist's working space was embedded in his private space, located as it was between his collection of curiosities and his living quarters. This layout suggests that, embracing the idea of living and working under the same roof, Boucher aimed at creating a larger representational continuum unified by a stylish decor. The content of the lodgings, inventoried in the sales catalog of Boucher's estate, confirms this. In addition to the extensive collection of art and natural specimens, it included expensive furnishings, such as the marquetry works by Boulle, and an abundance of decorative objects made of bronze, marble, ivory, and porcelain, arms and armors, and jewelry, in sum, the accoutrements of interior style and elegance that justify the praise Boucher's dwelling received from his contemporar-

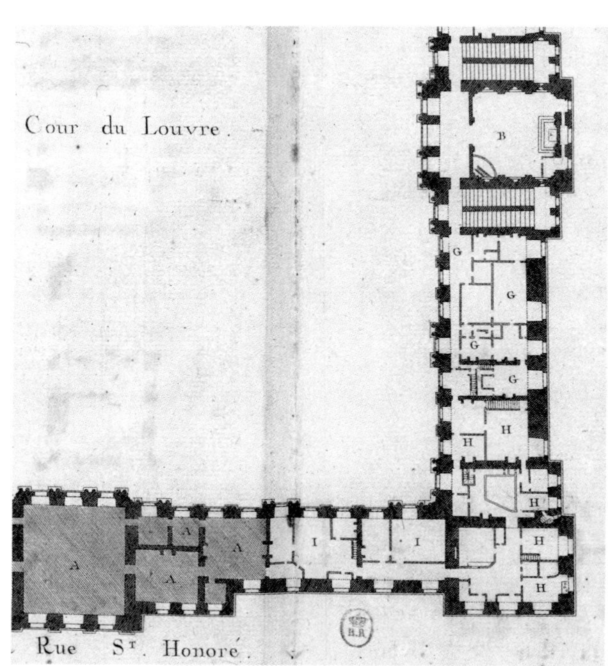

1.78.
Plan of Louvre with Boucher's apartment marked by letter "I." From Jean-François Blondel, *Architecture française* . . . Bibliothèque national de France, Paris.

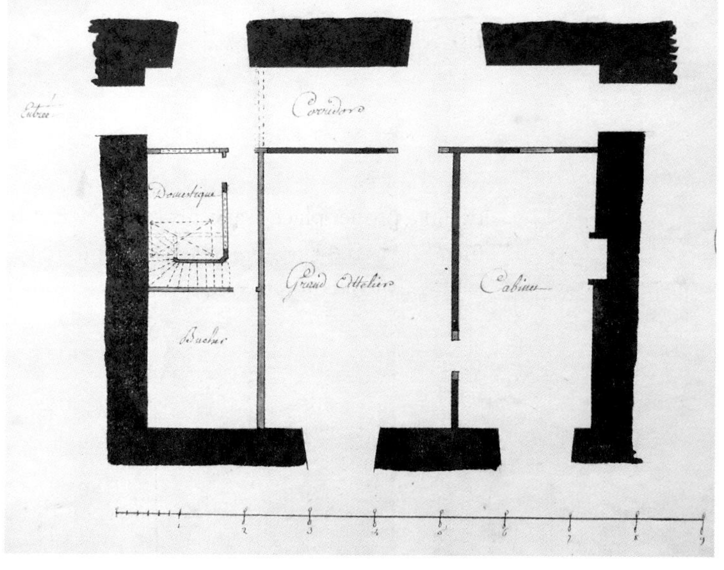

1.79.
Plan of Boucher's apartment in the Louvre. Archives nationales, Paris.

ies.[359] Although the inventory does not specify the furnishings' location, we may safely assume that the studio, situated between the cabinet and the apartment, was no less aesthetically ambitious in its decor than the adjacent spaces. Some of the inventoried objects that clearly belonged in it corroborate this idea. An elegant *boîte à couleurs*, or a box for pigments, in the form of a chest of drawers with a marble top listed in the inventory indicates the sense of style in the appointment of Boucher's working space. (A similar boîte was reproduced in the *Encyclopédie* [fig. 1.80].[360])

Boucher's insistence on renovating his apartment, even at a considerable personal cost, indicates that even as a lodger of the king, Boucher attached considerable importance to the new ideals of stylish and comfortable living. In his decorative ambition, he followed a broader trend in social behavior informed, as we have seen in his own paintings, by the new aspirations to well-being and the new understanding of social and personal identity based in appearances, from bodily appearance, defined by fashion, to the "look" of interior space defined by the new publications of architectural designs. But Boucher's expensive redecoration also suggests a recognition of the symbolic potential of his new space as a form of personal as well as professional self-representation. We know that Boucher kept his studio open to visitors, and we know that he led an active social life—Mannlich, among others, makes this amply evident—in which his private dwelling must have played a significant role.[361] The Louvre lodgings offered him the possibility to create a *decorative interior ensemble* encompassing both his life and his work and offering not only a proof of his good taste but also a certain image of himself as a person, and as an artist. He seems to have instantly grasped this opportunity. His insistence on changing the layout of his space—part of which, we may presume, having to do with the desire to situate his cabinet of curiosities in a proper place—and his careful selection of furniture and decorative objects point to it. In what way exactly did his new lodging represent him, then?

Much of Boucher's furniture and many decorative objects, such as those in the *goût Chinois*—from an exquisitely crafted miniature of a Chinese house acquired at Jullienne's sale, to numerous pagods and magots—offer proof, if we needed one, that Boucher's taste was honed by luxury merchants, such as Gersaint and later, after his death in 1750, other caterers to the growing taste for luxury commodities.[362] He clearly followed closely what their establishments

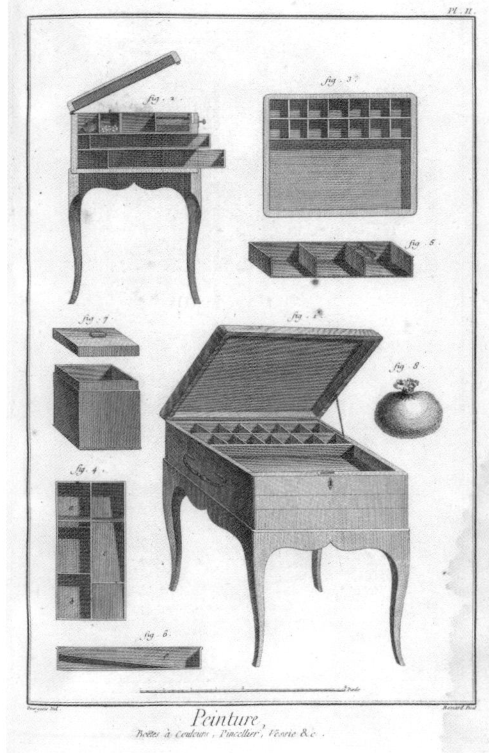

1.80.
"Boites à couleurs." Plate 2 of the entry "Peinture," in *L'Encyclopédie, ou Dictionnaire raisonné des sciences, des arts et des métiers*, 1771. Houghton Library, Harvard University.

offered for sale, conforming to the ideals of consumption that the merchants, but also Boucher himself (through his art and design), helped propagate. The artist's interior was a materialization of the kind of consumer dream that the marchand merciers aimed to foster, to which Boucher's own commercial activities as an artist and designer contributed, and which he represented in his art: a material realm unified by the notion of visual pleasure. In other words, his whole apartment was shaped by the aesthetic code that governed the formation of the *collections curieuses*, including his own.

In staging his dwelling as an aesthetic spectacle Boucher emulated not only the taste promoted by the marchands merciers but also the look of their shops and, to some extent at least, their function. In the period under discussion, concern for the aesthetic appearance of commercial space distanced the mercers from what they once were, that is, ambulant sellers with portable chests of drawers for the display of their wares carried on their bodies suspended from the neck.[363] Not only did the mercers choose strategic commercial urban locations for their boutiques (such as *La Pagode*'s Pont Neuf, or *Au Petit Dunquerque*'s quai de Conti), but they also made a conscious effort to turn these shops into elegantly appointed interiors with spectacular window displays that would attract buyers.[364] The decor of these boutiques resembled, in fact, the elite cabinets of the clients to whom they catered.[365] Combined with new advertising strategies, this emphasis on design and display was part of the marchands merciers' efforts to promote their products and draw a broader clientele.[366] The display of commercial goods also had a branding effect. The cultural historian Carolyn Sargentson, who analyzed the inventory of the *Petit Dunquerque*, a renowned boutique of the marchand mercier and jeweler Charles-Raymond Granchez, has argued that such elaborate interior design and display performed a specific commercial function, bestowing an identity onto the objects sold in it as being specifically "from the Petit Dunkerque."[367]

The analogy between these commercial spaces and the elegant interior Boucher created for himself suggests a functional similarity between them. The purpose behind the artist's emphasis on interior elegance may have been to arrive at a consistent aesthetic style that enhanced the sense of stylistic and authorial consistency of his productions. Given the capacious commercial imagination of the artist evident in the way he "designed" his own career, it is not surprising that he would have recognized the self-promotional potential of his own dwelling.[368] To think of Boucher's new premises at the Louvre in relation to the elegantly appointed interiors of the marchands merciers is to suggest the key role of the culture of consumption in defining the artist's personal as well as professional identity. Boucher's concern with decor and display, evident in both his apartment and his studio, points to consumption as the defining factor in the development of his sense of himself and his artistic persona. Not unlike the subject envisioned in his pictures of consumption of the late 1730s/early 1740s, this was a persona defined by a conspicuousness with a professional function. Boucher, unlike Voltaire's "worldly man" defined by the consumption of luxury, was not a man of leisure; his well-appointed rooms performed, if indirectly, a professional function—it was a space wherein he received his guests and his clients.[369] The taste and elegance of his dwelling and studio certainly aimed to impress his visitors but also, more importantly, to convey a certain *visual consistency* in his life and work. It was to create and sustain a style as a sign for both the person and the artist. In erasing the distinction between the personal and the professional sphere, this habitat made clear how commercial modernity changed the self-understanding of the artist.

POMPADOUR'S PAINTER

The view of Boucher as an essentially commercial painter—in the modern sense of the term—also helps to explain the mystery of his success with his major, and arguably most important, patron, Madame de Pompadour.[370] The defining aspect of their relation was luxury consumption. Both the painter and his patroness recognized commodities as means of self-definition: Pompadour, as a *bourgeoise* at court who mobilized art and decor in a vast effort of self-representation aimed to legitimize and solidify her status as the titular mistress to the king; Boucher as a provider of paintings and designs for her, but also, in a broader sense, as an artist who, as I have argued, defined himself aesthetically and professionally through the production of luxuries and the representation of their social and subjective effects.[371]

1.81.
François Boucher,
The Toilette of Venus, 1751.
Oil on canvas. Metropolitan Museum of Art, New York, bequest of William K. Vanderbilt, 1920.

Gersaint, who was important for Boucher's professional self-definition, was also a connecting figure between the painter and Mme de Pompadour. Like Boucher, Pompadour was one of Gersaint's clients, a fact made evident in *The Toilette of Venus* that Boucher painted for her in 1751 (fig. 1.81). Destined for the sumptuously appointed bathroom suite at Pompadour's château at Bellevue, the painting can be seen as, in a sense, her shop sign. The careful arrangement of precious things—luxury objects of the kind Pompadour bought from Gersaint or Lazare-Duvau, another dealer whom she used frequently—reminds us of Boucher's own elegantly arrayed collection and of his discernment as a decorator of his own studio and dwelling at the Louvre.

Boucher's painting was for and about Pompadour—in a particular way. Personified by Venus, Pompadour's body, presented here in the midst of precious things (the mirror in a gilded frame, the prominent bronze perfume burner, a pitcher, a silver tray, the jewels strewn about the silk and damask draperies, the sofa) acquires, even more literally than in Boucher's paintings for Derbais, the status of a commodity, a possession, one among many. Gersaint's trade card designed by Boucher in 1740, with its disordered assembly of goods over which a life-size magot presided, comes to mind (fig. 1.82). Venus is, in

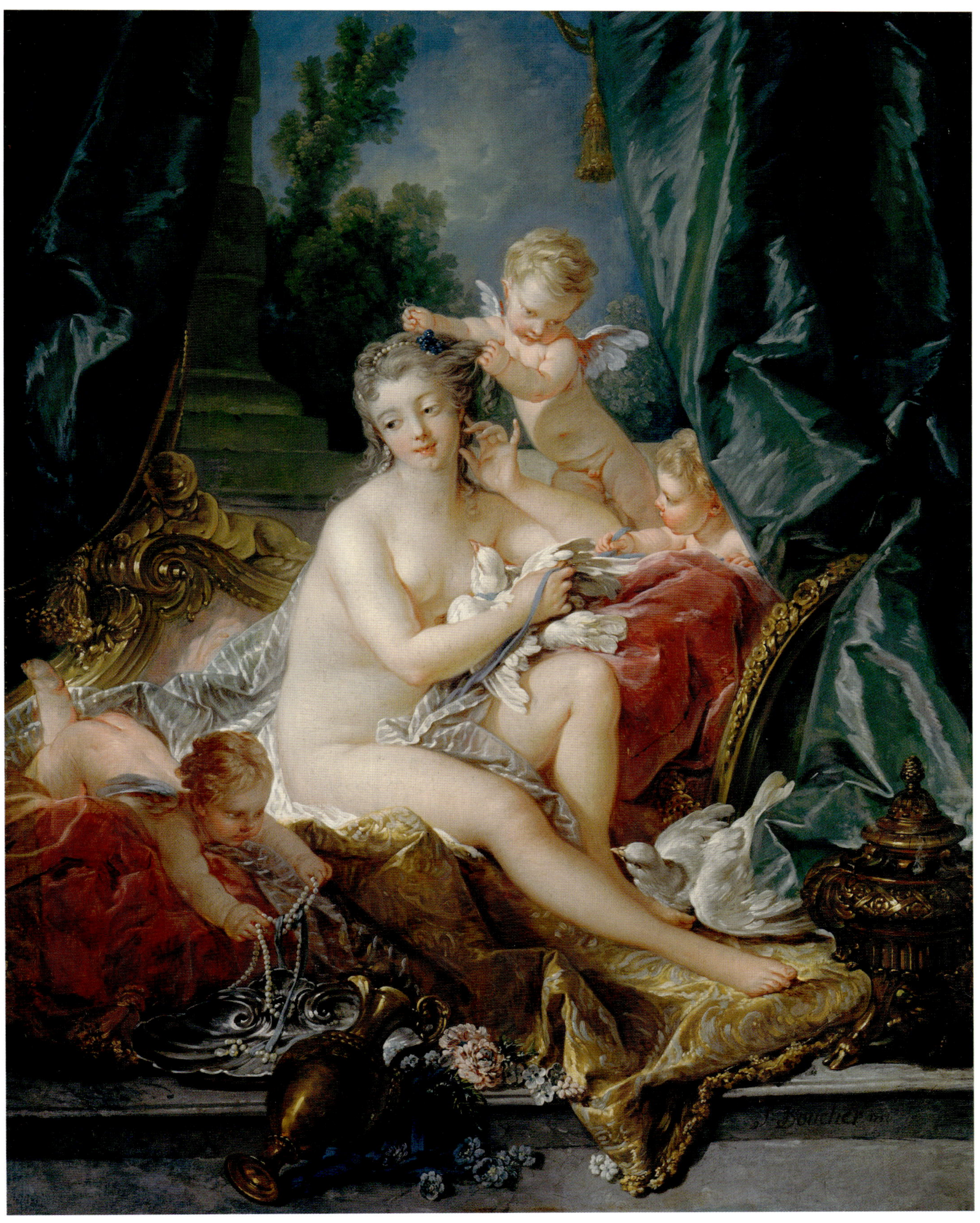

other words, a goddess of consumption. It is, however, not only the fact that she is surrounded by these various objects but also her *relation* to them, as this painting represents it, that is important: her body as itself an object, the flesh tucked in between the sheets of things. As such, Venus is a figure for Pompadour as a woman of taste who defined herself through material things, a collector of the luxuries and objets d'art of which she was brilliant orchestrator in space, the château de Bellevue, among them—to which Boucher contributed significantly.[372] It is precisely in its generic quality, its lack of physiognomic or anatomical specificity, that this mythological figure defines the patroness's identity in economically specific terms—Venus as a shopper. The canvas illustrates more literally than Derbais's the fate of mythology in the age of consumption. In this sense, *The Toilette of Venus* is also an indirect commentary on Boucher as an artist. It is not that Boucher identified with his patroness, but rather that the figure of Venus is an image of both Boucher's and Pompadour's abstracted identities, a portrait without a subject. (It is as empty as one of Boucher's designs for cartouches, with their accommodating void at the center waiting to be filled according to a specific commercial purpose [see fig. 1.26].) And it was this aspect—the subject as a cipher, identity as an empty field—that constituted the grounds of their affinity.

This affinity explains, in my view, the reason behind Pompadour's preference for Boucher as a portraitist, a choice that was far from obvious, given

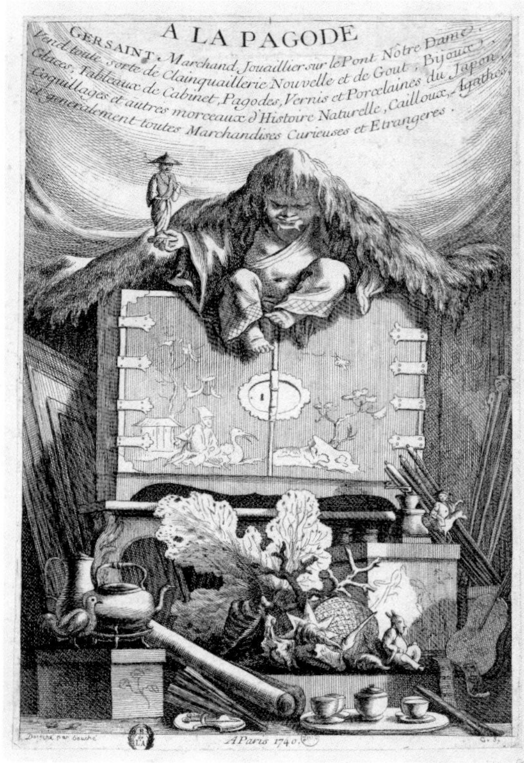

1.82.
Comte de Caylus after François Boucher, *Trade Card of Edme Gersaint*, ca. 1740. Etching and engraving. Bibliothèque nationale de France, Paris.

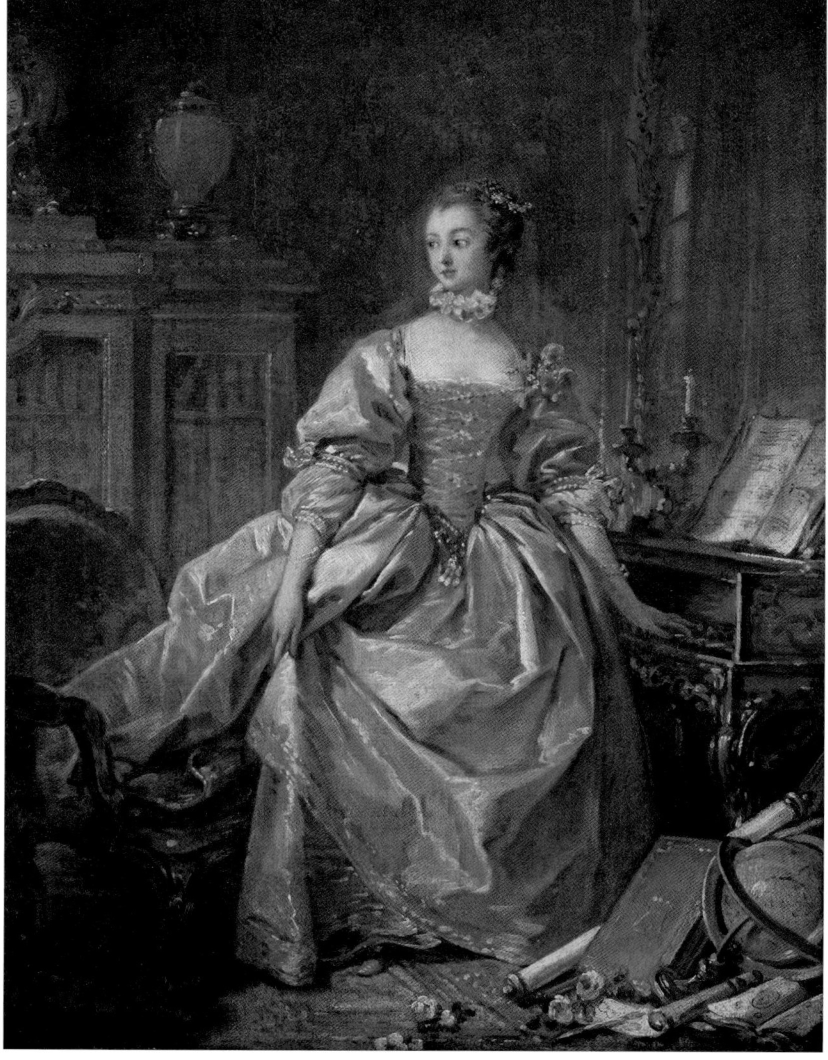

1.83.
François Boucher, *Madame de Pompadour with Her Hand Resting on a Harpsichord Keyboard*, ca. 1750. Oil on paper mounted on canvas. Musée du Louvre, Paris.

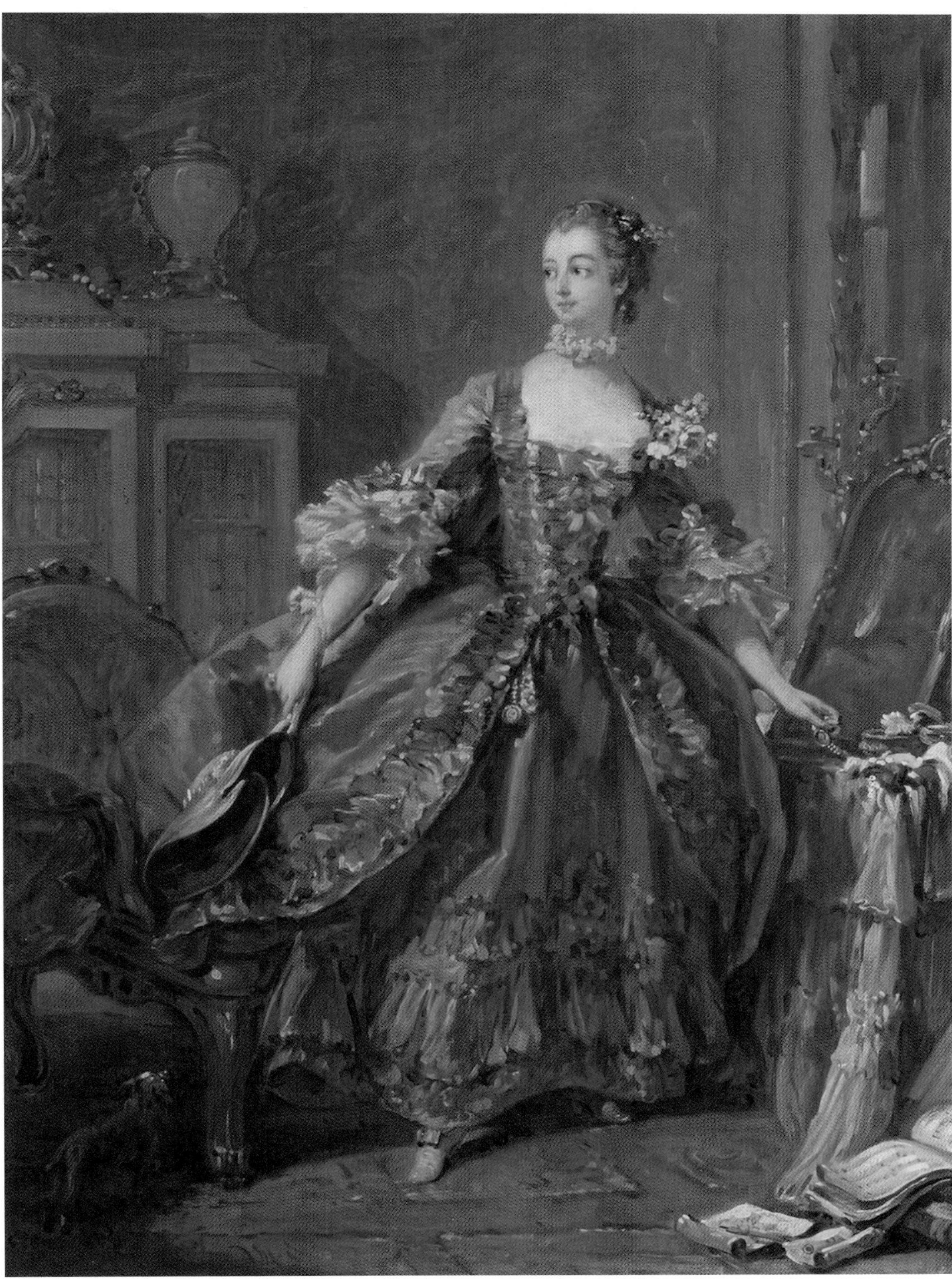

1.84.
François Boucher, *Madame de Pompadour*, ca. 1750. Oil on canvas. On loan from Rothschild Family Trust since 1995. Waddesdon Manor, Buckinghamshire.

the painter's notorious lack of skill in securing resemblance. Although Pompadour was well aware of his shortcoming—stating as she did in a letter written to her brother in April 1751 that the copy of Boucher's likeness she was sending to him in Italy "greatly resembles the original, less myself"—she seems to have been entirely satisfied with his results, multiplying her portrait commissions from him more than from any other artists.[373] There is a somewhat repetitive quality to these portraits, as the oil sketches for two of them demonstrate (figs. 1.83 and 1.84), and, judging from the ones that exist in finished versions (fig. 1.85), they demonstrate not only a flattering idealization of the sitter's features but also a curious evacuation of subjectivity. The self seems to have been displaced in these likenesses from the body onto the surrounding objects, the choice of

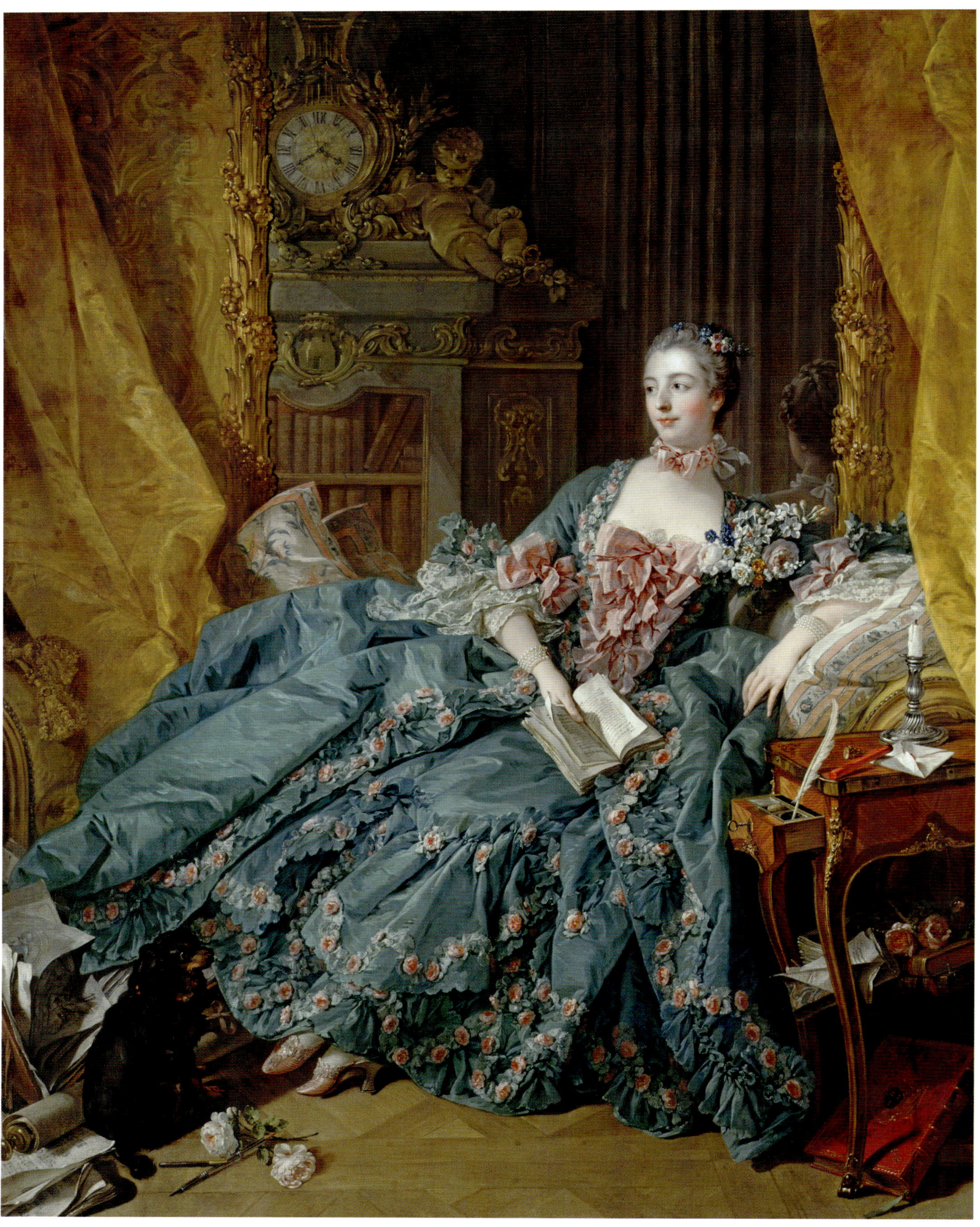

1.85. OPPOSITE
François Boucher, *Madame de Pompadour*, 1756. Oil on canvas. Alte Pinakothek, Bayerische taatsgemaelde-sammlungen, Munich.

1.86. RIGHT
François Boucher, *Madame de Pompadour*, detail of fig. 1.85.

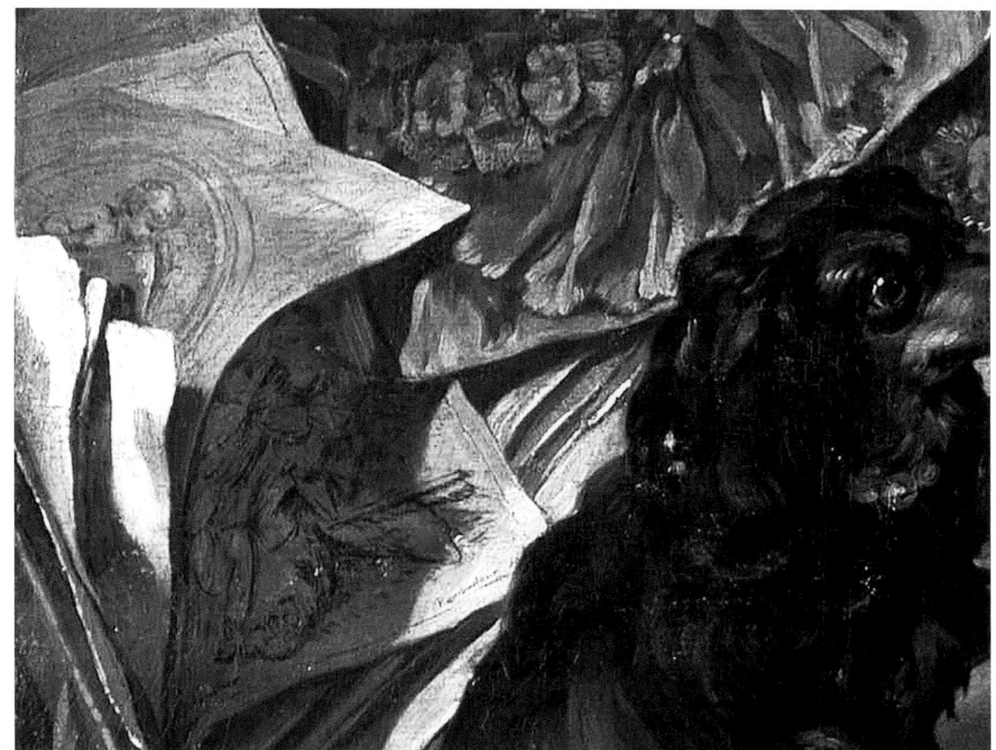

which was evidently determined by Pompadour herself. As I have argued elsewhere, Pompadour's contribution to the making of these portraits may be detected not only on the iconographic but also the formal level, in the patroness's "touch," which testifies to the sitter's implication in the painter's trace.[374] Pompadour, it must be remembered was an amateur artist herself, her drawing and etching skills honed by none other than Boucher, which is what the painter in his Munich portrait of her alludes to through motifs such as the intersecting etching tools lying on the floor, the prints scattered near them, and the double signatures—*Boucher* and *Pompadour*—visible on one of the prints that suggest the collaborative dimension of the sitter-painter relation (fig. 1.86). (The similarity of the signatures and reciprocal arrangement of tools on the floor in Pompadour's Munich portrait to the game of signatures in Watteau's portrait engraved by Boucher is striking.) These small but significant allusions, were, though, not only a deferential testimony to Pompadour's skills and her implied contribution to the portrait itself but also a reference to Boucher's particular talent, a quality that was most uniquely his own and that made the artist such a perfect match for Pompadour. This is what I have called his tact.

To have tact, as an artist, meant to be able to accommodate the other—an individual client, the market in general—but also to accommodate oneself, in a particular, always shared, way. It was to operate as an individual whose identity is dispersed, forever in representation, that is, nowhere. It was, in other words, to be a kind of self that exists for the sheer purpose of producing appearances—including the one called "Boucher."

Chapter Two

CHARDIN'S CRAFT

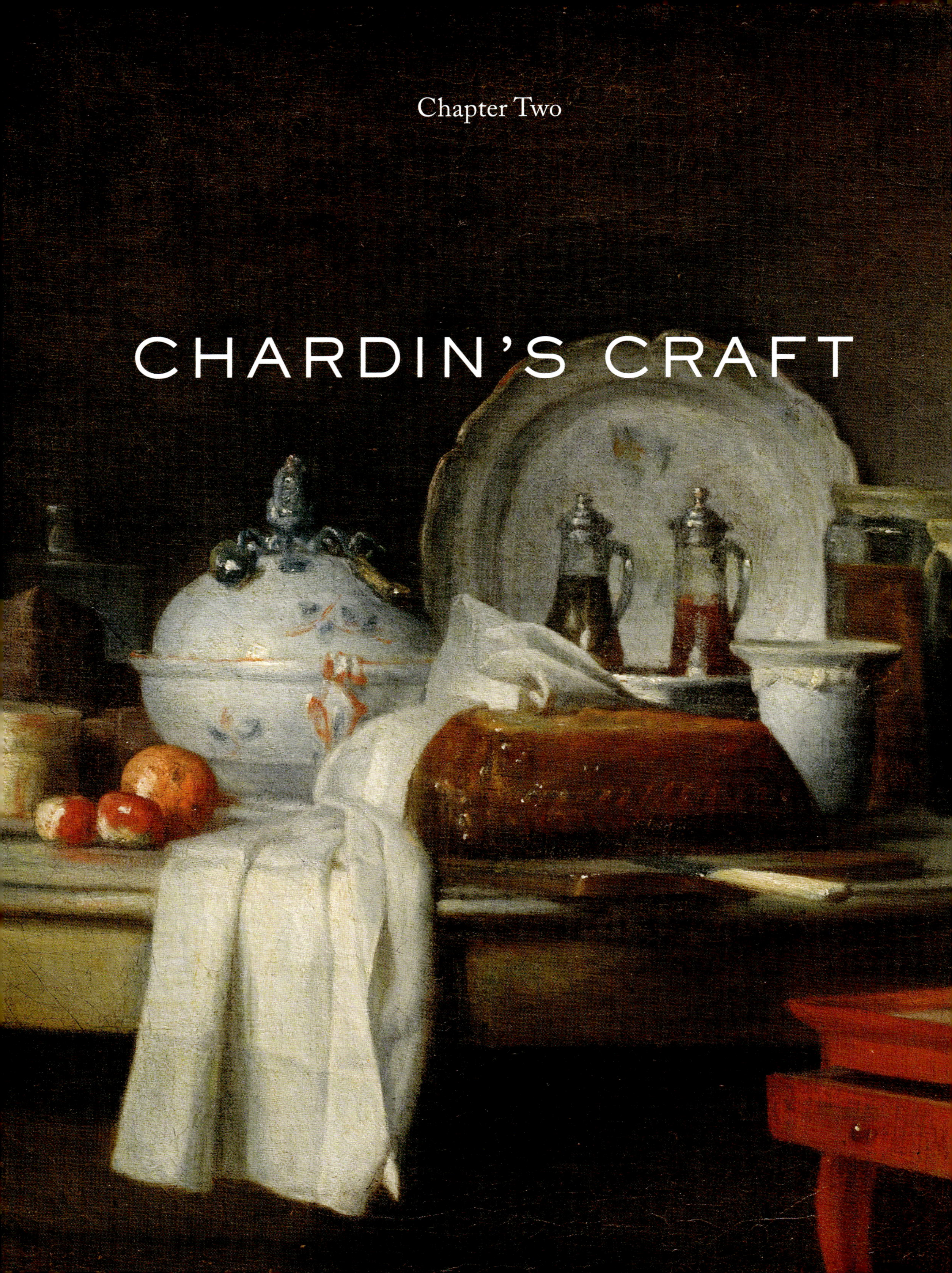

DEEP MATERIALITY

His mode of painting is entirely his own.

—Chevalier de Brunaubois-Montador

A few cooking utensils sit quietly on a stone ledge amid some raw ingredients for a simple meal (fig. 2.1).[1] A shiny copper pot with a ladle stuck under the handle of its lid and a white glazed pitcher are at the core of this random arrangement, with the smaller objects—a mortar and a pestle, a pepper mill, and a blue-green casserole with a handle jutting forward into view—distributed around them. The vessels create a barely discernible rhythm of vertical forms. A knife, a piece of raw meat, a plucked chicken, some kidneys or gizzards, an onion, and a swag of white cloth are balanced on the very edge of the table to secure the illusion of depth, that is, a sense of the objects emerging from within a space rather than simply appearing on the surface of the canvas. In their downward pull, however, they also provide a subtle planar effect of counterbalance to the upward verticals of the kitchen wares.

Featuring recognizable objects of everyday use rendered with an unassuming accuracy—no showiness, no feats of illusion, yet the object's presence unaccountably secured—Chardin's *Kitchen Table*, now in the collections of the Museum of Fine Arts in Boston, epitomizes the painter's uncanny skills. It was Chardin's fidelity to the object, the unforced harmony of his composition, and the ease of his delivery—the legendary "magic" of his touch—that most impressed his contemporaries. In *Dialogues sur les Arts* (1755), the writer and critic Pierre Estève spoke of Chardin's ability to capture "the most truthful nuances of the objects [bodies] with admirable accuracy."[2] Commenting on still lifes exhibited at the Salon of 1763, Diderot exclaimed: "Oh Chardin! The colors crushed on your palette are not white, red or black pigment; they are the very substance of the objects. They are the air and the light that you take up with the tip of your brush and apply to the canvas."[3] Others shared this high appreciation of Chardin's imitative gift, especially his superior use of color: "His eyes seemed to be like prisms capable of breaking down each object into its component tones, distinguishing the subtlest of transitions between light and shade," wrote the painter Antoine Renou in his eulogy of the artist.[4]

Immersed in the materiality of the object, faithful to its physical makeup to a degree that generated confusion between the substance of the thing and its image, capable of perceptual deconstruction and recomposition of the object on canvas through a magic use of color—these descriptions of the painterly method imply an unconventional intimacy with the world of things. Conveyed in these commentaries is the assumption that such a close engagement with the object amounted to a quasi-effortless representational mastery over it.

Yet Chardin's mastery was not easily achieved. A closer look at the surface of the canvas of the *Kitchen Table* suggests the effort needed by the painter to get things right: the mortar on the extreme right stands surrounded by a halo of pentimenti that indicate the ghostly presence of objects originally painted in its place. The radiograph of the painting confirms this, revealing a bowl-shaped vessel and a standing dish to have been where the mortar is now, and further making visible a whole geography of doubt about the placement and choice of almost all other objects (fig. 2.2). Thus the meat, originally placed on the piece of cloth at the very center of the image, in the final composition was moved to the side, while the mortar and the pepper mill were displaced to the right of their former location. Other elements, such as the casserole's handle, the pot's lid, and the ladle were also differently situated. We see the artist changing his mind quite considerably before settling for the final result, his extensive changes in the design necessitating substantial repainting.[5] The unforced harmony of composition with its casual organization of the objects was a result of a great deal of elaboration through trial and error.

Although making changes in the process of painting was a common enough practice in the eighteenth century, such an extensive internal reorganization of the canvas was unusual. It is the more surprising that the painting is not an example of the artist's early work, when he may have been expected to rehearse different solutions. The *Kitchen Table* was painted in 1755, when Chardin was fifty-six and at the peak of his artistic capabilities. Nor was the set of objects represented by any means new to the painter. On the contrary, the key elements—the copper pot, the mortar, the green-blue casserole with a jutting handle—appeared often in his paintings. They belonged to the artist—both his property and his props—and were featured in numerous other paintings, some of them compositionally close to the

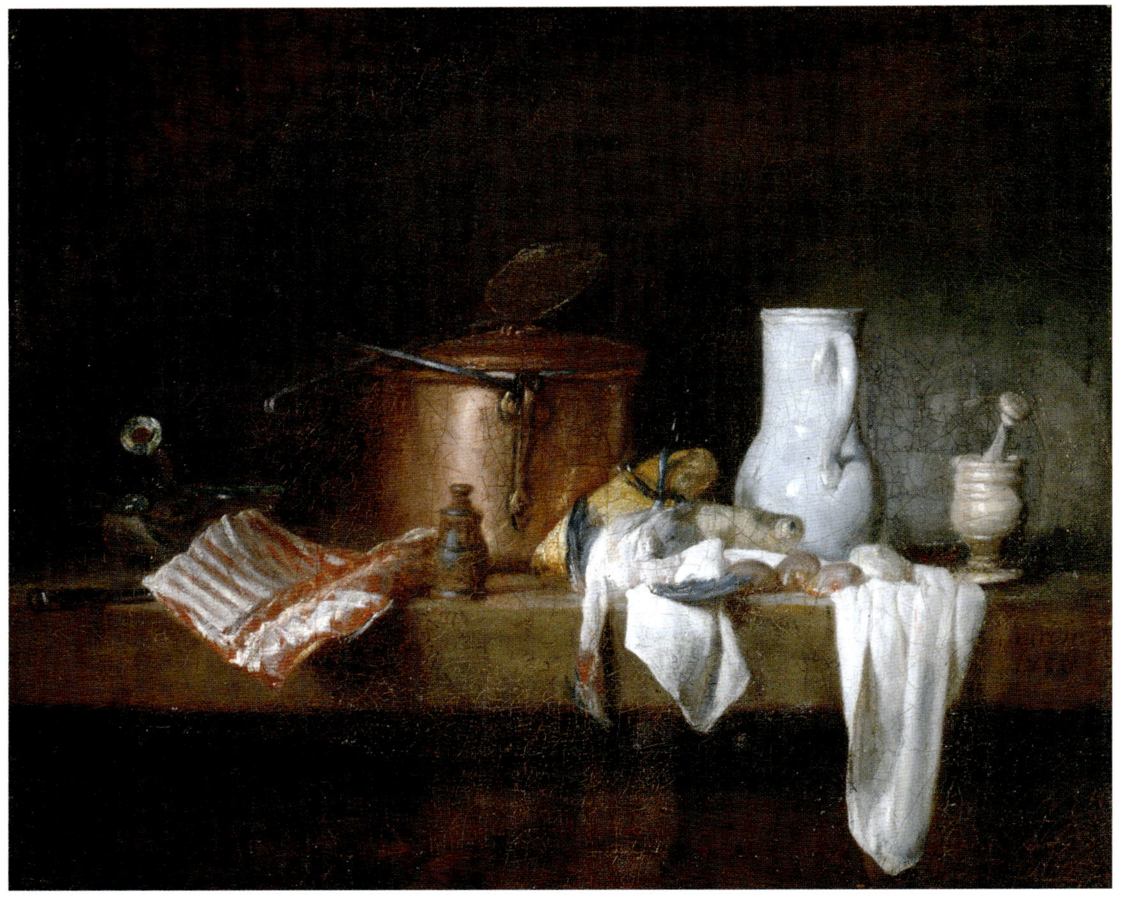

2.1.
Jean-Siméon Chardin, *Kitchen Table*, 1755. Oil on canvas. Museum of Fine Arts, Boston. Gift of Mrs. Peter Chardon Brooks.

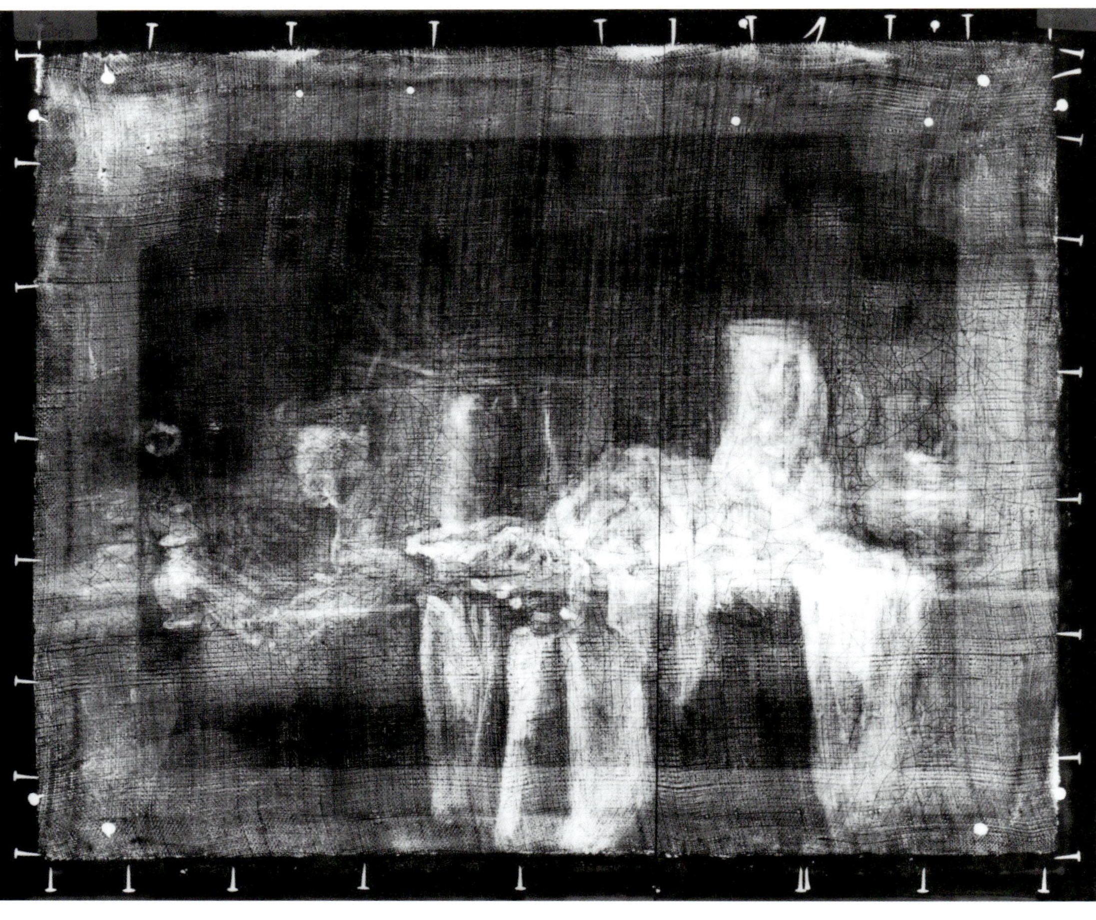

2.2.
Radiograph of Jean-Siméon Chardin, *Kitchen Table* (see fig. 2.1).

Boston picture.[6] Like a proto-minimalist, Chardin worked in series with variations, "recycling" things from earlier pictures. One would expect him to have the art of composing and recomposing these variables at his fingertips. Yet, as the radiograph indicates, each time it posed a challenge for him.

How does such a glimpse behind the curtains of representation affect our perception of the image? More generally, how is the process of painting an image, if we know anything about it, to figure in our account of its end result, the painting itself? To be sure, I am not thinking about the standard art historical procedure of considering preparatory work, such as drawings and oil sketches, as a document of the process of artistic invention. Given that Chardin was not in a habit of making preparatory drawings, and that his oil sketches are equally hard to come by, such a procedure would be difficult to employ consistently in his case.[7] Rather, I am interested in considering the painting itself as a repository of process, that is, as not only its final product—an image—but also material evidence of the history of its own making, a relic of creation. I will conduct a sort of archaeological exploration in order to recover what may be called the *deep materiality* of Chardin's painting, an aspect traditionally considered to be the domain of the expertise of painting conservators. What can an art historian do with this kind of evidence?

To return to the Boston still life, what do we make of the material depths of a painting that offer proofs of so much hesitation in the artist's search for a satisfying solution? Since it cannot be blamed on inexperience, doubt may well be recognized as inherent in his approach to the task of painting, specifically the painting of still life, though it stands in some contrast to those flattering assessments of Chardin's execution that focused on his natural painterly ease and knack for deception. It is not that such extensive repaintings may simply be taken, as they have been, to indicate "the care Chardin took in arranging his composition."[8] Instead, they suggest that behind the apparent mastery of execution, behind Chardin's capacity to render the "truth of the object," lies a more challenging and complex process than has been assumed.

Chardin's difficulty in painting did not go unnoticed by his contemporaries. Pierre-Jean Mariette, one of the very few eighteenth-century commentators who remained unseduced by Chardin's art, offered an unkind but intriguing assessment of the painter's craft:

> *One cannot deny that the paintings of Monsieur Chardin reveal too much fatigue and effort. His touch is heavy and undifferentiated. There is nothing easy about his brush; he expresses everything in the same way, with a kind of indecision that renders his work too cold. . . . Lacking a sufficient knowledge of drawing and unable to make his studies and preparatory sketches on paper, Monsieur Chardin is obliged to have the object he seeks to imitate continuously in front of him, from the very first touch of his brush on canvas to its very last, which takes a long time and would put off anyone other than him. Therefore, he always talks about how his work* costs him a great deal. *While he would like to hide it, his work signals it against his will.*[9]

The hostility of this judgment warrants some caution about its accuracy. Yet the theme of pictorial indecision Mariette stressed accords well with the material evidence of Chardin's doubt. What is more, the painter's excessive dependency on the object described by Mariette was also mentioned in other commentaries from the period, such as that of Chardin's friend and steadfast supporter Charles-Nicolas Cochin, though he viewed it more sympathetically. Rather than a result of poor training or a lack of imagination, Cochin suggested perfectionism as the reason for Chardin's difficulty of delivery. The painter's slowness and wavering was, in Cochin's view, due to his "cruel severity in chastising himself, which is natural for an educated man who does not allow himself to take any liberties and is not easily satisfied."[10] Even Diderot, otherwise more inclined simply to marvel at Chardin's pictorial wizardry, recognized the painter to be "a severe self-critic" who left some of his works incomplete because of his own excessively high expectations.[11]

The master of illusion was, then, also a kind of neurotic avant la lettre. His legerdemain concealed painstaking effort, procrastination, dissatisfaction, and a frequent inability to complete the task of representation. Suggested in these commentaries is a connection between the painter's character and his working method, his personality being seen as responsible for the idiosyncrasies of his process. While we know better than to assume such direct connection between the person and his or her work, these pronouncements are of interest insofar as they raise a broader question of the relation between painting and subjectivity. In what way exactly can a painting be said to speak of the subject, and to what extent can that subject be identified with the painter himself? It is clearly not a matter of finding out whether or not Chardin *was* actually a perfectionist, or for that matter a neurotic, compelled to produce his work in a certain way so that his particular mode of execution could be explained or "excused" by his character formation, as indeed it was by some of his contemporaries. Instead, one can ask how the painting itself produces a painter *as* a subject. To do so, one may well consider the personality of Chardin's paintings, to explore how they *behave*, not only as images but also as material formations, and how, in this capacity, they engage, imply, or construct their author.[12] One purpose of my discussion is to activate the painting in relation to the painter, to recognize its agency as not only an image but also an object that, in its very materiality, is capable of producing the *effect of a subject*. What kind of subject do these paintings propose?

To explore this question, we must cast a different look at what Chardin's paintings represent and how. This reorientation returns us to the commentaries on the painter's skills with which I began. One could say that Chardin's paintings raise the question of the painted object as a problem or challenge for the painter. This is what Mariette evoked when he stated that Chardin's work costs him a great deal ("sa lui coûte infiniment"). To pursue this question, we must recognize the elements of Chardin's still lifes not as mere physical things or their more or less convincing imitation. Nor is this a matter of an optical or perceptual phenomenon, as some of the nuanced modern readings of Chardin have proposed.[13] Rather, Chardin's still lifes suggest a strange romance with the object as at once a material thing and an imaginary, spectral entity, something experienced not only on a physical but also a psychic register, which is what may have rendered the process of its representation "infinitely complex" for the painting subject.[14]

In the critics' claims about Chardin's molecular fidelity to the object, in the notion, if only metaphorical, that he may have painted with the stuff or flesh of things, one can detect evidence of a complex involvement, an attachment that may have been at once a stimulus and the very source of the painter's difficulty.[15] This difficulty, let us be clear, is not reducible to the mistakes or gaucheries of execution observed in Chardin's work by his contemporaries as well as his modern critics—a teapot wrongly outlined, a leg drawn too long, or other inaccuracies of perspectival and anatomical rendering—though these aspects are important.[16] My point is that the object represented in Chardin reveals itself to partake in a kind of illusory game where the stakes are higher than the mere accuracy of rendition, where the subject—beginning with the subject who produces the illusion—is at issue.[17]

What I have called the "deep materiality" of Chardin's paintings refers not only to the physical depth of their surface, which, due to the particularity of the painter's procedures amounted to a thick, quasi-geological formation, but to also their *inner life*. For Chardin's paintings confront us with a dimension of interiority that, while generated by his technical procedures, is irreducible to them, a material register that must be examined as a domain of meaning.[18] To focus on the signifying dimension of materiality is to reverse the vector of interpretation that has defined the recent discussion of Chardin's work. The interpretive efforts of the past two decades have developed a richly contextualized understanding of the painter's work by examining its relation to, among others, empiricist epistemology, materialism, the educational ideals of the Enlightenment, and the period's religious practices, in particular Jansenism.[19] These analyses, notwithstanding their diverse hermeneutic purposes, have been predicated on the assumption of a homological relation existing between Chardin's painting and the discourses or practices of his time. While I am not questioning this assumption per se—and I will offer a fair dose of contextual and theoretical evidence to back up my own claims—I wish to put more weight on the work itself. We need, in my view, a more detailed account of the texture of Chardin's painting and a fuller articulation of the logic that governs its material and technical, rather than the merely visual or iconographic, dimension. While in and of themselves the technical aspects have not been ignored, how exactly they matter in the contextual exegesis of Chardin's work remains unclear.[20] What difference does a painting *qua* painting make in producing a vision of things? How painting complicates, exceeds, or bypasses the existing forms of knowledge—how its materiality produces its own discourse—is of key importance to me.[21] It is in this sense that I attend to Chardin's *craft*.[22]

Chardin's technical skill was notoriously inscrutable for his contemporaries. "This magic defies understanding," Diderot once announced in front of Chardin's still life shown at the Salon.[23] Because of the resolute privacy in which the painter worked, it may indeed not have been easy for Chardin's contemporaries to penetrate the mysteries of his procedures.[24] Yet even Diderot recognized that Chardin must have had a technique that was "clearly defined and delimited" and that could be comprehended if one made an effort to do so, "for man is not God and the artist's studio is not nature."[25] The aim here is to recover an approach to execution wherein pictorial mastery is inflected by the palpable sense of challenge or trouble, by the inherent *negativity* of Chardin's process pointed to by, among others, Mariette (although my understanding of the term is different from Mariette's literally negative assessment). What we need is a better grasp of the complex and contradictory aspect of Chardin's procedures that evinced both an advanced technical savvy and a certain *unknowing*, the nature and effects of which remain yet to be fully understood. It is in this ambivalent sense that I restore the centrality of craft to Chardin's aesthetic project.

—·—

In Chardin's time, the painter's craft became the object of renewed, if double-edged, attention. On the one hand, defined as "an exercise of mechanical art," craft was opposed to the intellectualized, professionalized, and increasingly autonomized pictorial practice that had been promoted by the Academy since its inception.[26] The Academy's elevation of painting to the status of liberal art, and its embrace of discourse as an explanatory and legitimizing basis of pictorial practice, either discredited or displaced any concerns with painterly craft. Moreover, associated with the guild structure, and specifically with the Académie de Saint-Luc from which the royal institution and its members were at pains to distinguish themselves, craft was cast as the attribute of the *maîtres peintres*, described in the Academy's early battles with the guild as "gross and harmful spirits," an "abject troupe," "grinders of colors," and "ignorants and mercenaries."[27] These strongly negative terms weighed upon the perception of craft in the collective imaginary throughout the eighteenth century.

At the same time, however, an alternative evaluation of craft was gaining traction. In the nuanced conception of pictorial practice formulated by André Félibien, the first secretary of the Academy, execution was inseparable from the faculty of intelligence and imagination.[28] Moreover, the issue of rendition and manual skill played a key role in the early attempts to establish the autonomy of painting as a medium, notably in the writings of Roger de Piles. Notwithstanding his support for painting's aspiration to liberal status, which entailed its assimilation into the larger domain of letters, de Piles insisted on painting's essentially different, visual character.[29] These early conceptualizations of practice had an impact on the understanding of craft that began to emerge within the new institutional context for the production and reception of art during the second quarter of the eighteenth century. The introduction of regular Salon exhibitions in 1737, the rapid development of the modern art market, and the emergence of cultural mediators such as critics, dealers, connoisseurs, and amateurs contributed to a new appreciation for painting as a material object. The forms of discourse generated in these contexts—Salon reviews, sales catalogs, and catalogues raisonnés—transformed the shared perception of the status and meaning of painterly craft.

With the establishment of regular Salon exhibitions as a platform for the public discussion of art, questions of execution and technical expertise acquired unprecedented relevance.[30] Initially, the critical discourse on painting challenged the importance of execution in favor of other criteria of aesthetic judgment, such as decorum, costume, and social purpose. Rather than the minutiae of handling, issues pertaining to the subject matter prevailed in the Salon reviews.[31] Yet at the same time, criticism precipitated a radical reevaluation of craft. Confronted by the critics' assumption of the right to aesthetic judgment, artists sought to regain control over their professional domain by denouncing the critics' incompetence and insisting on their own exclusive possession of technical know-how.

Some artists entered into polemical exchanges with critics to revindicate what they perceived as their prerogatives. "I call craft anything I don't know about," declares Phylakei, the protagonist of *Les Misotechnites aux Enfers* (The Technique-Haters in the Underworld), a satirical dialogue on the arts published anonymously in 1763 by Cochin.[32] Consisting of eight *entretiens*, the dialogue was an extensive argument with a real-life critic, abbé Nicolas Bridard de La Garde, featured as Phylakei (the Greek etymology of his name referring to "La Garde" in French), the author of Salon reviews that were particularly harsh on artists.[33] Cochin, the secretary of the Academy and a practicing artist, intervened in defense of the attacked. But beyond its immediate polemical purpose, his pamphlet addressed a larger question of technical knowledge in both the practice and understanding of pictorial art.

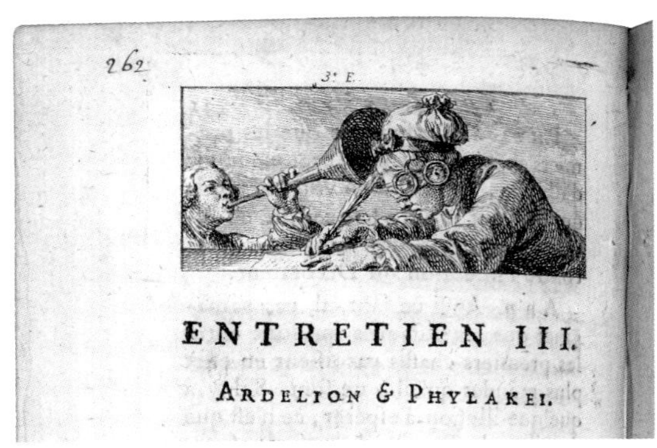

2.3.
Charles-Nicolas Cochin, *Phylakei écrit à tatons*, figure 4 from [Cochin], *Les Misotechnites aux Enfers, ou examen des Observations sur les arts*, 1763. Engraving. Bibliothèque national de France, Paris.

Phylakei's provocative avowal of his technical ignorance aimed to reveal the incompetence of critics at large. From the artists' perspective, men of letters like La Garde who took up writing about art were philistines who did not know what they were talking about. The vignette illustrating the third dialogue in which Phylakei offers his definition of craft, designed and engraved by Cochin himself, makes this point patently clear (fig. 2.3). Deprived of his glasses (which dangle by a ribbon in front of his ear) and blindfolded, the critic is shown writing to the tune of false opinion, personified by a man blowing an outsized trumpet into the writer's ear. Unseeing and biased, the figure represents a critic as a "voluntary blindman," an impostor in the realm of art.[34]

Blindness was one of the established visual tropes for deriding the incompetence of critics in the debates surrounding the early Salon exhibitions, as Watelet's well-known caricature of La Font de Saint-Yenne attests (fig. 2.4).[35] But in Cochin's tract, it is specifically the blind man's obliviousness to craft that is targeted, the neologism *misotechnites* of the brochure's title clearly pointing to the lack of *practical* expertise about painting as impaired judgment. The superiority of artists, in whose name Cochin speaks, resides precisely in their possession of empirical knowledge that comes only from practice and that may not even be translatable into words. Hence it is only the painters who can properly judge their productions.[36] And it is the painters—the imaginary tribunal of old masters consisting of Raphael, Guido Reni, Veronese, Poussin, and Rubens—whom Cochin convokes at the end of the dialogue to adjudicate the critics' opinions and pronounce the verdict—needless to say, against them.

Les Misotechnites aux Enfers offers insight into the role and meaning that technical competence had acquired in France by the mid-eighteenth century. Reclaimed as technical expertise, craft constituted the condition sine qua non of the practice of painting as well as its judgment, its integrity, and ultimately its autonomy. Practical knowledge of materials and procedures, joined by imagination and genius, defines for Cochin the essence of the medium, with the artist emerging as a sovereign expert of his or her own productions.[37] This was a novel argument and, we may note, a risky one for Cochin (as secretary of the Academy) to articulate, insofar as it potentially challenged the Academy's emphasis on the conceptual and discursive dimensions of pictorial practice.[38]

Cochin was by no means alone in his attempt to validate material execution. The bourgeoning art market generated its own new discourse of expertise on painting as a material object.[39] Transformed into a commodity, painting was submitted to a new kind of scrutiny that focused specifically on painterly skill. Aspects of execution came to be appreciated as the means of assessing the value of painting on the

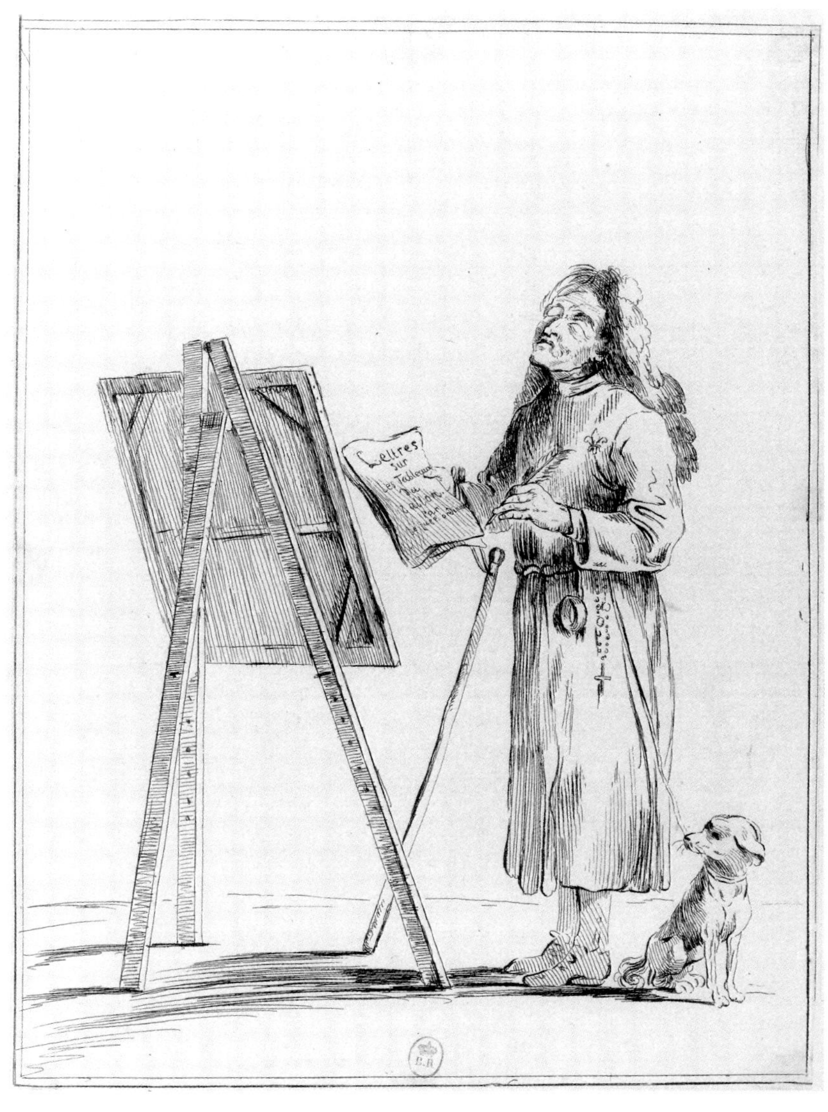

2.4.
Claude-Henri Watelet, *Caricature of La Font de Saint-Yenne*. Bibliothèque national de France, Paris.

art market, and it was, therefore, the evaluation of the painter's craft that a dealer or a sale commissary was expected to provide. An assessment of le faire proved, moreover, central to the formulation of style as the basis for defining the artist's oeuvre, as the efforts of dealers such as Gersaint, discussed in the previous chapter, make clear. The execution-oriented account of the object was disseminated through publications, such as sales catalogs and catalogues raisonnés, that consisted not only of a list of works but also of a "situating" preface, wherein an expert discussion of the artist's oeuvre was offered. Thus the development of the art market led to the emergence of the "regime of expertise" that was focused on the painter's craft.[40]

Parallel to the reevaluation of craft in the art world was a broader phenomenon of rediscovery and reevaluation of artisanal modes of production that we witness in Enlightenment discourse. Diderot's entry on craft ("métier") in the *Encyclopédie* (1765), epitomizes this perception. "I do not know why this term has been seen as vile: it is to crafts that we owe all the things necessary for living. If anyone would make an effort to go around the workshops, one would see nothing but utility joined with the greatest proofs of discernment."[41] While Diderot refers to a specialized skill involved in the production of useful objects, his entry, and the discussion of different crafts in the *Encyclopédie*, not only rehabilitated manual skill but also offered its radical reconceptualization. A new interpretive grid for understanding technical activity that emerged in the *Encyclopédie* did not only submit the operations of a skilled worker to rational understanding but also pointed to their cognitive dimension.[42] Inscribed within the larger matrix of Enlightenment rationality, this new epistemology of making, and a sense of mastery linked to it, had broader implications reaching beyond the practice of the trades into the domain of art.

It is in this context of the ongoing reappraisal of artisanship—a culture oscillating between disavowal and discovery of the meaning and merits of manual skill—that we must situate Chardin's effort to develop a highly individuated approach to execution. There is no doubt that his investment in painterly craft as the means of self-distinction was at least to some degree an attempt to position himself within the emergent field of public discussion on art wherein technical competence became an issue of critical importance. By developing a manner of painting that not only signaled manual competence but also appeared "magical," Chardin was making sure that his work would be noticed at the Salon. And it was. It is a measure of his success that once they entered the public sphere, his silent (nondiscursive), technically inscrutable paintings were studied attentively by critics, that his work was so often cited in the polemics about the relative merits of le faire, and that Chardin himself came to be recognized as a painter's painter.[43]

—·—

The Salon was, however, neither the exclusive nor the defining domain for Chardin's practice. While as a member of the Academy, he was expected to exhibit his work at the Salon, his paintings—not least because of their predominantly small scale—appealed less to the public at large than to a select audience of artists, connoisseurs, and *amateurs*.[44] His work was collected by sophisticated professionals, such as the journalist and editor of the *Mercure de France* Antoine de la Roque; well-known artists like the painter Joseph Aved and the sculptors Edmé Bouchardon and Jean-Baptiste Pigalle; distinguished amateurs, among them Carl Gustaf Tessin and Laurent La Live de Jully; and discerning noble and upper-class patrons in France and abroad, including the Swedish Crown Princess Louisa Ulrike and Russia's Catherine the Great.[45] If his paintings were sought after, it was because, notwithstanding the humble nature of his subjects, they were recognized as vehicles of aesthetic discernment, objects on which to exercise—or through which to prove—one's capacity for the appreciation of art.

But Chardin's idiosyncratic mode of execution also had much to do with his personal and professional background in which craft figured prominently. Having grown up in the artisanal milieu—his father was an established cabinetmaker, a member of a clan of *menuisiers* specializing in billiard tables; his mother came from a family of renown *paumiers* (racquet makers)—the young Chardin insisted on becoming a painter, a choice his father consented to only reluctantly.[46] Jean-Siméon received his first artistic training in the studio of an academic painter, Pierre-Jacques Cazes, an education that should have led him to the Academy. Instead, at the age of twenty-five, Chardin sought and obtained a *maîtrise*, or a license of a master painter, from a guild school, the Académie de Saint-Luc. Whether this was his own choice, or, as Chardin's early biographer Cochin suggested, a decision imposed on him by his father—who, apparently unbeknownst to his son, acquired the maîtrise for him by paying for it from his own pocket—is uncertain. However, the fact that four years later, Chardin decided to present himself at the royal Academy indicates that he aimed higher than the guild. He was not only admitted but, in an unusual manner, also instantly received as a full member of the Academy, which led him to renounce his maîtrise. Yet, notwithstanding this spectacular success, the rank that Chardin received upon his entry, the "painter with a talent for animals and fruit," placed him squarely at the lowest level of the academic hierarchy. The category of the *peintre à talents* smacked of guild nomenclature.[47] The shadow the guild had cast over Chardin's career was deepened by the tension between the royal Academy and the Académie de Saint-Luc, which ended only in 1776, that is, at the very end of the painter's life, with the latter's abolition.[48]

Chardin's sense of never having left the guild far behind must have also been reinforced, or exacerbated, by the fact that he had never extracted himself completely from the artisanal context of his childhood, living and working during his formative years and well into his maturity in his parents' house, together with his younger brother Juste, who followed in the steps of Chardin père, and his brother's family. While such prolonged cohabitation of parents and adult children was not in and of itself unusual for the bourgeois households of the eighteenth century, what made it more so was the difference between the father and son's respective professions and social standing.[49] The fact that Chardin's working space was located in the same house as his father's workshop must have functioned as a daily reminder of both the proximity and distance between their respective *métiers*.[50] It was likely also a source of some tensions, given the father's and the rest of the family's unfamiliarity with the nature of Chardin's pursuit and, if we trust Cochin, the history of disagreement between the father and son regarding the latter's choice of profession.[51]

In the context of Chardin's daily life, craft was not exactly a neutral realm of manual competence but a charged domain of experience in which domestic intimacy was mixed with paternal pressure. Living and working as an academic painter in the midst of artisans, the young painter had to conduct a complex negotiation to establish his personal and professional autonomy. Chardin's approach to his own craft had something to do with this negotiation. One can say that Chardin transformed craft, a defining activity of a maître peintre, into an attribute of an *artiste* in the emergent modern sense of the term referring to a professional image maker who takes his métier as a personal vocation.[52] This modern usage of the term was not fully established until the third quarter of the eighteenth century, and, in Chardin's time, artiste could still denote any kind of accomplished artisan, for example, someone who knew how to mix mercury, as well as an old master.[53] The painter's practice straddled these two domains, his craft retaining the older connotations of a carefully guarded and secretly deployed technical skill while also serving him as the means of artistic self-individuation.

In his self-conscious effort of self-individuation, Chardin is comparable to Boucher, with whom he shared an artisanal background and whom he knew as a colleague at the Academy. Yet their approach was very different. While Boucher, as we have seen, sought to define himself above all through the metonymic effects of the surface, developing a signature style and embracing mechanical reproduction to expand the scope of his oeuvre, Chardin's aesthetic distinction and recognizability were linked to the effect of depth, not only in the sense of spatial illusion that his still lifes were seen to convey, but also in the compelling effect of inwardness of the painting itself, in the complex, layered geology of his canvas. While Boucher operated under the auspices of the visual sign, privileging the effect of the signifier, Chardin was, emphatically, a haptic painter producing tactile surfaces that suggest the existence of a material depth beneath them. The problem raised by his work is, therefore, not how the signifier functions but how it is made, how object is turned into a sign. It is in the very *substance* of the sign that Chardin dwells. Through his mode of execution, he constructs a complex archaeology of the image that results in unique and mysterious forms appearing on its surface. This deep materiality constitutes, in my view, not only a zone of self-individuation but also a sphere of the painter's self-experience. What exactly was the nature of this self-experience, and how it contributed to the distinct quality of Chardin's work in different genres, are the central concerns of this chapter.

2.5.
Jean-Siméon Chardin, *Menu de gras (The Meat-Day Meal)*, 1731. Oil on canvas. Musée du Louvre, Paris.

2.6.
Jean-Siméon Chardin, *Menu de Maigre (The Fast-Day Meal)*, 1731. Oil on canvas. Musée du Louvre.

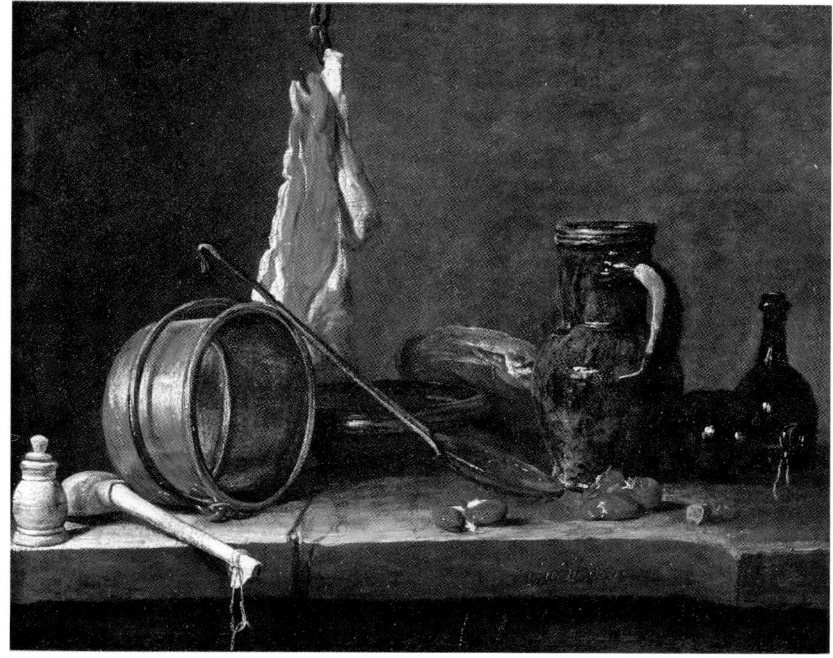

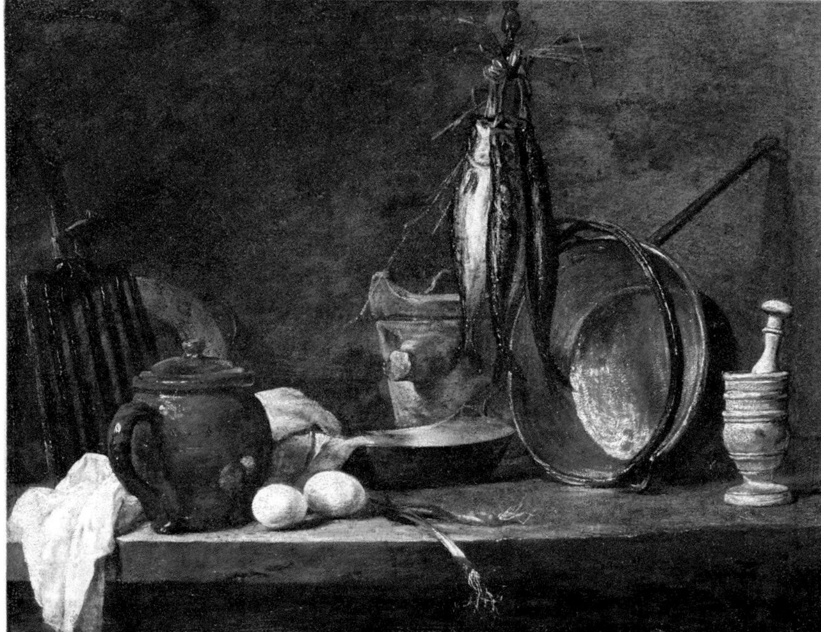

THE OBJECT (INSIDE/OUT)

It has been laid open and you can admire the beauty of its huge yet delicate architecture, tinged with red blood, with blue nerves and with white muscles, like the nave of a polychrome cathedral.

—Marcel Proust, "Chardin and Rembrandt," 125

It has been said that Chardin's still lifes differ from those of his predecessors in that he gives up on rendering the circumstances and accords the central place to things.[54] René Démoris noted "the singular investment of the painter in the objects," the more curious that these objects—simple kitchen utensils or standard food items—are often of no intrinsic interest.[55] Looking at Chardin's early still lifes painted from the mid-1720 to the 1730s, one gets a clear sense of an altogether different *relation* to the object than that seen in Dutch and Flemish painting. Drawing on Northern models, Chardin subtly transforms them by, first of all, repositioning the featured items. Placed on a narrow stone ledge, his pots, pans, mortars, knifes, and food items are often balanced precariously on its edge (figs. 2.5 and 2.6). To be sure, the motif of the protruding object was a standard device for securing pictorial depth—as is evident in Pieter Claesz's *Still Life with Stoneware Jug* (fig. 2.7)—but Chardin's deployment of it, as witnessed, for instance, in the *Kitchen Table*, makes the sense of *risk* involved in such placement come to the fore. Multiplied beyond necessity on the brink of the shelf, the knife, the piece of raw meat, the plucked chicken, and the suspended cloth produce a sense of material excess spilling out from this arena of display, posing a threat to the stability of the arrangement.

How different a lesson one could learn from the Dutch may be illustrated by the work of Chardin's younger contemporary, Anne Vallayer-Coster. In her masterful *Still Life with Ham, Bottles, and Radishes* (1767) (fig. 2.8), the tightness of the composition endows a similar grouping of objects with a sense of stability and evident utility—see the knife firmly stuck in the ham as if to demonstrate its function. Things are put *together* and remain there, only the hair-thin ends of the radishes venture out. By contrast Chardin's compositions are

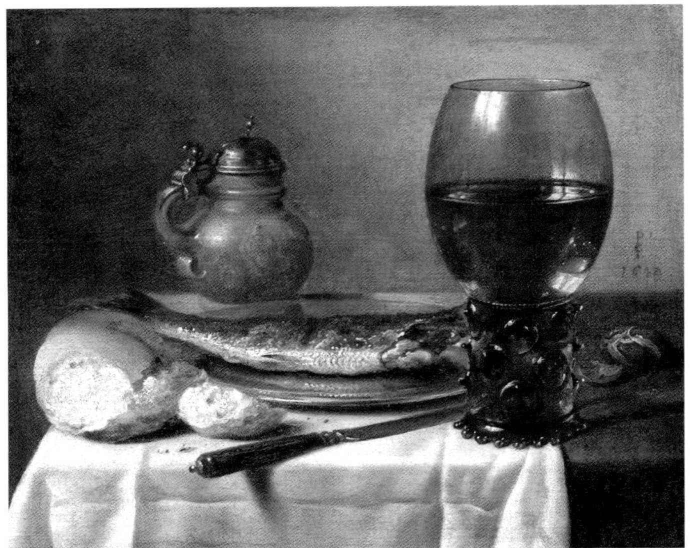

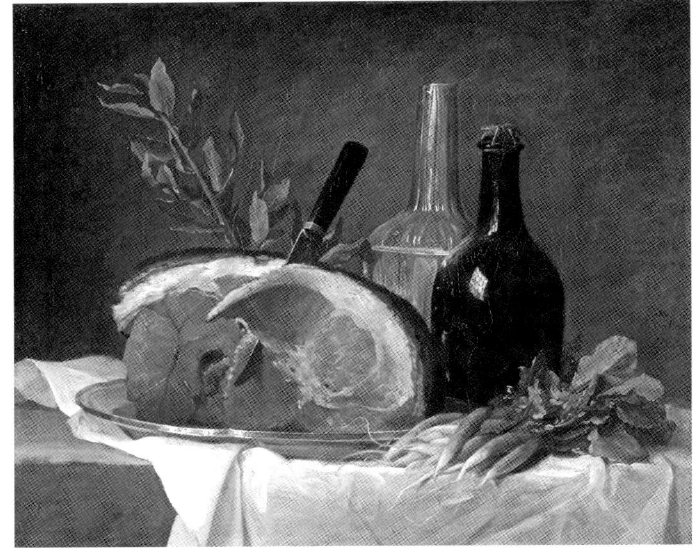

2.7.
Pieter Claesz, *Still Life with Stoneware Jug, Wine Glass, Herring, and Bread*, 1642. Oil on panel. Museum of Fine Arts, Boston, Bequest of Mrs. Edward Wheelwright.

2.8.
Anne Vallayer-Coster, *Still Life with Ham, Bottles, and Radishes*, 1767. Oil on canvas. Staatliche Museen zu Berlin

often marked by a sense of an outward spill, what could be called an "inside/out" effect. This effect is manifest, literally, in the upturned objects so frequently encountered in Chardin's early still lifes, such as the motif of the copper cauldron turned over on its side that appears in numerous paintings, among them *Kitchen Still Life with Loin of Mutton* (1732) (fig. 2.9), where, moreover, a piece of raw meat—not unlike that in the Boston painting—placed on a white cloth cascades downward as if the overturned copper pot had just spilled its yet uncooked content.[56] But the "inside/out" may also be recognized, more broadly, as a structuring principle that governs the composition of the painter's many early works. One could say that in these works Chardin *activates* the standard tropes of still life, endowing his arrangements with an internal dynamism, such that his paintings do not merely present a set of objects but also enact what the composition *does*, the action of pulling the image itself inside-out, almost disgorging it.

Disgorgement comes to mind not only because of the comestible nature of the displayed objects but also because of the violence some of them represent or are marked by, as in the chicken with its throat cut, its head dangling sadly on a long neck, its body deflated, a motif featured in several canvases painted around 1730–31 as well as the Boston still life.[57] We are far from the tactfully vanitative signifiers of decay in Dutch still life, such as the bees and caterpillars marking discreetly the inevitable erosion of life in the paintings of Balthasar van der Ast, one of the masters of the genre (fig. 2.10). With Chardin, death enters the image more explicitly and, more importantly, it penetrates the very process of painting. While the project of the seventeenth-century Dutch painters was marked by a thorough sense of separation from the suggested intrusion of death on live matter—the eating away of life in van der Ast had nothing to do with the painter's own process—in Chardin, death becomes inseparable from the very materiality of the painting.[58]

Consider the way Chardin rendered the throat and neck of the chicken in the Boston still life, like a mottled wound, slightly blurred. Although the term "relaxed focus" has been used to describe this type of blurring in Chardin, it has nothing relaxed about it.[59] It looks as if blood has been mixed with the pigment, as if the painter, as Diderot suggested, indeed dipped his brush in the dead chicken's flesh. Then there are those slabs of flayed meat appearing in several early still lifes, such as the one in the Musée Jacquemart-André, tilted forward as if to invite our touch and yet repelling it at the same time by the suggestive rendition of raw flesh[60] (see fig. 2.9). The effect produced by the thick materiality of pigment—the white smudges of the bone conveyed through unblended strokes of gray and red, with some dabs of pinkish red in between—enhances the meat motif's ambiguous address. The protrusion of Chardin's thick and sticky marks, typical of these early still lifes, echoes and reinforces the sense of expulsion conveyed by the arrangement of some of the objects on the edge of the ledge, suggesting also its reversibility. It is as if the canvas were a mouth both spilling its content and threatening to suck it back in, the idea of ingestion

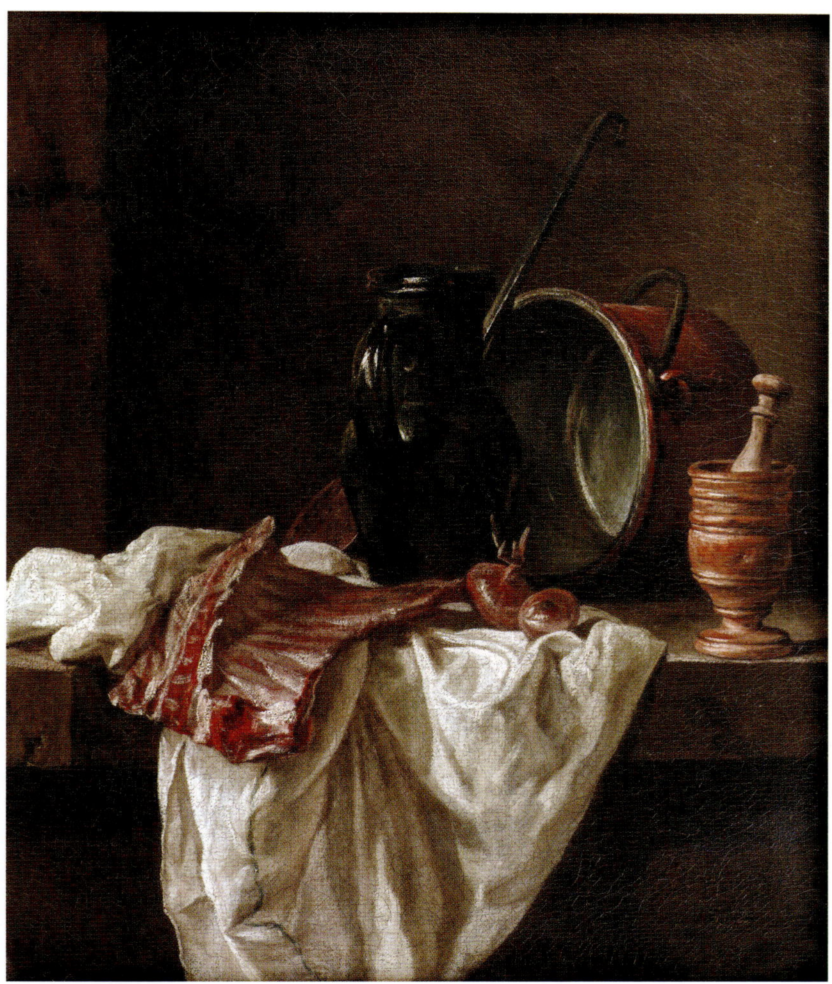

implied by the displayed food moving back and forth between the possibilities of eating and being eaten at the same time.

Nowhere is this ambivalent mode of address more explicitly, and more violently, spelled out than in Chardin's famous painting of *The Ray* (fig. 2.11). The whole composition revolves around the eviscerated body of the fish suspended on a hook, its voided inside rendered with a kind of chromatic fury in all its glistening details. Monumentalized by the scale of the canvas—unusually large for Chardin—this wedge of violent chroma, driven in between the foodstuffs on the left and the kitchen utensils on the right, produces an imposing image of both the object and the process that went into fleshing it out.[61] Its whitish rectilinear form dotted with clots of pigment evokes the very support on which the fish was painted, while the extraordinary spectacle of its entrails reads as an allusion to the painter's process, the placement of this "canvas" between the raw materials for a meal and the meal-making tools reemphasizing the suggested analogy between the act of painting and culinary preparation.[62] Defined as a compositional core of the canvas turned inside/out, the giant fish makes evident the structural centrality of the trope of representation as evisceration in Chardin's vision. It literalizes and magnifies the

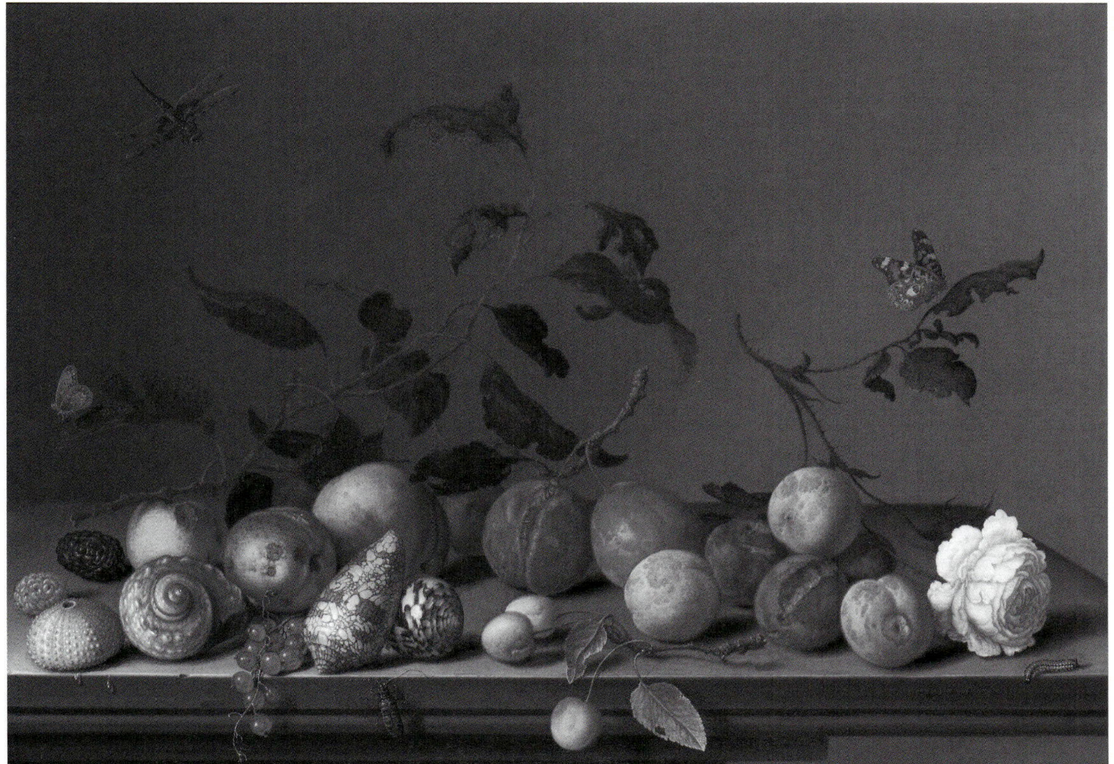

2.9.
Jean-Siméon Chardin, *Kitchen Still Life with Loin of Mutton*, 1732. Oil on canvas. Musée Jacquemart-André, Paris.

2.10.
Balthasar van der Ast, *A Still-Life of Fruit and Shells with a Rose and Various Insects upon a Stone Ledge*. Oil on panel. Private Collection, United States (by courtesy of David Koetser).

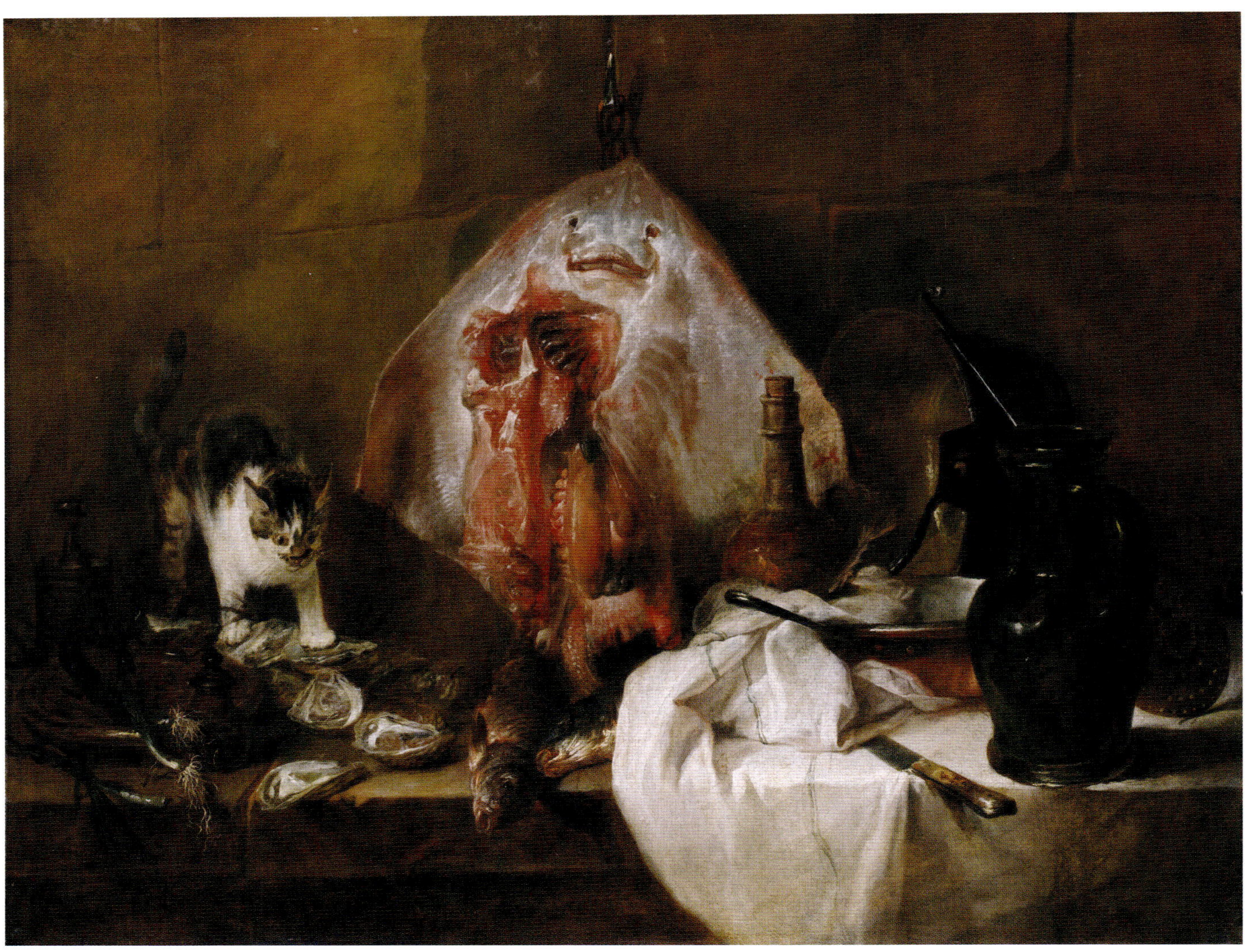

violence entailed by the visualization of the object—the principle of inside/out—that informs Chardin's early work as we have seen, albeit on a smaller scale, in other still lifes.

But if *The Ray* represents the very object of representation, it also offers a suggestive image of its subject. The anthropomorphic dimension of the fish, standing erect, its "face" appearing right above the disemboweled cavity, with its Mona Lisa smile and its "eyes" (which are in fact its gills) staring out at the viewer, turns it into a human figure of sorts, a version of an academic *écorché*. This suggestion is compounded, and complicated, by the figure's animated mode of appearance, and the violence entailed by it. Erupting onto the stage of representation, this vicious écorché violates the space of the subject, both the viewer's and the painter's. The violence of its incursion is what the painting performs and reflects upon, with the cat alarmed by the oysters acting as an internal commentary on the viewer's—or the painter's—fright vis-à-vis the canvas. But the canvas also testifies to the painter's own violence, giving us some sense of how Chardin experienced the act of representation envisioned in *The Ray*.

This violence is reciprocal and transitive; it defines the object and the subject of representation interchangeably, as its agent and target. The fish is both its symptom and its site: the effect of the subject's close encounter with the object and a frontier at which this encounter takes place. An interface of mutilated flesh, the ray thus erects the boundary between the subject and the object and also renders it precarious—violated—in bodily terms. It is the oral dimension of this bodily violence that is most intriguing. Torn apart, the fish looks as if some giant mouth has bitten into it, pulling its contents out. Yet, at the same time, it comes across as being a giant *gueule* itself, with some of its bulbous innards lined up in rows

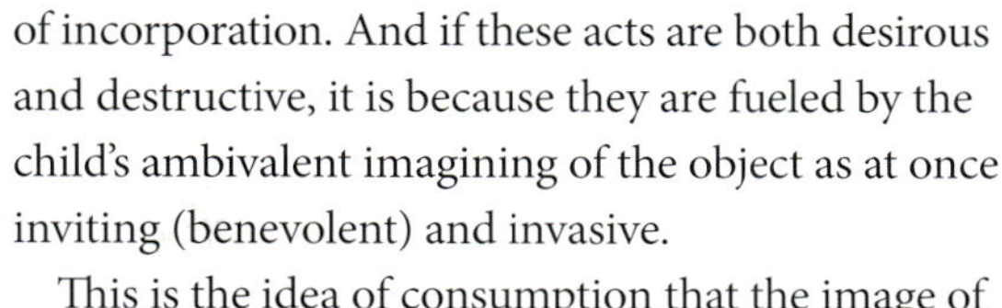

2.11. OPPOSITE
Jean-Siméon Chardin, *The Ray*, 1725–26. Oil on canvas. Musée du Louvre, Paris.

2.12. BELOW
Jean-Siméon Chardin, *The Ray*, detail of fig. 2.11.

like teeth (fig. 2.12). This vision evokes eating as a brutal physical act, the way animals eat—a cat or a dog sinking its teeth into flesh—or as a primitive human mode of consumption unmediated by tools, the way a baby or a young child might gulp things up without using a fork and knife. But it is oral also in the sense of evoking a basic psychic operation of a subject defining itself in relation to an object through an act of ingestion that is also an act of incorporation.[63] Think, again, of the way babies use their mouths not only to eat but also to relate to the surrounding world, to know and possess things by *internalizing* them. Theirs is a messy mode of contact, at once passionate and aggressive, driven as it is by the contradictory desires for both fusion with and separation from the object. The violence that characterizes these oral engagements stems, we are told, from the child's uncertainty about its own bodily and psychic boundaries at this stage of development, boundaries that the child attempts to chart in relation to the object precisely through these acts of incorporation. And if these acts are both desirous and destructive, it is because they are fueled by the child's ambivalent imagining of the object as at once inviting (benevolent) and invasive.

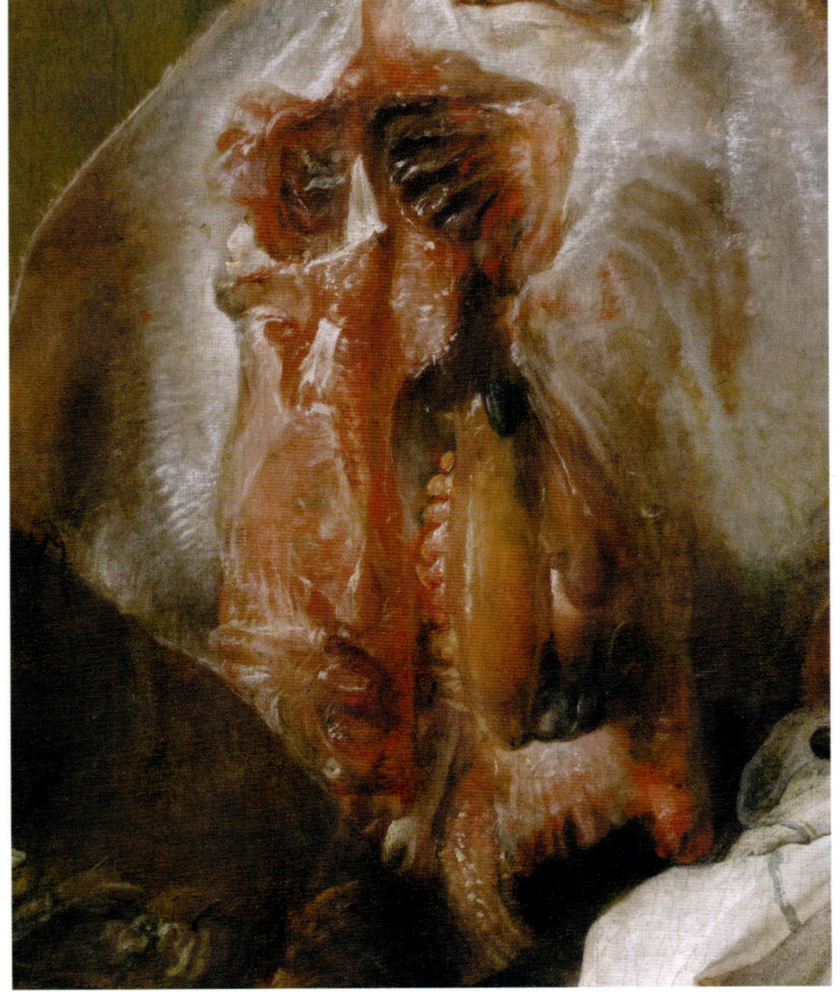

This is the idea of consumption that the image of the ray calls up; it is primitive in a sense of being unmediated or uncivilized, as animals eat, but also in a sense of harking back to the way the mouth is used by a child in the early stages of its development and to the infantile fantasies that underwrite this mode of oral engagement. The way Chardin painted the ray enhances these oral connotations. Delving into the depth of the cavity, the painter unleashed his brush in a mode that is brilliant and masterful but also primitive and messy. With the white, black, and red pigments of different intensity, he slashed, smudged, and smeared the canvas to bring forth the spatial complexity of the ray's bodily interior. In some places, the fish's corpus appears to have been painted directly with the painter's own body, which left its indelible traces on the canvas's surface: for instance, the row of "teeth" along the shiny vesical form in the center has been most likely produced by the fingertips, and the dabs of curdled white defining the upper right edge of the cavity also seem to be a product of a hand rather than a brush. The sticky chewiness of pigment in some places—the white highlights in particular—heightens the impression of the painter's direct bodily contact with the canvas—a way of painting Chardin came to be known for—thus also underscoring the notion of the painting subject's entanglement with the object.[64]

If this painterly performance may be called oral, rather than visual, it is not because Chardin actually painted with his mouth, but rather that his particularly tactile mode of painting—not unlike a bite— suggests both the physical and the psychic dimensions of his process. Aggressive but also affectionate in its attention to the object rendered lovingly in all its horrifying details, this oral performance does not only serve the purpose of depiction, fleshing out as it does the contours of the fish. It is also involved in the task of drawing the bodily and psychic boundary of the subject involved in this act.

The at once passionate and aggressive touch that brought forth *The Ray* has another, sexual dimension. It is hard to ignore that if the cavity of the fish is an image of a voracious mouth, half-devoured and devouring, it also comes across as a gruesome visual fantasy of a genital organ. For an eighteenth-century viewer this association was put on the table,

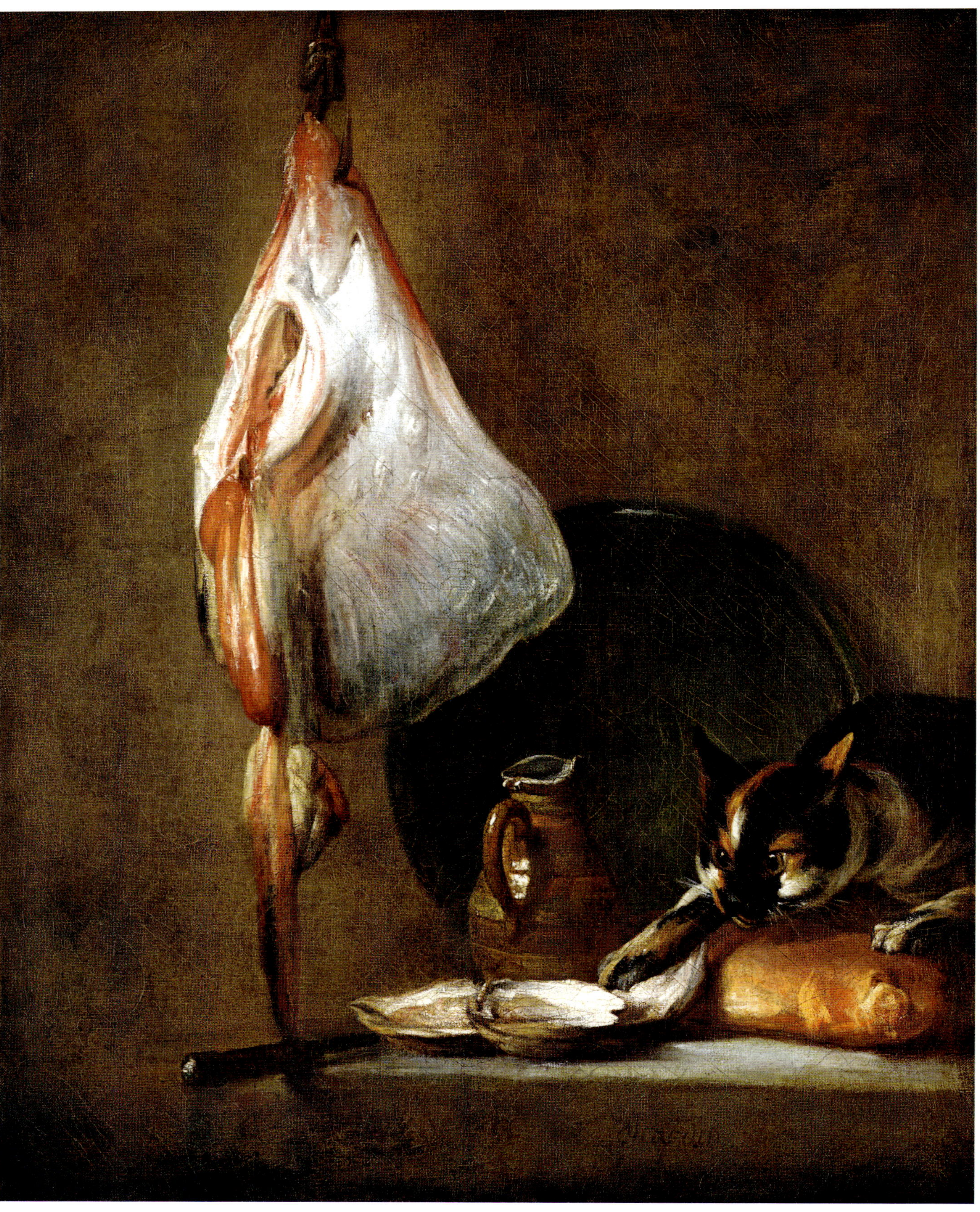

2.13.
Jean-Siméon Chardin, *Cat with Ray, Oysters, Pitcher, and Loaf of Bread*, 1728. Oil on canvas. Thyssen-Bornemisza Museum, Madrid.

so to speak, from the start, by the very name of this still life's protagonist, *la raie*, which in the period's common parlance referred to female genitals.[65] The way Chardin painted the fish played up its connotations as a sexually charged image of mutilated and mutilating femininity that reveals itself as a fantasy of an injured masculinity, an image of male risk. For from the depth of this ghastly image of a bodily wound suggestive of a female organ rise up pendulous elongated forms that evoke a male body. This sexually suggestive and bi-gendered interpretation of the ray, a standard motif of seventeenth-century Flemish still lifes, recurs in Chardin's early work, notably in *Cat with Ray, Oysters, Pitcher, and Loaf of Bread* of 1728 (fig. 2.13).[66] Although the fish, suspended from a hook, is shown in profile, its gutted orifice is in full view, a product of a brush that seems to have been particularly interested in conveying its gory aspect. Here the orifice is nestled in an oval shape produced by vigorous slashes of red and white pigment that form something disturbingly close to the shape of a vulva exhibiting its wounds. Rendered in vivid red, the pendant forms that appear below the orifice—similar to the shiny tubular vesicle at the center of *The Ray*'s cavity—place masculinity at the core of this genital spectacle. What these spectacular renditions of mutilated organs amount to is an anxious vision of femininity as a domain of male self-identification, a vision that speaks of both a loving attachment to and a violent repulsion of the female body as a site of subjective self-definition.

As such, *The Ray* not only reenacts on a monumental scale the logic of inside/out that governs the appearance of the object in Chardin's other early still lifes but also envisions the violence subtending the *subject's* emergence into the visual field. If the cavernous innards of the fish open up to a kind of interior within the painting, it is not exactly, as Proust described it, an aesthetic space, a cathedral to admire and wonder about, but an architecture of a violent subjective experience, a space of the painting subject anxiously charting its confines within and against those of the painted object.

—.—

What led Chardin to develop this approach? How are we to understand the relation between the object and the subject implied in this process and what, in particular, are we to make of the mixture of violence and passion marking this relation?

I would suggest that the violence of *The Ray* had much to do with the conditions—both professional and personal—in which it was made as well as the original function of this canvas. Chardin painted *The Ray* in his parents' house. Located at 21 rue du Four, on the corner of rue Princesse, in the Saint-Germain district, it was a place where the painter lived and worked throughout his youth and well into his middle age.[67] He remained there even after his first marriage in 1731, moving out only when, sometime after his first wife's death, he remarried and relocated to his second wife's house right down the street.[68] He was about forty-eight years old at the time. Throughout the 1720s and early 1730s, that is, when he embarked on painting still lifes, Chardin's studio was situated next to the household's kitchen on the third floor.[69] It is from this space, its physical proximity enhanced by the smells and noises that must have penetrated his workspace, that the painter culled some of the things and foodstuffs that repeatedly appear in his early works, including the glazed earthenware jug, pepper mill, mortar, and skimming ladle featured in *The Ray*, and probably the fish itself.

To bring such ordinary things into representation was not only a matter of convenience, that is, a result of these items being close at hand. It was also, no doubt, a self-conscious attempt to *make a place* for these things, and for the kind of life that they stood for—modest bourgeois, the life of Chardin's family—within the space of representation. Inscribing the commonplace objects from the Chardins' kitchen within the tradition of Northern still life, *The Ray* makes the elevating aspect of this gesture especially clear, reinforcing it by virtuoso rendition and uncommonly grand scale. At the same time, the confrontational logic of this kitchen scenery and the aggression at its center suggest some ambivalence inherent in this inclusive gesture, aggrandizing and elevating as it may be. Not exactly an embrace, but a more conflicted engagement with the domestic sphere is staged in *The Ray*.[70] If this is so, it is because the objects we are looking at are not mere tokens of bourgeois life but more ambiguous signifiers of how Chardin lived in his family house and what he made of it. To get some idea of Chardin's household experiences we must consider what was entailed in living where he did.

First and foremost, it meant being embedded in a professional context that was not his own. A household of a cabinetmaker, 21 rue du Four was defined by his father's métier in more than one sense. It was, to begin with, an arena of Chardin père's professional activity. The father's billiard table-making workshop

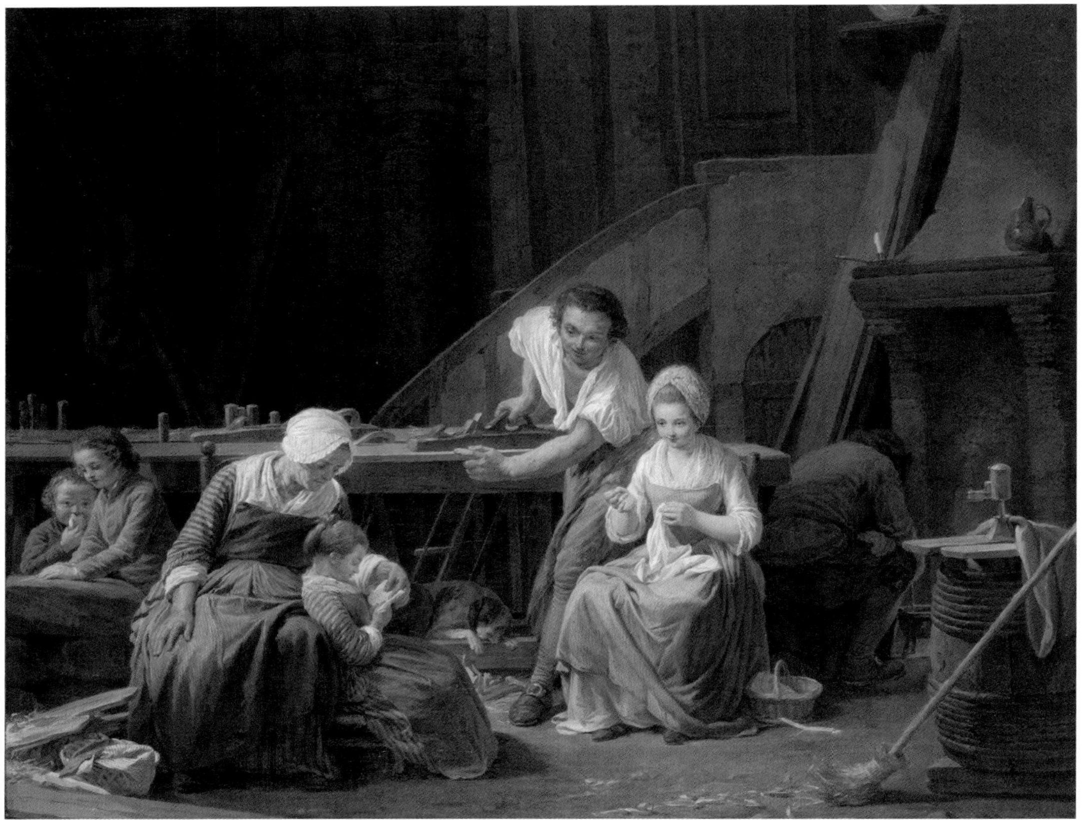

2.14.
Nicolas-Bernard Lépicié, *Joiner's Family*, ca. 1780. Oil on canvas. Wadsworth Atheneum Museum of Art, Hartford, Connecticut. The Ella Gallup Sumner and Mary Catlin Sumner Collection Fund.

was most likely located on the ground floor of the house and, following the custom established in artisanal households in the eighteenth century, opened directly to the street, making the work conducted within it publicly visible. It also identified the dwelling that housed it with the profession of a *menuisier*.[71] Chardin's younger brother Juste, who followed in his father's footsteps, must have worked in the workshop as well. The presence of the workshop was not only a physical fact, however, but also an interior space that imposed a certain rhythm and ethos of labor on family life.[72] Moreover, it was a workspace governed by rules of professional hierarchy, discipline, and a distinctly paternalistic principle of complete subordination to the master who functioned as a father figure for the apprentices and journeymen employed in it.[73] It was precisely in order to ensure his paternal function that the workshop was integrated into the master's home and his family, with apprentices most often living on the premises and participating in the family life.[74]

The paternalism of the artisanal workshop was modeled on the eighteenth-century family structure within which the father occupied a privileged and powerful position.[75] In this period, it was fathers who decided all matters regarding the professional and economic status of their children, retaining their right long after the children had become adults.[76] In artisanal families, where the father's legal authority was combined with his status as a master, the father's enhanced sense of paternal entitlement sometimes led to serious conflicts. The life story recounted by an eighteenth-century master glazier, Jacques-Louis Ménétra who was able to forge his own career only by escaping the grip of his father, is instructive. The young Ménétra's apprenticeship with his father led to a clash, precipitating the son's identity crisis and ultimately driving him out of the parental household.[77]

Ménétra's account, though itself a literary construction rather than a document of its author's experience, may serve as a historical antidote to the idealized depictions of the artisanal household as a happy family that began to appear after the mid-eighteenth century, in the wake of Rousseau's writings. Among the examples of this iconographic trend are two scenes depicting a workshop of a menuisier, not unlike that of Chardin's father: Nicolas-Bernard Lépicié's *Joiner's Family* (fig. 2.14) and Noël Hallé's *Education of the Poor*. In these scenes, the transmission of professional knowledge between fathers and sons is couched in harmonious and affectionate terms.[78] Moreover, they offer a vision of congenial and normative gender relations, with sons aligned with their fathers in pursuit of their profession while daughters are aligned with their mothers. These visual constructions of the artisanal workshop stand in stark contrast to what Ménétra had to say about it, the comparison suggesting that the affective relations obtaining within the artisanal household were in reality far more complex than those presented by the painters.

Unlike Ménétra, Chardin was not his father's apprentice. Yet he too was caught in the structure of paternal authority that governed the mutually imbricated professional and familial lives of his household. The more so that he was financially dependent on his father. That Chardin continued to reside in his parents' house well into adulthood, despite the fact that he exercised a métier different from his father, was surely due to the fact that he could not afford to do otherwise.[79] The income of a young painter barely starting out was not high enough to permit living on one's own, and Chardin was not in possession of an independent fortune. This is confirmed by the marriage contract he signed at the age of twenty-four with Marguerite Saintard, a daughter of a well-to-do "*marchand bourgeois*" from a family higher up on the social scale than Chardin's own, in which the future groom is listed as having owned at the time only "some furniture and 2000 livres of which he is supposed to pay his master painter's license."[80] The marriage, though, was postponed, as was the custom at the time in cases when a young man could not immediately afford to set up an independent household.[81] In Chardin's case it took eight years for the nuptial ceremony to occur, by which time a new marriage contract had to be signed because of a significant change in the financial status of the bride whose father had lost his fortune.[82] While the new conditions under which the marriage took place certainly marked a financial setback for Chardin, the period of prolonged expectation that preceded it was probably equally taxing, if in a different sense. It meant that for an extended period of time, Chardin's civil status remained undecided, his social ascent and access to financial independence postponed, thus also weakening his standing within the parental household.[83] Suspended between celibacy and marriage, Chardin found himself in the position of not-yet-a-man, an eternal son, a situation the more encumbering given his continuing economic dependence on his father. A promise of change in this situation occurred when, in 1730, the painter received his first significant private commission from Count Conrad-Alexandre de Rothenbourg, an event that must be related to the finalization of his marriage not long afterward.[84] But the fact that even after his marriage, Chardin continued to reside on rue du Four rather than setting up his own household—likely because of the shortage of means—indicates that his financial status remained fragile and that he remained susceptible to his father's authority, not only in an economic but also in a legal and moral sense.

Chardin used painting as the means to situate himself in the material and symbolic realm of his own house, the domestic sphere of craft that was practiced in the context of his own family and that defined its life. It provided him with the means to imagine himself as a member of this household, and the objects featured in it were records of this imaginary negotiation.

That Chardin initially saw painting as the means to define his place within the paternal domain of craft is indicated by one of his very first canvases, the *Game of Billiards* (fig. 2.15).[85] Painted around 1720, when Chardin was twenty-one years old, this genre scene depicts a group of men playing billiards on the kind of table Chardin père supplied. The painter studied the players carefully, including making some preparatory drawings for the individual figures, a procedure that was highly unusual for him and that he abandoned later on.[86] Yet it is not the players but the billiard table itself that seems to be the main protagonist of this scene. Placed at the center of the composition, the object of his father's mastery is the very core around which Chardin choreographs the whole arrangement. The table's balusters define the rhythm and shape of the lower legs of the players gathered around it, while the squared substructure of joints sustaining its top, though invisible, is reenacted by the squared floor that serves as a ground plan of the scene.[87] And it is around this primary object that the painting seems to conduct a kind of conversation with Chardin's father, formulating a message along these lines: "while you make billiard tables, I paint pictures of them." The *Game of Billiards* is a kind of wager; by both evoking and differentiating himself from his father's craft, Chardin stakes his professional identity on the painting. Let us note, though, that, notwithstanding its self-confident tone, the painting still remains immersed—thematically, compositionally—in the symbolic domain of his father. The striking figure dressed in black that looms in the foreground surveying the scene—not unlike a master joiner supervising the making of the billiard tables—may even be seen to embody the watchful

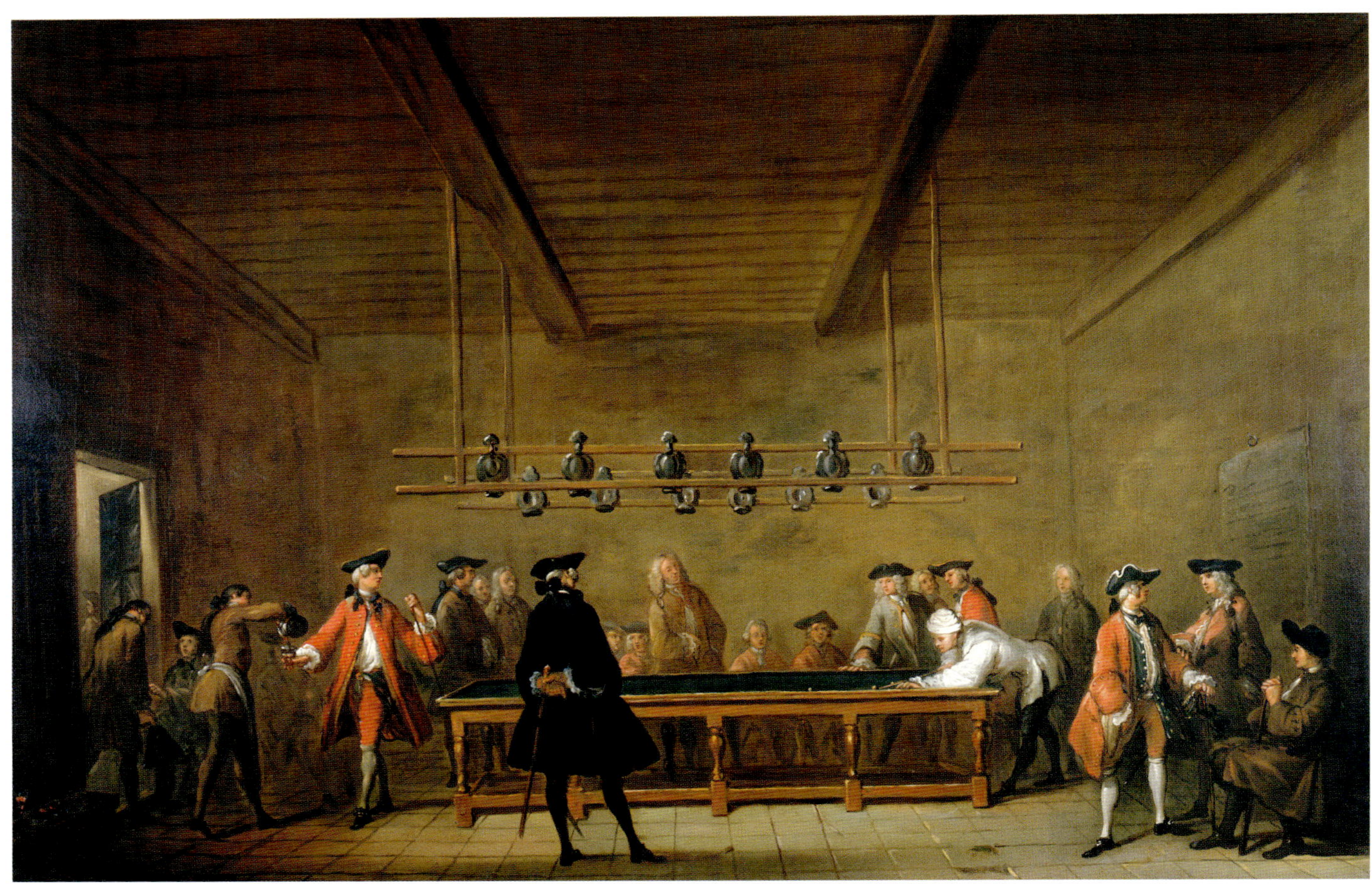

gaze of the father as the symbolic authority under which Chardin paints.

—·—

As an exercise in paternal thematics, the *Game of Billiards* had, though, no suit. In fact, soon after having painted it, Chardin renounced genre scenes altogether, at least for a time being, settling instead for a different type of painting: still life. Adopted as his chief means of artistic self-definition, still life engaged Chardin in a different dialogue with the domestic context, relocating it from the domain of his father, in which the *Game of Billiards* was steeped, to the physical and symbolic realm of the kitchen which, in eighteenth-century bourgeois households, was a distinctly feminine sphere.[88]

It is with this feminine realm that *The Ray* engages, if ambivalently. The domestic objects were summoned by Chardin not for the purpose of mere description but to conduct a complex negotiation for his own professional and personal identity. The painting gives the impression that the ray had to be *wrested* from its context in order to enter the visual field, an impression epitomized by the motif of disembowelment. It further suggests that the transformation of a thing (the fish) into a sign (*The Ray*) entailed a physical act of pulling the object from some internal depth onto the representational surface—and that this act has something to do with the object's mission to situate Chardin, as a painter and as a person, within his household as a domain of artisanal craft and family life. As staged here, this fragment of a household interior is a space, at once material and imaginary, of self-identification. Hence, what is being "wrested" in *The Ray* is not the thing per se but the contours of the body and self of its painter, Chardin. The dynamic of push and pull, of inside/out enacted by *The Ray* conveys, on this level, the sense in which, for Chardin, painting at this stage was an act of self-description underwritten by an unresolved combination of attachment to, and separation from, the parental domain. Thus the torn-out fish had to perform a double operation in order to represent Chardin. On the one hand, it had to be distanced from the household as the paternal realm of craft, to enter the domain of a different kind of expert making, namely art. On the other hand, it also had to be torn away from the feminine/maternal sphere in order to con-

2.15.
Jean-Siméon Chardin, *Game of Billiards*, ca. 1720. Oil on canvas. Musée Carnavalet, Paris.

vey its painter's masculine identity, a matter of particular importance within the artisanal context of Chardin's self-definition. The artisanal identity was defined in gendered, distinctly male terms, the status of the master having been tied to the social and familial ideal of the father.[89]

How was Chardin's sense of masculine mastery inflected by his household experiences, what challenge did his status as an "eternal son," and his prolonged existence as a not-yet-husband in his parents' house, pose to his self-definition as a gendered subject, what kind of pressure did it put him under—we cannot know. But what we do have is the visual evidence of some tension around gender identity involved in his self-representation, a sense that masculinity has to be *revindicated* as opposed to being simply asserted, and of the equivocations of this self-defining process. *The Ray* speaks of some anxiety attending the painter's strategic immersion in the maternal kitchen. The fantasy of aggressed and aggressive femininity that it bodies forth testifies to an identification with the feminine underwritten by fear of emasculation, and by violence. And so does *The Ray*'s "oral" mode of execution, the effect of fusion laced with aggression in this mode of rendition producing the effect of an anxious intimacy with the maternal object.

Staging the painter's identity in situated and relational terms—in the eighteenth century, identity, as it was articulated in philosophy, notably by Locke, was conceived precisely as a relation—*The Ray* defines it as *neither/nor*: neither in the domain of the father's craft, nor that of the mother's body.[90] As a testimony to gender relations within an artisanal household, *The Ray* is evidently more complex than what we have seen in the paintings of Hallé and Lépicié. Sexual difference does not define the structure of the family as it did in these paintings, aligning the boys with the father, the girls with the mother, but cuts *through* the subject.

What *The Ray* offers, then, is an image of the *costs* of self-representation as they were experienced by Chardin in the early stages of his professional career. The painting suggests that while ensuring the object's visibility and meaning, the process of representation also endangers it, the voided corpus of the fish conveying vividly and palpably the physical loss incurred by the object. At the same time, insofar as the gutted fish in *The Ray* is also a specter of the subject involved in this process of depiction, it visualizes "the pound of flesh" that the subject must pay upon entering the symbolic realm of painting.[91] Mariette's dictum about Chardin's painting process—"sa lui coûte infiniment"—comes to mind. But what we witness is not quite what Mariette meant. It is not a matter of the effort involved in getting things right but rather of a more complex, not only technical but also symbolic challenge posed by the painter's attempt to develop a language of objects, to make things speak—*for him*—in the specific circumstances of his early career. What *The Ray* makes clear is that the domestic sphere on which Chardin draws was not a serene domain of inspiration but a more pernicious realm of negotiation that was at once aesthetic and subjective, in which the painter's professional and personal identities were at stake.

The distinctly subjective and affective tone of this painting must also be situated in relation to the institutional circumstances of its production. It has generally been assumed that the painting, which is not dated, was executed by Chardin soon after he obtained his license as a master painter, around 1725–26.[92] The ambition and size of this canvas, matching almost exactly the prescribed dimensions of the so-called masterpiece that painters were obliged to submit upon their admittance to the guild, makes one wonder if it weren't, in fact, Chardin's chef-d'oeuvre. While this tempting hypothesis may not be likely—had it been so, the painting would have remained in the possession of the Académie de Saint-Luc, which it did not—*The Ray* was certainly the very work in and through which the young painter tried to take stock of his new professional status, to represent himself as a newly minted maître peintre to himself and to the world.[93] The fact that as soon as he could, in June 1728, Chardin exhibited the painting at the annual outdoor exhibition at the Place Dauphine—the only place where art could be publicly shown before the return of regular Salon exhibitions in 1737—confirms his investment in it as the means of professional self-representation.[94]

Hence *The Ray* became, in a sense, a public version of Chardin's chef-d'oeuvre, a document of the painter's craft that he used to position himself in the larger public realm. Yet in its spectacularly staged execution, *The Ray* also exceeded the parameters of what one would expect then of an artisan of the brush. It was not that it was necessarily better than a typical masterpiece—the guild's expectations regarding the quality of execution were high enough, and the corporation counted many brilliant painters among its members—but rather that it proposed an understanding of craft that was different from the notions of manual expertise and brio cultivated by the guild.[95] In Chardin's hands, craft became self-reflexive and interiorized; it spoke of affect as much as skill. Performing the very process that brought it about, *The Ray* produced an image of a skill that was at once self-aware and unknowing, capable of reflecting upon itself but also transmitting, as if unwittingly, the (oral) impulses of the body. A tour de force of execution, *The Ray*'s magnificent cavity interiorized craft literally, by concentrating on a bodily interior, but also figuratively, by opening up a dimension of interiority within the painting, a material and subjective depth wherein both the shape of the painted object and the boundaries of the painting subject, including his sexual identity, were negotiated. (That the aesthetic and technical prowess of the masterpiece was, in the corporate male culture of the guild, also a proof of manhood, may have contributed to the anxiety evident in this negotiation.[96]) This was more than the painters' guild asked from a start-up painter. And it also implied an idea of the painter that exceeded the guild's definition—not only, or not quite, a *master*, but rather someone more complexly and more ambivalently involved in pictorial practice and also ambivalently identified with the institution that defined its parameters, the guild. The push and pull, the inside/out enacted by *The Ray* can be seen as Chardin's double-edged declaration of allegiance to and rejection of the guild as the institutional frame of his practice, or, in its affective tone, a declaration of his love and horror of the guild.

In the complexity of its ambition and its delivery, *The Ray* was a form of a wishful farewell to the guild, a work that, while representing Chardin as its member, was also on some level intended to situate him elsewhere. The painting ended up doing just that when it became Chardin's entry ticket to another institution. The painter's decision to present himself at the Academy may have been directly linked to the attention *The Ray* attracted when it was shown at the 1728 exhibition at the Place Dauphine. According to one source, some academicians who visited the exhibition were so impressed by Chardin's work that they encouraged the young painter to seek admission to the Academy, which is what he did in September of that year.[97] In another account, repeated by several sources, the painter used subterfuge to draw attention to his work and gain academic admission. He placed his paintings, *The Ray* among them, in a hallway leading to the academicians' meeting room to take them by surprise. One of them, Nicolas de Largillière, himself a portraitist and still life painter, unsuspecting of Chardin's ruse, took the paintings to be by a Flemish master. When Chardin revealed himself to be the author of these works, he was unanimously accepted into the Academy's ranks and received as a full member on the same day—an unusually speedy reception.[98] How accurate this account is remains uncertain, but the very fact that it circulated in Chardin's time suggests that the painter was recognized as a "surprise invader," a man of talent who strategically uses his status as an outsider vis-à-vis the royal institution to enter it.[99]

It is worth noting how congruent this strategy was with the arresting, confrontational logic of *The Ray*, with its eagerness to impress the viewers by shocking them. This logic suited *The Ray*'s new institutional purpose: it succeeded in getting the academician's attention and was one of two paintings they chose from among other works submitted by Chardin as his *morceau de réception*. The second one was another unusually large-scale still life, the *Buffet* (fig. 2.16). The painting, which Chardin most likely produced specifically for the occasion of his institutional coup, is worth considering if we are to get a better sense of what was at stake for him in his quest for professional advancement. If *The Ray* represented Chardin's relation to the guild, the *Buffet* gives us some sense of how the painter imagined himself vis-à-vis the Academy.

— . —

A complex dynamic of want informs the *Buffet*. It is not only an impressive assembly of well-rendered things but also a self-reflexive image of a threshold of representation, not unlike *The Ray*. In this case, the threshold, marked by the stone buffet, is the meeting place of two social and aesthetic realms: the world of entitlement and leisure represented by the sumptuous display of food, drink, and fruit topped by a parrot perched on a brass ring, and the world of raw materiality and labor evoked by the copper cooler with simple flasks of wine and radishes and a dog looking up at the displayed food from below. These two domains—the salon, or some such space of elite pleasures, versus the kitchen—are mapped onto two different approaches to still life: the aristocratic buffet with its elaborate displays of fruit pyramids and shiny silver platters that was practiced in France, notably by Chardin's older contemporary, Alexandre-François Desportes; and the low, mostly Dutch and Flemish depictions of kitchen stuff, both in still lifes and genre scenes, such as those by Gerard

2.16.
Jean-Siméon Chardin, *Buffet*, 1728. Oil on canvas. Musée du Louvre, Paris.

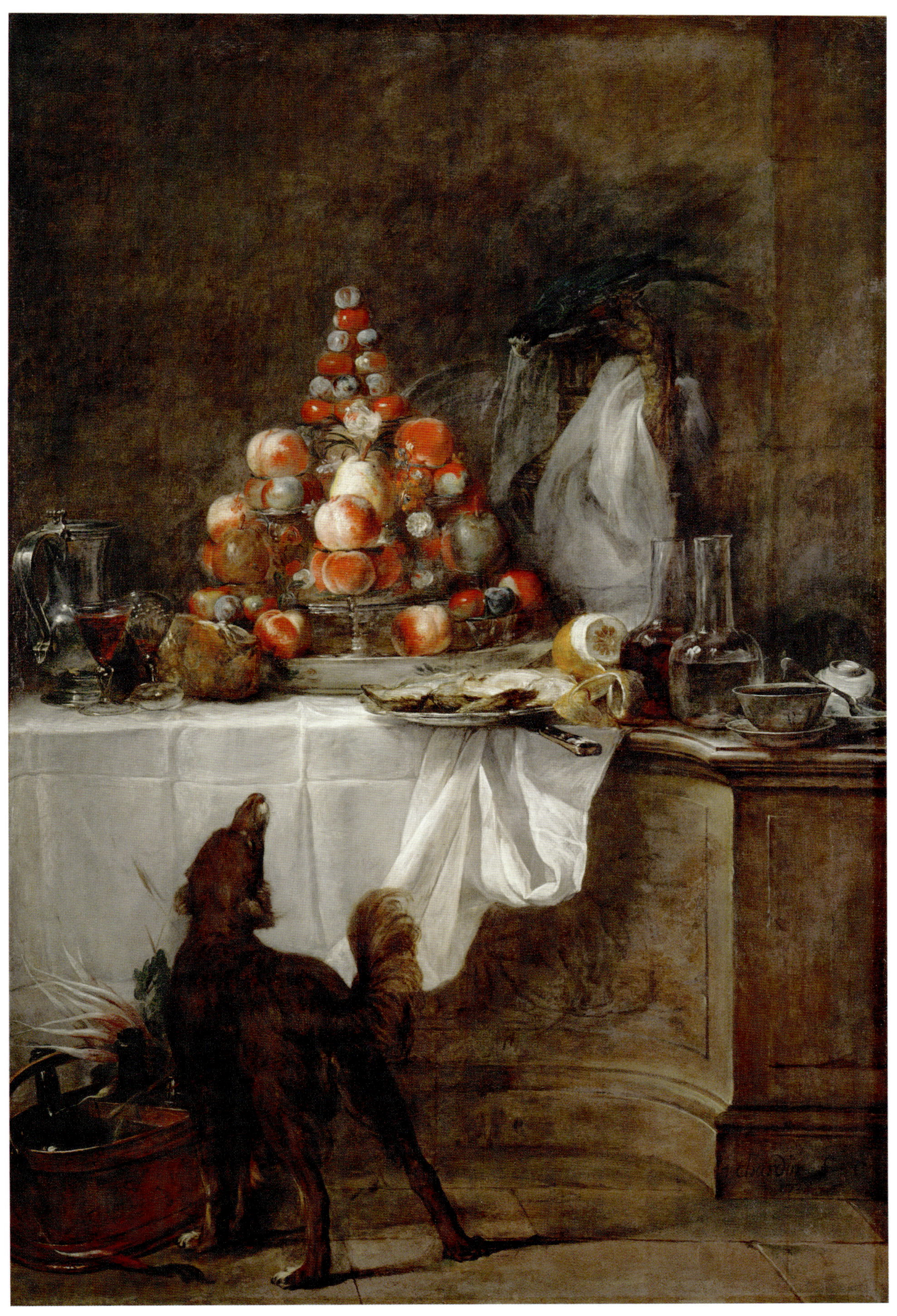

Terborch. Situated in between these two realms of high and low, the dog, an intruder from the kitchen, represents both appetite and aggression, a desire for, and a potential threat to, this display of luxury. These connotations belong with the canine motif commonly used in hunt-related still lifes but, by transposing it into a domestic domain, Chardin alters its meaning. While in hunting imagery the dog's attention is focused on the hunting trophy—the dead game eagerly sniffed by a spaniel in Melchior d'Hondecoeter's *Still Life with Peacock, Rabbit, and Spaniel*, for instance (fig. 2.17)—Chardin's canine is attracted to something it did not hunt for and in which it cannot partake, for dogs do not eat oysters or fruit.[100] But insofar as these comestible objects are also tokens of pictorial expertise—the pyramid of peaches right above the dog's muzzle is a classic motif of the buffet still life à la Desportes (fig. 2.18)—what this dog pines for is the access to still life as a representational tradition. And, as the painting suggests, it may well try to get it as dogs do, by snatching the fold of the tablecloth and pulling down the whole elaborate arrangement. The prominent knife sticking out from underneath the silver platter with oysters right above the folded tablecloth parallels the position of the dog's body, reinforcing its status as a carrier of potential destruction.

Like the ray, the dog is a threshold figure, one through which Chardin, in this case, situates himself in relation to the artistic establishment, the animal's posture pointing to the ambivalence of this attempt at self-definition. While the young painter seems eager to assert his mastery over existing aesthetic models, he also defines his position as a threat to them. With one snap of his teeth, the dog can cause the whole triumphant construction to tumble down. As represented by the dog, the young Chardin describes himself not only as an able latecomer to the still life tradition but also as its potential disruptor. The purpose of the animal's inclusion in the buffet scene seems to be precisely to signal the possibility of a violent upending of tradition, to suggest the potential threat Chardin's practice poses to the aesthetic status quo. (Let us note, in passing, the oral dimension of his threat, the dog's muzzle, though its violence is only proleptic, being not unlike the phantasmatic "mouth" of the ray.)

But this kitchen dog who has wandered into a salon alludes also to the artist's professional standing, signaling its *basesse* in terms of social as well as aesthetic hierarchy.[101] His claim to a place within the establishment is, in other words, launched from a position of lowliness that evokes his status as a maître peintre perceived as inferior. From the elite point of view, artisans were seen as lowly for the reason of both the manual and commercial nature of their labor. As the author of a seventeenth-century *Traité de la noblesse* put it, "the assiduousness of the manual labor of artisans and the appetite for gain necessary for their subsistence renders them as slaves, inspiring in them only the sentiments of baseness and subjection."[102] This sentiment persisted in the perception of the guild painters, especially in the minds of their academic counterparts for whom they remained an "abject troupe."[103] By situating himself—not without some irony—in the lowly place of a dog salivating at the buffet, Chardin inverts this basesse, recasting it as a position of some power, of potential threat.

Combined with the ambitious scale of the *Buffet*, the latent aggression that underwrites its display of pictorial mastery suggests an interestingly contentious mode of submission to aesthetic authority. In this regard, *Buffet*, though different in tone, comes close to *The Ray*. If *The Ray* situated Chardin's practice in the domestic realm of the kitchen, *Buffet* spells out what painting practiced from this position (a position of the kitchen dog) can *do* to the aesthetic tradition of still life and to the Academy as its guardian. In this sense, the *Buffet* offered a quasi-allegory of Chardin's practice poised on the threshold of change.

As for *The Ray*, in its new institutional context,

2.17.
Melchior d'Hondecoeter, *Still Life with Peacock, Rabbit, and Spaniel*, ca. 1660–69. Oil on canvas. Fine Arts Museums of San Francisco, Museum Purchase, William H. Noble Bequest Fund.

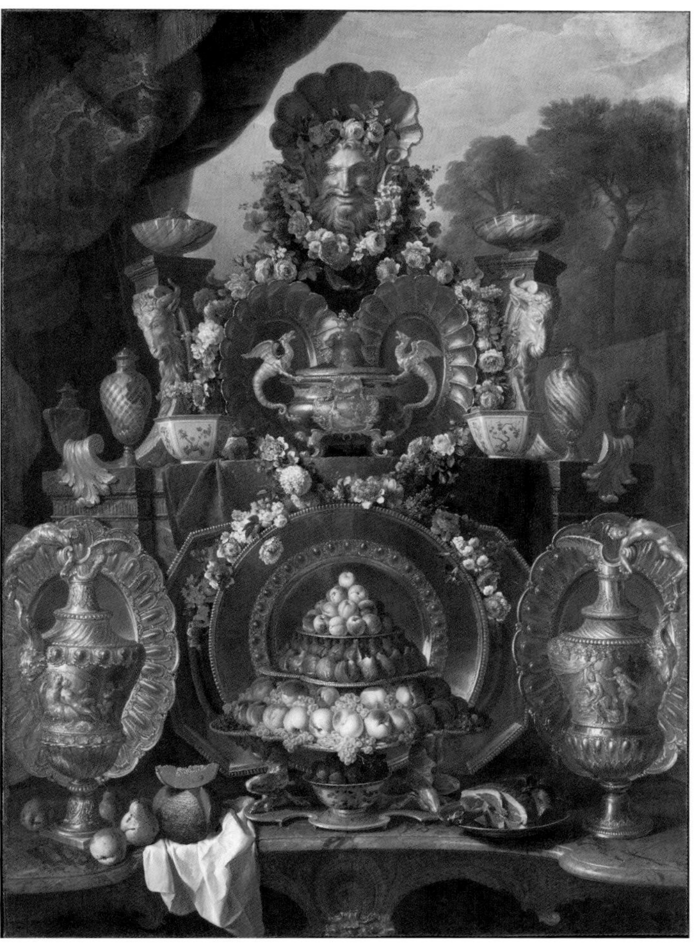

2.18.
Alexandre-François Desportes, *Still Life with Silver.* Oil on canvas. Metropolitan Museum of Art, New York, Purchase, Mary Wetmore Shively Bequest, in memory of her husband, Henry L. Shively, MD, 1964.

the painting acquired another resonance, closer to the institutionally subversive tone of the *Buffet*. By elevating an ordinary object to the status of a human figure, this monumental proof of pictorial mastery not only pitched Chardin's claim at a level higher than still life but also, potentially, challenged the academic order of aesthetic importance.[104] The painting's transitive violence enhanced this sense of challenge. Aggressive and aggressed, the ray could be seen as a vengeful écorché that threw the academic privileging of the human body in the Academy's face. (This new institutional resonance of the painting was sustained by the fact that, as a *morceau de réception*, *The Ray* remained exhibited on the premises of the Academy. Diderot, who saw it there in 1763, recognized its import precisely in these terms, using Chardin's still life to launch an attack on the boring and insignificant genre of history painting as he saw it practiced at the Academy, notably by its future director, Jean-Baptiste Marie Pierre.[105])

Mixing eagerness to impress with a drive to aggress, a longing for belonging with a desire to subvert, both paintings speak of Chardin's complex self-awareness as an artist early on in his career. Both also make clear the larger issue at stake in Chardin's early work, the issue of access to representation understood not only as a field of vision but also as a realm of professional and social privilege and—for Chardin specifically—a realm of autonomy, both artistic and subjective. Still life, or what he made of it early on in his career, was the means through which he negotiated his entry into these realms. The logic of inside/out that governed his works—and that *The Ray* and *Buffet*, the painter's two most ambitious canvases of this period, epitomize—was the very mode of conducting this negotiation. The way in which the painter staged and rendered his motifs introduced the register of affect into both the thematics and the morphology of still life, thus *interiorizing* this established type of representation. This personalized, individuated, and affective use of still life distinguished Chardin's work within the genre as it was practiced by the Northern painters and by his French predecessors and contemporaries. This is how Chardin's early still lifes made evident his approach to painting as "entirely his own."[106]

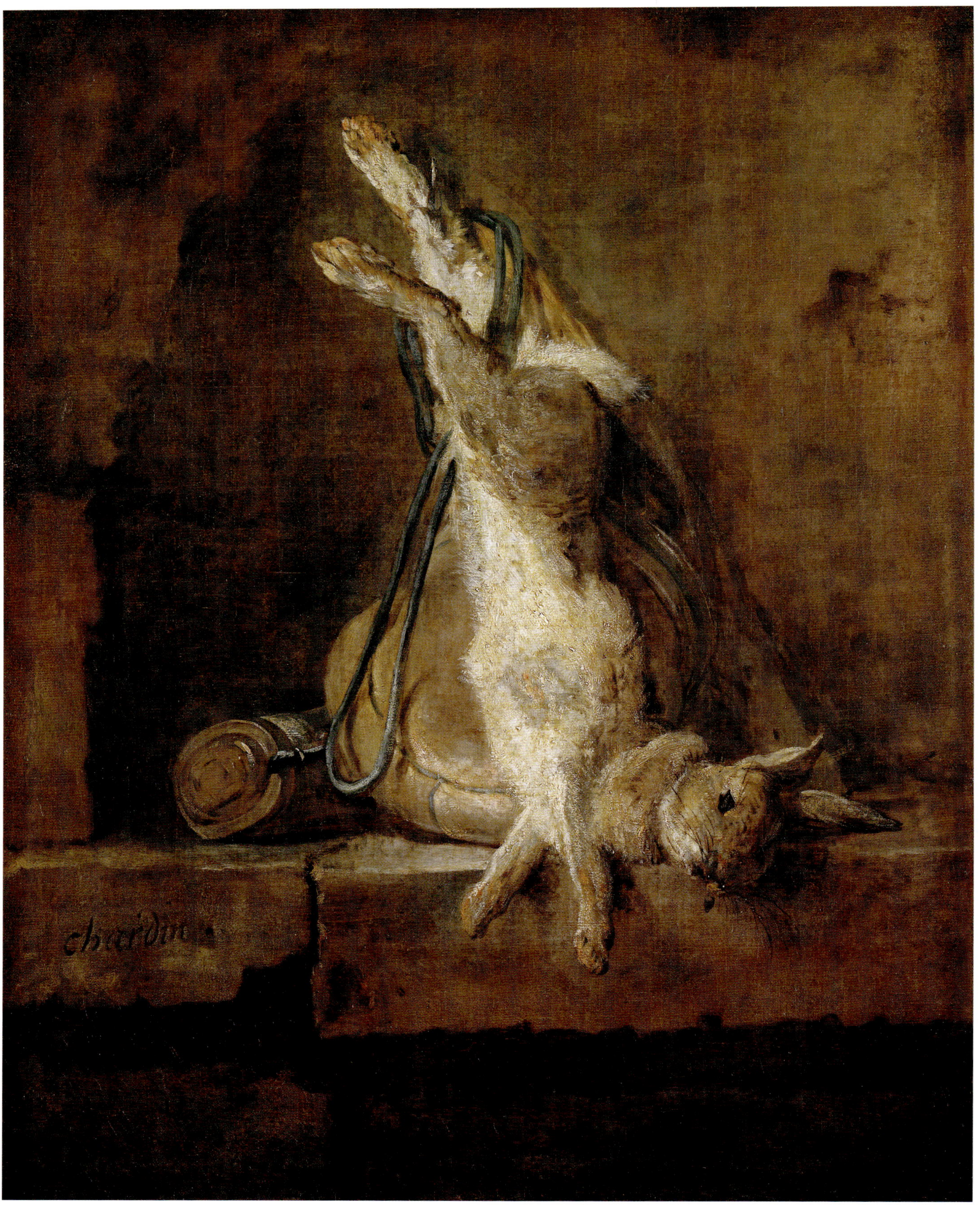
chardin

2.19. OPPOSITE
Jean-Siméon Chardin, *Wild Rabbit with Game Bag and Powder Flask*, ca. 1729. Oil on canvas. Musée du Louvre, Paris.

2.20. BELOW RIGHT
Jean-Siméon Chardin, *Wild Rabbit with Game Bag and Powder Flask*, detail of fig. 2.19.

THE BLIND TOUCH

I see nothing; my eyes are at my fingertips.

—Roger de Piles

Within Chardin's early output, still lifes featuring hares and rabbits form a group apart.[107] In these paintings Chardin took up an established subgenre within the still life tradition, the hunting trophy, and redefined it. The difference of his approach lies not only in his rejection of the abundant display of dead game amid fruit and flowers in a landscape setting—a format practiced by Chardin's Dutch and French predecessors—but in an altogether different mode of representing dead game itself.[108] This difference was noted by his contemporaries. Cochin, providing an account of Chardin painting a rabbit for the first time, summed up his approach in the following way:

> *The object appeared unimportant; yet, the manner in which he wished to render it turned it into a serious study. He wanted to depict it with the greatest veracity in all respects, yet tastefully, giving no appearance of servitude that might make its execution dry and cold. He never painted fur. He realized that he should not paint it hair by hair or reproduce it in detail. "Here is the object," he was telling himself, "that must be rendered. In order to represent it truthfully, I have to forget everything I have seen, including the ways in which others treated similar objects. I have to place it at some distance so that I no longer see the details. I should take care to imitate well and with greatest veracity its general mass, the tone of its colors, its roundness, the effects of light and shadows." He managed to achieve it, demonstrating the premises of that taste and that magic handling that, from then on, always characterized his distinctive talent.*[109]

As Cochin saw it, the rabbit posed the specific pictorial challenge of capturing the phenomenological truth of its appearance, its fur in particular. This entailed a rejection of the existing conventions of representation in favor of a direct engagement with the object in its immediate and contingent physical presence. At the same time, it necessitated a distanced and abstracting gaze, an approach based in translation, or interpretation, rather than a literal transcription of the object's appearance. We see what that meant when we look at one of Chardin's early trophy still lifes, the *Wild Rabbit with Game Bag and Powder Flask* (ca. 1729) at the Louvre (fig. 2.19). The painting makes palpably evident how the painter obtained the rabbit's "general mass, the tone of its colors, its roundness, the effects of light and shadows": his chromatic, seemingly chaotic, and performative touch. A detail of fur on the rabbit's belly epitomizes it: the layers of rapid, messy strokes superimposed on one another, the uppermost strata of crusty white drips and slashes registering both the illuminated texture of the fur and the movement of the painter's brush across the canvas's surface (fig. 2.20). It is the tactile quality of tone displayed in this detail that is characteristic of Chardin's approach. Color is a texture, a substance, as much as a visual effect.

How different this interpretation of the subject was from the more common approach may be gauged by considering the work of Chardin's older and highly successful colleague, Jean-Baptiste Oudry. Aiming at the highest degree of verisimilitude, Oudry's *A Hare and Leg of Lamb* (1742) emphasized the contrast between the glistening fat of the meat and the furry pelt of the animal, producing a trophy of both the hunter and the painter's mimetic skills (fig. 2.21). The success of this demonstration relied on the invisibility of the artist's hand; for the trompe l'oeil to succeed, the traces of its production had to be carefully hidden. Oudry understood this well, his hare conveying a preponderant sense of pictorial control over the represented object. Yet this is precisely

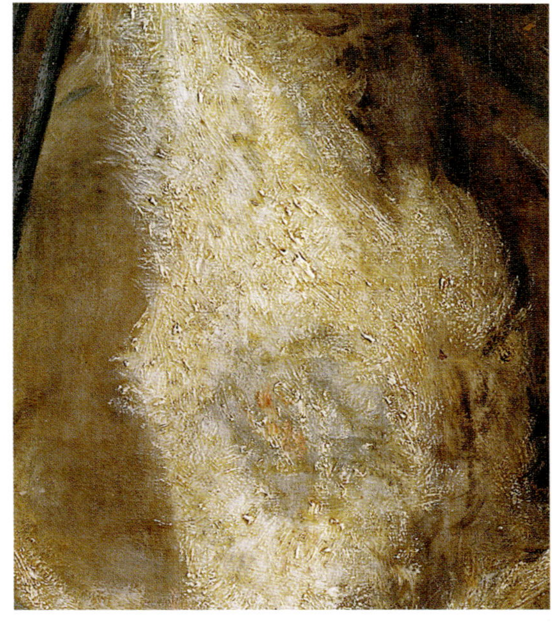

what Chardin, in Cochin's telling, worked *against*, as the Louvre's *Wild Rabbit* makes clear. In contrast to Oudry's sharply outlined contours of the hare's stiffened corpse, Chardin offers us the soft, palpable lump of a body deposited gently on a ledge. While Oudry anchors and stabilizes his motif by showing it nailed against a neutral background, Chardin presents it ensconced within a chipped stone niche from which it emerges, but only gradually and incompletely, into view, its body still half buried in the material folds of representation. The quasi-monochrome ocher-brown tonality of the entire painting, enlivened by some red and creamy-white highlights used for the rabbit's pelt, enhances this effect of tactile immersion.

The difference between Oudry and Chardin can be described in terms of an opposition between vision and touch. What appears in Oudry's painting to be the result of a traceless transmission of visual facts is in Chardin's work an insistently material, tangible product of the brush. And this is not only because Chardin's *Wild Rabbit* foregrounds the painter's manual labor. It is also because touch appears to be the very cause of the animal's emergence into view; it is as if the painter's brush has "sculpted" the shape of the rabbit from the undifferentiated stone mass, bringing it up from the monochromatic, barely modulated background into light.[110] This impression is particularly strong in *Rabbits and Partridge* (1731), where the gentle sweeps of the painter's brushes—still visible on the canvas—seem to have scooped out the motif from the palpable depths of stone to pose it at the center of a parapet (fig. 2.22).

This tactile rendition not only creates softer formal effects than those of Oudry but also introduces a dimension of affect into these representations. The way in which Chardin puts the elements of his trophy together, as he does, for example, in *Rabbits and Partridge*, suggests a sense of care, almost affection for the dead game. Unlike the Oudry, the bodies of Chardin's rabbits are not yet stiffened by rigor mortis, having been deposited gently on the ledge, the painter's touch mediating between their soft fur and the hardness of the stone. The rabbits look almost asleep rather than dead, even if the blood dripping from the mouth of the one in the center suggests otherwise.[111] With Chardin, empathy seems to have entered the trophy and complicated its effect.

The depictions of dead game differ also from Chardin's own domestic still lifes, where we have witnessed similarly tactile execution and affect, though of a different kind. The touch evident in both *Rabbits*

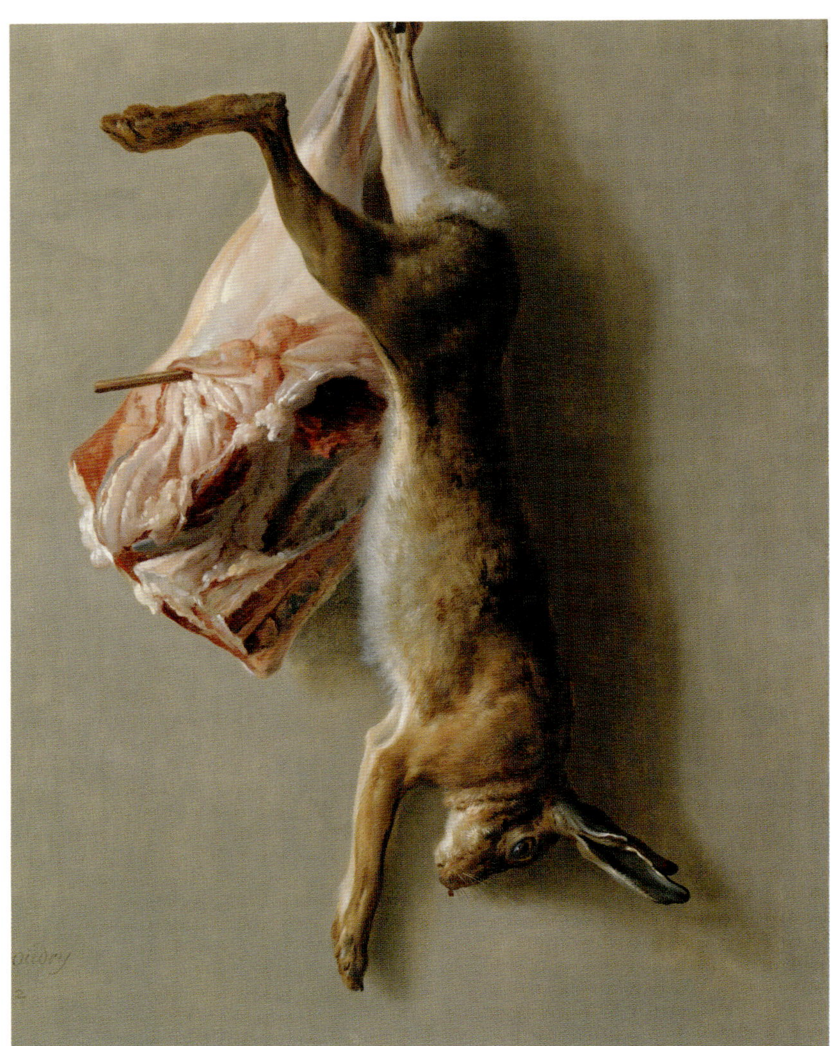

2.21.
Jean-Baptiste Oudry, *A Hare and a Leg of Lamb*, 1742. Oil on canvas. The Cleveland Museum of Art, John L. Severance Fund.

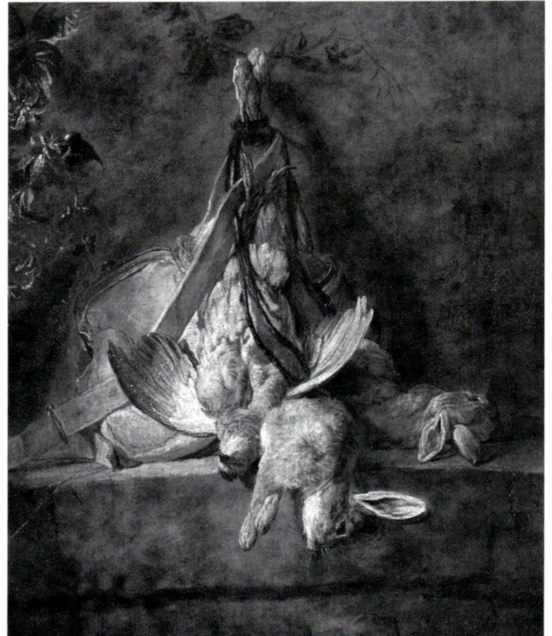

2.22.
Jean-Siméon Chardin, *Rabbits and Partridge*, 1731. Oil on canvas. National Gallery of Ireland, Dublin.

and Partridge and the Louvre's *Wild Rabbit* is much gentler. The latter, though the rabbit's body is twisted slightly, its front paws dangling from the ledge, lacks the structural violence of inside/out that governed Chardin's domestic still lifes, in particular *The Ray*. It produces a sense of a quieter, less conflicted intimacy with the object. To be sure, aggression is not entirely absent from this imagery. It is implied by the thematics of the hunt, and, in some cases, also by the mode of execution. Take a closer look at Chardin's *Dead Hare with Powder Flask and Game Bag*; instead of the animal's hair, we see a flurry of the painter's brushstrokes that are especially agitated in the area of the hare's chest and its wounded loin, places where the painter seems to have forgotten himself in his process, buried himself in it, his brush burrowing and sniffing like a hunter's dog (fig. 2.23). We are reminded of the animal protagonist of Chardin's *Buffet*, painted two years earlier, who acted as a stand-in for the painter's relation to the still life tradition. But if we discern a similar alignment of the painter's stance with that of the dog in *Dead Hare*, its implications are different. There is no suggestion of orality inherent in the dog's relation to the arrangement of comestible objects in the *Buffet*, or enacted by the disemboweled *Ray*. (There are, we may note, no disembowelments staged in Chardin's hunting trophies.) Rather, what comes to the fore in the *Dead Hare* is the *unseeing* dimension of the painter's touch. Looked at up close, the painting produces a sense of confusion, the movement of the painter's brushes lacking direction—a chaotic, disoriented touch that nonetheless produces a compelling image of the animal's body.

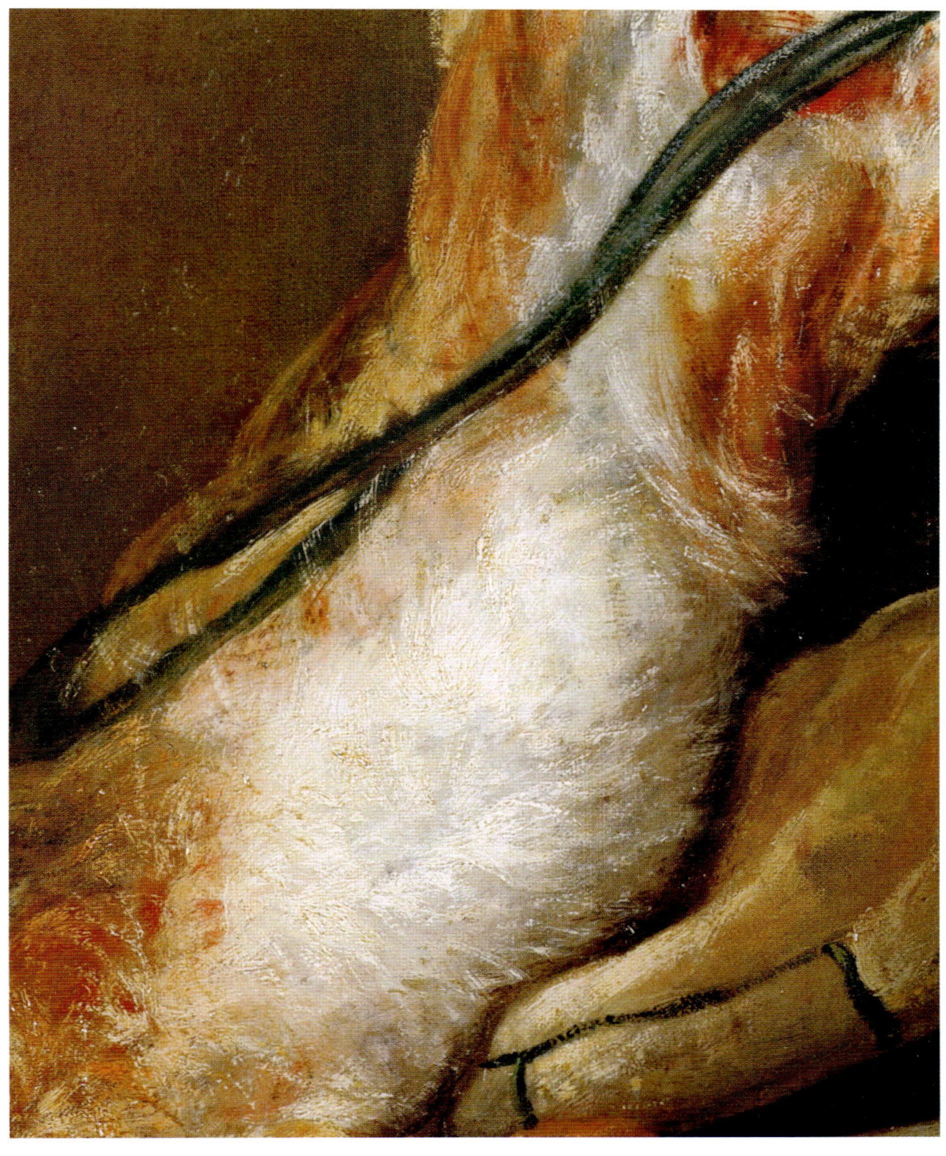

2.23.
Jean-Siméon Chardin, *Dead Hare with Powder Flask and Game Bag*, detail of fig. 2.24.

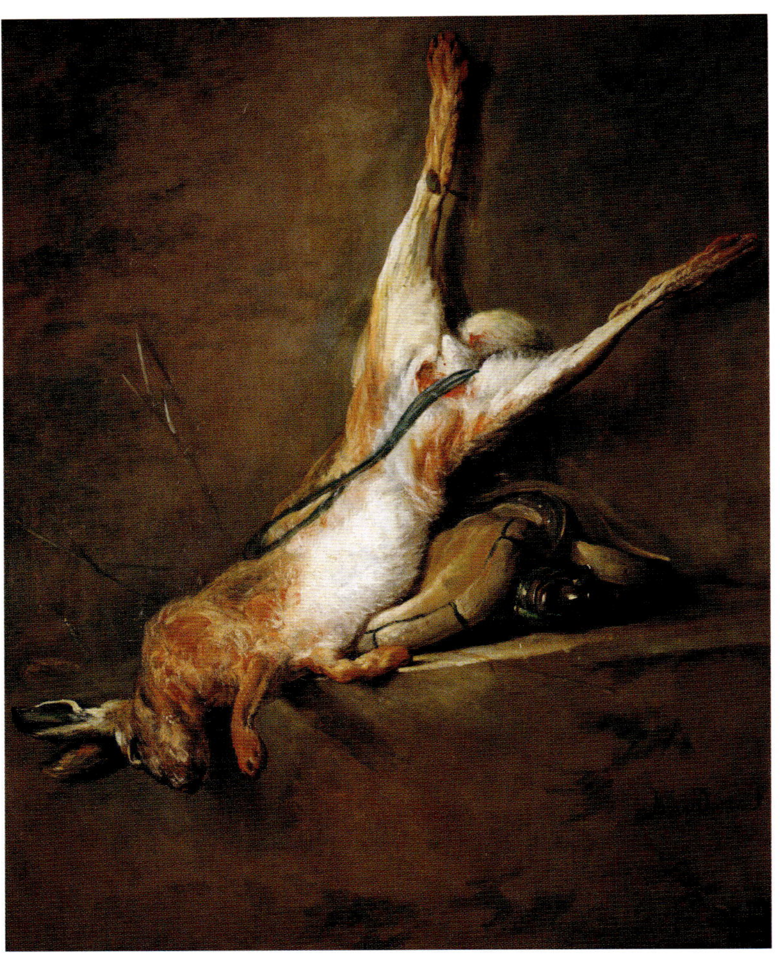

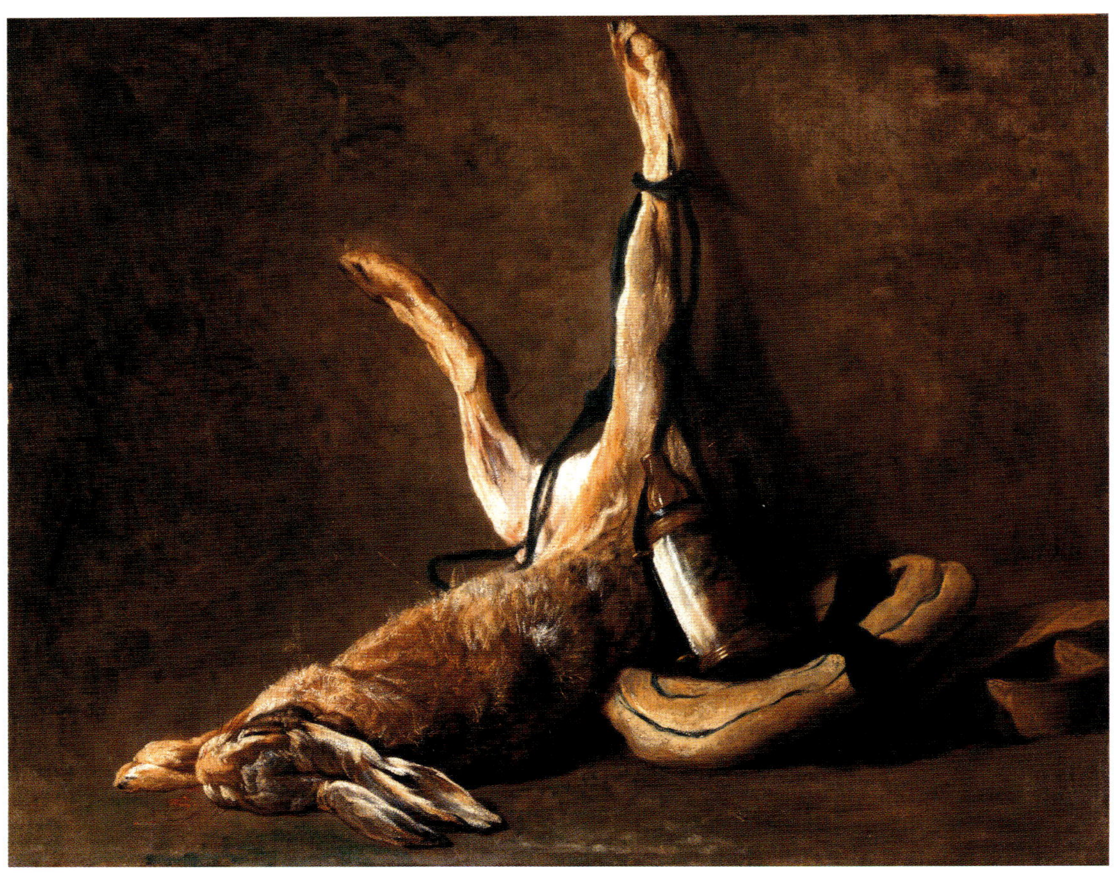

2.24.
Jean-Siméon Chardin, *Dead Hare with Powder Flask and Game Bag*, 1730. Oil on canvas. Musée du Louvre, Paris.

2.25.
Jean-Siméon Chardin, *Hare with Game Bag and Powder Flask*, ca. 1730. Oil on canvas. Philadelphia Museum of Art, Gift of Henry P. McIlhenny, 1958.

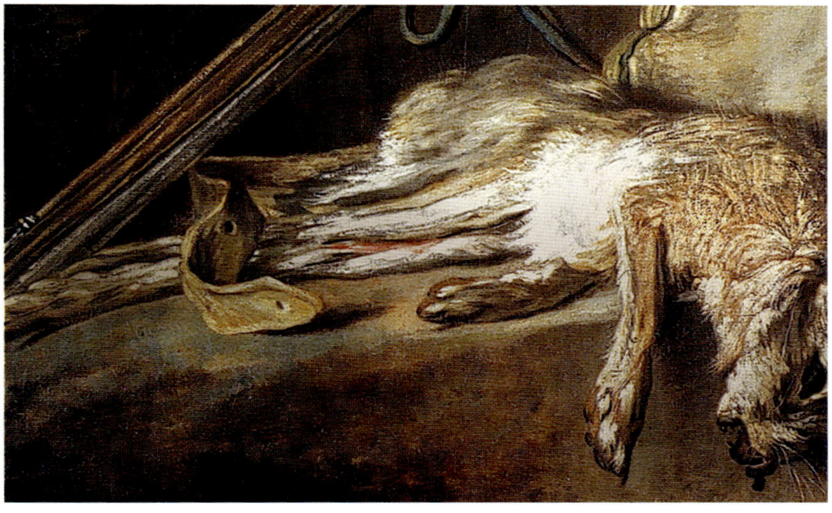

2.26. ABOVE
Jean-Siméon Chardin, *Dead Hare with Rifle*, ca. 1730 (detail). Oil on canvas. Musée de la Chasse et de la Nature, Paris.

2.27. BELOW LEFT
Jean-Siméon Chardin, *Wild Rabbit with Game Bag and Powder Flask*, detail of fig. 2.19.

2.28. BELOW RIGHT
Jean-Baptiste Oudry, *A Hare and a Leg of Lamb*, detail of fig. 2.21.

This sense of disorientation is evident not only in the morphology but also in the very structure of Chardin's tactile vision of dead game. Striking in some of these paintings is the spatial uncertainty in the presentation of the motif. It is not only that much of his dead game emerges from a penumbral space, its location at once specific—no abstract backgrounds à la Oudry—and underdescribed. It is also that the animal's position is often unstable, its body dislocated. Such is the case of the Louvre *Dead Hare*: its body twisted, its legs indecorously splayed, the hare threatens to slide off the ledge at the very place where the artist's interest in securing the illusion of space seem to have momentarily slackened (fig. 2.24). The ledge loses its edge and disappears halfway through the painting—as if the painter literally lost his vision.

Similar spatial inconsistency and dislocation characterize the *Hare with Game Bag and Powder Flask* (fig. 2.25). Here the animal's limp corpse has been thrown across an otherwise unmarked and undifferentiated space, neither a pantry nor an abstract space of the trompe l'oeil but a more opaque, temporal realm of a process that renders the body present without *situating* it.[112] Instead of assigning it a place in vision, Chardin suspends the hare's tactile body in a field of touch. It is difficult to find one's way in such a field. Aside from the body of the hare, there is nothing to orient our gaze. Only the blue strap attached to the hunter's powder flask and wound around the rabbit's leg snakes toward us like a leash for the eye to find its way in this palpable but sightless space.

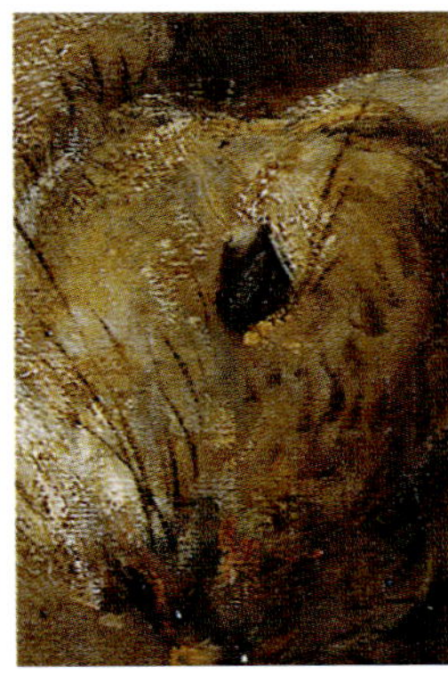

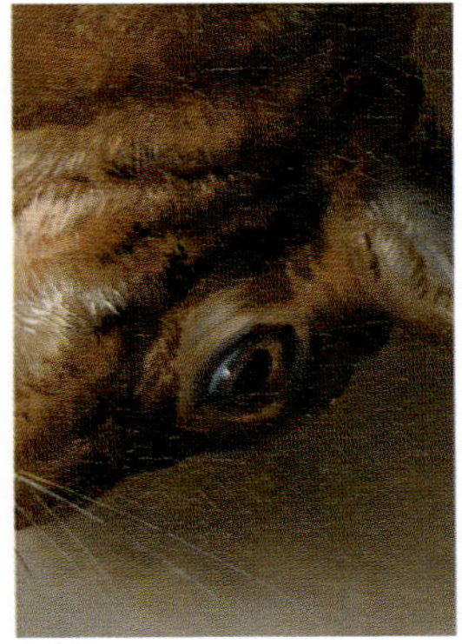

The hare's disoriented position poses the question of how the painter navigated this haptic space in the process of making the image. Painting directly on the canvas, without a preparatory drawing—rarely if at all used in still lifes and, in Chardin's case, never used—he followed no direction but the chromatic intuition of his fingers and brushes. A close-up look at the fur of the Louvre *Wild Rabbit* and *Dead Hare* makes this clear (see figs. 2.20 and 2.23). The sense of shape, volume, and texture is generated by the seemingly random, unstructured application of pigments, as if by a hand that, going over the canvas's surface, brings forth shapes much like a sculptor's fingers would. In addition to tonal modeling, it is the sheer thickness of paint that produces the effect of the fur. There are no contours or lines in the animal's body—except those that describe the whiskers—but only stains, smudges, smears, and blobs of pigment that cohere only when viewing the fur from a distance. This is conspicuous in the *Dead Hare with Rifle* (fig. 2.26), where the legs of the animal are rendered in thick smudges of ocher, red, and white pigment running parallel to each other in unintegrated streams that peter out at the end, as if mimesis ran out of steam at the rabbit's paws. What I am suggesting is that this mode of chromatic approximation not only conveys the contingency of Chardin's vision but also points to the dimension of blindness at its core.

This unseeing is registered explicitly in the eyes of some of the rabbits and hares. It is curious how Chardin chose to render them. In the *Wild Rabbit*, an opaque area of almost entirely unmodulated dark pigment marks the animal's eye—no pupil, no iris, just a pitch-black unreflective patch amid the textured chroma of the rabbit's fur (fig. 2.27). A quick glance at Oudry's *Hare* will remind us how differently a painter could represent this anatomical detail. Playing the illusionistic game to the hilt, Oudry turns the rabbit's unseeing pupil into a shiny globe that has trapped light (fig. 2.28). Chardin, on the other

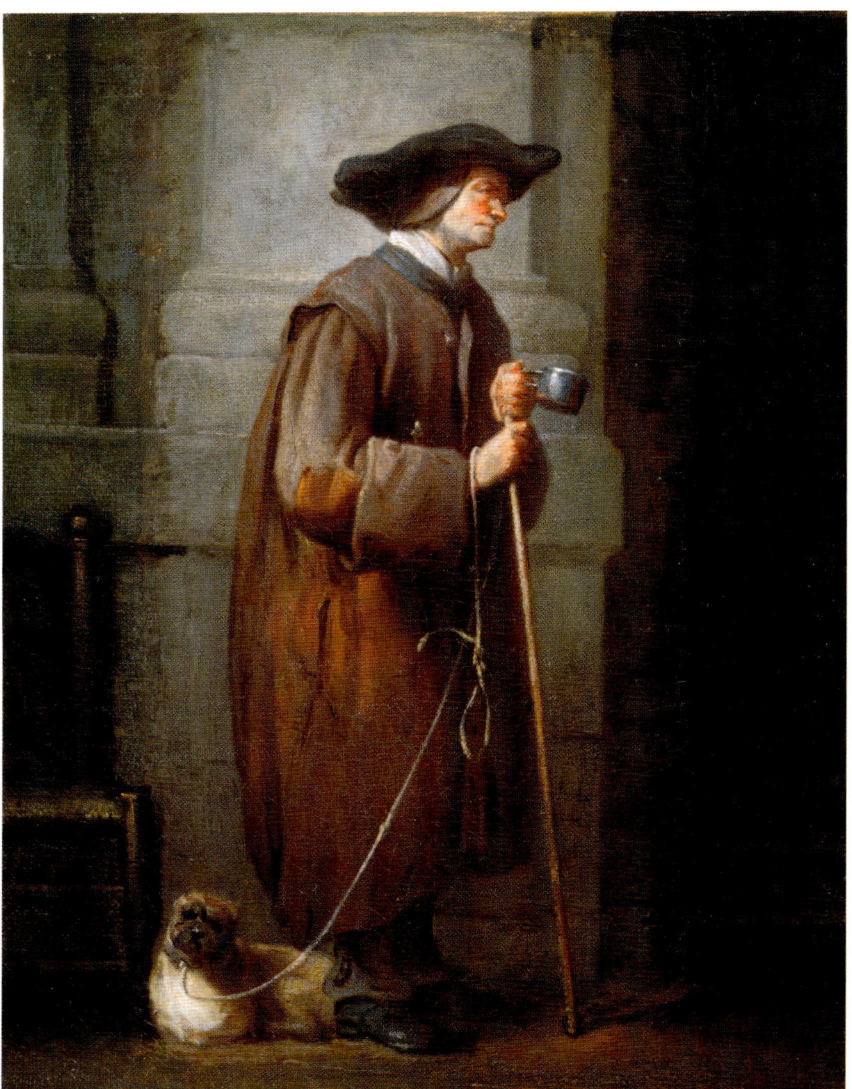

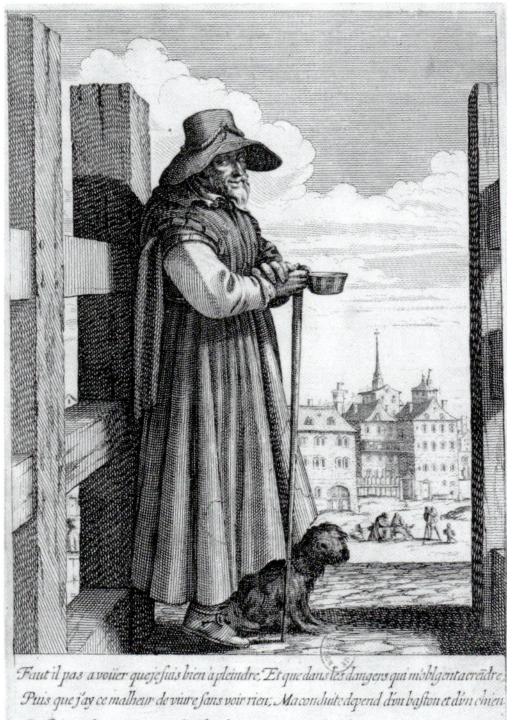

hand, plants an undifferentiated, amorphous blot of sooty pigment in place of the sightless eye, turning this anatomical part into a kind of blind spot in representation—no color, but sheer darkness opening up into the unseeable and unseen. Mimesis has stopped, there is *nothing* there. In another example, the *Dead Hare*, Chardin takes great care to outline the drooping rim of the hare's eye socket only to display its empty content, as if the eye were gouged out. Some modulation of black was necessary to suggest the hole-ness of this hole, but it is minimal in comparison to the tonal differentiation of the rest of the body.

—.—

Blindness was both thematized and enacted in a small but important painting Chardin produced around this time: the *Blind Beggar* (fig. 2.29).[113] An outdoor scene, it was an unusual work for Chardin, as was its male protagonist.[114] The painting's importance for our purposes lies in the connection it reveals between blindness and subjectivity, which is relevant to Chardin's trophy still lifes.

While drawing on the established iconography of the urban poor represented earlier by, among others, Jacques Callot and Abraham Bosse, Chardin departs from it in important ways (fig. 2.30).[115] Depicted with the requisite attributes of a blind beggar—the walking stick, the cup for the alms, and a dog—his protagonist is not a social type, but, as his costume and the fleur-de-lis badge pinned to his coat indicates, a specific individual, a member of the community of Quinze-Vingts, a well-known Parisian hospice for the blind.[116] Founded in the thirteenth century by Saint Louis, King of France, this confraternity inhabited a large enclave in the middle of Paris, between the rue Saint Honoré and rue Saint Nicaise.[117] Its blind members were officially authorized to beg by a papal

2.29.
Jean-Siméon Chardin, *Blind Beggar*, ca. 1733. Oil on canvas. Harvard Art Museums/Fogg Museum, Cambridge, Massachusetts, Bequest of Grenville L. Winthrop.

2.30.
Abraham Bosse, *The Blind Man*. Engraving. Bibliothèque nationale de France, Paris.

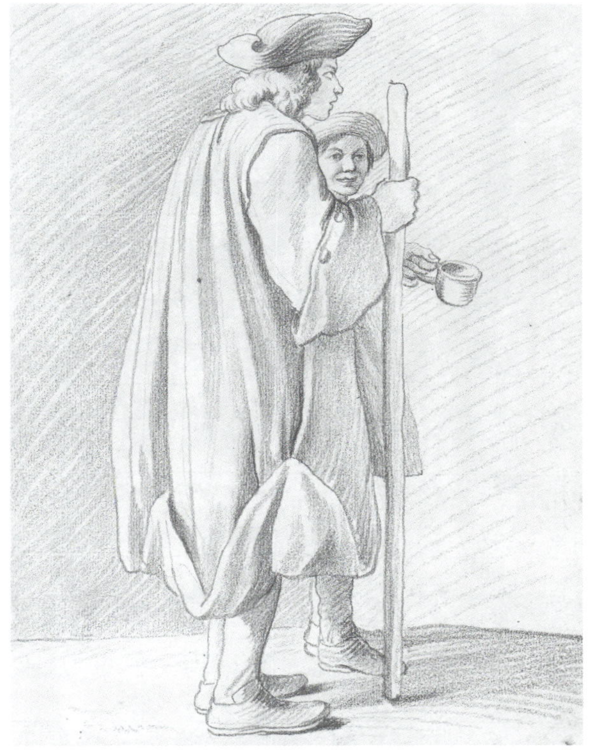

2.31. ABOVE
Edmé Bouchardon, *Blindman of Quinze-Vingts*, ca. 1732–37. Sanguine. British Museum, London.

2.32. BELOW LEFT
Jean-Siméon Chardin, *Blind Beggar*, detail of fig. 2.29.

2.33. BELOW RIGHT
Jean-Siméon Chardin, *Blind Beggar*, detail of fig. 2.29.

edict that distinguished them from the legions of beggars on the streets of Paris who were subject to arrest and imprisonment.[118] Moreover, the Quinze-Vingts brothers possessed an exclusive privilege of collecting alms in front of Paris churches, which is where Chardin's protagonist most likely stands.[119]

The dignity with which Chardin endows his blind beggar speaks to his subject's relatively entitled status within the social hierarchy of the Parisian poor. Notwithstanding his humiliating task, the blind man appears neither subdued—as was Callot's protagonist, with his head bent downward and his face hidden under his hat—nor eliciting pity.[120] Notable also is the solitude of Chardin's figure; the Quinze-Vingts blind were customarily accompanied by a sighted guide whose assistance in collecting alms was required by the regulations of the confraternity.[121] This is how Bouchardon depicted the *Blindman of Quinze-Vingts* in his drawing, produced at about the same time as Chardin's painting, for the *Cris de Paris*, a compendium of prints illustrating different urban trades (fig. 2.31).[122] The difference between the two works emphasizes Chardin's beggar as a solitary sentinel posted at the gates of an interior, a man onto himself. Most importantly, what differentiates Chardin's blind is the treatment of blindness itself.[123] His unseeing gaze directed slightly upward, his mouth firmly shut—he is not a street crier like Bouchardon's *Aveugle*—the *Blind Beggar* seems not blind so much as turned in upon himself.[124]

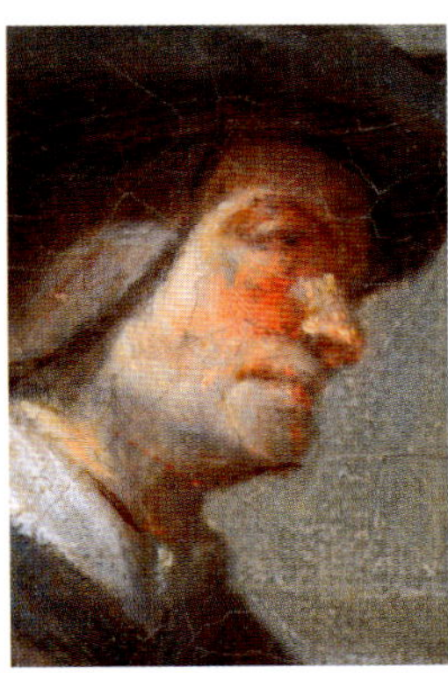

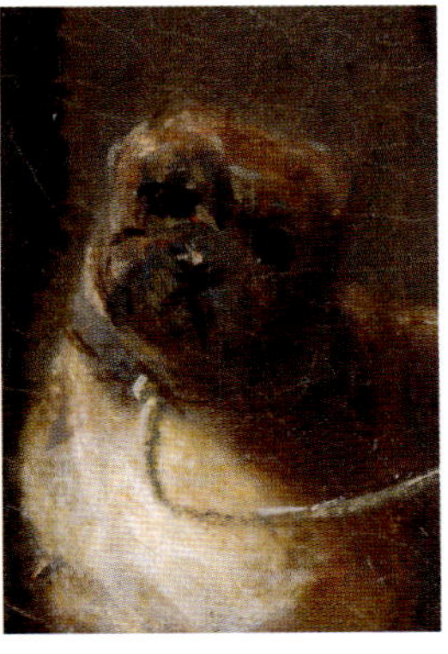

Chardin's mode of execution, admired by Salon critics, contributed to this effect of interiorization.[125] Note the handling of the beggar's face that emerges into light from underneath the large dark rim of his hat, built up by patches of pigments laid next to one another, and especially the way his sightlessness was conveyed by a thin swath of gray-white pigment that rises up from below the lower eyelid toward the dark pupil, not to blot but to veil it—a treatment markedly different from the blank eyes of the blind men of Bosse and Bouchardon (fig. 2.32). A withdrawal is suggested: visible but unseeing, the eye appears as an instrument of vision directed inward. Rather than the beggar, it is his dog who seems to be blind: the wisps of pigment that render its canine "face" circumvent the dark hollows of the eyeless sockets (fig. 2.33). In their mute blackness, they resemble the *Wild Rabbit*'s dead eye.

Conveyed by Chardin's idiosyncratic handling of paint—the unintegrated slashes and strips of pigment that build up shapes thickly, suggesting material depth—is a sense not only of the beggar's but also of the painting's inaccessible interior. This self-reflexive dimension is reinforced by details such as the patch of lighter, orangey-brown pigment deposited on the beggar's right sleeve. While it represents an actual patch sewn onto the beggar's threadbare coat, the thickness of pigment used to render it also acts as a deliberately posed barrier to our gaze. Another eloquent detail is the empty loop of the dog's leash dangling from the beggar's wrist, an ocular opening that, while leading our eye into the depth of the canvas, offers no entry into it.

What this up-close perusal of the painting reveals is how chroma in Chardin's work may act as a deterrent or marker of the painting's interior as impenetrable—for our gaze as much as that of the painter's.

His experience of the process of arriving at this effect may be called a "blind touch" insofar as, for him, the coherence of form it produced was palpable but not visible, except from a distance.[126] Painting as he tended to do directly on a blank canvas, without recourse to underdrawing, that is, with no "road map" for his brush to follow, the painter proceeded not unlike a blind beggar walking with his stick without the assistance of a *guide voyant*—by feeling his way about the canvas's surface.[127]

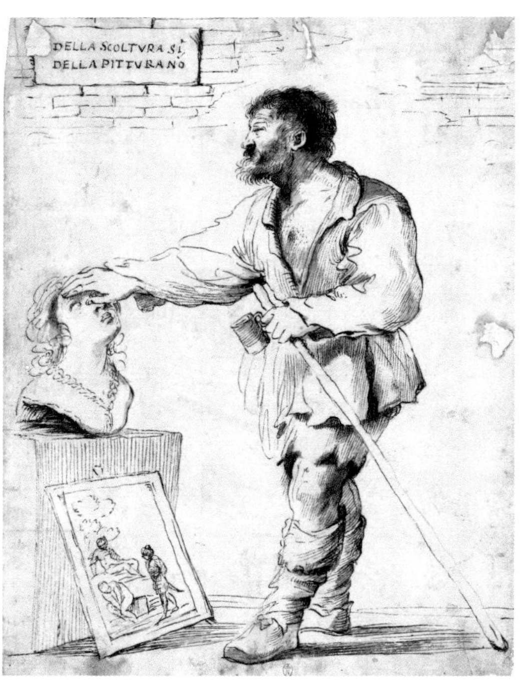

2.34. LEFT
School of Guercino, *Allegory of the Superiority of Sculpture over Painting*, early seventeenth century. Pen and brown ink, over black chalk. Musée du Louvre, Paris.

2.35. OPPOSITE
Jean-Siméon Chardin, *Attributes of the Arts*, 1731. Musée Jacquemart-André, Paris.

Blindness is then a condition of interiority that this painting describes and performs, declaring itself to be a self-reflexive commentary on Chardin's practice as a blind man's craft. It was "blind" in the sense that Chardin's mode of applying pigment produced the impression of what I have called earlier "deep materiality," the effect of material depth that was impenetrable to others, not only physically (no access to the layers of paint that constitute a given tonal impression) but also cognitively (no one could figure out how he painted and, above all, how he obtained such unusually compelling chromatic effects). It is telling that to describe the effect of mystifying depth in Chardin's works exhibited at the Salon of 1753, among them the *Blind Beggar*, one critic chose to address Chardin precisely by invoking a language of blindness: "The eye, deceived by your apparent lightness and facility of execution would like, by its repeated yet vain efforts, to learn its secrets; but it ruins itself, loses itself in your touch."[128] The *Blind Man* both illustrates and materializes an original conception of painting in which the operations of chroma are associated with touch rather than sight and are defined by inscrutability, at once material and subjective.

This view of the *Blind Beggar* is even more justified if we consider that blindness was an important intertextual trope in contemporary discourses on art and human subjectivity. Appearing in early eighteenth-century arguments about the specificity of painting as a medium, the problem of blindness was also a touchstone of later debates on the role of the senses in the constitution and subjective functioning of a human being.

In his *Cours de peinture*, a foundational text on painting based on his lectures delivered at the Academy, Roger de Piles evokes a blind man to make a point about the distinct nature of painting as a medium. In his view, what defines painting is its decidedly visual aspect linked to its reliance on color. Opposing the views of advocates of drawing as the defining, intellectual basis of painting—notably Charles Le Brun, who notoriously claimed that "pigment grinders would have the same rank as painters if drawing did not differentiate them"[129]—de Piles dissociated color from the purely material means of execution by introducing the concept of *coloris*. Defined as a mode of using pigments "in order to imitate the appearance of colors" on the canvas, coloris was a form of pictorial knowledge; it required the understanding of color harmonies and of the light and shade.[130] As such, coloris established painting as a distinctly visual activity; whereas pigments were tangible, the effect they produced was visible. Color determined the superiority of painting over other mediums, such as sculpture and drawing, both of which de Piles associated with an inferior sense of touch. Addressing itself to the hand rather than the eye, drawing, like sculpture, required no mental or physical distance but contact.[131] Even a blind man could discern, by touching, the contours of things and recreate them, a fact confirmed, in de Piles's view, by the existence of blind sculptors. De Piles recounted the story of a wax sculptor who, though blind, was capable of producing portraits of astonishing likeness. In response to the incredulous viewer questioning the degree of his blindness, the sculptor responded: "I see nothing; my eyes are at my fingertips."[132]

The *Blind Beggar* may be seen as Chardin's own bid to define painting's specificity, an image of what painting was *for him*. Enlisting the figure of the blind man to appropriate touch as the defining aspect of

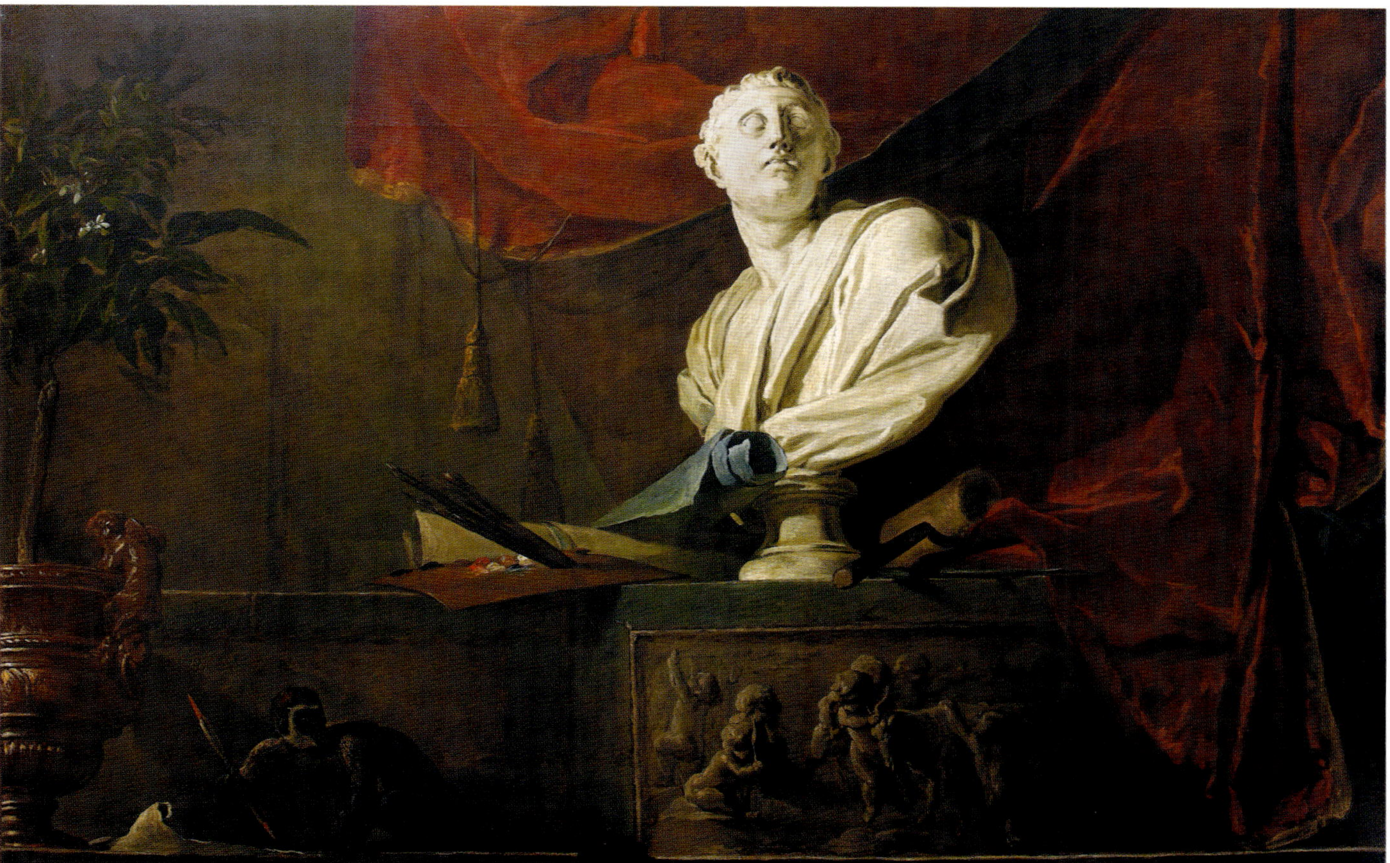

painting rather than sculpture, Chardin distinguished his stance from de Piles's and from the standard arguments illustrated by the long iconographic tradition of *paragone* between the arts. This tradition was exemplified by a drawing from the school of Guercino wherein the trope of the blind man's touch served (differently than in de Piles) to elevate sculpture over painting; whereas sculpture could be known and practiced by touch, painting could not, which is the reason for its lower status signaled by its placement below the sculpted bust (fig. 2.34).[133] Chardin's practice demonstrated the reverse: in his hands, it is painting that amounts to a performance of touch. Both iconographically and morphologically, the *Blind Beggar* announces itself to be a work of an artist who painted as if his eyes were "at his fingertips."

Chardin resorted frequently to the trope of blindness when staging his version of paragone between painting and sculpture. Such is the function of the conspicuously blind-eyed sculpted busts featured in his numerous still lifes with the attributes of the arts, the most spectacular one being the large-scale canvas painted for Comte de Rothenbourg's library (fig. 2.35).[134] Here a giant plaster bust, most likely based on the Hellenistic marble of the so-called *Diomedes*, dominates the composition as if to convey the superiority of sculpture over painting (evoked by the palette and brushes) and drawing (represented by an anatomically inaccurate monkey). But the bust is also a monochrome spectacle of *pictorial* mastery. Staring out with its emphatically unseeing eyes, the *Diomedes* may be seen as an emblem of the painter's palpable practice epitomized by his image of the blind man.

The *Blind Beggar*, though, evokes not only the haptic use of pigment but also the state of inwardness. By establishing the connection between the inaccessible material and interior depth of both its protagonist and the painting itself, the *Blind Beggar* represents the subjective dimension of Chardin's chromatic practice. Color was traditionally associated with subjectivity because there were no established rules governing its application. In seventeenth- and early eighteenth-century theoretical reflections on painting, its use was described as individually determined, depending on personal preferences rather than rationalized principles.[135] In Chardin's case, however, the individualized (subjective) dimension of chroma is suggested in a particular way: by the blind man as both a material product and a figure of touch.

—·—

Chardin's protagonist may be situated in the ranks of blind men who, as both real persons and rhetorical tropes, made repeated appearances in the Enlightenment discourse on the senses.[136] This discourse challenged the Cartesian belief in the superiority of vision—a belief that led de Piles to align painting with sight—by reconsidering the position of touch in the hierarchy of the senses and by reassessing its cognitive function. The accounts of the recovery of sight by those who were born blind provoked new inquiries into the role of the senses in human cognition, and especially into the relative importance of sight versus touch.[137] Haptic apprehension came to be considered as an alternative mode of experiencing and knowing both the world and oneself. A distinct possibility emerged that the cognitive capacity of a person born blind, based as it was exclusively in touch, was not impaired but different.

This possibility was most provocatively explored by Diderot in his *Letter on the Blind for the Use of Those Who Can See* (1749).[138] His exploration centered on an actual person, a certain man-born-blind of Puiseaux, who was, however, largely Diderot's own invention, a hybrid figure combining the features of different blind men that had appeared in the texts of Diderot's predecessors, among them Montaigne (whose *Essays* included a story of a blind man hunting hares!) and Descartes.[139] Diderot's "interviews" with the man-born-blind of Puiseaux provided evidence of how knowledge obtained through touch was not only sufficient but could be superior to that provided by sight.[140] Openly opposing Descartes, who, while evoking the possibility of "seeing with hands," placed vision firmly at the top of sensorial hierarchy, Diderot sketched out an understanding of touch as an alternative mode of cognition. In doing so, he "recycled" the image of a blind man walking with sticks from *La Dioptrique*, where Descartes used it to explain his geometrical conception of human vision, to illustrate an altogether different, tactile mode of encountering and knowing the world (fig. 2.36).[141] In Diderot, the blind man's condition appeared not as a deprivation but as an alternative mode of perception that may indeed be of use to "those who can see." Moreover, raising the issue of perceptual and subjective self-sufficiency of the blind, the *Letter* also pointed to the need for reevaluating their position in society.[142]

Parallel to Diderot's explorations was the philosophical work of Étienne Bonnot de Condillac.[143] In his *Traité des sensations* (*Treatise on Sensations*, 1754),

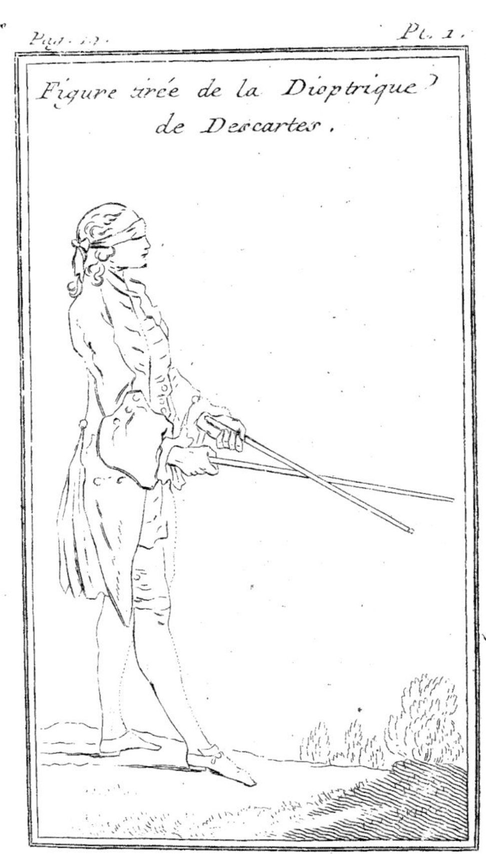

2.36.
A Blind Man Performing "Natural Geometry." Figure drawn from Descartes, *La Dioptrique,* Plate I, Denis Diderot, *Lettre sur les Aveugles*, 1749. Wellcome Library, London.

Condillac systematically examined the respective roles of the senses in the constitution of the human subject. Resorting to a rhetorical device of a statue, he described its gradual acquisition of all five senses, establishing the paramount role of touch in its experience of itself and the world. It is through touch, argued Condillac, that we discover our body's continuity and apprehend its difference from other objects, both discoveries being key for the recognition of our body as the locus of self.[144]

The eighteenth-century debate on blindness and on the role of touch in the makeup of the human sensorium provides the discursive parameters within which the *Blind Beggar*'s own argument must be situated.[145] Dignified, individuated, and interiorized, Chardin's image of the blind man is not only a respectful representation of the mendicant of the Quinze-Vingts but also a testimony to a new understanding of blindness. Chardin's foregrounding of touch in this painting—his illumination of the blind man's firm grip on his cane and on his tin cup, his finger wrapped around its handle—combined with his palpable mode of execution suggest an affinity between the blind man's mode of being in the world and Chardin's mode of painting. Inscribed in the succession of blind men through whom, from the late seventeenth century on, arguments about the touch of the unsighted were articulated, Chardin's protagonist speaks to the epistemological dimension of the painter's own "blind touch." This small canvas—itself a tactile object that can be held in one's hands—thus offers a self-reflexive image of Chardin's practice, an exercise of a tactile rather than visual intelligence that, while unseen, is nonetheless an interiorized form of knowledge.[146] Moreover, it suggests a connection between his tactile practice and subjectivity. The solitary, self-absorbed figure embodies touch as the blind beggar's means of self-experience, which may also be seen as the painter's self-experience: a mode of being inside oneself, and in the depths of the painting during the process of making it.

As such, the *Blind Beggar* offers us some insight into Chardin's hunting trophies, the feats of his blind touch. The painting helps us realize that the originality of his interpretation of this motif had to do not only with the task of representing the animal—the naturalist ethos evoked by Cochin—but also with Chardin's understanding of himself as a painter. This self-conception differed radically from how Desportes, a master of trophy painting, imagined himself. As *Self-Portrait as a Hunter* (1699) makes clear, Desportes's practice was predicated on a fantasy of the painter being himself a hunter (fig. 2.37). By assuming the hunter's garb and identity, the trophy painter suggested himself to be a man of leisure, thus elevating his social status. Chardin's aspirations, as communicated, if only indirectly, by the *Blind Beggar*, are far humbler. It is with the men of small urban trades, such as the mendicant of the Quinze-Vingts, that Chardin aligns his practice. Posted outside the church, this solitary member of artisanal confraternity may well have accommodated Chardin's sense of himself as a professional outsider, a peintre à talents within the Academy. His respectful depiction of the mendicant may be seen as a mode of validating his own marginal position. Unlike Desportes, Chardin seeks recognition exactly for what he does—and how he does it. He embraces not the outward appearances of social and professional success, but the condition of inwardness. It is as a figure of interiority that the *Blind Beggar* speaks of the painter.

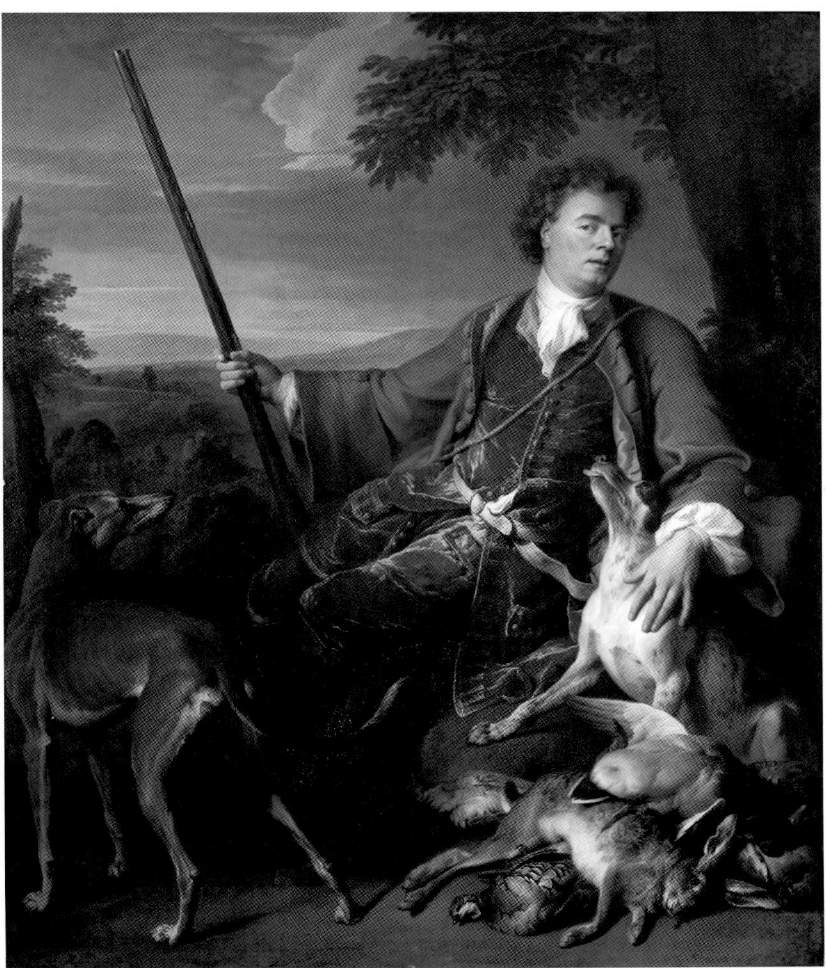

2.37. Alexandre-François Desportes, *Self-Portrait as a Hunter*, 1699. Oil on canvas. Musée du Louvre, Paris.

This brings us back to the rabbits and hares. They too have a kind of interiority. For Sarah Cohen, Chardin's injection of interior life into the bodies of dead game reflected the growing recognition of the rabbits and hares as sentient beings.[147] Yet I would argue slightly differently that aside from representing the animals, these paintings are also self-reflexive representations of Chardin's distinct tactile "talent." This is manifest in the animals' eyes. The mute black spot in the furry head of the *Wild Rabbit* depicts neither life nor death. A signal of the eye's absence, it is *not* a sign but an instance of semiotic rupture—a zero degree of representation—that refers to nothing but painting itself, at its most sophisticated and crudest.[148] This semiotic breach indicates not only the painter's self-consciousness about his handling but also a certain limit in his practice. The epitome of Chardin's touch as the hallmark of his "distinct talent," the rabbit's eye opens up to the material dead end of his painting, hinting at the painter's particular impediment: his blindness to himself.

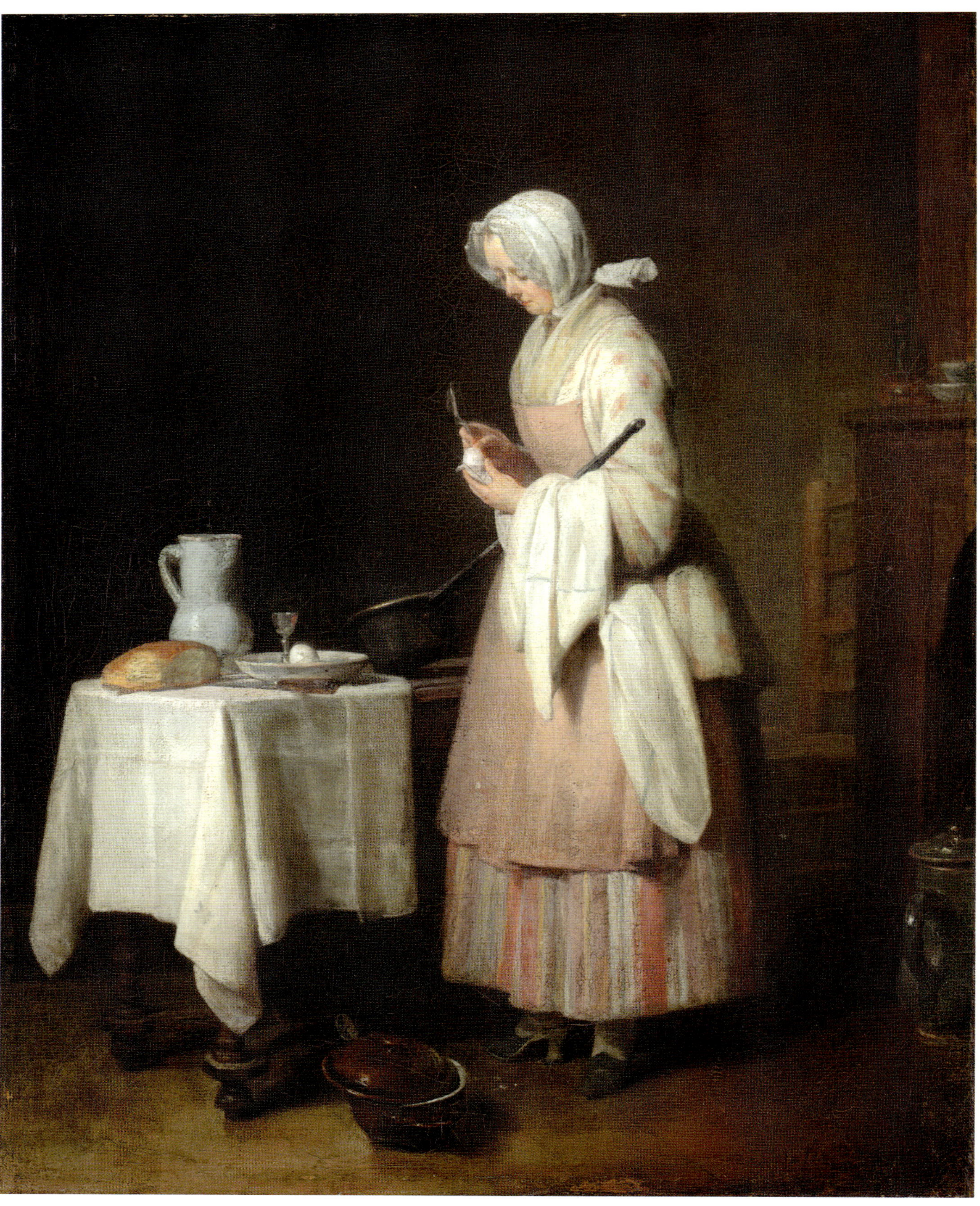

UNDERNEATH THE VISIBLE

For the generations of rococo and beyond, the art-work is beginning to be considered as an instrument that permits vivid hallucination.

—NORMAN BRYSON, Word and Image

2.38. OPPOSITE
Jean-Siméon Chardin, *Attentive Nurse*, 1747. Oil on canvas. National Gallery of Art, Washington, DC, Samuel H. Kress Collection

2.39. BELOW RIGHT
Jean-Siméon Chardin, *Study for the Attentive Nurse*, ca. 1747. Oil on canvas. Private Collection.

The *Blind Beggar* was a harbinger of an important shift in Chardin's career during the early 1730s: the painter turned to genre scenes.[149] This was an unexpected move, given the limits of the eighteenth-century painter's professional specialization, and it called for an explanation.[150] Pierre-Jean Mariette provided one in a by-now-familiar anecdote. In it, Chardin witnesses his friend Joseph Aved's refusal to paint a portrait of a woman who had offered to pay him too little money for it. He admonishes Aved for having missed a good opportunity, to which Aved responds with a taunt that could not but pique Chardin's professional pride: yes, indeed, it would have been a good opportunity, had it been as easy to paint a likeness as it is to paint a sausage. "Aved's remark"—Mariette tells us—"made a strong impression on Chardin. . . . There and then he resolved to give up his first talent; then he had to choose another."[151]

The reasons for Chardin's resolution sound compelling enough: a combination of spurred artistic ambition and promise of financial gain. As has been pointed out, other factors may have also contributed to the painter's decision, among them the return of regular Salon exhibitions in 1737.[152] Chardin, who had previously shown his work only at the open-air art displays held at the Place Dauphine, may have been encouraged by this new opportunity. Changes of a different kind that occurred in the painter's family life in the early 1730s may have led Chardin to pursue a more ambitious career course: his postponed marriage finalized in early 1731; the death of his father in the spring; and the birth of his first child, a son, at the end of that year, followed by the birth of his daughter in 1733.[153] Still, the boldness with which, at the age of thirty-four, he decided to "upgrade" his practice cannot be overestimated. The painter's decision to change his "talent" is even more intriguing given that, having achieved remarkable critical and commercial success in practicing it—he was seen as the inventor of a new kind of painting, and had prominent European elite patrons lined up to buy his works as soon as they came off his easel—Chardin gave up on it almost as abruptly as he took it up: in 1748, he returned to still life, and in 1751 he painted his last genre scene.[154] What do we make of this mysterious interval in the painter's career, an experiment that was rewarding but renounced? What was at stake in Chardin's turn to genre?

I want to suggest that genre painting performed a key function in Chardin's process of self-individuation, in both an artistic and a subjective sense. The engagement with the human figure offered the painter not only the means of professional advancement but also an opportunity to reimagine himself. The situations he staged in his paintings allowed him to reconfigure the relation between the object, the canvas, and his own body, ultimately providing him with the framework within which to envision himself as an embodied self. At the same time, the human figure proved to be a representational challenge for the painter, his depiction of domestic scenes serving as a stage for negotiations that, while different from those Chardin conducted in his early still lifes, were no less complex. This challenge had to do with Chardin's training, with his methods and the conditions of his work, to which I will attend in due course. First and foremost, though, we need to examine the paintings themselves.

The *Attentive Nurse*, known also as *Convalescent's Meal* (fig. 2.38), is a good place to start. In the middle

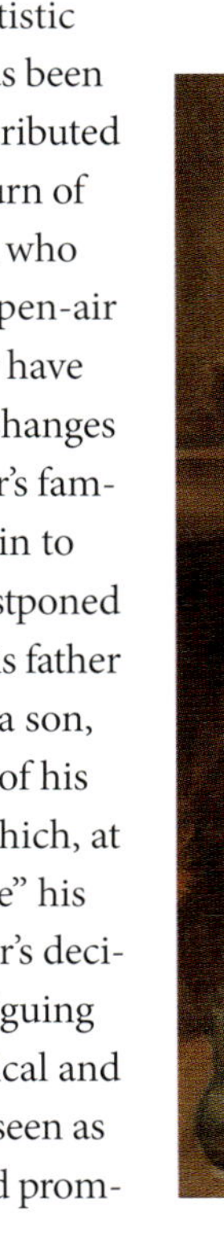

of a sparsely furnished room, a woman is shown peeling a freshly boiled egg. Cradling the egg in one hand, she lightly pinches the shell with the fingers of another, her spoon, suspended in midair, catching a glint of light like a blade. Wrapped in light-colored clothing that matches the whiteness of her object and resonates with the white tablecloth and white jug, she looks not unlike a friendly ghost, a luminous apparition in this darkened, windowless interior. But if she is a ghost of sorts, so is the deliberate arrangement of things on her table, a phantom of the still lifes Chardin used to paint and will return to again.[155] A reminder of the past and of the future, the still life appears to be as important an actor in this picture as the figure. It is as if these two aspects of the painting were related to each other, their similar shapes and chromatic consonance underscoring their reciprocity, the white jug with its "bent" arm echoing the woman's arm; the table cloth rhyming with aspects of her dress, especially with her towel.

How deliberate the suggestion of this dialogical relation between the figure and the still life was can be gauged from a preparatory sketch for the painting, a rarity in Chardin's oeuvre (fig. 2.39). Compared to the final version, the sketch makes evident the considerable amount of visual editing involved in the production of this effect. The woman's figure has been lightened: her bonnet turned from black to white; her brown dress enlivened by white and pastel stripes; the kitchen towel repositioned across her arm, better to accord with the shape of the tablecloth's swag. At the same time, the objects on the table were rearranged to rhyme subtly with the figure. Having migrated from the floor onto the table, the green jug became white and a loaf of bread was placed next to it, the shape of both producing a rough equivalent of the silhouette of the woman in her light-colored garments—two elegantly bulbous, slightly leaning forms framing their respective eggs.

The comparison of the *Attentive Nurse* with its sketch suggests that Chardin's embrace of genre did not simply launch him into a new territory of professional expertise but involved a negotiation of the relation between what Mariette called his two "talents." This hypothesis is borne out by Chardin's other genre paintings, especially the single-figure compositions, such as the *Scullery Maid* (fig. 2.40), the basic structure of which may be defined as a "figure + still life" combination. It is almost as if the painter lifted the arrangement of kitchen utensils displayed in many of his earlier still lifes, laid them

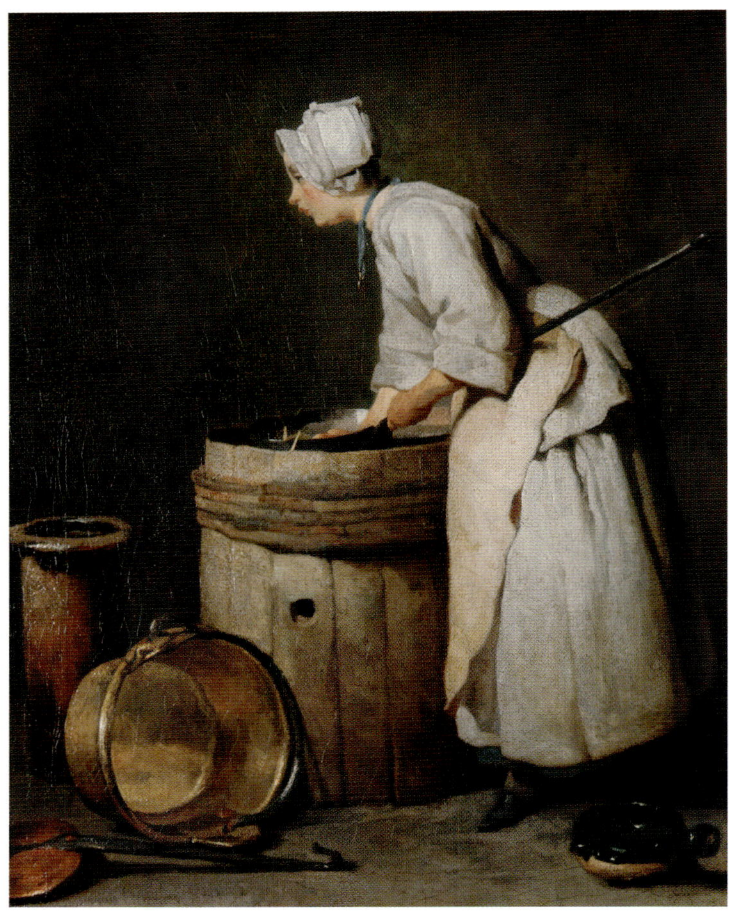

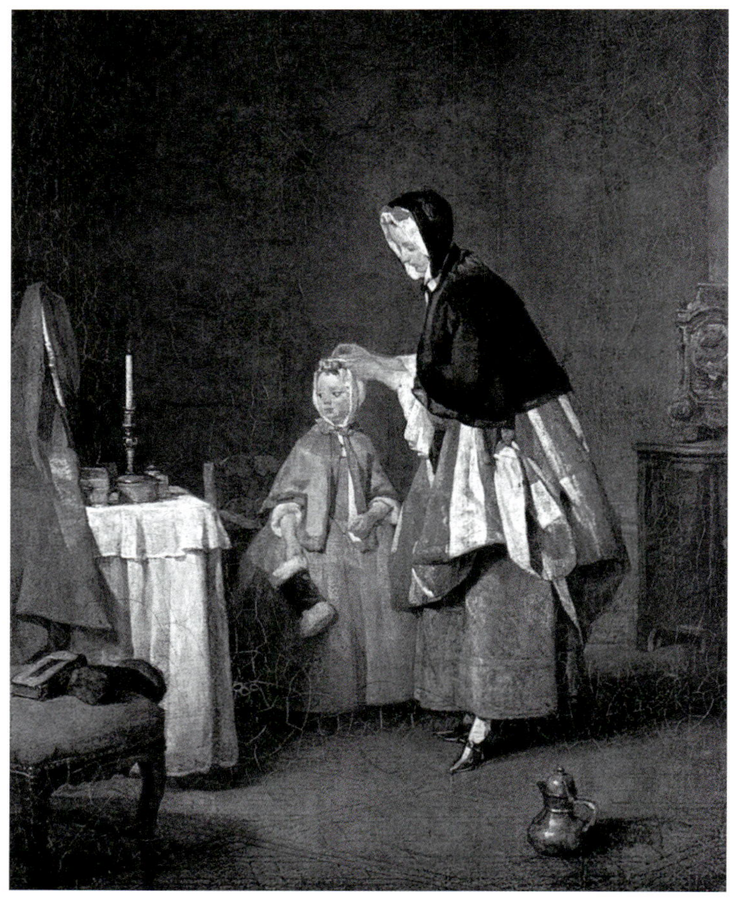

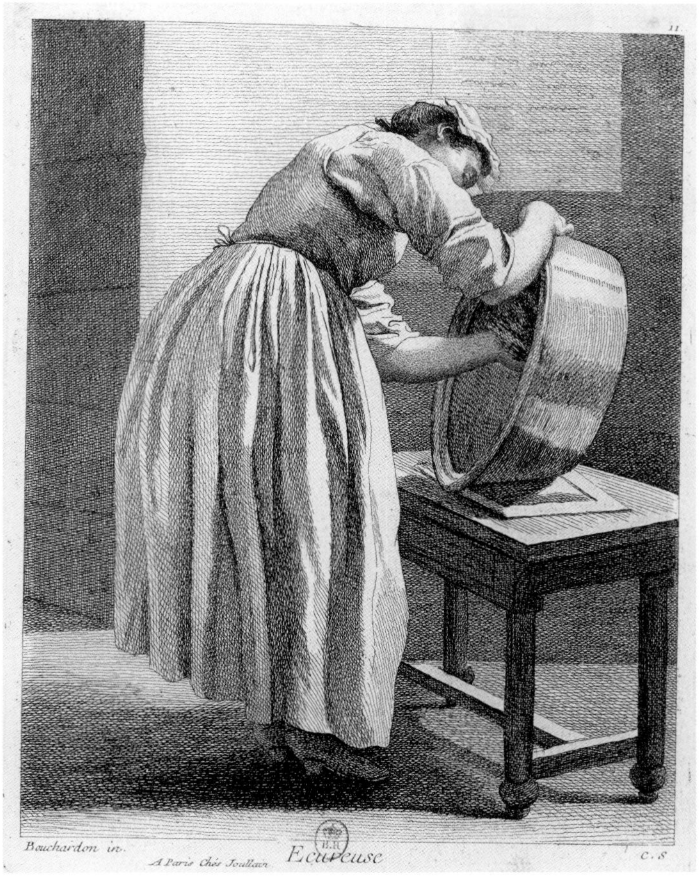

2.40. OPPOSITE TOP
Jean-Siméon Chardin, *Scullery Maid*, 1738. Oil on canvas. The Hunterian Museum and Art Gallery, University of Glasgow.

2.41. OPPOSITE BOTTOM
Jean-Siméon Chardin, *The Morning Toilette*, 1740. Oil on canvas. Nationalmuseum, Stockholm.

2.42. ABOVE
Comte de Caylus after Edmé Bouchardon, *Scullery Maid*, from *Cris de Paris*, 1737. Etching and engraving. Bibliothèque nationale de France, Paris.

out on the floor in his new canvas, and inserted the figure of the maid in between.[156]

The insistent and deliberate staging of these recognizable items from the painter's still life repertory, as well as their odd placement in relation to the figures, is intriguing. One wonders, for example, what the earthenware boiling pot, with its lid precariously balanced on its rim, is doing at the feet of the nurse. The motif is a remnant of the messy kitchen interiors by Dutch painters, such as Willem Kalf or David Teniers, on whom Chardin trained his eye, but here, in the caring nurse's room, it appears out of place. Together with a large lidded jug placed right behind her, the pot on the floor produces a sense of precariousness that disturbs the serene reciprocity between the figure and her objects laid out on the table. One cannot help noticing that if the attentive nurse makes a step forward or backward, that is, if she is inattentive, she risks knocking down one of these domestic utensils. The recurrence of such curiously placed objects in almost all of his genre scenes is clearly not a result of Chardin simply registering what was before his eyes. Their presence is sometimes hardly plausible, as in the case of the prominent coffee pot (*marabout*) standing on the parquet floor in the foreground of *The Morning Toilette* (fig. 2.41). One is reminded of Louis-Sébastien Mercier's descriptions of the interiors of the Parisian poor wherein the kitchen utensils rolled around on the floor together with chamber pots.[157] Yet the presence of such arbitrarily placed items in the households of the well-to-do indicates that we are not dealing with a savvy use of the "reality effect" à la Flaubert, but rather with something else.[158] One could say that the oddly placed motifs perform the effect of *unreality*, constructing a space of experience irreducible to the social nature of acts or the forms of labor that take place in it. How does this space relate to the protagonists of these scenes?

The uncommon character of Chardin's figures had not gone unnoticed by his contemporaries. The seriousness and solemnity with which his protagonists perform their daily tasks—those "moments in the business of life, without the least interest, which in themselves merit no attention," as the critic La Font de Saint-Yenne put it—were seen to rescue them from the baseness associated with Northern examples of such scenes, and to distinguish Chardin's version of genre painting from that of his Dutch and Flemish predecessors.[159] However, it is not only the gravity of their performance but the way in which they are *distanced* from it that is perhaps the most striking. Philip Conisbee noted how different Chardin's "ambiguously distracted" *Embroiderer* (ca. 1733–35) was from Casper Netscher's 1644 version of a similar subject.[160] We can also see how Chardin's depictions of household tasks differed from the French examples by casting a quick comparative glance at Bouchardon's rendition of a scullery maid for the *Cris de Paris* (fig. 2.42).[161] While Bouchardon's *récureuse* is entirely absorbed by the act of scouring, Chardin captures a moment of suspension in the maid's performance conveyed by the unseeing look of the woman and underscored by the pendant hanging down from her neck—its medallion, like her face, catching a glint of the incoming light and making this temporal interval more visible. We see a similar effect in the *Turnip Scraper* (fig. 2.43), who is shown taking a pause from her work, with her knife stuck in her hand and looking elsewhere with a certain stupor. The half-scraped turnip in her hand dangles loosely, like the scouring maid's medallion, accentuating the effect of a gap that opens up in her experience—of her task, or of herself.

One can say that it is not only the performance of daily routines but also a space of subjective experience that Chardin gives us to see. The question is, *whose* experience, and of what kind? René Démoris

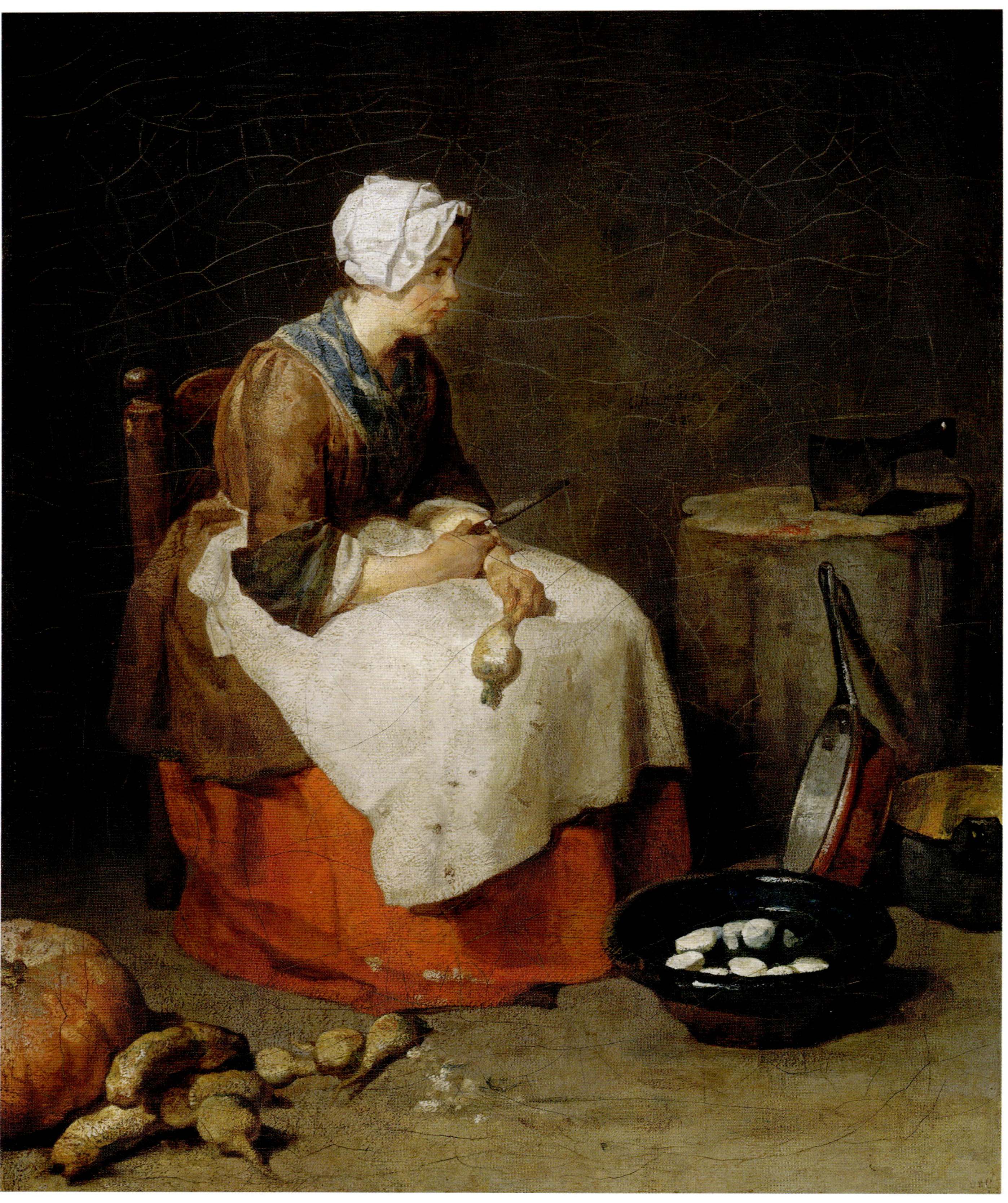

2.43. OPPOSITE
Jean-Siméon Chardin, *Turnip Scraper*, 1738. National Gallery of Art, Washington, DC, Samuel H. Kress Collection.

2.44. BELOW LEFT
Jean-Siméon Chardin, *The Washerwoman*, 1734. Oil on canvas. Nationalmuseum, Stockholm.

2.45. BELOW RIGHT
Jean-Siméon Chardin, *Woman Drawing Water from a Fountain*, 1733–35. Oil on wood. Nationalmuseum, Stockholm.

offered a persuasive interpretation of Chardin's genre works as constructions of "l'espace de moi": a nonrelational, asocial, that is, essentially, narcissistic space.[162] While in dialogue with Démoris's, my own interpretation proposes a different account of the nature and meaning of this subjective space, specifically, the role of the figure in it, ultimately suggesting its broader implications for Chardin's practice.

—·—

As has been noted, the domestic realm depicted by Chardin is dominated by the figures of women and children, in the near-total absence of men.[163] Whatever else these paintings are about, they construct a space of primary relations between mother, or a maternal figure, and child, a space of initial subjective experiences based in duality that seems yet unaffected by a third party, be it a paternal presence, language (the exchanges, when they do occur, are muted), or social experience. What I find striking is the sense of disconnection that consistently defines these maternal figures' relation to their tasks and to children, when children are shown.

The protagonist of *The Washerwoman* (fig. 2.44), for example, one of Chardin's earliest essays in genre, does not only seem distracted from what she is doing. She is also oblivious to the bubble-blowing child hidden behind her washbasin. It is this at once physical and psychological hiatus between the woman's body and that of the boy that the painting insists on, both through the lighting that accentuates the wooden vessel separating the two figures and through a discontinuous compositional structure. The scene is interrupted by the gap of the door frame opening up to the adjacent room where another woman hangs clothing. In *Woman Drawing Water from a Fountain* (fig. 2.45), we are confronted by another figure of withdrawal: turned away from us, a woman stoops to fill her jug with water. The presence of a child, an eerie witness of the servant's daily routine, makes the scene even more intriguing. Removed to another room, and clearly ignored by the other woman who is sweeping the floor, the child appears like a phantom immobilized within the door frame, which, moreover, cuts off almost half of its body from view. The distance separating this faraway infantile apparition from the turned-away figure in the foreground contributes to the disjunctive, resolutely antinarrative structure of this image, which, in the absence of any gestural cues, discourages any anecdotal inferences regarding the relation between the figures we may have.

Hiatus, again, is at the core of both the situation depicted in *La Pourvoyeuse* (fig. 2.46) and its tacit libidinal dimension.[164] A perspectival plunge similar to the one we have seen in *Woman Drawing Water from a Fountain* at once establishes the connection and divides the protagonist of this canvas from a woman in the background, who interacts with a

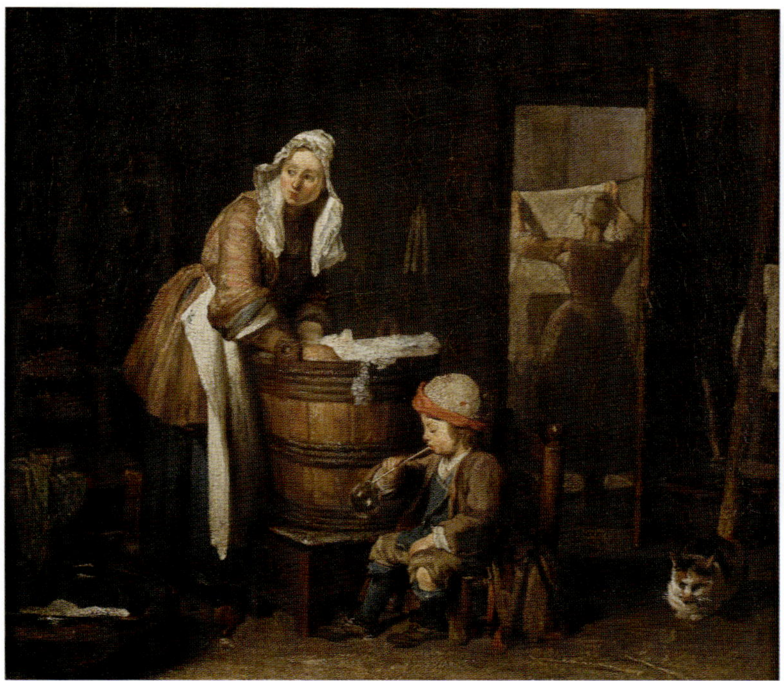

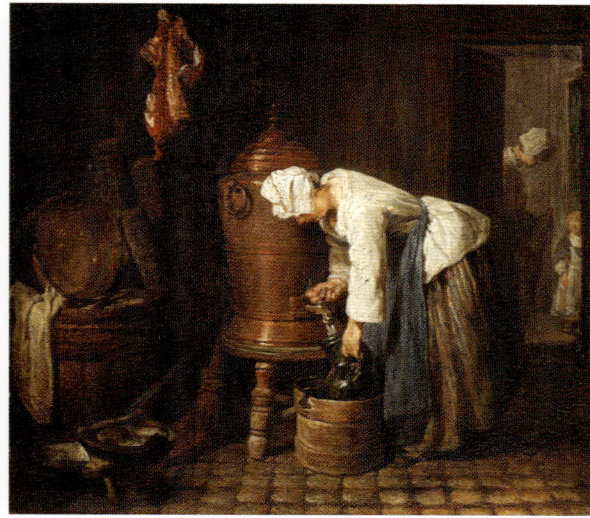

barely visible male intruder hovering on the threshold of this domestic enclosure. In the absence of a clear physiognomic expression on the face of the ambiguous protagonist—there is only a hint of affect slightly differentiating the figures in the three extant versions of this painting—we are left with the spatial distance itself as the main carrier of meaning in this scene.[165] Through it, this servant's ambiguous position within the structure of the painting's erotic allusion is conveyed: is she the object of the male intruder's pursuit (he may have followed her from the market), or an eavesdropper on his dalliance with another woman? Placed halfway between the distance separating the female figures, the water fountain, the exaggerated scale of which makes it appear as another actor in this scene, reemphasizes the spatial split between them, enhancing the vagueness of the erotic intrigue in which they are involved.

This sense of figural disconnection—or subjective withdrawal—reemphasized by the internal spacing of the scenes, is even more striking in the paintings that feature figures who explicitly interact. Such is, for example, *The Diligent Mother* (*La mère laborieuse*; fig. 2.47). Its ostensible subject is parental instruction: the mother is evidently pointing out to her daughter some shortcomings in her embroidery work. A caption under the engraved version of this painting by François-Bernard Lépicié spells it out thus: "A trifle distracts you my girl / Yesterday this foliage was done / I see from each stitch you have made / How distracted your mind is from work" (fig. 2.48). And yet it is not the girl but the mother who is visibly distracted. Her legs extended, her body slack—a curiously languorous pose for someone defined by the title of this painting as "laborieuse"—she casts an empty, unanchored look in space. (The deliberateness with which the painter produced this effect is evident if we look closely at the mother's face: a glaucous patch of whitish pigment was applied directly over her eyes in order to amplify the effect of an unseeing gaze. The *Blind Beggar* comes to mind [see fig. 2.32].) It is as if the mother has momentarily absented herself from her context, her daughter, and her parental function. Proust, for one, saw deliberation in the mother's eyes: "the mother, eyes filled with the past of the one who knows, who calculates and foresees."[166] But the woman's look is rather strikingly inattentive and unaware, a mark of momentary absence or withdrawal from a full subjective existence and also a withdrawal from her daughter, which is mutual: the girl looks down. The slightly crooked, outward-bent

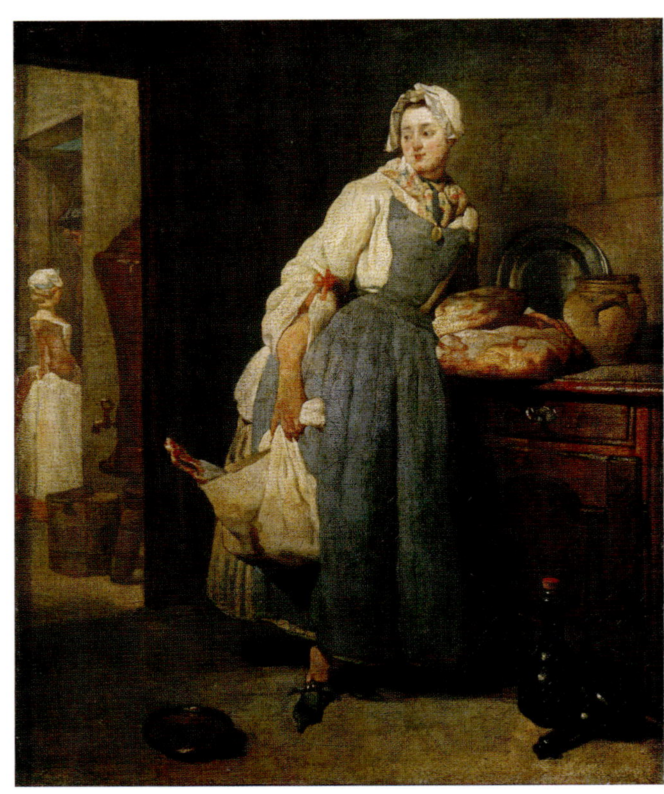

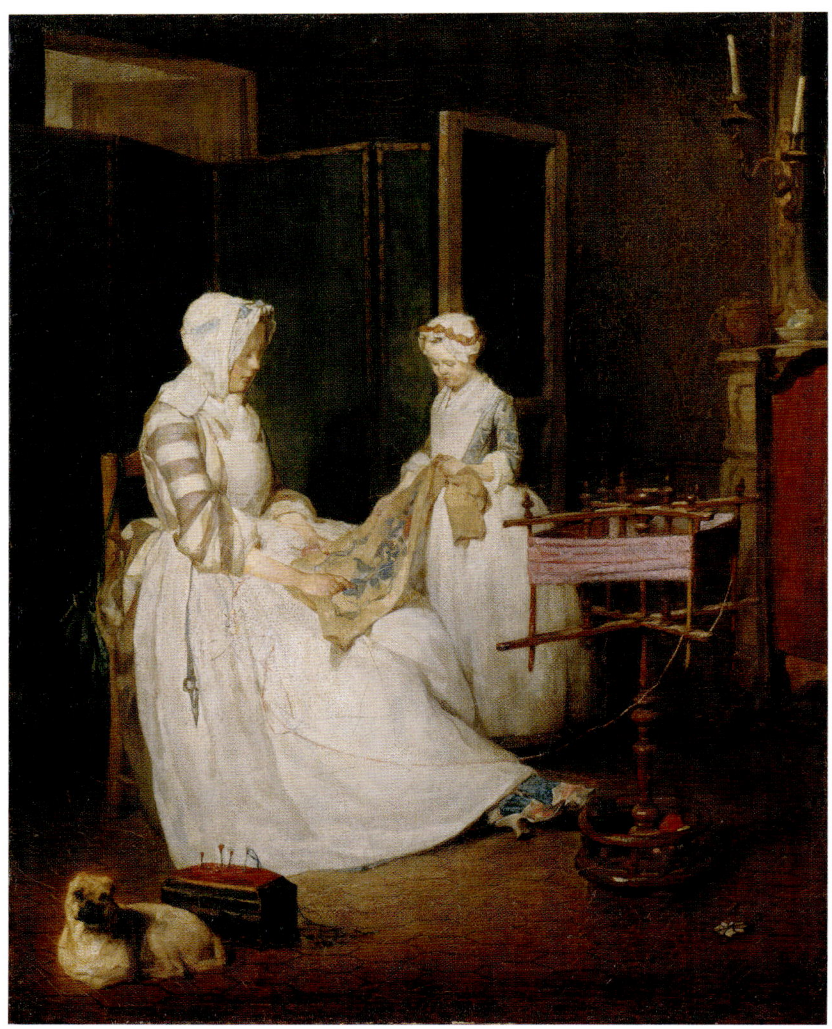

2.46. OPPOSITE TOP
Jean-Siméon Chardin, *La Pourvoyeuse*, 1738. Oil on canvas. Musée du Louvre, Paris.

2.47. OPPOSITE BOTTOM
Jean-Siméon Chardin, *The Diligent Mother* (*La mère laborieuse*), 1740. Oil on canvas. Musée du Louvre, Paris.

2.48. RIGHT
François-Bernard Lépicié after Jean-Siméon Chardin, *The Diligent Mother* (*La mère laborieuse*), 1740. Etching and engraving. Bibliothèque nationale de France, Paris.

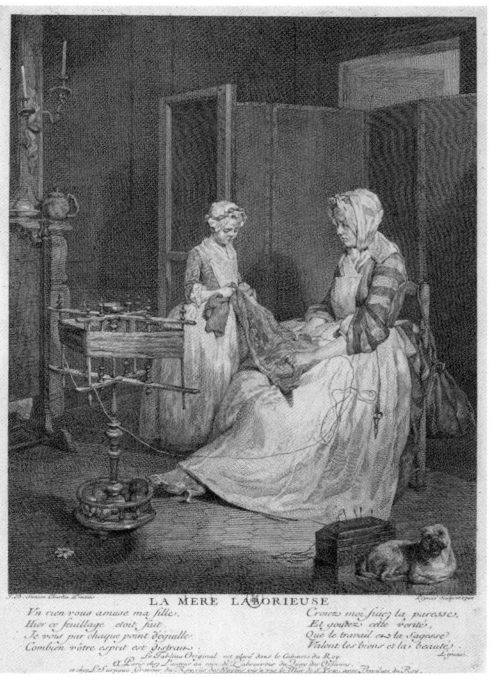

candles in the sconce in the background echo the bodily divergence of the figures, emblematizing the sense of the physical and psychological disconnection between them.

What do we make of the sense of distance, detachment, or distraction that so consistently mark the women featured in Chardin's genre scenes? To my mind, these symptoms signal a lack of internal content, a dimension of blankness or negativity within the self. The inert *Turnip Scraper* and the distracted mother are figures of subjective evacuation; it is not only silence or a retreat from language, but a kind of emptiness, an absence of interiority that they convey.[167] What is the nature of this subjective experience that is based on the subject's absence?

To answer this question, let us step back for a moment from the specific iconographic roles of these women as washerwomen, servants, or mothers to consider the shared imaginary function they perform in Chardin's painting. This function may be compared to that performed by apparitions or ghosts. Chardin's predilection for white tones in the depiction of these women—almost monochrome in the *Scullery Maid*, *The Diligent Mother*, and the *Attentive Nurse*—encourages such association. But it is especially their bracketed existence within their surroundings, their disconnection from others when others are shown, and, most emphatically, their evacuation from themselves that suggest their apparitional state.

In Chardin's time apparition was understood as a perceptual experience synonymous with subjective vision, only that while the latter was produced internally, through an act of imagination, the former was experienced externally, as a delusion that the object existed outside of the mind while it was generated and sustained by it.[168] Its psychic dimension was captured by the term *hallucination*—from Latin *alucination-em*, or *hallucination-em*, noun of action *alucinari*—to wonder (in the mind), dream, talk unreasonably—the use of which can be traced back to the early seventeenth century, though it came to be identified with psychic disorder only in the early nineteenth century.[169] While in art history the term has already been associated with painting in Chardin's time—notably by Norman Bryson, to describe the vividness of illusion provided by rococo painting[170]—I will use it differently, to account for the elusive presence of Chardin's figures, in a visual and a subjective sense.

Helpful for understanding this mode of figural appearance is the way hallucination was conceptualized by the psychoanalyst André Green in his account of a psychological process wherein the whole figure first emerges in the mental realm of the child. This process occurs in the early stages of subjective formation when the infant first perceives the mother—or a care-giving figure—as a whole person. As Green has observed, this perception is predicated on the infant's recognition of the mother's *absence* from its own body—until then the child had imagined the maternal body to be part of its own—an absence that the infant, in an attempt to make sense of it, visualizes as a phantom, a "negative hallucination," in Green's words.[171] This hallucination is not yet a fully fleshed visualization of another person but an intermediary or provisional image, a sort of visual placeholder—or as Green has put it, a representation of the absence of representation—for what the child recognizes to be no longer part of itself.[172] It is negative because it acts as a voided frame—like memory without content—of the mother's absent body, but also because it functions as the child's own "negative" image, an empty contour within which the infant begins to imagine itself. This negative image is salutary insofar as it provides an imaginary frame for the child's autonomous corporeal existence; separated from the child and self-enclosed, it allows the child to perceive its own separateness from the world, its own completeness. But as a voided structure, it is also precarious, inscribed by a sense of loss and instability, which the child internalizes and has to cope with in the process of negotiating its bodily and psychic autonomy.[173]

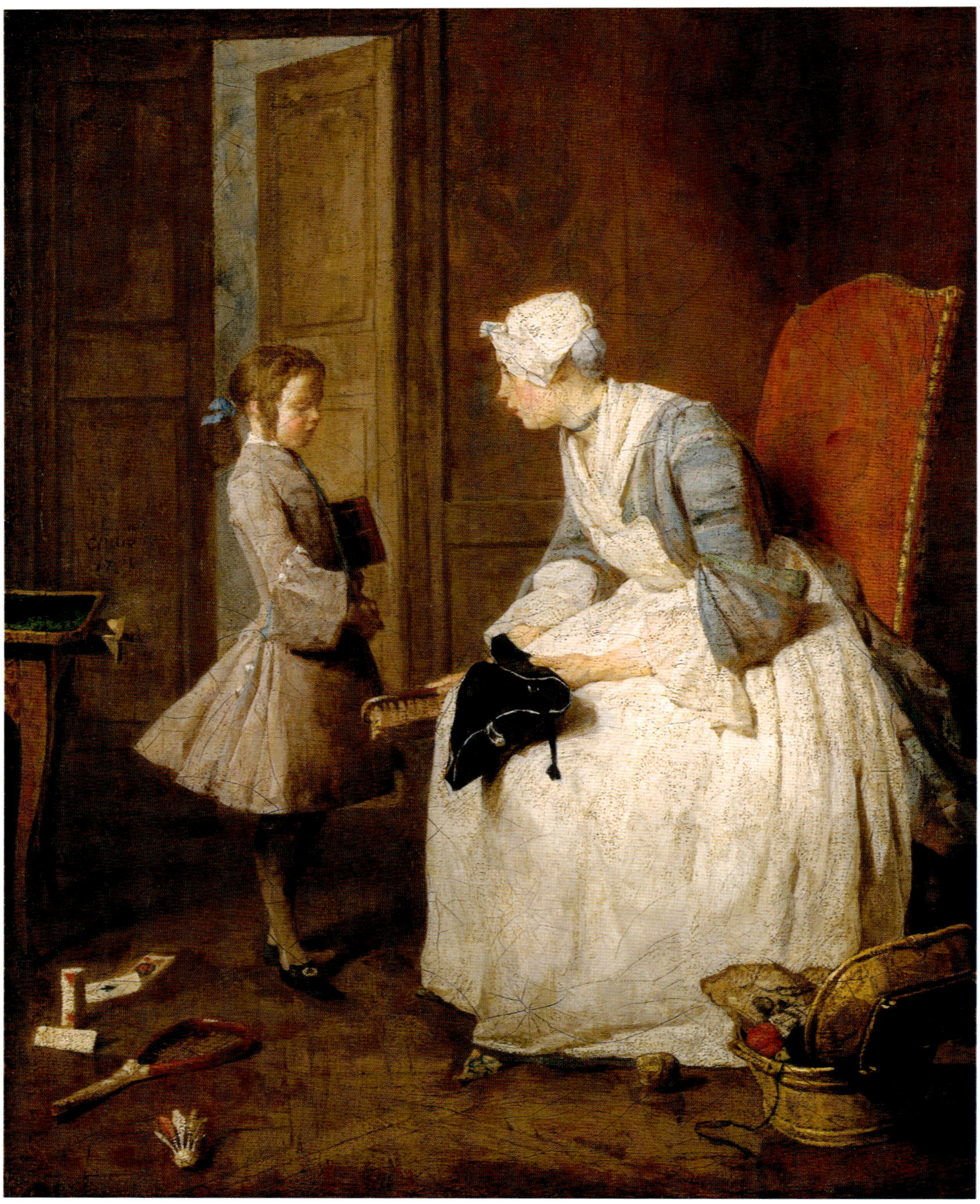

Green's account complicates the classic psychoanalytic description of primary narcissism as a stage of psychic development by suggesting that the process of forming one's self-image, which is at the core of narcissism, is underwritten by a fundamental negativity.[174] Before investing in one's own bodily image, one engages with an image of an absence in a series of defensive back-and-forth interactions with the maternal frame. One projects oneself into the empty visual sheath of the maternal and, like on a Möbius strip, one returns to oneself. It is in the course of the back-and-forth passages between the residual vision of the mother and what the child begins to visualize as itself, that the contours of human subjectivity first emerge.

Green's insight into the founding import of the hollowed-out maternal image for the figuration of one's own self is relevant for our discussion, as is his insistence on the double sense of negativity as both a formal and affective relation that the nascent subject establishes with the apparitional image of the mother. For something similar may be said about the function of the maternal figures, and female figures more generally, in Chardin's pictorial realm. Their elusive

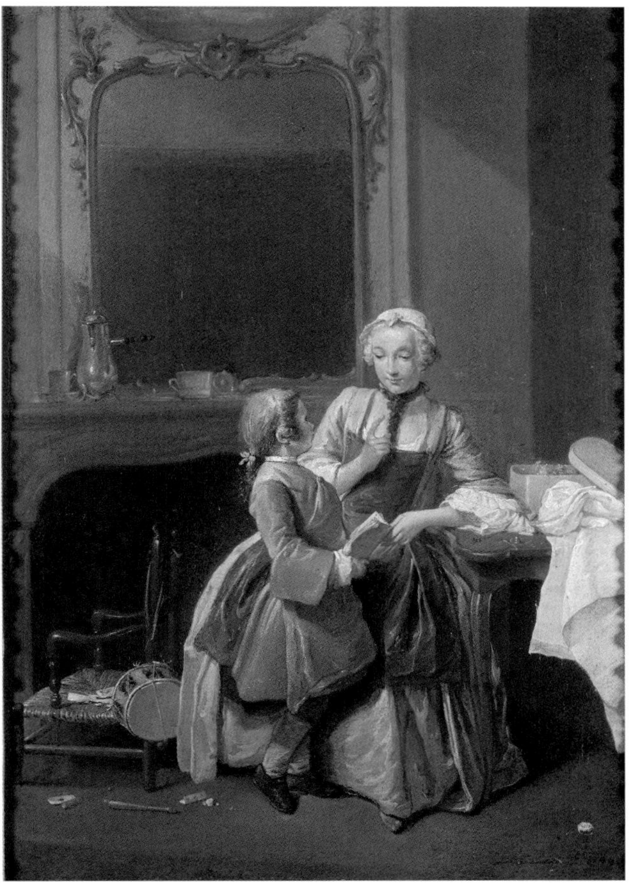

2.49. OPPOSITE
Jean-Siméon Chardin, *The Governess*, 1738. Oil on canvas. National Gallery of Canada, Ottawa.

2.50. ABOVE
Louis Aubert, *The Reading Lesson*, 1740. Oil on panel. Musée de Picardie, Amiens.

appearance on the canvas may be likened to the introjected visions of the maternal corpus, to negative hallucinations, in Green's sense of the term. The notion captures their status as visual forms given to the perception of absence that consistently marks these figures as withdrawn, distracted, or split off from their contexts and from themselves. It accounts for their spectral appearance, enhanced by Chardin's propensity to represent his figures in white or light-colored clothes, their bodily stasis, and their inexpressive physiognomies. If they may be called hallucinations, it is then precisely in the negative sense: not because they are vividly, exceedingly present in vision, but because they are only residually there.

In paintings in which these apparitional figures are shown to interact with children, negativity defines the affect of the depicted situation and also its compositional structure. For in these interactions—the mother reproaching her daughter; the governess scolding the boy in her care (fig. 2.49)—the women are shown discontent, the children resistant, the negotiations they conduct unresolved. The protagonists of these paintings appear at once connected by a physical object—the embroidered fabric held by the daughter and spreading on the mother's lap; the brush used by the governess to dust off the boy's hat—and set apart, the split between them underscored by the background motifs, such as the folding screen in *The Diligent Mother*, or the door jamb in *The Governess*. These motifs help situate the principal characters in their separate spaces, but they also suggest a potential reversibility of their respective positions. In *The Diligent Mother*, the motif of the screen, both unfolding and, with its last flap, doubling over in reverse, evokes, not unlike a Möbius strip, a possibility of a back-and-forth movement between the mother and her daughter. In *The Governess*, the door jamb serves as a vertical axis along which the figures' positions may be reversed, the door wing swung open enhancing, by its movement, their potential reversibility.[175] (The particularity of Chardin's axial, hieratic, and potentially reversible arrangement of figures is the more evident in comparison to another depiction of a governess with a child, *The Reading Lesson*, painted contemporaneously by Louis Aubert [fig. 2.50].) What I am suggesting is that Chardin's scenes of child formation are visually articulated as a relational structure revolving around a hiatus or a split that sets the protagonists of these scenes apart while also suggesting the incompleteness of their separation, that is, their continuous codependence. Both thematically and structurally, *The Diligent Mother* and *The Governess* testify to the link between the visual and affective negativity of the maternal figure and the problem of separation evoked by the tense, unresolved relation between a mother (or caretaker) and a child.

Taken as a whole, the scenarios of domestic life staged in Chardin's genre scenes are inscribed by phantoms of a subject in the process of separation. I propose that this process has something to do with the painter's own separation—not from the object, as in his early still lifes, as much as from a certain type of representation of the object, the still life. If, for Chardin, as we have learned earlier, still life was never a merely imitative exercise but a product of his repeated attempts to situate himself as a painting subject in the at-once material and imaginary world of the object, his engagement with human figures brought to the fore the question of this subject's own visual form, its visual intelligibility. That this was so had to do with Chardin's particular working methods, which were related to the nature of his training.

Since, unlike Boucher, Chardin did not receive a formal artistic education, he lacked extensive schooling in the representation of the human body. We

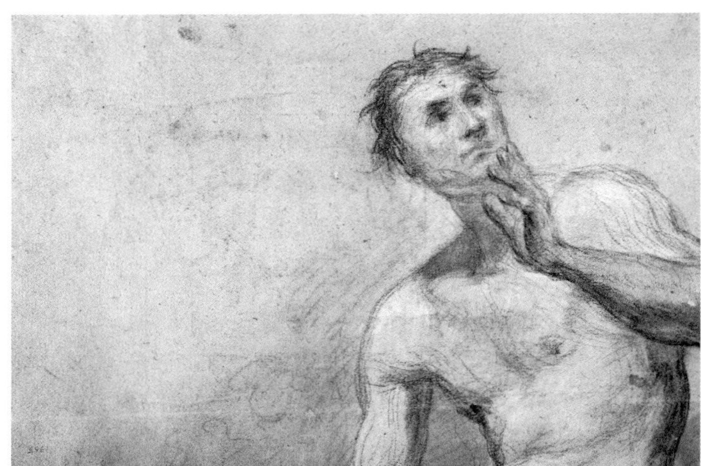

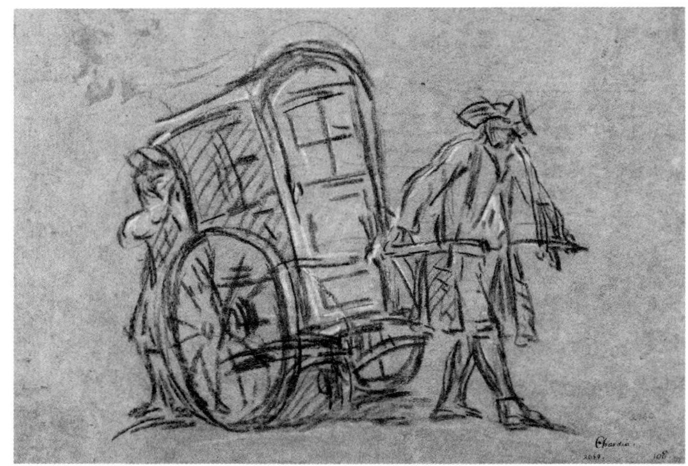

2.51.
Jean-Siméon Chardin, *Male Nude*, ca. 1720. Drawing. Nationalmuseum, Stockholm.

2.52.
Jean-Siméon Chardin, *The Sedan Chair* (recto of fig. 2.51), ca. 1720. Black and white chalk on thick buff-colored handmade paper. Nationalmuseum, Stockholm.

are told that he did not have enough opportunities to draw from the life model in the studio of the history painter, Pierre-Jacques Cazes, with whom he took private lessons, as Cazes did not pose models often for lack of money.[176] Although recently uncovered documents suggest that Chardin also attended drawing classes at the Academy—most likely through Cazes's protection—and even won some term prizes for his results, nothing indicates that he pursued a full course of drawing instruction.[177] Moreover, Chardin did not take the drawing courses until he was twenty or twenty-one years old, that is, relatively late in life, given that the usual age for students to begin such instruction was seven or eight.[178] This meant that the painter lacked the sustained exposure to the human body that young students at the Academy had over several years: first by copying from prints and drawings of old masters, then by drawing from plaster casts of bodily fragments (*la bosse*), and finally working daily for two hours with a live model.[179]

The tentative quality of Chardin's early male nude drawing, now in the Nationalmuseum, Stockholm, gives us some sense of the shortcomings in his training and his shaky figural beginnings in Cazes's studio (fig. 2.51). The indecision evident in the multiplying outlines of the model's left shoulder, the disproportionate, awkwardly drawn hand, the anemic, tapering torso—a result of inadequate mastery of foreshortening—all signal the young Chardin's lack of anatomical knowledge and his inexperience as a draftsman.[180] The recto of the same sheet contains a sketch for an early work, the *Surgeon's Shopsign*, that, while drawn with a certain panache, displays a similar degree of anatomical incertitude—notice especially his fumbling with the right arm and hand of the porter holding the rods of the sedan (fig. 2.52).

Another important consequence of Chardin's limited training was that he lacked an interiorized bodily image of himself. The prolonged, multistaged training at the Academy was a process of not only artistic but also subjective formation. By the repeated recreation of bodily form, students not only acquired a capacity to draw a human body but also internalized its image—first in fragments, and then as an integrated whole—which helped them imagine their own. Through what we would now call the psychic mechanism of introjection, an academic conception of the body entered the students' minds, establishing not only an internalized repertory of forms on which they could draw in their subsequent careers but also their personal imaginary, a bodily *imago* to which they could relate their own corporeal existence. The very young age at which they began their artistic training made its formative function also in this sense the more propitious. What I am suggesting is that the repeated exposure to, and mimetic engagement with, artistic representations of the body allowed these young individuals to develop a self-image as an embodied form. This was one of the ways in which academic training contributed to the young artists' personal formation. While we have a good understanding of the Academy's role in forging a new professional identity of the artist over the course of the eighteenth century, we have not yet fully examined how this institution shaped the artist's personal identity.[181] Yet there is in this period evidence that points in this direction. Diderot, for one, recognized the role of interiorization in pedagogical experience when he described the contrived figures that academic instruction instilled in students' minds as the "limp phantoms" impeding their imagination and creativity.[182] (Note Diderot's choice of a hallucinatory term.)

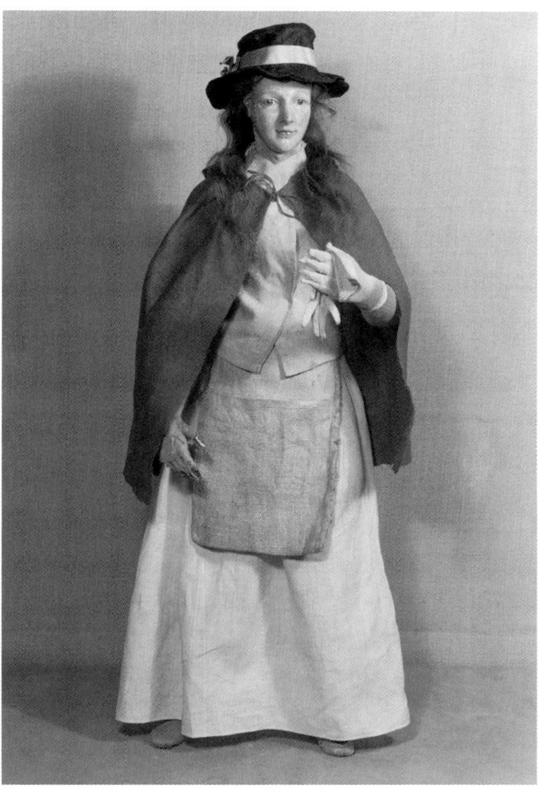

2.53.
Lay figure in women's clothes belonging to Louis-François Roubiliac. Museum of London.

One can say that Chardin's lacunar artistic formation installed *an absence* at the core of the painter's practice and of his self—not the phantom of the training routine that Diderot saw haunting the academic artist, but, on the contrary, a ghost of its lack.[183] It is this ghost that the painter confronted when, turning to genre subjects, he engaged with the human figure. How did he go about painting it?

To begin with, instead of professional models, Chardin used the members of his household and extended family—the maids, his sister-in-law, her children, his first wife, and later, after her death, his second wife, and possibly other female family members who lived in the house at different points in time.[184] The proximity of his studio on rue du Four to the household kitchen facilitated his use of women working there as models for his genre scenes. While painters have always been known to use their family members, wives, or lovers for models, Chardin's exclusive dependence on the female inhabitants of his house was unusual, insofar as it brought real-life supporters who cared for him in different ways, both affective and practical, into the figural support of his aesthetic project.[185]

The stasis of their appearance may have been due to Chardin's use of the intermediary of the lay figure. Ubiquitous in artists' studios since the Renaissance, these smaller than life size, fully articulated human figures made of wood, wax, or stuffed upholstery were a convenient substitute for the live model.[186] Their bodies often androgynous, they could serve as models for depicting both men and women with just a change of clothes. One surviving example from around the mid-eighteenth century, which belonged to the artist Louis-François Roubiliac, has two sets of male and female costumes complete with wigs, hats, and shoes to fit it (fig. 2.53).[187] While we have no direct evidence that Chardin owned a mannequin, the consistent immobility, repetitious poses, and expressionless faces of his figures suggest that he used one. What corroborates this suggestion is the exceptionally small scale of most of his figural paintings, with the protagonist of, say, the *Attentive Nurse*, barely the size of Roubiliac's mannequin.[188]

The most important reason for Chardin to resort to the intermediary of the lay figure, the most patient of models, would have been the unusually long time it took him to produce the shape of the human body on the canvas. For lacking the traditional preparatory means of figural representation, namely, the habit of drawing, Chardin developed an idiosyncratic procedure of painting directly on the canvas (as we have witnessed in the *Blind Beggar*), conjuring the figure up out of nothing, from within an empty frame by means of purely chromatic suggestion.[189] Devoid of the armature of drawing underneath, his figures materialized on the surface of his paintings unbound by lines, through the process of slow build-up of pigment, its modeling accomplished by the gradation of color and by varying the physical thickness of paint. This was not, let us note, a procedure that one could learn at the Academy, where color was not taught except in the private ateliers of its members. It was closer to the tricks of the trade that were being passed on in the master painters' workshops at the guild school where Chardin got his license. His habit of mixing chalk with oil paint, a procedure that thickens the white pigment and, when mixed with oil, renders it more transparent than using a traditional gum or glue binder, was one of the tricks he could have learned there.[190] It allowed Chardin to obtain subtle textural effects: superimposing the films of pigment on top of one another, he was able to build up a complexly textured surface, often by dragging a loaded brush over layers of paint as they dried out, as witnessed in the bonnet of the *Attentive Nurse* (fig. 2.54).[191] The bonneted head of a woman in another painting, the *Housekeeper*, offers us a glimpse underneath the top layer of paint, into

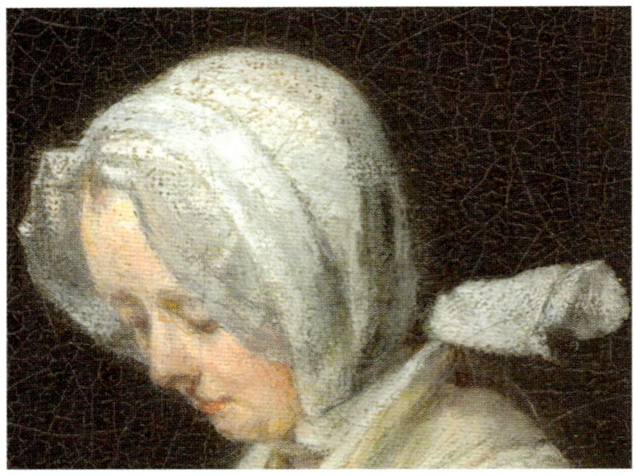

the complex stratification of pigment revealed by the abrasions the painting suffered due to excessive exposure to light (fig. 2.55).[192] It is from this material thickness, the invisible but palpable depth of the canvas, that Chardin's spectral figures emerge, like chromatic ghosts, into view.

This uncommon effect of Chardin's paintings was most eloquently remarked upon by Pierre Estève in his *Dialogues sur les Arts*. A series of imaginary conversations in the tradition exemplified by Roger de Piles's *Dialogue sur le coloris* (1699), on which Estève drew, the *Dialogues* restaged the older debate on the relative merits of drawing versus color for a new purpose of reassessing artistic education in France.[193] Chardin featured in them prominently because Estève saw his work as an alternative model to the drawing-based conception of art promoted by the Academy. His views were expressed in the *Dialogues* by a fictitious Peruvian painter who challenged the opinions of a French *amateur* promoting the idea of painting founded in the "science of drawing." According to the Peruvian, the direct imitation of the visible world that constituted the mission of painting could only be accomplished by the means of color rather than drawing. Addressing his interlocutor, the Peruvian asserted:

> *When studying nature, I observed only the roundness of shapes ["la rondeur de chairs"] and never the distinct contours enclosing them. What do you mean, then, . . . by the science of drawing? Could one represent a body by other means than the gradation of colors that give volume to its parts? In a beautiful picture I see figures that have volume but are not contained by lines and that, while maintaining their roundness, retreat, so to speak,* underneath what is visible.[194]

Pointing to the irrelevance of line for the representation of nature, the Peruvian extolled Chardin's power of chromatic suggestion—the "beautiful picture" referred to Chardin's work—which made his figures appear to hover on the threshold of the visible. The French *amateur*, for his part, appreciated the piquant effects of Chardin's method but deemed his art to be "low" in comparison to the conceptually more elevated, drawing-based practice of a history painter. Committed to the depiction of common things and people, Chardin was, in his view, unable to imagine, contrast, or compose, and thus to enter the higher aesthetic register of painting. Moreover, the *amateur* dismissed Chardin's transcription of contingent effects as uneconomical and too slow.[195] In the end, the Peruvian painter prevailed by demonstrating the superiority of Chardin's method and formulating a program of educational reform based on the model of his chromatic practice. Referring to the Academy as a "republic of monkeys," the Peruvian proposed to found an alternative establishment offering education in color, the most natural means of representing the visible world, and, moreover, insofar as color engaged the senses rather than the intellect, a universally appealing one.[196]

For us, the significance of Estève's assessment of Chardin's chromatic method lies specifically in the connection he establishes between what I have called the hallucinatory appearance of Chardin's figures and his rejection of line and contour in favor of color.

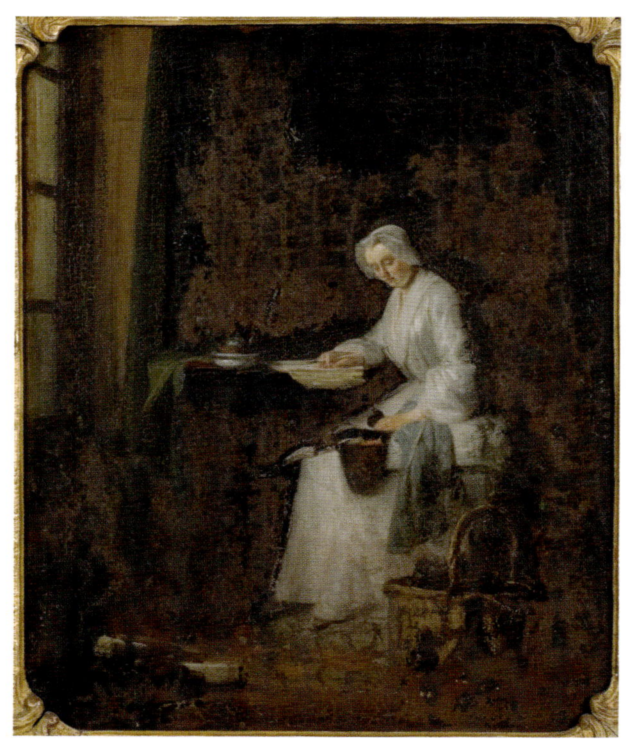

2.54. LEFT
Jean-Siméon Chardin, *Attentive Nurse*, detail of fig. 2.38.

2.55. BELOW
Jean-Siméon Chardin, *Housekeeper*, 1747. Oil on canvas. Nationalmuseum, Stockholm.

2.56. OPPOSITE TOP
Jean-Siméon Chardin, *La Serinette* (*Lady with a Bird-Organ*), ca. 1751. Oil on canvas (lined). The Frick Collection, New York.

2.57. OPPOSITE BOTTOM
X-ray radiograph of Jean-Siméon Chardin. *La Serinette* (*Lady with a Bird-Organ*) (fig. 2.56).

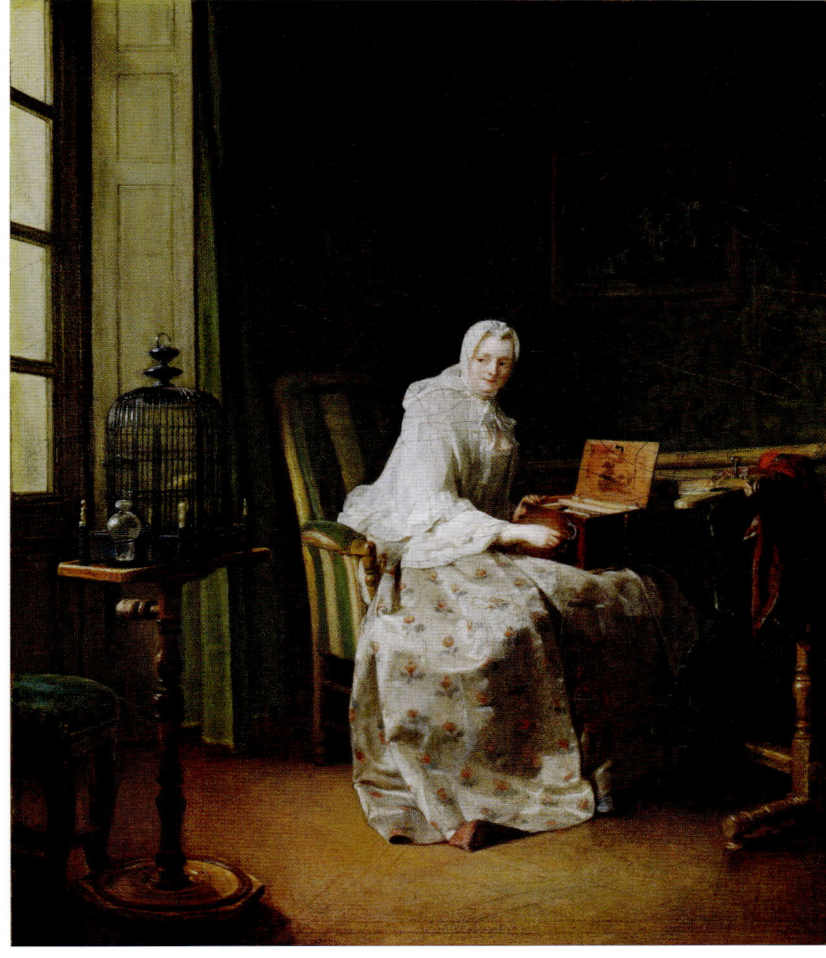

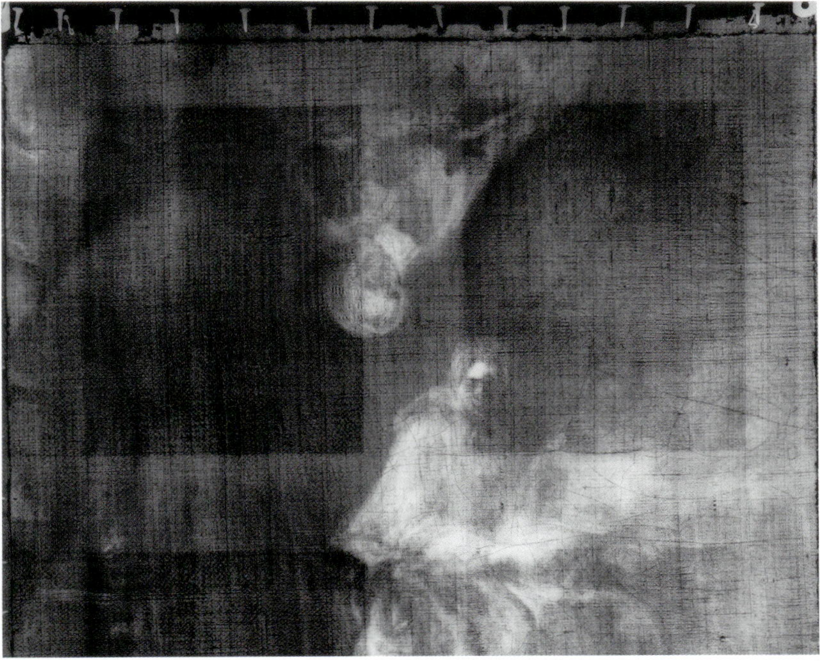

It is the painter's painstakingly slow process of building up "la rondeur de chairs" through the application of layers of pigment on the surface of the canvas that produced, as Estève recognized, the impression of the figure's hesitant, incomplete passage into the sphere of the visible, an effect evident throughout his figural oeuvre. For Estève, this mode of appearance was closest to how we see things in reality, leading him to support the chromatic method and dismiss drawing as "unnatural" and irrelevant for artistic training and practice. But in focusing on its effects, Estève did not consider the *painter's* experience of his chromatic procedure.

We have evidence that while generating such evocative effects, Chardin's chromatic method also posed some problems. One was that it rendered the figure elusive for the painter himself, making the process of securing its presence on the canvas challenging. The extent of the challenge may be gauged from an X-ray radiograph of Chardin's last genre painting, *La Serinette* (*Lady with a Bird-Organ*) (figs. 2.56 and 2.57). Granting us indeed a peak "underneath the visible," the radiograph provides material proof that the practice of painting directly on the canvas, without using a preparatory drawing, exposed Chardin to extensive and time-consuming corrections.[197] It appears that at first he made a false move and was obliged to turn the canvas upside down and start anew. Even then, it took him some time before he settled on the position of the figure, shifting it from the right to the center. Clearly, even if the painter resorted to the intermediary of the mannequin, as he seems to have done in some cases in order to relieve his models from prolonged sittings, it could not stabilize his process of transcribing the mannequin's shape onto the canvas. The radiograph exposes the extreme volatility of the figure in Chardin's pictorial realm, the ghostliness of the X-ray image enhancing this effect.

This elusiveness of the figure must have had not only practical consequences for the painter's studio practice but also psychological ones affecting the way in which the painter's own body "figured" in the painting process. We may speculate that Chardin's habit of direct negotiation of the surface of the canvas as an arena on which, as if from nowhere, the figure was expected to appear—a habit documented by our radiograph—generated a peculiar dynamic of *self-involvement* in his genre practice. Because this practice was unmediated by preparatory work, it repeatedly threw the painter back onto his own resources, that is, onto his own body not only as a physical tool but also as an imaginary basis of corporeal representation. It caught him in a relation of mutual dependence on the figure, one that involved a continuous back-and-forth, imaginary interaction between his own body and the body he was fleshing out on the canvas. On the one hand, it involved imagining the figure in relation to how he imagined himself, in rapport with his own body as a physical and psychic boundary mobilized to retrace another corpus on the canvas. On the other hand, it generated a reverse dependence of the painter on the figure.

The radiograph of *La Serinette* offers us a glimpse into what may be called the "inner life" of Chardin's genre paintings, that is, both the history of their making and its subjective implications. A complex morphology of figural noncoincidence, the X-ray image represents—if inadvertently—what was at the core of Chardin's painting of genre: the self's pursuit of its image, a form of individuality in search of embodiment.

This brings us to the question of the import of Chardin's turn to genre scenes. The discussion of the paintings offered so far suggests that if the figure came to perform a crucial function in Chardin's pictorial realm, it was not only as the token of the professional advancement he aspired to but also, more importantly, as the means through which he could reimagine himself in relation to the professional and institutional realm of painting, in particular in relation to still life. What was at stake was not simply leaving the painting of objects behind—the very persistence of still life motifs as key actors in his genre scenes belies that—but of repositioning oneself in relation to it. The question of acquiring new representational skills entailed by Chardin's move to a new type of image proved inseparable from the question of acquiring a new self-image, as a painter.

This is the complex mission that the female figures in his paintings perform. They are not only the markers of the painter's ambition but also forms through which he tries to situate himself in relation to the painted object—the hallucinatory representations of the painter himself. To put it differently, the women in his canvases are the *framing structures* for the emergence of the figure as both the new subject of Chardin's work and Chardin himself as a painting subject. This is precisely what the painter did not possess in the exercise of his "first talent" as a still life painter: the sense of a distinct place, the embodied position from which to undertake the task of imitation, a sense one arrives at by recognizing the boundary separating one's own painting body from the painted object. It was this lacking sense of the imaginary confines of the body and self that produced the confusion manifest in Chardin's earlier work. (For example, his "blind" groping of the object, the logic of inside/out that governed the object's appearance on the representational stage.) Offering him the missing sense of bodily contours, the figure provided him with the first, negative frame of the physical and psychic sense of the self, ultimately producing, as we shall see, the conditions of possibility for the emergence of the painter's own body into the visual field. It is this sense of physical and subjective emergence as if from within an empty frame that the figures themselves enact in paintings such as the *Attentive Nurse*, with their hazy, soft-contoured silhouettes gradually coming into view from within the dark background. Luminous and withdrawn amid their objects—which are also the objects of the painter, the props of his still lifes—they embody the possibility of representing a whole person and also imagining oneself as an embodied whole—the very possibility of the painting subject's visual and subjective existence.

—·—

Inasmuch as this process of "shepherding" the figure into view confronted Chardin with its volatility, it could not but bring up the specter of the painter's own elusiveness to himself, his tenuous hold on his own self-image. It opened up a dimension of blankness, or negativity, in his experience of himself as a painting subject, a quality with which he in turn endowed his figures. The painter's negative self-experience in the process of representing the figure may account for the subliminal aggression that we witness in some of Chardin's genre scenes.

Consider the knife-wielding *Turnip Scraper* sitting listlessly beside a blood-stained cutting block with a butcher's cleaver driven ominously into it (fig. 2.58). It is not clear what the object of this violence is—except for the blood traces, the cutting block remains conspicuously empty—nor, for that matter, who is its subject. The manifest passivity of the knife-wielding maid puts her function as an "executioner" in brackets. Aggression is also hinted at in the *Attentive Nurse* —probably painted as a pendant to the *Ratisseuse*—though it is barely discernible, the figure more ambiv-

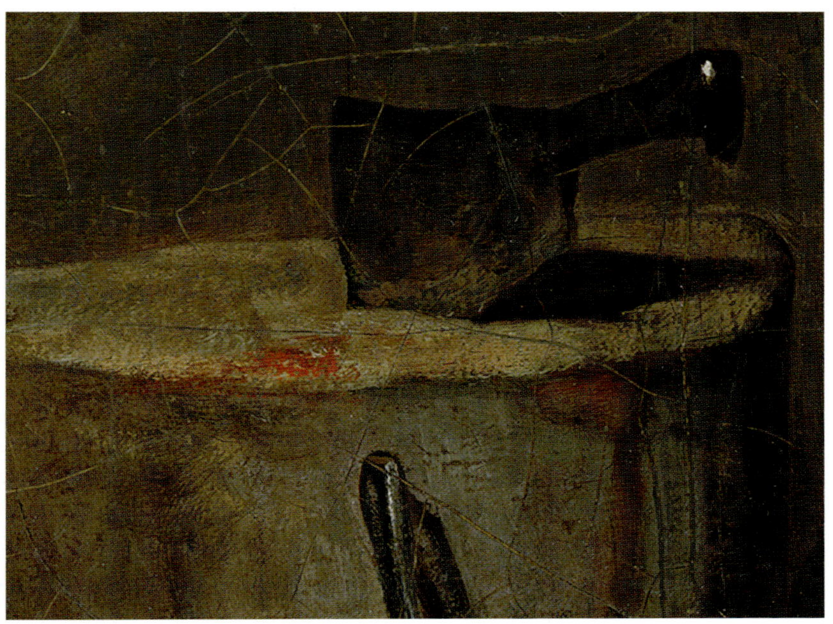

2.58.
Jean-Siméon Chardin, *Turnip Scraper*, detail of fig. 2.43.

alent.[198] The nurse's pose and gesture epitomize this ambivalence, conveying both tenderness, in the way she is holding the egg, and a capacity for a rougher kind of handling. Her touch—pinching the egg to get the shell off—is in itself a bit ambiguous, a kind of cruel caress. Another comparison with the sketch for this painting (see fig. 2.39) makes it clear how deliberate the painter's choice of it was. He exchanged the gesture of the woman's hand tapping the egg with the spoon for one involving a more direct contact between her fingers and the egg's surface.

The comparison also allows us to appreciate the deliberate choice of the painter's own touch, his substitution of the fluid, creamy strokes with which he rendered the figure of the nurse in the sketch for the highly textured and at times coarser treatment he used to secure her shape in the final version of the canvas. Drier, occasionally patchy, in places harshly rubbed in, elsewhere dragged across the visible layers of underpainting, it is a rougher version of the "blind touch" that became Chardin's hallmark ever since the chevalier de Brunaubois-Montador in 1738 dubbed it admiringly a "brutal and rugged" manner ("du brut, du raboteux").[199] In the parts of the nurse's torso and especially her bonnet, you can almost hear the dry brush scraping the surface of the canvas. It is as if what the nurse was doing to the egg, so too the painter did to the surface of the canvas: she pinches and peels, he scratches and scrapes. This impression of reciprocity of touch is augmented by the formal and chromatic affinity between the oval shapes of the egg and the woman's head, both rendered in Chardin's signature chalky hues. These tactile, chromatic, and formal affinities suggest an analogous, and reversible, relation between the painted figure and the painter—comparable to the reciprocal and reversible relation between the female figure and the child in some of his other paintings—a relation also marked by ambivalence evident on the level of form and (brutal) handling.

This subliminal brutality may be linked to the combination of dependence on the figure and its "unreliability"—anatomical, compositional, both due to the unreliability of Chardin's training—in the painter's experience of it. It has been observed that in psychic life, the perception of an unreliable object may cause the aggression of the subject against itself, triggering a kind of deadly narcissism, a self's cruel turning upon itself. For insofar as the subject identifies with the deceiving object, it directs its anger, caused by the object's deception, onto itself.[200] One can say that, in Chardin's work, we witness a similar kind of phenomenon.

It is precisely such an ambivalent rapport that we find thematized in *La Serinette*. An interior scene of domestic pastime, this painting was also, as it has been noted, a meta-commentary on art making: an image of the mechanical, repetition-based training associated with the Academy.[201] The canary that this lady teaches how to sing by cranking a bird organ may be seen to allude to those protracted exercises in imitation that eighteenth-century aspiring artists had to withstand to become academic professionals. As such, *La Serinette* may be related to more overt examples of the iconography of artistic instruction in Chardin's oeuvre, such as *The Drawing Lesson* (fig. 2.59). The recurrence of this imagery in Chardin's output is, as I have argued elsewhere, intriguing, given that it represents the kind of practice Chardin himself had only to a limited degree.[202] Far from being straightforward records of instruction, these are imaginary "scenes" seeking, in different ways, to position Chardin's own practice in relation to the training envisioned in them.

It is also an image of artistic education inflected by Chardin's personal experiences that we witness in *La Serinette*. Here the instructional scene of confrontation with the figure has been staged in a domestic context, the privileged locus of Chardin's own practice, with his own wife serving as a model for its protagonist. The role its female protagonist performs is ambivalent. Insofar as the bird in the cage is a surrogate of an art student submitted to a training

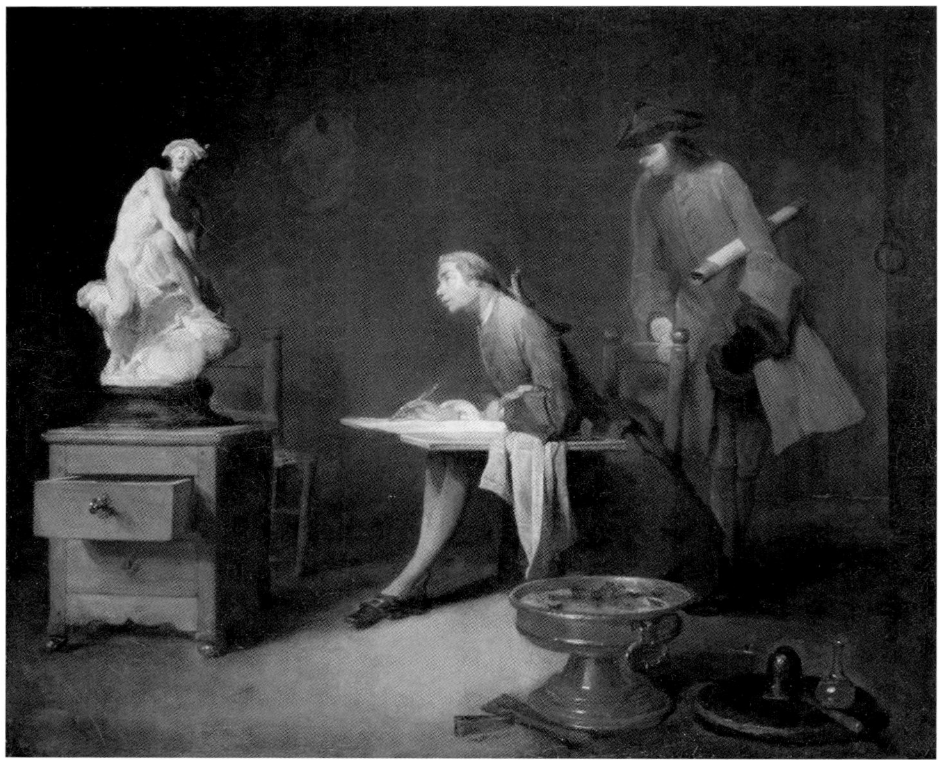

routine, the woman represents a student's model, her apparitional whiteness not unlike the spectral figure of Pigalle's *Mercury* serving a similar purpose in Chardin's earlier *Drawing Lesson*. But the woman also acts as the Academy in domestic disguise. As such, she appears to be both accommodating, coaxing her pet to performance, and merciless, her activity revealing the tedium and even violence inherent in the kind of training that submits the young artists, like birds trapped in a cage, to the torturous task of quasi-mechanical reproduction.[203] The sly smile on the woman's face hints at her awareness of the dubious nature of her occupation.

Yet if the woman personifies the Academy, she is also the result of a performance that blatantly ignored it. Rendered in Chardin's signature whites, she is a chromatic manifesto of the painter's nonacademic (contour-less) figurality. But while displaying Chardin's customary technical bravura, she also bears traces of the painter's troubles with figural representation. One cannot miss the inaccuracies of her anatomy, her head being disproportionally small, and her feet, attached rather arbitrarily to the hem of her dress, seemingly discontinuous with the rest of the body discernible under her gown's folds.[204] At once utterly suggestive and marred by evident deficiencies, this white apparition may be seen as a kind of *negative hallucination* of the Academy, simultaneously a figure of the painter's defiance of academic training and the unintended testimony to the effects of its absence in his work.

But the bird trainer is also a figure of the domesticity to which Chardin devoted his art, a symptom of the painter's immersion in his own household and its inhabitants. As such, she represents the importance of women in Chardin's aesthetic enterprise but also, in the role he assigns her—the sly and subtly cruel trainer—the ambivalence in his reliance on femininity, the negative dimension of his dependence on it. The bird owner epitomizes Chardin's strange romance with the figure—which is, to a large extent, a romance with himself. *La Serinette* offers an ingenious, layered vision of Chardin's complicated and ambivalent rapport with the institutional and domestic parameters of his practice. Repeating the combination of figure + still life that constituted the basic composition of Chardin's genre scenes, *La Serinette* hints also at the ambivalent results of Chardin's experiment with genre. While the cage spells out the sense of entrapment that may be associated with academic training and with a certain mode of representation—still life—the woman points to the ambivalent function of the figure—and of femininity—in the painter's practice as a means of both emancipation and constraint.

2.59. ABOVE
Jean-Siméon Chardin, *The Drawing Lesson*, Salon 1753. Oil on canvas. Tokyo Fuji Art Museum.

2.60. OPPOSITE
Jean-Siméon Chardin, *The House of Cards*, ca. 1736–37. Oil on canvas. National Gallery, London, bequeathed by Mrs. Edith Cragg, as part of the John Webb Bequest, 1925.

THE SUBJECT

But what is it to exist?

—Encyclopédie

A young boy leans gently against a table.[205] Holding his breath, his cheeks flushed, his eyes cast down, he slowly places a card on top of his fragile construction (see fig. 2.60). The presence of the two board game tokens lying on the table emphasizes the hazard involved in his performance. He, though, seems unaware of it. Dressed with manifest propriety, in a long jacket with a blue velvet collar unfastened for comfort and a freshly washed shirt, his hair tied neatly in a ponytail, the boy appears calm and concentrated. Traced in a thin line of light yellow pigment, the rim of his hat forms an arabesque loop that, while helping to describe the complex volume of the *tricorne*, also highlights the sense of self-containment conveyed by its wearer's inscrutable face.

Utter absorption also characterizes the child who, standing by his table, watches the spinning toy he has just launched, his two fingers still grasping the absent object (see fig. 2.61). Transfixed by its movement, the boy is oblivious to the instruments of learning—his books, the inkwell, the scroll of writing paper on his table, and the porte-crayon sticking out of its open drawer—that clearly cannot compete with the attraction of the game. His eyes tied by an invisible thread to the spinning object, the boy is enthralled by this exercise of chance.

The House of Cards (fig. 2.60) and *Child with a Top* (fig. 2.61) belong to distinct group of paintings in Chardin's oeuvre. Representing children amusing themselves in various ways, these paintings differ in character from his depictions of women performing

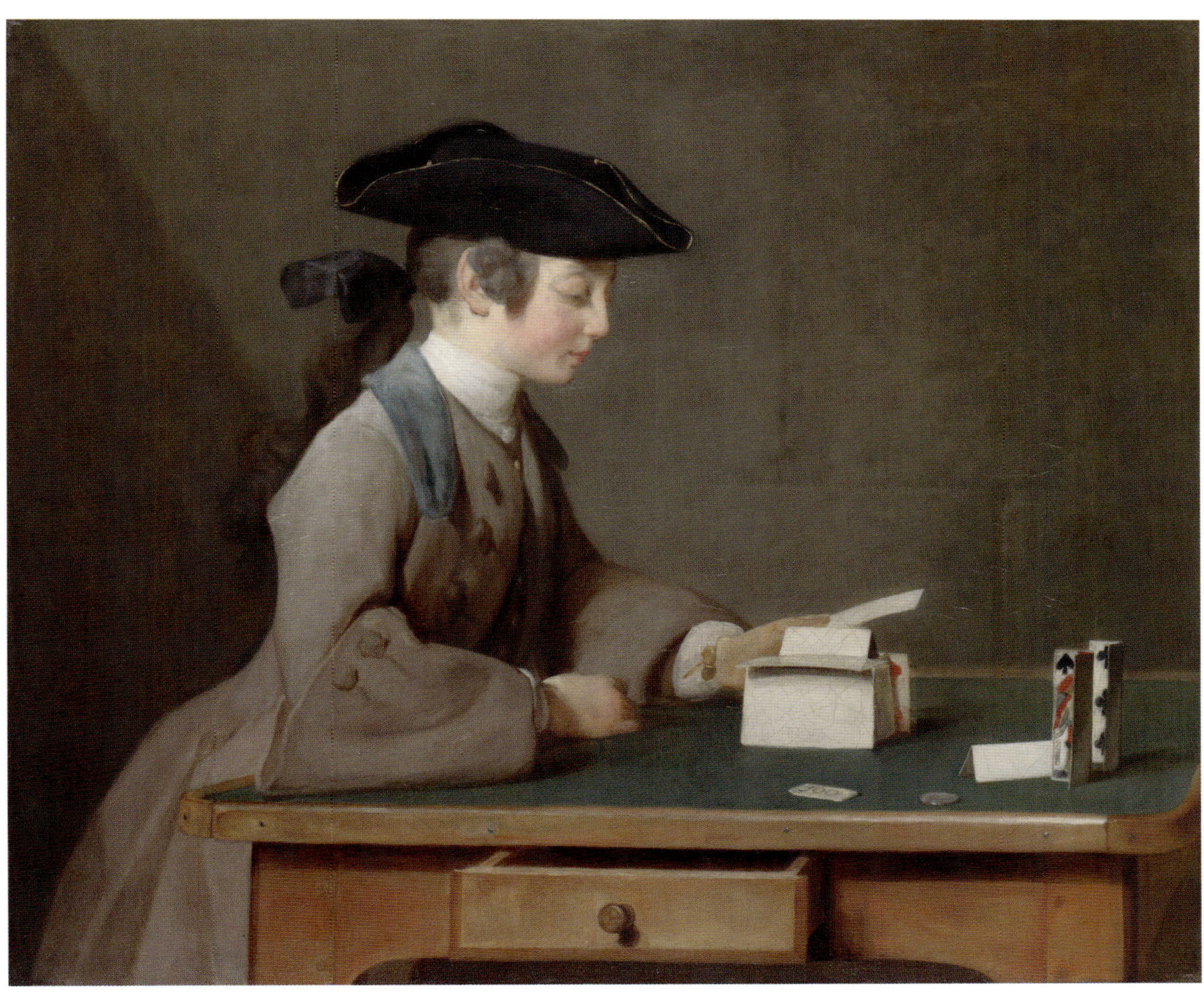

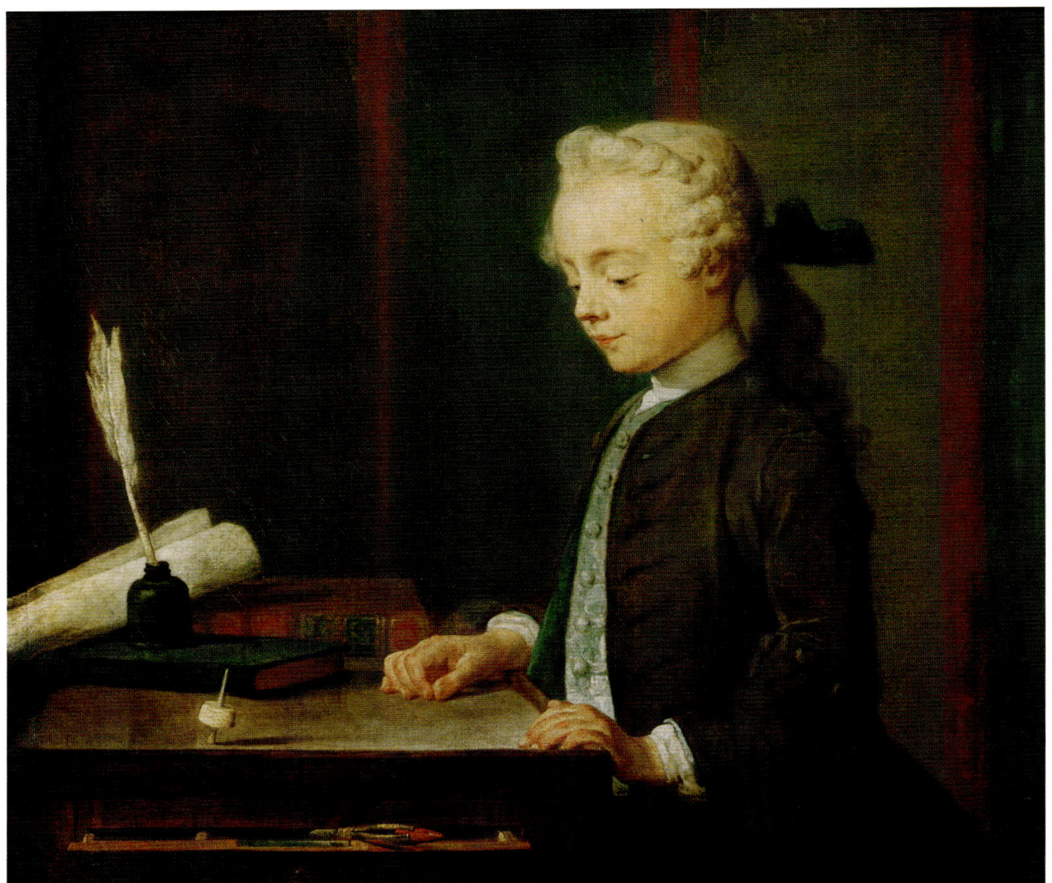

2.61.
Jean-Siméon Chardin, *Child with a Top*, ca. 1737–38. Oil on canvas. Musée du Louvre, Paris.

various household chores. Significantly larger in scale, the figures of children are endowed with a subjective presence that stands in contrast to the effect of evacuation that characterizes his paintings of women shown momentarily detached or distracted from their tasks.

And yet one feels that, executed in the period between 1733 and 1738, that is, contemporaneously with the images of women, these representations of children *are* related to those of women from which some of the children's figures may have been directly derived. Take, for example, *Soap Bubbles* (fig. 2.62), whose protagonist is but an older version of the boy in *Washerwoman* (see fig. 2.44). What, though, is the nature of this relation? What can these depictions of children tell us about Chardin as a painter of genre scenes?

To begin with, who are these absorptive youths? Are they little masters, as opposed to the female servants that Chardin's genre scenes, especially those of the early 1730s, represent? Or are they usurpers of their masters' pleasures, as may be the case of the boy wearing an apron in the Washington, DC, version of the *House of Cards* who, it has been claimed, interrupts his cleaning chores to play cards left by the others on the table (fig. 2.63).[206] The identity of some of these individuals *is* known, for at least two of the paintings were intended as portraits: the London version of *The House of Cards* (1736–37) depicts the son of Monsieur Lenoir, a Parisian furniture maker and Chardin's close friend, while the *Child with a Top* (ca. 1737–38) portrays Auguste-Gabriel, the younger son of another friend of the painter, the jeweler Godefroy, whose older son Chardin had painted some years earlier. Yet if these paintings are portraits, they eschew the traditional portrait formula, *en face*, which Chardin adopted for the portrait of the older Godefroy but did not repeat in other images of children. Engrossed in their banal yet irresistible distractions, Chardin's "sitters" do not bother to look at us, nor, for that matter, do they care about being looked at, entirely immersed as they are in their activities.

Unorthodox as portraits, these images also have little in common with other depictions of children in the genre painting of the period.[207] For if they inscribe themselves within the iconographic tradition of "children's games," they depart from it by de-emphasizing narrative. The sense of self-presence and self-sufficiency exuded by Chardin's remarkably immobile protagonists—this immobility being perhaps a side effect of using a lay figure—stems

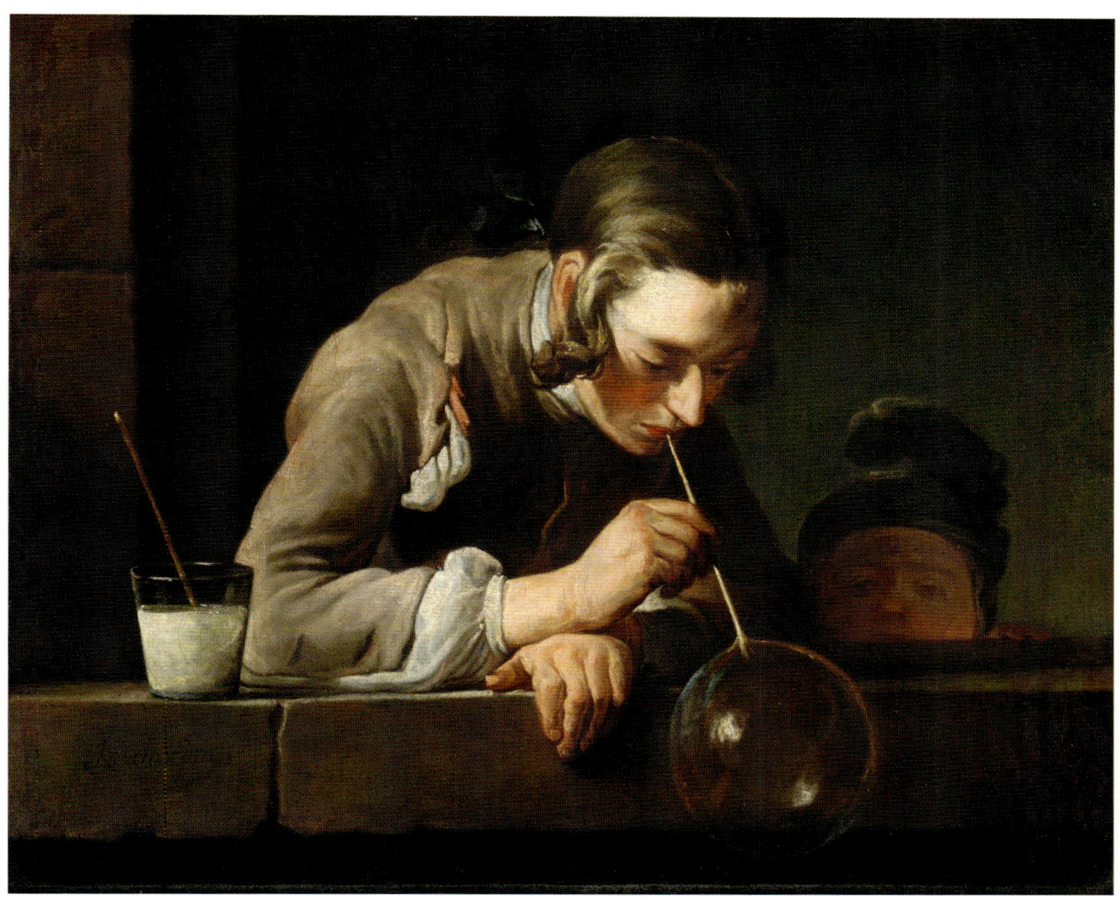

2.62.
Jean-Siméon Chardin, *Soap Bubbles*, ca. 1733–34. Oil on canvas. Los Angeles County Museum of Art, Gift of The Ahmanson Foundation.

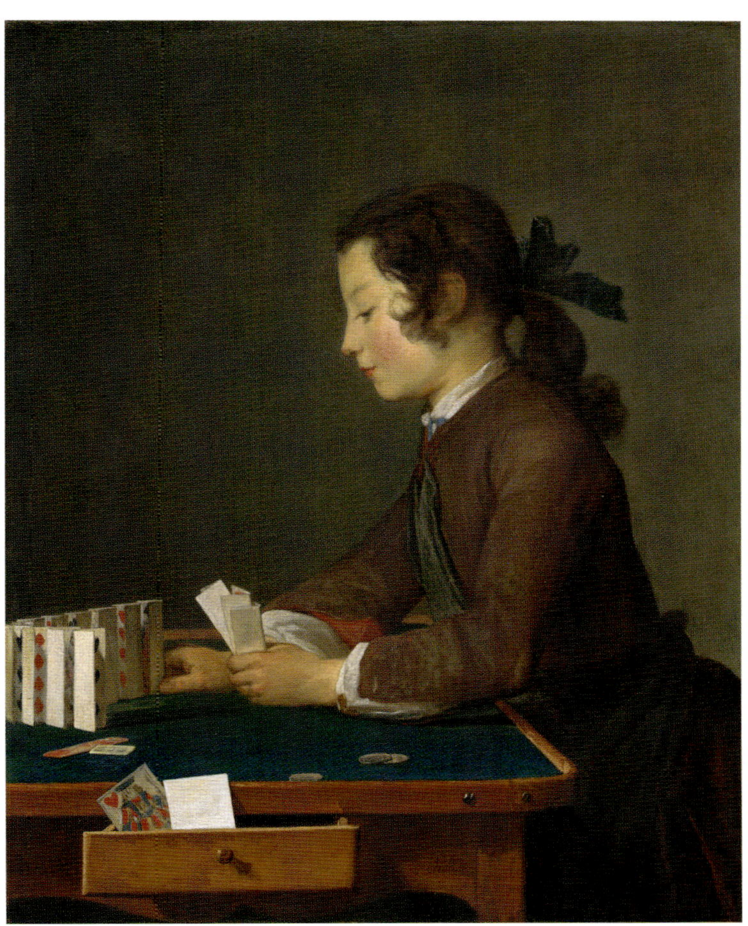

2.63.
Jean-Siméon Chardin, *House of Cards*, 1737. Oil on canvas. National Gallery, Washington, DC, Andrew W. Mellon Collection.

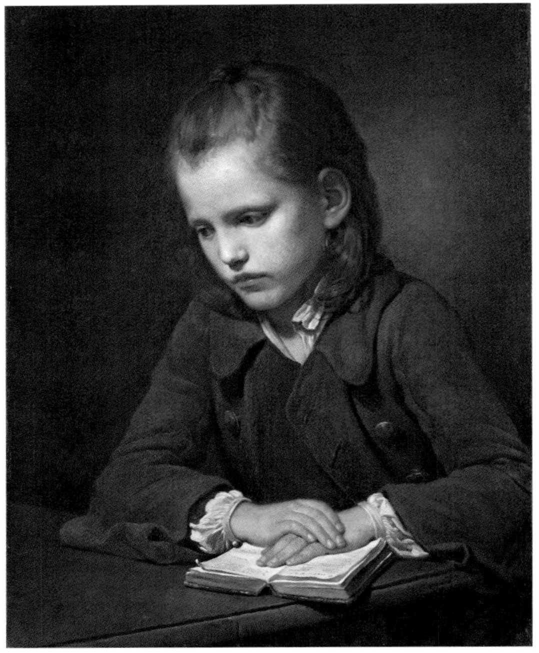

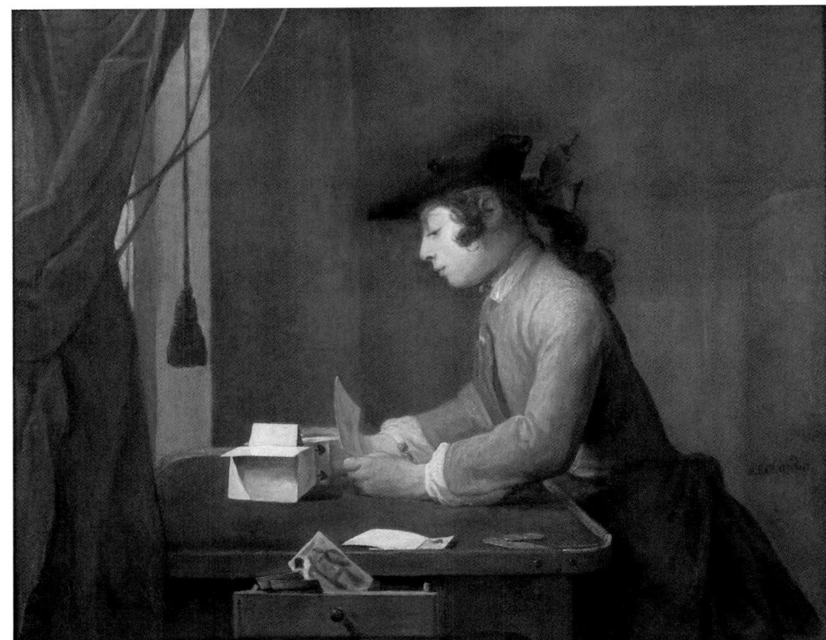

2.64.
Jean-Baptiste Greuze, *Schoolboy Learning His Lesson*, 1757. Oil on canvas. National Galleries of Scotland, Edinburgh.

2.65.
Jean-Siméon Chardin, *Boy Building a House of Cards*, 1735. Oil on canvas. On loan from Rothschild Family Trust since 2007, Waddesdon Manor, Buckinghamshire.

also from the absence of a larger story or discursive context that framed the appearance of children in the work of Chardin's contemporaries.[208] For example, although Greuze was evidently inspired by Chardin's models, he used them to different ends, as his *Schoolboy Learning His Lesson* (fig. 2.64) makes clear. Tense with the effort to memorize his lines, the body of Greuze's youth is caught in the disciplinary net of pedagogy that deprives him of the benefit of choice between work and leisure that the protagonist of Chardin's *Child with a Top* enjoys.

The uneasy fit of Chardin's images of children within both portraiture and the narrative format of genre scenes brings us to the problem of their meaning. Despite the lack of extensive critical commentary on these paintings in Chardin's time, they have been the subject of numerous and rich interpretations in the modern literature.[209] To my mind, the importance of this thematic subgroup within Chardin's output lies in their emphasis on the youths' interiority and especially on how they show the emergence of a sense of self to hinge on the subject's relation to his or her object. It is by representing these children's engagement with things that these paintings construct a certain vision of subjective self-sufficiency, a fantasy of being everything to oneself. As such, they made, in my view, a unique contribution to the cultural understanding of individuality in the eighteenth century. But they were also of crucial importance for the painter's developing sense of his own individuality. If the depictions of women in Chardin's genre scenes provided the imaginary frame for the emergence of the painter as a subject, the process of painting children offered him an altogether different, embodied mode of self-experience. How and why this became possible is what we need to explore.

Despite the different kinds of activities in which Chardin's young protagonists engage—playing cards, spinning a top, blowing bubbles—the paintings reveal some shared basic qualities. One is their strikingly rudimentary definition of space. The interiors these figures occupy are conspicuously empty, except for the basic prop on which they lean, like a table, with a few accessories necessary for the performance of their tasks. That this effect of spatial evacuation was deliberate is confirmed by comparing the London *House of Cards* with earlier versions of the same subject. As the first painting of this series, now in Waddesdon Manor, indicates, initially the boy faced a window that was eliminated in subsequent versions (fig. 2.65).[210] In the London canvas, the unadorned squared stone walls of the boy's room produce a sense of airtight austerity, an almost prison-like containment.

This carceral appearance of space reminds us of Hannah Arendt's observation that privacy, before it acquired its modern connotation of individual enrichment, "meant literally a state of being deprived of something." In ancient Greece, for example, it signified deprivation of the human capacity to participate in public life.[211] Yet in my view Chardin's depleted interiors have to do with a specific stage in the life of an individual that precedes the socializing immersion in the public sphere. They offer a setting for the most basic occupations through which a young person first begins to rehearse his relation to the world, and to himself.[212]

Playing games is one of those self-defining occupations, and those illustrated by Chardin are remarkably consistent in one respect: they all entail letting go of an object, testing to see if it will return, and thus acquiring a basic sense of mastery over it, a mastery that provides enjoyment for the depicted subject. Envisioned in these games is the young subjects' readiness to confront the contingency of the object, its unreliability—will the top remain on the table or will it roll off and disappear? Will the house of cards continue to stand when another card is added to it? What these rudimentary exercises in relating to and separating oneself from objects represent are also rehearsals in relating to and separating from oneself.

However, if the games these children play allow them repeatedly to enact their separateness from things, they also produce their intimate connection to them, a connection intriguingly registered on the bodies of the young players. In the *Soap Bubbles*, the shape of a balloon balanced on the tip of the boy's straw corresponds to that of his head, with its *bombé* hairdo and drawn-out features highlighted just like the soapy globe, while the action of bubble blowing is echoed by his white shirt sleeve puffing out from the tear in his sleeve. A similar idea is conveyed by the hand of the top-spinning boy, whose two fingers touching each other form a void that marks the absence of the toy he has just launched (fig. 2.66). It is these basic interactions with a thing, Chardin's paintings suggest, that lead to the formation of a discrete space within the self—not unlike the little gap between the boys' fingers—wherein the self can establish rapport with itself.

2.66.
Jean-Siméon Chardin, *Child with a Top*, detail of fig. 2.61.

In the eighteenth century, the key mechanism responsible for the development of this internal space was the "inner sensation," also known as the sixth sense.[213] This notion referred to what empiricist philosophy recognized as the internal sentiment on which our sense of our own existence, or, in Locke's words, "an internal infallible Perception that we *are*," depends.[214] Locke's "inner sense" was linked to the philosopher's broader recognition of the senses as the source of knowledge and of sensory experience as vital to the formation of the self. Processed very early on in France, Locke's empiricist legacy contributed to the development of sensationism that received its full articulation in Condillac's work of the late 1740s and early '50s.[215] The concept of the inner sensation was taken up by a number of mid-eighteenth-century French thinkers, among them abbé Lelarge de Lignac, who described it as a sentiment of "coexistence" with one's body," and Rousseau, who, in his *Reveries of the Solitary Walker,* recounted how, sitting by a lake and listening to the lapping of the waves, he would become aware of his existence "without troubling myself with thought."[216] In Rousseau's account, it is specifically the object—the waves and their sound—that touch him, awakening his self-awareness.

Eighteenth-century discussions on the inner sense were summarized and expanded in an important article on "Existence" written by the economist and social philosopher Anne-Robert-Jacques Turgot for the *Encyclopédie*.[217] Turgot established a connection between the idea of inner sensation and the body through what he called *le tact intérieur* (the inner touch). As Turgot defined it, the "inner touch" referred to the internal experience of the self produced by a group of sensations linked to the joint physical and psychological experience of one's own body, specifically pleasure and pain. The two key distinguishing features of this group of sensations—thirst, hunger, nausea, and all kinds of bodily aches and pleasures, including the *frissonnement* of sexual gratification—are their continuous presence and their special intensity due to the affective nature of the reaction they produce. As Turgot puts it, "this multitude of confused sensations that never abandon us and that, in a sense, circumscribe our body, render it always present to ourselves."[218] It is through the faculty of the inner touch, which produces a perception of one's own body as a palpable boundary, that we arrive at the sense of the "self" (*moi*), an interiority located in "that little space circumscribed by pleasure and pain."[219]

But if the inner touch is a gauge of our own being, it is also crucial to our recognition of the existence of external objects, for it activates our passive internal impressions of objects and moves us to pass judgment on them.[220] Turgot's complex discussion may be summarized the following way: if we recognize that objects exist, it is, first of all, by perceiving the difference between the perceptions they produce and those produced by our own body. While our internal sensations are continually present and intense, those generated by objects are unstable and fleeting, especially since the objects that are their source may not even be present. Yet with the help of memory and imagination, we are able to interiorize and retain the sensations they produce so that, even in their absence, we are aware that objects exist. Through inner touch, we are also able to distinguish between those objects that produce pain and others that are a source of pleasure and, having stored this sensory information, we behave accordingly, avoiding some objects and seeking others. We have thus established a relation between the consciousness of the self and the objects surrounding it that is not based in pure perception, but rather in what Turgot calls a "connexity [*sic*] which links together the changes of every object and our own sensations as the causes and effects of one another."[221] We may add that like Locke, Turgot found supporting evidence for his thesis in the psychology of children, who "lend feeling to all they see," by which he meant that they make more evident the affective relation that imbues our experience of things.[222]

Turgot's notion of the tact intérieur throws into sharper relief what Chardin represents in his images of children.[223] What these paintings evoke is not simply a tactile experience of the object but its internal processing through touch, the very basis of interiorization. Recording the emergence of a child's interior realm as a function of sensory experience, these images point to the ways in which the relation to the object produced by this experience structures the child's relation to his or her own body and self, the reason for it being Turgot's "connexity." The state of deep concentration in which these children are shown has to do not only with their attention to the vagaries of the thing they are playing with but also with their perception of their own self emerging within that "little space" of their own body as a result of its engagement with the object. At stake in these paintings—*pace* Michael Fried—is not exactly absorption but rather a question of acquiring a sense of self that makes absorption possible in the first place.[224]

The *Child with a Top* suggestively conveys the role of the "inner touch" as a mechanism through which, by grasping an object, one gets a grasp on oneself. His two fingers touching each other as if they were still holding the absent toy visualize a connection between the experience of one's own body—its "coexistence" with one's self—and the experience of that which exists outside of it. The similarity between the shape of the object and the boy's hand suggests this formative reciprocity, and the fact that the roughly circular hole between the boy's fingers is echoed by the shape of the buttons on his vest, and, farther up, by the oval of his lidded eyes, reinforces this experiential—tactile and visual—connection between the body, the object, and the self. As depicted by Chardin, the "inner touch" amounts to a mode of self-experience in which the object performs a crucial mediating role: it is by engagement with the object that the child arrives at the realization of its "own peculiar being."[225] What we see in these paintings of children is their recognition—intuitive as it may be—of an inviolable interior space within which the self can be experienced.

—.—

Yet if what Chardin paints corresponds to Turgot's conception of the "inner touch," it is also different in its emphasis. Whereas Turgot spoke of the risks involved in the subject's encounter with the object, which he compared to treacherous rocks that the self, sailing on the seas of self-discovery, must learn to avoid, Chardin focuses on the satisfactions and pleasures such encounter provides, including the intimations of sexual pleasure. That sexuality is tackled in these paintings is not surprising. The age of these young people hovers around the time of puberty, a moment when sexual self-awareness begins to emerge, its existence having become in this period a subject of increasing concern.[226] Their careful attire signals, moreover, that they have already entered the social field and are, therefore, potential objects of others' desire.[227] But it is the children's internal process of realizing their own desirability on which these paintings focus.

In *Child with a Top*, for example, the self-experience of the youth is laced with latent eros. Closing upon a void, the boy's hand acts as a potential receptacle—not only of the object, but also of his own

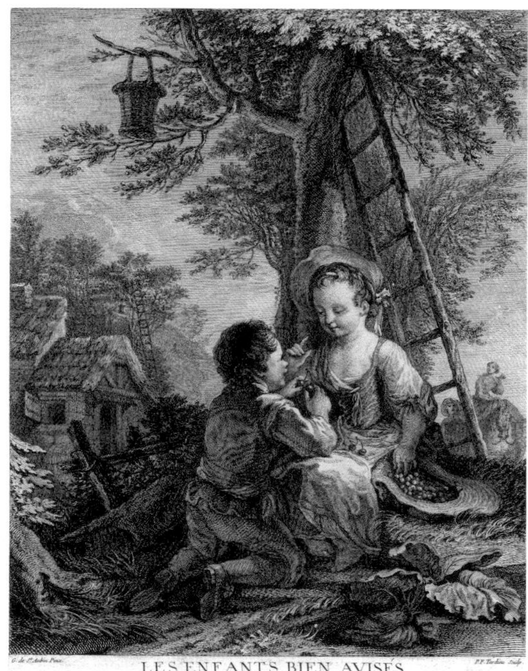

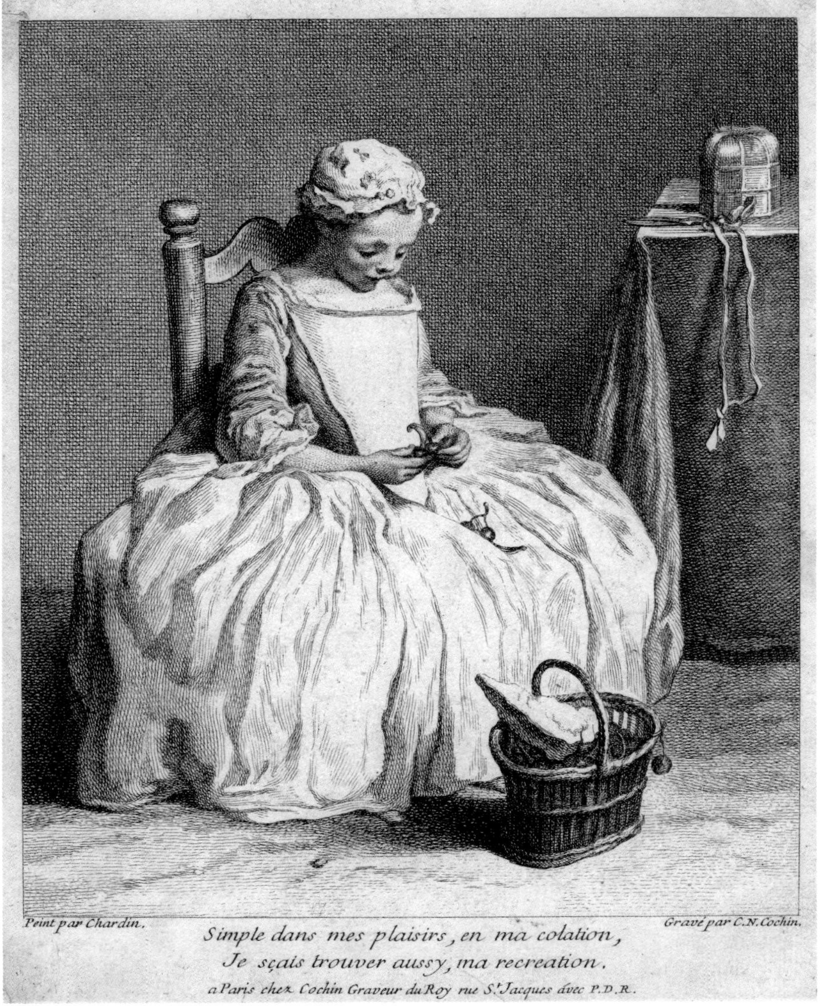

2.67. BELOW
Charles-Nicolas Cochin after Jean-Siméon Chardin, *Little Girl Enjoying Her Lunch*, 1738. Etching and engraving. British Library, London.

2.68. RIGHT
Pierre François Tardieu after Gabriel de Saint-Aubin, *The Well-Advised Children*, 1760. Etching and engraving. British Museum, London.

body. Touching itself, it hints at the possibility of another kind of touching whose explicit aim is to produce a bodily pleasure. Thus an allusion is produced to the relation between spinning a top, taking pleasure in the object, and taking pleasure in oneself. The emphasis is placed, though, on the internal rather than the physical dimension of this pleasurable self-experience (Turgot's *frissonnement intérieur*), and on the connection that emerges between the gratifying experience of one's own body and the discovery of oneself as a self. To put it in yet stronger terms, pleasure, including self-pleasure, is suggested to be not only internal but also *constitutive* of interiority. A solitary experience with the object creates a space, at once physical and mental, in which self-reflection and taking pleasure in oneself become inseparable.

This idea is suggestively communicated by the little girl in a small painting, now lost, that was exhibited at the Salon of 1737 and engraved by Cochin a year later (fig. 2.67). It is not her having a simple lunch of bread, cheese, and cherries but rather the girl's internal processing of the pleasure thus experienced, and, moreover, the way in which this sensory delight returns her to herself, that Chardin represents through her self-contained figure.[228] Again, this self-involvement has some erotic resonance—the consumption of cherries was an established motif in the iconography of lust, manifest, among others, in the eighteenth-century imagery of preadolescent flirtation (fig. 2.68)—but here, unlike more traditional depictions, it is discreet, self-oriented, and internalized.[229]

What is important, in my view, is that the bodies of these young protagonists—the top-spinning boy, the cherry-eating girl—allude to sexuality as an area of experience that is not yet fully accessible, neither to the viewers nor to the protagonists. If their figures have sexual appeal, they are not yet fully aware of its consequences; instead, they are shown to be in the process of discovering it, first and foremost for themselves. The *Girl with a Shuttlecock*, which, like the *Little Girl Enjoying Her Lunch*, was exhibited at the Salon of 1737, speaks to this idea of libidinal self-discovery with special eloquence (fig. 2.69).

While the girl's status as a game player, as well as the visible signs of budding sexuality in her body, indicate this girl's entry into the field of social and potentially libidinal interactions, it is her tools and how she handles them that ultimately define her position in this field as still precarious and negotia-

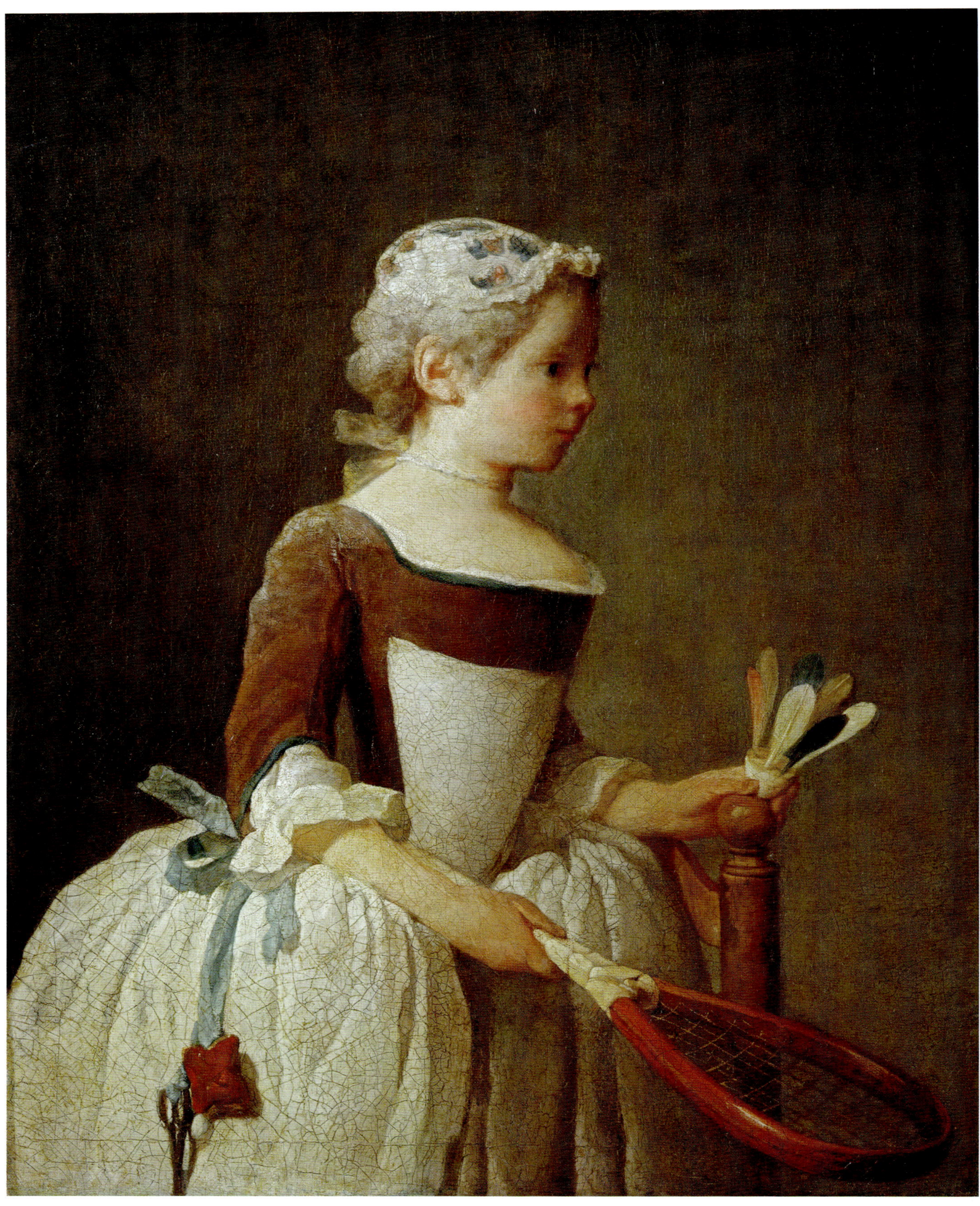

2.69. OPPOSITE
Jean-Siméon Chardin, *Girl with a Shuttlecock*, ca. 1737. Oil on canvas. Private Collection, France.

2.70. RIGHT
Jean-Siméon Chardin, *Girl with a Shuttlecock*, detail of fig. 2.69.

ble. Presented as extensions of her body and as its defining attributes, both the racket and the shuttlecock suggest the idea of readiness combined with a sense of resistance.[230] The racket's role is telling in this regard; placed, as if strategically, right at the level of the girl's lower abdomen and pointing downward, it acts as a symbolic reiteration of her reproductive organs. Drawing attention to what is buried underneath the folds of the girl's dress, the racket defines the function of this body part in ambiguous terms, as a potential receptacle that remains resolutely inaccessible, the impression conveyed by the deterrent function of the racket as much as by the proliferating milky folds of the player's skirt that suggest yet withhold her anatomy from view. The girl's hieratic presentation enhances this sense of corporeal self-containment and unavailability epitomized, if we look up close, by the rendition of such details as her ear, its orifice both opened up to our view and "plugged" by a blob of opaque reddish pigment (fig. 2.70).

Yet the attributes of the player not only position her in the field of the gaze but also mediate her own relation to her body. In this regard, it is curious to note a certain awkwardness with which the girl holds these instruments, the stiffness of her arm grasping the racket, its maladroit appearance exacerbated by the summary modeling of the flesh and her paw-like hand, and the demonstrative way in which she holds the shuttlecock balanced on the globe-shaped finial on the back of her chair. Does she know how to play yet, or is she merely measuring herself up to the game's prospect? Monumentalized and dignified, she appears also quite fragile, poised on the verge of play that, given the sexual eloquence of her attributes, must also be understood as a threshold of desire—others' and her own. She seems to occupy this liminal position hesitantly. Her awkward pose and her tentative hold on the racket and the shuttlecock seem to formulate a question: What does it mean to be a player in the field of desire and what may be the consequences of entering it?

These were also the questions that Chardin's audience was likely to have asked when the painting was shown at the Salon of 1737, the same year that a sexual scandal involving a thirteen-year-old girl abducted by a much older man erupted in Paris. The affair, which was the talk of all Paris, was especially scandalous because the "abduction" was performed by the girl herself—with considerable aplomb, she had escaped from a convent and traveled alone, accompanied only by her female servant, across the country in order to reach her older lover hiding in his provincial estate.[231] The adventure of the girl became the subject of a novel published in 1739 by Charles de Fieux, chevalier de Mouhy, which enhanced its notoriety while raising the more general question of erotic activity and sexual autonomy of young women.[232] The public discourse surrounding the affair offered context in which to consider Chardin's painting, featuring a girl of approximately the same age as the novel's heroine, displayed at the Salon.

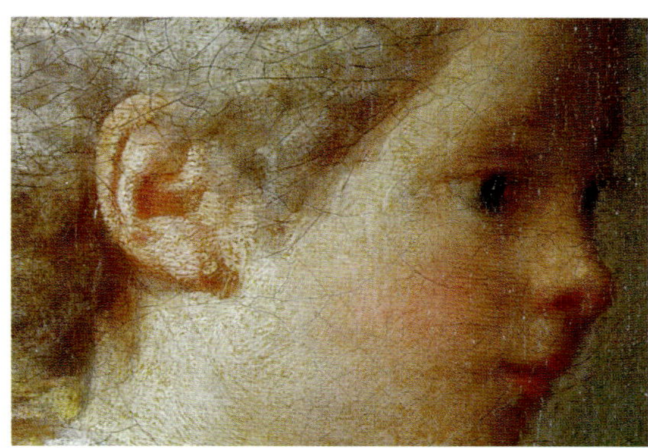

Mouhy's *Mémoirs d'Anne-Marie de Moras* is of interest for us in revealing the complicated psychological process through which its protagonist, between the ages of eight and thirteen, becomes aware of the sexual potential of her body and the familial and societal pressure put on it. Enclosed in a convent following her father's death, Anne-Marie was subjected to her manipulative mother's efforts to marry her to an advantageous party, notwithstanding her tender age. The maternal maneuvers backfired, though, precipitating the girl's *prise de conscience* of her own sexuality and ultimately resulting in her attempt to take charge of her fate as a woman, against her mother's designs. What Mouhy shows is the fragility of his heroine's position in this complex process of sexual self-discovery.[233]

Offering us a glimpse into the early eighteenth-century perceptions of adolescent female sexuality, Mouhy's *Mémoires* conveys the idea that although access to sexuality is (as we would put it today) culturally and socially mediated, it is also a matter of individual internal negotiation. As the episodes of Anne-Marie's creative recasting of herself into a sexually mature young woman demonstrate, sexuality is predicated on the development of an *imaginary*, interpretive relation to one's anatomy and is, therefore, irreducible to the anatomy itself.[234] Moreover, sexuality is also a self-individuating tool. The story of Anne-Marie launching herself into the hazardous game of desire in the pursuit of both individual identity and personal independence speaks to this idea eloquently.

Brought to bear on Chardin's *Girl with a Shuttlecock*, the story of Anne-Marie de Moras accentuates the notion of sexuality as a process of internal reflection in which the girl is shown to be immersed. But de Moras's bold move from ideas to action also makes us appreciate the *caution* exhibited by Chardin's protagonist. Poised on the brink of her game, our player takes her time considering its stakes. The painting's most intriguing aspect lies in the effect of suspension that characterizes this image of an individual about to enter the domain of sex. The way her body is presented conveys a sense of tension between, on the one hand, the girl's apparent unawareness of her status as a sexed and sexual being and, on the other, her self-consciousness about it. Yet, unlike de Moras, this girl, at once clueless and knowing, is not telling us anything; her "story," if there is one, is withheld from us by Chardin. If Salon viewers did bring the questions raised by de Moras's case to the painting, the painting itself did not provide them with any definite answers. The girl remains inscrutable.

It is this sense of subjective inscrutability that so sharply distinguishes Chardin's protagonist from those featured in Greuze's later representation of adolescent sexuality. Unlike Greuze's visually garrulous young girls who "offer" their bodies, framed by the telltale signs of physical and moral damage, for the viewer's inspection—as in the *Dead Bird* (fig. 2.71), or, later, the *Broken Jug*—Chardin's protagonist, dignified, inapproachable, is a child whose universe remains inaccessible to adults.[235] Diderot would not have been able to engage its protagonist in an imaginary dialogue, at once solicitous and patronizing, which he conducted with the protagonist of Greuze's *Dead Bird* when it was exhibited at the Salon of 1765.[236] The *Girl with a Shuttlecock* offers no grounds for such imaginary projection. Unlike the damaged adolescents featured by Greuze, she is not presented as an object of someone else's desire as much as a subject negotiating her own relation to it. In sum, Chardin envisions sexuality as an attribute of the emergent subject, not as an activity—as in Boucher's *Lady on a Day Bed*—but as a mental process of coming to terms with oneself as a sexed being.

Taken as a group, Chardin's paintings body forth interiority as a hidden and inviolable space of self-experience and budding sexual imagination, a space where the child's body begins to experience itself as pleasurable. They are, in other words, about childhood as a process of getting to know how to be with oneself and how to appreciate it. As such, these paintings contributed to the discourse on childhood as a discrete moment in the life of a human being that began to emerge in the early modern period and that manifested itself in a variety of concerns regarding the well-being and education of children. Yet, in my view, Chardin's paintings are not, as it has been argued, pedagogical in a sense of advocating the benefits of play versus learning in children's formation.[237] Rather, they are about the emergence of children into subjectivity, that is, about the formation of the subject as a self-sufficient entity onto itself.

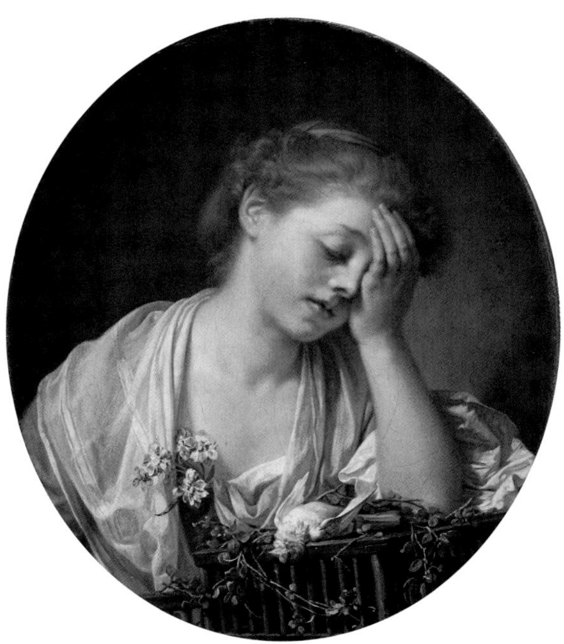

2.71.
Jean-Baptiste Greuze, *The Dead Bird*, 1765. Oil on canvas. National Galleries Scotland. Edinburgh.

Pedagogy does enter the picture—though even then only ambiguously—when these young protagonists are inserted into the scenarios played out in some of the genre scenes. It is as if one of the key functions of these scenes were precisely to test how these newly minted young subjects would fare in familial or social contexts. And, in the light of our analysis, it is hardly surprising that what Chardin emphasizes is the children's resistance to instruction, their unwillingness to cooperate, and their dissent in the face of even the most encouraging or solicitous parental figures. Thus, if the boy in the *House of Cards* (1736–37) was merely absorbed in his activity, when confronted with the governess in the later painting (*The Governess*, 1738), he becomes defiant (see figs. 2.60 and 2.49). Dressed in a *redingote* similar to that worn by the protagonist of the London canvas, this figure, holding himself very straight and looking down, visibly refuses the woman's pedagogical discourse, whether it is a reproach or encouragement. His body is his shield, he remains immutable. Even more pronounced is the transformation of the girl featured in *The Good Education* who, in comparison to her figural predecessor, the *Girl with a Shuttlecock* (see fig. 2.69) retreats further into herself when confronted with the interrogations of her mother (fig. 2.72). If the protagonist of the earlier canvas was inscrutable, the heroine of the later, overtly pedagogical scenario is recalcitrant. We are told that she is trying to recite the gospels and is embarrassed by the failings of her memory.[238] This may well be. Yet with her head slightly bent downward, her eyes cast down, she appears to be also a figure of mute resistance. If this is an image of pedagogy, it would be safe to say that it depicts its frustrations: notwithstanding the title, given to the painting by the engraver, it is not about a "good education" but rather about the obstacle to it posed by the uncooperative child.

—·—

If these paintings of children contributed to the cultural discourse on the self and, specifically, on its early development in childhood, they had also some effect on the internal development of the painter. Depicting these young persons' arrival at the realization of their own subjectivity through the exercise of inner touch, Chardin developed his own bodily self-awareness. While the children are shown gaining an intuition of their bodily self-presence through their self-reflexive engagement with objects, Chardin, painting them, arrived at a sense of his own embodied existence by engaging with *his* object, the canvas. One can say that having repeatedly visualized the occupations of children, painting became for him, too, a kind of play that, like the infantile diversions he depicts, had a formative effect. By producing the interiorized images of children, he arrived at the recognition of his own interiority, an embodied sense of himself as a painting subject separate from the painted object. It is in these paintings, in other words, that we witness a transformation of Chardin's blind touch into an "inner touch"—an instrument of subjective self-discovery.

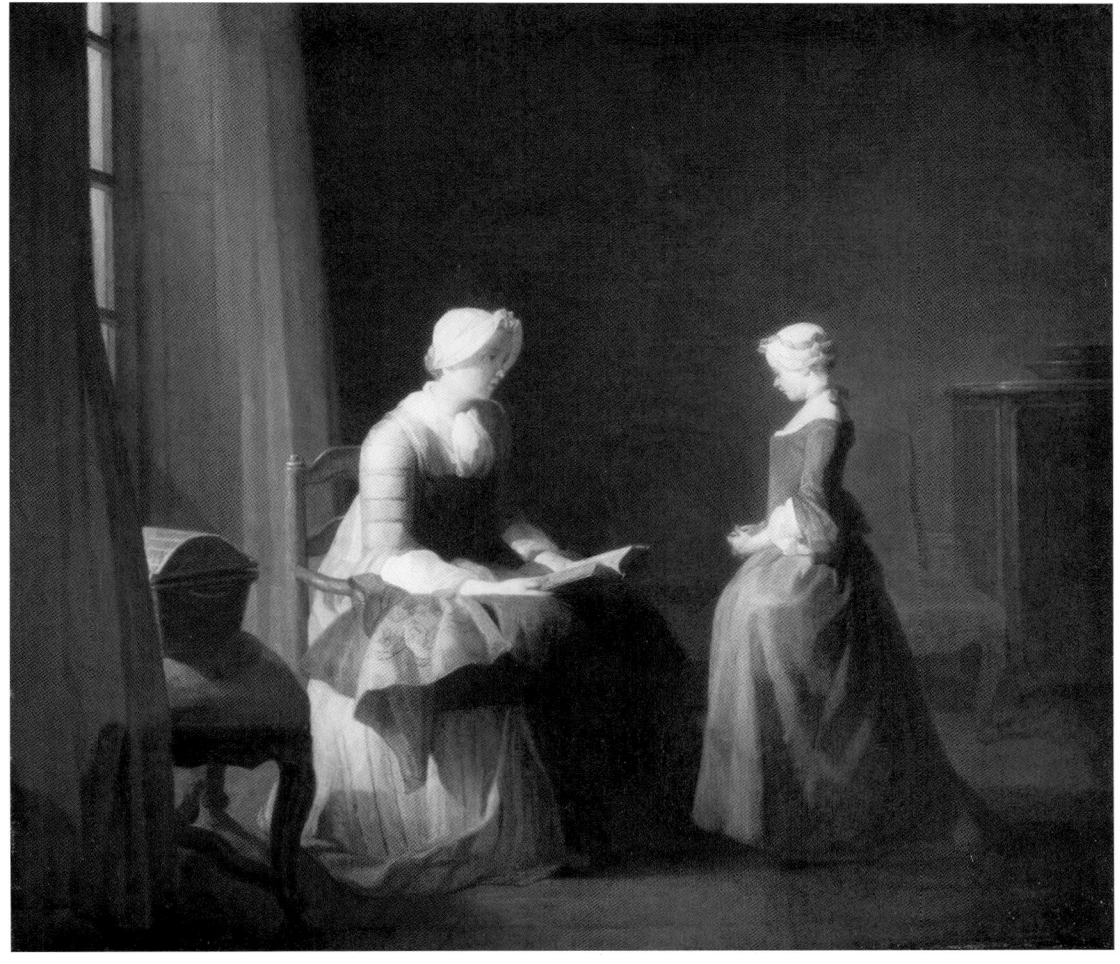

2.72.
Jean-Siméon Chardin, *The Good Education*, ca 1753. Oil on canvas. Museum of Fine Arts, Houston, Gift in memory of George R. Brown by his wife and children.

This new dimension of self-reflexivity is most clearly manifest in the *Soap Bubbles* (see fig. 2.62), a painting that, by establishing an analogy between the activity of the depicted youth and that of the painter, both thematizes and performs the connection between touch and vision. Shown in the process of producing a soap bubble, which swells into a brilliant globe at the tip of his straw, the young boy evokes a painter's process of generating forms that descend from the tip of his brush onto the canvas. The way Chardin paints the boy's body reinforces this analogy. Registering the light hitting the boy's face from the side, the thick, curdled white pigment, mixed with some pinks and blues, accrues in one spot on his forehead, its tangible crust rising above the surface of the canvas.[239] These textured whites, Chardin's signature pigment, have also been used for the boy's shirt, its collar and sleeves sticking out from under his jacket, and, in thinned smudges mixed with blue, for rendering the transparency of the soap balloon dangling from his straw. The chromatic correspondence between the two signals the connection between what the boy does and how Chardin paints him, the activity of blowing a bubble into a shape suggesting itself as similar to how the painter builds up the surface of his canvas to convey volume through varying degrees of thickness. The glass with soapy water standing next to the boy on the ledge, and the elongated brush-like shape of the straw, helps to drive home the analogy between the occupation of the boy and that of Chardin.[240]

It is the dimension of interiority in both these activities that Chardin emphasizes. In this aspect the painter departs from his numerous Dutch predecessors who rendered such scenes, among them Gerrit Dou and Willem van Mieris. Dutch painters often used the motif of the window as an exteriorizing device, as a painting by van Mieris's pupil, Mathijs Naiveu, makes clear, its elaborate, illusionistic form underscoring the activity of bubble blowing as a feat of illusion comparable to the painter's own (fig. 2.73). In Chardin's rendition, however, the window becomes a frame of an interiorized performance.[241] The concentrated effort of Chardin's protagonist to maintain the transparent globe suspended at the end of his straw is markedly different from the showy gestures of Naiveu's youths sending their soap bubbles out into the world. And so is Chardin's conspicuously paired down stone encasement framing the boy's act. Such recasting of the standard Dutch motif deflates both its narrative potential and any emblematic resonance—the vanitative dimension of the soap bubble typical of emblems such as *Quis Evadet* or *Homo sicut bulla*—drawing attention to the absorptive dimension of the boys' activity. As others have observed, this preoccupation mirrors both the deep engrossment of the painter himself in the act of painting and the absorption of the beholder contemplating the work.[242] But there is also something more specific that Chardin achieves. By eliminating decorations and details, and by closing in on his protagonist, the painter shifts emphasis away from the trappings of illusion to the internal logic of imitation. We have witnessed a similar treatment in Chardin's rendition of rabbits and hares, their radical difference from the approach of the painter's contemporaries, notably Oudry, residing in Chardin's avoidance of illusionism in favor of tactile imitation. But in the *Soap Bubbles*, the imitation takes on a theoretically more explicit meaning.

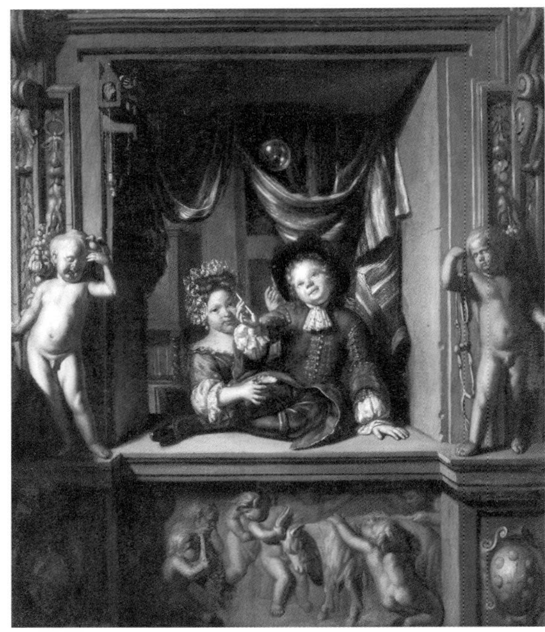

2.73.
Mathijs Naiveu, *Boy and Girl Blowing Soap Bubbles*. Oil on canvas. Museum of Fine Arts, Boston, Museum purchase with funds donated by contribution.

Closely following Roger de Piles's recommendations regarding the imitative process, Chardin secured the visual unity of his painting by clearly locating his main object, the bubble-blowing youth, directly on the principal axis of our vision: the straight line from A to B in de Piles's diagram from *Cours de peinture* (1708) (fig. 2.74). He reinforces this demarcation through the use of stark chiaroscuro to model the youth's head and through the much weaker tonal definition of the peripheral objects, notably the younger boy's head with its blurry features rendered in halftones.[243] Chardin foregrounds his exemplary deployment of light and shade, moreover, in the ren-

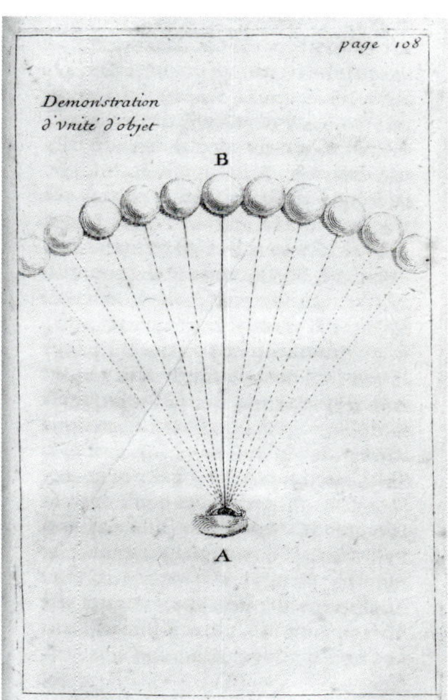

2.74. RIGHT
Plate I, "A Demonstration of the Unity of the Object," from Roger de Piles, *Cours de peinture par principes.*

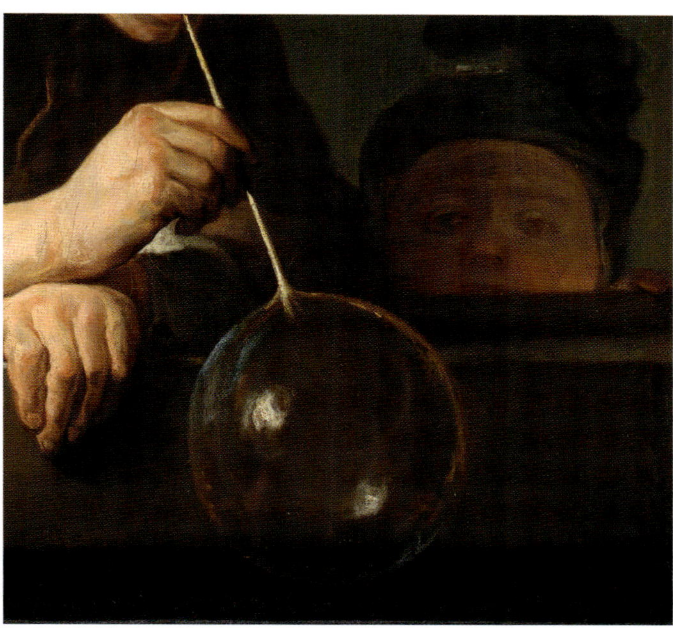

2.75. FAR RIGHT
Jean-Siméon Chardin, *Soap Bubbles*, detail of fig. 2.62.

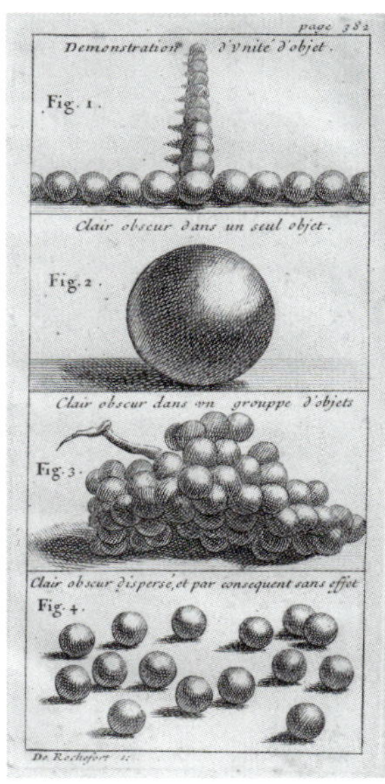

2.76. BELOW
Plate II, from Roger de Piles, *Cours de peinture par principes.*

dition of the soap bubble. The transparent globe (fig. 2.75) is an almost by-the-book illustration of de Piles's recipe for how to handle an individual object "in order to give it relief; which is to use, in the fore-part, the most lively light and the strongest shades, always preserving the reflected lights near the turning on the side of the shade" (fig. 2.76, see especially the second figure from the top).[244] In Chardin, this recommendation is realized by the two white patches of the "most lively light" on the surface of the bubble and by the articulation of its contours through chromatic modulation (a combination of ochers and reds).

Yet the de Pilesian concept of pictorial unity was not the only organizing principle of Chardin's image. For if *Soap Bubbles* presents us with a visually coherent and unified surface, it also draws our look beyond or behind it, into the depths of painting, both in the literal and the figural sense of the word. It does so through a combination of an interiorized staging of the main motif emerging from the unarticulated depths of the niche and a thematic emphasis on inwardness conveyed by the figure of the boy engrossed in his act. The *Soap Bubbles* insists on the link between imitation and subjectivity, which, though already suggested by de Piles, was more fully theorized later in the century by none other than Chardin's friend and supporter, Cochin.[245]

In his important polemical discourse of 1764, Cochin sought to establish the superiority of imitation over illusion by valorizing the painter's performance inherent in imitation.[246] The particular importance of his argument lies in his emphasis on the subjective dimension of the imitative act. Imitation, Cochin argued, was distinct from illusion because it involved a more sophisticated, nuanced, and individualized approach to execution (le faire), which he understood not as a matter of mere technical skill but as an "emanation of creative personality."[247] The key factor that inflected the process of imitation was the painter's *sentiment*, which was, in Cochin's words, what "moves the artist at work."[248] An effect of sensation, but not reducible to the organs that produced it, sentiment was a kind of interior sense—not unlike Turgot's "inner touch"—a mode of perceiving nature that was at once receptive and active. The work of art was seen as the effect of sentiment in that it represented nature as it has been *felt* by the artist, the feeling made manifest in his or her very mode of representation.

This idea was new. While the term *sentiment* was used earlier, notably by the abbé Dubos, to refer to a viewer's response to a work of art, Cochin understood it to be part and parcel of the artistic process, including its material and technical dimensions.[249] Sentiment was a principle of subjectivity that entered the process of imitation and distinguished it not only from simple copying but also from illusion. To illustrate his point Cochin—not surprisingly—evoked the work of Chardin. In Cochin's eyes, Chardin was an extraordinary painter because he was able to produce a kind of beauty that exceeded even the best illusionistic effects: "alien to illusion," it shunned exactitude in favor of ingenuity, instinct, magic, in sum, le sentiment.[250] Cochin's description echoes Chardin's oft-cited dictum about how one should paint. Responding to a younger colleague who was bragging about his capacity to use colors, Chardin asserted that "one uses colors, but one paints with the feeling [le sentiment]."[251]

It is this understanding of imitation that the *Soap Bubbles* puts into practice. That it does so had to do, no doubt, with Chardin's rising ambition as a figural painter, his desire to elevate the status of his work by a manifest display not only of his theoretical savvy—in the construction of the pictorial space à la de Piles—but also of his unique and inimitable craft as a practice of subjectively inflected imitation. But this demonstration speaks also to the personal dimension of Chardin's engagement with the image of the interiorized subject and to its effect on his own practice and on himself. It is this dimension that the *Soap Bubbles* communicates more directly than other paintings, and, in order to find out how it does so, we must examine it one last time.

It is, as we have noted, the rendition of the *Soap Bubbles*' main protagonist that speaks to the subjective bases of imitation most eloquently: the posture and expression of this introspective figure suggest his impenetrable interiority to be the very font of imitative process. But what the painting also insists upon is the inextricable connection between the youth's "presentness" to himself and the action he performs, and especially its product, the soap bubble. Chardin's composition hints at how the boy's experience of the object helps him arrive at his bodily self-awareness, at a recognition, that is, of his own body as a distinct boundary analogous to, but separate from, his soap bubble. By witnessing the bubble gradually swelling into a globe, the boy appears to realize his own embodied existence, the visual rapport between the curving surface of the soap bubble and the inverse curve of the boy's own face—not unlike the analogy between the oval formed by the fingers of the top-spinning boy and his toy—making evident this aspect of his self-experience.

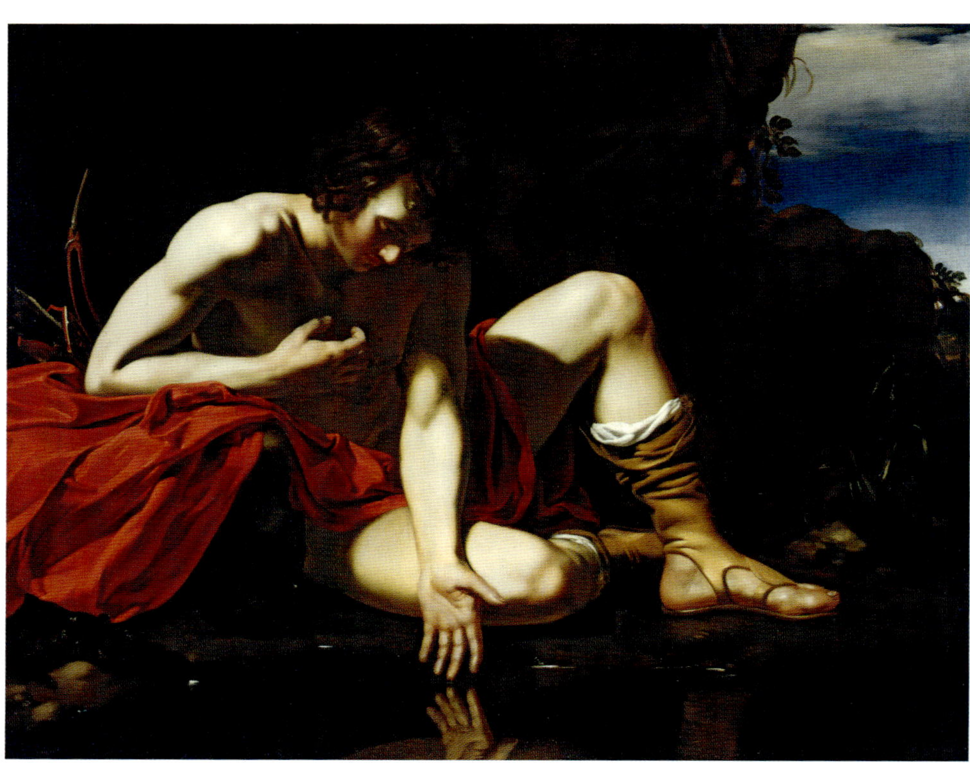

2.77.
Attributed to a Dutch artist active in Rome, *Narcissus*, mid-1640s. Oil on canvas. The John and Mable Ringling Museum of Art, Sarasota, Florida, Museum purchase, 1969.

If the rapport established is visual, it is also emphatically tactile, in terms of what the painting does and in what the boy is shown doing, his hand grasping the straw in a gesture that reinforces the tactile connection between his body and his object materialized by the straw. It is this gesture—a vehicle of the inner touch—that fastens the notion of quotidian diversion to the idea of self-experience.[252] Like the lapping waves of the lake that prompted Rousseau to realize, without thinking, his own existence, bubble blowing leads Chardin's protagonist to recognize the emergence of his own interiority. At the same time, the painting may be said to "exteriorize" the subjectivity involved in the painter's own performance. It is a multilayered self-reflexive commentary on Chardin's practice of imitation inflected by sentiment. But it is also, speculative as this claim may be, a representation of the sentiment at which the painter himself arrived by painting this and other pictures of inward-bound children: the sense of his own embodied existence acquired through the "inner touch" of his painting. The soap bubble is also an image of the painter's interiority.

It is as such that this image epitomizes the critical shift in the relation between the subject and the object that occurs in Chardin's paintings of children. This new relation is underwritten—and reinforced—by the *Soap Bubbles* latent evocation of the iconography of Narcissus. Whether by accident or design, the pose of Chardin's bubble-blowing youth evokes the mythological figure, who is usually represented in a leaning posture. The resemblance comes to the fore in comparison to a painting by an unidentified Dutchman working in Rome in the mid-seventeenth century, which Chardin may have known through an engraving (fig. 2.77). The bubble blower's leaning posture, the position of his upper torso, especially his bent right arm, and his head, with his face thrown in sharp relief by the strong light coming from the side, seem close enough to the protagonist of the Roman painting to propose an analogy between the two. Whether it was established via this or another work, the importance of the *Soap Bubbles*' connection to the iconography of Narcissus lies in the relation between the subject and the object conveyed by it—a relation different from that which we have witnessed in Chardin's depiction of women.

Narcissus's problem resided not so much in his falling in love with his own reflection as in his inability to recognize this reflection for what it was—not his body but an image, *an object* that was separate from himself. The Dutchman's painting alludes to this problem by the extended gesture of Narcissus reaching out with his hand to touch what he takes to be himself, but what *we* see only as a reflection of his hand in the water. His gesture speaks, in other words, of his inability to distinguish his own body from its image. If Chardin's absorbed youth evokes the mythic figure, it is clearly a Narcissus of a different kind. If his youthful posture contains a residue of a narcissistic attachment and a pleasure taken in one's creation, the subject thus envisioned is separated from his object, the straw sustaining the soap bubble announcing itself as a measure of his distance from it. It is important to note that, though reflective, the surface of the soap bubble does not provide the reflection of the boy's face; unlike the pool's or the mirror's surface, it does not lure him with his own image. Rather than seeing it as a reflection of himself, he can see the object for what it is. If the bubble is defined as an autonomous object, a product of imitation about to be released into the world, the painter, too, is shown as capable of his own independent embodied existence. The act of painting—like the bubble-making activity of the boy—provided him with a sense of his own body, the touch of his brush having become a vehicle of "inner touch." In this sense, the *Soap Bubbles* emblematizes the shift in Chardin's understanding of himself as a painter brought into being by his depictions of children.

This returns us, at long last, to the vexing question of why, notwithstanding the success of Chardin's figural compositions, the artist abandoned genre paintings as abruptly as he took them up. Several factors may have been involved. It has been suggested that Chardin's decision had to do with the progressive discrediting of genre painting in the critical discourse surrounding the Salon exhibitions from the mid-1740s on, which the painter may have taken to heart. This possibility strikes me as unlikely, given that his genre scenes continued to be in high demand. More probably, Chardin simply no longer needed it. Genre painting had accomplished its mission by demonstrating the painter's capacity to represent something other than an inanimate object—a mere sausage, to evoke Aved's taunt—and by establishing his domestic and international reputation. Most importantly, it produced a fundamental change in his practice, allowing him to experience the object—and himself—in an entirely different way and thus to return to his original vocation as a still life painter.

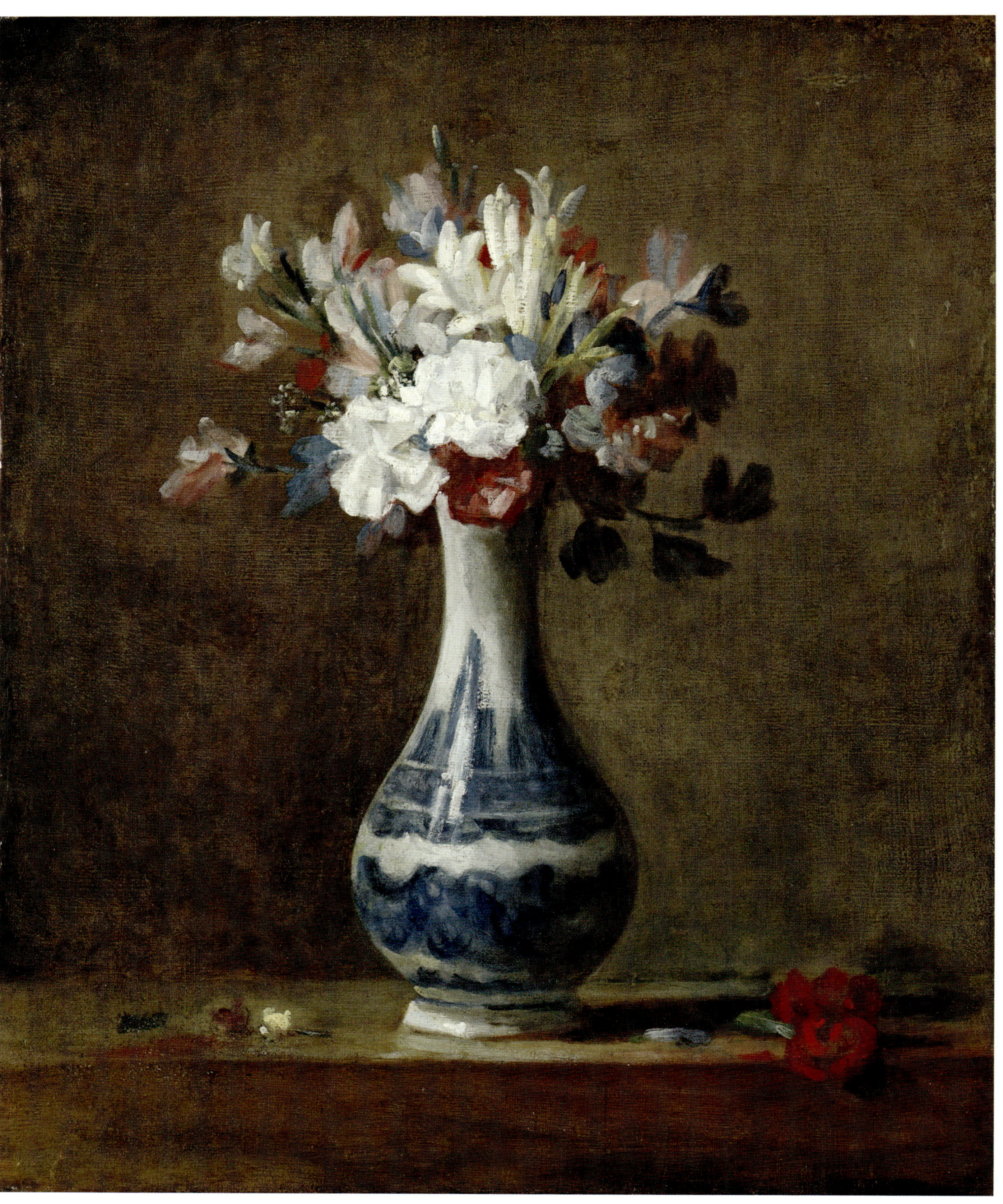

THE RETURN TO THE OBJECT

Here you are again, great magician, with your silent arrangements!

—Diderot, Salon of 1765

2.78. OPPOSITE
Jean-Siméon Chardin, *Bouquet of Carnations*, early 1750s. Oil on canvas. National Galleries of Scotland, Edinburgh. Purchased with the aid of the Cowan Smith Bequest Fund 1937.

2.79. RIGHT
Ambrosius Bosschaert, *Still Life with Flowers*, 1619. Oil on copper. Rijksmuseum, Amsterdam.

The Salon of 1753 marked Chardin's official return to still life.[253] The painter had not exhibited publicly for a while—he was notably absent from the Salon of 1751 and showed only one work, the *Drawing Lesson*, at the Salon of 1748—and critics reproached him for indolence.[254] As if to appease them, Chardin sent nine works to the Salon of 1753, five of which were still lifes.[255] Although it is not clear how many of them were newly painted, the prevalence of still lifes among Chardin's submissions signaled his renewed interest in this genre and his desire to revive his public image as a painter of things. But it also marked a considerable change in Chardin's approach. Featuring refined accessories of domestic pleasures and comforts rather than the kitchen stuff typical of the earlier still lifes, these new paintings represented their objects in a remarkably different way. It would be more correct to say, in fact, that the still lifes of the second period announced a reinvention of the object rather than a return to it.

We can get some sense of Chardin's new approach by considering briefly the *Bouquet of Carnations* painted in the early 1750s, now in Edinburgh (fig. 2.78).[256] Here the motif itself, an elegant Delft vase filled with flowers, indicates, first of all, a change of location. Leaving behind the rough and raw domain of the kitchen depicted in the earlier paintings, the painter has moved to the more refined territory of a household parlor. But the Edinburgh painting also makes evident a greater emphasis on the autonomy of the object. Standing erect at the center of the composition, the flower vase declares its presence with an assertiveness that reminds one of a human figure. Gone is the sense of inversion that defined Chardin's compositional arrangements earlier on, exemplified in the *Kitchen Still Life with Loin of Mutton* (see fig. 2.9) by the combination of things spilling from the edge of the ledge, the turned-over copper pot, and the strap of flayed meat. The solitary flower vase appears self-contained, a serene and imperturbable protagonist of the canvas.

A record of the object's sovereign existence, the *Bouquet of Carnations* suggests that a separation has taken place; the painter seems to have distanced himself from the object, which enabled him to see it for what it was. This distanced vision should not be confused, however, with striving for objectivity. Enough to look at the work of one of Chardin's predecessors, Ambrosius Bosschaert's *Still Life with Flowers* (fig. 2.79), to realize the difference of Chardin's approach. The Edinburgh *Bouquet* was painted by someone sitting right in front of it, its appearance having been modified by the viewpoint this position afforded its painter. The approximated shape of the flower petals dissolved by the incoming light, its reflections also registered in the rose tints of the vase's white-and-blue surface, and the blurry outlines of the vase's decorative pattern, point unmistakably to an embodied subject perceiving the object from a particular vantage point, rather than from Bosschaert's unspecified place suspended somewhere in mid-air.

But if the Edinburgh still life is a vision of a situated eye, it is also a product of a specific hand. The flowers appear as a bouquet of pigments that not only registers contingent appearance rather than the taxonomic reality of Bosschaert's flowers but also bears the traces of the body and tools involved in painting it. Note the whites applied with a mid-size

square-tipped brush that make the petals of tuberoses look almost like the indexical traces of the painter's tool.[257] Notice also the loose structure of the carmine strokes representing a fallen carnation at the base of the vase, the standard trope of Dutch still life that Chardin turns into swirls of unprocessed pigment, like a note scribbled to himself: "red here." This morphological reciprocity between the object and the brush makes evident the painter's participation in producing this vision of the object.[258]

The *Bouquet of Carnations* differs radically from seventeenth-century Northern models of representation based in observation, offering as it does a record of sensory experience wherein vision is inseparable from touch. But this aspect also distinguishes the *Bouquet* from Chardin's earlier still lifes. There is no sense of mutual entanglement of the subject and the object, no aggression manifest in the painter's touch, as was often the case in those earlier works.[259] Rather, touch and sight, subject and object appear to *coexist*, and to reciprocate, bound together by something close to Turgot's "connexity," that is, a relation of interdependence between separate and autonomous entities. While the painter's gaze envelops the flower vase, leaving visible and palpable marks on the vase's surface, the vase seems in turn to extend toward the painter and the viewer due to the effect of aeration; applied in small, tangible strokes, the brown and ocher pigments render the void around the vessel palpable and animated, a markedly *shared* space. The object, as Diderot observed, appears to "breathe" in it, which implies that it "breathes" the same air as the subject.[260]

The radical change in Chardin's perception of the object witnessed in *Bouquet of Carnations* amounts, then, also to a new vision of the subject. The subject we have witnessed in Chardin's earlier still lifes, wrestling with the object in an anxious attempt to chart its own boundaries—pushing and pulling, turning the object inside out in an effort to separate itself from it—has been replaced by someone who, looking at it from a safe distance, conducts a relaxed, silent dialogue with the thing. This dialogue brings to mind the engagement of Chardin's children with the instruments of their diversion; the painter may be said to see the bouquet of flowers as the protagonists of his earlier paintings saw a spinning top or a dangling soap bubble. Inherent in the children's look was the touch that had preceded it—the top having been spun before it could be observed spinning—and that defined the import of their engagement, the tactile contact with the object and the sensory recognition of its boundaries leading the subject to corporeal and subjective self-recognition. It is this generative reciprocity of touch that defines the painter's gaze on the flower vase in the Edinburgh painting. The sovereign mode in which the bouquet claims its place in the space of representation, its erect, quasi-human presence, speaks not only of the bouquet's autonomous existence but also of the autonomy of the subject who envisions it.

This change in Chardin's vision was, in my view, due significantly to his experience painting genre scenes. The figural interval in his practice allowed the painter to develop a new approach to still life not only because it placed him at some distance from things, but also because it led him to develop a sense of his own body, providing a sense of physical and subjective independence from which he could cast a different look at what he was painting. Thus if the new still lifes point to a different mode of experiencing things, they also testify to a new mode of self-experience. The distinct quality of Chardin's new still lifes can be linked to the painter's newly acquired "inner touch," a faculty that enabled him to generate an effect of coexistence between subject and object, as well as a combination of the seemingly contradictory qualities of autonomy and relatedness in the object's appearance. It is this mechanism that defines the subject of these new paintings as at once independent and connected to the represented things. Devoid of tension, this new type of connectivity and relatedness made space for the emergence of pleasure in the subject's experience of the object. And it is this pleasure that the still lifes of the second period imply—not only in the choice of objects but also in their mode of rendering.

That Chardin was able to take stock of his own practice in this way had to do with personal circumstances and with new developments in the artistic culture of his time that accompanied his return to still life. In the late 1740s, the painter finally left his parents' house to establish himself on his own. This important development was precipitated by the death of his mother in 1743—Chardin père had died twelve years earlier—resulting in the division of the family's fortune between Chardin and his siblings. The painter's younger brother Juste ended up acquiring the family house, which included the workshop of the *maître menuisier* he had inherited from his father.[261] Chardin, meanwhile, within a year of his mother's death married his neighbor, Marguerite Puget, a widow of a merchant considerably more affluent than Chardin himself. Sometime afterward, he moved from rue du Four to live in his new wife's house located nearby, on 13 rue de Princesse.[262]

It was in his new dwelling that Chardin painted most of the still lifes of the second period. The kind of everyday objects and foods that entered the painter's work at the time—Delft vases, Meissen porcelain, crystal cruets, pâtés, pomegranates, brioches, and *bombonières*—indicates the artist's access to a more refined bourgeois lifestyle than he had known in his parents' household. But Chardin's relocation also had deeper consequences, entailing as it did his separation from the familial and artisanal context of his earlier life and work. Distancing him from both his father's artisanal milieu and his mother's domestic sphere, Chardin's second marriage afforded the painter greater material comfort but also a fuller sense of autonomy. It created the conditions of possibility for Chardin's new autonomous vision of the object.

Another important factor was the critical response to his later still lifes, especially Diderot's. From the late 1750s, Diderot commented consistently on the originality and import of Chardin's painting. Attending to Chardin's faire, and especially to his inimitable chromatic skill, Diderot sought to translate the unusual effect of his depictions of objects on the viewer—their subjective appeal—by developing a language of vivid description unprecedented in the critical reception of still lifes.[263] In his attempt to capture the originality of Chardin's work, Diderot developed a discourse of still life as a genre worthy of serious reflection despite its lack of narrative and of historical dimension. Moreover, in his analysis of Chardin's still lifes, Diderot formulated a distinctly philosophical notion of aesthetic pleasure. Although the circulation of Diderot's *Salons* was limited, they impacted the public discourse of art in Paris, the reception of Chardin's work, and, one should think, the painter himself.[264]

Diderot was not the only commentator who recognized the originality of Chardin's vision. Many others offered insights into his work exhibited at the Salons of the 1750s and '60s.[265] The favorable reception of Chardin's still lifes was not only important to the painter himself, reconfirming him in his pursuit, but it also contributed to the elevation of the genre at the Salon. Chardin himself may have contributed to this elevation as the Salon's *tapissier*. From 1755 (officially from 1761), he was responsible for hanging all the paintings at the Salon, a function that granted him the power to determine their arrangement on the walls.[266] It also allowed him to see his own work in a different, distanced, and contextualized way.

In sum, the transformation in Chardin's vision did not simply come about as a result of a "natural" process of artistic maturation but was a self-conscious shift in the painter's approach to the task of representation, a shift enabled by his experience of his own work of the preceding decade and facilitated by the new material, symbolic, and discursive conditions of his practice from the late 1740s on.

That Chardin's reinvention of the object was linked to his representation of subjects, specifically his depiction of children, is signaled already by the *Smoker's Case*, an undated still life assumed to have been painted in the late 1730s (fig. 2.80). This dating has been established on the basis of the painting's chromatic and morphological affinities with the *Girl with a Shuttlecock*, with which the *faïence* jug and lidded porcelain cup at the center of the *Smoker's Case* share their white and blue tonality and unctuous texture (see fig. 2.69).[267] But the connection between these two paintings runs deeper, in my view, manifesting itself in the similarity between the objects' thematic and formal "relatedness" to the subject and the girl's rapport with her accessories in the 1737 canvas. It is precisely the way in which the *Smoker's Case* calls up the subject that distinguishes this painting from Chardin's earlier still lifes.

To begin with, rather than the raw materials of meals, or other common household items depicted in Chardin's early still lifes, the *Smoker's Case* features the accessories of a specific individual—the smoker.[268] We know that these are, in fact, the personal belongings of the painter, their very status pointing to a shift in his understanding of still life: the motif has been individuated and personalized.[269] The interest of the *Smoker's Case* lies in its capacity to evoke a subject who, though outside the painting, is its raison d'être. The embers glowing in the bowl of the pipe and the smoke it emits indicate the user of these objects is nearby. He may even be seen inscribed in the very form of things: the prominent vertical shape of the white faïence jug around which the whole scenography of the *Smoker's Case* revolves produces the effect of subjective presence within the painting. At the risk of literalization, one could say that it is as if the jug itself were "smoking" the pipe, the diagonal placement of the pipe's long stem, its end almost touching the figure-like jug, reinforcing this impression.

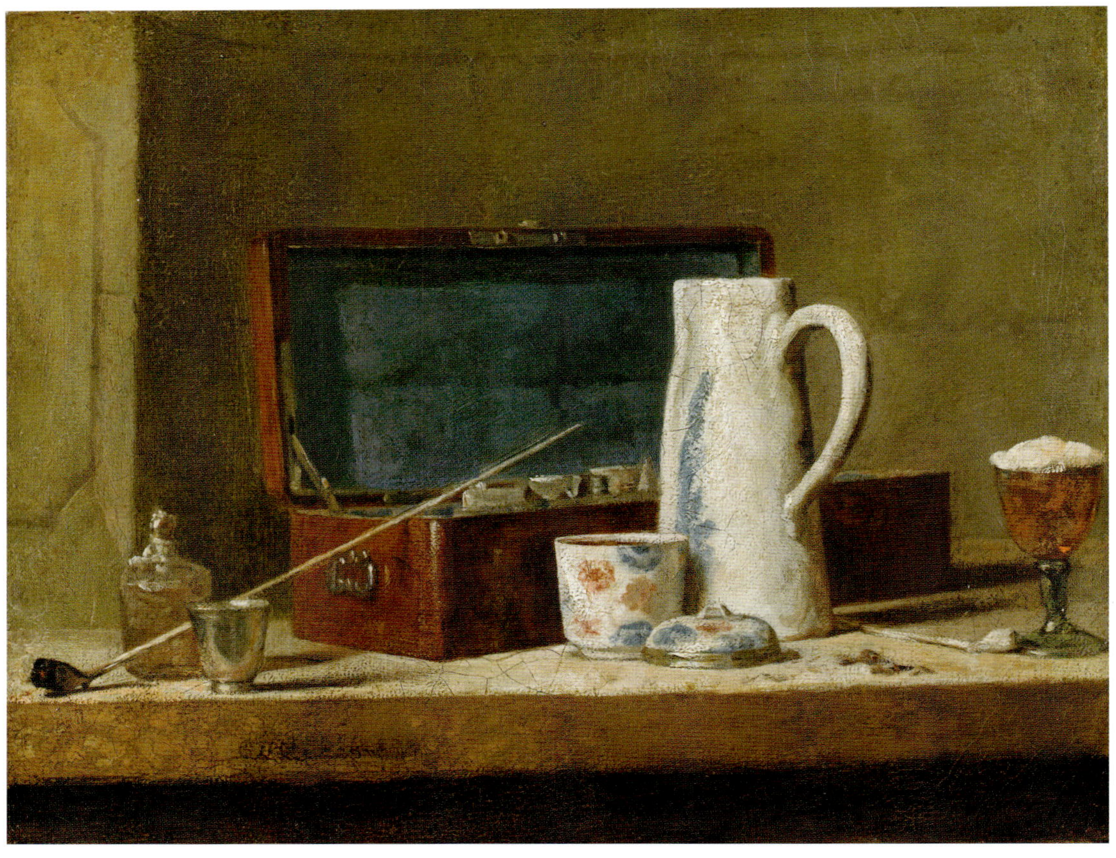

2.80.
Jean-Siméon Chardin, *Smoker's Case*. Oil on canvas. Musée du Louvre, Paris.

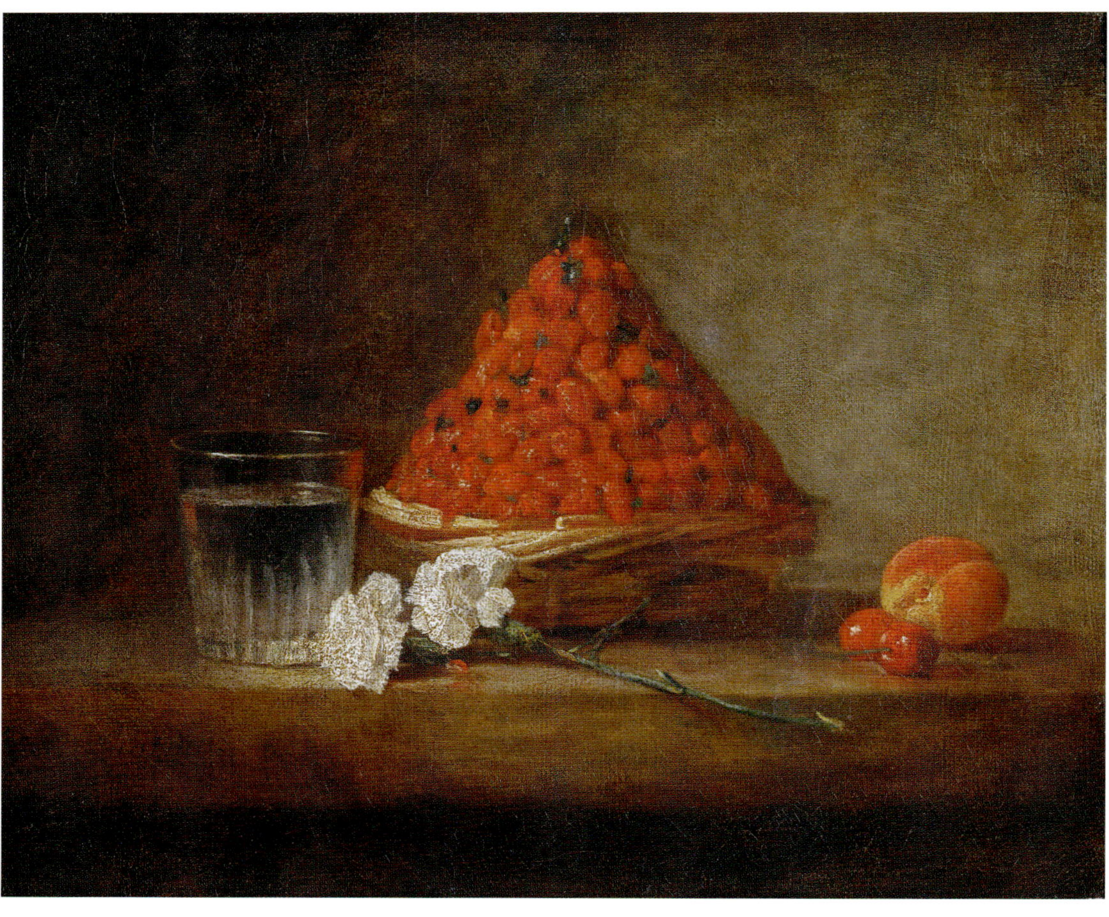

2.81.
Jean-Siméon Chardin, *Basket of Wild Strawberries*, ca. 1761. Oil on canvas. Private Collection, France.

Beyond its tonal and morphological analogy to the *Girl with a Shuttlecock*, the *Smoker's Case* makes evident how the engagement with the figure enabled Chardin to approach still life in a different way, that is, to personalize it. My point is that it was precisely the image of this self-reflexive young woman—and the representations of children in general—that enabled the innovations evident in the *Smoker's Case*. It was by painting children engaged in a silent dialogue with their objects—and, through their objects, with themselves—that Chardin's gaze was diverted away from the goods and utensils in the household kitchen to the things in his immediate surroundings that had more personal relevance to him.

The nature of his gaze also changed, as the structure of presentation in the *Smoker's Case* makes clear. One is struck by the effect of harmonious coexistence of things in this small painting, its composition lacking the precarious and confrontational quality of the earlier arrangements. Instead of the logic of inside/out, it is the discreet interconnection between things that the painter conveys by proximity—the long-stemmed pipe that, resting on the case, extends toward the silver containers that stand on the left— and by chromatic consonances between them. Nestled inside the case, the smoker's silver accessories echo the containers on the far left while the case's blue-green lining accords with the color of the ornaments of the lidded cup and the jug. The white wisps of highlights enveloping these objects create a sense of chromatic unity, of harmonious togetherness of things.

Testifying to the close relation between two distinct areas of Chardin's practice, genre painting and still life, the *Smoker's Case* is an important transitional painting that announces the key concerns shaping Chardin's still lifes of the second period, namely, personal experience and pleasure. The connection is most evident in the *Basket of Wild Strawberries* from around 1760 (fig. 2.81). Its composition is anchored by a vertical object, the pyramid of berries, that engages in a kind of dialogue with the subsidiary element, a glass filled with water. Because there are far fewer things on display here than in the *Smoker's Case*, the relation between the mound of berries and the glass predominates, encapsulating a sense of this still life as an offering of refreshments—or of the painting representing these refreshments—to an individual receiver. The painting serves as a delectable reward for the person who stands in front of it, be it the painter or the spectator.

The placement of the objects in the *Basket of Wild Strawberries* accentuates their status as seen by a specific individual. As in the *Bouquet of Carnations*, Chardin adapted the motif from a long-established iconography.[270] While his painting shares the key elements that constitute the motif—the combination of carnation and berries—he transforms their display into a scenography of individuated sensory experience. In contrast to his Dutch predecessors' elevated viewpoint, Chardin places himself on a par with the object, and this is how we too are invited to look at it. The strawberries are meant *for* us, targeting our sensory pleasure. The way Chardin depicts them invites an association with a body that would taste the aromatic berries, sip water from the glass, smell the white carnation, or touch the skin of the peach.

A connection can be made between the individuated mode of address in this painting and the way Chardin represented the simple pleasures of individual children—one at a time. The painting's inconspicuous and intimate display of life's simple rewards—fruit to be eaten, water to be drunk, flowers to be smelled—brings to mind the gratifying experience of Chardin's earlier *Little Girl Enjoying Her Lunch* (see fig. 2.67). It is the object as a source of such rewarding experience that the painter now depicts, as if, having represented someone else's pleasure, he became capable of partaking in it. What I am suggesting, again, is that the *Basket of Wild Strawberries* is in an important sense connected to the figural interval in Chardin's practice, that the experience of the object this painting registers echoes the experiences of the children recorded by the painter. This is how *Basket of Wild Strawberries* declares itself to be a product of the "inner touch."

Chardin's emphasis on the sensory dimension of things as a source of individual experience can be related to the larger epistemological shift that recognized the role of the senses in constituting subjectivity. To say that the *Basket of Wild Strawberries* is a product of the "inner touch" is to suggest that it does not merely evoke consumption and its attendant pleasures, but instead speaks of the kinds of experiences and pleasures that contribute to one's sense of self. At stake is not simply finding a reward in eating—or in imagining oneself to eat—but a matter of realizing one's own existence through such experiences. This is where the painting's affinity with *Little Girl Enjoying Her Lunch* resides. The ways in which the objects of Chardin's still lifes address themselves to the different sensory faculties—enlisting as they do sight, taste, and touch—brings to mind

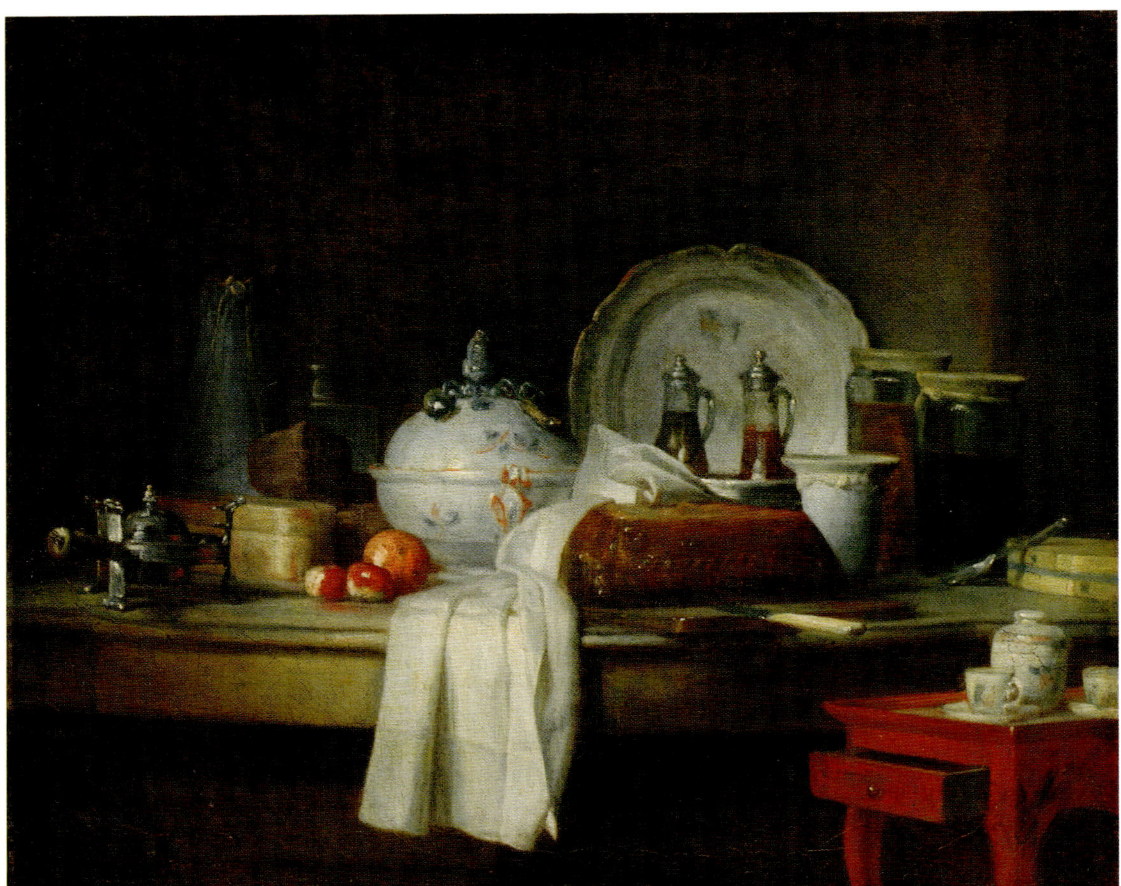

2.82.
Jean-Siméon Chardin, *Butler's Table*, 1756. Oil on canvas. Musée du Louvre, Paris.

Condillac's experiment with the statue that comes alive by acquiring her senses one by one, demonstrating the role of the sensory apparatus in the formation of human subjectivity.[271] The *Basket of Wild Strawberries* may be seen to illustrate the premise of Condillac's discourse and of eighteenth-century French sensationist philosophy at large. But the sensory experience afforded by this painting is not sensationist in a generic sense; it is individually determined, its unity more precarious and contingent than it may seem.[272] Unlike his Flemish predecessor, Jacob van Hulsdonck, who painted the same motif, Chardin emphasizes the presence of a specific body involved in, and defined by, its sensory engagement with the object, as if to say: "I have touched these things, and they in turn have touched me. And this is what I have painted." It is not an image of the sensationist subject as such but a record of Chardin's particular subjective experience as a still life painter who has reinvented himself through the experience of an object—by painting it. The individual pleasure that is at the core of the *Basket of Wild Strawberries* was, to begin with, the painter's own.

The concept of personal pleasure that inscribed the sparse display of things in the *Basket of Wild Strawberries* also defines the more complex multi-object arrangements of the 1750s and 1760s. To begin with, these works testify to a shift in the painter's interest toward the representation of things that evoke consumption rather than preparation or that, more generally, focus on the rewards of the senses. Pâtés and cheeses, soups and sauces, fruit and preserves, wines and desserts, and other ready-to-eat items begin populating his still life arrangements from this period. It is not that Chardin entirely abandons kitchen scenery. He does return to some of his earlier culinary compositions, though, upon revision, they appear different, markedly paired down.[273] But it is the new assortments of things that the painter invests in. This is evident, for instance, in the *Butler's Table* (fig. 2.82). The very fact that the first version of this painting, now in Carcassone, was painted as a pendant to the Boston *Kitchen Table* indicates that the artist consciously established the rewards of consumption as an alternative to the thematics of his earlier still lifes (see fig. 2.1).

In fact, Chardin may have been interested in exploring the aesthetic contrast between the two. The

2.83.
Jean-Siméon Chardin, *The Jar of Apricots*, 1756. Oil on canvas. Art Gallery of Ontario, Toronto.

2.84.
Jean-Siméon Chardin, *The Jar of Olives*, 1760. Oil on canvas. Musée du Louvre, Paris.

dining room set up in the *Butler's Table* offers not only a different group of objects but also an aesthetic alternative to the culinary scenery of the Boston painting.[274] It is the pleasure of use rather than the rituals of making that this new aesthetics of the object revolves around. But it is a pleasure of a particular kind. It is intimate and individuated, in both its scale and character. Improvised, pointedly practical (note the portable stove for warming the dishes, *la réchaud*, on the extreme left), and cozy rather than ostentatious, it identifies itself as bourgeois rather than aristocratic. Eschewing the splendor of Chardin's own earlier *Buffet* (see fig. 2.16), the *Butler's Table*, though well equipped, features no elaborate pyramids of fruits and silver platters but the simpler rewards for a bourgeois palate evoked by a pâté and a *pot à oile*, some fruit and preserves in their jars, a sugar mountain wrapped in blue paper hovering in the background, and a tea set on a red-lacquered table on the side. While they speak of comfortable life, these items are not tokens of social privilege nor of aesthetic entitlement. They testify, rather, to someone's everyday pleasures. The person thus evoked is socially situated—a relatively well-to-do middle-class individual—but it is the pleasure rather than the status of this person that Chardin brings to the fore. The small format of the painting—minuscule in comparison to the giant scale of the *Buffet*—emphasizes the at once modest and individuated dimension of the pleasure its aims to provide. Measuring 38 × 46 cm, it seems, moreover, only large enough to accommodate the gaze of one person at a time.[275]

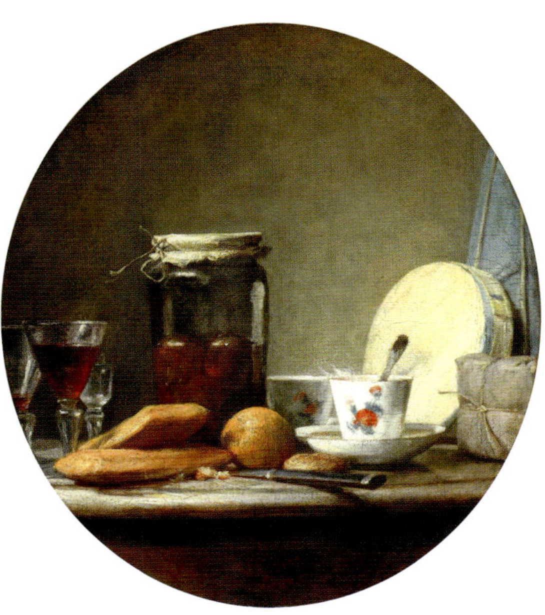

Similarly rewarding assortments of things can be found in other still lifes of the second period, notably in the oval pendants *The Jar of Apricots* (fig. 2.83) and *The Sliced Melon* (1760, private collection), both shown at the Salon of 1761; *The Jar of Olives* (fig. 2.84), *Grapes and Pomegranates* (1763), and *The Brioche* (1763).

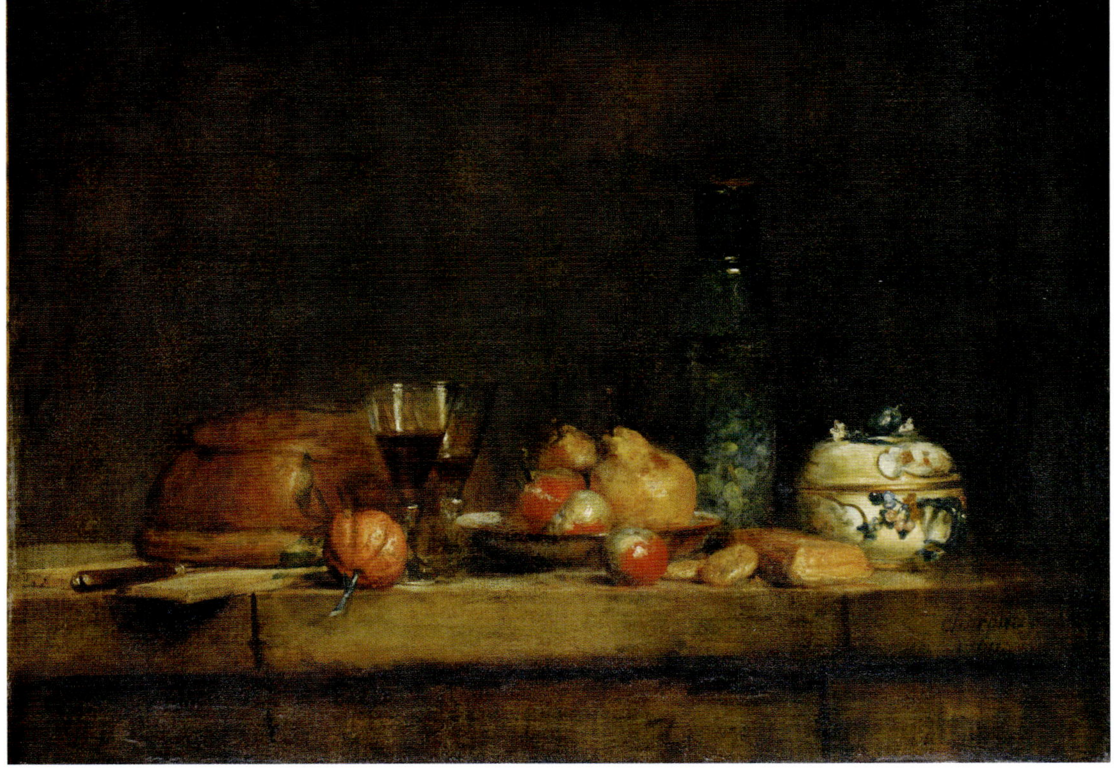

Several distinct traits shared by these still lifes define the difference of Chardin's approach. One is the way in which distance materializes in these paintings, producing the effect of aeration we have already witnessed in the *Bouquet of Carnations*. Produced by tonal gradation, in some cases by scumbling, this effect can be seen in *The Brioche* and the *Grapes and Pomegranates*, where the principal object in both compositions appears surrounded by a halo of air, its particles moving as if the object were indeed breathing. In other paintings, something like a mist, a vapor, or a foam is emitted by the objects.[276] These formal devices emphasize the autonomy of the thing, its existence onto itself, but they also suggest their connection to the subject. Exuding warmth that materializes in the steam rising from it, the tea in the white porcelain teacup in *The Jar of Apricots*, with a spoon plunged in it, is evidently being consumed. The teacup, in other words, is there *for* someone, the pleasure of its contents is to be enjoyed.

Such is also the function of the wrapped or sealed objects that appear increasingly in Chardin's still lifes from this period, such as the bombonière shown to the right of the steaming cup in *The Jar of Apricots*, or, next to it, the little brown package of uncertain content, tied with a string, and, behind it, the sugar loaf in its blue paper, a motif that reappears in other works. Little visual secrets, these wrapped-up items epitomize the object's separateness from the subject, its impenetrability. But these visual gifts are also obviously meant to be used and appreciated: the box of sweets is to be opened, the sugar mountain unwrapped, the jar with apricots unsealed. The wrapping and sealing has the double-edged function of suggesting both the inviolability of the thing—and, by extension, of the painting—and its availability for sensory gratification, its connection to the viewer whom the painting defines as an individuated subject of the senses.

What is the most striking about this group of still lifes is the subjective mode of address manifest in the character of the represented object as a source of bodily pleasure and in the status of the painting itself as an object of visual and tactile gratification. The paintings invite our gaze to wrap itself around the painted things, to traverse the shadowed background in search of additional pleasures. It is our look that they materialize.

It is this aspect that Diderot recognized at length in his response to Chardin's still lifes. From 1759, when Diderot first began writing his accounts of the Salons, he singled out Chardin's still lifes for the novelty and originality of their vision, and he continued to comment on the painter's work until the early 1770s. One of the most salient aspects of these commentaries is their personal tone: "You come just in time, Chardin, to refresh my eyes after your colleague Challe mortally wounded them," announced Diderot in his review of the Salon of 1765.[277] The familiar tone is symptomatic of the critic's response to Chardin's work throughout the *Salons*, wherein the notion that the still lifes appeal to him personally—as if they were painted *for* him—is frequently repeated. The idea of being interpellated by these paintings, that is, of being at once addressed and constituted as an addressee, is the defining trope of Diderot's commentaries on Chardin.[278]

Speaking of *The Jar of Olives* exhibited at the Salon of 1763, Diderot described how he found himself tempted by the edibles displayed in it: "these biscuits need only be picked up and eaten, this Seville orange opened and squeezed, this glass of wine drunk, this fruit peeled and this pâté sliced."[279] It was not only what they were but also how they were depicted that made them so appealing. Diderot takes their mode of representation to be exceedingly natural, a record of things "as they are," such that one is, precisely, tempted to reach out for them.[280] Yet at the same time, he repeatedly acknowledges this effect to be a result of an artifice, extolling Chardin's extraordinary technical skill in producing it, especially his chromatic craft that he finds magical, even sublime.[281] Throughout Diderot's writing on Chardin, the idea of nature displaying itself in his still lifes appears side by side with nuanced discussions of the painter's craft. In Diderot's view, Chardin is in fact not only "the finest colorist of the Salon, and perhaps one of the finest in all painting," as he stated in his *Salon of 1765*, but *the* painter tout court.[282] It is, therefore, how they were *painted* that makes the objects in *The Jar of Olives* so appealing. Considering Chardin's handling in still lifes in general, Diderot declares: "This magic defies understanding. The thick layers of color are applied one on top of the other and the effect transpires from below. At other times the effect is like a vapor breathed lightly on to the canvas; elsewhere a delicate foam has been scattered onto it. . . . Approach the painting and everything blurs, flattens out and vanishes; step back and everything comes together again and reappears."[283]

What comes to the fore in this description is not only material specificity of the painter's faire, but also the way in which this handling solicits the viewer's attention and produces a certain kind of subjective experience. What the passage implies is that this mode of rendering *calls* for its viewer's attention in a particular way, that it is meant to be seen not just as an image—as was the case in de Piles—but also as a material object. The implication of viewing the painting as both an image and a thing is that the viewer is, to some extent, like the painter, first coming up close, and then taking a distance from the canvas as he paints. This identification of the viewer and the painting subject is evident in the trope of vision evoked by Diderot. In an earlier, particularly telling passage of his review, Diderot states à propos *The Jar of Olives* that, in looking at other painters' work, he has "an impression of needing different eyes," but when he looks at Chardin he can simply make use of his own.[284]

It is not just a new phenomenology of looking but the subjectivity involved in looking that Diderot articulates. His interest in the still life is fueled not just by personal attraction but, more precisely, by a kind of scopic drive.[285] The back-and-forth movement drawing the critic in toward the painting amounts to a pull of desire, a force of attraction registered on a psychic level that is not entirely under his control. He recounts being drawn to the painting as if it were a sexual object, or else a primal scene. And the way in which the critic "animates" Chardin's objects and his manner of painting confirms the nature of his attraction to it: "thick layers of color" become layers of flesh, painting transformed into an imaginary body that exerts its sensual attraction on the viewer. On another occasion, Diderot explicitly vaunts Chardin for "painting flesh at his will."[286]

Diderot's insistence that these depictions of inanimate things imply a human subject—that is, that they make sense when experienced by someone in particular—ascribes an unprecedented importance to Chardin's still lifes and to still life as a genre. The critic's recognition of the subjective dimension of these paintings takes different forms, as in a passage in his *Salon of 1767* where he compares the viewer to a tired traveler sitting down in front of a Chardin painting in order to take respite, just as one does during a walk in nature to enjoy its greenery, its silence, and fresh air.[287] Still life, like the landscapes by Vernet that the critic once described in similar terms, is seen as an imaginary location of pleasure. The position in which it places the critic is comparable to that of the little girl in Chardin's earlier painting: he enjoys painting like a refreshment, his pleasure in it comparable to the pleasure of the girl enjoying her simple lunch of cherries and cheese.

For Diderot this pleasure is philosophical. Looking at some of the still lifes Chardin showed at the Salon of 1765, Diderot suddenly feels the urge to share his thoughts with his readers:

> *I must, my friend, communicate to you an idea that's just come to me and that I might not be able to recall at a different moment. It's that the category of painting we call genre [that is, still life] is best suited to old men or to those born old; it requires only study and patience, no verve, little genius, scarcely any poetry, much technique and truth, and that's all. You yourself know that the time we devote to what's conventionally known as the search for truth, philosophy, is precisely when our hair turns grey, when we'd find it very difficult to write a flirtatious letter. Regarding, my friend, these grey hairs, this morning I saw that my entire head was silvered over, and I cried out like Sophocles when Socrates asked him how his love life was going: "A domino agresti et furioso profugi." I am free of that savage and merciless master.*[288]

Chardin's paintings inspire Diderot to make a larger claim about still life as a genre, his definition hinging on the distinct kind of pleasure such images—when they are painted as well as Chardin's—elicit. Describing in a mock-deprecating way the simplicity of skills involved in painting a still life, the critic elevates this type of painting to the domain of philosophical experience. His evocation of philosophy—and Diderot realizes how unusual the association of still life painting with philosophy is[289]—aims to distinguish the kind of sensory gratification provided by still life from the most common type of carnal pleasure. That Diderot saw still life in these terms was precisely the effect of the transformation in Chardin's practice after the figurative interval, when he returned to his "first talent." It was Chardin's paintings of the 1750s and '60s that led Diderot to formulate the idea of the subject constituted by still life (which is what in the quoted passage the critic refers to by the period term "genre"). But the critic's notion of subjectivity as a function of still life must have also been significant for the painter himself. It fostered, or quickened, a recognition of himself as an embodied person posited by these displays of rewarding things.

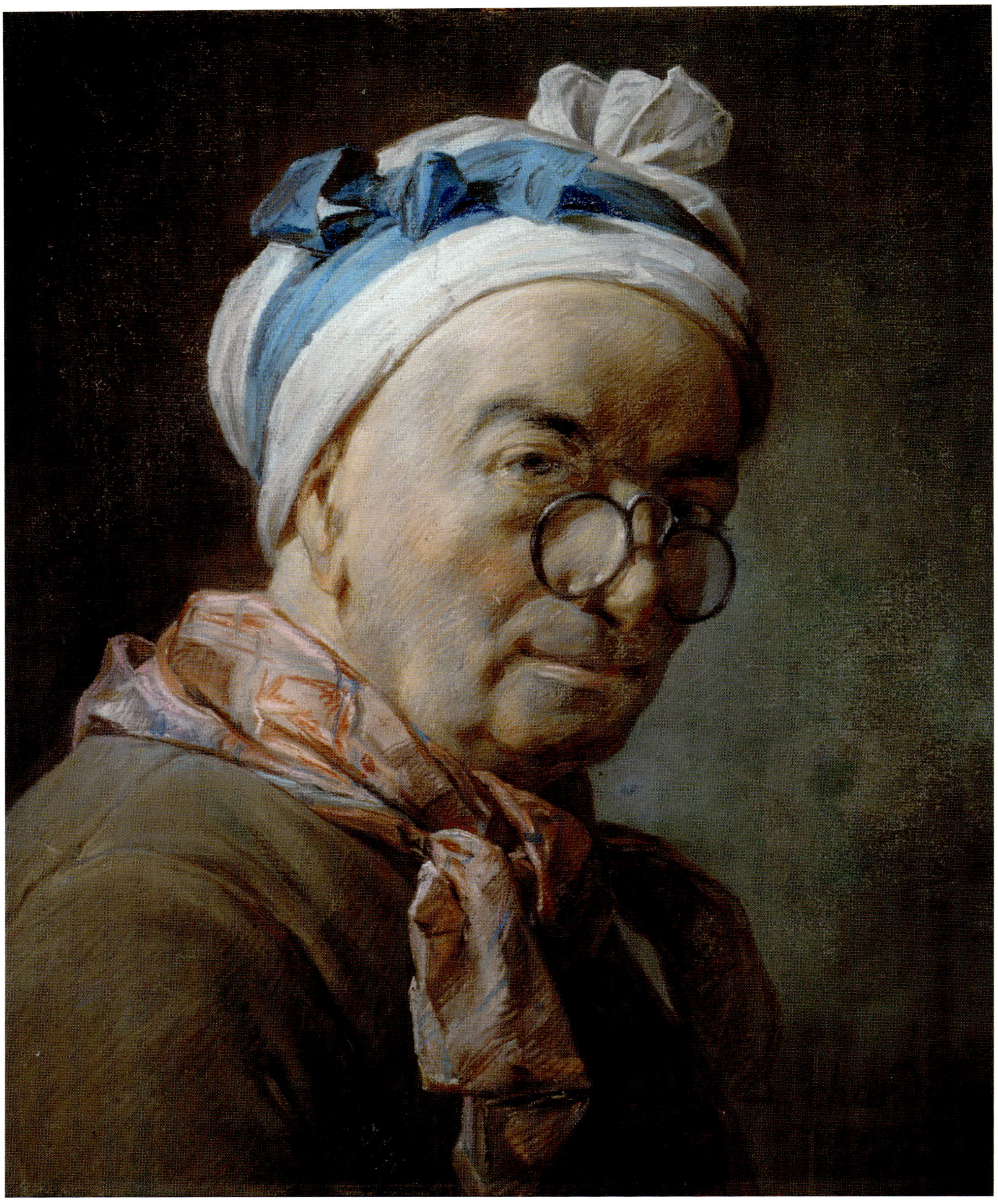

2.85. OPPOSITE
Jean-Siméon Chardin, *Self-Portrait Wearing Spectacles*, 1771. Pastel on paper. Musée du Louvre, Paris.

2.86. RIGHT
Maurice Quentin de La Tour, *Jean-Siméon Chardin*, 1760. Pastel. Musée du Louvre, Paris.

2.87. BELOW
Jean-Siméon Chardin, *Self-Portrait Wearing an Eyeshade*, 1775. Pastel on paper. Musée du Louvre, Paris.

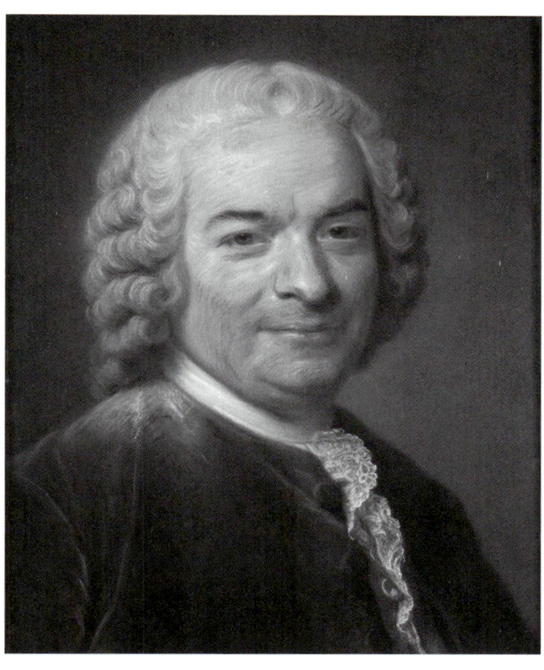

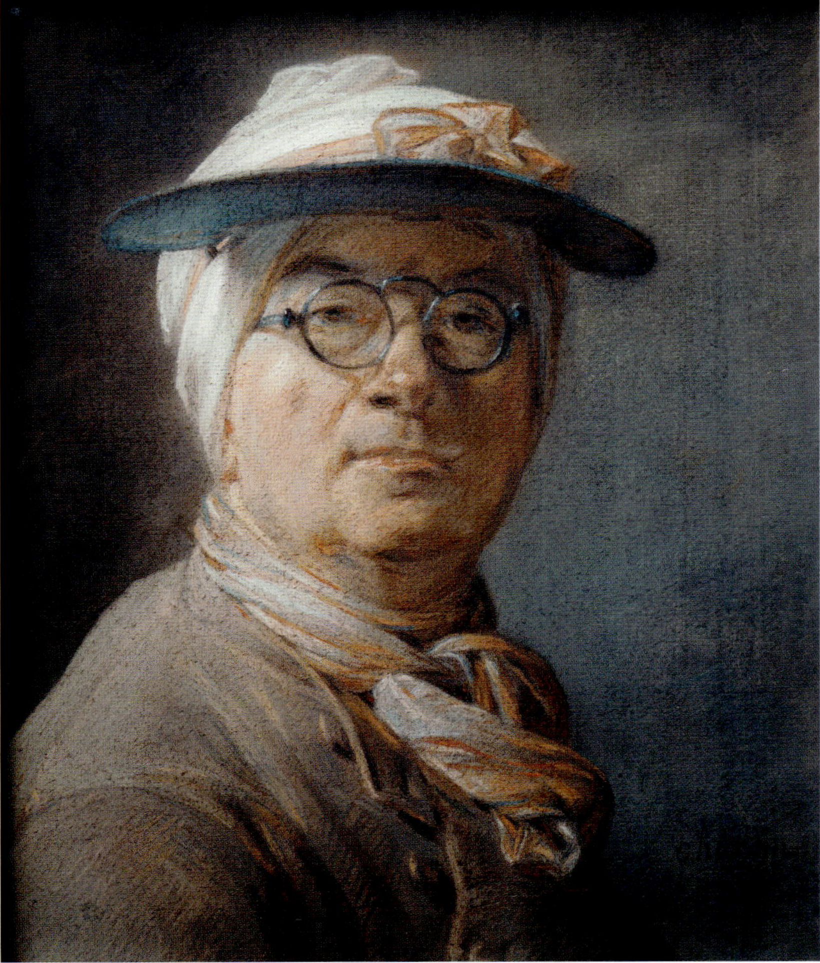

THE PAINTER

It is my own self that I am painting.

—MONTAIGNE, Essays

Late in life, his sight failing, Chardin finally turned his gaze on himself (fig. 2.85). Until then, the painter seems to have had neither interest in, nor need for, self-portrayal. Although he sat for others, notably for Maurice Quentin de La Tour, who produced a pastel likeness of him in 1760 (fig. 2.86), the painter himself evidently did not feel the need to assert his status or promote himself by means of self-depiction.[290] It was only when the threat of blindness caused by his lifelong exposure to lead in oil pigments forced him to turn to pastel that he engaged in self-portrayal.[291] A portrait medium par excellence, pastel may have offered Chardin a technical incentive to depict himself. But his new undertaking must also have been motivated by other factors. What led Chardin to self-portraiture in the late stage of his career? What was at stake in these self-representations?

Between 1771 and 1779, Chardin produced his likeness three times (figs. 2.87 and 2.88; see fig. 2.85) The first two of his self-portraits were displayed at the Salons of 1771 and 1775, and the third one, which is unsigned and undated, may have been among the *têtes d'étude au pastel* the artist sent to the Salon of 1779.[292] The painter's foray into pastel garnered much praise from critics who lauded his truth in depiction, his mastery of color, his bold and knowing touch, and his overall technical excellence in handling a medium that was new to him. Few Salon commentaries engaged specifically, though, with the self-portraits.[293] One of the most intriguing, if posthumous, assessments of their importance was offered by Cochin, who remarked that the technical facility manifest in Chardin's late pastels belied the deep reflection involved in producing them. Cochin saw greatness comparable to history painting in these works.[294]

Yet the idea of greatness hardly comes to mind when one looks at Chardin's self-portraits. Modest in scale, they offer a strikingly intimate vision of the painter. His appearance is remarkably informal: wearing the same plain light-brown jacket, a pink-and-blue madras scarf tied loosely around his neck, his head wrapped up in a white fabric held by a rib-

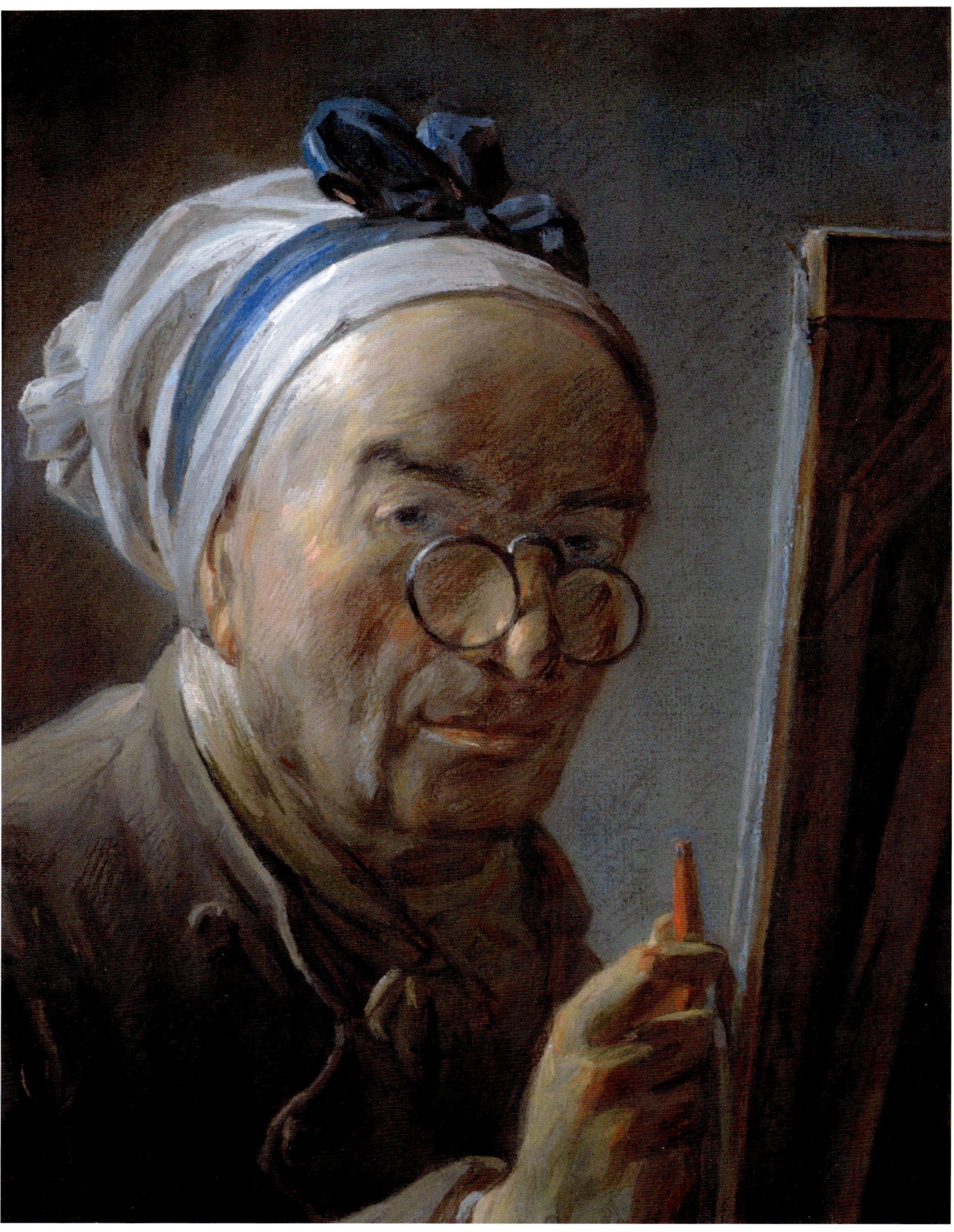

2.88. OPPOSITE
Jean-Siméon Chardin, *Self-Portrait (at His Easel)*, ca. 1779. Pastel on paper. Musée du Louvre, Paris.

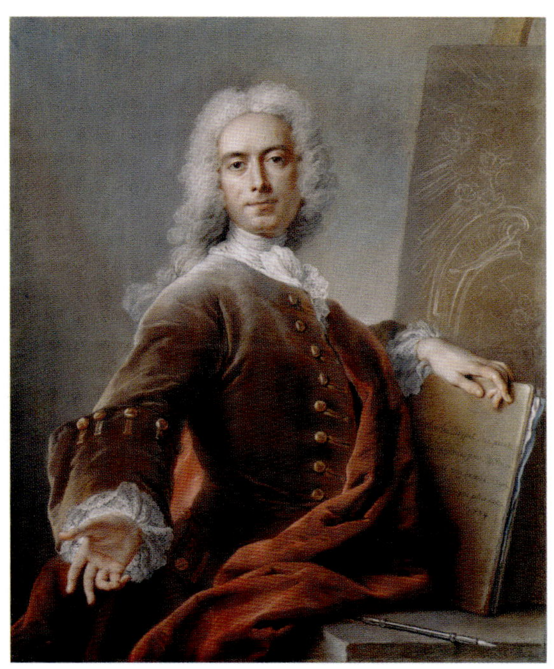

2.89. RIGHT
Charles-Antoine Coypel, *Self-Portrait*, 1734. Pastel on paper. The J. Paul Getty Museum, Los Angeles.

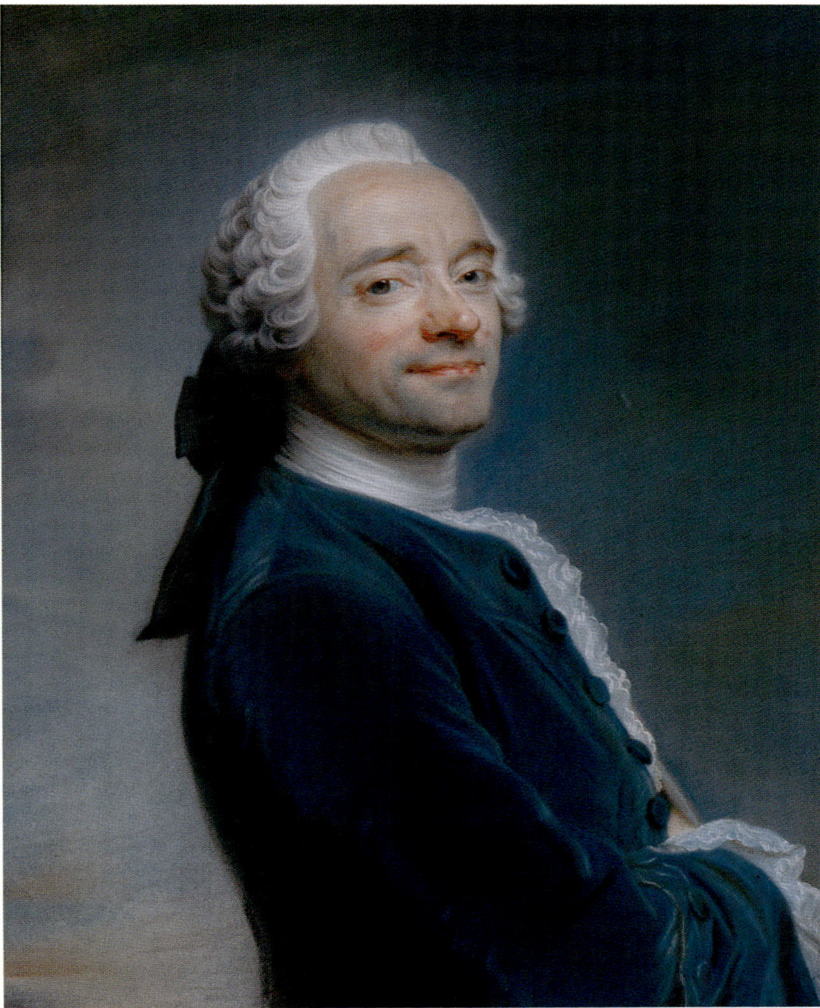

2.90. BELOW
Maurice Quentin de La Tour, *Self-Portrait*, 1751. Pastel. Musée de Picardie, Amiens.

bon, the artist portrays himself in the quotidian simplicity of his working clothes, his mode of self-presentation devoid of any pretension or claim to status. Having chosen a bust format, Chardin avoided the grandiose tone and rhetorical gestures typical of portraits of academicians, such as Charles-Antoine Coypel's pastel *Self-Portrait* of 1734 (fig. 2.89).[295] He also shunned the academic formula of the portrait bust illustrated by Roslin's portrait of Boucher (see fig. 1.1). His body slumped, his face bearing visible marks of aging confirmed by the presence of eyeglasses on his nose, Chardin presented himself with a ruthless accuracy.[296]

This emphasis on truth in self-description was not unique to Chardin. It exemplified the new naturalist trend that emerged in French portraiture around the mid-eighteenth century. Claudia Denk has related Chardin's self-portraits to a broader shift in artists' self-representation that emphasized professional status rather than social rank and institutional prestige.[297] Yet there is, to my mind, a marked difference in tone and purpose between Chardin's self-portraits and those of his contemporaries. It is not only that with the exception of his last likeness, Chardin does not bother to display his tools or directly reference his work. His portraits also show a lack of interest in self-promotion or self-flattery of any kind. Unlike colleagues such as La Tour, who portrayed himself in a fancy blue velvet jacket and powdered wig in his 1751 *Self-Portrait* (fig. 2.90), Chardin eschewed sartorial opulence that would suggest his prosperity or elevated social status. He presented himself in unassuming, private, and distinctly domestic terms. One could say that his is an image of an artist not as a bourgeois professional but as a bourgeois tout court as he would appear at home, a creature thoroughly ensconced in the trappings of domesticity. While such a domesticated appearance was not unheard of in portraiture at the time—one thinks of François-André Vincent's 1774 portrait of his patron, Bergeret de Grancourt, in white deshabille and a wig-less head protected by a satin cloth—it was far from being accepted or even common (fig. 2.91).[298] The few references Chardin does make to his professional occupation—such as the blue-green visor in his second self-portrait, an accessory used by artists at work to shelter their eyes from light, as well as the canvas, blue paper, and pastel stick he grips in his final portrait—are overshadowed by accoutrements of domesticity, most notably the luminous white bonnet tied with a vivid blue ribbon that he wears in two of his self-images, which appear as important for Chardin's self-definition as his professional tools.

The domestic character of the self-portraits—enhanced at the Salon of 1775 by the presence of his wife's portrait, also in pastel (fig. 2.92)—is matched by their private mode of address. For in all three of them Chardin appears unconcerned with engaging the viewer, as portraitists were advised to do. In his *Cours de peinture*, de Piles recommended that portrait painters should try not only to render the distinct traits of their sitters—or, as the case may be, of themselves—but also strive to interpellate the viewer directly: "Stop, look at me, I am [that famous artist,] the unique one in my profession!"[299] La Tour evidently took de Piles's advice to heart, as observed in his self-portrait of 1751. Chardin's gaze, on the other hand, remains resolutely unsolicitous. It is self-examination that his self-portraits speak of. Attentive and deadly serious—there is not even a shade of smile—the painter is looking at himself, or, to be precise, at his reflection in the mirror. The prominence of the eyeglasses, appearing consistently in all three self-portraits, supports the idea of self-scrutiny. They enhance the vision of a painter who is involved in the process of trying to *see* himself.

Yet it is not only sight but also touch as the means of self-representation that Chardin's pastels bring to the fore. This is due to a singularly open mode of execution that by leaving the traces of the pastel crayons unmerged and visible turns the painter's self-image into a map of his process. This approach, as the nineteenth-century critic Lady Dilke asserted, distinguished Chardin from other pastelists of his time. Writing in 1889 about his 1775 *Self-Portrait*, which she saw at the Louvre, Dilke observed: "Chardin used the colored chalk in a manner totally different than La Tour. He was not afraid of leaving his stroke as he had placed it and did not strive for the velvety effects which account for the ordinary charm of the master pastelist."[300] This is also what we witness in Chardin's first *Self-Portrait*, where the painter covers the surface with rhythmic unblended traces of blue pigment interspersed with touches of red, pink, gray, black, and white. While this approach was, to an extent, necessitated by the very nature of the medium, which called for a lateral spread rather than a layered accumulation of color on the surface, Chardin's interpretation of it was remarkably loose.[301] It stands in stark contrast to the approach of Liotard, who not only carefully hid his touch but also declared his method to be the only viable means of using pastel.[302]

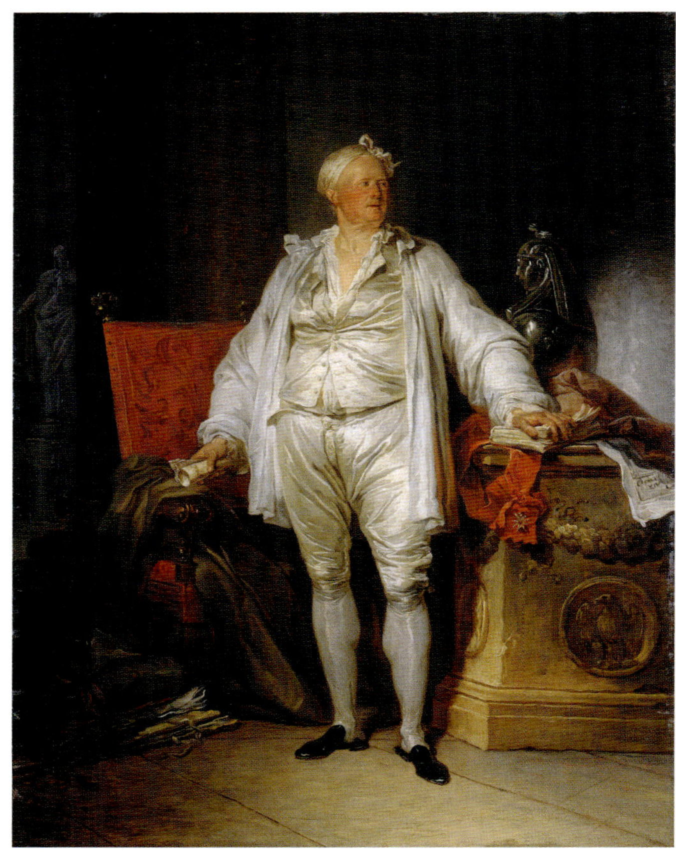

Placing bits of different hues side by side, Chardin set up a chromatic dialogue between them, a strategy admired by, among others, Cézanne, who dubbed Chardin a "cunning craftsman." Writing to Emile Bernard, Cézanne commented on the 1775 *Self-Portrait*: "Haven't you noticed that by letting a plane of light ride across his nose at an angle the values are better established for the eye? Verify this fact, and tell me if I am wrong."[303]

In her discussion of Chardin's self-portraits, Denk has observed that through his masterful and idiosyncratic deployment of the medium, Chardin "portrayed" himself.[304] In the absence of his tools or paintings, it was his creative approach to technique—close to Diderot's conception of execution as interpretation rather than transcription of the sensory data received from nature—that spoke of his work, thus asserting his artistic individuality. Yet if Chardin's pastel technique—like his handling of oil paints—was no doubt a means of self-individuation, more must be said about its idiosyncrasy in the self-portraits. For there are aspects of the painter's brilliantly tactile interpretation of the medium that do not easily square with visual mastery. At times his open, deliberately unintegrated mode of handling reveals pastel to be a technique of undoing,

2.91. OPPOSITE
François-André Vincent, *Monsieur Bergeret de Grancourt*, 1774. Oil on canvas. Musée de Beaux-Arts et d'Archéologie, Besançon.

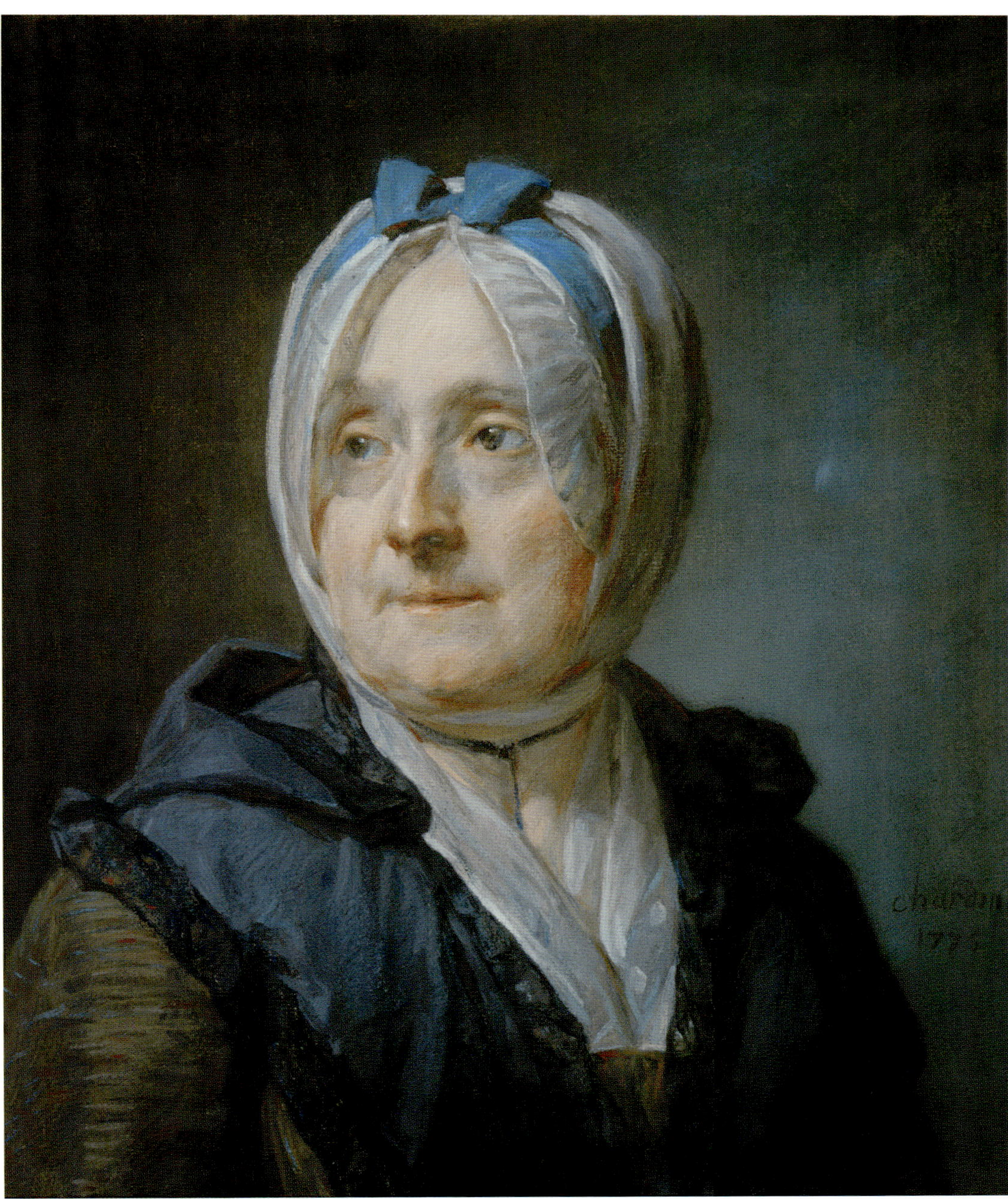

2.92. RIGHT
Jean-Siméon Chardin, *Madame Chardin*, ca. 1775. Pastel. Musée du Louvre, Paris.

or unseeing, especially in the last self-portrait, where the nearly autonomous strokes loosen the bonds of resemblance almost to the point of illegibility.

Nowhere is *seeing* put into question more intriguingly than in the rendition of the painter's eyeglasses. They evoke sight as a problem, not only in the sense that they are a telltale sign of the painter's impaired vision due to old age—Chardin was seventy-two when he painted his first self-portrait—and the noxious impact of oil pigments, but also in that their very presence casts doubt onto the idea of visual perception as the basis of this self-image. How Chardin depicts these visual aids at once brings up the idea of vision and puts it into question. In all three portraits, the featured devices—the *besicles* he wears in his first and last self-portraits, and the *lunettes à tempes* that appear in his second likeness—are his defining attributes.[305] But their rendering defines their function ambivalently. The besicles sliding off the tip of the painter's nose appear as the eyes' double that replaces but also potentially *displaces*, if not obstructs, sight. Chardin's use of obfuscating grays and, in the last self-portrait, darker, even less transparent ochers, turns the lenses into opaque disks, reinforcing the effect of sight impeded rather than sharpened. Alberto Giacometti recognized this effect when, copying the 1771 self-portrait, he repeatedly went over the round metal rims of the besicles, the insistent, dark circles traced by his pencil turning this accessory into the principal actor of Chardin's likeness (fig. 2.93).

The spectacles perform a key function in Chardin's self-portraits. Far from merely a token of faithful self-description, they epitomize the non-mimetic dimension of the painter's approach to self-representation. Testimonies not only to the impairment of Chardin's vision but also to the role of touch as an alternative to sight, they evoke blindness as a pervasive trope for the painter of "deep materiality." If they are Chardin's attribute, it is not only because they refer to his living body—or to his very act of representing it—but also because they evoke one of the key aspects of his pictorial practice at large, the task of self-individuation in and through representation. The presence of the eyeglasses underscores that it was the painter's relation to himself, rather than his relation to the viewer, that constituted Chardin's main preoccupation in these portraits, not only in a sense of being his own first viewer but also as the *maker* of his own image.

"Ce moi que je peins" (It is my own self that I am painting), declared Michel de Montaigne in the prefatory note to his *Essays*.[306] Although undertaken at a different historical moment, Montaigne's attempt at self-representation offers an instructive comparison for Chardin's own project.[307] Written between 1580 and 1592, the *Essays* illustrate their author's pursuit of self-knowledge, a project to which he devoted himself upon his retirement from public life. It was to "assay himself," the tentative nature of this undertaking being reflected by its very title ("essai" in French meaning a trial or an attempt), that Montaigne engaged in describing his nature, habits, thoughts, and opinions, whether these regarded philosophical matters or bodily activities, such as eating, sleeping, or having sex, in order to arrive at a sense of his own personality.[308] His pursuit was marked by a desire for truth that led him to record his appearance and actions in the context of his everyday life rather than the public domain. He announced: "If my design had been to seek favor of the world I would have decked myself out better and presented myself in a studied gait. Here I want to be in my simple, natural, everyday fashion without striving or artifice: for it is my own self that I am painting."[309] In other words, it was how he appeared to himself rather than to others that concerned Montaigne. To look at himself in the privacy of his home, in the simplicity of his quotidian dress and habits, was understood by the author as the condition of getting to the truth of his self.

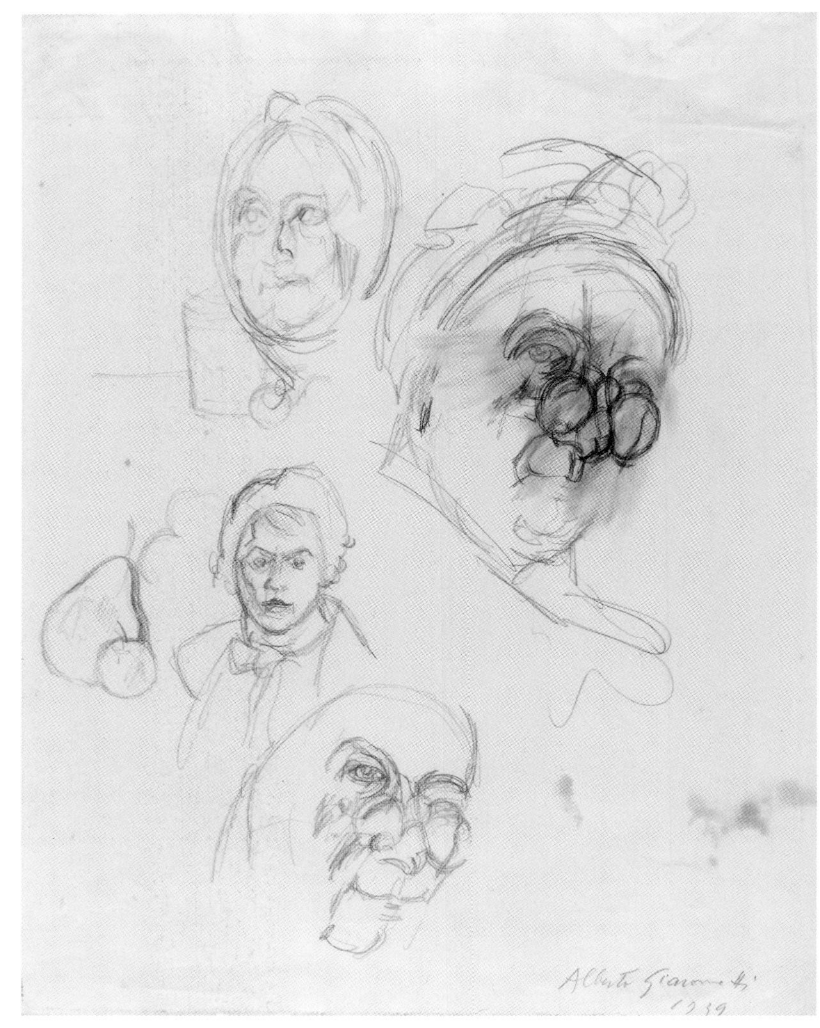

Yet Montaigne's *Essays* were not merely a vehicle of truth but also a means of self-invention. He wrote not to disclose what he knew about himself, but rather to find out who he was, to develop his identity through writing, the very title of his project indicating the tentative and open-ended nature of such enterprise. As such the *Essays* constitute a paradigmatic example of early modern literary self-fashioning. The self that Montaigne was "depicting" was a kind of fiction crafted in words.[310]

Chardin's self-portraits seem to echo Montaigne's succinct statement of purpose: "C'est moi que je peins." Undertaken late in life, around the time when he retired from his administrative duties at the Academy, Chardin similarly emphasized "naturalness" and "simplicity."[311] Like Montaigne, Chardin seems to have been interested not in how others saw him but in how he appeared to himself, as an object of his own gaze. Although the painter exhibited his self-portraits at the Salon, they were remarkably intimate

2.93.
Alberto Giacometti, *Copies of Heads of Chardin, Madame Chardin, and Jacques-Louis David*, 1939. Graphite, with touches of stumping, on cream wove paper. Art Institute of Chicago, Gift of Louis Goldenberg with balance from members of the Committee and Staff in honor of Mrs. Joseph Regenstein.

in their address. Montaigne's intentions in publishing his *Essays* were stated clearly: "I have dedicated this book to the private benefit of my friends and kinsmen so that, having lost me (as they must soon) they can find here again some traits of my character and my humours."[312] Chardin's self-portraits seem also to have been intended largely for the benefit of a limited audience—his family, his friends, and himself.[313] (That, upon his retirement, Chardin's parting gift to the Academy was his 1760 pastel portrait by La Tour rather than any of his own self-portraits produced at that time confirms their private character.[314]) I focus on their importance for the painter himself.

While Montaigne's *Essays* help us recognize the deliberate nature of Chardin's self-construction, they also underscore essential differences between the two projects. Chardin represented his self not by describing the life of his mind and body, as did Montaigne, but by painting—in his case literally—his body stroke by stroke. This task of self-embodiment was, in my view, in a crucial sense enabled and sustained by Chardin's own art.

Self-portraits are always in one way or another engaged with the artist's work. The very invention of the genre during the early modern era signaled the recognition of the painter's identity as a function of his or her own art. In his discussion of Albrecht Dürer, Joseph Koerner has argued that from the moment of its inception as a distinct pictorial genre, the self-portrait constituted an indirect commentary on the artist's work.[315] Yet Chardin's self-portraits occupy a distinct place within this tradition, particularly in their relation to the artist's earlier paintings, which in my view constituted the "conditions of figurability" that enabled Chardin to transform his body image into a figure of his self.[316] It was because he experienced *himself* in making art—if differently at the different stages of his career—that late in life Chardin was able to arrive at self-representation. Hints of their connection to the painter's earlier practice can be found in the self-portraits themselves.

One connection is the emphatically domestic attire that the painter adopted in all three self-portraits. The prominence of his bonnet rendered with attention to its elaborate details, and the conspicuous presence of the blue or pink-rimmed ribbons tied carefully into large bows, cannot be explained solely by the painter's sartorial habits.[317] Clearly the choice of this curious headgear for a self-portrait was part of Chardin's self-fashioning—the care and chromatic brio with which he painted it confirm this. In all three pastels, in addition to the face and the glasses, it is the bonnet that engaged the painter's crayons the most. Chardin's choice of the attribute is especially interesting in that it establishes a relation between the painter's body and the bodies of all the bonneted female protagonists of his genre scenes, such as *The Diligent Mother* or the *Attentive Nurse* (see figs. 2.47 and 2.38). While on the head of *The Diligent Mother* the ribbon was veiled by the semi-transparent wrap around the woman's bonnet, in Chardin's self-portraits it is one of two principal chromatic accents, the second being the madras scarf tied around his neck like a feminine *fichu*, such as that worn by the servant in *La Pourvoyeuse* (see fig. 2.46).

These sartorial correspondences could hardly be accidental. To my mind, they are residual traces of the painter's investment in the female figure that marked his foray into genre painting. Chardin's embellished headgear conjures up the domestic sphere of femininity that once constituted the very domain of his professional—and personal—self-definition. This was, as we have seen, the domain the artist embraced early on in an effort to situate himself within, and distinguish himself from, the paternal realm of artisanship; it is from this sphere of domesticity that his work emerged, first the early still lifes and then the genre scenes focused on the women and children of his extended family. It was Chardin's family home rather than the institutional context of the Academy that provided the material and symbolic basis for the artist's self-definition throughout most of his career.[318] The feminine aspects of Chardin's attire express his sustained connection to this sphere, a symptom of the role of the female figure as the imaginary armature of his self-representation. As his self-portraits suggest, Chardin had finally *inhabited* the figure.

The image of the painter's body is, then, not merely a document of himself at a specific moment in time, but the result of prolonged self-reflection—involving memory and imagination—that could not be reduced to sight. This idea returns us to the painter's eyeglasses as an ambivalent sign for vision in Chardin's self-portraits. In eighteenth-century France, corrective glasses were more frequently represented as an attribute of an incompetent critic—as in Cochin's vignette illustrating *Les Misotechnites aux Enfers* discussed earlier—than an accessory of a painter (see fig. 2.3). None of the French artists of Chardin's generation portrayed themselves in eyeglasses, and it may well be that some of the painters who did so later

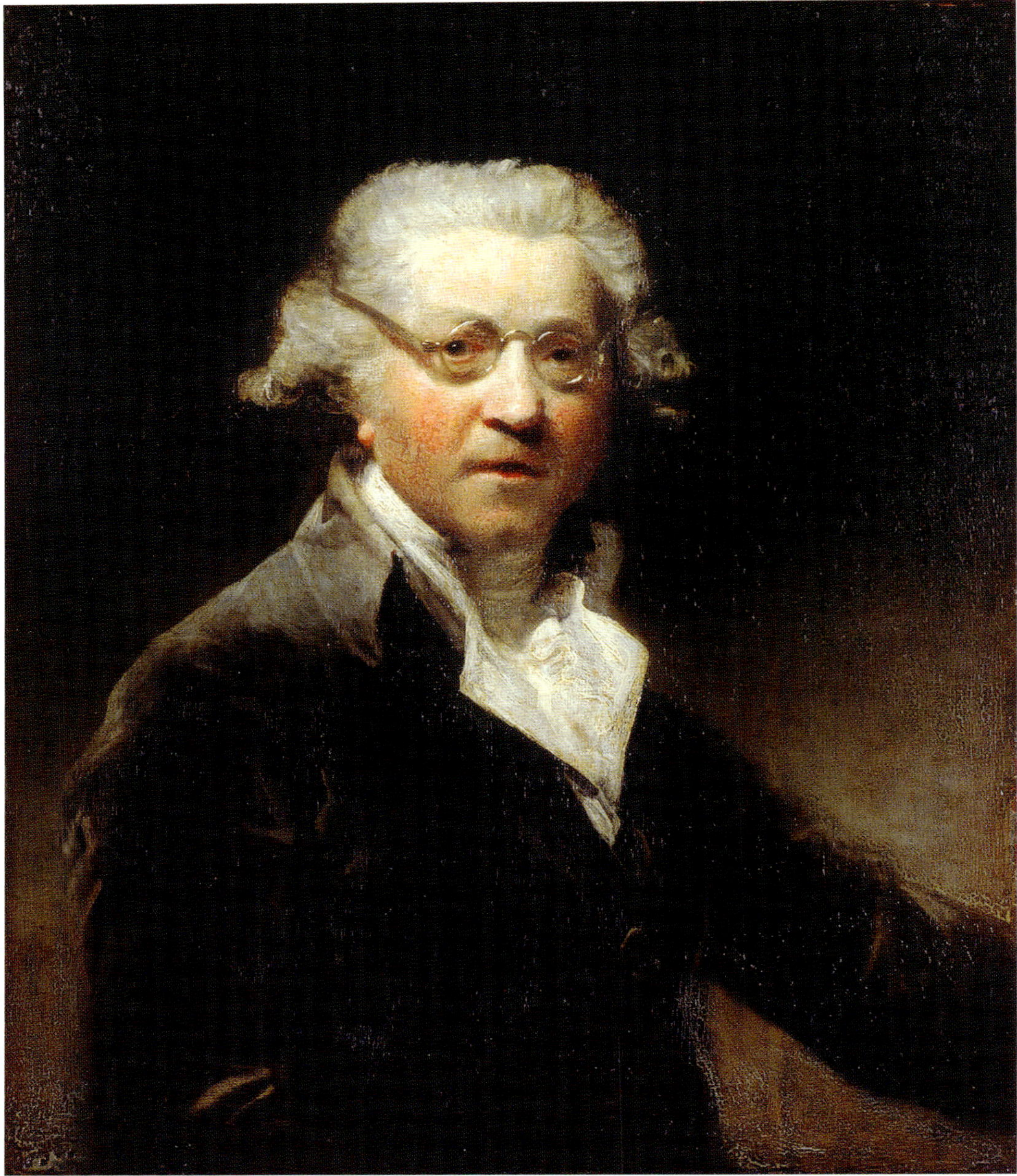

2.94.
Joshua Reynolds, *Self-Portrait with Glasses*, 1788. Oil on panel. Royal Collection Trust, London.

on—for example, Joshua Reynolds in his *Self-Portrait with Glasses* (fig. 2.94)—were inspired by Chardin's example.[319] Unusual before Chardin, the choice of spectacles as an element of an artist's self-definition signaled the artist's social position. Besicles, relatively cheap to produce in the eighteenth century, were popular among the lower classes but were rarely worn by the elite, and never in public.[320] At the theater or in another social context, members of the upper class preferred to use a monocle, considered more elegant. The inclusion of the besicles in Chardin's self-portraits was something of a class act—one the matched the defiantly common character of the painter's attire.

A sign of class, the spectacles also defined Chardin's vision of himself in these self-portraits. Note, in this regard, the relation he sets up between his eyeglasses and his eyes. Chardin's look in all three likenesses seems slow or delayed, aimed at his object—himself—yet somehow unfocused. His eyes, moreover, do not perform the traditional function of apertures into the soul. Instead of suggesting his subjective presence by marking the light coming through his eyes—as painters commonly do by placing a small dot of white pigment on the iris right above the pupil—Chardin does the opposite: he opacifies his eyes, displacing the light from the eyes to his eyeglasses. In all three self-portraits, his eyes are presented as neither the source nor the recipient of light. In his first and last pastels, Chardin's irises and pupils, half-hooded by his lids, appear blotted, and, in the second,

2.95.
Jean-Siméon Chardin, *Self-Portrait Wearing an Eyeshade*, detail of fig. 2.87.

2.96.
Joshua Reynolds, *Self-Portrait with Glasses*, detail of fig. 2.94.

the light dances on the metal rim of the besicles while the eyes, smudged behind the lenses, remain dark, the impression enhanced by the shadow cast on his face by the blue-green visor. This rendition of the eyes cannot be explained by the mediating effect of glass, as a quick glance at Reynolds's *Self-Portrait*, where the sparkle in the painter's eyes is clearly visible behind his lenses, attests (figs. 2.95 and 2.96). Rather, it is an alternative way of suggesting interiority, similar to the way Chardin conveyed it in his early painting of the *Blind Beggar* (see fig. 2.29). In the latter, the condition of blindness was represented as inviolable interiority; in the self-portraits, it is interiority itself that is represented as a kind of blindness. Not simply a suggestion of impaired sight, the painter's bespectacled and obfuscated eyes may be seen as a commentary on the origins of these self-representations not in vision but in the interior life of the depicted subject. They evoke a subjective space in which Chardin's transformation into the object of his own vision had occurred.

This transformation hinged on a distance that the painter acquired from himself in and through representation. The eyeglasses, a mediating object, stand for it. Shown at some remove from the painter's eyes, the besicles in particular announce themselves as a measure of that distance—a hiatus between the painter's position as a seeing subject and as an object of his own vision. As such, they hint at a psychic separation that must have occurred for Chardin to be able to recognize himself as an object, that is, an entity separate from himself. We have witnessed a similar process of subjective separation in Chardin's scenes of adolescent diversions that became, in his hands, representations of self-discovery through the experience of objects both related to and distinct from oneself. Like the young protagonist of the *Soap Bubbles* (see fig. 2.62), Chardin too seems to have arrived at such self-recognition, acquiring a sense of his own body as an entity separate from and thus visible to himself. It was his own practice that, by providing him with an experience of the body he had not received through training, made his self-representation possible. This is why Chardin embarked on self-portraiture only late in life.

Working in pastel may have contributed to the painter's self-recognition insofar as the medium exteriorizes touch: in pastel there is no hidden depth, everything is on the surface. Chardin made the most of this quality, adopting an even looser mode of application than other artists, which enabled him to see his own touch. There was, however, also an invisible dimension to his tactile operations. An instrument of anamnesis, touch brought the artist into contact with his own pictorial past. This process involved vision but also a kind of blindness, not only because self-representation, due to its mediated nature, obfuscates as much as reveals its subject—a point made at length by Jacques Derrida in his discussion of blindness as the defining trope of the self-portrait—but also because of the challenge of "figuring" himself out that was uniquely Chardin's own.[321]

The presence of the eyeglasses evokes this particular challenge. As instruments of seeing and non-seeing

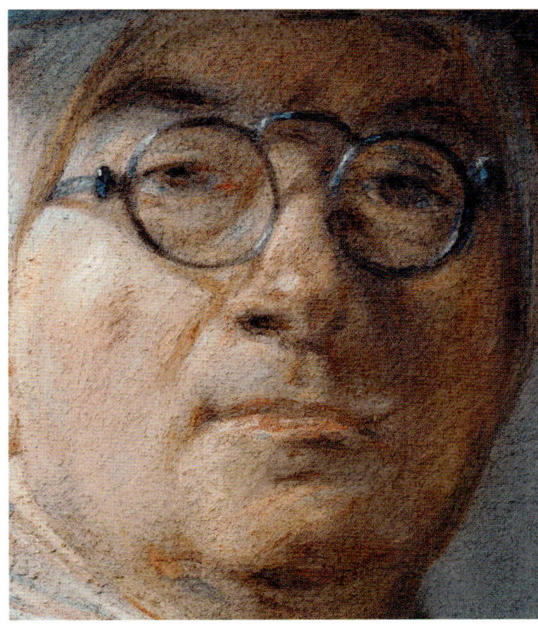

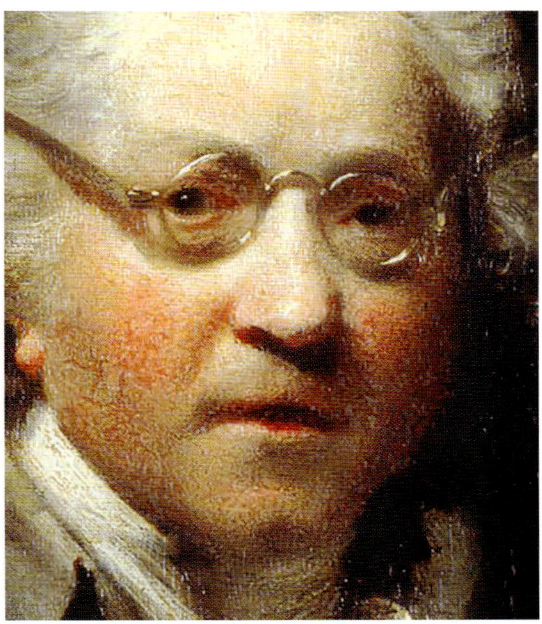

they help us recognize the connection between the late self-portraits and Chardin's larger aesthetic project. In evoking both sight and blindness, they look back to the artist's earlier practice of bringing up forms as if from "underneath the visible" to the surface. They define their wearer as the painter of the invisible in an aesthetic and social sense, evoking both the chromatic, contourless existence of his elusive figures and their "invisible" or unassuming social status, which was also the painter's own. In this sense, they are the signs for the painter's "inner touch" acquired through representation.

—.—

Among the three self-portraits, the last one, produced in 1779, strikes a slightly different note (see fig. 2.88). Compared to his earlier versions, Chardin has visibly aged, his hunched body appearing closer to the surface of the image, as if the painter had to lean forward to see himself in the mirror, his sight having evidently deteriorated. Moreover, by showing himself brandishing a pastel crayon, as if to make a point, he opens up the possibility of a dialogue with the viewer, or with himself. Rendered with two contiguous slashes of red hue—one stark crimson, with a grain of blue on top, another muted ocher-red—the crayon in Chardin's hand may be seen as a reference to the making of this image, echoing as it does the rough, unblended strokes with which the painter portrayed his body and especially his face, his ruddy cheeks fleshed out by touches of different colors, red hues prominent among them. But, oddly held, the red stick also suggests an argument of some sort, if formulated with chroma, without words.

What point is Chardin making? To begin with, let us consider the external circumstances that may have been relevant to the making of this work. Throughout the 1770s, Chardin's health had gradually deteriorated, leading to his death in December 1779 at the age of eighty.[322] The last decade of Chardin's life was marked by disappointments, a sense of not being sufficiently appreciated by his peers and by economic difficulties. These setbacks were linked to changes at the Academy, to the monarchy's renewed investment in history painting, and to an aesthetic shift toward neoclassicism, resulting in the devaluation of the kind of art Chardin was making and, therefore, of Chardin himself.[323]

By the mid-1770s, the painter's institutional career was coming to a close. In July 1774, citing bad health, Chardin resigned his post as treasurer of the Academy after having served in this function, joined to that of tapissier, for twenty years.[324] Although he remained an active member of the Academy, Chardin seems to have had a hard time accepting his diminished importance within the institution.[325] Moreover, the Academy's power structure had changed, resulting in a loss of influence of Chardin and his supporters. In 1770 Jean-Baptiste Marie Pierre became the director of the Academy, and under his rule—judged by many as autocratic and arrogant—its priorities shifted. With the support of the new *directeur général des Bâtiments*, the comte d'Angiviller, the Academy committed itself more rigorously to the support of history painting and solicited royal patronage almost exclusively for this purpose. To ensure his control over the institution, Pierre forced Cochin to resign his position as secretary, assigning him a function of mere advisor (*conseilleur*). Chardin took it upon himself to protest what he perceived as mistreatment of his friend and advocate. In March 1777, he wrote a long and bitter letter to d'Angiviller opposing Pierre's disrespectful attitude toward Cochin as well as himself. Reporting Pierre's insensitivity, Chardin complained that is was "unjust to mistreat an old man [meaning himself] pensioned by the King."[326] But d'Angivillier, while expressing deep respect for the painter, defended Pierre's actions.[327] Having made an enemy of the new director, Chardin's later requests for financial support went unheard.[328] When in June 1778, citing "the mediocrity of his fortune," the artist wrote to d'Angiviller asking for a pension commensurate with the salary he had received earlier as the treasurer of the Academy, his request was refused. Pierre drafted d'Angiviller's response.[329]

Although Chardin's financial situation may not have been as bleak as his letters suggest—though not as well off as Boucher or Oudry at the end of their respective careers, he was far from destitute—the refusal of his superiors to comply with his requests must have disappointed and demoralized him.[330] Situated in the context of these diminished and demeaning professional circumstances, Chardin's last *Self-Portrait* takes on the air of a rebuttal accentuated by the presence of the stretcher and the pastel stick in the painter's hand. These professional attributes, absent from the earlier self-portraits, transform the 1779 image into a more explicit commentary on Chardin's talents and show him engaged in a dialogue with the very institution with which he found himself at odds: the Academy. These aspects of the *Self-Portrait* would have been highlighted by its dis-

2.97.
Jean-Siméon Chardin, *Self-Portrait (at His Easel)*, detail of fig. 2.88.

play at the Salon, the Academy's domain, where the painting doubtlessly served to demonstrate that Chardin had kept up his work despite his advanced age, in addition to reasserting his professional autonomy in relation to the royal institution. Combined with his defiantly domestic attire, the painter's attributes locate his practice squarely at home. Rejecting the apparatus of self-presentation typical of the institutional portrait, Chardin offers viewers an image of an artist with no visible affiliation with the Academy. "It is *myself* that I am painting"—he seems to be declaring, his statement, within the context of the Salon, taking on a specific, anti-institutional charge.

Moreover, this self-image may be seen as an avowal of aesthetic independence, a declaration of chromatic defiance vis-à-vis the Academy. The stick of red pigment interrupting the field of vision aggressively puts forward color rather than drawing as the means of representation. One could see this assertive vertical bar of red as a distant echo of the bloody innards of the fish slicing open the pictorial space of *The Ray*, the painter's earlier pledge of allegiance to color (see fig. 2.11). Thrust at the viewer, the stick of red in the *Self-Portrait* acts as the condensed sign of who Chardin was within the institutional context of the Academy and within the artistic culture at large. (One thinks of Estève's explicitly anti-academic interpretation of the painter's chromatic method.) By establishing chromatic correspondences between his tools and his body—between the red crayon and its traces on his face; between the blue paper on his stretcher and the blue ribbon and the highlights on his bonnet—Chardin revindicates his professional identity as a painter of color unconfined by the Academy's rules or discourse.

To read the 1779 *Self-Portrait* exclusively as a form of professional revindication, however, would be to ignore its function as the means of the painter's dialogue with himself. That dialogue manifests itself above all in the stick of red pigment that, splitting this space of self-representation, acts as a differential mark, commenting on Chardin's divided identity—the difference *within* himself—and on his medium, pastel, as the means of negotiating it. A bar of red that resonates yet resists integration with the rest of the picture, the crayon spells out the painter's conception of himself as inseparable from the materiality of his craft.

The dialogue between the painter and his medium the last self-portrait sets up, also reveals the risks of his reliance on his craft. This is most evident in Chardin's rendition of his face, a tour de force of the making and unmaking of the self. The dense pattern of hatchings that simultaneously secures the painter's features and threatens to unmoor them, make his face appear as if it were about to slide off, following the movement of the besicles down his nose. The evanescence of the medium, its dust barely adhering to the paper's surface, enhances this effect. Note, for instance, the scrap of blue pigment in the lower left of the painter's face that looks as if it were about to peel off, threatening to pull down the fold of flesh with it (fig. 2.97). A kind of flaying—a *defacement*—is being produced. Self-representation is no longer an instrument of self-fashioning but the very means of losing the self. The ambivalent, half-admiring, half-disparaging praise offered by a critic of Chardin's work shown at the Salon of 1777 comes to mind: "Monsieur Chardin reminds me of those athletes who, tottering after a terrible combat, gather all their forces to mount on the arena to expire."[331] Yet what the last *Self-Portrait* suggests is something differently ambivalent: the promise and the limits of the painter's craft as a tool of self-definition. If his mode of execution suggests the impermanence of this self-representation, hinting at the possibility of imminent defacement, the red crayon gripped by Chardin's hand strengthens this discomfiting suggestion. Sparkling on its very tip are some material traces of the *object* that has just been depicted, or undone: the painter himself.

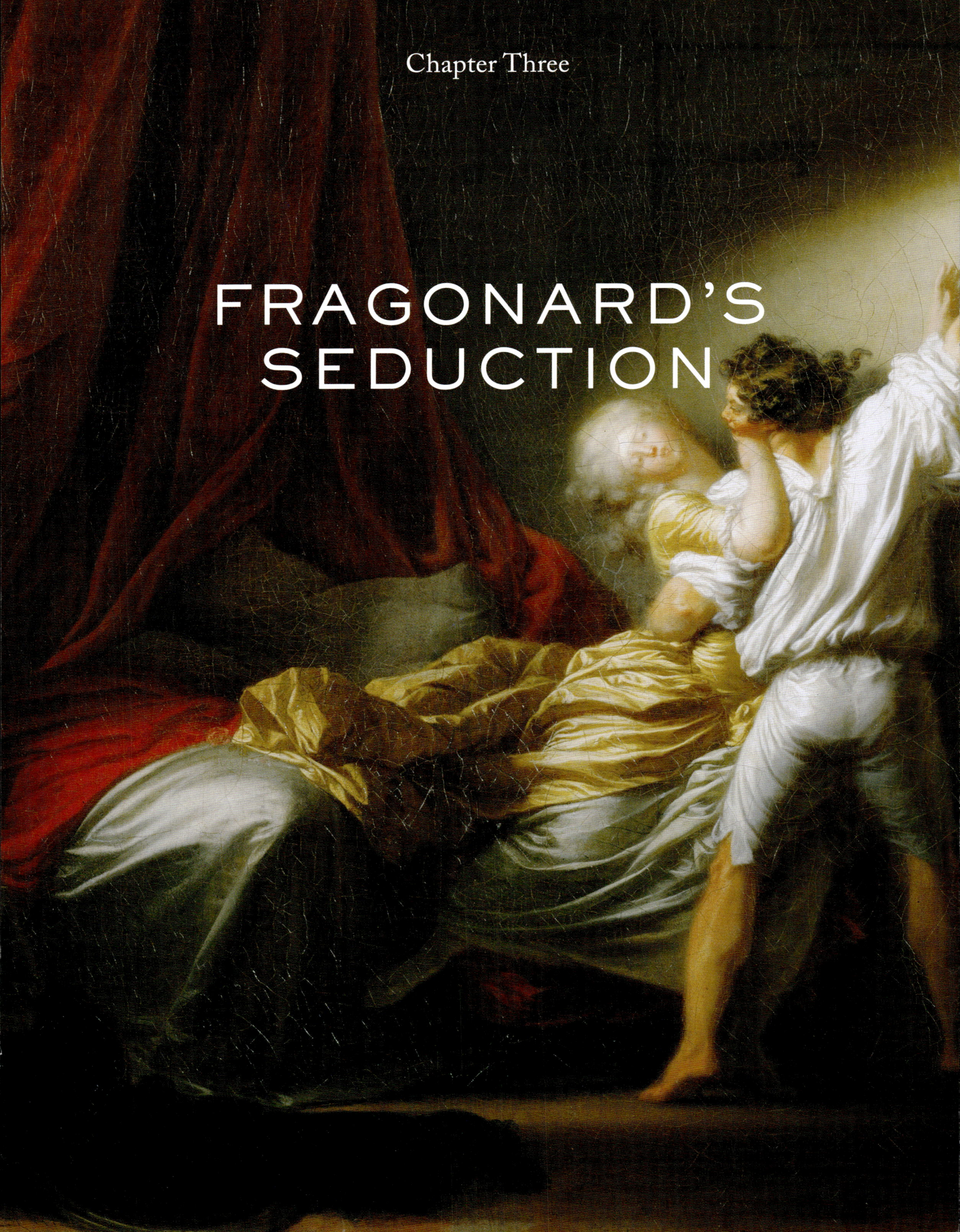

Chapter Three

FRAGONARD'S SEDUCTION

EROS AND INDIVIDUALITY

To achieve happiness, everyone has to grasp the type of pleasure that is proper to him.

—Thérèse Philosophe

There has hardly ever been a painter whose work would be as extensively and as consistently committed to eros as was Fragonard's.[1] The meaning and import of this visual commitment has been a subject of extensive scholarship.[2] Yet the radical originality and even strangeness of Fragonard's arousing art continue to elude us. Notwithstanding Mary Sheriff's groundbreaking work, and the more recent scholarship on the subject that has productively situated the aesthetic enterprise of the painter in the artistic and libertine culture of his time, the existing models of interpretation have not fully accounted for the ambitious and highly idiosyncratic nature of his erotic project nor for its pictorial and material specificity.[3]

We do not get much help in this regard from Fragonard's contemporaries, whom he disappointed by opting out of a promising career as a history painter despite the institutional and critical encouragement he had received early on to pursue it. Fragonard was groomed for success like few before him—certainly neither Boucher nor Chardin, both of whom were his teachers, were thus prepared.[4] Having won the prestigious Prix de Rome in 1752, at the age of twenty, the young artist entered the École des Élèves Protégés, the newly created finishing school for the most promising history painters, where he was trained in drawing for four years. In 1756 he departed for Rome, where he spent five years as a *pensionnaire* of the French Academy, proving both his extraordinary talent and inclination to follow his own path.[5] In 1765, after his return from Rome, Fragonard exhibited a large-scale, ambitious history painting, *Coresus Sacrificing Himself to Save Callirhoë*, which gained him provisional membership in the Academy and the recognition of the Salon critics (fig. 3.1).[6] The painter turned his subject, based in an obscure tale from Pausanias's *Description of Greece*, into a sweeping neo-baroque drama of love-driven sacrifice, its bold composition, gestural panache, expressive range, and chromatic brilliance recognized as a tour de force of execution. The painting's spectacular suggestiveness led Diderot to dream in his review of the exhibition.[7]

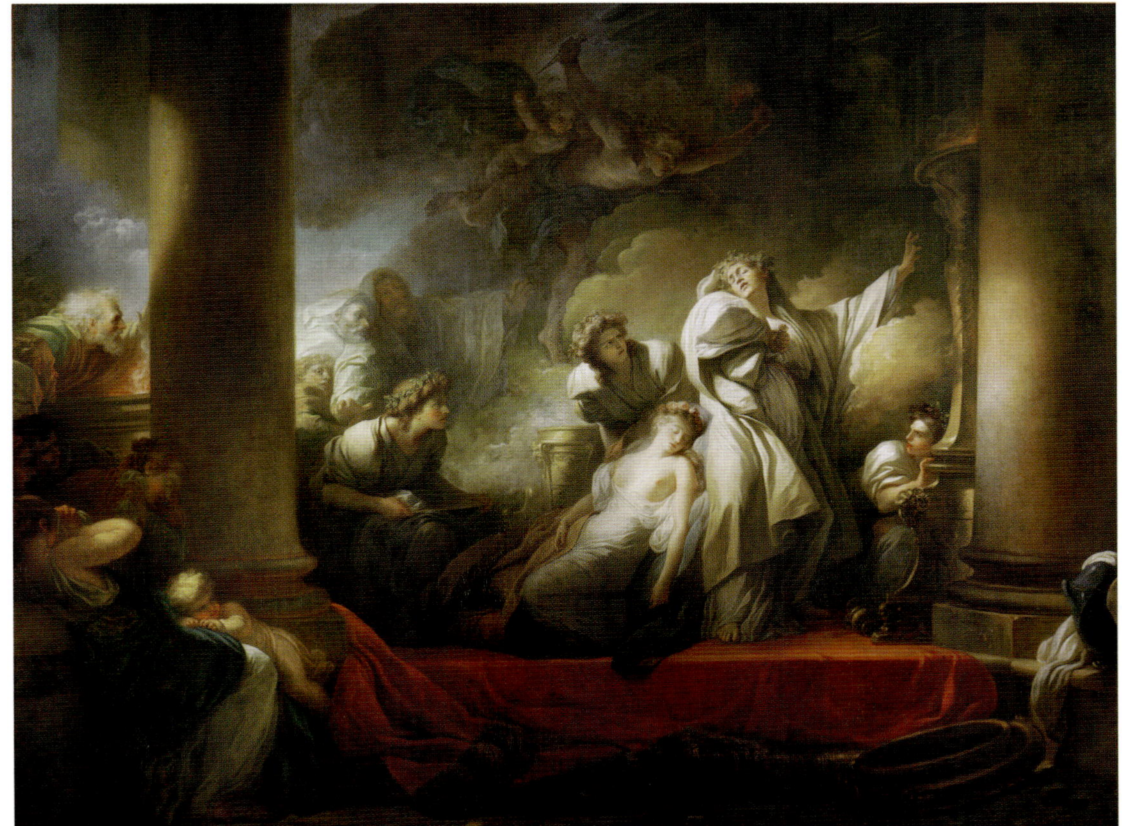

3.1. Jean-Honoré Fragonard, *Coresus Sacrificing Himself to Save Callirhoë*, Salon of 1765. Oil on canvas. Musée du Louvre, Paris.

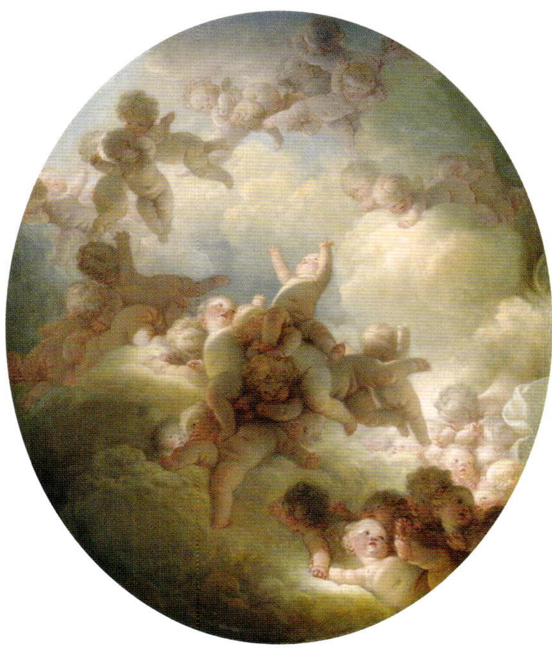

3.2. LEFT
Jean-Honoré Fragonard, *Groups of Children in the Sky*. Oil on canvas. Salon of 1767. Musée du Louvre, Paris.

3.3. OPPOSITE
Jean-Honoré Fragonard, *The Swing*, 1766. Oil on canvas. The Wallace Collection, London.

The painter, however, went on to dash the high hopes both the Academy and the critics had for him. Two years after his public success all he could come up with for his main entry at the Salon exhibition was the *Groups of Children in the Sky*, a painted ceiling decoration quite understandably dismissed by Diderot as a "beautifully prepared omelet, moist, yellow, and slightly burnt" (fig. 3.2).[8] This odd compositional lump of plump putti, to which I shall return in due course, marks Fragonard's more or less voluntary exit from the main arena of aesthetic scrutiny. After his failure to impress the critics in 1767, the artist renounced exhibiting at the Salon, turning increasingly to private commissions and effectively removing himself from the public forum of artistic debate.[9] Stalling with and ultimately failing to deliver his *morceau de réception* to the Academy, he also forfeited his chance to become a permanent member of this institution.[10] Fragonard's withdrawal from the sphere of artistic officialdom did not mean that, from then on, his work passed unnoticed. On the contrary, he continued to be recognized as a painter of exceptional, if mostly squandered, gifts. Commenting on his absence from the Salon of 1769, the *Mémoires secrets* sarcastically reported that "instead of working for the glory and for posterity, [Fragonard] contends himself to shine today in the boudoirs and in the closets."[11] And, in 1771, Mme d'Épinay echoed a largely shared view when she quipped dismissively: "M[onsieur] Fragonard? He wastes his time and his talent: he earns money."[12]

As these comments attest, Fragonard's involvement with erotic subjects, combined with his reliance on private patrons, placed him in an awkward position as an artist. While his paintings and drawings were sought after by the renowned collectors and amateurs of the period, and they fetched high, at times even notoriously exorbitant prices, they were not the object of any sustained critical examination.[13] Many admired Fragonard's sheer technical brio—his "magical execution," and "the lightness and wit of his touch" (echoing the terms of praise used earlier for Chardin and Boucher)—but no one was interested in articulating what were the specific aesthetic merits, if any, of his erotic art.[14] In vain shall we look for an extensive contemporary discussion of paintings such as *Bathers* (see fig. 3.13) or *The Swing* (fig. 3.3)—only a deprecating anecdote survived about the origins of the latter as a commission contemptuously passed on to "M[onsieur] Fagonat" [*sic*] by the history painter Doyen, who deemed its licentious subject unworthy of his time.[15]

The critical disregard for Fragonard as an erotic painter was historically overdetermined. Erotic subjects ranked very low in the established hierarchy of genres, discouraging any serious assessment of works that took them on—the *tableaux licentieux* or *obscènes* as these were called at the time—whether or not they were shown at the Salon.[16] It was history painting that occupied the privileged position in the official discourse on art. The hope for extensive critical consideration, let alone *gloire* and regard of posterity, were reserved almost exclusively for painters who, like Doyen, resisted the temptation of what were thought of as lucrative but frivolous commands. Furthermore, Fragonard's career choice rubbed against a drastic devaluation of private patronage in the official art discourse of the second half of the eighteenth century. While the leading art critics advocated the public as both an actual audience and an ideal, private art sponsors were often explicitly taken to task for commissioning art for their own pleasure, and for keeping it out of public sight.[17]

Curiously, the most prominent among the critics responsible for de-legitimizing eros as a subject of worthy aesthetic explorations, Diderot was himself ardently committed to promote a new appreciation of sex elsewhere. On the pages of his *Encyclopédie*, the writer campaigned for the recognition of sexuality and of sexual pleasure as natural aspects of human life that needed to be studied, discussed, and better known. In his entry on "Jouissance" (enjoyment, par-

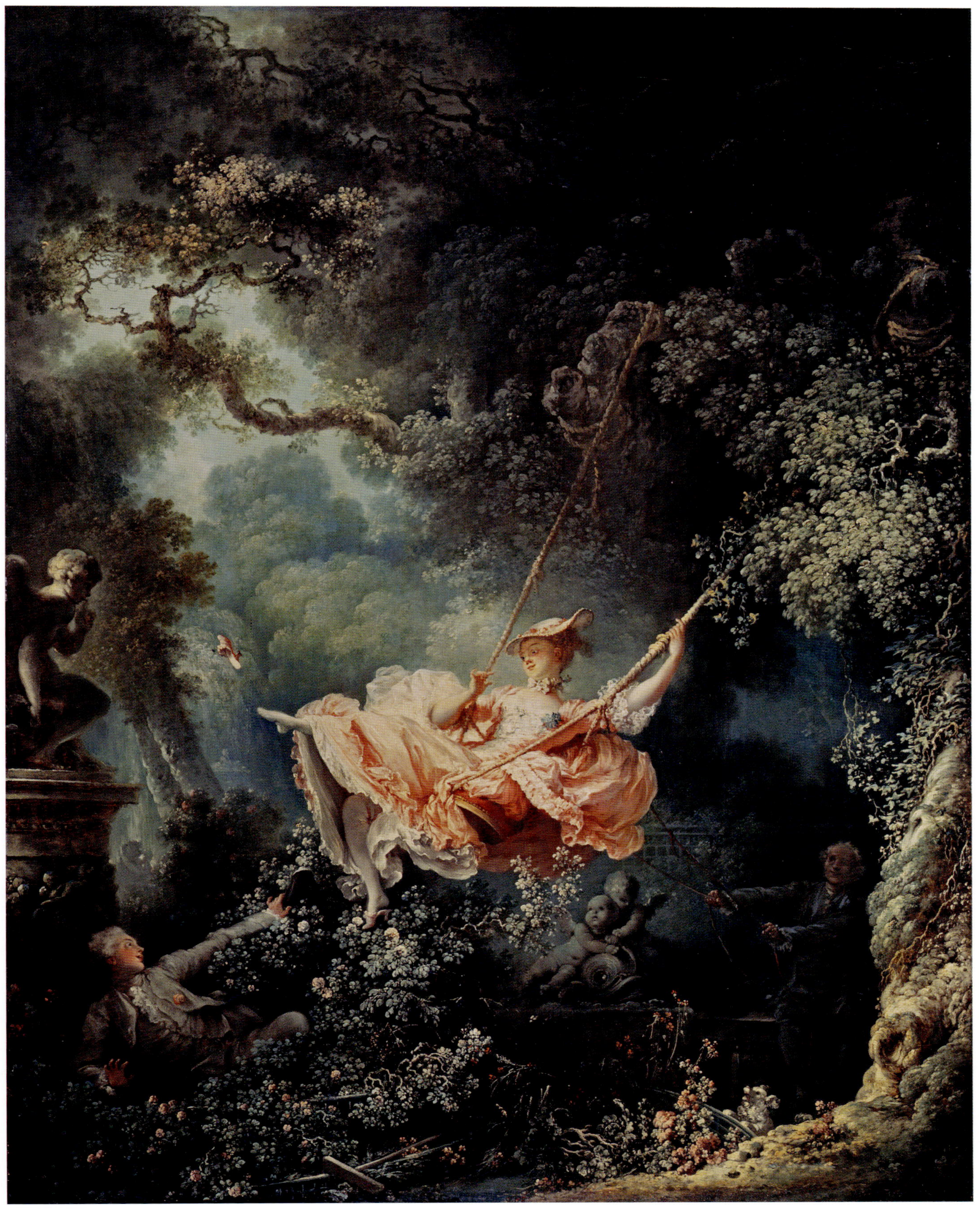

ticularly sexual), he specifically inveighed against the prudes who would oppose such open discussion: "If there is some perverse man who would be offended by the eulogy that I am making of the most venerable and the most basic of passions, I would evoke nature for him, I would make it speak to him."[18]

Nonetheless, painters committed to depicting this "natural and venerable passion," such as Fragonard, could not gain Diderot's public acceptance. (Recall also the care with which the critic sought to distinguish the pleasures induced by Chardin's painting from sexual satisfaction.) In his scheme of things, it was enlightening to write about sex, but it was morally defective or, at best, artistically irrelevant to paint it.[19] An artist refusing the new ethos of art—didactic in purpose, public in address, morally sound in subject matter—that had been articulated by Diderot and has subsequently been adopted by art historians as the quintessential criterion of artistic modernity, could not but be seen as *retardataire*.

A different historical assessment of Fragonard's work is possible, however, if we consider it in a broader context of an intense cultural concern with sex and sexuality in this period, a concern that Diderot-*philosophe* was only one among many to express. For the very reason of its extensiveness and variety, Fragonard's erotic opus may be recognized as a sizable visual file in the vast cultural archive of sexual pleasure that Michel Foucault saw opening up in Western culture in the wake of the Counter-Reformation. The rapid growth of that archive in the eighteenth century, manifest in the outburst of erotic literature and in the development of the distinct modes of describing sexual experience, marked, in Foucault's view, the advent of modern understanding of both sex and self—the beginning of the "age of sexuality."[20] For modernity, as he declared in a much-cited passage, "managed to bring us almost entirely—our bodies, our minds, our individuality, our history—under the sway of a logic of concupiscence and desire."[21] The surge of the confessional mode in eighteenth-century literature was one manifestation of the process in which the connection between sex and the "truth" of self was being repeatedly asserted.[22] Individuality per se came to be defined in terms of one's particular sexual inclinations, and the goal of the confessional narrative was to reveal it as extensively as possible. As a result, in the course of the century, the understanding of sex shifted from what one does to who one *is*. As Foucault was quick to assert, the cultural individuation and personalization of sex also led to the emergence of an erotic discipline; it entailed a use of sexual discourse as the means to distinguish between licit and illicit practices and between what is—and who is—normal and what/who is not.[23]

Notwithstanding some shortcomings of Foucault's analysis—it was meant, after all, as a provocative sketch rather than a comprehensive history of sexuality—its merit, for our purposes, lies in the description of modernity as a formation that has turned eros into a key element of subjective self-definition.[24] While we may be wary of the predominantly discursive (as opposed to visual) and disciplinary emphasis of Foucault's argument, it provides a useful point of departure for our reconsideration of Fragonard's erotic enterprise and for the reassessment of the artist's position in the artistic context of his time and in the art historical narrative of the eighteenth-century origins of modernity. Rather than taking Fragonard for granted as a belated artist caught up with the waning aristocratic ethos of libertinage, or, alternately,

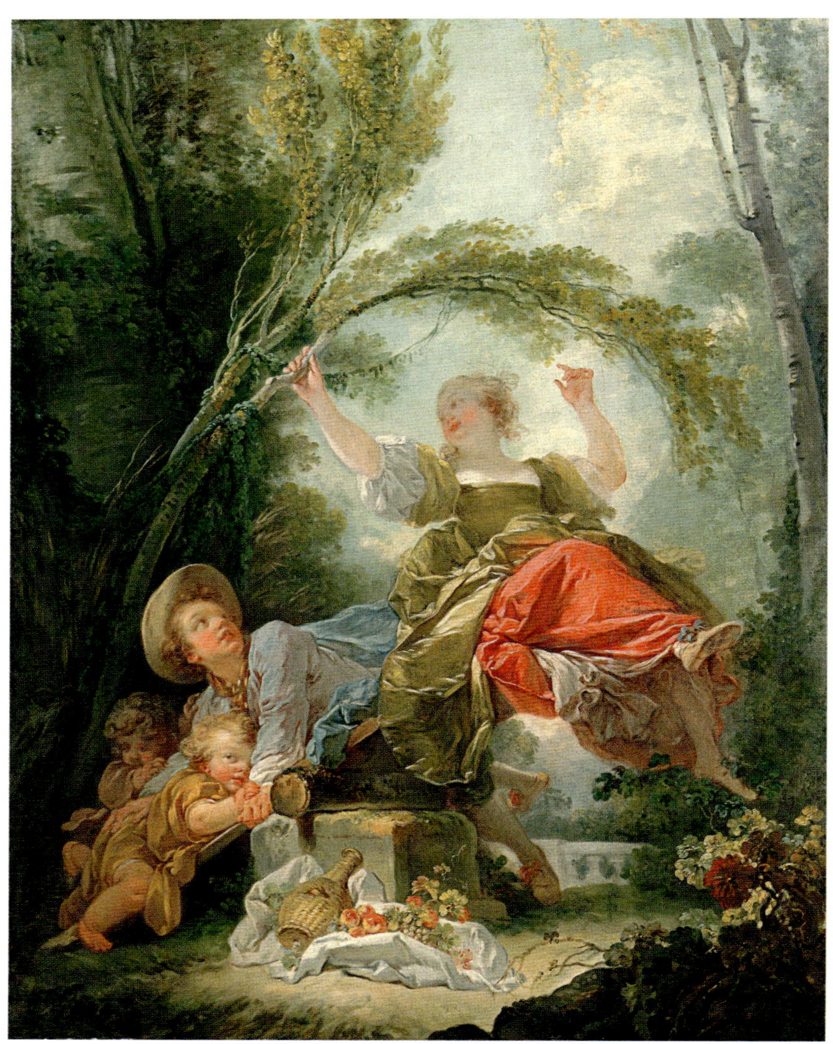

3.4.
Jean-Honoré Fragonard, *The Seesaw*, ca. 1750–52. Oil on canvas. Museo Thyssen-Bornemisza, Madrid.

3.5.
Jean-Honoré Fragonard, *The Bolt*. 1778. Oil on canvas. Musée du Louvre, Paris.

3.6.
Jean-Honoré Fragonard, *Happy Lovers*, ca. 1770. Oil on canvas. Georges Ortiz Collection, Switzerland.

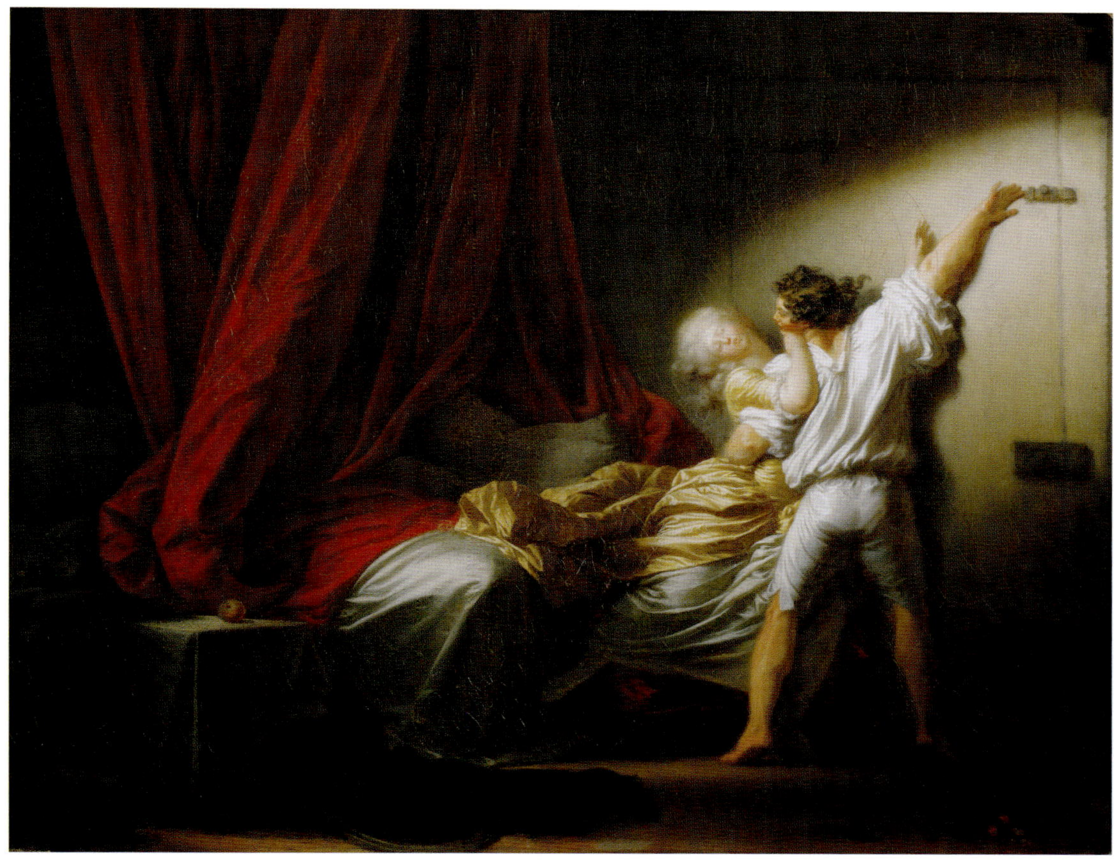

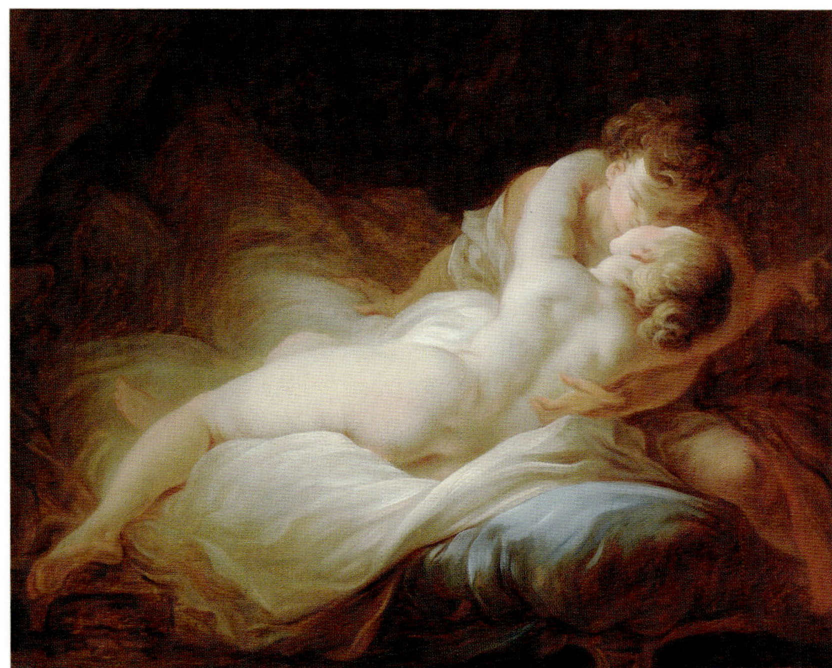

as a mis-recognized proto-romantic painter of passion—which is how his project has most often been construed—it seems more fruitful to consider the painter's entire erotic oeuvre as a symptom of the pressing cultural need to figure out the relation between sex and self.[25] The question is, how did Fragonard's work, *as painting*, address this new need, and how exactly, in this capacity, did it contribute to the period's discourse of sexual pleasure? If modernity is indeed a cultural formation that insists on sex as the truth of self, what are the truths—and the self—that Fragonard articulated?

We may begin, in art-historical terms, by asking about the position Fragonard occupied in relation to other eighteenth-century painters of sexual themes. Where does his work stand in relation to his teacher, Boucher? Although in the beginning of his career Fragonard followed Boucher closely, as his early *The Seesaw* (fig. 3.4), demonstrates, he came to develop an entirely different approach to eros, in the character of the represented scenes and in their pictorial rendition. Shortly put, Fragonard's oeuvre formulates a new sexual imaginary in which erotic experience is redefined in individualized, privatized, and thoroughly physical terms.

Most obviously, Fragonard's licentious scenarios tend to feature contemporary rather than the mythological figures or pastoral characters that prevailed in Boucher's repertory. Moreover, Fragonard's figures tend to be anonymous individuals as opposed to socially situated actors. It is relatively difficult to pin down their class insofar as the markers of social status are inconspicuous, inconsistent, and ultimately unconvincing. For example, if the identity of the ravished woman swathed in yellow satin in *The Bolt* (fig. 3.5) is unmistakably upper class, the social standing of her partner remains uncertain.[26] In the *Happy Lovers* no social identification of any kind is possible: all one can say is that these are two bodies engaged in making love (fig. 3.6).[27] One may also note that the individuation of these figures is kept to a minimum: their physiognomies are conventional and summarily rendered—a dot for the eye, a crescent for the mouth—just enough articulation to suggest the movement of emotion or desire across the face, without implying character or personality.[28] It is as the generic man and woman that these individuals wrestle in amorous combats.[29] Subjects of desire rather than social class, their rapport is defined by remarkable reciprocity.

Furthermore, one is struck by the heightened intimacy of Fragonard's scenes staged, prevalently, in interiors. In bolted rooms, on unmade beds, under the shade of a canopy, sexual activity, be it an interaction between two people or an autoerotic performance, is repeatedly defined in Fragonard's paintings as a guardedly private act. The voyeuristic position that these images tend to accord the viewer only emphasizes the privatized character of these scenes. Fragonard's work evidently contributed to the important cultural change that occurred in the course of the eighteenth century when sex came to be understood as an activity apart, an experience that requires privacy.[30] The bolt has clicked, the couple has been locked in a room where no one else, except our gaze, can enter, and the new cultural location of desire as a discrete space—a spatial secret—came visually into being.

Notable also is that while Fragonard works essentially within a genre format, traditionally used for gallant scenes, he shifts its usual emphasis; it is not the elaborate social rituals of seduction that he represents, as did earlier Antoine Watteau or Jean-Francois de Troy (see fig. 1.59), but an intimate physical engagement, the dynamics of sex as bodily motion, as friction between material surfaces. One may also note that far more nudity appears in Fragonard's pictures compared to the work of his predecessors, helping define the notion of direct physical contact between bodies as a key aspect of the erotic encounter.

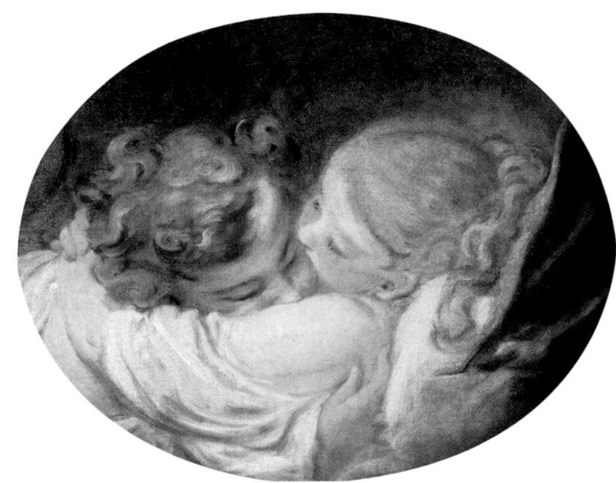

3.7.
Jean-Honoré Fragonard, *The Kiss*, ca. 1770. Oil on canvas. Private Collection.

Even such a cursory overview makes clear that Fragonard did not simply paint sex but sketched out the contours of a historically specific argument about it that may be roughly defined as materialist, in the eighteenth-century sense of the word.[31] His very emphasis on the physical dimension of sex suggests a materialist understanding of desire as a physiologically specific force of attraction between bodies rather than souls. It is precisely in these physiologically specific terms that Diderot defined the idea of sexual pleasure as a natural bodily phenomenon in the *Encyclopédie*: "An individual presents himself to another individual of the same species and of different sex, the feeling of any other need is suspended; the heart palpitates, the limbs quiver; the voluptuous images wander in the brain; the torrents of energy run through the nerves, irritate them, before surrendering under the siege of a new sensation, insistent and tormenting. The sight becomes blurred, the delirium is born; reason, the slave of instinct, limits itself to serving it, and nature is satisfied."[32]

This passage could almost serve as a caption for the *Happy Lovers*, their bodies painted as if they were indeed animated by some internal torrent of energy, their cheeks flushed with rushing blood, their embracing limbs melting into each other while the couple, oblivious to the world surrounding them, engages in their natural pursuit. Or take *The Kiss*, a small oil sketch rendered in whorls and smudges of pigment, where the upper torsos of the lovers seem to have sunk into each other with a force of suction so strong that you can almost hear it—here, too, sexual encounter is constructed in terms of sheer physical energy (fig. 3.7).

I am not suggesting that the *Encyclopédie* or the materialist philosophy of the body were the direct *sources* of Fragonard paintings, but rather that his aesthetic project might be situated within a larger cultural field of inquiry into sexuality as a basic human activity in need of reappraisal. That the meaning of sexual experience must be reevaluated was, for example, the main message of pornographic literature, which in this period became an important tool for disseminating philosophical materialism.[33] Explicit descriptions of sexual acts were often interspersed in these publications with sophisticated expositions of materialist philosophy, the task of arousal mingled with the didactic purpose of "naturalizing" eros. Thus the single most popular eighteenth-century pornographic novel, *Thérèse philosophe*, first published in 1748, offered an account of sexuality that echoed the arguments of such Enlightenment writers as Julien Offray de La Mettrie and Diderot (so much so that the latter was even believed to be its author).[34] The sexual vicissitudes of a young woman were presented as a pursuit of pleasure following the implacable laws of nature, a human body understood, in La Mettrie's terms, as a *machine à jouir* (machine for enjoyment). The main emphasis of the novel was, though, on the individual—and individuating—dimension of sex. As one of its protagonists put it succinctly: "To achieve happiness, everyone has to grasp the kind of pleasure that is *proper to him*."[35] Thérèse's erotic adventures were to be understood not as mere diversions but as a pursuit of her erotic truth, her own unique kind of sexual satisfaction.

Fragonard's paintings share with *Thérèse philosophe* this materialist emphasis on the individuality of sexual experience, and such illustrated pornographic novels may well have served as the mediating factor between philosophical materialism and Fragonard's vision.[36] Indeed, quite a few of Fragonard's paintings seem close in their iconography and character to the openly licentious visual repertory of these publications. For instance, the heroines of the pendants *The Stolen Shift* and *All Ablaze* (figs. 3.8 and 3.9), whose bodies are subjected to the obscene pranks of the putti, bring

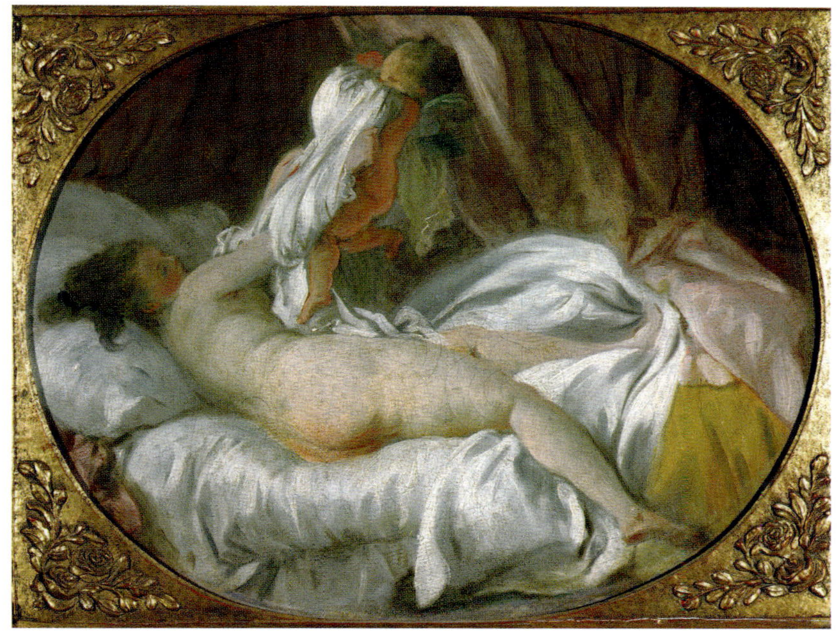

3.8. BELOW
Jean-Honoré Fragonard, *The Stolen Shift*, ca. 1765. Oil on canvas. Musée du Louvre, Paris.

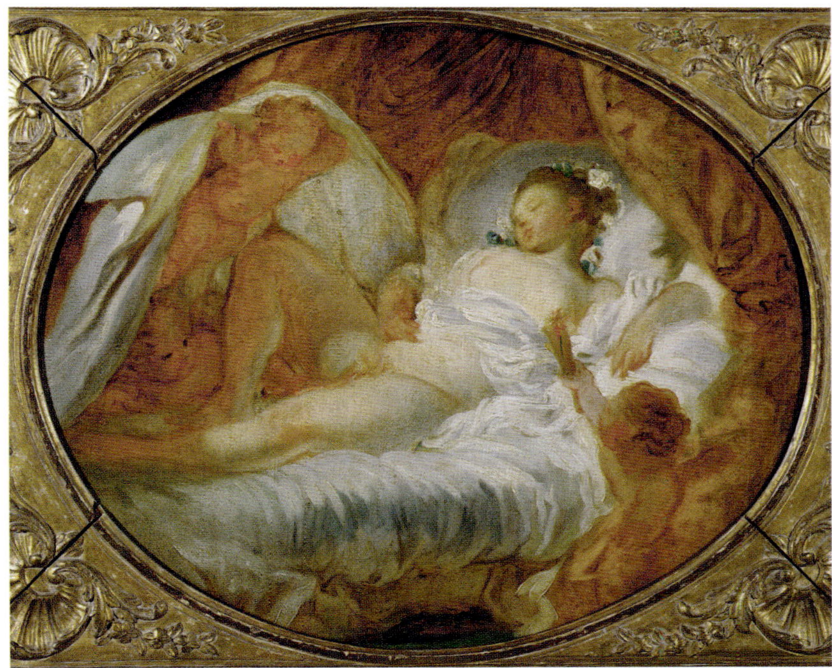

3.9. BOTTOM LEFT
Jean-Honoré Fragonard, *All Ablaze*, ca. 1765. Oil on canvas. Musée du Louvre, Paris.

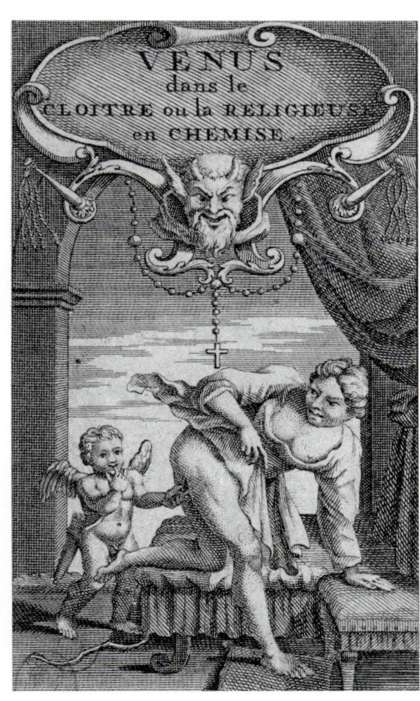

3.10. BOTTOM RIGHT
Frontispiece for Jean Barrin, *Venus dans le cloître*, 1746, engraving. Bibliothèque national de France.

to mind the frontispiece of the 1746 publication *Venus dans le cloître* (fig. 3.10), where the woman's body is shown being prompted, so to speak, by an irreverent cupid.[37] From the materialist perspective, espoused by pornographic authors as well as the philosophes, the games depicted by Fragonard could not but be seen as the thinly veiled metaphors of the physiologically specific symptoms of sexual arousal—witness the heating up of the body, the quickening of blood circulation evident in these women's flushed complexions. The torches of the young pranksters may even literally bring to mind the "flambeaux de la volupté" that the most radical promoter of the materialist eros, La Mettrie, evoked as the necessary instruments of erotic enlightenment.[38]

Yet these voluptuous paintings cannot be seen as mere translations of the pornographic repertory onto canvas—they are, for one, never quite as explicit as pornography. (Enough to compare the *Happy Lovers* with an illustration from the first edition of *Thérèse philosophe* [fig. 3.11], representing the heroine with her aristocratic lover to appreciate the painter's tactful avoidance of genital explicitness.) Nor, for that matter, are they simply *illustrations* of the materialist notions of sexuality. There is more than mere physiology or mere mechanics of sex in Fragonard. An engraving from a late eighteenth-century German erotic manual offers us an exaggerated, derisive example of what La Mettrie's idea of the human being as the "machine for enjoyment" may look like when applied to the everyday life of a bourgeois couple (fig. 3.12). In contrast to this mechanistic satire, Fragonard formulates the erotics of the body ravished by a desire understood as an *internal* force that not only animates but also subsumes or overtakes its physical reality—witness the woman's body almost bleached by the light of physical attraction in the *Happy Lovers*, or the merging bodily contours of the magnetically bonded couple in *The Kiss*.

This internalized construction of eros had to do with the mode of painting peculiar to Fragonard, a manner that, as his contemporaries acknowledged, was "uniquely his own."[39] The connection between this distinct handling and the erotic character of the painter's work has not gone unrecognized by Fragonard's scholars. The painter's cultivation of formal incompleteness, for instance, has been understood as a strategy of erotic appeal that opened the visual field to the participatory or possessive play of the viewer's imagination.[40] In particular, Sheriff has argued that the painter's open manner combined with an inviting presentation of female flesh—a combination epitomized by his *Bathers* (fig. 3.13)—was geared specifically to secure the male viewer's pleasure and control over the image, generating a sense of possession at once visual and erotic.[41]

I suggest that Fragonard's mode of painting importantly complicates rather than simply reinforces the ostensible erotic effect of his canvases. To begin with, it is not only the open character of his forms and image-structure but also their dynamic aspect that calls for more sustained consideration. It is not simply

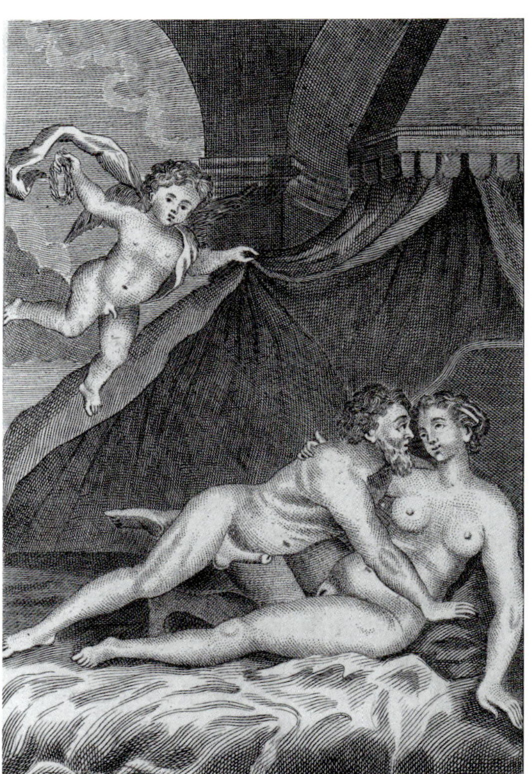

3.11.
Plate from Jean-Baptiste de Boyer, Marquis d'Argens, *Thérèse philosophe*, 1748 (first edition). Engraving. Bibliothèque national de France.

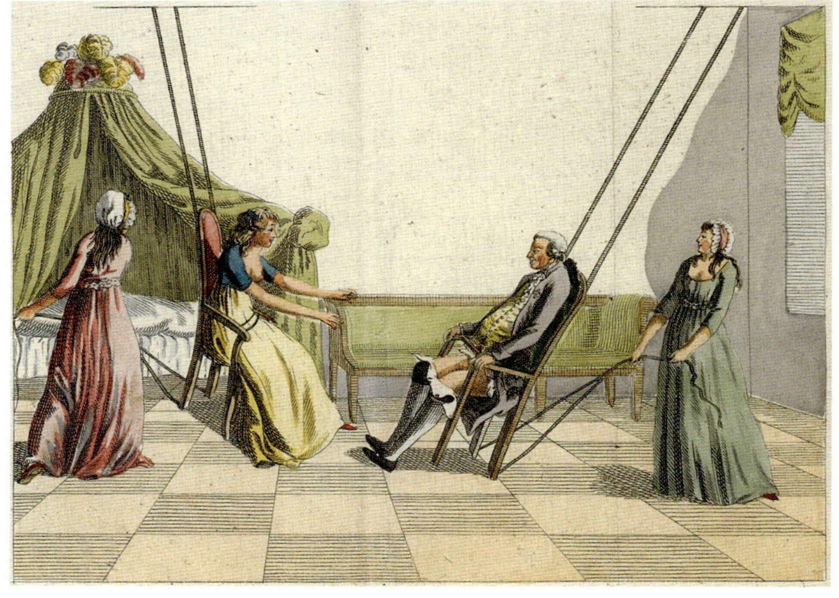

3.12.
The Mechanical View of Intercourse. Illustration to *Amors experimental-physikalisches Taschenbuch*, 1798. British Library, London.

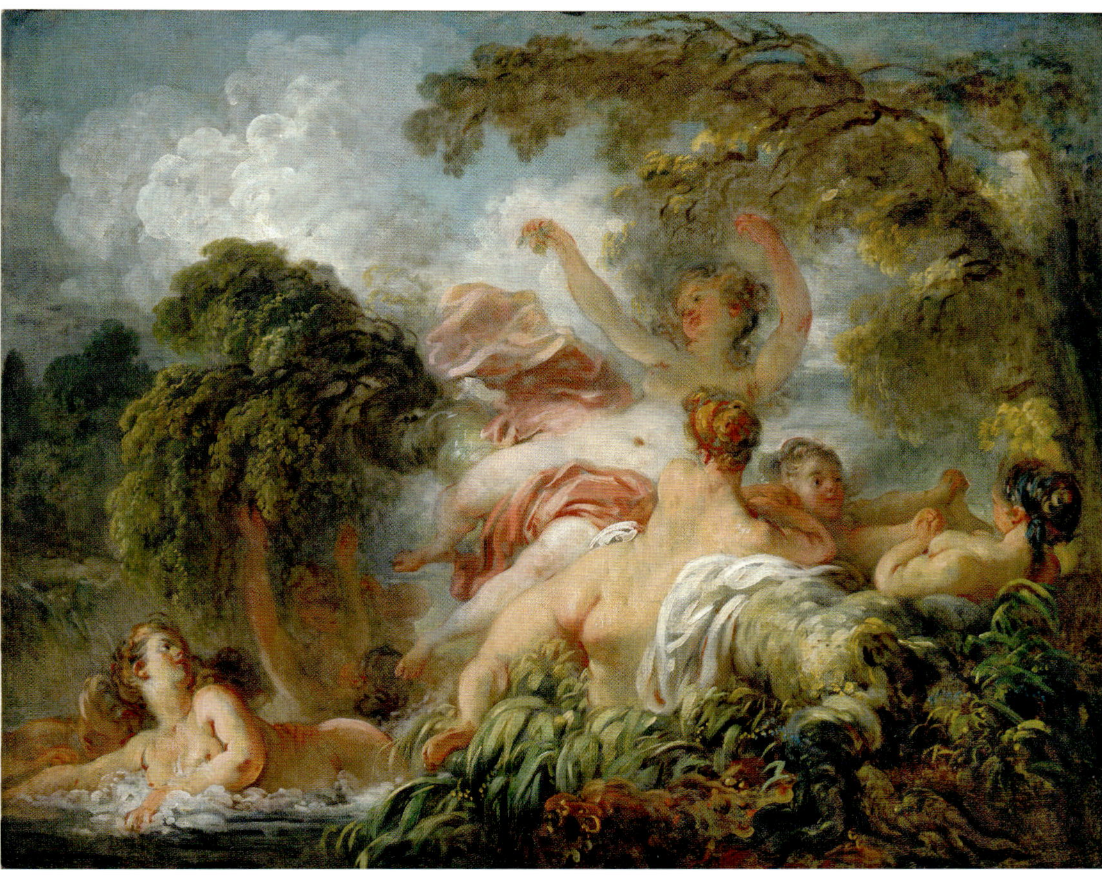

3.13.
Jean-Honoré Fragonard, *Bathers*, 1763–64. Oil on canvas. Musée du Louvre, Paris.

that Fragonard makes a point of displaying his craft, drawing attention especially to the chromatic virtuosity of his faire. Nor is it that, in its tangible quality, his touch simply reenacts and enhances the palpable availability of flesh for imaginary erotic possession. Rather, the surface of his canvases often seems to have a *life of its own*, as if it were animated from within. This is what the Louvre's *Bathers* conveys suggestively: the frothing, ebullient forms in this painting testify to an internal agitation, as if some force were pushing the masses of pigment from behind, carrying forth the nude bodies of women entangled in a tree branch and, through them, materializing the canvas's surface. The two figures in the center that seem to be versions of the same body flipped around by the mass of water surging from behind underscore this internal dynamism, as do the figures on the right with their push-and-pull gesture.

The agitated morphology of this and other works suggests that the play of pleasure and sexual difference in Fragonard's painting cannot be fully accounted for in scopic terms, be it in the sense of relations obtaining within the field of vision defined by these compositions or in their mode of address to an imaginary viewer. The behavior of form in these compositions testifies to something far more deeply ingrained and ultimately more important for which their visual staging of female seduction or abduction by the forces of irresistible (and presumably male) desire is only a facade, or a pictorial effect. To begin to realize this, one needs to consider the function of the female body in these compositions not from the point of how it relates to the viewer as much as *where it comes from*, so to speak, to address us. The insistently forward movement poses the question of its source or cause—however we may want to call the pressing sense of it being somehow internally motivated—that seems worth investigating. What exactly is it that propels Fragonard's *Bathers* into view, what informs the very mode of their appearance and, by extension, the mode of emergence of the image itself?

These questions evoke the broader project of this chapter, which shifts the focus of analysis of Fragonard's paintings from the visual to the material register of making in an effort to recover their particular kind of *bodiliness*. This specific corporeality cannot be understood without considering the role played by the painter's own body in the process of representation. I will situate this corporeal dimension of painting in relation to the broader cultural concern with the body as the locus and agent of sex and to its emergent understanding as a force of nature, an idea linked to the radical reconceptualization of the natural realm in Fragonard's time. Relating Fragonard's practice to this broader cultural domain, I will explore how the painter mobilized his own body as the means of artistic individuation, his different modes of doing so, and their effects and meaning. Moreover, I will consider Fragonard's bodily practice in relation to the artistic culture and social world in which he operated to assess how his embodied conception of painting, and of the painter, defined his social position and artistic standing.

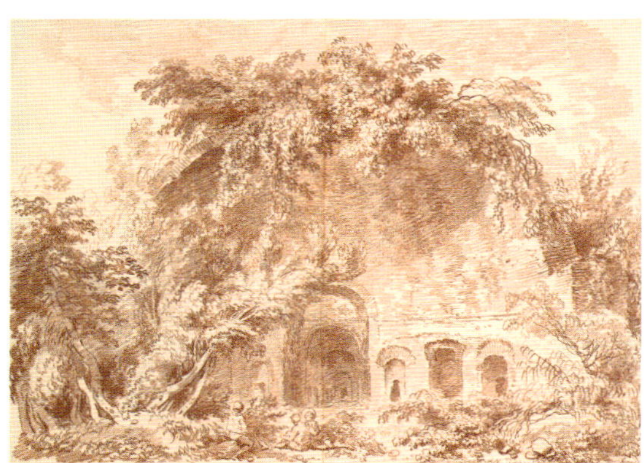

THE UNSEEN

It is, unexpectedly, from Fragonard's landscapes that we get a better grasp of how in his practice a picture actually emerges into being. The artist started to draw from nature in Rome, during his stay at the French Academy. Its director, Charles-Joseph Natoire, encouraged students to sketch outdoors, and Fragonard did so extensively together with Hubert Robert, another young French artist who was in Rome on a privately funded visit.[42] The sheer amount of landscapes Fragonard produced in Italy and over the course of his career—both paintings and drawings—testifies to a sustained interest in exterior views, particularly in a certain kind of view to which the artist repeatedly returns: usually parks, many of them around half ruined Italian villas, where vegetation and architecture mingle in studied disarray and where nature is always constructed as a peculiarly intimate setting (fig. 3.14). What I focus on is a curious structuring habit that Fragonard displays in the construction of many, if not all, his views, a compositional strategy that he tends to use to secure the effect of intimacy.

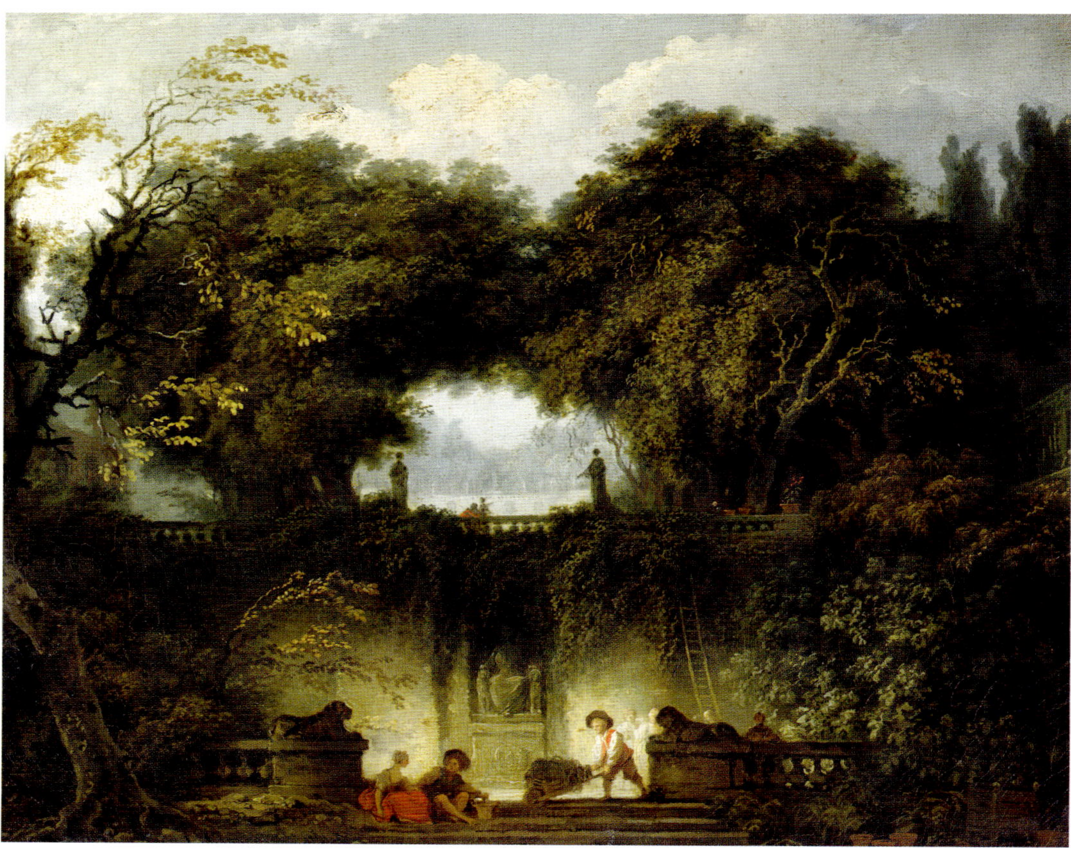

3.14. OPPOSITE TOP
Jean-Honoré Fragonard, *The Ruins of the Hadrian Villa*, ca. 1760. Fondation Custodia, Frits Lugt Collection, Paris.

3.15. OPPOSITE BOTTOM
Jean-Honoré Fragonard, *Gardens of the Villa d'Este*, also called *The Little Park*, ca. 1762–63. The Wallace Collection, London.

3.16. BELOW LEFT
Jean-Honoré Fragonard, *The Great Cypresses at the Villa d'Este*, 1760. Red and black chalk. Musée des Beaux-Arts et d'Archéologie de Besançon.

3.17. BELOW RIGHT
Jean-Honoré Fragonard, *Shaded Avenue*, 1773–74. Wash with brown ink. Musée du Petit Palais, Paris.

Based on Fragonard's summer of sketching in and around Rome, the Wallace Collection's *Gardens of the Villa d'Este,* also called *The Little Park* (fig. 3.15) epitomizes this habit.[43] The whole scene is centered on a voided core topped by the arching trees and illuminated from within. Split in half, this arcade of inner light bustling with life is governed in the lower register by the presence of a seated female statue, her head swathed in the veil of darkness, while the upper oval opens up to a distant view, with silhouettes of some strollers etched against it.

It is not just the way in which Fragonard makes such an exterior setting look cozy, but, more specifically, the effect of interiority it produces that deserves our attention. Note the care Fragonard puts into fleshing out the richness of the leafy thicket, the secret life of the tree branches forming the niches wherein hover the matchstick human figures. On the left, a Ruisdaelian tree with yellow remnants of life withering on its branches acts as a *repoussoir* leading our gaze inside this protected enclave of interiority. But above all, note the odd light that comes from below, as if from underneath the retaining wall, installing an enclave of a luminous elsewhere at the core of this image, a kind of hearth that heats up this representation from within.

What we may first take simply for a topographical accident returns as a morphological principle of Fragonard's numerous landscape drawings and sketches. In the tunneled view of the Villa d'Este in Tivoli (fig. 3.16), the thick waves of cypresses frame a barely defined architectural specter in the background, its dissolving contours producing a sense of spatial and temporal distance. Then there are the several drawn and painted versions of the *Shaded Avenue*, such as the sheet at the Petit Palais in Paris (fig. 3.17), elegantly receding into the abyss of emanating light.[44] The Horvitz collection's *Garden of an Italian Villa, with a Gardener and Two Children* (fig. 3.18) offers a decentered and dispersed version of this view. If the composition is far less structured—no plunging perspective, the gardener's tools scattered in the foreground as if to reinforce the sense of randomness of the whole arrangement—it too is infused by background light. We get a sense of this view as being informed by something that cannot be seen but whose implicit presence can be felt—the statues point to it, turning toward the incoming light. The drawing was produced after Fragonard's return from his second visit to Rome, and, as Eunice Williams has observed, it is an imaginary composition comprising all the most desirable features of an

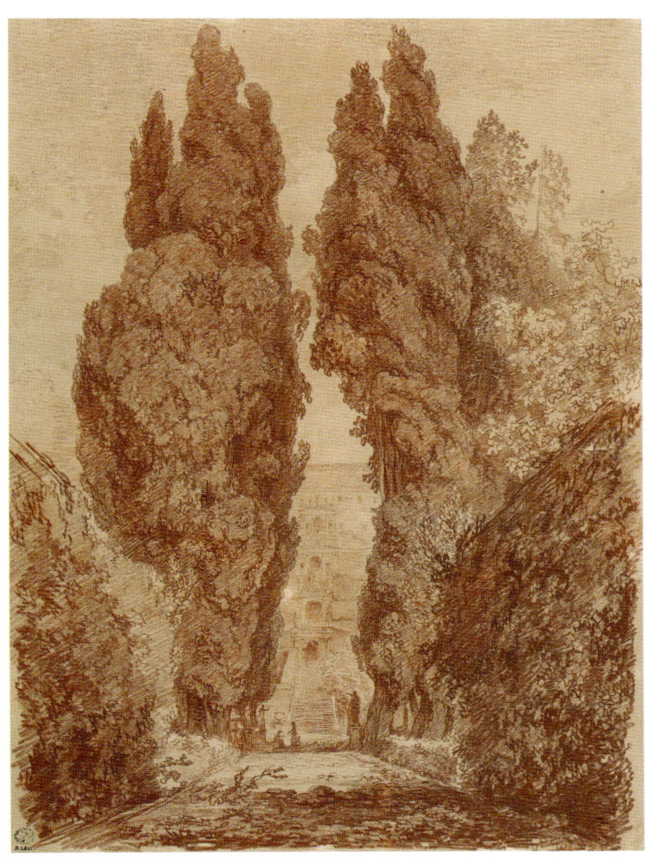

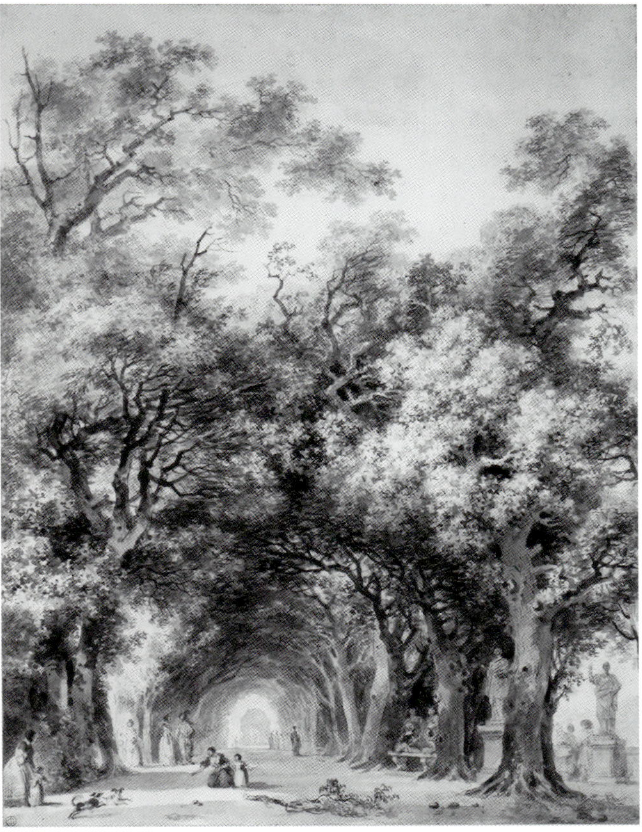

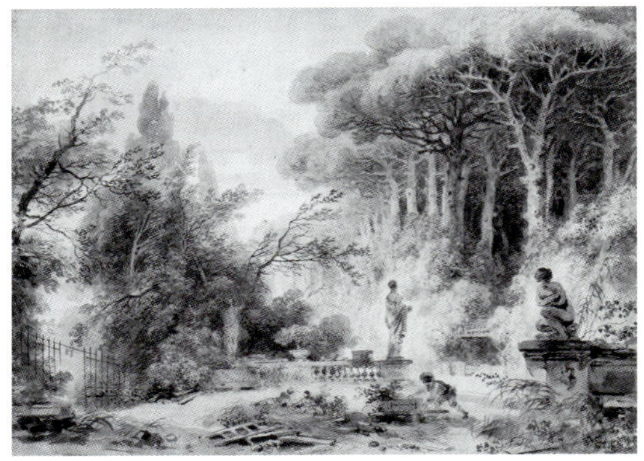

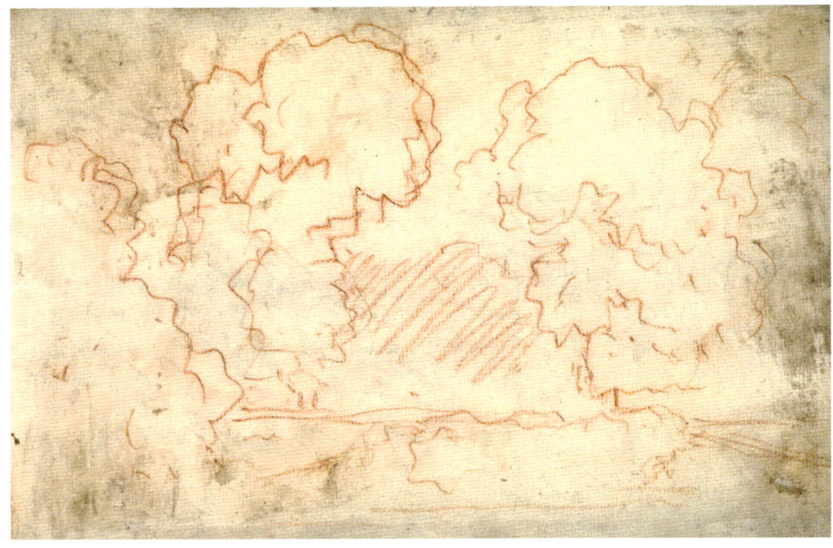

Italian park.[45] Yet as the light that impregnates it suggests, the memory that informs this scene may not be of Italy, to which it ostensibly refers, flaunting all the typical signifiers of Italianicity, such as the scattered remnants of antiquity and the overgrown vegetation of its informal parks, but of something it does not show, the unsaid or unseen of this image.

A rough drawing from Fragonard's sketchbook now at Harvard Art Museums gives us insight into the fundamental role of that "unseen" in the construction of a view (fig. 3.19). The site has just barely been blocked out in red chalk lines that divide the space into the "here" of the trees and the "not here" of the empty center framed by their scalloped outlines. It is the primal compositional division that we see in this embryonic "sketch before a sketch" that clearly matters most to the artist. The artist starts out from the edges, building up around a nucleus of a vacuum that he seems to need to establish as such (marking it by a non-mimetic scribble), in order to proceed further, a necessary void that may be seen not simply as the reserve but as the *generative* core of the image.

Technical analysis of another drawing confirms this recognition: the infrared photograph of the Baltimore Museum of Art's *Temple in the Garden* has revealed a black chalk sketch underneath the pen and ink drawing (figs. 3.20 and 3.21).[46] The pattern of these tangled chalk lines indicates that the artist first sketched around the empty center before brushing in, with ink, the shapes of the architecture, as if to warm up around the hearth of an absence necessary for the image to emerge. What the infrared glimpse into Fragonard's process demonstrates is the structural importance of the lacuna buried in so many of his compositions, the blank antecedent around which his images coagulate.

There is a connection between this structuring absence at the core of the process of representation to which Fragonard's drawings attest and the effect of interiority produced in his paintings by the motifs of canopied statues, shaded alleys, and architectural coves. More or less conspicuous traces of this structural principle can be found in two of Fragonard's most intriguing and commented upon paintings, the *Fête at Saint-Cloud* (fig. 3.22), and the so-called *Fête at Rambouillet* retitled as *The Island of Love* (fig. 3.23).[47]

3.18. ABOVE LEFT
Jean-Honoré Fragonard, *Garden of an Italian Villa, with a Gardener and Two Children*, late 1770s. Brush with brown wash over traces of graphite on off-white antique laid paper, laid down on Japan paper. The Horvitz Collection, Wilmington, Delaware.

3.19. ABOVE RIGHT
Jean-Honoré Fragonard, *Landscape*, ca. 1758, sheet 28r in Fragonard's *Sketchbook from the Italian Period*, ca. 1759–61. Red chalk on off-white antique laid paper. Harvard Art Museums/Fogg Museum, Cambridge, Massachusetts, Louise Haskell Daly Fund.

3.20. BELOW LEFT
Jean-Honoré Fragonard, *Temple in the Garden*, ca. 1760. Pen and brush and brown ink, watercolor over black chalk. Baltimore Museum of Art, The Peabody Art Collection, Collection of the Maryland State Archives.

3.21. BELOW RIGHT
Infrared photograph of Jean-Honoré Fragonard, *Temple in the Garden* (fig. 3.20).

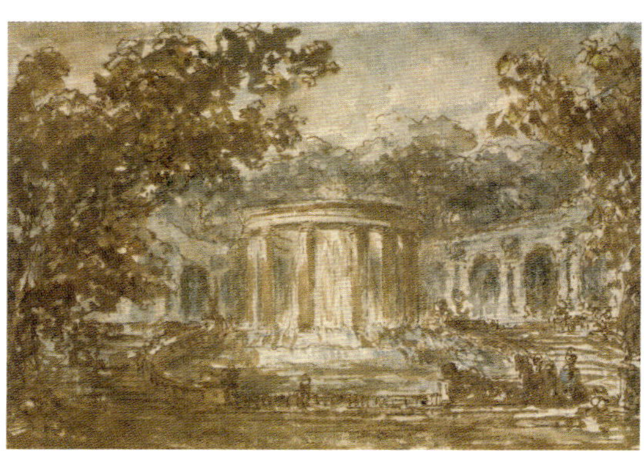

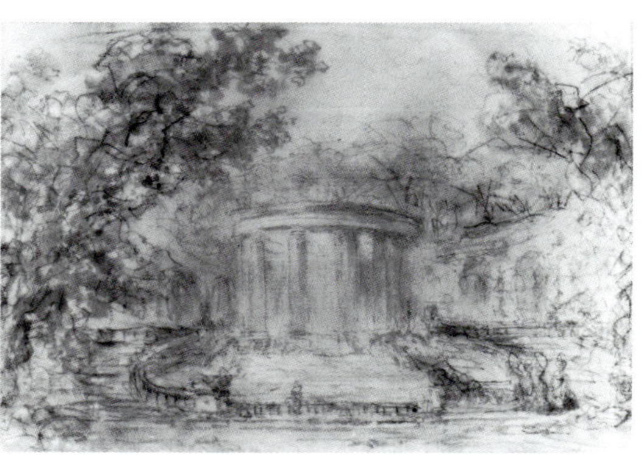

3.22.
Jean-Honoré Fragonard, *Fête at Saint-Cloud*, mid- to late 1770. Oil on canvas. Banque de France, Paris.

3.23.
Jean-Honoré Fragonard, *The Island of Love*, ca. 1768–70. Oil on canvas. Museu Calouste Gulbenkian, Lisbon.

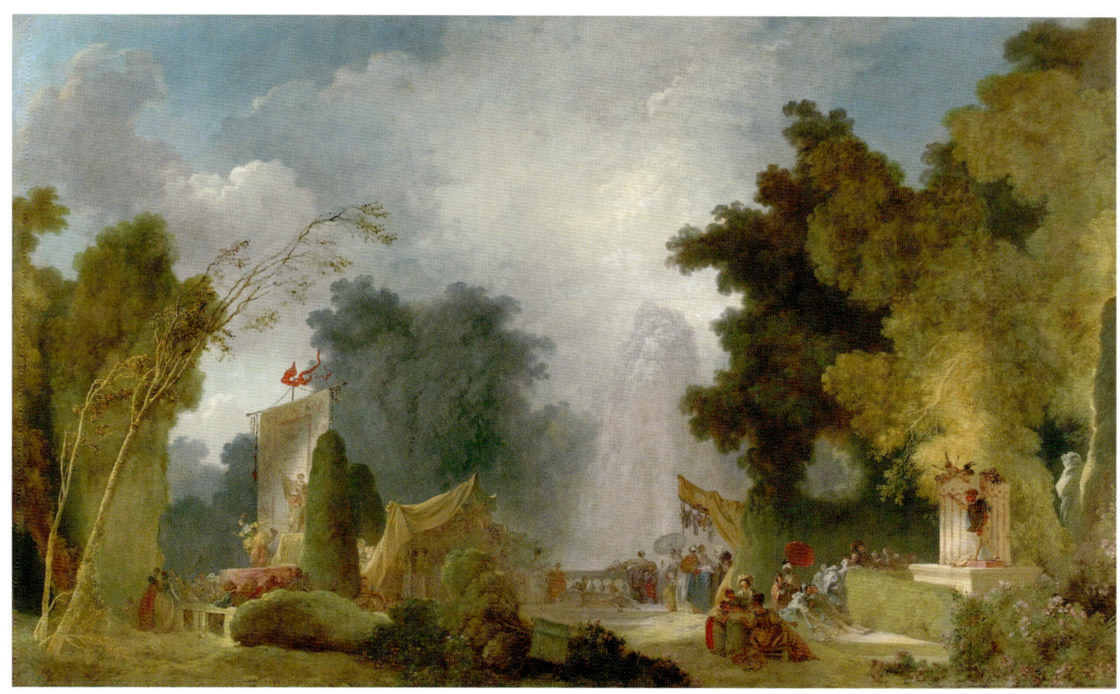

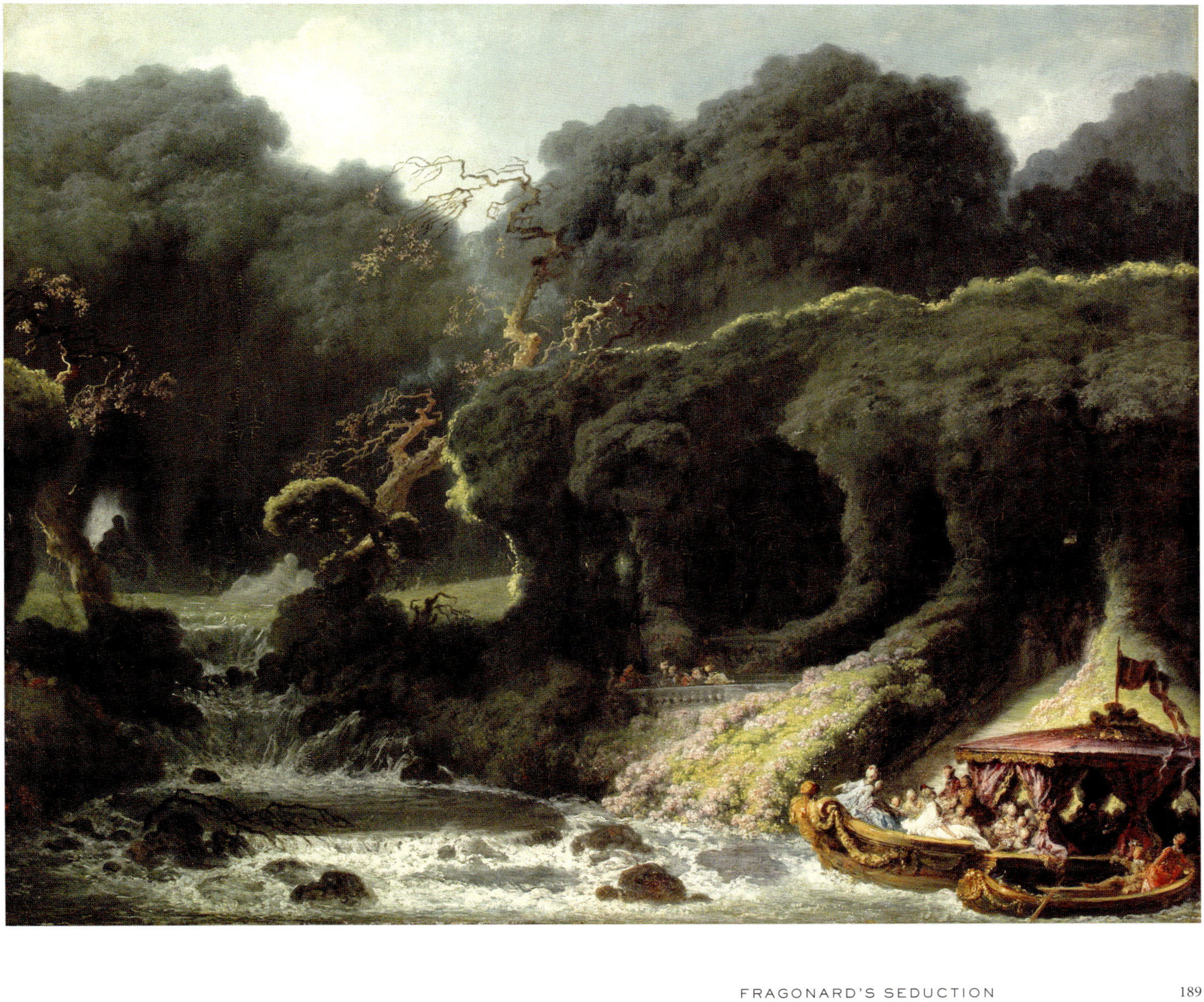

Both produce a sense of presence that exceeds the field of the image and yet remains key to it. Thus, in the midst of the *Fête at Saint-Cloud* a gigantic fountain surges up like a geyser from behind the balustrade at the center. Cut off from its source, which is located in the invisible lower terrace, this jet of water appears excessive or unwarranted, a silver-white mound of nothing that marks the liquefied center of this composition. It competes with the major attraction of the fair, the makeshift theater performers and puppet sellers hawking their wares. Its effervescence, although not incompatible with the insouciant mood of the gathering, conveys also a sense of unmotivated excess. The function of the surging water as the immaterial structure that focuses the scene is even more pronounced in the watercolor sketch related to the central portion of the painting (fig. 3.24).[48] Here, the entire gathering of strollers appears captivated by the gush of whiteness in the middle of the scene—the jet of a fountain so forceful that it obliterates its own origins and part of its sculptural setting. Flanked by the two standing statues—the only visible remnants of its elaborate architectural framework—this powerful font seems to "rain" blank spots on its surroundings, clothing the statues and the human figures in aqueous sacs of light. It is as if the whole composition, painted in light and liquid strokes of wash, floated on a surface of water.

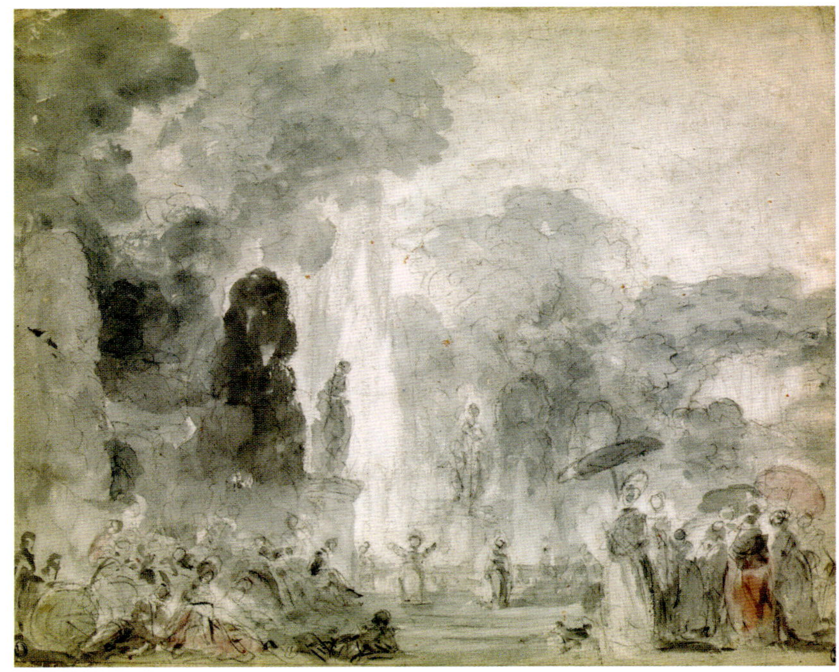

Cavities are the most prominent structural elements of *The Island of Love* in the Goulbenkian collection in Lisbon, a painting of a very different mood from the insouciant serenity of the *Fête at Saint-Cloud*. The whole space buckles under the weight of the bizarre, cavernous mass of the hedges, so suggestive that they, rather than anything else, seem to constitute the very *subject* of this representation.[49] The usual

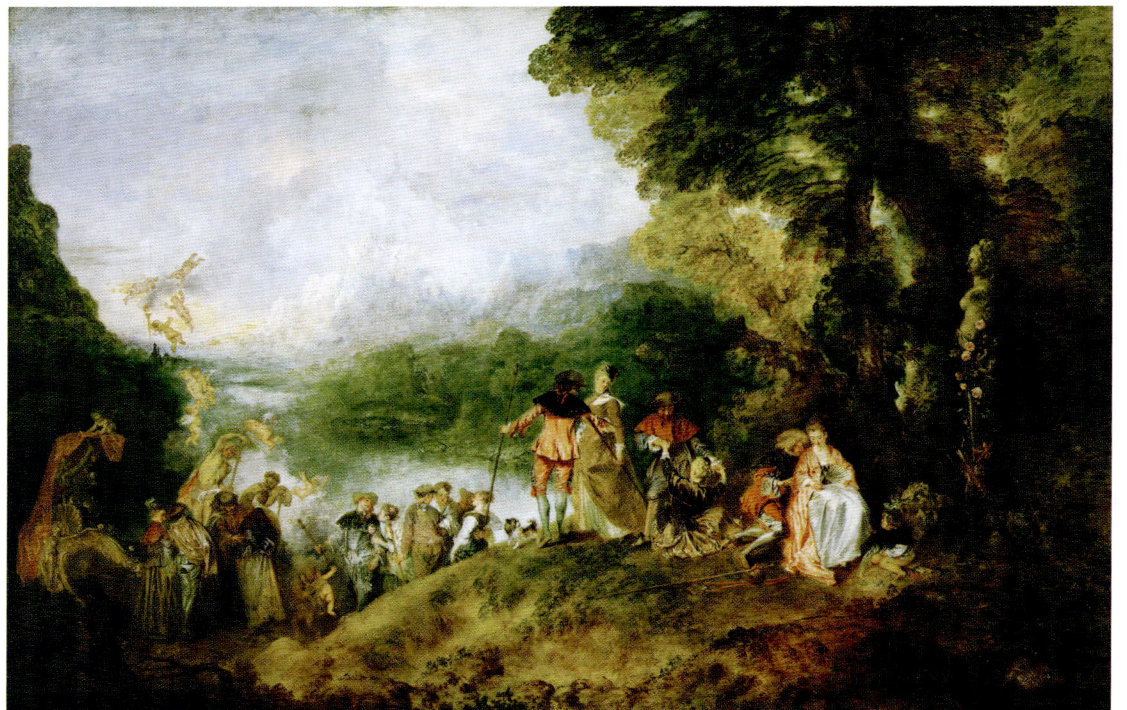

3.24.
Jean-Honoré Fragonard, *View of the Park*, late 1770s. Black chalk with gray wash and touches of green and pink watercolor over pencil underdrawing; verso: black chalk. Metropolitan Museum of Art, New York, Robert Lehman Collection, 1975.

3.25.
Antoine Watteau, *Pilgrimage to the Isle of Cythera*, 1717. Oil on canvas. Musée du Louvre, Paris.

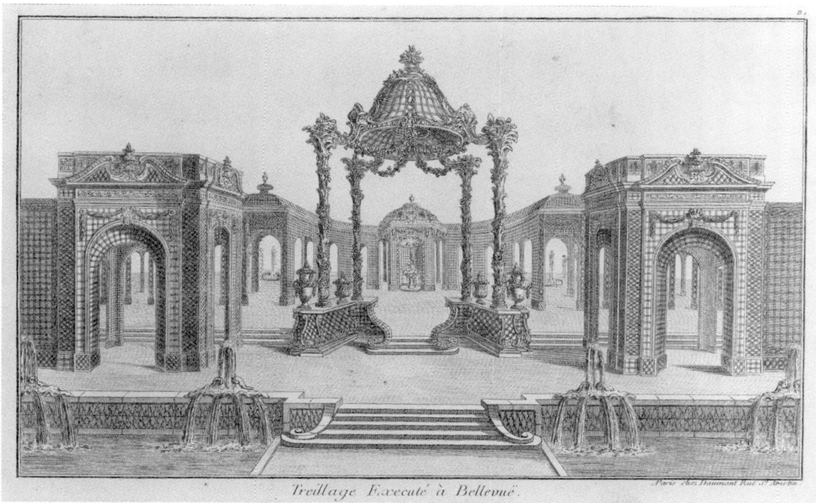

3.26.
Trellis Work Made for the Château de Bellevue. Etching Châteaux de Versailles et de Trianon.

comparison made between this scene and Watteau's *Pilgrimage to the Isle of Cythera* makes clearer the paramount importance of scenery over people in the Fragonard (fig. 3.25).[50]

What exactly are these huge, dark-green spongy-form molds limned by light and soaring above the small human figures scattered on the terrace? They have nothing to do with the standard forms of garden architecture—enough to cast a quick glance at the design for trellis work for the park at the château de Bellevue to realize it—or the known topography of gardens (fig. 3.26).[51] And what are we to make of the vastly overgrown and foaming vegetation spreading like lava down the stairs and into the river? Nothing that a mere neglect by the gardener could ever have produced: there is a sense of excess, of things spilling out of control, heightened by the drama of the storm conveyed by the lightning that strikes the withered tree in the background. In a clearing at the back of the picture a by now familiar motif of a shaded female statue looms ominously in a hollow—as if in a kind of cave.

What kind of island is this? What love thus imagined, from within this odd setting? It seems that the little pockets of interiority that, as we have observed, organized space in Fragonard's landscape sketches had taken the upper hand: the whole scenery became in *The Island of Love* a sort of phantasmatic interior. It is not enough to say, however, that it represents a fantasy world—so does, if differently, Watteau's *Pilgrimage to the Isle of Cythera*. What we see in the Fragonard is, more specifically, an epigenetic fantasy of nature as at once a theater and a force of life.

BEING AND BECOMING

Few commentators failed to notice the prominence given to vegetation in Fragonard's work as well as its peculiar rendition, not just in the Lisbon painting but also in his oeuvre at large, where one encounters, as the poet Yves Bonnefoy put it, "these insane trees with crowns toppling like snowdrifts."[52] But the attempts to make sense of it rarely went beyond only the most general remarks. Pierre Rosenberg has described the Gulbenkian picture as "an ode to the forces of water in which the luxuriant vegetation triumphs," though he also declared that this "enchanting" painting was "disquieting, and even somewhat frightening."[53] One feels that Rosenberg is on to something, but what does such description imply? Is this indeed a pantheistic vision, as he has suggested?

In my view, the unusual and compelling aspects of Fragonard's landscape vision—so distinct from the work of his predecessors, such as Watteau, and, more immediately, his teacher, Boucher—had to do with a major shift in the understanding of nature that was taking place at the time he was painting. To put it briefly, God was making his exit from the natural realm as Enlightenment thinkers submitted its expanse, both visible and invisible, to scientific scrutiny. This is not to say that eighteenth-century natural science was entirely or uniformly atheistic—far from it—but that it switched the focus of attention from the Creator to the creation and to the specific laws that governed its functioning. God as such had ceased to be a sufficient explanatory principle for the existence of the natural realm.[54] It would be hard, therefore, to assume that a painting of nature produced at the time could be in any straightforward or traditional sense "pantheistic." Rather, one may reasonably expect the opposite: some version of the materialist view of the world permeated not by an omnipresent God but by new principles discovered through scientific inquiry.

The key figure in the formulation of this new view was George-Louis Leclerc, comte de Buffon, both because of the scope of his enterprise—the forty-eight volumes of his *Histoire naturelle*—and because of its intellectual ambition. The superintendent of the Jardin du Roi from 1739 until his death in 1788, Buffon undertook an enormous project of writing a new "biography" of nature, an extensive new account of its life.[55] Produced with the aid of a team of collaborators and published between 1749 and 1789, his *Histoire naturelle* has been compared in its status and effects to the *Encyclopédie*, and it even exceeded the latter in popularity.[56]

Buffon's major contribution consisted in the description of nature as an enormous living whole, a vast continuum of organic life the different forms of which depended solely on the mode and degree of organization of matter.[57] Such a view, of which Buffon was not the only but certainly the most articulate and influential promoter, marked an important shift within the materialistic outlook on the world. In place of the earlier mechanistic view of nature as an immutable, perfectly ordered, and self-maintaining system—a clock made by the Divine Clock-Maker, as Voltaire put it—there emerged a vision of nature as, in Buffon's words, "a living power, immense, which embraces everything, animates everything."[58] The understanding of the natural order as a static *form* imposed from without was displaced by a new concept of a creative *force* operating from within.[59] The major goal of this creative force was, as Buffon recognized, the production of life. His recognition was part of the fundamental eighteenth-century discovery that the animate sphere constituted a discrete realm unto itself.[60] But if the domain of life was indeed a realm unto its own—at once a material fact and a special *kind* of materiality—the question was, what were the principles of its organization? How to define the distinctive mode in which life functioned became the great epistemological challenge of eighteenth-century science: how does life, to begin with, come about?

Two kinds of answers could be given to this question following the two dominant theories in the scientific discourse at the time: preformation and epigenesis. Preformation assumed life to originate from preexisting germs that were either dispersed throughout the world at creation (*dissémination*), or encapsulated in one another like Russian dolls (*emboîtment*), and which contained the organs of generation.[61] Whether through *dissémination* or *emboîtment*, the future organism was understood to have been formed in all its parts before conception. As one scholar noted, "nothing new, therefore, ever emerge[d], in the preformationist realm of forms; nature [was] bereft of any productive energy."[62] The epigenetic theory, on the other hand, conceived of generation as a process of gradual organization of unformed matter caused by the action of vital powers that involved no preexistent forms.[63] In this view, the living organism developed after conception *from within itself*, through internal division and differentiation, and this process implied a serial addition of parts rather than a mere enlargement of a preexisting total shape, as was the case in preformation. Epigenesis emphasized the organic capacity of self-generation and self-formation that followed no prior script, engaged no preexisting external authority.

Buffon's theory of generation, explained in detail in the second volume of the *Histoire naturelle* (published in 1749), aligned itself with epigenesis, offering, though, a particular version of this view.[64] Buffon believed procreation to be a common phenomenon for all natural forms, from vegetation to animals, with the same laws governing the reproduction of vegetables or polyps and also sexual reproduction of mammals and birds. He developed a tripartite scheme to explain it. According to this scheme, life originates in small irreducible particles, called organic molecules (*molécules organiques*), that form the matter of all living beings. Ingested by the living body with nourishment, these molecules are transformed into parts of the new organs by the action of an interior mold (*moule intérieure*), a kind of internal formative agent that Buffon defined by drawing an analogy between human art and the art of nature: "In the same way that we can make molds by which we give whatever shape we please to the exterior of bodies, let us suppose that Nature could make molds by which she defines not only the external shape [*figure extérieure*] but also the internal form [*forme intérieure*]."[65] If the term may appear to us as contradictory, insofar as the mold is commonly associated with exteriority, it is, Buffon asserts, because we are used to looking only at the surface of things. Our eyes lack the capacity to see through the external appearances and to understand the unseen. Yet behind every surface of life there is an internal structure responsible for its material organization, for its nutrition, and for growth. It is this internal mold, aided by the penetrating forces (*forces pénétrantes*), its executive agents, that configures all living forms, providing their individual structure and securing their identity.[66]

Buffon's theory of life as a result of the internally generated arrangement of material particles accorded with the main emphasis of the epigenetic view, even if it was not entirely consistent with it. His concept of the moule intérieure was ambiguous and could be seen as a lingering preformatist assumption, although, as the historian of science Jacques Roger has noted, his contemporaries were largely unable to perceive these inconsistencies.[67] The key aspect of his approach

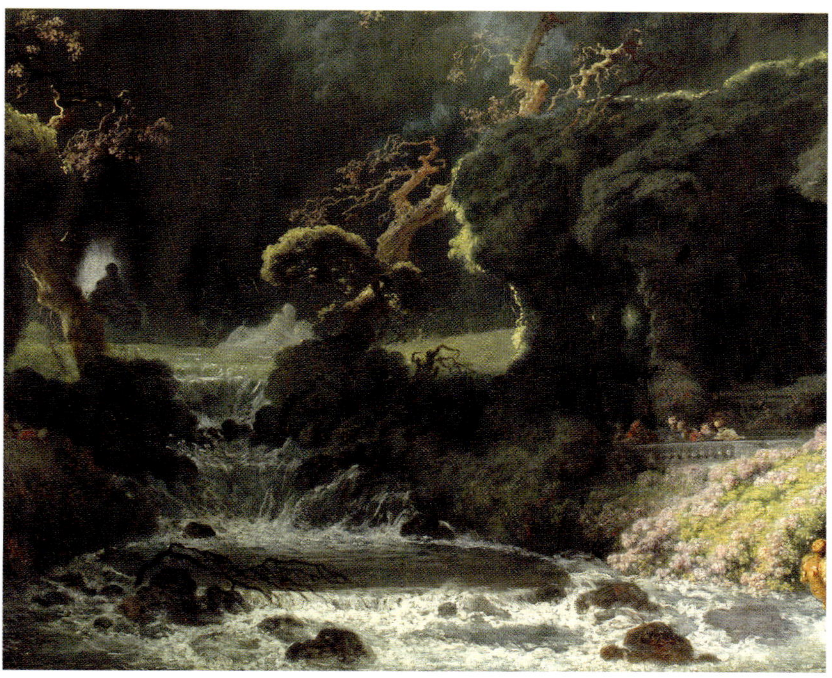

3.27.
Jean-Honoré Fragonard, *The Island of Love*, detail of fig. 3.23.

was his rejection of the idea of preexisting germs, a belief that was at the core of preformation, in favor of the notion of "organic matter, ever active, ever ready to mold itself, to be assimilated, and to produce beings similar to those that receive it."[68]

What we see in the Gulbenkian picture is what such recognition of nature as active matter may look like when put into paint: a molecular continuum animated from within, in constant movement and ceaseless proliferation, a realm where being is clearly announced to be a function of a larger, all-encompassing organic process of becoming.[69] Under Fragonard's brush the landscape setting appears to generate itself from within itself, demonstrating not only a visual but also morphological affinity with the Buffonian conception of nature. It is as if some kind of invisible penetrating forces were pushing from within the space of the painting, resulting in the spontaneous mushrooming of life, the foaming vegetation that dominates and marginalizes the human figures. Fragonard's very process of picture-making in *The Island of Love* appears permeated by the idea of nature as a living, creative force, the sense of space having been secured not by geometry but by efflorescence, not by rational construction but by something like organic growth. (In this lively context, the withered tree, notwithstanding its Ruysdaealian pedigree, must be seen not as a foreboding vanitative symbol but, more literally, as an instance of dead matter that is there only to make the ebullience of the surrounding life the more evident.)

Just as Buffon and his followers departed from the idea of nature as a system in favor of a more mobile conception of an organic whole in which everything was dynamically interconnected, so did Fragonard depart from the traditional academic notion of painting as a system based on preparatory drawing and governed by the principles of linear composition in favor of a more unscripted approach. The basic academic principles of picture-making, such as *ordonnance* and *distribution* (referring to the composition of the whole and the coordination of figures), that made visible a certain hierarchy of meaning are replaced in Fragonard by what may be called an *epigenetic* understanding of painting—one that rejects preexisting structures of organization in favor of a more spontaneous procedure, a self-generated materialization of the image.[70]

Yet to say that this is an essentially Buffonian vision does not do full justice to this strange painting. If there is, as it has been noted, a foreboding or frightening dimension to *The Island of Love*, it is because it formulates what haunts this newly emergent conception of the natural realm: the question of who or what is behind it. If not God, what is responsible for this continuous molecular growth, this ceaseless natural production of life as matter? Buffon, as for him, spoke of nature's "propensity for generating life," but he did not explain the reason for this tendency, leaving his contemporaries querying the origin of nature's incessant reproductive activity. Were the organic molecules a result of a spontaneous generation from inanimate matter and, if not, how to account for their existence?[71] The female figure looming in the background of the Lisbon canvas performs a similar interrogative function (fig. 3.27). The statue calls forth the idea of presence but refuses fully to deliver it, its shape remaining vague and distant, impossible to identify. Is this some sort of divine effigy, like the reclining river god in front of it, on the right? All we can say is that this looming figure resembles the female statues that repeatedly appeared in Fragonard's landscape sketches, a sign—or cipher—of femininity presiding over this ambiguous visual "ode" to nature as a force of life. What it intimates is that this interior landscape is a woman's domain, a feminine interior.

And it does so not only in a symbolic but also a morphological sense. Placed at the vanishing point of this composition, the statuary phantom of femininity not only suggests itself as a symbolic source of this foaming tunnel of forms but also inscribes the whole view with the allusion to female body. Underwriting this unusual cavernous landscape is an inter-

Prima figura fœtus duodecim dierum. 141

A A *Placenta, in qua ſunt radices & trunci venæ & arteriæ vmbilicalis.*
B *vaſa vmbilicalia.*
C *fœtus duodecim dierum.*

3.28.
Figure II in Séverin Pineau, *Opusculum physiologum et anatomicum*, 1597. Middle Temple Library, London.

nal anatomy of a woman; seen in relation to the originary femininity at the core of this image, the vast oval enclosure with its walls covered by what resembles the barnacles of bodily tissue, and its frothing secretions flowing from the hollow compartments into the main basin below, doubles as the inside of some imaginary womb.[72] What may have been the purpose of such anatomical construction of a view? To answer this question we need to make a brief excursus into the domain of the eighteenth-century anatomical imagination.

There was a long tradition, reaching back at least to the late Renaissance, of imagining the woman's body, and specifically the womb in topographical terms, as a landscape or location where life originates. One example is Séverin Pineau's late sixteenth-century medical treatise where the uterus is represented as a sort of lake with a small fetus floating in it (fig. 3.28).[73] In the eighteenth century, though, the understanding of the female interior as the origin of human life underwent a significant transformation conveyed by the anatomical illustrations from this period. While earlier the womb was imagined as a separate world in which the fetus lived dissociated from the rest of the woman's body, by the mid-eighteenth century this discrete chamber has been integrated with feminine anatomy and the fetus's existence shown to be dependent on the bodily apparatus of the mother. A sequence of large-scale color plates from the French anatomist Charles-Nicholas Jenty's *Demonstration of a Pregnant Uterus of a Woman at Her Full Term* (first published in London in 1757, its French translation following two years later) suggestively conveys this newly embraced concept of material continuity between the womb with its fetus and the mother's flesh through a gradually "peeled away" presentation that begins with a view of the woman's distended belly, proceeds through the outer walls of the womb, and ends in the section showing the curled-up unborn fetus inside (figs. 3.29, 3.30, and 3.31).[74]

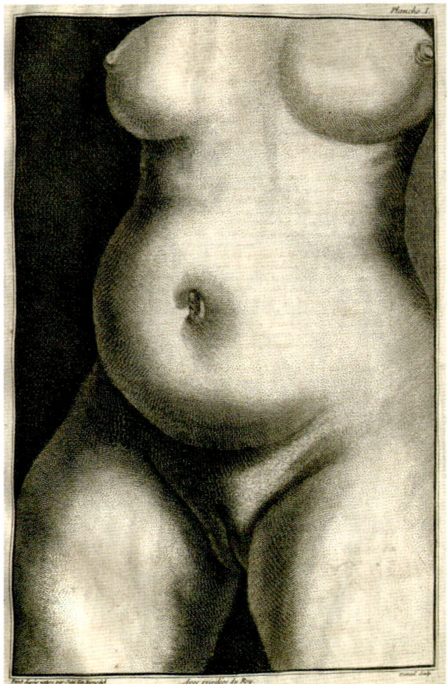

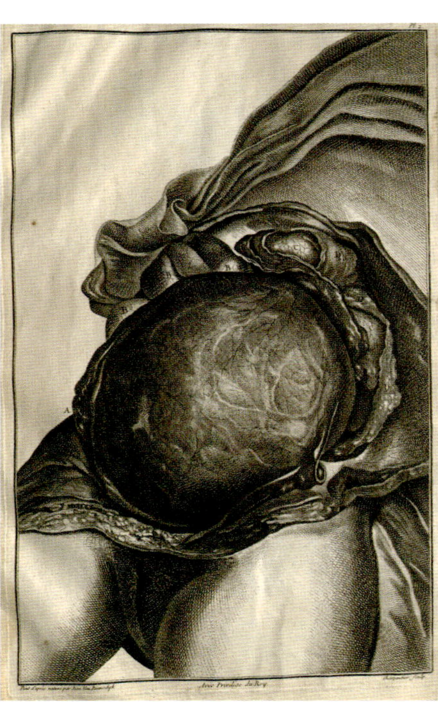

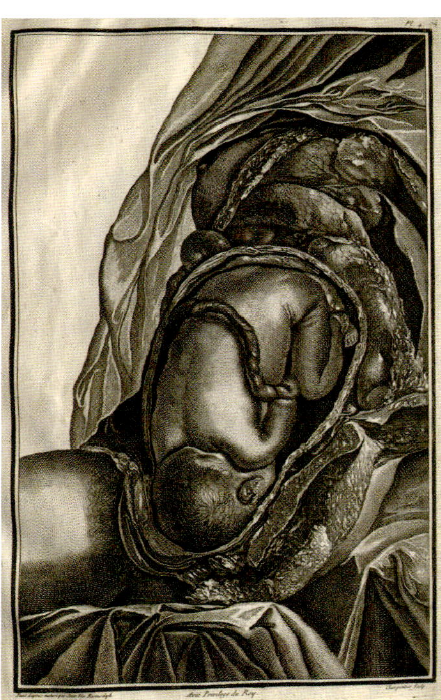

3.29. TO 3.31.
Charpentier after Jan van Rymsdyke, Figures I, II, and IV in Charles-Nicholas Jenty, *Démonstration de la matrice d'une femme grosse et de son enfant à terme . . .* (Paris: Chez Charpentier, 1759). Engraving. The Francis A. Countway Library of Medicine, Harvard University.

3.32.
Plate XXII (II) to "Anatomie," entry in *L'Encyclopédie, ou Dictionnaire raisonné des sciences, des arts et des métiers,* 1762. Houghton Library, Harvard University.

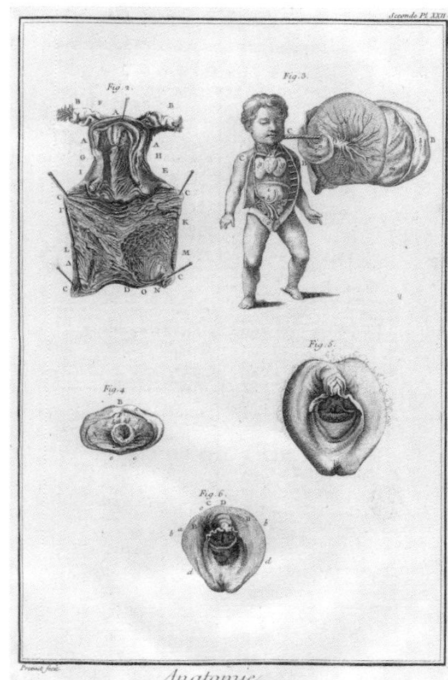

It has been noted that these new renditions of the pregnant body did not simply represent a step forward in anatomical accuracy and obstetric knowledge but had broader cultural and philosophical ramifications. They contributed to the new cultural construction of the woman as mother, making evident the importance of the maternal body and consistently positioning it as a violable object, the effect enhanced by the seeming aliveness of the dissected pregnant cadavers.[75] Moreover, it has been argued that these illustrations impinged on the emerging notions of individuality and subjective autonomy. Situating the male viewing subject in the position of epistemological control and comfort, these illustrations defined the maternal corpus as a mere support of the individual represented by the fetus.[76] One of the only two plates devoted to female anatomy in the *Encyclopédie* epitomized this view: the woman's body was synecdochically reduced to her reproductive organ and genital parts (the image of uterus plus three different types of hymen); furthermore, these organs shared the page with a figure of an incongruously free-standing newborn still attached by the umbilical cord to the disembodied placenta (fig. 3.32).[77] Such representations have been seen to epitomize a specific "cultural logic of individualism" that sacrificed the maternal body to fetal subjectivity by defining it as the invisible background, thus disenfranchising the mother, and by extension, the woman, as a subject.[78]

Other conclusions, however, may also be drawn from this visual material. One could speak of the *surging* of the maternal body into view, both in a sense of its pervasive presence as an image in the new, richly illustrated anatomical treatises and in terms of the internal dynamics of these representations. For example, the distended belly in the Jenty, with its fleshy excess rushing forth and threatening to spill out its contents, its effect enhanced by the near-life size of these plates and the new color print technology, may be seen as an image of the maternal body's autonomous creative capacity.[79] Such visions fed both the new materialist recognition of the formative power of the woman's body expounded in the epigenetic theory of generation and the older beliefs and prejudices about its mysteries, which continued to linger on in the rationalist culture of the Enlightenment.[80] At that time, enlightened minds such as Voltaire's still subscribed to the old myth that the mother had a mysterious capacity to shape her fetus, and even the better informed advocates of the new bodily science, such as Diderot, did not have a very clear idea about how the uterus actually worked and how exactly it contributed to the process of conception.[81] These unsolved "secrets" of generation constituted a persistent epistemological challenge throughout the eighteenth century, contributing to the production of a cultural enigma of the womb.[82]

Returning now to Fragonard's Lisbon painting: in the context of the discussed anatomical views, the extreme arbitrariness and eccentricity of its cavernous setting becomes even more striking. It is hard not to notice the shallowness of the basin of water and its flat, rocky bottom that make it difficult to imagine how any boat could sail in these waters without getting wrecked. The boats are indeed pushed to the side, as if to make a place for the surging flatness of a circular plateau of the riverbed, an oddly unmotivated shape that bears an uncanny resemblance to the topography of the uterus in some of the illustrations we have just discussed: an internal bed swathed in a slimy film of something like a placenta being slushed away, as if the birth waters had been broken and were spilling out (see fig. 3.27).

In the quasi-molecular continuum of this eccentric *Island of Love*, matter seems to have morphed into an etymologically related term: mother. The result of this morphological transformation is, though, not an illustration of the old cliché of Mother Nature but rather a visual recasting of the new materialist conception of active nature *as* mother. Ernst Cassirer's term for nature in the new philosophical discourse as a "womb of becoming" comes to mind.[83] We may perceive Fragonard's intra-uterine landscape as a vision of nature *impregnated* by the new understanding of the maternal body as a material, anatomical, and physiologically specific site of generation of life. The sense of a womb as a locus of activity, of continuous molecular production, is what the Lisbon landscape shares with the new maternal anatomies, its topography performing the generative function of Buffon's *moule intérieure*. Yet there is one fundamental difference between our painting and most of the considered anatomical illustrations: there is no fetus, this "uterus" is empty. What the distended cavity with the arena-like plateau at its center stages—quite dramatically—is an absence.

This absence suggests a link between what *The Island of Love* implicitly articulated as feminine morphology and that generative hollow of the unseen around which Fragonard, as we have seen, tended to construct his landscape views (see figs. 3.15 and 3.16). What his drawings and paintings often only hinted at as feminine—for example, by the inclusion of the female statues in them—may now be comprehended in more specific terms, as a maternal interior, a space of becoming. Notwithstanding its unusual aspects, the Gulbenkian canvas reveals something more general about picture-making according to Fragonard, an association at work in his process between the reproductive capacity of the mother's body and the representational capacity of art, between the generation of life and the generation of an image.

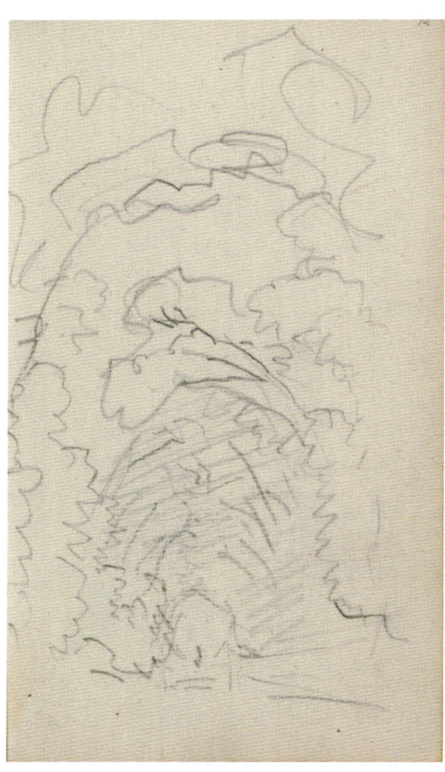

3.33. BELOW LEFT
Jean-Honoré Fragonard, Amsterdam Sketchbook, Folio 12r. Pencil. Rijksmuseum, Amsterdam.

3.34. OPPOSITE
Jean-Honoré Fragonard, *Blindman's Bluff*, ca. 1775/80. Oil on canvas. National Gallery of Art, Washington, DC, Gift of The Samuel H. Kress Foundation.

Some intuition of this connection emerged in the earlier commentaries on Fragonard's work; it informs, for instance, the Goncourt brothers' description of his landscape sketches as "furious embryos," a term referring to the energy inherent in some of the draftsman's most rudimentary notations.[84] One such "furious embryo" may indeed be found on a page from Fragonard's sketchbook, now in the Rijksmuseum in Amsterdam (fig. 3.33). It is a view of one of those shaded alleys that we have seen repeatedly rendered in Fragonard's work, as in the Petit Palais drawing (see fig. 3.17), or in the more elaborate structure of *The Island of Love*. But this particular folio allows us to catch a glimpse of how he did it, shedding more light on the artist's process and on the reasons for his fascination with this particular motif. It seems to have been done while the artist was walking under the canopy of the trees, pencil in hand. The jagged, angular, interrupted lines, so different from Fragonard's usually fluid strokes, speak to it quite bluntly—traces of the draftsman's hand unsteadied by the movement of his body.[85]

Why would Fragonard have needed to sketch as he walked? Evidently, there was no topographical necessity to do so, the site having been much easier to render while sitting or standing under the trees. But if the artist chose to walk, was it not because he was interested in capturing precisely that movement *from within* that was then perceived as being at once nature's and mother's? By simulating the quasi-natural growth of the shape of the alley from the inner core—a hollow—at the bottom center, the draftsman let the page itself give birth to an image. By drawing as he moved, Fragonard was coming as close as he could to enacting the process of generation, his sequence of progressing or receding arches mapping out an act of becoming—of an image. What I am saying is not that this page looks like a maternal body but rather that it *behaves* like one, the process of image construction being defined in terms of growth and parturition. As such, the sketch provides, in a roughest possible form, an image of what may be called, in Buffon's terms, the *internal mold* of Fragonard's epigenetic vision, a matrix or pattern that is the "mother" of this view and that defines the artistic process as, in a sense, a maternal production.

The Amsterdam sketch sheds more light on the purpose behind the latent structure of the Gulbenkian landscape as a voided womb: if this landscape invokes the maternal body, it is as the site of the origins of the painting itself, an instrument of *its* generation. Put

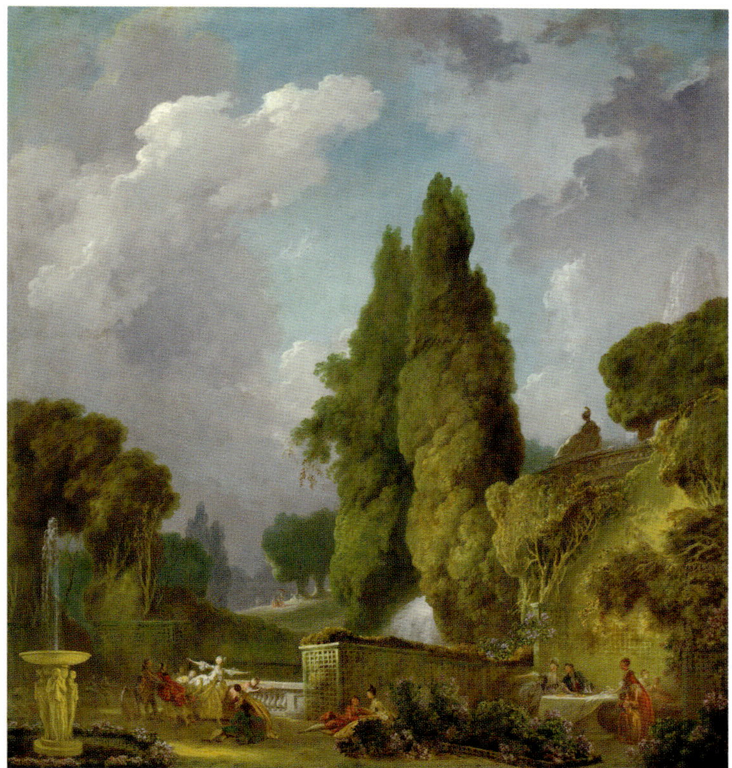

otherwise, this highly idiosyncratic vision declares itself to be the very product—the substitute "fetus"—of its own implicit "womb." But, as a meta-commentary on the very process of image construction typical for Fragonard, *The Island of Love* says more, amplifying the effect of the Amsterdam sketch: there is a sense of drama and a discernibly mysterious mood to this pictorial restaging of the internal/maternal mold of Fragonard's vision. What the Rijksmuseum sheet presented as the bare compositional matrix acquired in the Gulbenkian canvas a semantic thickness, having been infused with a subjective meaning that is as insistent as it is obscure.

The maternal body embedded in this painting is not unseen or hidden as much as presented *enigmatically*, as the inherent structure that shapes this composition and yet remains unintegrated with its ostensible content and meaning. The statue looming at the distant outlet of this composition encapsulates the enigmatic mode in which the maternal body informs this view: an underarticulated, as if half-suppressed incarnation of a female presence that we cannot fathom but that this painting, too, is unable to fathom itself. Buried at the very core of this image, the phantom statue seems to belong to a separate, only vaguely articulated—one may say unconscious—register of this image. And it is precisely this enigmatic form of maternal allusion that produces the strange mood and the unmotivated quality of this view—festive *and* foreboding, scenery *and* anatomy, all at once.

What we have recognized, in Buffonian terms, as the internal mold of *The Island of Love*—and, more generally, of Fragonard's process of constructing an image—may be more precisely described as an enigmatic signifier: a thing-like representation that lacks a signified, and is, therefore, incapable of direct communication.[86] In the Lisbon landscape, the maternal body signifies in such a mysterious way, as the material bedrock of the composition—like the round rock surging at the center—that insists on it from within and yet is unable to communicate its meaning. The message of pleasure conveyed by *The Island of Love* acquires, too, an enigmatic twist. Emphasis shifts from gallant innuendo to erotic inscrutability. What Watteau's *fête galante* (see fig. 3.25)—an inspiration for Fragonard's canvas, judging from his figures' outmoded costumes—conveyed allusively, through elegant concatenations of men and women shown in half gestures and profiles perdus, Fragonard renders more inscrutably, as a secret of nature erupting at the center of the composition and disrupting all the narrative links.[87] Human frivolity is displaced by a more powerful, more attractive, if obscure, erotic "thing" at the center to which the figures are related, albeit in an unclear way.

As such, this extraordinary painting illustrates in an extreme form a larger concern with the place of human pleasure within the epigenetic vision of nature in Fragonard's work. This issue frames his depictions of gallant subjects staged outdoors, games such as hot-cockles or the blindman's buff, of which he painted several versions. In these compositions human activity is often dwarfed by suggestive natural settings. Thus it is the twin cypresses—a motif harking back to Fragonard's views of Villa Tivoli brought from his first Italian trip—that appear as protagonists in the Washington *Blindman's Buff*, their dominant shapes flanking the abundant cascade of water presided over by a looming female statue (fig. 3.34). Below the statue, an overgrown trellised area illuminated as if from within provides a monumental shelter for the figures preparing an improvised meal. In other paintings, the figures nestle comfortably in a landscape setting, as does a group of young people engaged in a guessing game in *Jeu de la palette* (fig. 3.35). Surrounded by the typical motifs of the artist's Roman repertory, including the overgrown cypresses (their crowns cut off) and the ubiquitous female statue, this group produces a very different

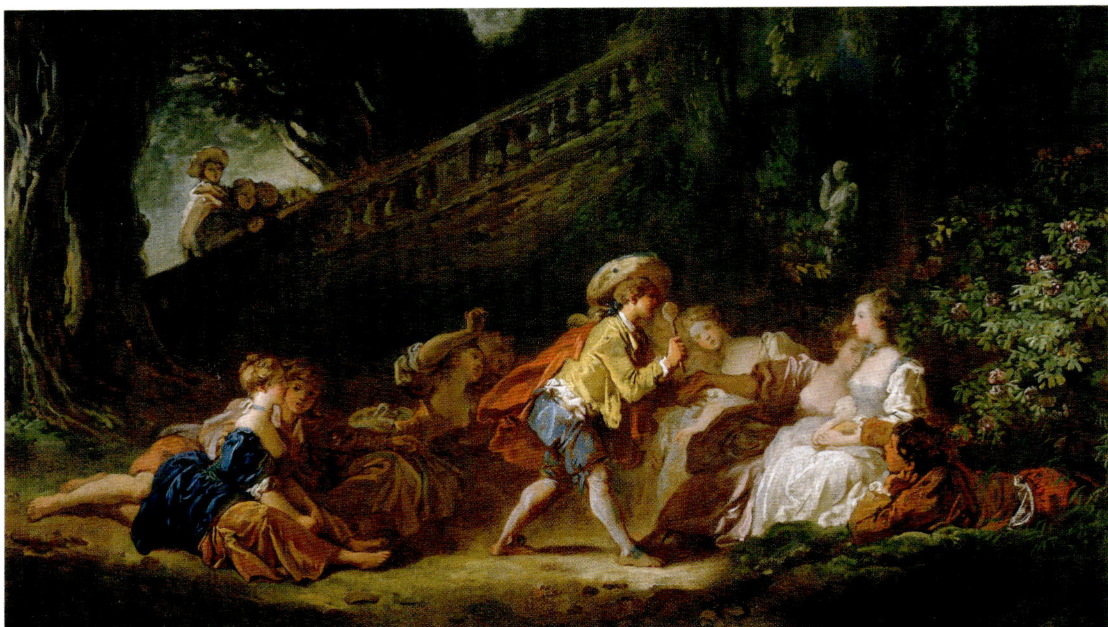

3.35.
Jean-Honoré Fragonard, *Jeu de la palette*, ca. 1757–59. Oil on canvas. Musée des Beaux-Arts de Chambery.

effect from Boucher's earlier rendition of a similar scene, *Delights of Life in the Country* (fig. 3.36): while the latter is staged against a composite, quasi-theatrical backdrop, Fragonard's youths are tucked into a corner of a continuum of nature that both contains and exceeds them.[88]

In comparison to these paintings—whose chronology remains, as usual with Fragonard, uncertain, making it hard to gauge if they preceded or postdated *The Island of Love*, itself of uncertain date—the Lisbon canvas performs a compositional reversal, the effect of which is to give prominence to the eros inherent not in human activity but in the natural setting itself. The painting's enigmatic signifiers—the "anatomical" rock, the spectral female statue, and the light illuminating the whole scene mysteriously, from behind—point to the presence of that which cannot be seen, known, or understood: an incomprehensibly erotic object.

The enigmatic eroticism of this scene is a product of the overlapping cultural and individual fantasies of the female body as the site of reproduction. It partakes in a larger confusion of the Enlightenment culture about the meaning of the woman's body as the locus of eros and as an agent of life. (This is the erotic aspect of the cultural "enigma of the womb" in the period when women's sexuality was still being confused with the exigencies of reproduction.[89]) At the same time the nature in *The Island of Love* is also a highly individualized, idiosyncratic vision, a construction of the maternal body as interred core of both nature and painting. The enigmatic object of an infantile imagination buried in this composition speaks also of the artist's conception of painting and his process of representation; it is a belated echo of the mother's body understood as a force that produces not babies but a symbolic form, an image. And it is from this maternal hollow in the scene of love, this fantasy of an unembodied uterus (essentially psychic, rather than sensu stricto anatomical space), that eros in Fragonard's oeuvre emerges—as a kind of souvenir from the womb, the founding fantasy behind the painter's seductive vision. As such, *The Island of Love* helps us understand the nature of seduction at stake in Fragonard's art and reconsider some of his thematic predilections. Moreover, it raises the question of the role of the painter's own body, and of his pleasure, in the pictorial process.

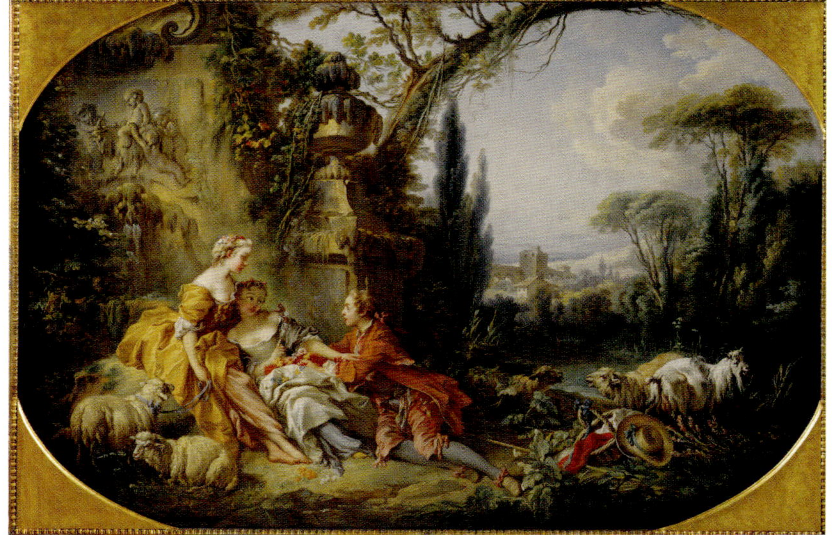

3.36.
François Boucher, *Delights of Life in the Country*, ca. 1735–40. Oil on canvas. Musée du Louvre, Paris.

PICTORIAL SEDUCTION

I would paint with my ass.

—Fragonard

The idea implicit in *The Island of Love*—that what really counts in the painter's erotic vision is the body that is *not* there—can be detected in a number of Fragonard's works.[90] One is the suggestive sketch of an empty bed that amounts to a tour de force staging of an absence (fig. 3.37). A version of that canopied arena where so many of Fragonard's women are shown engaged in auto- or para-erotic acts—as are the protagonists of the *Stolen Shift* and *All Ablaze*—this soft object rendered in animated strokes of pen reasserts the importance of eros as an internally generated production originating in the unseen space behind its billowing cloud-like shapes.[91]

This insight may be brought to bear also on the *Bathers* (see fig. 3.13), whose morphological affinity to *The Island of Love* is quite striking.[92] What the Lisbon landscape spelled out as the obscured but visible maternal font of representation may be seen to operate in the *Bathers* as the unseen but nonetheless visibly and palpably effective anteriority—an interior prior to representation—that "shows" in the distention of the painter's brushstrokes and that generates forms with an energy that did not escape some of the painting's eighteenth-century commentators.[93] The whole scene seems due to the effect of this internal force producing forms that burst forward from somewhere beyond and toward the canvas's surface where they settle into a crust—not unlike the flowery burst of vegetation spilling down the stairs from one of the bizarre molds of greenery in *The Island of Love*. There is a mobility to these forms that, notwithstanding the diagonal of the fallen tree trunk that indicates a feeble attempt at some compositional organization, is resolutely nondirectional, that spreads like foam; the word that comes to mind is effervescence. Within the dynamic and dispersed structure of this canvas, the texture of the women's bodies appears to be morphologically close to the vegetation surrounding them—note the golden "foliage" of hair growing on the head of the uppermost bather that looks exactly the same as the leaves of the tree she is holding on to. Moreover, their unstable postures and gestures reemphasize the dispersed dynamics of the composition, as in the two figures pushing and pulling each other, on the right; the central figure tugging at the foliage above her; and, on the left, the one submerged in the water and reaching to the branches of the fallen tree as if to pull herself up.

The *Bathers*' bodies seem to be part of a landscape in formation, propelled by a force that engenders life—theirs as well as their setting's.[94] An essentially epigenetic image, it generates itself from within itself and, by doing so, stages its own becoming. If Fragonard took up the standard eighteenth-century trope of woman as nature, he gave it a particular interpretative twist, aligning the female body more specifically with organic growth, with the power to engender form—natural and artistic—of which this body, as he envisions it, is at once a cause and effect.

We should also look again at Fragonard's notorious *Swing* to recognize, beyond or besides its voyeuristic aspect, the role of its dynamic morphology (see fig. 3.3). The deep recess and quasi-aquatic coloring of this painting's improbably lush vegetation flesh out the walls of a kind of organic interior within which the figure of the swinging woman acquires a more intriguing status than has been traditionally acknowledged. It is not only, as it has been argued, a voyeuristic object for her lover peeking from below (which is not, in any case, the position from which we look at her body), but also a function of the dynamics of this space that, like a swing, propels her forward into view.[95] The moving woman's body announces itself as an effect of the haptic interior from which it emerges

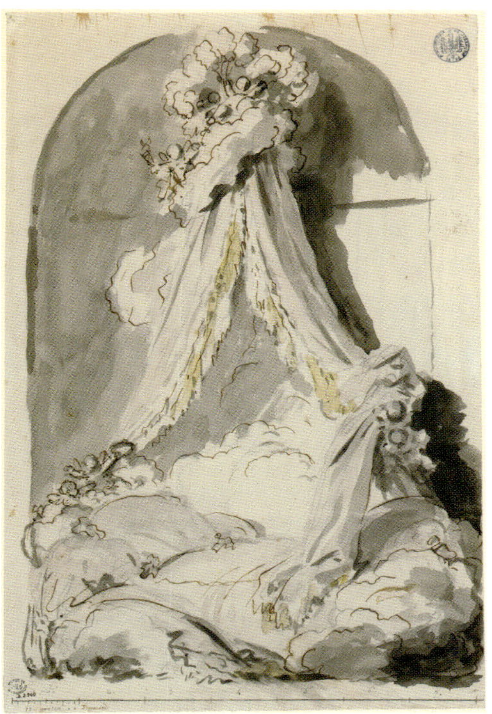

3.37.
Jean-Honoré Fragonard, *Bed with Cupids*, ca. 1765–70. Pen, brown wash, and watercolor over black chalk underdrawing. Musée des Beaux Arts et d'Archéologie, Besançon.

in full bloom and that grants the depicted men only half existence; note the subdued, nearly *grisaille* tonality of their impassive bodies resembling the statues in this painting, except for the visible blush on the reclining man's cheeks, which seems but a reflection of the amorphous pink creation he sees hovering above him. This creation itself, a bundle of creamy textures and whirling molecules, is morphologically akin to the organic life swelling around her, her erotic charge only a token of the more extensive tactile sensualism of this space. (That is, while men are reified, the woman is aligned with life.) Brightly lit, a centerpiece of the composition, this figure ensconced in the womb of nature is a phantasmatic amalgamation of fetus and mother, an imaginary product *and* an impersonation of the generative power of the maternal eros behind this scene.

My point is that the particularity of Fragonard's erotic paintings has to do with the absent body, a body behind the scenes, that functions as their enigmatic source and, as such, exerts pressure on their appearance and meaning. The internal agitation of many of these compositions testifies to the effect of the force that exists beyond the realm of the visible and outside the ostensible signifying economy of these paintings: the unseen maternal body that functions as an eclipsed signifier, lacking a signified. It is as such that this body makes its rounds in Fragonard's oeuvre where we find numerous and diverse testimonies of its subcutaneous existence. If in the *Bathers* and *The Swing* it manifested itself in the overall morphological effect of these paintings, in other works it appears as an insinuation of an alien carnal presence that underwrites and subtly alters the meaning of the visible.

In the Louvre's *The Bolt*, besides the embracing bodies of the lovers, we find a bed that looks positively like some gigantic thighs from which the female protagonist seems to have been ravished by her muscular partner (see fig. 3.5). Its evident if unexplainable presence, highlighted by the shine of the satin sheets that cover it, becomes even more insistent in comparison with the painted sketch for this seduction scene, now in private collection, where the bed appears in its conventional shape, without alluding to the human body.[96] Fragonard's anthropomorphic rendition of the inanimate object reminds one of the widely read eighteenth-century libertine novel by Crébillon fils wherein a speaking sofa narrates a series of erotic adventures taking place on its cushions. In the case of our painting, though, the purpose of this metamorphosis and the gender of the object are different. In Crébillon fils, the sofa—a masculine noun in French—is a man in disguise; it stands for a certain Amanzei condemned by the god Brahma to reincarnate as a piece of furniture to pay for his transgressions.[97] In the Fragonard, on the other hand, the bed suggests itself in a woman's form, its thighs parted in a feminine, simultaneously erotic and birth-giving position, consonant with the erotic/generative construction of the maternal body we have witnessed in Fragonard's work earlier on. In the light of our discussion, the bed's giant satin-covered "thighs" cannot but belong to the invisible mother that haunts Fragonard's pictorial universe and that this painting declares to be, quite literally, the erotic font as much as the locus of seduction depicted in this scene.

Similarly, it is the pronounced carnality of the bed featuring a young woman playing with her lap dog that is most striking about the Munich variant of the so-called *La Gimblette* (fig. 3.38): the large, pliant and palpable pouch of her bed's canopy resembles an interior of a giant uterus as it was depicted in the *Encyclopédie* (see fig. 3.32).[98] It is not only the bodily allusion per se but the way in which it inscribes the whole composition and frames its content that distinguishes Fragonard's approach to the erotic pictorial assignment from that of other contemporary painters who took it on. While in the works of Boucher (see fig. 1.45) and other contemporary artists, such as Le Prince and Lépicié, the bed functions as a more or less elaborate setting for an eroticized display of a female body, in the Fragonard it becomes an aesthetic factor that redefines the erotic import of the scene.[99] Cropped at the top, the yellow-ocher, soft materiality of its canopy dilating to fill the whole space, it suggests a bodily enclave in which the depicted woman's own body is ensconced with her legs bent not unlike a fetus in its womb.

Therein lies Fragonard's seduction: it is the painting itself that is caught up in the grip of desire, attached to the maternal space from which the image and its subject—insofar as we understand the subject as an effect of representation—emerge without quite being able to separate. Seduction is not just what the painting is "about" but, more to the point, it is what secures its existence and shapes its appearance. In that sense, what we witness is a redefinition of the de Pilesian idea of the seductive call of painting familiar to Fragonard's contemporaries.[100] In defining a successful painting, de Piles emphasized the attraction its form must exert on the viewer. "True painting, there-

3.38.
Jean-Honoré Fragonard, *La Gimblette*, ca. 1770. Oil on canvas. Alte Pinakothek, Bayerische taatsgemaelde-sammlungen, Munich, on deposit from the Collection of the HypoVereinsbank, Member of UniCredit.

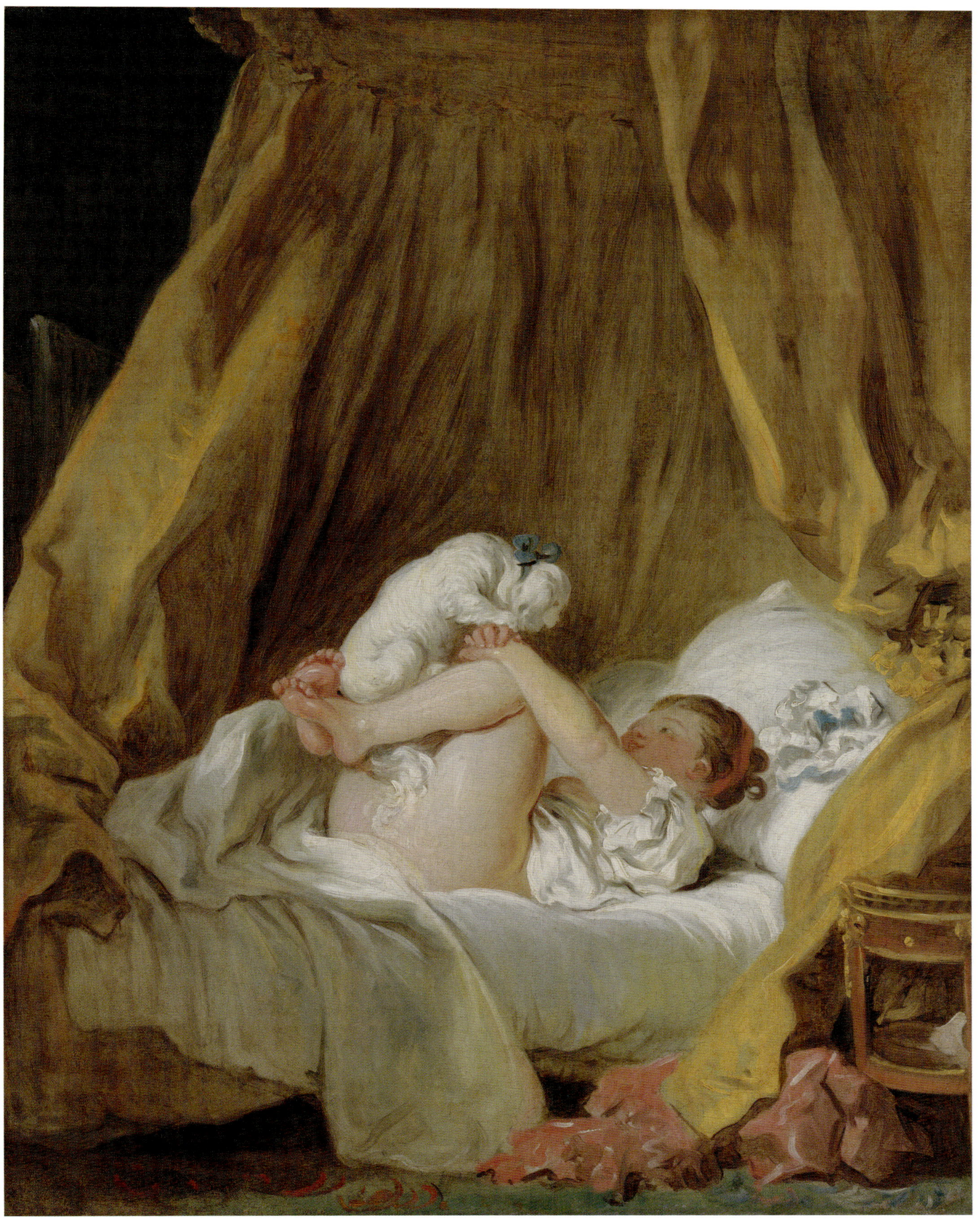

fore, is such as not only surprises, but, as it were, calls to us, and has so powerful an effect that we cannot help coming near it, as if it had something to tell us."[101] This interpellating effect was described by de Piles literally in terms of visual but also physical seduction of the viewer, as a seizure resulting in his or her amorous transport. Terms such as "séduire," or "flatter les yeux," "tromper agréablement," and "imposer" (to seduce or flatter the eyes, to trick in a pleasing way, to impose), all referring to a newly conceived eroticized notion of pictorial illusion, were common in the aesthetic lexicon of the eighteenth century.[102]

Yet the seduction at work in Fragonard's painting—and the body it invokes—is of a different kind. To begin with, it is the artistic process, not only its product, that is defined in Fragonard as erotic, though in a rather idiosyncratic sense. This process implicates the painter himself, and it does so through his own body insofar as this body is directly engaged in the process of representation. Fragonard is supposed to have once declared: "Je peindrais avec mon cul" (I would paint with my ass).[103] It may seem a surprisingly crass declaration from someone renowned for the lightness and sophistication of his touch, but whether or not he actually uttered it, it captures well a distinctly bodily relation of the painter to his work. Contrary to what one may expect, however, there is nothing phallic or even manly about it. Instead, this relation is rather childish: I could paint in whatever way; it's a matter of play, a child's game, as in an infant's first bodily experiments in self-articulation. Fragonard's statement conveys a sense of amused abdication from the position of manual control associated with painterly mastery, a voluntary regression into the realm of infantile sign-making. But in its very infantilism, it also signals an important recognition: I am not in charge of the painting process; my body is drawn into it by the process itself, and any bodily part would do in this blind and driven activity (we could say it is an activity *of* drives understood as psychic forces), the more unthinkable—and unthinking—the better. In sum, I paint as much as I am *painted*, I succumb to the process of the emergence of form from and through my own body, a process of which I am both an agent and a mere witness.

What Fragonard's dictum evokes is the unconscious dimension of le faire, the register of picture-making that eludes the rules of painting as a codified form of representation and that is grounded instead in the primary processes of the body. This alignment of painting with instinct rather than instruction does not imply that Fragonard painted as if he were utterly untrained—which he was not—or that he cultivated vulgarity of expression—far from it—but rather that he willingly accepted the dimension of *un*learning in his embodied process of making. He intuitively perceived this process as a kind of submission necessary for an image to acquire a tangible form.

Evoked by such an approach to picture-making is an infantile subjectivity harking back to that early stage of psychic development when one experiences one's own body as yet unorganized by language but already capable of semiotic activity *in its entirety*. Such is the experience of an infant who, before the acquisition of speech, produces primitive, inchoate bodily signals (including emission of bodily waste) that have, though, a specific aim: they are the means of articulating the child's relation to the mother's body and constitute a mode of communicating with the mother (or a caretaker performing that function). Implied by Fragonard's mode of sign-making is a subject who opens up the gates of conventional language to the flow of signs from the anterior, more primitive stage of self-articulation. He formulates a semiotics based on traces that palpably translate the internal psychic pressure of the drives, an aesthetic of anteriority that, though rooted in his own body, rings back to the mother's interior as the space of his origins, both material and imaginary.[104]

The seduction at work in Fragonard's paintings may be understood as a form of mimicry of the other, as the literary theorists of desire from René Girard to Jean Baudrillard would insist, but of a specific kind: a mimicry of maternal interior.[105] This is what their dynamic morphology repeatedly suggests: a quasi-compulsive attempt to recreate what is no longer there, the missing inside from which the painting subject emerges and on which it continues to *lean*—the unconscious maternal object-source of Fragonard's erotic art.[106] Fragonard's canvases articulate their deep implication in the very space of desire they repeatedly flesh out, if for different purposes and to different ends. The position occupied by the subject of eros in these representations is not an adult male voyeur seeking control over his field of vision but an imaginary infant seeking to reach *before* language and vision, into the tactile realm of the womb conceived as the phantasmatic font of representation.

THE EROTIC MOTHER

I was intoxicated with delight at having a young and pretty mamma whom I loved to caress.

—Rousseau, The Confessions of Jean-Jacques Rousseau

3.39. BELOW
Jean-Honoré Fragonard, *The Good Mother*, ca. 1773–74. Oil on canvas. Museum of Fine Arts, Boston, Bequest of Robert Treat Paine 2nd.

3.40. RIGHT
Jean-Honoré Fragonard, *Sappho Inspired by Love,* ca. 1780. Oil on canvas. Private Collection.

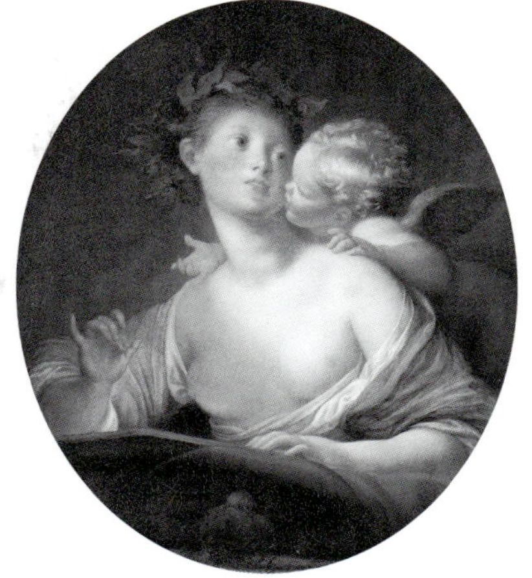

It is through the prism of this argument about Fragonard's seduction that we may consider the painter's multiple engagements with the iconography of the so-called Happy Mother. Under different titles, images of maternity and especially of maternal bliss are among the most frequent in Fragonard's oeuvre. Since Carol Duncan's groundbreaking study, these paintings have been considered predominantly in relation to the new Rousseauian ideology of maternal virtue, articulated most extensively in his *Emile*, though it has also been noted that they propagated this ideal quite ambiguously.[107] No doubt painted in response to the demand for such pictures, Fragonard's works were nonetheless remarkable for their special emphasis—iconographic and morphological—on the erotic dimension of the bond between mother and child. In my view, his paintings were not messages "about" the normative social ideal of motherhood as much as love letters *to* the Mother, tactile evidence of an attachment that was more singular than the Enlightenment ideology of the maternal prepares us for.

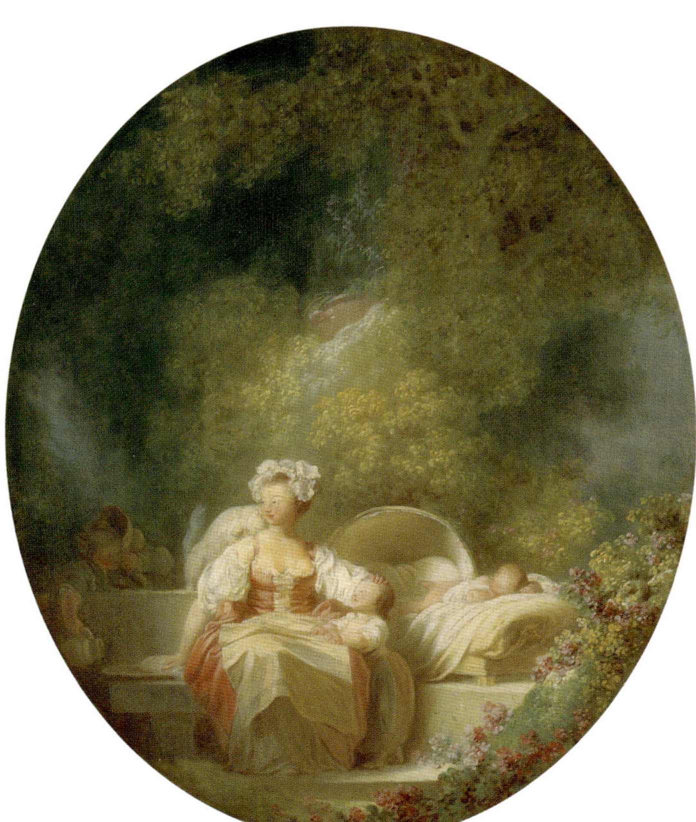

Take, for example, *The Good Mother* (fig. 3.39).[108] The woman tending the children is not just the guardian of her charges but a human sentinel at the gates of exuberant nature, foliage pouring down from behind her, flowers spread on the ground, a vision of unrestrained generation, of which her body is but a contributing part. This scenery resembles that in one of the painted sketches for Fragonard's *Progress of Love* cycle (see fig. 3.66), the ostensibly moral argument about motherhood being framed as an amorous tryst. With no lover—or father—in view, it is the encounter between this maternal figure and her children that is implicitly eroticized. Other aspects of the painting also hint at it. The mother's sexual appeal is evident: her full breasts, emphasized by her tight corset, suggest both nourishment and sensual gratification, and the furry white cat rubbing itself against her neck reinforces the idea of sensuous appeal. Note also the quasi-theatrical display of the infant lying in the crib suggestively exposed, its uncovered bottom up in the air—similar to Boucher's *Girl on the Sofa* (see fig. 1.46)—the crib itself having been raised on a stone platform, brightly lit like a stage for an erotic argument. There is also a naughty little boy peeking from behind his hat, ready to do some mischief—an avatar of so many other playful youngsters engaged in more or less sexually explicit pranks with older, maternal women in Fragonard's work.

Such are the figures of Venus with the little cupids and the versions thereof, such as *Sappho Inspired by Love* (fig. 3.40), or women coming undone by the naughty putti, as in the already mentioned *Stolen Shift* and *All Ablaze*, but also genre scenes with no

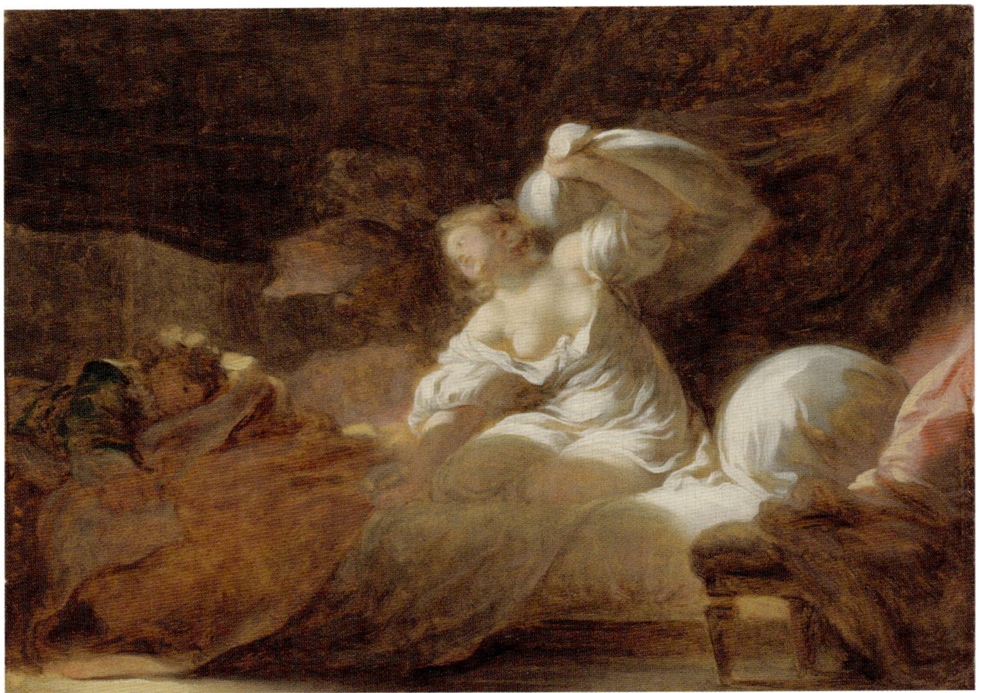

3.41.
Jean-Honoré Fragonard, *The Useless Resistance*, ca. 1770. Oil on panel. Fine Arts Museums of San Francisco, Mr. and Mrs. E. John Magnin Gift.

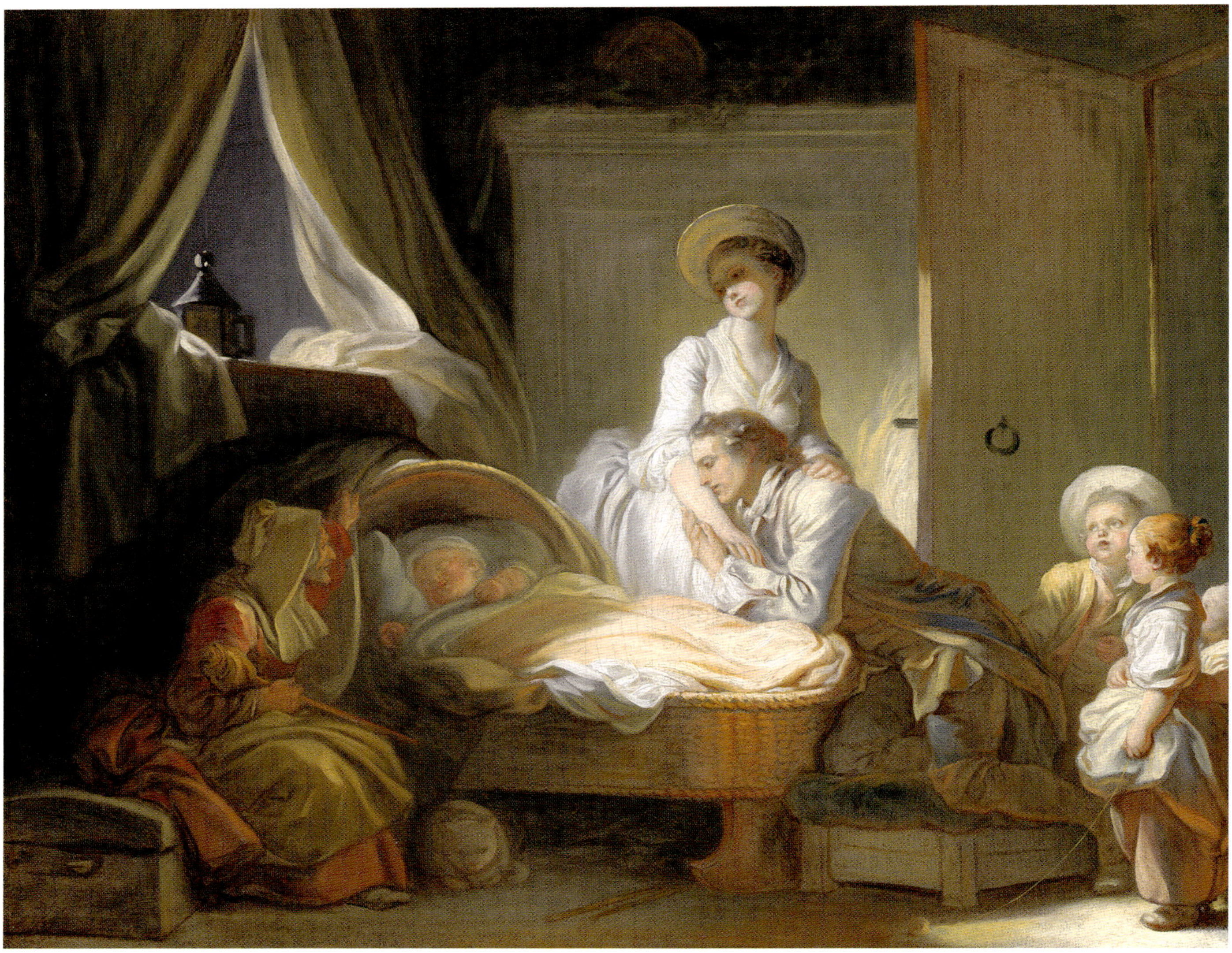

3.42.
Jean-Honoré Fragonard, *Visit to the Nursery*, ca. 1775. Oil on canvas. National Gallery of Art, Washington, DC, The Samuel H. Kress Collection.

mythological or allegorical pretext, such as San Francisco's *The Useless Resistance*, in which a young woman, her bosom exposed, pummels a boy buried in her unmade bed with a pillow (fig. 3.41).[109] In regard to paintings such as these, it is the Rousseau not of *Emile* but rather of *The Confessions* that seems more relevant. Speaking of his friend and mentor Mme de Warens, who took care of him after he left his father's house, Rousseau described there just this kind of unorthodox, at once affective and sensual, maternal attachment of himself as a young boy.

> *From the first day the sweetest intimacy was established between us, and it continued to prevail during the rest of her life. "Little one" was my name, hers was "Mamma," and we always remained "Little one" and "Mamma," even when the passage of the years had almost effaced the difference between our ages. The two names, I find, admirably express the tone of our behavior, the simplicity of our habits, and, what is more, the relation between our hearts. . . . And if there was a sensual side of my attachment to her, that did not alter its character, but only made it more enchanting. I was intoxicated with delight at having a young and pretty mamma whom I loved to caress.*[110]

Like Rousseau's Mme de Warens, Fragonard's "good mother" and other grown-up women engaged in para-erotic games with the eager male youths in his genre scenes are figures of maternal seduction, objects of puerile desire—not just of their putative sons' but of the subject implied by these paintings. It is precisely a male child's look, cast stealthily from the side, at the mother—presumably the child's own—that may be seen responsible for the sexualized definition of her body in the *Visit to the Nursery* (fig. 3.42).[111] While this rendition of the woman may have been, as Sheriff has argued, incongruous in the period's terms, combining as it did two then irreconcilable definitions of the woman's role as a sexually attractive and even aroused object of her husband-lover's attention *and* as a nursing mother to her child, it is actually quite consistent with the logic of Fragonard's maternal fantasy: the loving gaze of an infant, at once his mother's child *and* her lover.[112] In other words, if this mother's body was defined as both nurturing and erotic, it was because she was an object of an enamored infantile fascination.[113] Let us also notice that the husband's gaze, and even his body, has been visually merged with, if not subsumed by, the maternal corpus of his wife, kneeling as he is just below her swelling breasts, at the level of the womb, in a position of her quasi-offspring. The erotic attraction that the husband represents vis-à-vis his wife is predicated on his positioning as her child, on her status as *his* mother.

Important, too, is the morphological register at which the erotic fantasy manifests itself in Fragonard's representations of mothers. One painting, the *Italian Family* (fig. 3.43), testifies to it with a remarkable painterly eloquence. A radiant maternal figure with an infant in her arms emerges as if from the inner core of this painting, against the bleached whiteness of the door in which some other barely articulated shapes hover about. Because of the light that accompanies her entry, the mother has the quality of an apparition, her status reflected by the reaction of other figures, one of them dropping to his knees in front of her like a shepherd adoring the Virgin Mary in Nativity scenes, including Fragonard's own.[114] It is, though, the formal staging of her entry that is the most striking; it is as if, with her arrival, the picture itself emerged into view. The sheer thickness of pigment applied in fat, buttery strokes makes the surface of the canvas appear like a crusted membrane on which things are only just beginning to take shape, as if summoned into existence by the physical pressure of the incoming light. What is striking is not simply the unusually thick textures but the dynamic deployment of paint, especially the movement of the billowing white shapes that seems to push the maternal figure forward into view. Representation acquires an organic quality, the generation of forms being likened to a kind of growth.

In this aspect, the *Italian Family* bears also some morphological similarity to *The Island of Love*. It too declares itself to be motivated from within, by a dynamic internal process. The promise of an image that has not yet fully taken shape, this work lets us into the kitchen of that process through the back door. Both thematically and formally, the painting exposes the grounding of the artist's trace in the maternal body understood as an anteriority, a luminous "elsewhere" that pushes this image into existence, its imaginary source of which the figure of the entering mother is a cipher. The inarticulate density of pigment, the randomness of its application, the almost blindly dabbed-on paint—as if by the painter's own bodily part rather than his brush—flesh out a child's haptic fantasy of its own originary space as the origin of this artistic vision. This fantasy issues from the

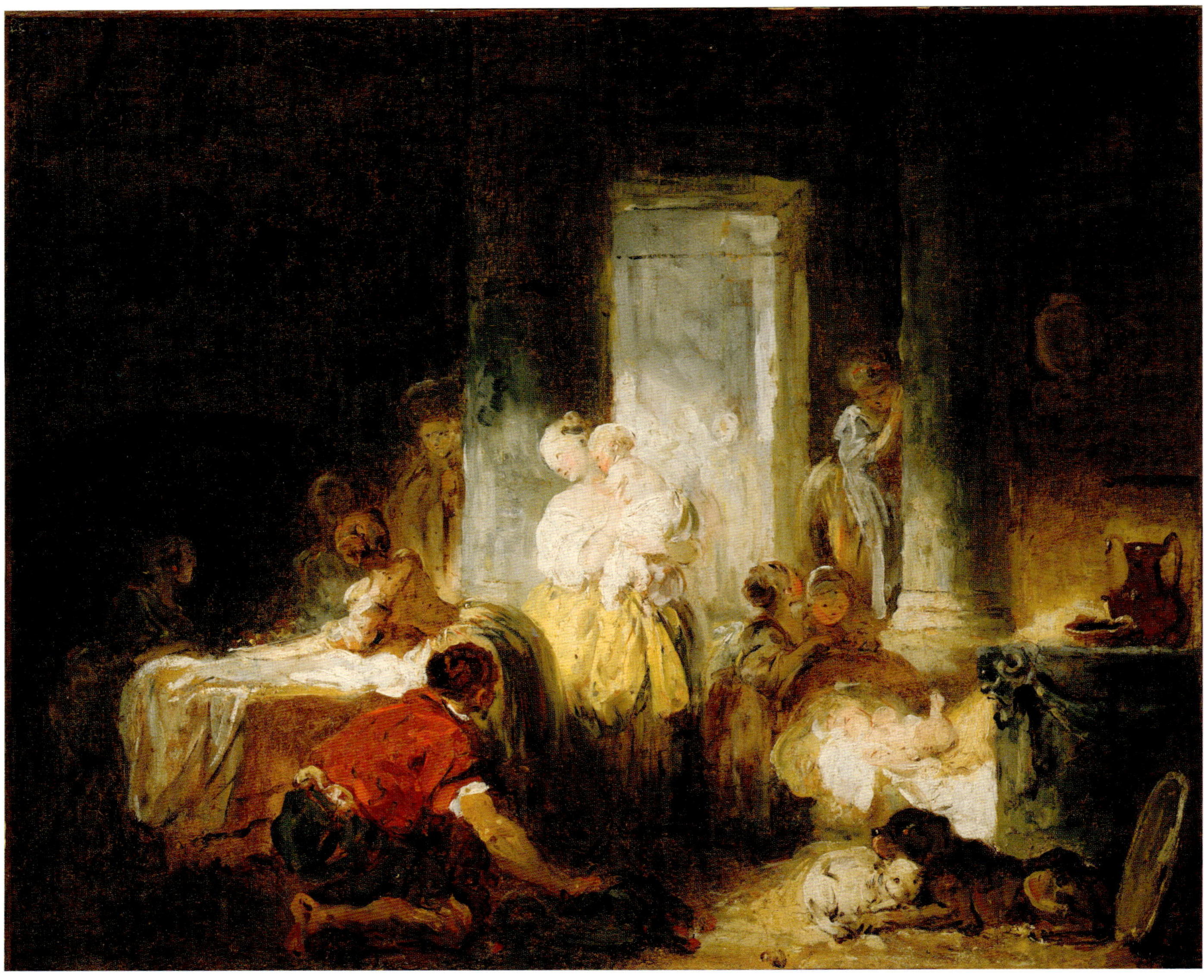

imaginary corpus of the Mother that secures the morphological coherence of this field of representation and creates a glowing gap of light (the unseen) within it. The emphasis, unlike in *The Island of Love*, is not on this active source per se as much as its dynamic effect on the canvas's surface, extraordinarily sketchy and cogent at the same time.

Offering us a glimpse of the painter's process, the *Italian Family* brings to mind a brief commentary on the painter's working method left by Pierre-Jean Mariette who reported that in making an image, Fragonard proceeded by repeatedly erasing and repainting—"il efface et revient sur lui-même"—a method the connoisseur ascribed to the artist's lack of self-confidence and the resulting continuous dissatisfaction with his productions.[115] This habit of perpetual wiping away and retracing his own steps may also be seen as a symptom of an attachment, at once physical and imaginary, to the support of the image, an indication of an unconscious reluctance to separate from the material ground of representation to which the artist's hand keeps being drawn back, as if by an invisible thread.

This kind of touch is thematized in the *Young Child Standing on the Windowsill*, an image of a child propped on the body of the invisible mother that belongs to a group of exceptionally intimate small-scale renditions of the mother and child theme (fig. 3.44).[116] Filling up the whole canvas, the little boy, his still uncoordinated body supported from behind so that he appears standing on his own, is shown with an unmitigated frontality. This mode of presentation generates a sense of conflation between his body and the surface of the canvas, with his hands edged by light and flattened as if against the invisible window pane emphasizing this effect. The painting

3.43. OPPOSITE
Jean-Honoré Fragonard, *Italian Family*, ca. 1760. Oil on canvas. Metropolitan Museum of Art, New York, Harris Brisbane Dick Fund, 1946.

3.44. BELOW
Jean-Honoré Fragonard, *Young Child Standing on the Windowsill*, ca. 1775. Oil on canvas. Private Collection.

is, in other words, not unlike a child supported by a mother who is withdrawn from view. Hovering in the background of this picture, the maternal figure—almost entirely eclipsed except for her highlighted hands framing the red-shod feet of the child in a gesture of worried protection—may be seen to personify the maternal anteriority that precedes and guarantees the form of this painting, and, as the painter's other works diversely suggest, of his aesthetic project at large. We may say that if the *Young Child Standing on the Windowsill* depicts a toddler as he sees himself, sovereign, even if in reality dependent on the behind-the-scene maneuvers of the mother, it also conveys how the painter sees his work, as autonomous yet dependent on the maternal precedence. The toddler's portrait literally embodies a sui generis infantile conception of the picture that underwrites Fragonard's vision.

The question of autonomy raised by this vision, idiosyncratic as it may be, was related to then current cultural concerns with the individuality of infants and children. To perceive this relation, the *Young Child Standing on the Windowsill* may be compared to the wishfully autonomous newborn from the anatomical plate in the *Encyclopédie* standing on its own while still being linked by the umbilical cord to the placenta (see fig. 3.32). Just as the illustration for the *Encyclopédie* offers a cultural construction of the individual subject based on the relation of dependence, at once avowed and disclaimed, between the infant and the maternal body, so does Fragonard's practice convey a vision of autonomy based in a similar dependence. For if Fragonard's epigenetic conception of painting posited a notion of artist as a subject *engendered* by the very form of his paintings, it also anchored the painter's touch in the maternal anteriority of the image. As in the case of the encyclopedic newborn still attached to the remnants of the maternal body, his works bear the material residues of their maternal dependence.[117]

In this sense, Fragonard's depictions of maternal bliss, while illustrating a broader interest in affective motherhood, are also the articulations of a particular creative intimacy at the core of Fragonard's aesthetic enterprise. The figure of the Erotic Mother fleshed out in these canvases embodies the very condition of representation for Fragonard, the ground of his bodily understanding of both the image and the process that brings it about.

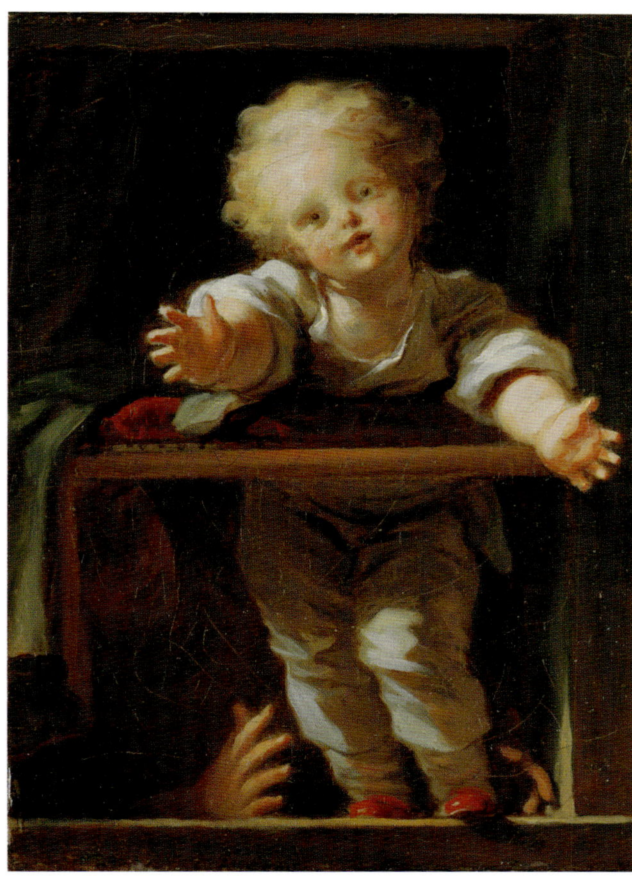

THE ARTIST'S PLEASURE

Pleasure is the essence of man, and of the order of the universe.

—La Mettrie

It is in the context of this imaginary link between the bodies of mother and child that inscribed the painter's approach to pictorial representation that we may now reconsider Fragonard's bizarre entry to the Salon of 1767, the *Groups of Children in the Sky* (see fig. 3.2).[118] The artist's contemporaries and modern scholars alike have been puzzled by Fragonard's decision to submit such an anticlimactic picture in the wake of his stunning *Coresus and Callirhoë* shown at the previous Salon. The iconography of this canvas—a study for a ceiling decoration painted for a private patron that exemplified many other commissions of this kind the painter received at that time —was not unusual.[119] Fragonard followed Boucher's example, his painting being a more complicated version of such decorative works as the *Spring*, one of the ceiling panels executed by his teacher for the Salle du Conseil at Fontainebleau (fig. 3.45).[120] But what was surprising was that Fragonard would present so inconsequential a work after a promising debut on the most important public arena of art display. For an artist at the early stages of his career, before his full acceptance as a member of the Academy, this was certainly a misstep. The more so that, even for a purely decorative painting of this type, the *Groups* was oddly conceived, with its compositionally unconvincing arrangement of chubby toddlers entangled with one another to form a clump of flesh hovering in the clouds—it looked as if Fragonard tried to combine the putti from *all four* of Boucher's Fontainebleau panels into one swarm. Diderot's disappointment—"Monsieur Fragonard, this is devilishly feeble work"—was echoed by others who judged the *Group* to be an artistic letdown, if not an outright failure.[121]

Yet the artist's decision may not appear as puzzling if we consider this painting as a symptom of a certain logic of pleasure evident in Fragonard's practice at large. Given the painter's investment in the figure of a child as a form of indirect self-representation, the *Groups of Children in the Sky* may be seen as an unwitting manifestation of Fragonard's artistic entanglement in the imaginary realm of the maternal body. The singular inarticulateness of this composition, its sense of knotted irresolution, testify to a painter's brush unable, or reluctant, to bring off the embryonic forms still buried in the amorphous maternal grounds of this image. The strong light emanating from the depth of the painting—suggesting an off-stage presence of Aurora—only underscores the messy tightness of this cherubic cluster, their bodies being too enmeshed with one another to make any clear compositional or iconographic sense. It is significant that while neglecting and ultimately failing to produce an official commission of a similar kind—the *Allegory of Spring* for the ceiling of the Galerie d'Apollon at the Louvre which, assigned to him in May 1766 as a requirement for a full membership in the Academy, was still pending at the time of the Salon of 1767—the young artist saw it fit to exhibit a version of this assignment painted for a private individual, "M. Bergeret" (Pierre-Jacques-Onésyme Bergeret de Grancourt who became one of the painter's most important patrons).[122] Thus, whether or not it was intended as such, the display of the *Group* effectively marked an important shift in the artist's professional life, representing his renunciation of history painting and his commitment to private patronage as an alternative to an official career. It has now been largely accepted that this shift need not be seen merely as a sign of Fragonard's abandonment of aesthetic ambition, but, on the contrary, should be recognized as the painter's self-conscious adoption of an alternative mode of operation that allowed for a greater degree of aesthetic experimentation than a practice conducted under the auspices of the Academy ever could.[123] In this regard, Fragonard could be seen to have followed the examples of his teachers, Chardin and Boucher, who developed differently individuated styles largely by relying on private clients and the art market.[124] If his investment in private patronage suggested that he opted for a greater aesthetic freedom, might it not have also indicated the artist's desire to pursue his own professional and personal pleasure?

In the idiosyncrasy of its articulation, the *Group of Children in the Sky* may suggest just that. If the confused fleshiness of this canvas is a symptom of the gratifying involvement of the painter's own body in it, may we not see his pleasure as a factor not only in the process of producing this image but also in his decision to exhibit it? The question is how did the painter's enjoyment in painting relate to that of the patron

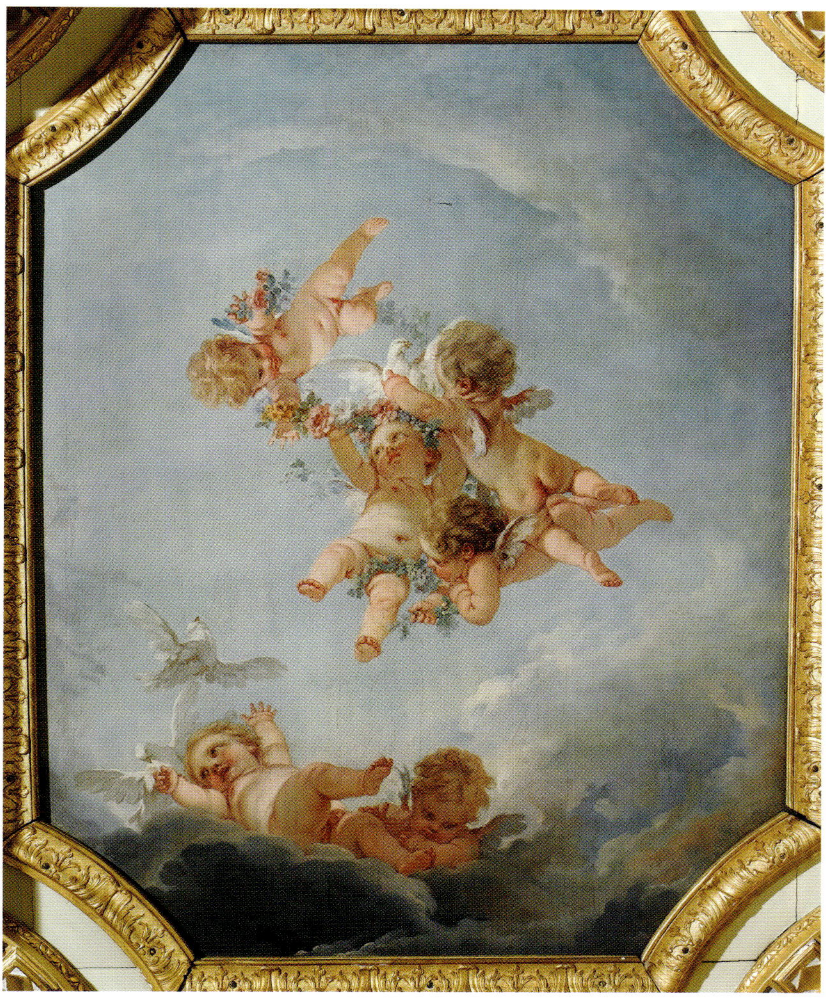

3.45.
François Boucher, *The Four Seasons: Spring*, 1763. Oil on canvas. Salle du Conseil, Fontainebleau.

for whom the painting was made? Was Fragonard's gratification in executing this work similar to that of Bergeret in receiving it? This question touches on a larger issue of the relation between Fragonard's bodily conception of painting and his professional and social functioning as an artist. How did his particular mode of practicing painting—embodied and gratifying—figure in his relations with his patrons and clients? How did the artist negotiate his preferences with their specific demands? We know that despite his extremely successful career, Fragonard's relations with his clients, including Bergeret, were not free of tension and conflict.[125] The more reason to reflect on the consequences of the painter's particular approach to painting for establishing his position in the artistic culture and the social world of his time.

To consider the artist's pleasure as a factor in his mode of practice and professional functioning is not the same as assuming that, as the Goncourt brothers would have it, Fragonard simply followed his Southern temperament in choosing an individual career path.[126] Nor is it, as the painter's late nineteenth-century biographer, Roger Portalis, asserted, to define his practice as an essentially hedonistic pursuit.[127] Far from wishing to revive the myth of a proto-romantic painter in pursuit of self-fulfillment and self-expression or engage in psychobiography, I would suggest that what we witness in Fragonard's practice is the emergence of the painter's *bonheur* as a historically viable artistic preoccupation.

"One must try to let pleasure break through all the gates that lead to the very depth of our selves; there is nothing else for us to do," declared the *femme savante* Emilie du Châtelet in her *Discours sur le bonheur* written in the late 1740s.[128] Her pronouncement encapsulates the new importance and meaning the ideal of personal *bonheur* acquired in France in about the mid-eighteenth century.[129] Declaring happiness to be the chief human aspiration, the discourse of the Enlightenment redefined its earlier, Christian, and philosophical sense by associating *bonheur* (happiness, well-being) specifically with pleasure, referred to as *plaisir*, *jouissance*, or *volupté*.[130] It was a kind of happiness that was felt rather than known, linked to perception and sensual experience as opposed to intellectual knowledge, and, as such, defining the self.[131] As Rousseau's Julie asserted, "to feel and to enjoy [*jouir*] are for me the same thing, I live simultaneously in all that which I love, I grasp myself in happiness and in life."[132] The sensual bases of *bonheur* were emphasized most insistently by La Mettrie, who, as we have seen, conceived of pleasure, particularly sensual pleasure—his term was *volupté*—as an important and defining aspect of selfhood.[133] With the flair of a *provocateur*, La Mettrie committed his work entirely to the advocacy of happiness based in pleasure as the motor of human functioning, that is, as the key component of individual identity and the motivating principle of life. He insisted that such a notion of bonheur was essentially democratic and amoral: it is "open to the ignorant and the poor as much as to the learned and the rich; there is a happiness for all classes and—this will revolt prejudiced minds—for the wicked as well as the good."[134] The radical social implications of La Mettrie's materialist notion of bonheur went against the grain of the mainstream humanist ideals of the Enlightenment.[135] They may have suited Fragonard, whose position within the Enlightenment culture was oblique. Among Fragonard's more immediate contemporaries, men his own age, Giacomo Casanova distinguished himself in putting this ideal of bonheur as a self-defining principle into practice. His lifelong, indefatigable pursuit of pleasure during his travels across Europe, including several stays in Paris, became a goal in and of itself that shaped his life and his writing about it.[136]

It seems reasonable to expect that such widespread cultural concern with bonheur, and the democratic turn in its conception, impacted not only how people thought of themselves as private individuals but also how they functioned as professionals. While it would be historically and economically naive to claim that pleasure constituted the sole motivation in the eighteenth-century artistic practice, it could certainly be considered as a factor in professional self-definition and conduct. It has been argued that the eighteenth century marks the beginning of a transformation of the artistic profession into a vocation. Analyzing this complex historical process, the sociologist Nathalie Heinich has noted that the artists' pursuit of professionalization differed from that of the writers; while the latter sought to distinguish themselves from the amateurs, the former wished to separate themselves from other professionals, from the practitioners of art as a métier.[137] The institutional bases of this transformation—especially the key role of the Academy—are well understood. What has not yet been considered, however, is the role of personal gratification in the artist's vocational self-definition.

Fragonard may be seen as the first significant case in this historical process of vocational transformation. While his early association with the institution and his academic training must have helped him develop a sense of professional dignity and autonomy that distinguished his self-conception from that promoted by the guilds, endowing him also with more authority vis-à-vis his patrons, he recognized the incompatibility of his particular talent with the traditional expectations and mode of operation of an academic artist. Fragonard's professional bonheur lay in this recognition. Claiming his right to pursue his own goals and gratifications—the right advocated in the writings of his contemporaries, especially La Mettrie's—he recast the institutionally grounded idea of professional dignity and autonomy. As such, Fragonard's approach may be seen as an early form of artistic individualism, a practice of *self-accommodation* through painting. This practice implied an increased sense of artistic self-awareness that was typical of an academic artist at the time but that was, in his case, grounded in a set of methods and procedures developed largely on his own and in relation to a different, private audience. In this regard his approach was close to that of his teacher, Chardin. Although Fragonard received full academic instruction in drawing at the École des Élèves Protégés—an institution created specifically to address the lacunae in training of the young artists before they departed for Rome—he made use of it in his own way. Subjected to the strict pedagogical regime at the French Academy in Rome, the young artist became quite notorious for following his own paths and frustrating the expectations of the authorities by his uneven progress and unpredictability.[138]

Facilitating the young artist's self-discovery in Rome was no doubt his encounter with the art *amateur* Jean Claude Richard, abbé de Saint-Non, who took him under his wing. While remaining a student at the Academy, Fragonard traveled with Saint-Non to Tivoli and Naples and accompanied him on the *amateur*'s return trip to Paris, making art-related stopovers in the major cultural centers along the way. Much has been said about Saint-Non's importance as a steadfast supporter of the artist.[139] I would emphasize that Fragonard's encounter with Saint-Non opened up to the young pensionnaire of the French Academy a different perspective on his work that the Academy followed with a mixture of admiration and concern, as the correspondence between the director of the French Academy, Natoire, and the *directeur des bâtiments* Marigny demonstrates.[140] It was the interest and pleasure that the *amateur* took in Fragonard's art that must have encouraged and validated the young artist's own satisfaction with his productions, while opening up the prospect of an audience, and a market, for his work. As it has been acknowledged, the extensive period of sketching from nature enabled by Saint-Non's support—the two months Fragonard spent with him in Tivoli, a shorter stay in Naples, and the six months of drawing while traveling back with him to Paris (April–September 1761)—was crucial for the development of the young artist's style.[141] What has not been considered was the role of this experience for the development of the artist's self-awareness, especially about the gratifying dimension of his work. Made largely for the pleasure of Saint-Non's eyes, the bulk of the artist's Italian work may well have helped him to develop a sense of his work as a source of his own pleasure.

Individual pleasure was precisely what amateur practice and discourse on art were centered on.[142] Initiating the young Fragonard into this personally rewarding realm of art appreciation, Saint-Non also helped him locate his ambition in and connect his

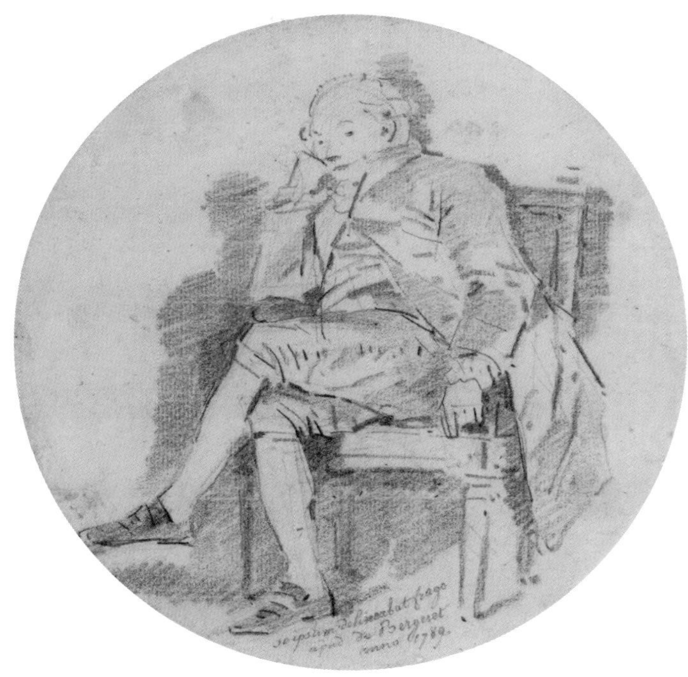

3.46.
Jean-Honoré Fragonard, *Self-Portrait*, 1789. Black chalk on paper. Fondation Custodia, Frtis Lugt Collection, Paris.

professional self-understanding to the milieu of his benefactor. The artist may have come to aspire to the social position equivalent to that of the *amateurs* who became his most important clients. The hallmark of the social world of the *amateurs* was the interconnectedness between them and artists, the sense of shared interest—the love of art—and the rhetoric of friendship that glossed over the actual social inequality between these two groups.[143] Fragonard's immersion in this social context may have consolidated his habits of self-accommodation through art. Yet the professional character of the painter's association with the *amateurs* must have also raised for him the issue of difference—and the necessity of self-differentiation. It hardly needs to be stated that he was not an amateur—art was for him not a pastime, but a profession and career. His life depended on the income generated by his involvement in the relaxed sociability of the *amateur* milieu, among men of independent means and different, sometimes exceedingly lavish, lifestyles. He may have been Saint-Non's "friend," but theirs was not a relationship of equals. It is telling that, appreciative as he was of Fragonard, Saint-Non never even mentioned the young artist in the diary he kept during their travels in Italy.[144] Even more instructive are the artist's close relationship with another *amateur*—incidentally, Saint-Non's brother-in-law—the fabulously wealthy financier, Bergeret, with whom the artist traveled to Flanders and to Italy, for his second trip, in the early 1770s.[145] Their "friendship" ended in a dispute over the rights to the drawings Fragonard produced during their joint travels, which his sponsor, assuming they were his, appropriated. The artist brought Bergeret to court, won the case, and was remunerated.[146] Clearly the pleasure his protectors took in his art was not always compatible with the artist's own interests and pleasures. It is essential to keep in mind the difference in the social and economic status of the *amateur* and the artist, and the difference in the position from which they appreciated and enjoyed art, to properly assess the meaning and implications of their amicable interactions. Formative and sustaining as it may have been for Fragonard, his financial and social dependence on the *amateur* circles evidently also posed some problems. It necessitated acts of self-protection, such as the artist's legal battle with Bergeret, and also other, more subtle but vital gestures of self-assertion through which the artist claimed his rights to *his* bonheur.

It is exactly this purpose that one may detect in one of the painter's rare self-representations, a small tondo drawing now in the Lugt collection in Paris (fig. 3.46).[147] Looking from some distance, the artist shows himself seated in an armchair, relaxed, pensive, his face resting on his arm, his leg swung over the other. The Latin inscription at the bottom of the drawing attesting that it was produced in 1789 "at the home of Bergeret" defines this work as a testimony to the artist's lasting connection to the *amateur* and his family.[148] Despite their falling out, Fragonard reconciled with his patron by the late 1770s, and after the death of Bergeret père in 1785, continued to enjoy a close rapport with his son, Pierre-Jacques, who hosted the artist and his family in his château de Cassan, near l'Isle-Adam.[149] While it is uncertain whether the artist portrayed himself at Cassan or elsewhere—Bergeret's elegant Parisian residence, Folie Beajon, has been suggested as another possible location—the fact that the drawing was executed in the domestic context of his patron's house is an important factor for considering its purpose and meaning.[150]

With the artist's facial features barely marked by summary dots and bars—Jean-Pierre Cuzin describes the face as "ghostlike vague"[151]—it is the artist's body that defines him, the choice of its pose suggesting that Fragonard was interested above all in conveying a sense of being at ease with himself. Presenting himself in this way—as an embodiment of domestic bonheur—the artist also, if indirectly, positions himself in his patron's house, asserting his right to personal comfort on a par with his host. His mode of self-depiction harks back, in fact, to the informally domestic self-presentation adopted by Bergeret père in Vincent's 1774 portrait of him, well known to Fragonard as it was painted in Rome during their joint sojourn there (see fig. 2.91). The choice, which was most certainly the sitter's own, to be depicted in a white satin *déshabillé*, unbuttoned vest, shirt baring his chest, and, in lieu of a wig, a scarf wrapped inelegantly around his head, suggests Bergeret's understanding of sartorial comfort as a sign of entitlement compatible with the tokens of cultivation and amateur skills (antiquities, books, prints, and drawings, the latter likely including Bergeret's own) that surround and define him.[152] It is in this sense that Fragonard too adopts the informal mien, slumped in the *fauteil* in his unbuttoned coat, although, by comparison to his patron's appearance in Vincent's portrait, his is far more gracious. Although small and casually executed, this self-image clearly demonstrates not only the artist's capacity for self-accommodation but also his desire to make a point of it. That the artist produced this self-image as Bergeret's guest, and that he offered it to Pierre-Jacques as a gift, enhances its self-assertive dimension, as does the history of Fragonard's complex professional and personal relations with Bergeret père.[153] If this image of domestic bonheur speaks of the reciprocity—actual, desired, or only imagined—between the artist and the *amateur*, it does so in a subtly assertive tone that reaffirms his sense of entitlement to personal comfort. What this suggests is that, if art was for Fragonard a means of positioning himself—of *representing* himself—in relation to his patrons, the issue of pleasure and of the body as its site and agent played a significant role in it. It was indeed a practice of self-accommodation.

THE PAINTER'S TOUCH

I am an inexhaustible bag of tricks.

—Diderot, Rameau's Nephew

Nowhere is the artist's use of his body as a tool of self-distinction more apparent than in an intriguing series of portrait-like paintings Fragonard produced in the late 1760s. Featuring half figures of men and women in historical costumes, and similar in format and handling, the paintings form a distinct group the origins, function, and meaning of which have long been debated.[154] Although some of the figures were tentatively identified—among them the *amateurs* abbé de Saint-Non and his older brother, Louis Richard de la Bretèche; the artist Naigeon (figs. 3.47, 3.48, and 3.49); the critic Diderot; and the dancer Mlle Guimard—the prevailing opinion among scholars is that they are *figures de fantaisie*, a well-established genre of imaginary representation of human subjects. "Portraits of portraits," as Mary Sheriff aptly put it, they are self-conscious visual commentaries on the conventions of portraiture that harken back to the old masters, such as Rembrandt.[155] While some scholars considered them a consistent group commissioned by a specific patron or patrons, others have challenged this idea, suggesting that the paintings were most likely produced for the market, in response to the growing connoisseurial demand for such pictures, and to the thriving culture of performance.[156] In both the anachronistic garb of their characters and in their sketchy mode of rendering, the paintings testify to the rising fashion for pastiche and travesty associated with the circles of amateurs.[157] Displaying the painter's imitative skill expressly for the connoisseurial gaze, these examples of a pictorial performance on demand were symptoms of elective affinities and social interconnectedness between *amateurs* and artists at the time.[158] Such was the nature of the relation between Fragonard and one of the identified subjects of his "portraits," abbé de Saint-Non (see fig. 3.47), who etched many of Fragonard's drawings and some paintings (fig. 3.50).[159] By depicting Saint-Non as a fantasy figure, the painter engaged his supporter in a game of self-recognition that involved both the model for this fantasy and himself as its author.[160] Testimonies to the self-reflexive relation between the artist and the amateurs, Fragonard's *figures de fantaisie* have been seen as tokens of cul-

3.47.
Jean-Honoré Fragonard, *Abbé de Saint-Non*, 1769. Oil on canvas. Musée du Louvre, Paris.

3.48.
Jean-Honoré Fragonard, *Louis Richard de la Bretèche*, 1769. Oil on canvas. Musée du Louvre, Paris.

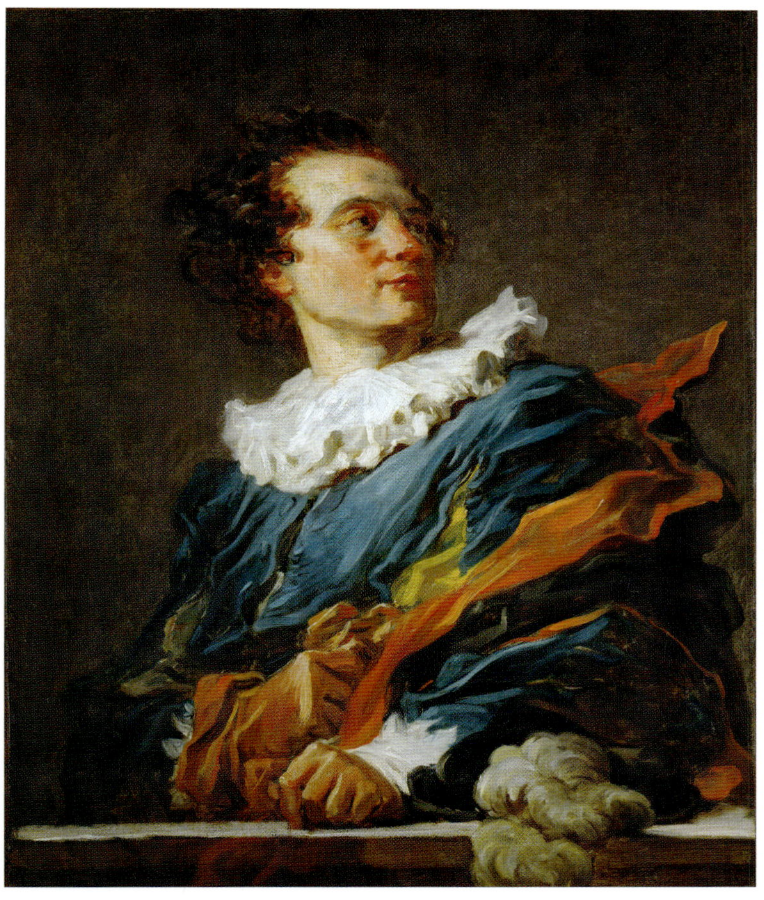

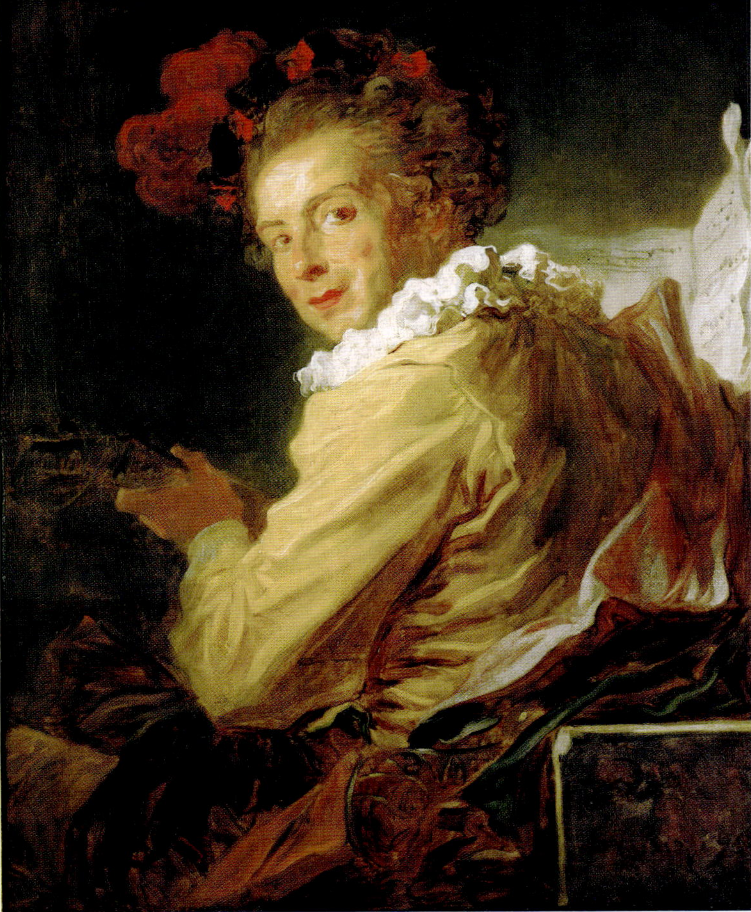

tural collusion and the mutual social valorization in and through art.

An important recent discovery has prompted further reflection on these paintings. In 2012, a sheet containing the painter's summary sketches of most, if not all, of his figures de fantaisie resurfaced on the art market, challenging some of the assumptions about these works (fig. 3.51).[161] The names scribbled by the artist under his thumbnail renditions of each likeness confirmed the identity of only two figures—abbé de Saint-Non and Monsieur de la Bretèche—and contradicted most of the others. The presumed Diderot and La Guimard have proven false. Other known members of the *amateur* circle have emerged, for example, Gabriel-Auguste Godefroy, portrayed as a child by Chardin (see fig. 2.61), who has been identified as the man earlier called *The Actor*.[162] While we do not know why the artist made these sketches—and the function of the sheet is in and of itself intriguing—they open up new interpretive possibilities. The recovered drawing confirms that the eighteen paintings sketched on it were indeed representations of specific individuals, and that they constituted a group, although it is unclear whether they were originally produced as such or only put together on paper by the artist afterward. The drawing also indicates the group was intended to be displayed together, either physically, or as reproductive prints, possibly a type known as the *gravure de société* practiced by the *amateurs*.[163] Last but not least, the *Sketches for Portraits* suggests the role of the artist in conceptualizing the mode in which these works were to function as an ensemble. While much about the paintings is still unknown—even the identity of some of the figures, to which Fragonard referred only in a summary way, by their last name, remains unconfirmed or unknown—the discovery of the sheet has certainly provided the ground for reconsideration of their purpose and meaning.[164]

I will focus on the significance of Fragonard's project for the painter himself. Whether it was his proposal for the manner in which the paintings were to be exhibited or a preliminary design for a reproductive print, the discovery of the *Sketches* brought to the fore the importance the painter attached to these works as an ensemble. It is thus Fragonard's conception of, and his relation to, the figures de fantaisie as an aesthetically cogent group that the page of thumbnail sketches invites us to ponder. In doing so, however, we must not lose sight of the particular character of these portrayals. While the discovery of the sitters'

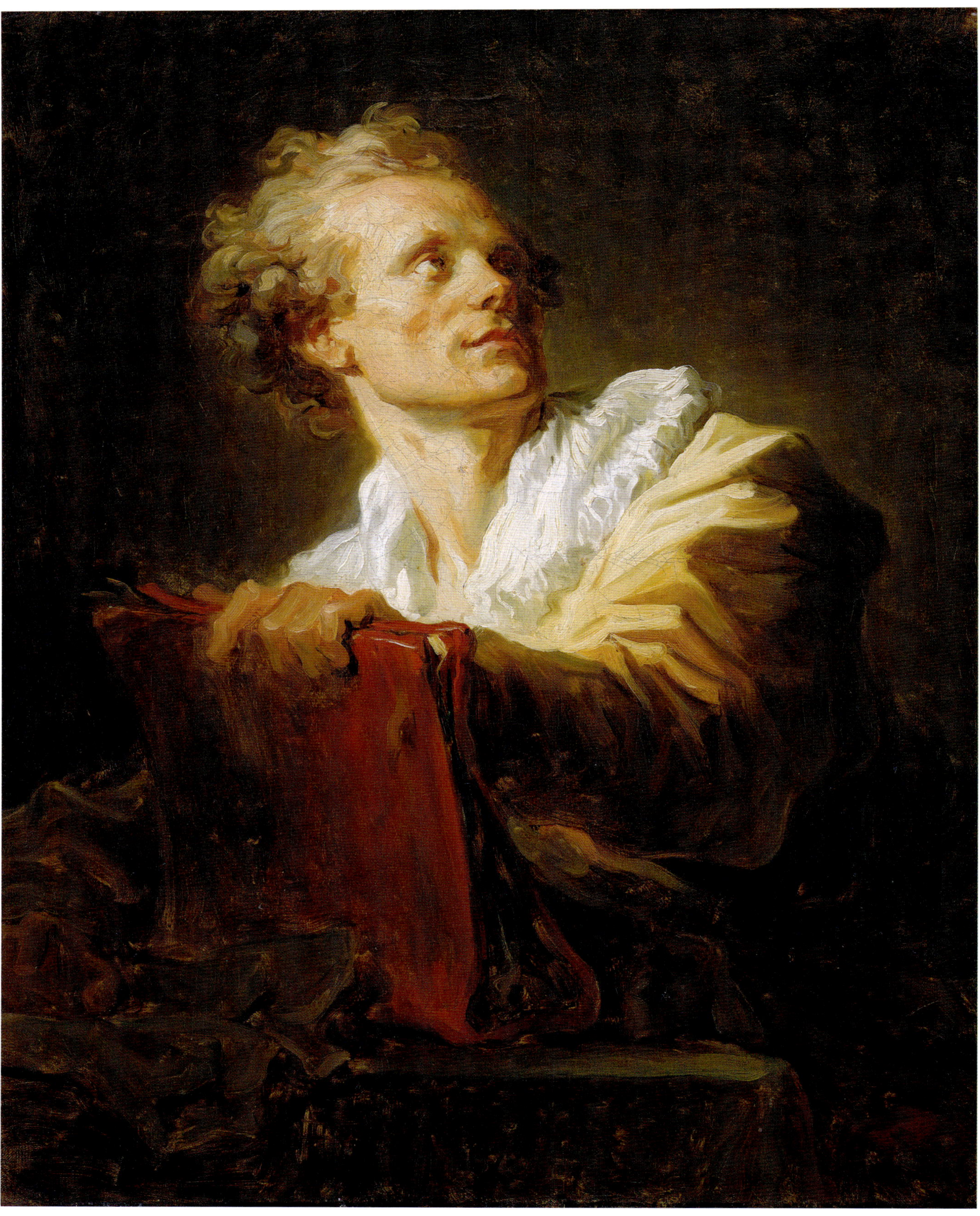

identities facilitated by the sheet of *Sketches* is clearly important, it does not contradict the key aspect of these "portraits": their function as self-consciously manufactured pictorial *fictions* of the self. Nor does the evidence of the sheet contradict the view of the *amateur* milieu as the main point of reference for these paintings, even if most of its members, with the exception of abbé de Saint-Non and his brother, turned out to be different than previously assumed.[165]

I see no reason to challenge the view of these paintings as the products of Fragonard's productive immersion in the amateur culture of his time, but I suggest a slightly different account of the way in which they speak of and for the artist. They are, to my mind, more complex testimonies to the interdependence between *amateurs* and their painter than the existing interpretations have allowed. In different ways, these figural fantasies signal tension and even antagonism in the artist's relation to this particular community, materializing his distinct fantasy of it, and of himself. It is in fact the painter's concern with self-differentiation that strikes me as paramount in these pictures. Rather than exemplifying the presumed aesthetic affinity and social equality between him and his clients—an equality that was in any case only a fiction masking a socioeconomic dependence and uneven status[166]—the figures announce themselves as agents of a complex negotiation that may be defined as ironic rivalry. They speak of the artist's desire to assert his superiority over the *amateur* through the means of a witty performance that is at times pushed to its limits, verging on refusal of cooperation, on non-representation.

The painter's body performs a crucial role in this agonistic negotiation. The way the painter deploys or, more accurately, unleashes his touch does not secure a stable identity but puts into question the relation

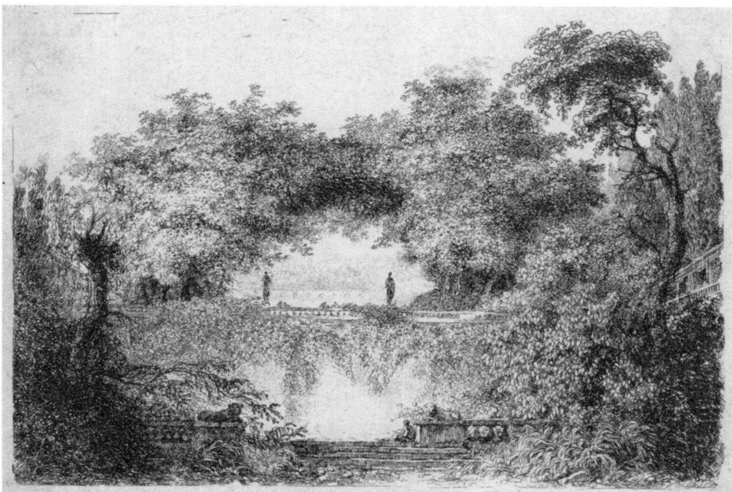

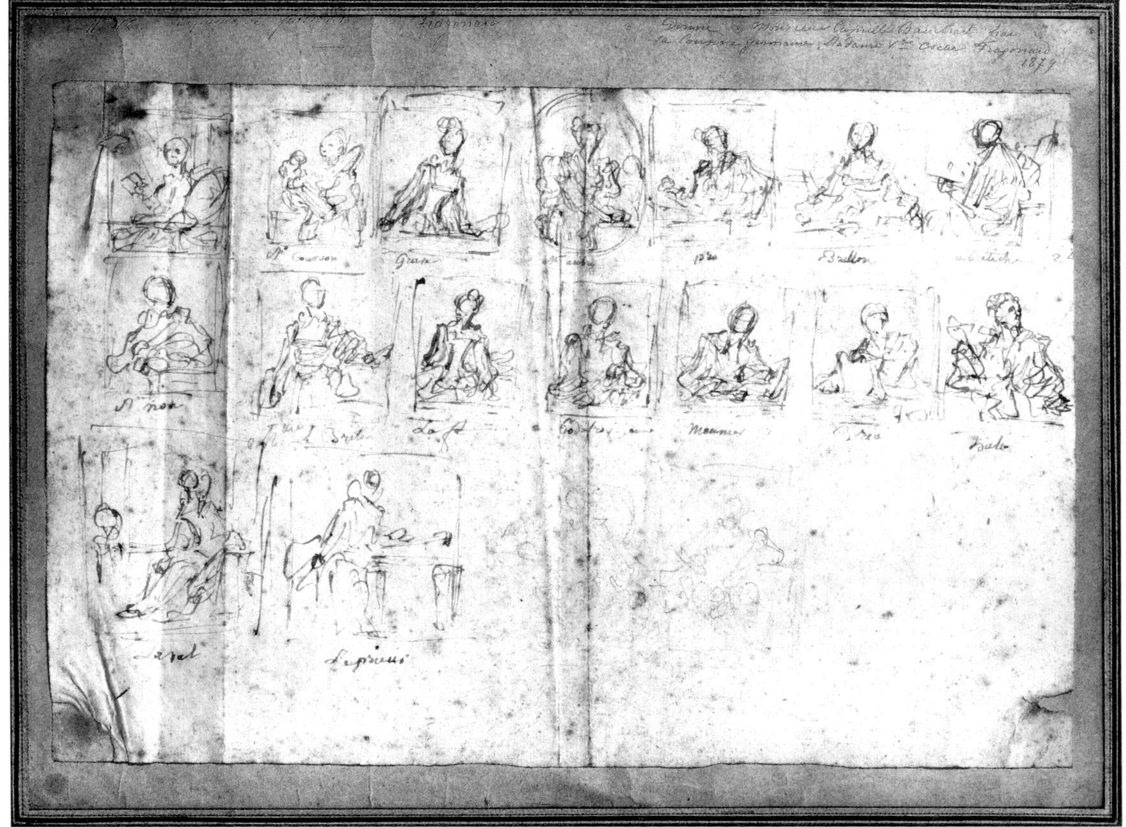

3.49. OPPOSITE
Jean-Honoré Fragonard, *Charles-Paul-Jérôme Bréa* (previously known as *Naigeon*), ca. 1769. Oil on canvas. Musée du Louvre, Paris.

3.50. ABOVE
Jean Claude Richard de Saint-Non after Jean-Honoré Fragonard, *The Little Park*, ca. 1763–65. Etching. The Baltimore Museum of Art.

3.51. RIGHT
Jean-Honoré Fragonard, *Sheet of portrait studies*. Private Collection.

between the body—both that depicted on the canvas and that implied by the very mode of depiction—and the self. It has been said that Fragonard's demonstrative faire in these paintings produces a tantalizing impression on the viewer "akin to seduction," but what have not been sufficiently attended to are its disconcerting effects.[167] One can say that the paintings reveal the *hazards* of the painter's touch, the risks of self-individuation—both for the models and for their painter. If the figures represent a relation between the two, it is, in other words, not as a hand-in-glove fit (though the frequency with which gloves appear as male accessory in these depictions may invite such an idea), but a more dissonant relation. At once asserting the person's presence and exposing its radical contingency, they reveal the precarious life of the self in representation—an existence based solely in the painter's touch. In sum, Fragonard's fantasy figures were, in my view, more complexly self-conscious and *differently* self-reflexive than the existing interpretations have suggested.

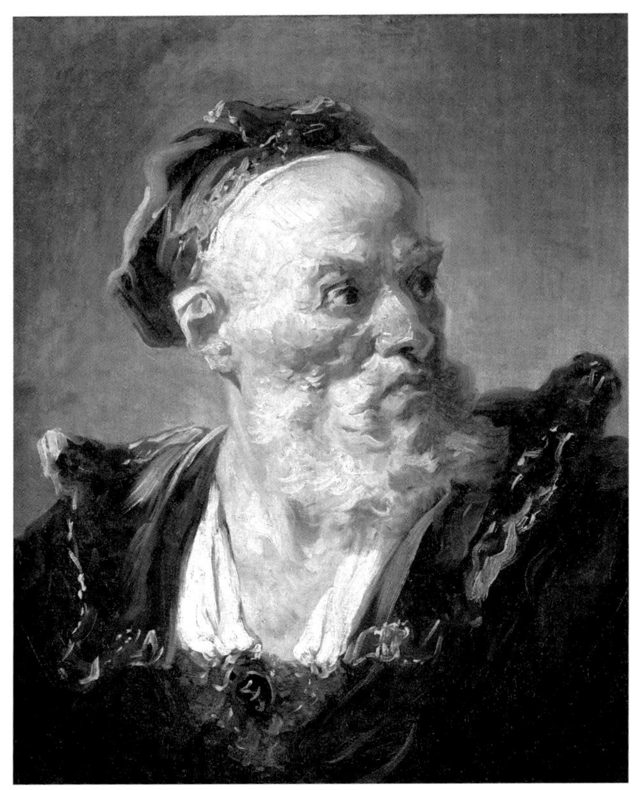

To begin with there is the question of the implications of Fragonard's chosen mode, pastiche, for a representation of the self. It has been assumed that this mode of address was seductive and solicitous, aiming to generate in his models/viewers the pleasure of self-recognition in pictorial masquerades. Yet pastiche is an ambivalent mode, potentially subversive, rather than merely playful and appealing. It is one thing to offer the style-savvy gaze of an *amateur* an image of an entirely invented character—for example, a stock figure of an old man traditionally referred to as a Philosopher or a Prophet, such as Fragonard's own *Bust of an Old Man* (fig. 3.52)—it was another to present such a privileged viewer with a travesty of him- or herself.

It was precisely the ambivalence—and risks—of pastiche as a mode of (self-)representation that Diderot explored in one of his literary experiments, *Le Neveu de Rameau*. Written roughly at the same time that Fragonard painted his series, this satirical short story illustrates a new literary convention of anchoring fiction in an actual person, an approach the writer shared with the painter.[168] In Diderot's satire, the narrator, defined simply as "Moi" ("I"), engages in continuous, sparring interchanges with a quasi-fictional character who performs the role of an authorial counterpart. This character, "Lui" ("He"), evokes a specific individual, Jean-François Rameau, the nephew of the famous composer, Jean-Philippe Rameau, who led a precarious existence as a music and singing teacher and a hanger-on in the houses of the Parisian elite.[169] The dialogue between him and the narrator follows their chance encounter in the gardens of the Palais-Royal. Its informal character exemplifies a novel type of creativity fostered by the social life of the salons—improvised, short, witty, and essentially dialogical forms that reflected the conversational mode of interaction between the participants of these gatherings. *Rameau's Nephew* is a self-conscious travesty of these exchanges. As shifting as the form of its dialogue is the character of its protagonist, who "lives for the day, gloomy or gay according to circumstances." And so is his appearance, and ultimately identity: "Today, in dirty linen and ragged breeches, tattered and almost barefoot, he slinks along with head down and you might be tempted to give him money. Tomorrow, powdered, well shod, hair curled, beautifully turned out, he walks with head high, showing himself off, and you would almost take him for a gentleman."[170] Rameau's nephew is, in other words, a living pastiche of the self. You can't pin him down, his very person is a performance. As such, he destabilizes the notion of social and cultural identity, but this dimension of the figure is shown to be particularly problematic for him, because, in the very real, unperformed sense, this drifter does not have a stable place in society. And it is he who bears the costs of his condition.[171]

3.52. OPPOSITE
Jean-Honoré Fragonard, *Bust of an Old Man*, ca. 1765. Oil on canvas. Musée Jacquemart-André, Paris.

3.53. BELOW
Jean-Baptiste Greuze, *Ange Laurent de La Live de Jully*, probably 1759. Oil on canvas. National Gallery of Art, Washington, DC, The Samuel H. Kress Collection.

If Rameau's lesser relative is the *habitué* of the salons whose very forms the dialogue imitates, it is because he lives off the diversion he provides in these establishments. Describing his role as high society's entertainer to the narrator, he boasts: "I am an inexhaustible bag of tricks. At every moment I had some quip ready to make them laugh till they cried. I supplied them with a complete madhouse."[172] The narrator is well aware that these performances were also a good source of income: "I: And that's why you had bed, board, coat, waistcoat, breeches and shoes found, plus one *pistole* per month." But his interlocutor has to remind him about the liabilities involved in this kind of occupation: "You should have seen how I was treated when I failed to bring it off! I was a clod, a fool, a lump, good for nothing and not worth the glass of water they gave me to drink."[173] And when the lesser Rameau made one mistake by saying a wrong thing about his benefactor's mistress, he was unceremoniously thrown out of doors.

Rameau's nephew embodies, as one scholar put it, a "wobbly concept of being and identity" that speaks not only of himself but also of the society in which he operates.[174] Through his protagonist, Diderot reveals the effects of social hierarchies underpinning the performative culture of his time, his text laying bare the relations of power that inscribe the realm of sociability in which the tricksters rub shoulders with the privileged and where pastiche is a mode of being at large. In his constant sparring with Rameau, the narrator is shown jockeying for position in the dialogue. Among others, they spar about the rules of the world as game of appearances in which the stake is power as much as pleasure. It is the radical unevenness in position between the elite members and their entertainers—artists, performers, tricksters—that Diderot's story exposes.

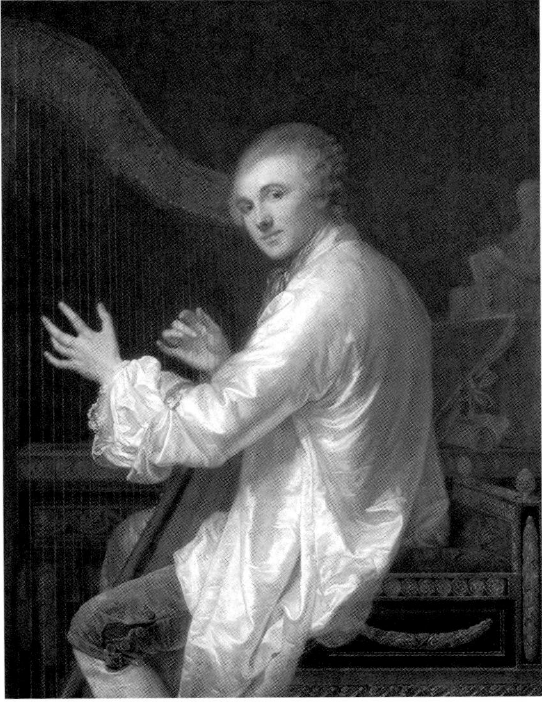

There are evident affinities between *Rameau's Nephew* and Fragonard's figures de fantaisie, both of them being testimonies to the performative culture of the time. One is the dialogical and playful mode of their presentation—both in their poses and gestures, and in the mode in which they were rendered. Such is, for example, *Monsieur de la Bretèche*, a Diderotian character in his mode of appearance and in the informal quality of his musical performance—he is shown playing a guitar—which has been momentarily interrupted by an invisible interlocutor (see fig. 3.48). Unlike Jean-Baptiste Greuze's portrait of *M. La Live de Jully*, whose eager pose leaves no doubt about his skill and commitment as an amateur musician—both underscored by the artist's eager display of his own mimetic skill—La Bretèche's likeness presents the idea of performance, both the model's and the painter's, in ironic brackets (fig. 3.53). Just as La Bretèche's action is interrupted, so is the texture of Fragonard's painting inconsistent, the body of his sitter rendered brilliantly but sketchily, especially in the lower part. Interruption and inconsistency define both the sitter's pose and the artist's mode of painting, suggesting also the idea of an inconsistent self, similar in that to the character of Rameau's nephew.

It is also the visibly ironic quality of the masquerade exemplified by the Williamstown *Warrior*—identified by Fragonard as "Hale," a name still unmatched with any specific individual—that makes one think of him as a version of Diderot's anti-hero (fig. 3.54).[175] Disheveled and distracted, *The Warrior* lacks a cogent appeal, his assertive pose contradicted by his facial frailty, his pursed lips, and his eyes casting a sideways, somehow anxious glance.[176] His heroic attire, complete with a sword, its phallic hilt protruding from under his arm, comes across as patently makeshift, a costume assumed for this particular occasion and evoking the possibility of a dramatic change (hinted at by his uncombed hair), as was Rameau's appearance: "Today, in dirty linen and ragged breeches, tattered and almost barefoot, . . . tomorrow, powdered, well shod, hair curled, beautifully turned out, he walks with head high, showing himself off."[177] A sense of contingency of both the body and the person is what our *Warrior*'s ragged elegance, and Fragonard's sketchy rendition of it, evoke, and a sense of grandeur that is thoroughly provisional—not that of the famous composer Rameau, but of the social drifter of his nephew; not of a truly heroic warrior but of a sort of self-inflated (and deflatable) Don Quixotic personage.[178]

What does this inconsistency of appearance and representation, and the shifty self it suggests, imply for Fragonard's models? What kind of understanding between the sitters and the painter do these fictions of identity convey? It has been offered that their sketchiness—what Norman Bryson has called the "cultivated insufficiency" of the sign—signaled the painter's deliberate attempt to engage, even seduce, the gaze of his sitters—amateurs, artistically inclined *salonières*, and artists—who were able to recognize themselves in and cherish such style.[179] The pictorial pastiche has been seen as a cultural code of complicity between the artist and the amateur, providing the ground for rehearsing their respective competences and thus reinforcing their respective professional and social identities. Yet this explanation has not taken into account the potentially disruptive dimension of such visual underdescription and subjective under-definition and their potentially disturbing effect on the receiver (the person thus described).

Consider the painting known as the *Lady with the Dog*, which we now know to represent Marie-Émilie Coignet de Courson, a well-known Parisian salonière

3.54.
Jean-Honoré Fragonard, *The Warrior*, ca. 1770. Oil on canvas. Sterling and Francine Clark Art Institute, Williamstown, Massachusetts.

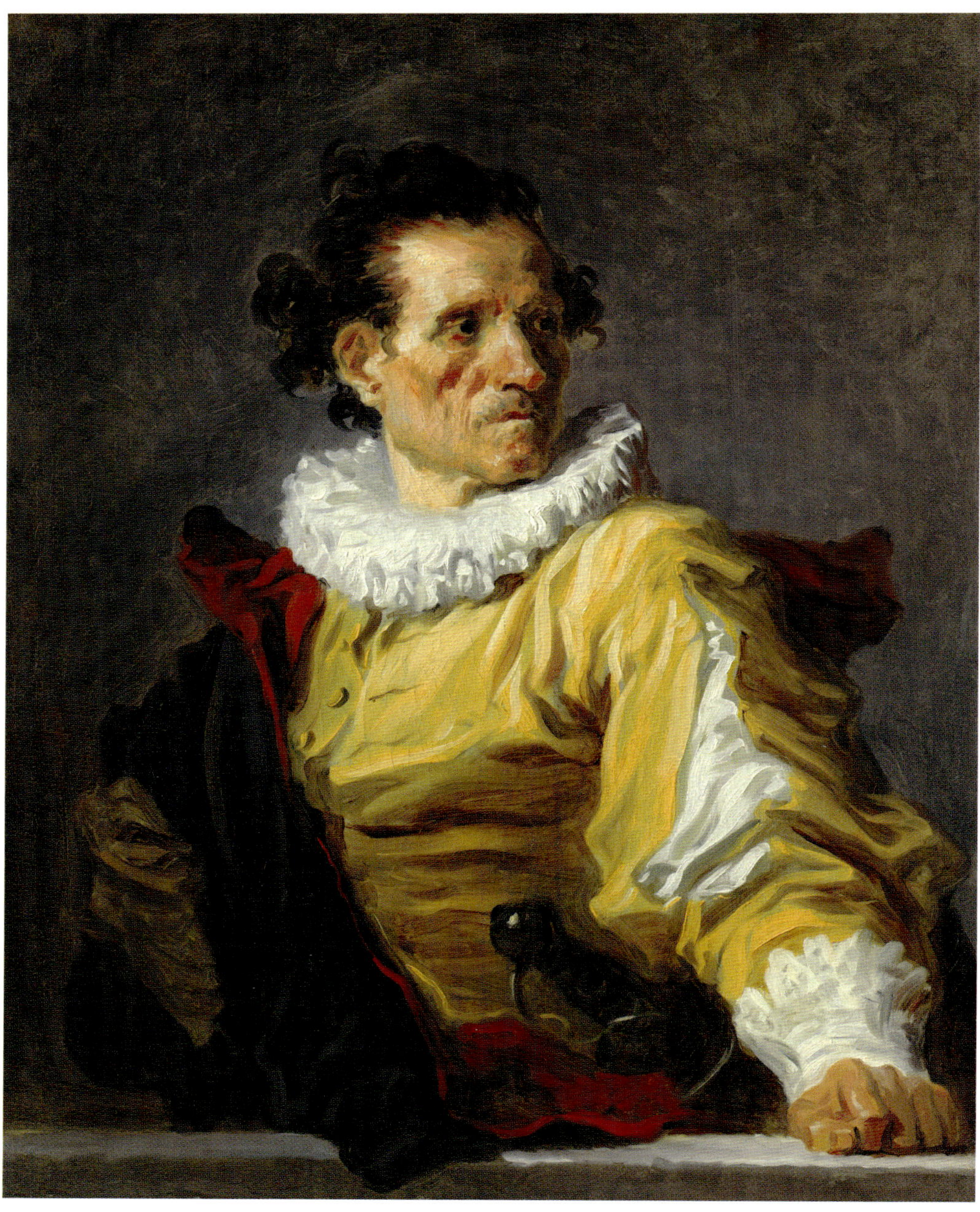

whose house on rue Saint-Dominique was famous for hosting the literary and artistic elite (fig. 3.55).[180] The garish splendor of her dress à la Marie de Medicis makes more noticeable the simultaneous undoing of her elaborate attire from behind: look at her ermine coat where the crudely smeared-on pigment produced thick smudges of teal blue and brown, and where the threads of representation come apart showing the inarticulate ground. These are obviously neither boastful nor even suggestive passages; they produce a sense of disturbing discontinuity that raises questions about the meaning of this painterly performance. As does the pose of Madame de Courson holding her dog as if it were her interlocutor, and her leering gaze. It may be a look of someone who acknowledges her awareness of the game in which she participates, a sign of her collusion with her painter. But what does it tell us of the painter's relation to her? Does his mode of representation bring his sitter into his game or is he laughing at or taunting her? The effect is ambiguous, it can be either—or both.

Fragonard's idiosyncratically uneven handling witnessed in the *Lady with the Dog* is consistent with his approach to the whole series. It is manifest in the highly abbreviated and schematically brushed-in foreshortening of the arm of the *Singer* who has been identified as Anne-Pauline Le Breton, wife of chevalier Séguiran and, after the latter's death, of his brother, marquis de Séguiran, known for her frequentation of the literary circles (and her widely publicized

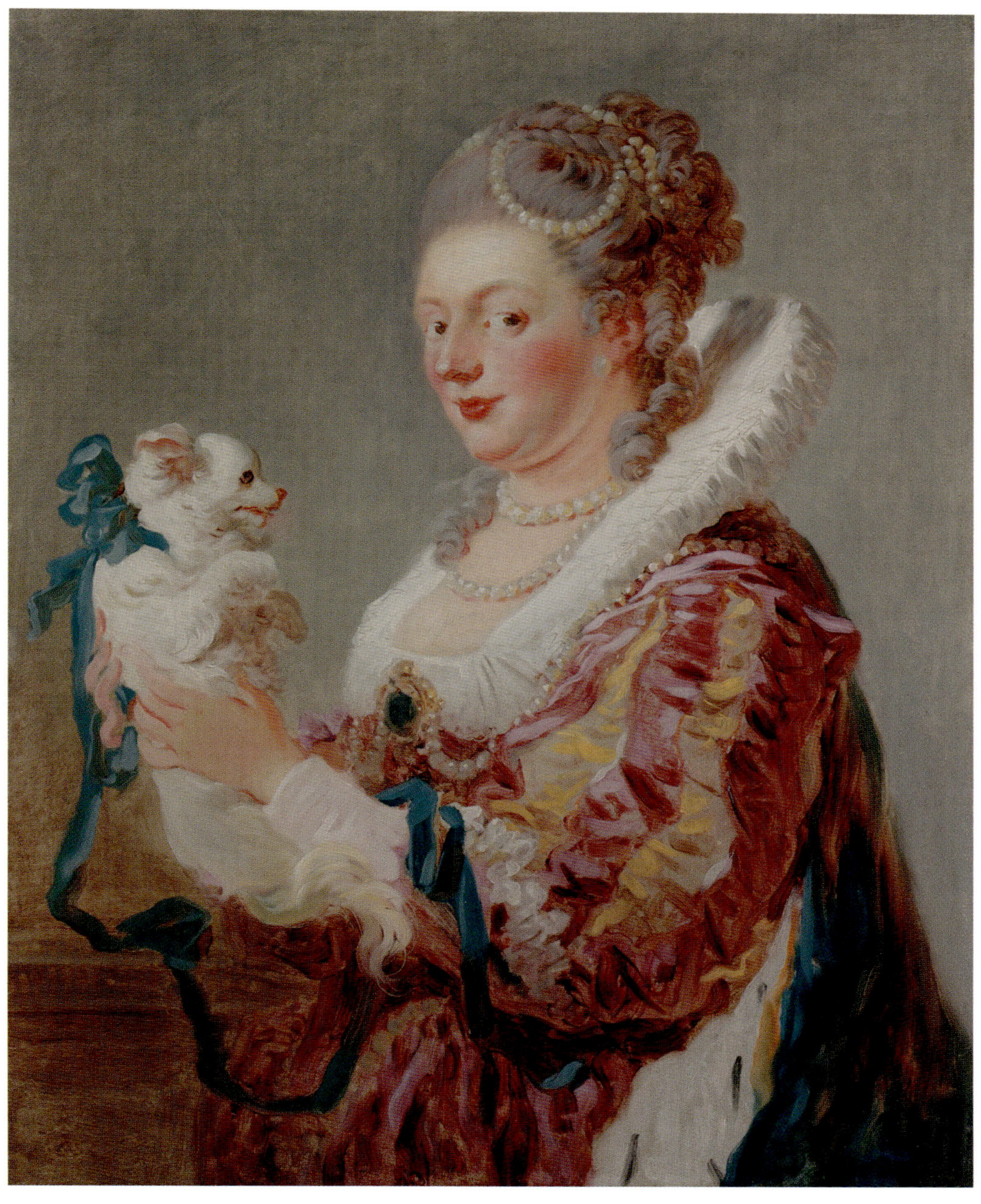

3.55.
Jean-Honoré Fragonard, *Marie-Émilie Coignet de Courson*, previously known as *Lady with the Dog*, ca. 1769. Oil on canvas. Metropolitan Museum of Art, New York, Fletcher Fund, 1937.

affair with Beaumarchais)—in sum, an elite woman dabbling in music as abbé Saint-Non dabbled in art (fig. 3.56).[181] Saint-Non's own corpus offers another example of performative handling, the slit of his Prussian blue sleeve opening up at the center of the composition to its yellow-ocher lining, the pigment used to render it having been carried sideways into a carmine flutter by the painter's sweeping brush. This gratuitous flourish shows off the painter's skill but also destabilizes the sense of his sitter's bodily presence: it suggests that Saint-Non is only provisionally in this *pochade*. In quite a few of these paintings, imitation seems to fizzle out altogether at the edges, as it does in the figure previously known as *Naigeon* and now identified as the miniaturist painter Charles-Paul-Jérôme Bréa (see fig. 3.49). The lower part of Bréa's body and the stone ledge on which he rested his thick portfolio—itself quite sketchily rendered—are fleshed out in thick, coarse, barely approximating strokes, an almost unformed matter. It produces stark contrasts with the sunny appearance of the painting's upper part painted with brio but more clearly articulated. It seems that in these lower parts, the painter's touch has altogether different connotations, imitation sliding into muddy inarticulateness, inelegant and unpleasant, that speaks of the less cultured aspects of bodily functioning than the stylishly attired, ruff-collared upper part. These rough passages could not have been a source of the viewer's easy delight in imitation. Rather than the pleasure of recognition, they provide a detour and challenge for the perusing eye.

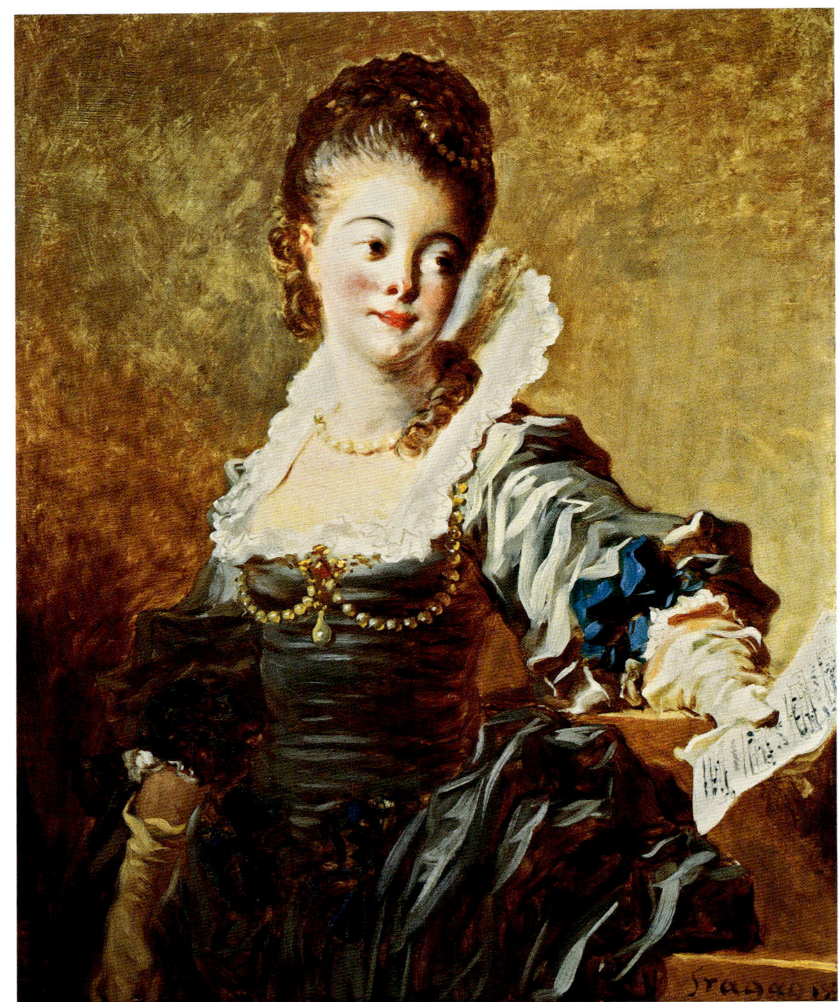

In all these cases, imitation reveals itself to be the means of securing form and identity and also of undoing it, its accomplishments displayed side by side its deliberate—even willful—inadequacy. This is not what the connoisseurial gaze can easily venture to complete—for one, there is too little there to go by. Nor is it just a self-conscious display of a *pasticheur*'s brio. One feels, rather, that such a degree of unfinish is staged to produce an argument. Far from an invitation for the viewer to participate in the process of representation, these moments of pictorial underdescription may be seen as instances of imitational refusal. "I could but would not pull it off because I don't want to"—they seem to say. In other words, they visibly put the sitter at the painter's mercy.

These aspects—and the tension they produce within the field of representation—point to a more complex purpose of these paintings than has been acknowledged. Although they may have been made to meet the existing demand for these kind of pictures—and made, therefore, to be accepted as such—these fantasy constructions allowed themselves to play with the established genre in a way that exceeded and may have frustrated the expectations. They engaged in a riskier game than did their contemporary counterparts, the portraits de fantaisie by artists such as Alexis Grimou, Jean-Baptiste Santerre, and Jean Raux, far more *sage*.[182] By the extent of their pictorial idiosyncrasy—most particularly in their inconsistent deployment of imitation—Fragonard's paintings not only reenacted but also pushed the limits of pastiche as a pictorial genre; despite their ostensible function, these *pochades* of the self subtly undermined the aesthetic competence and social standing of their models. And if they did, it was because of who his models in this series were—not just elite clients but, more specifically, individuals who, in one way or another, defined themselves through art. It is with this particular milieu—in which he operated and on which he depended—that Fragonard

3.56. OPPOSITE
Jean-Honoré Fragonard, *Anne-Pauline Le Breton,* previously known as *The Singer*. Late 1760s. Oil on canvas. Private Collection.

3.57. BELOW
Jean-Honoré Fragonard, *Louis Richard de la Bretèche*, detail of fig. 3.48.

engages in sparring exchanges, in agonistic intimacy. If they speak of his "friendship" with this privileged class it is as a kind of fiction, one that exposes the tension that underwrote this relation. They materialize a subtle sense of rivalry between the two parties of uneven standing, one, to put it crudely, having privilege and money, the other artistic talent. In other words, although fantasies, these complex canvases revealed something real about the artist's relation to the *amateurs*, making visible the anxious cultural self-positioning involved in this relation (on both sides) and hinting also at the question of economic survival (of the artist) entailed by it.[183] Testimonies to relatedness, they were also icons of (self-)estrangement.

Nothing speaks to this complex function more directly than the artist's use of signature in some of these paintings. In both the *Bréa* and the *La Bretèche* he signed in the muddiest, least articulated area of the painting. And the signature itself is a curious exercise in inarticulate self-representation (or misrepresentation). Abbreviated to the painter's nickname, "frago," it is buried in the thick materiality of pigment and quite difficult to find. It looks smeared on the canvas, like a graffiti. Moreover, the painter's nickname is disconcertingly misspelled. In *La Bretèche* it reads "*fraogo*" or "*fraggo*" (fig. 3.57); in *La Breton*, the misspelling is the more disturbing in that the signature is in plain sight, scribbled in darker pigment on the light-brown plinth of the pedestal on which the model's arm rests: "*fragao 17[69]*." Clearly, this is not a mistake—the deliberateness of the painter's gesture is striking. What to make of it?

Charlotte Guichard has offered an astute reading of these signatures as a particular kind of performance.[184] They are not there to claim the authorship as much as engage the viewer—specifically the *amateur*—in a playful dialogue with the author. Self-conscious in their form and content, they testify to Fragonard's awareness of his own image as an artist in others' eyes: his adoption of a nickname speaks to it, as does his touch, deployed in a manner that evokes how it was construed by the painter's contemporaries. Guichard sees the misspellings, too, as deliberate, a mischievous game with the *amateur*'s gaze, as is the embeddedness of the signatures in the pigment—it courts the *amateur*'s desire to inspect paintings up close.[185] In sum, like Fragonard's mode of execution, his signatures are signs of the painter's complicitous *jeu* with his clients.

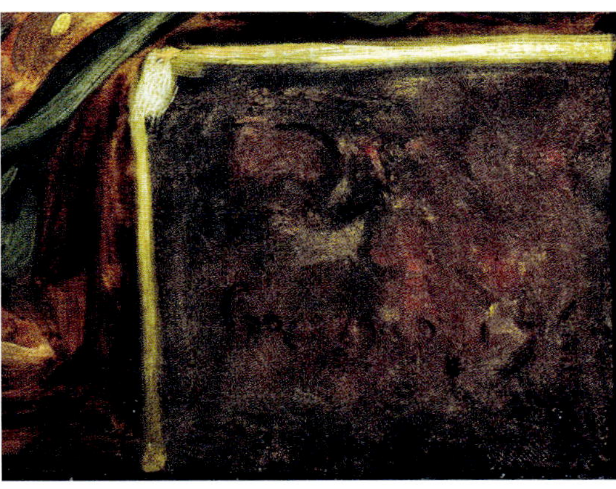

I see them a bit differently. If the signatures are no doubt self-consciously produced, they speak of a more provocative form of self-awareness. In their linguistic inaccuracy, their crudeness, and the base materiality that contrasts with the refined realm of his sitters' masquerade, they evoke a domain outside the cultural codes: the prelinguistic, bodily domain, the sphere of the abject a child erects to separate itself from the maternal as it tries to imagine its autonomous bodily existence. In *La Breton*, the signature looks literally as if it were smeared on the surface of the canvas by a child's finger dipped in some unappetizing primary substance. In the *Bréa*, it is scratched on, again by what looks like a finger, while the canvas was still wet—a negative inscription.[186] Fragonard's dictum "Je peindrais avec mon cul" comes to mind. These are the kind of signs—verging on disarticulation—that a bodily act evoked by the painter's remark would produce: thickly drawn, foreshortened, inarticulate. The refusal of orthography is indeed a game but a more primal and more dangerous one than Guichard's reading has allowed; it challenges, rather than teases, the onlooker's gaze. Buried in materiality, these signs of self do not encourage an up-close look as much as confuse it, threatening to trap the gaze.[187] If pleasure is implied, it is solely the artist's: a crudely material bodily pleasure—the pleasure of the drives—that contrasts with, if not opposes, the bonheur of the *amateurs*.

As such, the signatures pull these portraits into an altogether different realm—not that of the salons where art was talked about and Rameau's music could be heard, but a lower one, occupied by his nephew, the social drifter: a realm of crassness and vulgarity, of crude jokes and mean tricks, one in which one may not know how to spell. I am not saying it *is* actually the realm in which Fragonard belonged but rather that it is how he wished to *represent* himself, as the unruly natural body—the body as a force of nature (before language and other social codes)—and

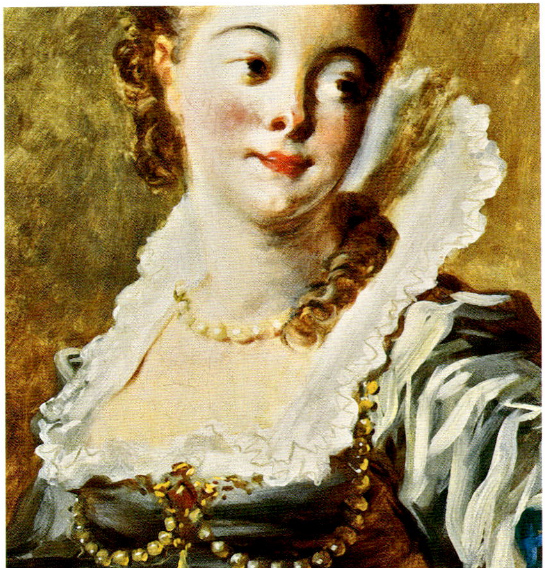

3.58.
Jean-Honoré Fragonard, *Anne-Pauline Le Breton*, detail of fig. 3.56.

thus to position himself, to stake his autonomy, in relation to the amateurs. His signatures are not signs of artistic self-consciousness as much as self-consciously staged *difference*, signs of perceived incompatibility between the painter's "bag of tricks" and the modest skills of an *amateur* dabbling in art.[188] They open up a hiatus of rudeness in the polite surface of representation. Unlike the more traditional forms of wit in signing exemplified by Fragonard's *Bust of an Old Man* (see fig. 3.52), where the painter signed with a stylish and legible "F" front and center on the medallion on his sitter's chest, these undecipherable signatures are the means of *sparring* with the amateurs for the place in—and control over—the space of art. They hint at these "portraits" being not only a field of play but also of subtle but unmistakable antagonism, of competition for access to self-representation. Is there more of Saint-Non or of Fragonard in the flimsy likeness of the abbé? Staging the painter's touch in such a manner, the signatures signal his deliberate effort to distinguish himself from his benefactors and models. The artist refuses to share the language of art with the *amateurs*.

This leads me to my last point about the morphology of these paintings: the notorious issue of their speed of execution. Two of the portraits bear inscriptions boasting the unusually short time of their execution on the back of the canvas ("Portrait de Mr de la Bretèche peint par fragonard en 1769 [corrected from 89?] en une heure de temps"; the same kind of inscription appears on the verso of the *Saint-Non*).[189] Whether or not these were the artist's own annotations—most likely they were not—there is no reason to doubt that they were based on the information that came from the artist. They sound like something he would like to be known about these paintings. These were indeed, as the conservators have affirmed, fast-painted canvases, often wet-on-wet.[190] But clearly the evidence of the painted surface was not enough for the artist—he felt he also had to brag about it. That he felt the need to do so is particularly interesting given whom he is painting "in one hour's time." The note is a sign of the artist's concern with asserting and distinguishing himself in relation to his models, to spell out the difference between his pictorial virtuosity and the *amateur*'s slow and belabored mode of working. Reflecting the lore associated with these paintings, the notes attached to two of them serve to make this point, if indirectly. Equivalent to these verbal commentaries is the painter's use of the handle of his brush to score the edges of the women's ruffs in the *de Courson* and *La Breton*, a mark of a certain cynicism of execution, a painterly laissez-faire that seems jarring, disrespectful, incompatible with the high-class status of his sitters and their "portraits" (fig. 3.58).

But if the fantasy figures signaled the painter's self-conscious estrangement from his sitters, they were also to some degree exercises in self-estrangement. They imply a particular conception of the creative self caught, as was said of Diderot's protagonist, "between attitude and authenticity, self-mockery and self-love."[191] Fragonard's figures evoke precisely such an exacerbated form of artistic self-consciousness that hovers between self-creation and self-estrangement. If there is an aspect of the paintings that communicates this particular kind of self-awareness most directly, it is the areas where the imitation slackens, the territory of the unformed wherein the artist chose to place his signatures, claiming these particular passages as his "own." Situating himself where his sitters were not, Fragonard defined *his* pleasure in picture-making as different from theirs, asserting his right to jouissance in a way that resonated with the reconceptualization of pleasure in this period and especially with La Mettrie's recognition of pleasure as a universal *right*.[192] The painter's claim to his own jouissance was part and parcel of his negotiation for artistic autonomy conducted in these canvases. It was, however, a pleasure of a particular kind. Conveyed by a materially "crude" and aggressive touch—a touch staged as a primitive force aligned with the force of nature as it was conceptualized at the time—this was a primal kind of eros, not unlike the unknowing, pre-verbal eros of a child "writing" on its mother's body. If it evoked the painter's body it was, in other words, as an infantile corpus, a seat of drives, poised on the threshold of culture.

There is something disruptive in this way of positioning oneself not just for the sitters but also for the painter. To define one's pleasure as a natural force is to assert its power but also avow oneself to be under its sway, not being entirely in control. The rough passages convey this, as does the mishandling of the painter's own name, a deliberate misrepresentation of oneself. What they signal is the painter's mastery—"I am in charge of how I paint and how I sign"—but also its potential loss: the end of representation and of himself as its agent. In this sense, the figures de fantaisie were a manifestation of a particular, potentially self-aggravating individualism.

Making palpable the tension between the "natural" corporeality—the body as an insubordinate force—and the social world, these "portraits of portraits" allow us to glimpse some risks inherent in the painter's understanding of himself as an unruly force, and in his practice's mission as a "natural" performance.[193] Moreover, what they make clear is that this "natural" form of pictorial jouissance does not simply collide with the cultured forms of satisfaction that define their models; as an attribute of an insubordinate body it may also run against the painter himself. It can be uncontrollable, unproductive, in both a social and psychological sense. In regard to the first, one can say that the figures de fantaisie speak of how the painter's "bag of tricks" may bring him trouble of which Rameau's nephew spoke—though in Fragonard's case, it would be a matter of having his own work, rather than himself, thrown out of his patron's house.[194] In the second, psychological sense, this mode of registering one's pleasure speaks to the dimension of the self beyond one's control, a subject of drives rather than of social and cultural conventions.

LOVE AND LIFE

Nature has the same interest in perpetuating all species. She bestowed on each one the same motivation, which is pleasure.

—Maupertuis

The most significant example of the fateful difference between the painter's and the patron's idea of pleasure is the story of Fragonard's most ambitious, if misunderstood and ultimately rejected, project, the cycle of paintings known as *The Progress* or *The Pursuit of Love* (figs. 3.59, 3.60, 3.61, and 3.62).[195] The paintings were commissioned in 1771 by the king's mistress, Madame du Barry, for her newly built garden pavilion at Louveciennes. Designed by Claude-Nicolas Ledoux, this "sanctuary of sensual pleasure" was an architectural landmark of the new neoclassical taste.[196] For reasons that are not entirely clear, not long after it had been installed on the walls of her salon, Fragonard's cycle was rejected by du Barry and replaced by the new decorative panels commissioned from Joseph-Marie Vien (fig. 3.63). The original commission was returned to Fragonard and after many vicissitudes ended up at the Frick Collection in New York, where it is now.

Much has been said about Fragonard's cycle, both regarding the possible reasons for its failure to please du Barry and its meaning.[197] I would like to shift emphasis away from either the stylistic or the iconographic exegesis of the depicted episodes, which have prevailed in the existing literature, toward analysis of the overall pictorial organization and the internal dynamic of these canvases—their pictorial behavior. The near-exclusive focus on style and iconography has resulted, among other things, in a misconception of Fragonard's Louveciennes project as rococo, and thus, given its relatively late date (1771–72), as a more or less complacent exercise in an outmoded genre.[198] Although such a view offers a convenient explanation of why the panels were dismissed by the artist's fashion-conscious patroness (they did not match the neoclassical decor of her new abode), it misses the point of these ambitious pictures. They are, in my view, far stranger and more disturbing than their interpretations so far have allowed.

First, let us recognize that, notwithstanding the nuances of their iconography, the basic semantic func-

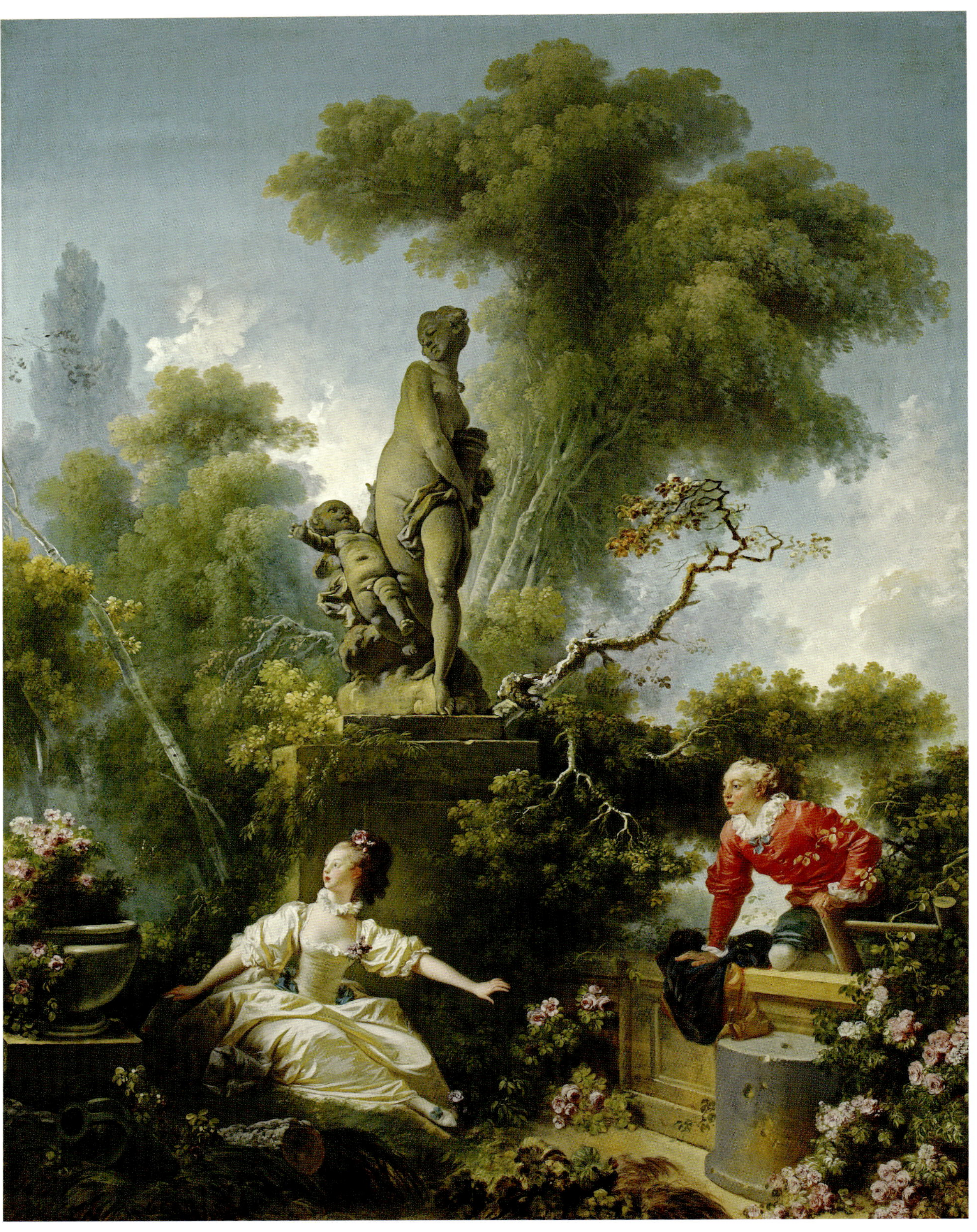

3.59. OPPOSITE
Jean-Honoré Fragonard, *The Pursuit of Love: The Meeting*, 1771–72. Oil on canvas. The Frick Collection, New York.

3.60. RIGHT
Jean-Honoré Fragonard, *The Pursuit of Love: The Pursuit*, 1771–72. Oil on canvas. The Frick Collection, New York.

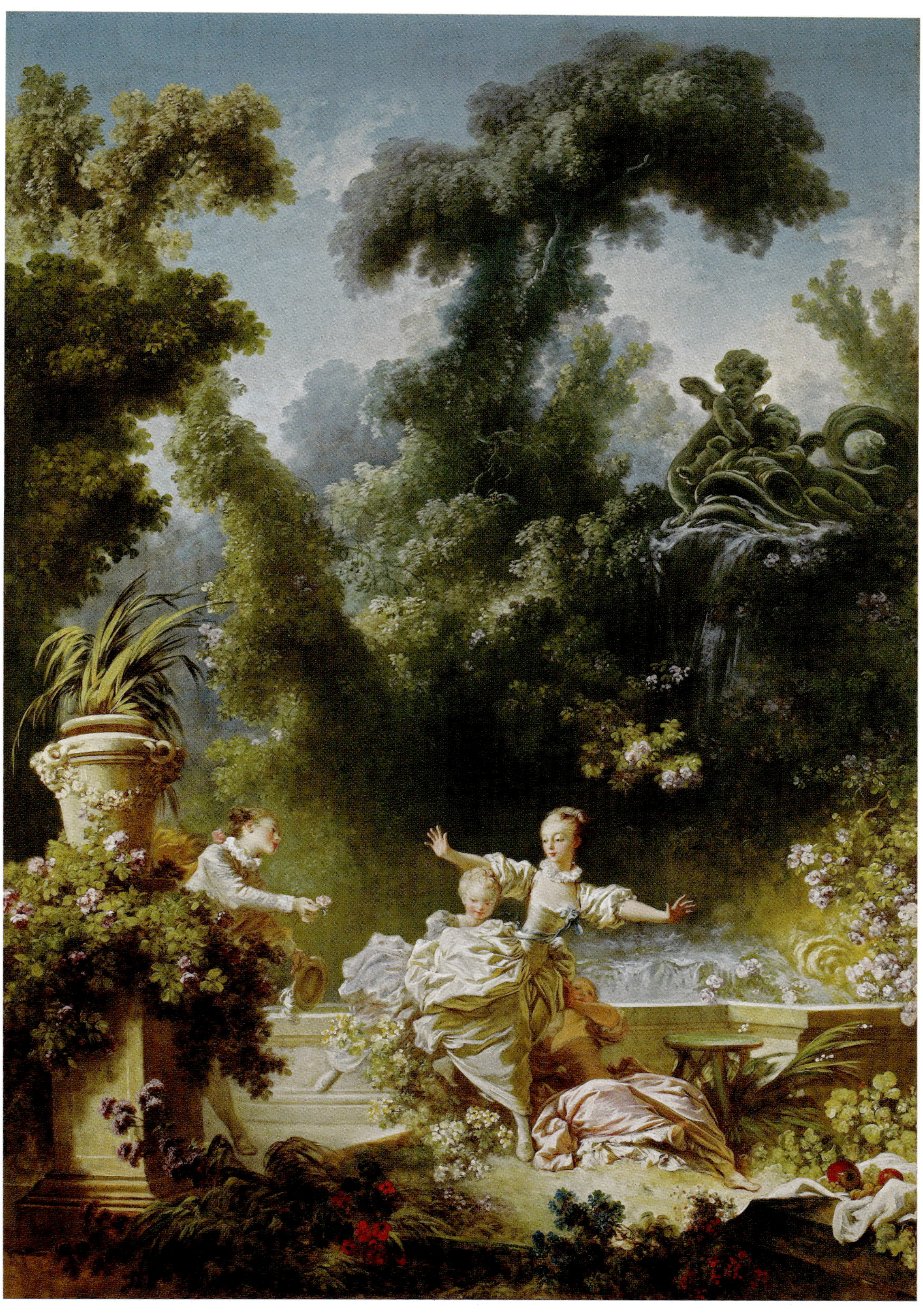

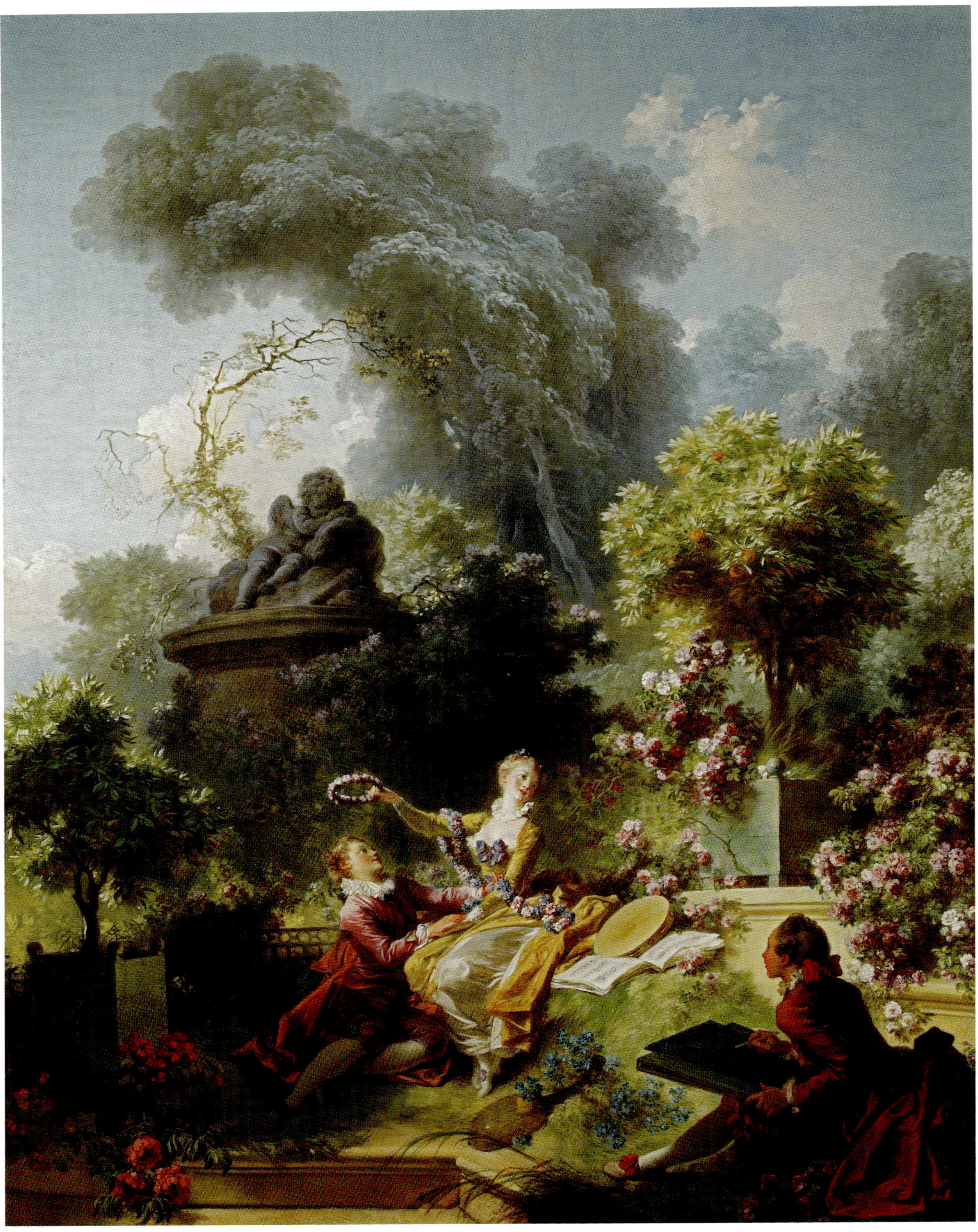

3.61. OPPOSITE
Jean-Honoré Fragonard, *The Pursuit of Love: The Lover Crowned*, 1771–72. Oil on canvas. The Frick Collection, New York.

3.62. RIGHT
Jean-Honoré Fragonard, *The Pursuit of Love: Love Letters*, 1771–72. Oil on canvas. The Frick Collection, New York.

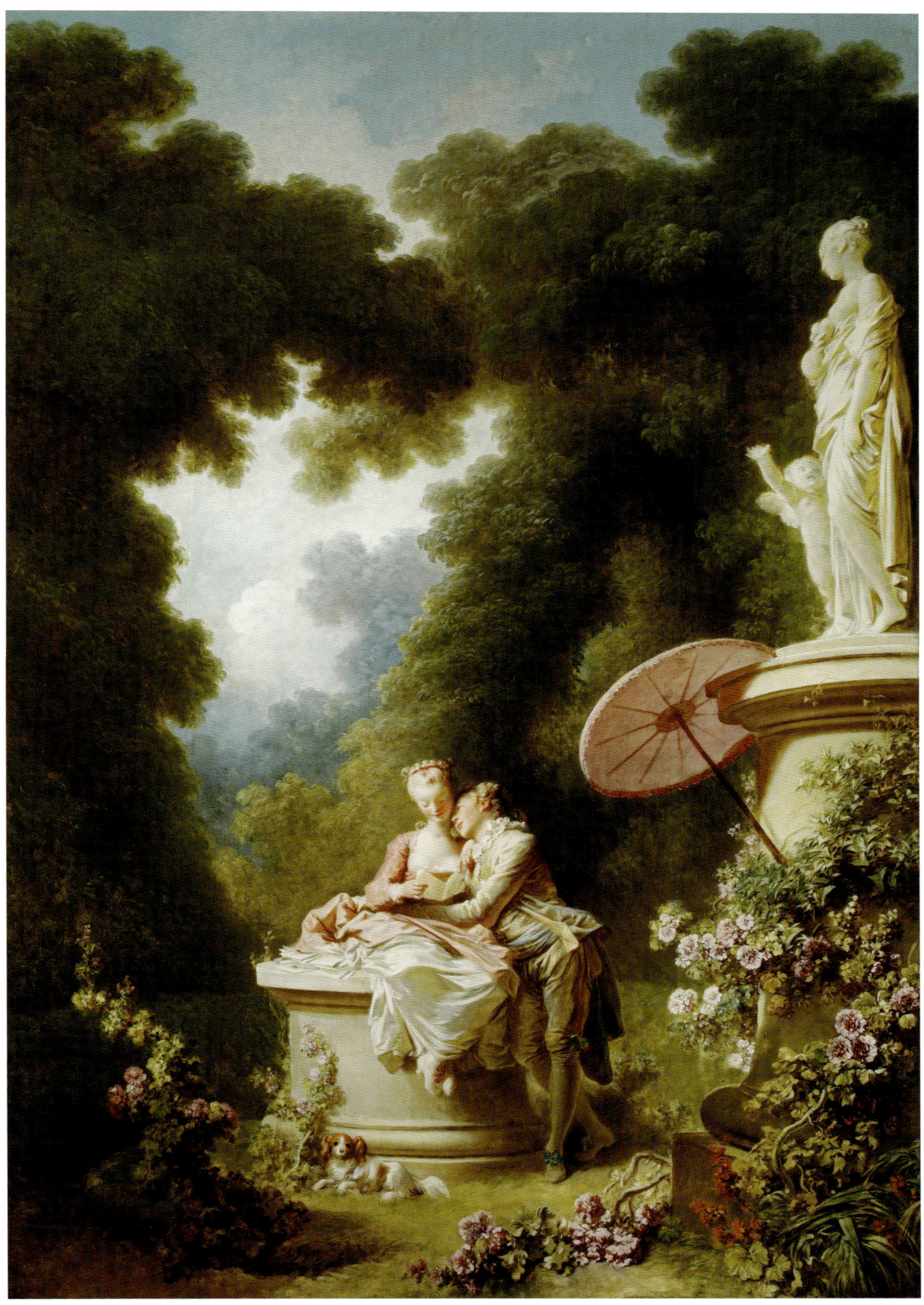

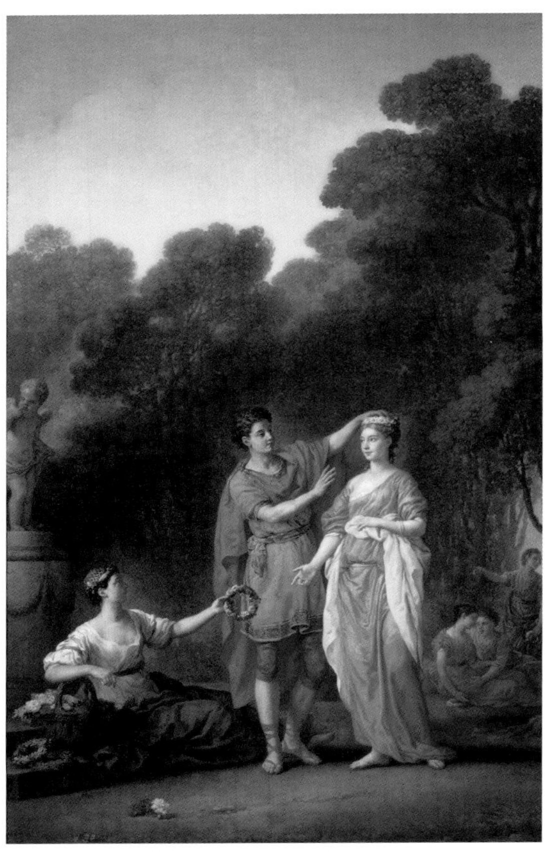

3.63.
Joseph-Marie Vien, *Lover Crowning His Mistress*, 1773. Oil on canvas. Musée du Louvre, Paris.

tion of the episodes depicted by Fragonard is intelligibly to convey a certain notion of Love, familiar at the time. Soon after the installation of these canvases at Louveciennes, one contemporary visitor reported that they "illustrate the theme of the shepherds' loves and seem allegorical of the adventures of the hostess of this place."[199] Fragonard's protagonists indeed rehearse the gallant rituals typical of *bergeries* in which Fragonard's teacher, Boucher, among others, had specialized (see fig. 1.28). A tryst between the two lovers is threatened by an invisible intruder (see fig. 3.59); a young man's pursuit is forestalled by his love-object's flight (see fig. 3.60); a pair of lovers stages the triumph of their love for a sketching artist (see fig. 3.61); and another pair of sweethearts is lost in a nostalgic reverie as they re-read their own amorous correspondence (see fig. 3.62). These scenes clearly follow the well-known, if not trite, eighteenth-century variation on the "boy meets girl" theme, including its predictable distribution of gender roles.

They are, moreover, remarkably proper, with nothing too sexually explicit or too serious at stake. Bodies are covered, embraces decent, physical love implied rather than described. We are far from what Fragonard could deliver on the subject of eros on other occasions around that time, for instance, in his *Happy Lovers* (ca. 1770), or *The Bolt* (1777–78), or in the rustic and far more sexually explicit version of the scene depicted in the *Lover Crowned* etched (*manière à lavis*) by Charpentier after Fragonard's drawing, *The Tumble* (fig. 3.64).[200] The function of these almost quaint scenes is to represent the idea of desire as the basis of an established sociocultural practice of courtship, a recognizable convention of sexual behavior, the emphasis being on conventionality and intelligibility rather than allegorical abstruseness of any kind.

Even if one could link these conventionally gallant episodes together in some sort of narrative sequence, as some interpreters have, this was manifestly *not* the concern of the artist. The actors in each painting are different, and there is nothing to suggest the necessity of a consecutive reading of these scenes. It is more productive to understand them, as few scholars have suggested, as four different aspects of love rather than stages in its progress.[201] What in my view truly matters is not the rapport between the depicted situations as instances of love as much as the complex and uneasy way in which they relate to the spectacle of nature offered in these paintings.

For, far from a mere setting, the surroundings of these figures appear as an autonomous theater of natural forms that competes with, rather than frames, the activities of the human beings. And this natural performance is quite extraordinary. This is where Fragonard fully unleashed his powers of pictorial suggestion. His execution is as striking in its brilliance as it is in the deliberateness of its emphasis. Clearly, this is nothing like the generic scenery of the traditional

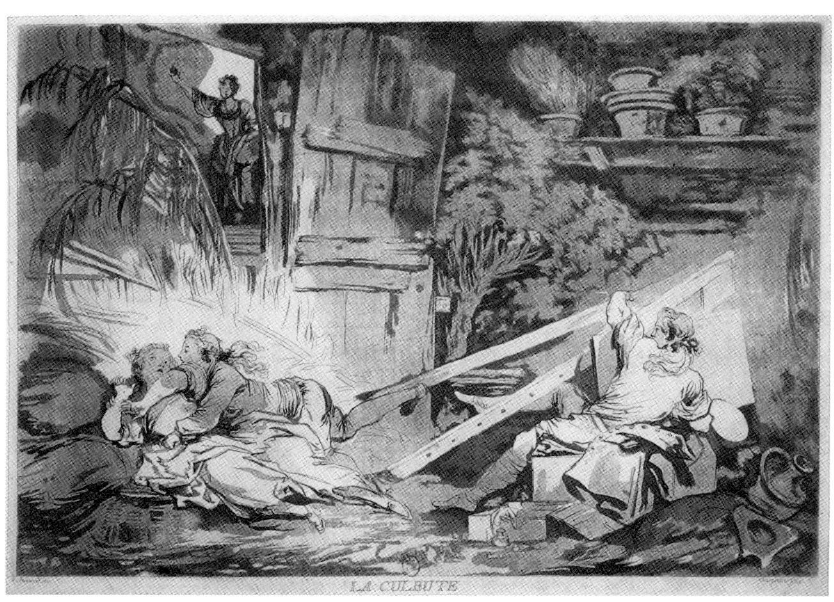

3.64.
François-Philippe Charpentier after Jean-Honoré Fragonard, *The Tumble*, ca. 1766. Wash manner engraving. Bibliothèque national de France, Paris.

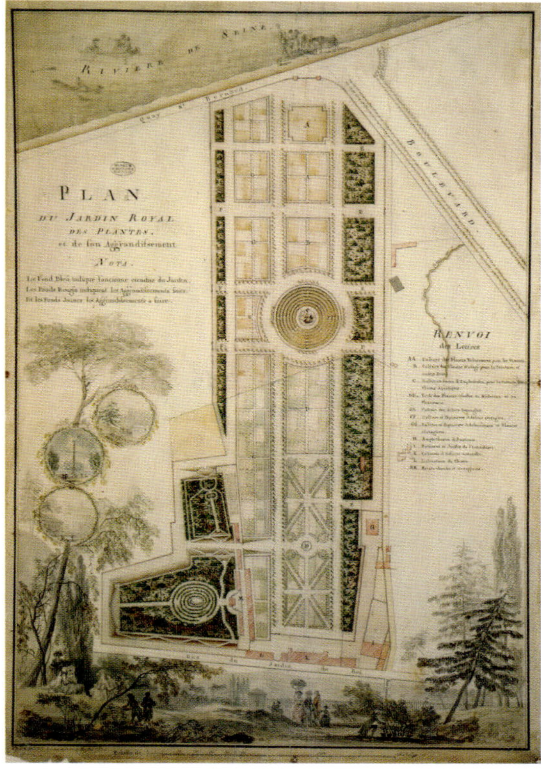

3.65.
Edme Verniquet, *Plan de Jardin des plantes*, 1783. Color engraving. Museum national d'histoire naturelle, Paris.

bergeries. Not only is nature given a vast amount of space; it is also rendered in an unusually dynamic way, its dramatic arrangements at times threatening to overtake the scenes and overshadow the actors in them. The trees themselves seem not so much to stand as to erupt into form, their foliage foaming, their branches shooting up in different directions. (The withered tree limbs in both the *Meeting* and the *Lover Crowned* seem to have no other function than to underscore the bursting energy of nature that frames them: the image of life that subsumes death.) The sheer proliferation of flora in every panel is remarkable, pink hollyhocks springing up, overgrown rose bushes gushing forth from their urns and spreading all over the place, as if they had been fed on some mega-fertilizer, the white-flowering shrub catching the fleeing girls in its snares (*The Pursuit*), while the blue and red hues of other flowers emerge from the ground elsewhere. Almost every inch of these paintings is covered by an amazing array of colors and textures with each single leaf blade glistening on the orange tree, every rose petal visible, different forms of vegetation exploding into view. An overall sense of continuous, uninterrupted *growth*, the hiss of which is almost audible, pervades these scenes.

This dynamic rendition of natural setting is not just a matter of compositional arrangement but of a distinct mode of painting. The structural and morphological emphasis on mobility—the gyrating swirls of flowers, the tree branches shooting up, the frothing foliage—was combined with a no less dynamic application of paint, a fact that did not escape Fragonard's contemporaries. In an imaginary conversation staged between three semifictional visitors to du Barry's pavilion, the character of an art expert describes the peculiarity of Fragonard's manner as "unsurpassed in roughness, in the rolled, the well-whipped, and the daubed," and he calls the painter a "veritable Dauber."[202] *Le heurté, le roullé, le bien fouetté, le tartouillis*—these were ambivalent terms for describing painterly technique at the time, so much so that our expert's interlocutor felt obliged to inquire whether they were meant as insults or praises.[203] What is interesting for us, though, is not so much the judgment value of these terms but the sense of unusual energy in the painter's manner, the *life* in his brush they conveyed, half-disparagingly as it may be. This jerky, abrupt mode of painting created the impression of pigment rolled and whipped into shape, as if things themselves were rubbed directly onto the canvas, leaving not strokes but smears or daubs on its surface. Heurté, roullé, bien fouetté: the passive form of these terms was well chosen. Lashed, rolled, and daubed by what? The energy of forms in these canvases appears as if they were *painting themselves*, without the help of the painter's brush, energy that makes these forms perform unusual maneuvers in an attempt to shortcut their way onto the canvas—a notion of process we have become familiar with in the course of this discussion of Fragonard's oeuvre. Here, though we are seeing perhaps its most consistent and dazzling application.

This *lively* manner was evidently not just a demonstration of the painter's technical brio; more importantly, it enacted a specific argument about nature that we have witnessed in his earlier work and that some of Fragonard's contemporaries would have no trouble recognizing. Through their organic and dynamic morphology, Fragonard's canvases proposed a Buffonian vision of the natural as a realm of Life, that is, a material continuum governed by the forces of ceaseless generation—a vision that we have already witnessed in the *Island of Love* and other works.[204] The Louveciennes sceneries appear less fantastic—they bring to mind a specific location, Buffon's Jardin Royal des plantes (fig. 3.65), a version of a picturesque garden that served as a popular place of promenades sketched by many artists, notably by Fragonard's close friend, the painter Hubert Robert.[205]

The Jardin's relevance for Fragonard was not though, in its picturesque quality per se but insofar as it was Buffon's own creation that promoted his understanding of nature.[206] For, designed and directed by Buffon, the Jardin became a showcase for a larger argument about life rather than art that the author of the *Histoire naturelle* was pressed to impose on his public.[207] Strolling in it, one was immersed in a theater of live forms—exotic animals were included—that made visible the notion of generation as a universal natural phenomenon of the living expounded by Buffon, as we have seen, in his writing.

Fragonard's natural realm in the *Pursuit* functioned, too, as a stage for an argument, one that can be articulated as a series of questions: How does sexuality as a form of conventional behavior *fit* in the processes of nature? What is the place of eros in the larger picture of life understood as a universal organic phenomenon? Does sexuality belong with the logic of nature and with the aims of natural reproduction or is it an independent human activity that should not be related to, much less subsumed under, the rubric of procreation, notwithstanding the ideological attempts to do so in this period?[208]

These were neither obvious nor innocent questions to pose at the time. The new discourse of natural philosophy, for one, left most of them unanswered, suggesting the connection between the universal phenomenon of reproduction and sexual activity of human beings as self-evident yet stopping short of providing a comprehensive account of its implications and meaning. It was left to other texts and visual forms, notably pornography, thoroughly infused as it was then by the new philosophical ideas, to explore the consequences of this connection, as did, for example, *Thérèse philosophe*. Among the natural philosophers, only Pierre-Louis Moreau de Maupertuis, a friend and interlocutor of Buffon, made an explicit attempt to connect the new materialist account of nature with the sociocultural realm of desire as human practice. Maupertuis's *Venus physique* (1745) followed by his *Système de la Nature* (1751) made this connection in its main argument and in the gallant rhetoric of its presentation.[209] Inherent in the smallest units of matter, desire was, in Maupertuis's view, the very force responsible for the dynamics of molecular organization.[210] While desire was presented as an explanatory model for how nature works, it was also repeatedly acknowledged by Maupertuis as the key aspect of daily human life. As the historian of science Mary Terrall has pointed out, these references to the dual registers, natural and societal, at which desire operated were part of the author's self-conscious strategy to address a general audience, and more specifically female readers who were, Maupertuis assumed, more tuned in to the narratives of seduction than to the rhetoric of burgeoning science.[211] But Maupertuis's mode of exposition also implied, on a conceptual level, the existence of a material continuum wherein the social and the natural spheres were united by the internal energy of attraction permeating and animating all.[212]

Fragonard's cycle offers a similarly energetic vision in which eros not only propels human action but also engenders the life of natural forms. But this vision differs from Maupertuis's "erotic science" in one key aspect.[213] It has to do with these paintings' not fully integrated mode of inscription of the gallant games of their protagonists in the context of nature, a mode suggesting that they both belong and do not belong with the natural order. What is most intriguing about these representations is their indecision, a subtle yet discernible compositional, morphological, and also conceptual irresolution rather than dynamic unity.

The evidence of the painted sketches for two of the panels gives us a better sense of the complexity of the final arrangement, providing a proof, if we needed one, that it was not accidental (figs. 3.66 and 3.67).[214] Striking in both sketches is the overall compositional and chromatic unity and especially

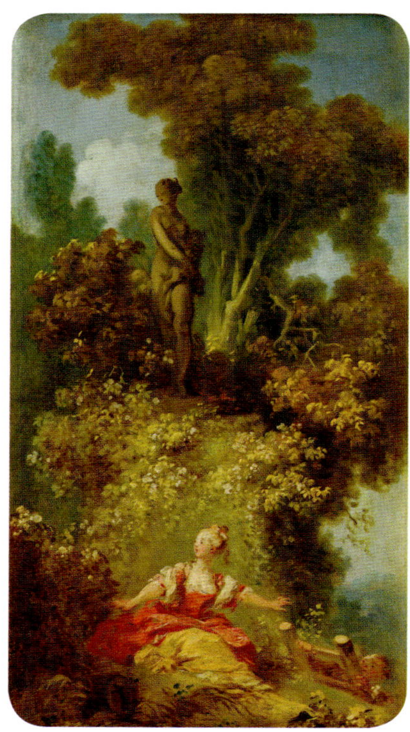

3.66.
Jean-Honoré Fragonard, *La Surprise*, ca. 1771. Oil on canvas. Musée des Beaux-Arts, Angers.

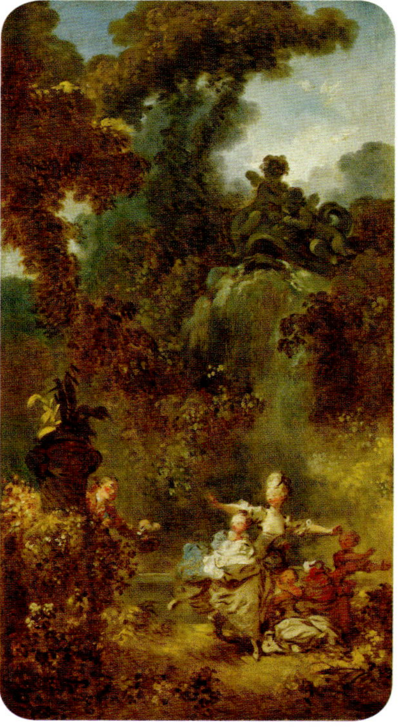

3.67.
Jean-Honoré Fragonard, *La Poursuite*, ca. 1771. Oil on canvas. Musée des Beaux-Arts, Angers.

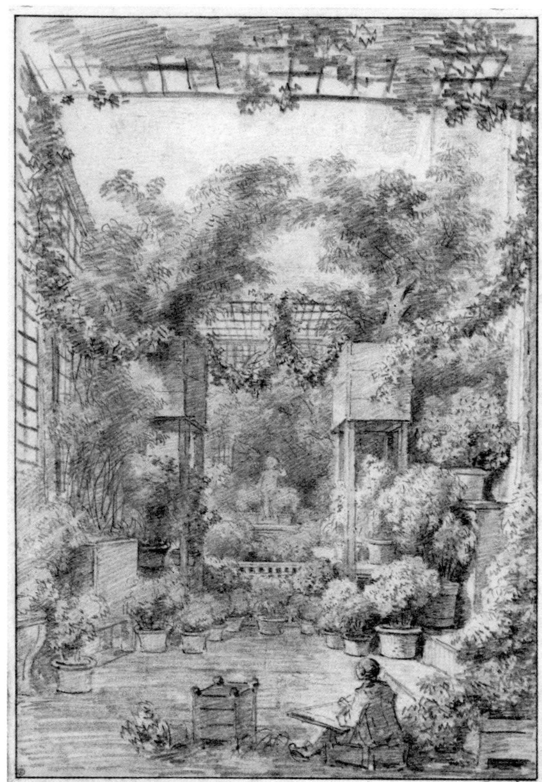

3.68.
Jean-Honoré Fragonard, *The Draftsman*, 1770s. Black chalk. The Metropolitan Museum of Art, New York, Robert Lehman Collection, 1975.

the integration of the female protagonists with nature. Both sketches are more pronouncedly vertical and the movement is one-directional—downward.[215] In each, the swirling female figure is caught in this strong downward flow of vegetation.

By contrast, in the final versions, visible effort has been made to render the figural groups more autonomous in relation to their setting, and to distinguish the female protagonists from their natural surroundings. In the *Meeting*, the woman is wearing a white, light-reflecting satin gown that marks her figure against the darker background, and the high pedestal of the statue was interjected between her body and the trees darting from behind. Her lover, a mere head scaling the ladder in the sketch, was also more fleshed out and he, too, wearing a crimson outfit, stands out from the natural setting. The final compositional structure further enhances the figure/ground separation, creating an effect of subtle tension. On the one hand, there is a tremendous forward surge of natural forms—the thicket of the shooting trees and the dynamic sculpture group planted at its core, the statue of Venus marching forward with Cupid falling behind, as if pulled backward by the sheer force of his mother's movement (an unusually energetic version of the iconography of the Chastised Love wherein Venus withholds the arrows from her son). On the other hand, there is the lateral pull of human desire carried forth by the figures of the man scaling the wall from the side and the woman with her arms extended sideways, her head turned away toward what appears to be some momentarily audible threat to their intimacy. These two compositional vectors remain essentially uncoordinated, an effect on which the suggestiveness of this panel relies.

Similarly, in *The Pursuit*, we witness noticeably discordant and abrupt movement—a compositional instance of the heurté quality mentioned before—with the young female protagonist rushing away in a considerable haste, at once toward us and to the side, her companions either pushing from behind or falling beside her, while her male partner leans forward to offer her a rose—so much movement in many directions at once. Most importantly, the figures in no way follow the trajectories of growth defined by natural forms; they are visibly animated by something other than nature, which has to do with the logic of the situation they are in.

The Lover Crowned presents an equally complex relation between the figures and their setting (see fig. 3.61). *The Draftsman*, in the Metropolitan Museum's Lehman Collection, without being strictly speaking a preparatory sketch for this panel, encapsulates what Fragonard may have originally tried to paint in this panel, and in the Louveciennes cycle as a whole, the idea with which he began: the notion of Love nestled in the heart of Life (fig. 3.68).[216] This idea is represented by the statue of Cupid standing at the center of a trellised garden, with potted plants arranged neatly around it, as if to suggest this stone personification of Love to be the core, if not the source, from which these stylized natural forms emanate and that the draftsman draws.

Brief comparison of this drawing to *The Lover Crowned* allows us to grasp instantly the far more complicated pattern of relations that the Louveciennes series stages between sex and nature, Love and Life. Here we find a similar figure of a sketching artist who confronts a far more complex spectacle. Not only is this a pronouncedly diagonal, more dynamic arrangement than the static, frontal structure of things in *The Draftsman*. It is also as if, once the live bodies of the lovers displaced the sculpted personification of Love as the artist's model—the stone Amour has been literally put to sleep—the relation between desire and nature became more complicated. All forms of life spurt into view, in a rich variety of shapes, colors, and substances, creating a widely

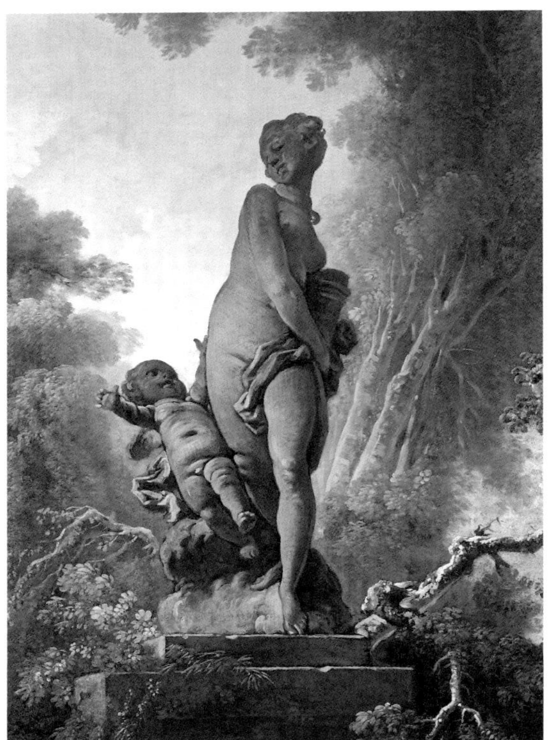

diversified, morphologically heterogeneous, and colorful visual field. The sheer variety of tone and texture of the greens—from lemony-green leaves of the potted plants to the blue-gray cotton-like substance of the trees—is striking. Whose triumph is being represented: Love's or Life's?

The point is that what seemed one and the same idea in the Lehman drawing—the force of Love identified as a force of Life—became in the final panel two coexisting but different registers. No alignment is possible; rather, human desire, embodied by the posing couple, is forever suspended between Nature and Art. A similar argument is made in the *Love Letters* (see fig 3.62), where the lovers are embedded in nature and yet seem radically separate from it, their quasi-sculptural arrangement on and around the empty pedestal and the limelight falling on them emphasizing that they are not a piece of nature but a piece of art.

There are, then, two worlds, two forces clashing with each other in these dynamic compositions, some relation between them proposed yet unresolved. The garden statues featured in these paintings underscore this irresolution. Inherited from Watteau's fêtes galantes, these motifs perform a differently ambivalent function: they are at once the symbolic auspices of Love under which the couples perform their gallant rituals *and* the ciphers of nature from which these actors emerge—the Venus in the *Meeting* who strides forward like Delacroix's *Liberty* avant-la-lettre epitomizes this (fig. 3.69). The poses of the couples and the statues are not coordinated, as they sometimes were in Watteau. Thus in the Dresden *Plaisirs d'Amour*, the pose of Venus, which evidently served as model for the one featured in the *Meeting*, is echoed in the pose of the woman below it, withholding her favors from a man (fig. 3.70).[217] Fragonard avoids such analogies. The embeddedness of the statuary overgrown by natural forms suggests a similar ambivalence in other panels. (The *Awakening of Nature*, a painting now lost, featuring a veiled personification of Nature at its center, confirms the status of Venus in both the *Meeting* and the *Love Letters* as the messenger of Life, not only Love.[218]) The distinct grisaille and white appearance of the statues increases the sense of heterogeneous materiality of these scenes: they are the silent markers of the seams between the worlds of nature and culture, of life and lust, visualizing the contiguity of these realms and their material and conceptual disparity.

How then, does the force of Love square with the force of Life? If this is, in a sense, a modern question (later pondered by, among others, Sigmund Freud), these canvases' modernity resides in their status as a query, in the way they pose the problem through their compositional irresolution and morphological diversity, without offering a simple answer. What the Louveciennes panels propose is a vision of nature as a realm of Life governed by Eros, a dynamic force of attraction that is distinct from—and compositionally incompatible with—the quaint gallantry of the human characters. It is this alternative form of desire that gives sense and direction to the proliferation of

3.69.
Jean-Honoré Fragonard, *The Pursuit of Love: The Meeting*, detail of fig. 3.59.

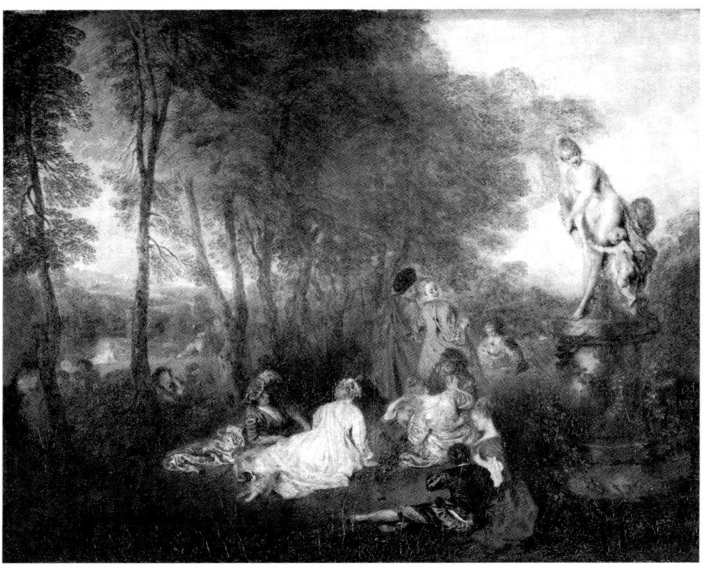

3.70.
Antoine Watteau, *Plaisirs d'amour*, 1717. Oil on canvas. Gemäldegalerie Alte Meister, Dresden.

3.71.
Jean-Honoré Fragonard, *The Vow to Love*, 1780–85. Oil on canvas. Private Collection.

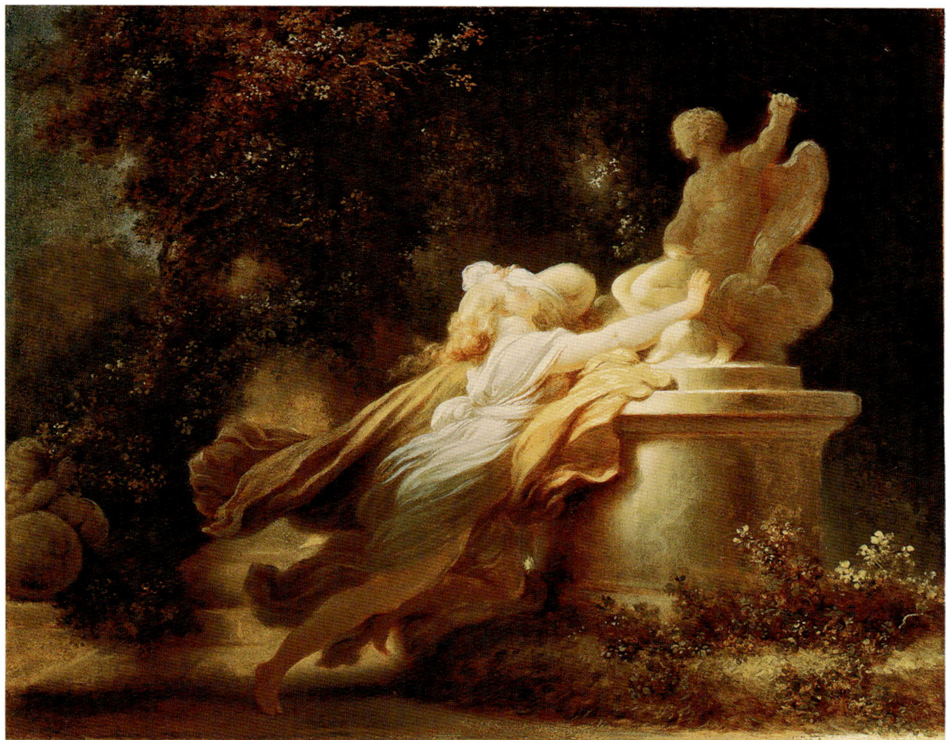

natural form in these dazzling panels, competing with, if not upstaging, the activities of men and women. The figure of Venus as the agent of the advancing nature in *The Meeting* epitomizes the powerful, irrupting, and distinctly feminine force of desire that ignores the sociocultural conventions. This is, ultimately, what surprises the protagonists of *The Meeting* where Nature itself proves to be the invisible intruder, the third party threatening to disturb their fairly tame games of love and chance.

Life is, in the Louveciennes cycle, not a particularly accommodating theater of human desire; it is instead an infraction or disruption in the established conventions of Love. That may have been too problematic a message for the panels to constitute a successful decoration. This staging of Nature as a realm of desire—the basic premise of Maupertuis's "seductive materialism"—that cannot be reined in by the codes of gallant behavior was, in my view, the key among the factors that made these paintings ultimately unacceptable for Fragonard's patron.[219]

—·—

Despite its failure as a commission, the Louveciennes cycle posed questions that remained resonant for Fragonard, echoing in his later productions. In his allegories of love painted in the 1780s, the key concern that had framed the Louveciennes cycle reappeared but was visualized differently, as the alignment of human eros with the propelling force of Life. Such is especially the case of *The Vow to Love* (fig. 3.71) and *The Fountain of Love* (fig. 3.72).[220] Both are extreme paintings, marked by a kind of dynamic excess, quite distinct from the relaxed motility of figures in Fragonard's earlier canvases, such as the *Bathers* (see fig. 3.13), and from the Louveciennes panels where agitation was predominantly nature's. The subject of love broached in these allegories was popular at the time, both in literature, particularly the Anacreontic poetry that enjoyed then a revival, and in the visual arts.[221] Yet even a brief glance at Jean-Baptiste Greuze's version of this iconography, the *Votive Offerings to Cupid* shown at the Salon of 1767, gives us a clear idea of how different Fragonard's approach to it was (fig. 3.73).[222]

Fragonard's paintings were recognized as images of the state of rapture, but the question is, as one scholar put it, "Is this rapture physical, spiritual or both?"[223] It was sensed that some realm of uncertain status, difficult to define, emerged in these passionate scenes, a realm that was more than physical and yet was not just spiritual. I suggest that these paintings were the intuitive representations of desire understood as a psychic force, and that their agitation, even a kind of violence—noted by a nineteenth-century commentator, Pierre de Nolhac, who discerned "sexual violence" in *The Vow*[224]—had to do with the emergent conception of desire as an internal agency that holds sway over the subject, male or female.

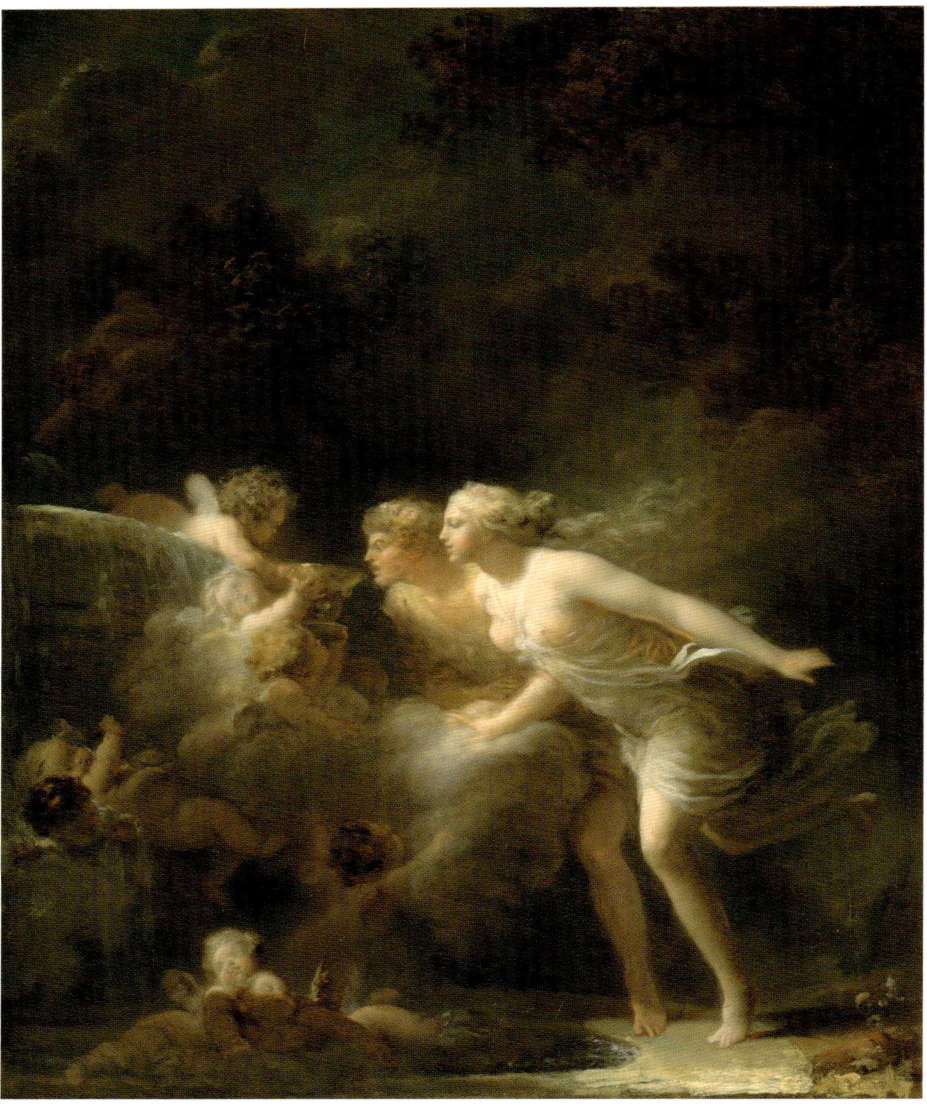

3.72.
Jean-Honoré Fragonard, *The Fountain of Love*, ca. 1785. Oil on canvas. The J. Paul Getty Museum at the Getty Center, Los Angeles.

In these overgrown, dark and clouded spaces, a drama of self ruled by what may be called libido avant la lettre unfolds. Freud, who introduced this concept, conceived of libido as the energy of sexual instincts—their executive function.[225] As for Fragonard, his energetic vision, while his own, may be related to what constituted the eighteenth-century discursive bases of Freud's later conceptions, namely, the emergence of the materialist understanding of nature and sexuality, and especially the speculations about the internal mechanism—Maupertuis's "principle of intelligence," La Mettrie's "motive principle"—governing all organic matter.[226] It was the allegories' relation to this discursive realm that constituted their radical novelty and originality. Patently discontinuous with Boucher's vision of sexuality on which Fragonard was trained, they are also distant from the episodes of Fragonard's Louveciennes cycle: eros is here not a convention, a codified practice articulated by the corresponding pictorial codes, but a kind of passion that governs both the body and the self. Whereas in his earlier work Fragonard's departure from Boucher was manifest in his emphasis on the physical and physiological dimensions of the body engaged in erotic pursuits, in these late paintings it is the inner force that overtakes and overrides the body that comes to the fore.

The painter's iconographic sources for these images have been well established.[227] It is, however, what Fragonard does with these sources that is most striking. The allegories convert the physical dynamism of their figural precedents—whether these were Antique bacchantes or the seventeenth-century sculptures of *Atalanta* and *Hippomenes*—into an internally motivated movement of the body that is, moreover, dramatically illuminated for emphasis. Lacking a visible source—no flambeaux de volupté in sight—the intense light seems to emanate from within the

3.73.
Jean-Baptiste Greuze, *Votive Offerings to Cupid*, 1767. Oil on canvas. The Wallace Collection, London.

3.74.
Jean-Honoré Fragonard, *The Vow to Love*, 1780–85. Oil on wood. Musée du Louvre, Paris.

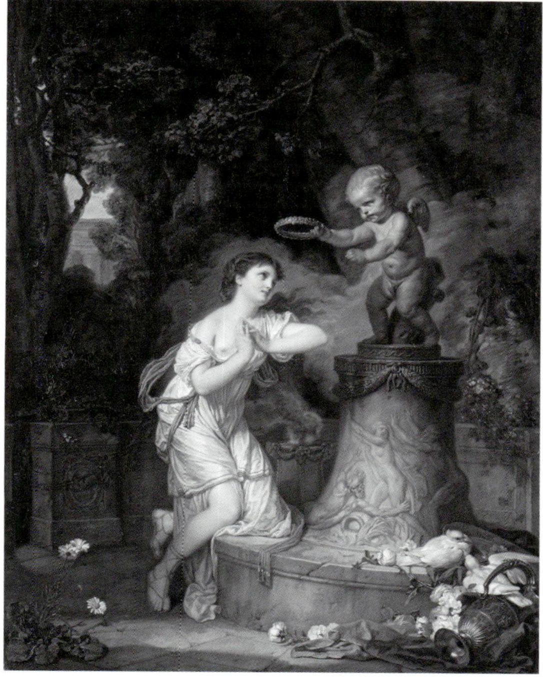

figures, heightening the internal origin of emotion that mobilizes them.

—·—

The staging of these scenes in a natural setting, rather than in an interior, as was typical of libertine iconography, underscores the connection between the conception of desire visualized in them and the new understanding of nature. But unlike in *The Pursuit of Love*, where the proliferating vegetation dominated over the conventionally gallant couples, here it is the human actors who come to the fore as the

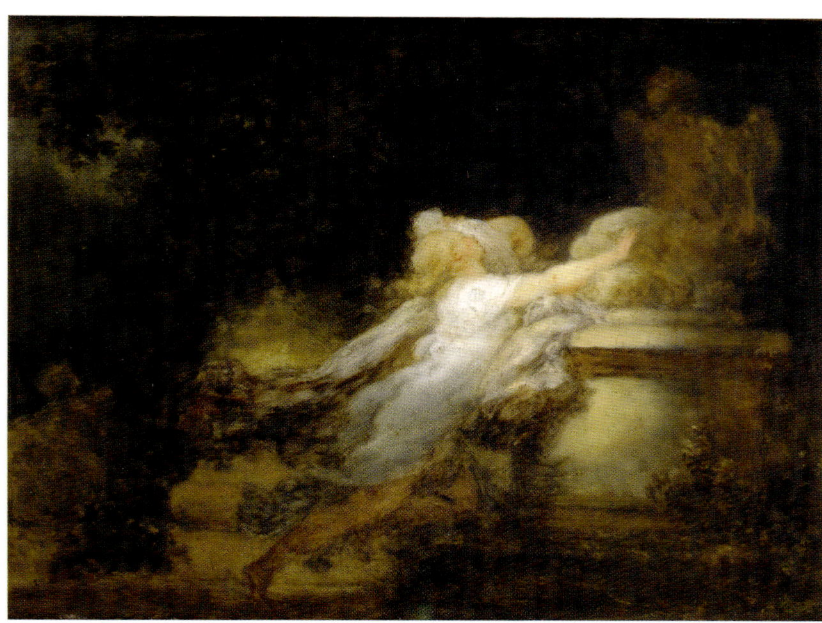

embodiment of an unruly vital force. Their bodies are vectors of the inner motion that propels them toward pleasure, but this is not, as it has been suggested, the Romantic, transcendent notion of Love.[228] What these figures represent is rather a kind of immanence: the power of desire as the principle that governs their actions not only from without (the statue of Love in one canvas; the swarm of amorini around the fountain in the other) but also, and more importantly, from within their own bodies. Although internal, it is not a state of mind, or what Fragonard's contemporaries referred to as *l'âme* (the mind or the soul), but rather a form of pressure exerted on the body from within. The small painted sketch for *The Vow to Love* (fig. 3.74), conveys suggestively this internal animation produced in the very substance of things, including the protagonist's body, painted in swirls of silver, gray, gold, and white tones. The dynamic molecular structure of the natural realm made manifest in the *Island of Love* encompasses the human realm in *The Vow to Love*. Although in the final version the woman's body is painted more smoothly than in the sketch, the sense of inner motion persists in her pose and gestures.

The same may be said of the couple in the *Fountain* shown propelled toward sensual fulfilment. The physical motion serves to convey their inner commotion. The couple's corporeal unison may indicate, as it has been suggested, the simultaneity of orgasms that was a constant concern in the erotic writings of the period.[229] But what these figures represent is not the physical dimension of sex but the notion of desire as a psychic force behind it. Caught in deadly haste, they precipitate themselves toward the cup of Love offered to them by one of the cupids as if it were a life-giving substance. The quasi-desperate expression on the face of the male figure—an echo of Le Brun's physiognomy of *Fright* (fig. 3.75)—and his voracious, impatient mouth opened to gulp the drink as if his life depended on it, underscore the idea of desire as an overpowering force.[230]

Both paintings interiorize desire as a form of internal energy, a blind drive (the blindfolded statue of Love hints at that) harnessing the body into a perpetual pursuit of pleasure that ignores social conventions. It was in the eighteenth century that the discursive ground for understanding eros as an internal force first emerged, as we have witnessed in Maupertuis, and when the question of how to conceive of its relation to the laws governing the realm of nature at large became urgent.[231] Fragonard's late allegories

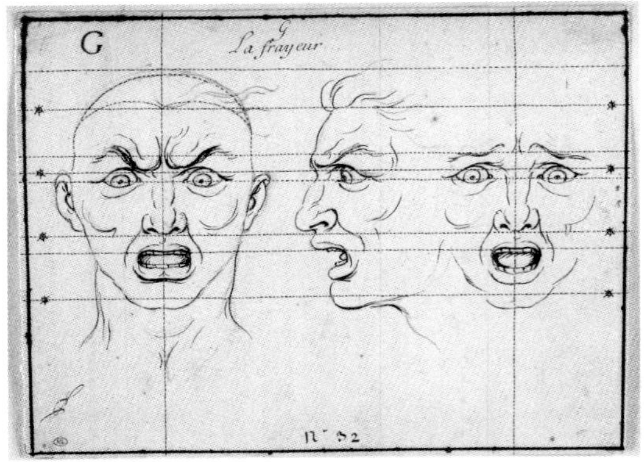

engage with the premise of the mutual imbrication of love and life, suggesting that eros constitutes the very principle of individual existence. Featured as an all-subsuming force that takes over these figures and permeates their being, desire is an attribute of the emergent modern conception of the self. The paintings make this point clearly, notwithstanding their cultural disguise. For if they evoke the ancient cult of love, they are not "about" the past. They stage Antiquity as the radical alternative to, and thus an example for, the present.[232] The vaguely Antique garb of the couple in the *Fountain of Love*, with the rose wreaths on their heads alluding to the cult of Venus, fails to situate them with any precision; these are neither specific mythological figures nor literary characters, but rather Antique ciphers for the modern individual. The couple at the fountain of love represents a Man and a Woman in the general sense posited by the Enlightenment, the young protagonist of *The Vow*, with her indistinct physiognomy blurred by light, is a figure of the self in the grips of desire. At the core of these allegories is the question of the relevance of such construction of human desire for the contemporary notions of individuality. They are ambivalent; they speak of desire as an at-once formative and destructive force. There is a distinct possibility of self-immolation at the altar of love that *The Vow* suggests, just as *The Fountain* opens up to a pernicious prospect for the rushing couple. (The frightened expression of the man hints at it.)

On this level, the paintings may be seen to allegorize the complex function of eros in Fragonard's practice: its productive, formative dimension as an aesthetic commitment that defined him as an artist, making his work desirable, and propelling his career, but also its darker aspect as the force of pleasure that ran counter to societal expectations and that proved subversive in his professional relations, with institutions (the Academy) and with patrons.[233]

ARS EROTICA

Eros functioned in Fragonard's practice as an agent of self-individuation in complex ways. It was neither simply an iconography nor only a mode of execution, but rather a principle that governed how the painter's own body materialized in his painting. This is not to say that it manifested itself in *all* of his paintings or that it did so always in the same way.[234] But it is to suggest that the particular bodily aspect of much of Fragonard's production should be seen as erotic in a particular, historically specific sense. I have aligned this eros with the eighteenth-century materialism and with the new science of nature that emerged in Fragonard's time, rather than, as it has been done, with the literary context of libertinage—not, to be sure, to deny the latter's importance, but to signal its insufficiency as a model for understanding Fragonard's palpable, bodily art. Individuality in his work has to do with the painter's willingness and capacity to tap the body as an intractable force, to develop a touch that could not be described as simply performative, or unfinished, that exceeded the period's polite aesthetic of *je ne sais quoi*.[235] This touch—and the corporeality it evoked on and in front of the canvas—is more direct, more insistently physical, at times deliberately crude or rough, and it is these qualities, among others, that link it with the new mode of thinking about the body and its place in the realm of nature in Fragonard's time. Neither painting merely "for money" nor heralding the conventional ethos of libertinage, Fragonard was a painter of the powerful but also ambiguous effects of the discovery of desire as a formative force and an agent of (self-)individuation. He painted what it meant to "grasp one's own pleasure," as the narrator of *Thérèse philosophe* urged its readers. To what extent could "one's own pleasure" constitute the basis of one's subjective and professional autonomy and to what degree could it limit, endanger, or constrain one's practice and oneself? These were the questions raised by Fragonard's *ars erotica*.

For *ars* it was. Inseparable from the Enlightenment's new knowledge of the body and nature, Fragonard's practice did not, however, amount to *scientia sexualis*.[236] Simply put, it was not a form of discourse, but a differently regulated form of art—a pursuit of pleasure that cannot be fully known but must be materialized.

3.75.
Charles Le Brun, *Fright*, 1678. Pen and black ink, black chalk, on white paper. Musée du Louvre, Paris.

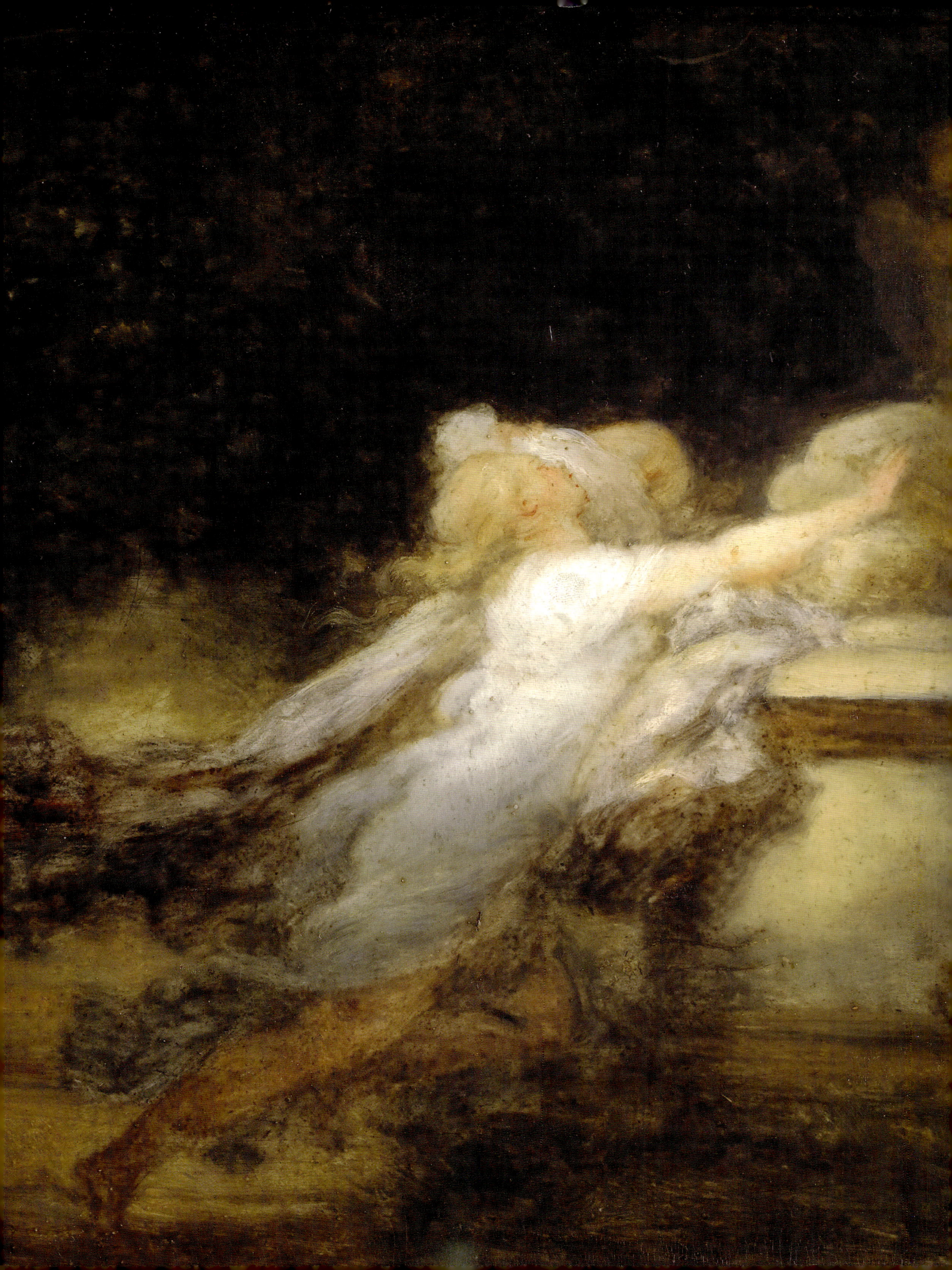

Notes

INTRODUCTION

1 See Edmond and Jules de Goncourt, *French Eighteenth-Century Painters.*

2 To be sure, I am only referring to the position these painters have occupied in the art historical accounts of the period as a whole and not to the extensive and varied literature on them as individual artists, which will be considered at length in the chapters below. Specifically, I am evoking the shortcomings of the stylistic category of rococo that proved ill-suited to accommodate the output of all three painters; to the limits of the semiotic notion of "visuality" that, while providing key insights into shared aspects of these painters' work, such as pictorial space, did not do justice to the distinct nature and complexity of their respective aesthetic projects, and to the sociocultural category of the public sphere that, as the criterion of artistic modernity, placed the three painters in a marginal position insofar as none of them could be said to have fully embraced or defined himself professionally by the condition of publicness. For the latter two models, see Bryson, "Transformations in Rococo Space," in *Word and Image: French Painting of the Ancien Régime*, 89–121; and Crow, *Painters and Public Life in Eighteenth-Century Paris.*

3 See especially, Comte de Caylus, "De la Légèreté de l'Outil," in *Vie d'Artistes du XVIIIe Siècle*, 149–59, esp. 155–56; and Cochin, "De l'Illusion" (1765). For the discussion of these texts and on pictorial touch and the notion of handling (*le faire*) in general in this period, see Démoris, "Le Comte de Caylus et la Peinture: Pour une Théorie de l'Inachevé"; and Michel, "Manière, Goût, Faire, Style: Les Mutations du Vocabulaire de la Critique d'art en France au XVIIIe Siècle."

4 For "le pinceau moëlleux," used by Watelet, see, *Boucher* 1986, 136; Chardin's "magic" was a term used commonly to describe his practice (e.g., by Diderot; see Michel, "Le Peintre Magicien," in *Le Goût de Diderot*, 235–56); and, in regard to Fragonard, "la touche spirituelle" or "l'esprit de sa touche," was also commonly used. (See PR *Fragonard*, 425.)

5 The extensive scholarship on Fragonard will be discussed in chapter 3. For the connection to literature, see especially Molotiu, *Fragonard's Allegories of Love*; and Faroult, *Fragonard Amoureux: Galant et Libertin.* For an important analysis of the technical aspects of the painter's practice, see Mary Sheriff's *Fragonard: Art and Eroticism.*

6 I am paraphrasing Baxandall's statement in *Patterns of Intention: On the Historical Explanation of Pictures*, 103. For the impact of British empiricism on French philosophy, see Yolton, *Locke and French Materialism.* For the notion of experience, O'Neal, *The Authority of Experience: Sensationist Theory in the French Enlightenment.*

7 For the new importance of experience in the reception of art, see Griener, *La République de l'oeil: L'Expérience de l'art au siècle des Lumières.*

8 *The Treatise on the Sensations* (1756). For a useful discussion of Condillac's treatment of touch, see Crampe-Casnabet, "Condillac: On ne touche que soi; Réflexion autour d'une Statue."

9 This aspect was emphasized by virtually all writers on the sense of touch, including Condillac. On the tactile sensation exhibiting "necessarily a *double* relation," see Cassirer, *Philosophy of the Enlightenment*, 117. For an exploration of this double relation in painting, see Lajer-Burcharth, "Pompadour's Touch: Difference in Representation."

10 "Chardin and the Bourgeois Ideals of His Time," 151.

11 For a useful summary, see Ann Thomson, "Materialism," in Kors, *Encyclopedia of the Enlightenment*, 3: 26–31. See also Desné, *Les Matérialistes français de 1750 à 1800*; and Yolton, *Thinking Matter: Materialism in Eighteenth-Century Britain.* For its broader cultural implications, see Jacob, *Cultural Meaning of the Scientific Revolution*, chap. 4, and Jacob, "The Materialist World of Pornography."

12 "Depuis la pierre formée dans les entrailles de la terre, par la combinaison intime de molécules analogues et similaires qui se sont rapprochées, jusqu'au soleil, ce vaste réservoir des particules enflammées qui éclaire le firmament; depuis l'huître engourdie jusqu'à l'homme actif et pensant, nous voyons une progression non interrompue, une chaîne perpétuelle de combinaisons et de mouvements, dont il résulte des êtres, qui ne diffèrent entre eux que par la variété de leurs matières élémentaires, des combinaisons et des proportions de ces mêmes éléments, d'où naissent des façons d'exister et d'agir infiniment diversifiées." D'Holbach, *Système de la Nature*, cited in Desné, *Les Matérialistes français*, 141. Translation, as everywhere else in this book, is mine except when stated otherwise.

13 For the term "period eye," see Baxandall, *Painting and Experience in Fifteenth-Century Italy: A Primer in the Social History of Pictorial Style.* I take Ann Thomson's choice of the title of her book, *Bodies of Thought*, to make a similar point in regard to philosophical discourse—namely, that materialism *embodied* thinking.

14 "Morphology" was a common word in the vocabulary of the eighteenth-century materialists. In his *Système de la Nature*, D'Holbach often uses the term "formation." See *Système de la Nature* cited in Desné, 138–42.

15 The *Salons* of Diderot, who was one of the exponents of materialism, abound with materialist terminology. See his discussion of Chardin's still lifes in chapter 2 below. On materiality as a broader methodological question, see also my *Chardin Material.* For attention to the material aspects of the work of art as a result of new "protocols of observation"

developed by the nascent science of connoisseurship, and related to the art market, collecting practices, and the displays of art at the Salon, see Griener, *La République de l'oeil*; Lafont, "Du Cabinet à l'Encyclopédie," in *1740, Un Abrégé du Monde: Savoirs et collections autour de Dezallier d'Argenville*; Guichard, *Les amateurs d'art à Paris au XVIIIe siècle*; and Smentek, *Mariette and the Science of the Connoisseur in Eighteenth-Century Europe*, esp. chap. 2. On the role of observation, see also Daston and Gallison, *Objectivity*. However, while the scholars who attended to these phenomena described them in terms of the advent of the "regime of the eye" (the term is Pascal Griener's), I would emphasize the materialist bases of these practices.

16 For the necessity to consider the historical existence of phenomena that had not yet entered language or made an appearance in the dictionaries, see, eloquently, DeJean, *Ancients against the Moderns: Culture Wars and the Making of Fin-de-Siècle*, xiv–xv.

17 As Peter Gay has observed, psychology was the foremost human science in the Enlightenment. (*The Enlightenment. An Interpretation*, vol. 2, 167.) On eighteenth-century empirical psychology, see also Vidal, *Sciences of the Soul: The Early Modern Origins of Psychology*.

18 See Binkley, *The Concept of the Individual in Eighteenth-Century French Thought from the Enlightenment to the French Revolution*.

19 It is not possible to cite the vast literature on this topic, which will be addressed at length in the chapters below, here. Among the most important for my discussion were: Perkins, *The Concept of the Self in the French Enlightenment*; Binkley, *Concept of the Individual in Eighteenth-Century French Thought from the Enlightenment to the French Revolution*; Wahrman, *Making of Modern Self: Identity and Culture in Eighteenth-Century England*; Seigel, *The Idea of the Self: Thought and Experience in Western Europe since the Seventeenth Century*.

20 Among the notable exceptions is Deena Goodman and Kathryn Norberg's edited volume *Furnishing the Eighteenth Century: What Furniture Can Tell Us About the European and American Past*, and in it, especially Goodman, "The *Secrétaire* and the Integration of Eighteenth-Century Self"; and Hellman, "The Joy of Sets: The Uses of Seriality in the French Interior."

21 For the methodological claim about paintings making their own arguments, see Bois, *Painting as Model*. For the eighteenth-century discovery that the work of art contains in itself something that doesn't reveal itself to discourse, see Démoris, "Chardin and the Far Side of Illusion"; and Griener, *La République de l'oeil*.

22 For the discussion of the new modes of art experience, see, most importantly, Crow, *Painters and Public Life*; Griener, *La République de l'oeil*; Michel, *Peinture et Plaisir: Les Goûts Picturaux des Collectionneurs Parisiens au XVIIIe Siècle*; Lafont, "Du Cabinet à l'Encyclopédie"; Guichard, *Les amateurs*; and Smentek, *Mariette and the Science of the Connoisseur*, among others.

CHAPTER ONE

1 The epigraph to this section is taken from Diderot, *Salon de 1761*, in Vernière, *Oeuvres Esthétiques*, 451. "Boucher a un faire qui lui appartient tellement que dans quelque morceau de peinture qu'on lui donnât une figure à exécuter, on la reconnaîtrait sur-le-champs."

2 For Largillière's portrait as a prototype vision of an academic artist, see McAllister Johnson, "Les morceaux de réception: Protocole et documentation." On academic portrait as a type, see also Williams, *Académie Royale: A History in Portraits*.

3 Boucher became the *premier peintre du Roi* in August 1765 at the age of sixty-two, replacing the deceased Carle Van Loo. Later that month he was also elected to Carle Van Loo's vacant post as the director of the Academy, which he ceded after only three years. See Michel, "Boucher Professeur à l'Académie Royale de Peinture et de Sculpture," 94.

4 Reported in Desboulmiers [Jean-Auguste Julien], "Éloge de M. Boucher," *Mercure de France*, September 1770, 181–89.

5 Desboulmiers speaks of his "astonishing fecundity" (étonnante fécondité), in ibid., 184. See also Diderot's ambivalent praise of Boucher's "inexhaustible fecundity" and "an incredible facility" of execution. *The Salon of 1765*, in Goodman, *Diderot on Art*, 1: 23.

6 J. F. Bastide, *La Petite Maison* (1758–60), quoted in Hedley, *François Boucher: Seductive Visions*, 37. See also Papillon de la Ferté: "Aucun artiste n'a été plus ingénieux [. . .]," in *Extrait des différens ouvrages publiés sur la vie des peintres* (1776), 659–60.

7 As in note 1 above.

8 *Cours de la Peinture*. For the seventeenth-century roots of this tradition, see Posner, "Concerning the 'Mechanical' Parts of Painting and the Artistic Culture of Seventeenth-Century France," 596. See also most recently, Delaplanche, *Un Tableau n'est pas qu'une Image: La Reconnaissance de la Matière de la Peinture en France au XVIIIe Siècle*. In a more general sense, the assumption that the work of art always in some sense bears the stamp of its maker goes back to Antiquity. See Wittkower and Wittkower, *Born under Saturn: The Character and Conduct of Artists*, chap. 17.

9 "De l'Illusion" (1765), "Réponse de M. C" (1760), "Lettre de Monsieur Cochin," and others. For the discussion of these texts, and especially the notion of *le faire*, see Michel "Manière, Goût, Faire, Style," and his *Charles-Nicolas Cochin et l'Art des Lumières*.

10 In Diderot's laconic phrase: "This man has everything but the truth." *Salon 1761*, in Vernière, *Oeuvres Esthétiques*, 449.

11 On the bias of Diderot's view of Boucher and its impact on the painter's later reception, see Brunel, "Boucher, Neveu de Rameau," in Sahut and Volle, *Diderot et l'Art de Boucher à David: Les Salons, 1759–1781*, 109; and Démoris, "Boucher, Diderot, Rousseau."

12 For notable exceptions from this entrenched approach, see Norman Bryson's discussion of Boucher in his *Word and Image*, 93–97; Crow, "Critique of Enlightenment in Eighteenth-Century Art"; and Lipton, "Women, Pleasure, and Painting (e.g., Boucher)."

13 *Journal Encyclopaedique* (1757).

14 The 1986 exhibition at the Metropolitan Museum of Art, New York, Detroit Institute of Arts, and Réunion des Musées Nationaux, Grand Palais, Paris, was curated by Alastair Laing, J. Patrice Marandel, and Pierre Rosenberg. (*Boucher* 1986.) Other important thematic exhibitions on Boucher included *Boucher* RMN 2003; *Boucher* ÉNSBA 2003; Joulie, *Boucher et les Peintres du Nord*; Joulie, *Esquisses, Pastels et Dessins de François Boucher dans les Collections privées*; Laing, *Drawings*; *François Boucher: Seductive Visions*, Wallace Collection, London, 2004, with an accompanying book by Jo Hedley; and more recently, *Boucher* Gammel Holtegaard.

15 For the methodological shift in Boucher's studies, see Hyde and Ledbury, "The Pleasures of Rethinking François Boucher." For arguments about Boucher's modernity, see ibid., and especially Schieder, "Between *Grâce* and *Volupté*: Boucher and Religious Painting"; Scott, "Reproduction and Reputation: 'François Boucher' and the Formation of Artistic Identities"; and my own "Pompadour's Dream: Boucher, Diderot, and Modernity." For new discussion of Boucher's work, see also Hyde, "Confounding Conventions: Gender Ambiguity and François Boucher's Painted Pasto-

rals"; Hyde, "The 'Makeup' of the Marquise: Boucher's Portrait of Pompadour at Her Toilette"; and Hyde, *Making Up the Rococo: Boucher and His Critics*; Lajer-Burcharth, "Pompadour's Touch"; Ledbury, "Boucher and Theater"; and Stein, "Les Chinoiseries de Boucher et leurs Sources: L'Art de l'Appropriation."

16 "Né sensible, aimable et voluptueux, il se vit presque toujours entraîné vers le grâces, dont il fut généralement appellé le Peintre." Bret, "Éloge de M. Boucher," *Nécrologe des Hommes Célèbres de France* 6 (1771), in Ananoff, 1: 135.

17 The notion of grace was common in the artistic vocabulary of this period. See Piles, *L'Idée du Peintre parfait* (1699), 75. Following de Piles, in painting, it was defined as pleasure generated by a fortuitous rendition of things. See Lacombe, *Dictionnaire portatif des Beaux-Arts* (1754). For Watelet it was distinguished from beauty in that, while beauty resided in the good rendition of bodily movement, grace amounted to a concordance between the movement of the body and the movements of the soul. *Réflexions sur les différentes Parties de la Peinture* appended to his poem *L'Art de Peindre* (1761); his entry on "grace" in Watelet and Levesque, *Dictionnaire des Arts*; and in the *Encyclopédie*.

18 "[. . .] il n'avait pas vu les grâces en un bon lieu; il peignait Venus et la Vierge d'après les nymphes des coulisses, et son langage se ressentait ainsi que ses tableaux des moeurs de ses modèles et du son atelier." Marmontel, *Mémoires*, 205. See also Diderot's vociferous commentary on Boucher's pastorals shown at the Salon of 1765. Accusing the painter of basing his shepherdesses on the actresses of the popular theater ("the prostitutes of the bases kind"), the critic claimed the deterioration of the painter's art to be a direct result of his debauchery. Goodman, *Diderot on Art*, 1: 22.

19 See Crow, *Painters and Public Life*.

20 See *Lettre sur l'Exposition des Ouvrages* (1747). Deloynes, no. 26.

21 La Font de Saint-Yenne, *Réflexions sur quelques Causes de l'État présent de la Peinture en France*, in Jollet, *La Font de Saint-Yenne: Oeuvre critique*, 43–94. On La Font's stance, see Jollet, "Le Citoyen, l'Oeuvre, le Monument," in ibid., 7–35. See also Crow, *Painters and Public Life*, 6–18 (on La Font and Le Blanc); and Démoris, "Le Coup d'État du Connaisseur délicat et sévère: Les *Réflexions de 1747*."

22 See Crow, *Painters and Public Life*, 7–11.

23 For the relation between artistic production and the market in other cultural contexts, see Alpers, *Rembrandt's Enterprise: The Studio and the Market*; and Solkin, *Painting for Money: The Visual Arts and the Public Sphere in Eighteenth-Century England*.

24 See McClellan, "Watteau's Dealer: Gersaint and the Marketing of Art in Eighteenth-Century Paris"; Scott, "Authorship, the Académie, and the Market in Early Modern France"; Glorieux, *À l'Enseigne de Gersaint: Edme François Gersaint, Marchand d'Art sur le Pont Notre-Dame, 1694–1750*; Michel, *Le Commerce du tableau à Paris dans la seconde moitié du XVIIIe Siècle: Acteurs et Pratiques*.

25 On the new mode of art experience linked to the commercial sphere, see Guichard, *Les amateurs d'art*; and Smentek, *Mariette and the Science of the Connoisseur*. Katie Scott's *The Rococo Interior: Decoration and Social Spaces in Early Eighteenth-Century Paris* opened up new avenues for the exploration of the commercial bases of aesthetic experience. The eighteenth-century term *amateur* refers to those collectors or connoisseurs who also practiced art for the pleasure of it. For the extensive discussion of this distinct social group and its cultural importance at the time, see Guichard, ibid.

26 For an earlier, shorter version of some of the arguments presented here, see my "Image Matters: The Case of Boucher."

27 A notable exception is Scott's relatively recent essay "Reproduction and Reputation."

28 Acccording to one, no doubt exaggerated, report, he earned 50,000 livres per year. (Crow, *Painters and Public Life*, 11, citing Alfred Babeau, *Le Bourgeois d'autrefois* [1881].) For comparison with the range of reveneus at the time—e.g., that of an average comfortable *bourgeois* being 3,000–4,000 livres—see Sgard, "L'Échelle de revenus."

29 See Brunel, *Boucher*, 35. According to the annotated copy of the sale catalog at the Bibliothèque Nationale de France examined by Brunel, Boucher's estate amounted to 152,618 livres. The sum obtained from the sale of the collection was 98,829 livres.

30 There is vast literature on the topic. Important for my discussion were, among others: Roche, *La culture des apparences: une histoire du vêtement (XVIIe–XVIIIe siècle)* (English edition: *The Culture of Clothing: Dress and Fashion in the Ancien Régime*); Roche, *Histoire des choses banales: Naissance de la consommation dans les sociétés traditionnelles (XVIIe– XIXe siècle)* (English edition: *History of Everyday Things: The Birth of Consumption in France, 1600–1800*); and Roche, *France in the Enlightenment*, esp. 519–640; Bermingham and Brewer, *Consumption of Culture, 1600–1800: Image, Object, Text*; Berg and Clifford, *Consumers and Luxury: Consumer Culture in Europe, 1650–1850*; and Shovlin, *The Political Economy of Virtue: Luxury, Patriotism, and the Origins of the French Revolution*.

31 Scott, "Reproduction and Reputation."

32 For the market as an imaginary construct as well as reality in eighteenth-century France, see Reddy, *The Rise of Market Culture: The Textile Trade and French Society, 1750–1900*, 1–18; and Sonenscher, *Work and Wages: Natural Law, Politics, and the Eighteenth-Century French Trades*, esp. 22–39.

33 The epigraph for this section is taken from *Nouveau Logogriphe* (1744), cited by Chatelus, *Peindre à Paris au XVIIIe Siècle*, 127. "He does not have sausage-like [literally: numb] fingers / This painter whose name contains / The shopkeeper who on Fridays / keeps his shop and his doors closed." The verses play on Boucher's name which means "butcher" in French. In eighteenth-century France, Friday was traditionally a fasting day, hence butcher shops were closed.

"touche facile, élégante, spirituelle." Desboulmiers, *Éloge de M. Boucher*, 188. In his *Dictionnaire des Artistes*, abbé de Fontanai spoke of "la légèreté d'une touche spirituelle et fine" (67).

34 Caylus understood the "lightness of touch" as the finishing touches the painter applies to the already completed painting to create an illusion of effortlessness. See "De la Légèreté de l'Outil," in *Vie d'Artistes du XVIIIe Siècle*, 149–59, esp. 155–56.

35 See chap. 2 below.

36 "Tact: le sentiment du toucher," in *Dictionnaire universel* (1708). Touch itself—*le toucher*—had in the eighteenth century multiple connotations. Among them "être joint, être proche l'un et l'autre." ("Toucher" [main entry on touch] in ibid.).

37 "Tact," *Encyclopédie*, entry by Chevalier Louis de Jaucourt, 15: 819–22.

38 Ibid., 820.

39 "Avoir le tact fin, sûr, etc. pour dire, Juger finement, surement en matière de goût." *Dictionnaire de l'Académie française* (1762), 794.

40 "Nous éprouvons un sentiment prompt d'estime, d'admiration, d'amour pour les actions vertueuses, et d' horreur pour les actions criminelles, dont nous connoissons au premier coup d'oeil la tendance et la fin. La promptitude avec laquelle cet instinct ou ce *tact moral* s'exerce par les personnes éclairées et vertueuses, a fait croire à plusieurs moralistes que cette faculté étoit inhérente à l' homme, qui l'apportoit en naissant; cependant il est le fruit de la réflexion, de l'habitude." *Système de la Nature*, 51, emphasis mine.

41 "J'ai là-dessus un tact qui ne me trompe jamais," brags the protagonist of Crébillon fils. See Crébillon, *Ah Quel Conte* (1751), in *Collection complète des Oeuvres de M. de Crébillon, fils*, 4: 21.

42 E.g., see "Tact," in *Trésor de la langue francaise informatisé*: "an intuitive, fine, measured and assured appreciation in the matter of conventions, tastes, and usages. Synonymous to politeness [among others]." See also Merriam-Webster: *Tact*: "French, sense of touch, from Latin *tactus*, from *tangere* to touch. A keen sense of what to do or say in order to maintain good relations with others or avoid offense. Skill and grace in dealing with others. Delicate and considerate perception of what is appropriate. Savoir-faire, poise."

43 *Salon de 1767*, in Versini, *Oeuvres*, 673.

44 Méré, *Lettres*, 55. On Méré and honnêteté, see Stanton, *The Aristocrat as Art: A Study of the* Honnête Homme *and the* Dandy *in Seventeenth- and Nineteenth-Century French Literature*.

45 "Quiconque sait complaire peut hardiment espérer de plaire." Faret, *L'Honnête Homme ou l'Art de Plaire à la Cour*, 70.

46 The term used by Domna Stanton in her discussion of Méré in *The Aristocrat as Art*, 132. She refers to Méré's "De la Conversation," in Boudhor, *Oeuvres Complètes du Chevalier de Méré*, 2: 107, and to his Sixth Discourse, "Suite du Commerce du Monde," in 3: 160.

47 "Il faut observer tout ce qui se passe dans le coeur et dans l'esprit des personnes qu'on entretient, et s'accoustumer de bonne heure à connoistre les sentimens et les pensées, par des signes presque imperceptibles. Cette connoisance qui se trouve obscure et difficile pour ceux qui n'y sont pas fait, s'éclaircit et se rend aisée à la longue." "De la Conversation."

48 "Du reste, on se plaît bien avec les personnes qui font tout ce qu'on veut, sans qu'on les en avertisse." Boudhor, *Oeuvres Complètes*, 2: 107–8.

49 "le personnage d'un honnête-homme s'étend partout; il se doit transformer par la souplesse du génie, comme l'occasion le demande, [. . .]" Boudhor, *Oeuvres Complètes*, 3: 157. Faret, who particularly emphasized *souplesse*, dubbed it "a sovereign precept." Faret, *L'Honnête Homme*, 70.

50 For example, in La Rouchefoucauld's understanding, insinuation amounted to a strategic use of a kind of receptiveness to the other. See La Rochefoucauld in Chauffier and Marchand, *Oeuvres Complètes*, 527.

51 "Suite du Commerce du Monde," in Boudhor, *Oeuvres Completès*, 3: 161. Stanton uses the term "the surface beneath the other." *Aristocrat as Art*, 132.

52 See Rosenberg, "The Mysterious Beginnings of the Young Boucher"; and Méjanès, "Le Séjour de François Boucher en Italie (1728–1731)."

53 The basic sources of information about Boucher's work for Jullienne are Dacier and Vuaflart, *Jean de Jullienne et les Graveurs de Watteau au XVIIIe Siècle*; Jean-Richard, *L'Oeuvre gravé de François Boucher dans la Collection Edmond de Rothschild*, 33–68 (for *Figures* and *Oeuvre gravé*); Roland Michel, "Watteau et les *figures de différents caractères*." See also Roland Michel, "De Watteau à Boucher: Formation d'une manière et d'un genre"; Tillerot, "Graver les dessins de Watteau au XVIIIe Siècle"; Tillerot, "Engraving Watteau in the Eighteenth Century: Order and Display in the *Recueil Jullienne*"; Scott, "Reproduction and Reputation"; and my own "Image Matters."

54 Dacier and Vuaflart, *Jean de Jullienne et les Graveurs de Watteau au XVIIIe Siècle*, 2: 8–9.

55 According to Jean-Richard, Boucher produced twenty-one prints for *L'Oeuvre*: nine after paintings or arabesques and twelve after decorative panels for the château de La Muette. See Jean-Richard, *L'Oeuvre gravé*, 63. Jean-Richard cataloged the prints of the copy of the *Recueil* that is at the Louvre. Dacier and Vuaflart's four-volume catalog refers to the copy of the *Recueil* at the Bibliothéque de l'Énsba in Paris.

56 Roland Michel, "De Watteau à Boucher," 38–39.

57 "Monsieur Jullienne who was in possession of most of Watteau's drawings, engaged Boucher to etch them and *to draw those that he lacked*; he did so with success and captured perfectly the grace, the lightness and the correctness of the Flemish Painter." Italics mine. *Galerie Française; ou, Potraits des Hommes et des Femmes célèbres qui ont paru en France . . . par une Société de Gens de lettres* (1771), quoted in Ananoff, 1: 133. Jullienne owned about 450 drawings by Watteau (according to the records of his sale in 1767). It has been suggested, however, that the *Recueil* was probably based mostly on the drawings from the collection of the abbé Haranger, one of Watteau's heirs, rather than Jullienne's own. See Dacier and Vuaflart, *Jean de Jullienne*, 2: 52.

58 The *Portrait de Watteau* was also sold separately after the publication of the first volume of the *Figures*. (For the Louvre version, see Jean-Richard, *L'Oeuvre gravé*, no. 33. Other examples are in the Cabinet des Estampes, BnF, Paris, Cleveland, and British Library.) Attribution of the drawing (Musée Condé, Chantilly) to Watteau is now considered untenable. (Roland Michel, "De Watteau à Boucher," 39, and n. 5.) For it being a Boucher drawing based on a painted portrait by Watteau, see Jacoby, *François Boucher's Early Development as a Draughtsman, 1720–1734*, 84–95. Other suggested authors of the drawing are Jullienne (Garnier, "Les Portraits de Watteau," 25–26), and François de Troy, Jullienne's teacher (Brême, *François de Troy, 1645–1730*, 184, n. 177). For the discussion of the attribution, see also Bailey, "'Toute seule elle peut remplir et satisfaire l'imagination': The Early Appreciation and Marketing of Watteau's Drawings," 69–70. As for the *Graces*, the etching is mentioned by most of the sources as having served as the frontispiece to the *second* volume of the *Figures*. (E.g., Dacier and Vuaflart, *Jean de Jullienne*, 2: 7–8; Jean-Richard, *L'Oeuvre gravé*, 48.) However, in the edition of the *Figures* that is at the New York Public Library the *Graces* frontispiece is inserted—erroneously?—in the first volume, after the *Portrait of Watteau*. (Bailey, "Toute seule elle peut remplir et satisfaire l'imagination," also lists it as the frontispiece to the first volume.) Boucher's original drawing for the *Graces* is preserved in the Queen's collections at Windsor.

59 Jean-Richard, *L'Oeuvre gravé*, 63; and Roland Michel, *Watteau*, 304.

60 Boucher finally undertook the trip at his own expense. See Laing, "Chronology," in *Boucher* 1986, 16–17, and Rosenberg, "The Mysterious Beginnings."

61 Dacier and Vuaflart, *Jean de Jullienne*, vol. 2, *Historique*; and vol. 4, nos. 5, 20, 85, 210, 211.

62 Ibid., vol. 3, 42, no. 85 (repr. in vol. 4); Jean-Richard, *L'Oeuvre gravé*, 63–64, no. 154; and Nicole Parmentier in Grasselli and Rosenberg, *Watteau, 1684–1721*, 238–39.

63 For Watteau's drawing, also referred to as *The Costumes Are Italian*, and its function as a *modello* for Watteau's etching, see Margaret Morgan Grasselli, in Grasselli and Rosenberg, *Watteau*, 122–24, no. 55. The drawing, long believed to have been by Watteau, has been recently de-attributed by Prat and Rosenberg (*Antoine Watteau, 1684–1721: Catalogue raisonné des Dessins*, 3: R60), though this de-attribution has not been widely accepted. Grasselli has argued, in my view convincingly, there is no reason to doubt Watteau's authorship. (Review of *Antoine Watteau 1684–1721: Catalogue raisonné des Dessins* by Rosenberg and Prat, 322–23.) Roland Michel also questioned Prat and Rosenberg's rejection of Watteau's authorship, pointing to, among other issues, the fact that Boucher's print was clearly marked as etched "d'après le dessin original." ("The

Rosenberg-Prat Catalogue of Watteau's Drawings," 754.) I am grateful to Meg Grasselli, and to Perrin Stein, for sharing their views on the drawing and its attribution with me.

64 For the suggestion of Boucher's retouching of Watteau's drawing, see Grasselli in Grasselli and Rosenberg, *Watteau*, 123. For the first state of Watteau's etching (reproduced here), see also Nicole Parmentier's entry E.8 in ibid., 238–39.

65 The information about Boucher's pay comes from Mariette. (*Abecedario de P. J. Mariette*, 1: 166.) By comparison, Boucher used to receive 60 livres *a month* (plus food and lodging) from Jean-François Cars for engraving frontispieces for theses.

66 While some of his prints were finished with a burin (notably the *Seasons*, retouched, according to Mariette, by Laurent Cars), Boucher himself worked exclusively in etching. For the *Seasons* and Mariette commentary, see Dacier and Vuaflart, *Jean de Jullienne*, 3: nos. 68–71.

67 See *De la Manière de Graver à l'Eau-Forte et au Burin*. The treatise, originally published in 1645, was reedited and augmented by Cochin who added eight theoretical chapters to it. See Courboin, *L'Estampe française: Graveurs et Marchands*, 32–39.

68 "Gravure"; "Gravure en taille-douce," *Encyclopédie*, 7: 877–903.

69 For Watteau's influence on Boucher's iconography and style, see Roland Michel, *Watteau*, 303–6, and Michel, "De Watteau à Boucher"; Brunel, *Boucher*, 81–89; Wintermute, "Pélerinage à Watteau: An Introduction to the Drawings of Watteau and His Circle," esp. 40–45; Brugerolles and Guillet, "Un de ces Hommes," in *Boucher* ÉNSBA 2003, 15–16; Joulie, "Formation et Culture de François Boucher," in *Boucher* ÉNSBA 2003, 76–87; Joulie, "Boucher, Bloemaert et Watteau: La Création d'un Monde"; and Hedley, *Seductive Visions*, 26–32.

70 Roger de Piles defined the quality of freedom in drawing as a habit of hand ("habitude que la main a contracté"). *L'Idée d'un peintre parfait*, 78. The entry on "tact" in the *Encyclopédie* insisted on habit in the development of touch. One had to *learn* how to touch, it was not an innate quality: "Le sense du *toucher* ne se développe qu'insensiblement & par des habitudes réitérées. Nous apprenons à toucher, comme nous apprenons à voir, à entendre, à goûter." "Tact," *Encyclopédie*, 15: 819.

71 "Sa pointe légère et spirituelle semblait faite pour ce travail." *Abecedario*, 1: 166. I follow the translation offered in Brunel, *Boucher*, 82, that gives "pointe," literally: (etching) needle, as "touch."

72 Boucher's etching is in vol. 2, no. 252 of the *Figures* (no. 118 in Jean-Richard's catalog of Boucher's works in the Louvre copy of the *Figures*). For the Clark drawing, see Wintermute, *Watteau and His World: French Drawings from 1700 to 1750*, no. 41.

73 Cochin compares the merits and challenges of etching and engraving in his "Préface de l'Editeur," in Bosse, *De la Manière de Graver*, xxi–xxiv.

74 This aspect differentiates training obtained through extensive practice of reproductive etching from the routine studio training through drawing after other artists' work.

75 For the relation between prints as images and mental process, see MacGregor, "The Authority of Prints: An Early Modern Perspective." I am concerned with the mental effects of the printmaking process.

76 Cf. Jacques Derrida's notion of writing developed in relation to Freud's notion of the "mystic writing pad" in "Freud and the Scene of Writing," *Writing and Difference*, 196–231. Freud likened the mystic writing pad—a device based on the principle similar to etching—to the operations of psyche wherein the traces of all our experiences persist latent and inaccessible, except as residual, memory-traces. See also Derrida, *Memoirs of the Blind: The Self-Portrait and Other Ruins*.

77 Roland Michel observed that Boucher was so minutely attentive to Watteau's figures that it was as if he wanted to "impregnate himself" with them. "De Watteau à Boucher," 39.

78 Bailey has suggested that the first edition of the two volumes of the *Figures* was intended as a pattern book or motif repertory for artists and decorateurs and that it was only the 1734 reedition of the *Figures* that aimed at a connoisseur audience. ("Toute seule," 69.) For a view of Jullienne's project as a construction of an oeuvre, see Scott, "Reproduction and Reputation."

79 On Crozat's *Recueil*, published in 1721, see Dacier and Vuaflart, 2: 18–19. For a lucid discussion of the *Recueil Crozat* and, more generally, the cultural functions of reproductive print, see Leca, "An Art Book and Its Viewers: The 'Recueil Crozat' and the Uses of Reproductive Engraving."

80 He contributed some etchings after Watteau to his *Recueil*. See Dacier and Vuaflart, 1: 134, nos. 271–72. On Jullienne as an aspiring artist, see Vogtherr and Tonkovich, *Jean de Jullienne: Collector and Connoisseur*.

81 "[. . .] On espère que le public verra d'un oeil favorable les desseins de Célèbre Watteau qu'on luy présente ici. Ils sont d'un goust nouveau, ils ont des grâces tellement attachée à l'esprit de l'auteur qu'on peut avancer qu'ils sont inimitables. Chaque figure sortie de la main de cet excellent homme a un Caractère si vrais et si naturel que toute seule elle peut remplir et satisfaire l'attention, et semble n'avoir pas besoin d'être soutenue par la Composition d'un plus grand sujet." Jullienne, "Préface" to the *Figures*, reprinted in Dacier and Vuaflart, 2: 6.

82 On Watteau's working method, see Comte de Caylus, *La Vie d'Antoine Wateau [sic], Peintre de Figures et de Paysage*, [1748], in Rosenberg, *Vies anciennes de Watteau*, 78.

83 For the eighteenth-century origins of the modern notion of authorship, see Michel Foucault's classic essay "What Is an Author?" (1969), in *Language, Counter-Memory, Practice*, 124–47. For a historically nuanced account of this multifaceted process of cultural invention, see Nesbitt, "What Was an Author?"; Hesse, "Enlightenment Epistemology and the Laws of Authorship in Revolutionary France, 1777–1793"; and Scott, "Authorship."

84 The term "author" was commonly used to describe anyone who created something original: "Auteur: Qui a créé quelque chose. [. . .] L'Auteur est celui qui n'a pris son ouvrage d'aucun autre; c'est celui qui l'a produit, qui l'a mis au jour. [. . .]" Furetière, *Dictionnaire Universel* (1743). Yet until the introduction of the notion of authorial privilege in France in 1777, such creators had no legal claim on their work. See Hesse, "Enlightenment Epistemology," 114–16. For the account of the system of royal privileges that regulated the production and circulation of texts and images under the Ancien Régime, see Birn, "The Profit in Ideas: Privilèges en Librairie in Eighteenth-Century France"; Fuhring, "The Print Privilege in Eighteenth-Century France, Part I"; Hesse, "Enlightenment Epistemology"; and Scott, "Authorship."

85 For Gersaint, see Glorieux, *À l'Enseigne*, 385–429. For the role of reproductive prints in this process, see Scott, "Reproduction and Reputation."

86 Regarding the double signatures, see also Hedley, *Seductive Visions*, 3, and Hyde, "Getting into the Picture: Boucher's Self-Portraits of Others," 26–28.

87 In this case, the copyright belonged to Jullienne who, on July 31, 1727, obtained the publishing privilege for Watteau's works in his possession. See Dacier and Vuaflart, 2: 23–24. On copyrights in print trade, see Fuhring, "The Print Privilege" esp. 185.

88 Fraenkel, *La Signature: genèse d'un signe*. For artists' signatures, see also Guichard,

Graffitis: Inscrire son nom à Rome XVIe–XIXe siècle, esp. 121–38; and Guichard "Fragonard et les jeux de la signature."

89 See "Écriture, Art Méchanique," (Diderot), *Encyclopédie*, 5: 371–72.

90 For this point, see Fraenkel, *La Signature*, 10, though she speaks of the sense of permanence rather than, as I want to emphasize, the consistency of the self.

91 Boucher does not sign his work for Jullienne consistently. The type of (the internal) signature he used for the frontispiece appeared on several other etchings that came from his hands, but others bore only an abbreviated form "bouch" or his initial, and some were not signed at all. (I have examined two complete editions that are in the print collections of the Metropolitan Museum of Art and the New York Public Library, both in New York.)

92 On Watteau's practice of not signing his work as linked to his employment in the commercial context, see Vogtherr, *Watteau at the Wallace Collection*.

93 For this association, see notably Crow, *Painters and Public Life*, chap. 2.

94 The epigraph for this section was taken from Grimm et al., *Correspondence litteraire*, 2: 282 (1753), cited in *Boucher* 1986, 106. "Il y a longtemps qu'on appelle ce peintre un peintre d'éventail."

95 Desboulmiers, "Éloge de M. Boucher," 184.

96 "les dessus-de-porte, les panneaux des voitures, la folie bisarre des pantins [qui] exercèrent ses pinceaux." Restout, *Galerie française*, in Ananoff, 134.

97 "[. . .] entrainé par les caprices de la mode et peut-être par la nécessité de se conserver des acheteurs, ils se livré quelque fois à des genres trop inférieurs à ces talens; [. . .] "imagination trop complaisainte," Restout, *Galerie française*, in Ananoff, 134.

98 His pupil, Fragonard, would be vilified for similar reasons. See chap. 3 below.

99 "les arts sont forcés de s'avilir." Bret, "Éloge de M. Boucher," in Ananoff, 134.

100 On prejudice or unease around the relation between Boucher and the milieu of "ornemanistes" persisting in the accounts of his career, see Brugerolles and Guillet, "Un de ces Hommes," 19–27.

101 The notable exception is Katie Scott's brilliant essay, "Reproduction and Reputation," although it addresses only a fraction of Boucher's output, namely prints. For an attempt to conceptualize Boucher's artistic identity in relation to an integrated notion of his practice, see my "Image Matters."

102 *Ornemaniste* commonly designated an artisan charged with the execution of an ornamental design produced by an artist, such as Boucher. In this it differed from *dessinateur* or *décorateur*, both referring to artists involved in the design of interior decorations, a function related to, and remaining in some tension with, that of an architect. On these terms and the tensions around them, see Fuhring, "Boucher et les Dessinateurs d'Ornement," esp. 246–50. The literature on Boucher as designer is considerable. Some of the fundamental sources are: Standen, "Boucher as a Tapestry Designer"; Faÿ-Hallé, "The Influence of Boucher's Art on the Production of the Vincennes-Sèvres Porcelain Factory"; Laing, "A Group of Boucher's Designs for Coach Panels"; Brunel, "Boucher: Le Corps et le Décor"; Joulie, "Boucher et les Arts Décoratifs"; and Joulie, "The Decorative Arts: Illustration, Invention, and Dissemination."

103 On Huquier's card, see Peter Fuhring in *Boucher et l'Art Rocaille*, nos. 67–68. On Huquier as a promoter of quality design and the publisher of the output of Meissonier and Oppenord, see Scott, *The Rococo Interior*, 261 and n. 101, 305; and Fuhring, *Boucher et l'Art Rocaille*, 278. See also Bailey, "Was There Such a Thing as Rococo Painting in Eighteenth-Century France?," 184. Following Fuhring, Bailey has suggested that the placement of Boucher's *Oeuvre* in the card indicates that Huquier planned to publish a complete print edition of his designs.

104 See Fuhring, "Boucher et les Dessinateurs," 250. For the eighteenth-century uses of the term "décorateur," see also Lavezzi, "The Encyclopédie and the Idea of the Decorative Arts," esp. 39–41.

105 On the meaning and ambiguities of "commerce" as a term, see France, "The Commerce of the Self," in *Politeness and Its Discontents: Problems in French Classical Culture*, esp. 99–101.

106 "Plaire est mon goult." [Alexis Piron], *Placet à Mr De Tourneant Directeur des Bâtiments, aux Fins d'obtenir pour Mr B(oucher) Professeur de l'Academie Royale de Peinture, un Logement au Louvre Vacant par la Mort de Mr Coustou Sculpteur*, February 1746. In Ananoff, 28, no. 255. Written on behalf of Boucher, Piron's was a petition addressed to the new *Directeur des Batiments*, Lenormand de Tournehem to obtain lodgings in the Louvre for the artist.

107 See Jacoby, *François Boucher's Early Development*; Jacoby, "François Boucher's Stylistic Development as a Draftsman"; and Stein, "Notes on the Boucher Exhibitions Marking the Tercentenary of the Artist's Birth."

108 For the *Boy Holding a Parsnip*, see Schoolman Slatkin, *François Boucher in North American Collections: 100 Drawings*, 41–42, no. 32; and Hedley, *Seductive Visions*, 61. For the painting from which it was derived (ca. 1735, in a private collection), see *Boucher* 1986, no. 28.

109 For the suggestion that the *Naiades and a Triton* was a presentation drawing rather than a study for the *Rising*, see Stein, "Notes on the Boucher Exhibitions," 173, and Hedley, *Seductive Visions*, 113.

110 For the vogue for drawing, and Boucher's role in it, see Jacoby, "François Boucher's Stylistic Development"; Bailey, "Toute seule"; and Laing, "Boucher—A Painter or a Draftsman Born?," in Laing *Drawings*, 20–37.

111 Boucher started exhibiting autonomous drawings at the Salon of 1745, following an earlier example of Bouchardon, who started the practice in 1737. See Jacoby, "François Boucher's Stylistic Development," 269.

112 See Joulie in *Boucher* RMN 2003, no. 3 (considered as a *Study for the "Rising of the Sun"*). Laing mentions another red chalk drawing of that motif, formerly in the collection of Madame Blondel d'Azincourt, now lost, of which he takes the Louvre *Naiads and Triton*, a property of her husband, to be a copy. (Laing *Drawings*, 194, and 251, no. 74, n. 7.) For Boucher's drawings in Blondel d'Azincourt's collection, see Laing *Drawings*, 35. For the Blondels, Sireuil, and Randon de Boisset as the foremost collectors of Boucher's drawings, see ibid., 31–35.

113 Jacoby, "François Boucher's Stylistic Development," 271.

114 For the discussion of these two works, see Schoolman Slatkin, *François Boucher in North American Collections*, nos. 35 and 44. Shoolman Slatkin dates the Fogg *Reclining Nude* for the late 1730s.

115 See Jacoby, "François Boucher's Stylistic Development," 277–78. On Glomy, see also Bailey, "Toute seule," 78.

116 Bret, "Éloge de M. Boucher." Similar testimony was left by English collector and connoisseur Charles Rogers, who visited the artist's studio in 1765 (*A Collection of Prints in Imitation of Drawings*, 2: 197).

117 Rosenberg and Prat, *Watteau: Catalogue raisonné des Dessins*, 3: 1427.

118 Mannlich, *Histoire de ma Vie: Mémoirs de Johann Christian von Mannlich (1741–1822)*, 1: 157.

119 "Ils nous occupà longtems a copier de ses plus beaux desseins qu'il vouloit garder dans son portefeuille. Ce sont ces copies que nous ne dévions que préparer sans y mettre les derniers touches qu'il rétouchoit pendant son

déjeuner, en fit des origineaux [*sic*] et les vendit deux louis piece." (He kept us busy for a long time copying those of his finest drawings that he wished to retain in his portfolio. These were copies that we only had to sketch out without finishing them and that he would retouch himself during his lunch time, thus turning them into originals to be sold for two *louis* a piece.) Mannlich, *Histoire de ma Vie*. For the discussion of this practice, see Michel, "Boucher Professeur," 98.

120 See François Boucher, *Triton*, ca. 1753–63. Black and white chalk with some stumping on light brown paper. Hertford House Library, The Wallace Collection, London, repr. in Hedley, *Seductive Visions*, 115. As a proof for this supposition, Hedley mentions an identical drawing, now in a private collection, much stronger in treatment, which she suggests was the original after which the Hertford drawing was copied.

121 [une suite d'estampes] "n'a été gravée que sur les desseins informes, furtivement tirés par les élèves de ce Peintre, le moins capables et les moins avancés, livré à son inçu au Graveur, lequel à son tour a terminé et mis en vente ces estampes sans la participation de l'auteur de ces tableaux, qui ne peut ni les reconnoître, ni encore moins les avouer dans des copies aussi infidèles." *Mercure de France*, March 1755, 145–46. For the analysis of Boucher's conflict with Duflos, see Scott, "Authorship," 36–37.

122 Scott, "Reproduction and Reputation."

123 On the crayon-manner technique and its role in the dissemination of drawings, see Bailey, "Toute seule," 83; Smentek, "'An Exact Imitation Acquired at Little Expense': Marketing Color Prints in Eighteenth-Century France"; and Raux, "La Main Invisible: Innovation et concurrence chez les créateurs des nouvelles techniques de fac-similés de dessins."

124 Smentek, "An Exact Imitation Acquired at Little Expense," 14.

125 On Louis Bonnet's first trois crayons engraving of Boucher, see Smentek, "An Exact Imitation Acquired at Little Expense," 15–16, and Raux in *Quand la Gravure fait Illusion: Autour de Watteau et Boucher, le Dessin gravé au XVIIIe Siècle*, nos. 28–30.

126 For Demarteau's alterations of Boucher's designs, see Griffiths, "The Search for Facsimile," 164–65. For Demarteau's *Naiades with a Triton*, see Raux in *Quand la Gravure*, no. 58. For the effect of Demarteau's reproductions, see Scott, "Reproduction and Reputation," 114–19.

127 Smentek, "An Exact Imitation," 16–17, and fig. 5.

128 On this, see Stein, "Notes on the Boucher Exhibitions," 172; and, at length, Scott, "Reproduction and Reputation," esp. 122–23.

129 For his early work for Cars, gathered in the so-called album Cazes in the Louvre, see Joulie in *Boucher* RMN 2003, 25–29. For Boucher's illustrations for an edition of Molière, published in 1734–35, for J. B. Guer's book *Moeurs et Usages des Turcs* (his drawings for it exhibited at the Salon of 1745), and, later in his career, notably for Ovid's *Metamorphoses*, see Joulie, in *Boucher* RMN 2003, nos. 75–76.

130 For Boucher's involvement in tapestry design, see Standen, "Boucher as Tapestry Designer," 325–44; Joulie, "Boucher Decorateur: Dessins pour la Manufacture de Beauvais"; and Joulie, "Boucher et les arts décoratifs," 84–90.

131 Standen, "Boucher as Tapestry Designer," 331.

132 See Faÿ-Hallé, "The Influence of Boucher's Art"; Savill, "François Boucher and the Porcelains of Vincennes and Sèvres"; and Savill, "Boucher: The Muse for Sèvres Porcelain and Gold Boxes in the Wallace Collection." For the engraving of Boucher's designs for porcelain published by Falconet at Joullains, see Jean-Richard, *L'Oeuvre gravé*, nos. 1233–36.

133 For the figure of *Jeune Suppliant*, see Préaud and Hallé, *Porcelaine de Vincennes*, 170, no. 491; and, with the reproduction of the drawing and a painting with the same motif, Préaud, *La Manufacture des Lumières: La Sculpture à Sevrès de Louis XV à la Révolution*, nos. 14, 14b, and 14c. The tea service was reproduced in Savill, "François Boucher and the Porcelains."

134 Sales catalog quoted in Savill, "François Boucher and the Porcelains," 162.

135 See Laing in *Boucher* 1986, 214–16; Joulie in *Boucher* RMN 2003, no. 45; and Ledbury, "Boucher and Theater," esp. 133–39 and 144–60.

136 For the Narbonne design, see Joulie, *Boucher* RMN 2003. See also Laing, *Boucher* 1986, no. 47, for the stage set designed for Charles-Simon Favart's *Les Amours Grivois*, now in Musée de Picardie, Amiens.

137 *Premier Livre de Fontaines* (1736) was engraved by Huquier, and the second volume published in 1738, engraved by Pierre Aveline. For the suggestion that Boucher did the drawings expressly for Huquier, see Joulie in *Boucher* RMN 2003, nos. 43, 93. For Boucher's fountains projects, see also her "Boucher et les arts decoratifs"; and Joulie in *Boucher* Gammel Holtegaard, no. 16.

138 *Nouveaux Morceaux pour des Paravants*, engraved by Charles Duflos, published in 1737, of which one original design by Boucher, *Rocaille*, has been preserved. See Fuhring in *Boucher* ÉNSBA 2003, no. 25. *Livre de Cartouches inventés par François Boucher, Peintre du Roi*, twelve of which were engraved by Huquier. For the cartouche design of *Neptune's Chariot* reproduced here, see Jean-Richard, *L'Oeuvre gravé*, 276, no. 1120. For the suite of vase designs by Boucher engraved by Huquier, see Fuhring, *Boucher* ÉNSBA 2003, 252. For clock designs, see Shoolman Slatkin, *François Boucher in North American Collections*, no. 86; and Joulie, "Boucher et les arts décoratifs," 89; and Joulie in *Boucher* Gammel Holtegaard, no. 17. For Boucher's numerous designs for *écrans* (a type of fan), many of them engraved by Huquier, see Jean-Richard, *L'Oeuvre gravé*, 127, nos. 397–400; and Brugerolles in *Boucher* ÉNSBA 2003, 64, ill. 3. For the fan design with Bacchus and Ariadne, see Schoolman Slatkin, *François Boucher in North American Collections*, no. 62. For a previously unpublished later stage design for this fan, and for discussion of Boucher's fan design in general, see Joulie, *Boucher* Gammel Holtegaard, 54–57, no. 15.

139 See Schoolman Slatkin, *François Boucher in North American Collections*, no. 87. She mentions Boucher designed a whole compendium of the *Tombeaux des Princes* (ibid., 20).

140 See Jean-Richard, *L'Oeuvre gravé*, nos. 12–20; 230–34, and 854. See also Stein, "Les Chinoiseries de Boucher," and David Pullins, "François Boucher's Activation of *Les Cinq Sens*," unpublished paper for my seminar "The Ethnographic Imagination" (Fall 2008), and delivered at the Frick Symposium in Spring 2009.

141 For luxury trades, see Sonenscher, *Work and Wages*, esp. 210–43; Thirsk, "Luxury Trades and Consumerism"; and Coquery, "The Language of Success: Marketing and Distributing Semi-Luxury Goods in Eighteenth-Century Paris."

142 See McKendrick, Brewer, and Plumb, *The Birth of Consumer Society: The Commercialization of Eighteenth-Century England*; Brewer, "'The Most Polite Age and the Most Vicious': Attitudes Towards Culture as a Commodity, 1660–1800"; Roche, *History of Everday Things*; Pardailhé-Galabrun, *The Birth of Intimacy: Privacy and Domestic Life in Early Modern Paris*; Berg and Clifford, *Consumers and Luxury*; and Coquery, "The Language of Success."

143 "Ainsi l'on voit en Angleterre, en France, / Par cent Canaux circuler l'abondance. / Le goût du Luxe entre dans tout les rangs." François-Marie Arouet [Voltaire], *Défense du Mondain*, in Morizé, *L'Apologie du Luxe aux XVIIIe Siècle et "Le Mondain" de Vol-*

taire: Étude Critique sur "Le Mondain" et ses Sources, 156.

144 Roche, *History of Everyday Things*, 53.

145 See ibid., and Roche, *Culture of Clothing*, esp. 67–85 and 501–20. For the erosion of the social and political concept of *répresentation* due to consumption, see also Shovlin, "The Cultural Politics of Luxury in Eighteenth-Century France."

146 See Roche, *The Culture of Clothing*; Roche, "Consumption and Appearance," in *France in the Enlightenment*, 548–77; and Shovlin, "Cultural Politics of Luxury in Eighteenth-Century France."

147 See Brewer, "The Most Polite Age," 345.

148 For the view of rococo as both product and symptom of commercial society, see Scott, *The Rococo Interior*.

149 Ibid., 252–65.

150 For a gold snuffbox based on Boucher's design, see Hedley, *Seductive Visions*, 77, fig. 61.

151 The design for this group, listed in the Vincennes inventory for 1752, has been lost, but it is assumed that it was provided by Boucher himself. See Castex, "L'utilisation de l'estampe et la peinture par les artistes et les ateliers," 61.

152 Joulie, "The Decorative Arts: Illustration, Invention, and Dissemination," 54.

153 See, however, Scott, "Reproduction and Reputation," for a related claim about Boucher's reliance on dissemination through print.

154 "beauty and, more difficult to render still, the graces, [were] reproduced by his brush in *thousand different forms*." ("M. Boucher vit toujours la beauté et les graces plus difficiles à saisir qu'elle se reproduire sous son pinceau *en mille formes differents*.") Bret, "Éloge de M. Boucher," italics mine.

155 For the "goût Boucher" in porcelain promotion, see Savill, "François Boucher and the Porcelains," 168.

156 Brunel, *Boucher*, 12.

157 For the changing mode of artisanal operation in this period, however, see Stürmer, "An Economy of Delight: Court Artisans of the Eighteenth Century," esp. 516 and 522. For the image of the artisan, see Sonenscher, *Work and Wages*, 42–72.

158 See Roche, *Culture of Clothing*.

159 Design for the frontispiece for the *Premier Livre de Groupes d'Enfants*. See Georges Brunel in *Boucher* ÉNSBA 2003, no. 24.

160 The location of the paintings was given in Derbais's posthumous inventory. See *Inventaire après le Décès de Mr. Derbais*, 2 Mars 1743, Minutier Central, LIX. 230 (item 56). For the discussion of these works, see Laing, "Boucher: The Search for an Idiom," and Laing in *Boucher* 1986, nos. 17–18; Brunel *Boucher*, 59–71; Bailey, *Loves of the Gods: Mythological Painting from Watteau to David*, nos. 43 and 44; and Hedley, *Seductive Visions*, 36–46.

161 Boucher was accepted as an associate member of the Academy in November 1731, but became a full member only in January 1734.

162 Mariette, *Abecedario*, 1: 165.

163 "Ses ingénieuses compositions attirerent un concours d'admirateurs, qui publièrent les talens de ce jeune artiste." Papillon de la Ferté, *Extrait des différens ouvrages*, 658.

164 Laing, *Boucher* 1986, 158, proposed the first possibility (private patrons), Bailey (*The Loves of the Gods*, 387) has suggested the second (tapestry manufacture). The works were indeed known to Boucher's contemporaries, e.g., Bachaumont, who saw them in situ. (Laing, ibid., 159.)

165 La Font de Saint-Yenne, *Réflexions*, 68–69.

166 The painting collection is listed in Derbais's inventory. Archives Nationales, *Minutier Central*, LIX, 230. On the *parlementaires* as collectors, see Bonfait, "Les Collections des parlementaires parisiens au XVIIIe Siècle."

167 For the consumerist fortune of the hôtel, see Coquery, *L'Hôtel Aristocratique: Le Marché du Luxe à Paris au XVIIIe Siècle*. See also Dewald, *Aristocratic Experience and the Origins of Modern Culture: France 1570–1715*, 146–73.

168 See Étienne, *Le Fabourg Poissonnière: Architecture, Élégance et Décor*.

169 Dennis, *Court and Garden: From the French Hôtel to the City of Modern Architecture*, 96.

170 *Inventaire après le Décès de Mr. Derbais*, folio 4.

171 Stürmer, "An Economy of Delight," 496.

172 On this issue, see Pons, *De Paris à Versailles, 1699–1736: Les Sculpteurs ornemanistes Parisiens et l'Art décoratif des Bâtiments du Roi*, 135–45; Scott, *Rococo Interior*, 15–47; and Bailey, *Loves of the Gods*, 386.

173 E.g., La Font de Saint-Yenne, *Réflexions*; Charles-Nicolas Cochin, "Supplication aux Orfèvres, Ciseleurs, Sculpteurs en Bois pour les Appartements et autres par une Sociéré des Artistes," *Mercure de France*, December 1754, 178–87, and La Font de Saint-Yenne, "Lettre à 'Abbé R[aynal]," ibid., February 1755, 148–71. See Scott, "Rococo and Its Critics," in *Rococo Interior*, 252–65.

174 Voltaire, *Temple du Goût*. On Voltaire, see Scott, *Rococo Interior*, 253–54.

175 For the relatively recent rediscovery of the *Birth of Venus*, which Laing suggests was painted first, see Laing, "La Re-Naissance de Vénus: Un Oeuvre de Débuts de Boucher Retrouvé à Paris," 77–81, no. 3. Because the paintings were listed in Derbais's inventory only by their titles, the exact number of Boucher's works is not absolutely certain, but we assume it was nine canvases, of which the five large-scale mythological subjects listed here hang in the billiard room and four others, featuring groups of Loves representing the Four Seasons, in the hall with the staircase. See Derbais's *Inventaire*, folio 4. Only one of the hallway overdoors, the Houston *Love the Harvester* (reproduced in Hedley, *Seductive Visions*, 45, fig. 61), is extant, the other three being known only through engravings by Lepicié, Aveline, and Fessard. For these, see Brunel, *Boucher*, 62–63, figs. 23, 25–27.

176 Laing, in *Boucher* 1986, 157.

177 All three are believed to have been executed before the vertical panels. See Laing, "The Re-Naissance of Venus," 78; and Duffy and Hedley, *The Wallace Collection's Pictures: A Complete Catalogue*, 50–51.

178 Virgil, *The Aeneid*, book 8, and Ovid, *Metamorphoses*, vol. 7.

179 On Lemoyne's impact, see Brunel, *Boucher*, 59–71, and for the Berger pendants in particular, see Hedley, *Seductive Visions*, 39.

180 For eloquent analysis of this aspect of the paintings, see Bryson, *Word and Image*, 95–96.

181 Ovid, *Metamorphoses*, 7: 391–93. Cephalus resisted Aurora's advances because he was in love with his own wife, Procris. His ambivalence was clearly registered in Lemoyne' s version of the same theme painted in 1724 for the duc de Bourbon's bedroom in the Hôtel du Grand Maître in Versailles (present Hôtel de Ville). For this overdoor, and the *modello* for it (private collection), see Bordeaux, *François Le Moyne and His Generation, 1688–1737*, 97–99, no. P50, fig. 46 and pl. 3. For the earlier Italian renditions of the subject, including Pietro da Cortona and Sebastiano Ricci, see also Bailey, *Loves of the Gods*, 64–65.

182 The watering can is held by a putto next to Cephalus, at the right edge of the canvas.

183 A preparatory drawing for the figure of Cephalus, in a private collection in Germany, was reproduced in Bailey, *Love of the Gods*, 389, fig. 3, and Laing *Drawings*, 27, fig. 18. A preparatory drawing for the figure of Mercury that was at Christie's was reproduced by Hedley, *Seductive Visions*, 43, fig. 29. Compositional oil sketches for the *Rape of Europa* and *Mercury* are in the Musée de Picardie, Amiens, and in the Cincinnati Art Museum, respectively.

184 Similarly, the *Rape of Europa* emphasizes the erotic prominence of the woman who is not so much being ravished as being shown. See repr. in Laing, "La Re-Naissance de Vénus."

185 This is especially clear in the comparison of Boucher's *Venus and Vulcan* to Charles-Joseph Natoire's far more *sage* rendition of the same theme. (*Venus Demanding Arms from Vulcan*, 1734, Musée Fabre, Montpellier.) See Bailey, *Loves of the Gods*, 384; and Janet M. Brooke, in *Les Peintres du Roi, 1648–1793*, 156–57, no. 12.

186 Laing, *Boucher* 1986, 136.

187 See Pomian, *Collectors and Curiosities: Paris and Venice, 1500–1800*, 52–53.

188 *Luxury and Capitalism*, 61.

189 Marx's notion of commodity fetishism does that too, but Marx believes eros is economically induced whereas Sombart thinks it is the other way around.

190 Laing, *Boucher* 1986, 133; Bailey, *Loves of the Gods*, 384.

191 Glazed *trumeaux* and large size mirrors (e.g., "Un grand miroir d'une seule glace de quarante-quatre pouces de haut sur vingt-neuf de large dans sa bordure en chapiteau (? illegible) noir de figures en ornement de cuivre dor prisé deux cents cinquante livres") appear repeatedly in the inventory. (*Inventaire*, folios 3–13, mirror f. 3.)

192 Mannlich, *Histoire de ma Vie*, 1: 157. (He is referring to Boucher's later pastorals.)

193 Bryson, *Word and Image*, 93. I am evoking Stürmer's argument in "The Economy of Delight."

194 La Font, *Réflexions*, 68.

195 The term "*pinceau moëlleux*" was used by Watelet, in response to Julien de Parme's diatribe against the *Venus and Vulcan*, both quoted in extenso in Laing, *Boucher* 1986, 136. (Laing translates the term as "charged brush.") See also Mariette's description of Boucher's "firm yet gracious touch" (*pinceau aussi firme qu'il est gracieux*), cited in Laing, *Boucher* 1986, 157.

196 As Bailey has noted (*Love of the Gods*, 381), Boucher conflated two scenes between Venus and Vulcan recounted by Virgil into one, which was not uncommon among artists. My point is that he also de-narrativized these scenes, transforming them into distilled images of an erotic encounter between individuals.

197 For the discussion of this issue in Marivaux (focused on *La Vie de Marianne*), see Russo, "The Self, Real and Imaginary: Social Sentiment in Marivaux and Hume."

198 *Le Paysan parvenu* appeared in installments between 1732 and 1735. See Deloffre, "Introduction," in Marivaux, *Le Paysan parvenu*, 3.

199 Marivaux, *The Upstart Peasant, or the Memoirs of Monsieur****, 197.

200 Ibid., 109, italics mine. I am altering Boyce's translation of the original "orgueil," which he gave, erroneously in my view, as "vanity." "Je voyais une femme de condition d'un certain air qui avait apparemment des valets, un équipage, et qui me trouvait aimable; qui me permettait de lui baiser la main, et qui voulait pas qu'on le sût; une femme enfin qui nous tirait, mon orgeuil et moi, du néant où nous étions encore; car avant ce temps-là m'étais-je estimé quelque chose? Avais-je senti ce que c'était qu'amour propre?" *Le Paysan Parvenu*, 135.

201 Jacob uses the term "amour propre" in a similar sense. On the eighteenth-century radical reevaluation of this notion, as, literally, the love of self rather than mere vanity, see Russo, "The Self, Real and Imaginary," 130–35.

202 For this formulation, see Reddy, *The Rise of Market Culture*, 1–3.

203 Ibid., 1–18.

204 For a psychoanalytic conceptualization of the Imaginary as one of the basic psychic functions, see Lacan, "The Mirror Stage as Formative of the Function of the I," in *Écrits: A Selection*, 1–7. For the construction of fictive subjectivity as an object of consumption in eighteenth-century literature, see Benrekassa, *Les Fables de la Personne*, and Russo, "The Self, Real and Imaginary."

205 See Rousseau, *Discours sur l'Origine et Fondements de l'Inégalité parmi les Hommes*, 235.

206 For Chedel's *Livre de Fantaisies*, see Scott, *Rococo Interior*, 249.

207 For this point, see Scott, *Rococo Interior*, 248–50.

208 In the Louvre painting he signs in the bottom right—*f boucher 1732*—that is, under Venus; in the Nancy painting, he signs—*boucher/173[3?]*— in the bottom center, which is on the axis of Aurora and the obfuscated putto.

209 For the argument about Boucher as an artist operating under the sign of Venus, see also Hyde, "Getting into the Picture," 21–25.

210 Scrutton, "Flesh from the Butcher," *Times Literary Supplement*, April 15, 2005, 11. Thanks to Jeffrey Hamburger for bringing this essay to my attention.

211 The putto behind a cloud thus illustrates the basic premise behind a semiotic conception of the self: insofar as the assumption of the visual sign involves a splitting of the subject between the signifier and signified, it also implies its partial eclipse by the signifier.

212 The *Leda and the Swan* was bought by Tessin in 1742, and is now in Stockholm, the version reproduced here is in the Resnick Collection.

213 See Joulie in *Boucher* RMN 2003, no. 62.

214 The epigraph for this section is taken from Marivaux's *La Vie de Marianne*, 114. "J'étais tout émue de plaisir de penser à ce qui aller en arriver [du mérite de ma petite figure], j'en perdais presque haleine."

215 On the growing taste for Dutch and Flemish paintings, both noted and deplored, see Bailey, *Patriotic Taste: Collecting Modern Art in Pre-Revolutionary Paris*, 18–20.

216 Laing spoke of "commercial speculation" being at the origins of *Le Déjeneur*, and he evoked Boucher's explicit intention to match or rival de Troy's productions of this kind. (*Boucher* 1986, 181.) On eighteenth-century genre painting, see Rand, "Love, Domesticity, and the Evolution of Genre Painting in Eighteenth-Century France"; Bailey, "Surveying Genre in Eigheenth-Century Painting"; and Michel, "Nature and Moeurs: Thoughts on the Reception of Genre Painting in France."

217 On the uses and meaning of commodity in eighteenth-century France, see Roche, *History of Everyday Things*, esp. 12–30; and Kwass, "Ordering the World of Goods." *Commodité*, which literally meant "convenience," was used in the French context to describe "the quality by which objects, such as pieces of furniture interacted with the body in pleasant way." (Ibid., 94.) In England, its equivalent was "comfort" (which, ironically, was adopted from the French word *confort*), a term the French did not use in this sense until the nineteenth century. *Commodité* predominated in eighteenth-century France, where it had a wider signification, denoting a broad range of objects, from tools of labor to objects of pleasure and taste. For comfort and *confort*, see also Crowley, *The Invention of Comfort: Sensibilities and Design in Early Modern Britain and Early America*; Roche, *History of Everyday Things*, 107–8; Perrot, "De l'apparat au bien-être: Les avatars d'un superflu necessaire"; and Vigarello in *Histoire des pratiques de santé. Le sain et le malsain depuis le Moyen Âge*.

218 For the *tableau de mode* as a term and a type of painting, see Leribault, *Jean François de Troy (1679–1752)*, 72, and Leribault, in *The Age of Watteau, Chardin, and Fragonard: Masterpieces of French Genre Painting*, 172. For its association with de Troy and earlier with Watteau, see Bailey, "Surveying Genre," 21–23.

219 "Mais qu'est-ce que le luxe, sinon une suite de bagatelles métamorphosées en choses de conséquence?" [Deslandes, M. (André François)], *Lettre sur le Luxe*, 33.

220 Diderot, *Encyclopédie*, 5: 635A. For the discussion of the instability of the term, see Rétat, "Luxe."

221 Veblen's analysis, offered in his *The Theory of the Leisure Class: An Economic Study in the Evolution of Institutions*, emphasized the pursuit of higher social status as the main motivation of consumption. For its impact and its critique, see McKendrick, Brewer, and Plumb, *Birth of Consumer Society*; and Kwass, "Ordering the World," 87. See also Berg and Eger, "The Rise and Fall of the Luxury Debates."

222 For the reception of Mandeville's *Fable* in France, see Ross, "Mandeville, Melon, and Voltaire: The Origins of the Luxury Controversy in France"; and Hundert, "Mandeville, Rousseau, and the Political Economy of Fantasy."

223 "Thus every Part was full of Vice, / Yet the whole Mass a Paradise." Mandeville, *Fable of the Bees*, 247. For the discussion of this point, see Hundert, "Mandeville, Rousseau," 37. It was Mandeville's recognition that Sombart developed in his political theory of the origins of capitalism as an alternative to Marx and Weber.

224 For the discussion of François Melon's *Essai politique sur le commerce* (1734), and Voltaire, see Ross, "Mandeville, Melon, and Voltaire."

225 Voltaire, *Le Mondain*, in Morizé, *L'Apologie du Luxe aux XVIIIe Siècle et "Le Mondain" de Voltaire*, 133. (I love luxury, even indolence, / All pleasures, the arts of all kind, / Propriety, taste, ornaments: / Every *honnête homme* [cultivated man] has such sentiments.)

226 In the stanza following the one quoted here, Voltaire evoked the "vile heart" of *le mondain* ("*mon coeur très immonde*") that echoed Mandeville's provocative insistence on the essential viciousness of man as the very source of social wealth and common good.

227 "le superflu, chose très necessaire," *Le Mondain*, 134.

228 For the moral reevaluation of self-love and vanity, see Russo, "Self, Real and Imaginary." Voltaire himself was more critical of a certain version of commercial personality when, in his *Temple du Goût*, mentioned earlier, he ridiculed the vulgar taste and false cultural ambition of the newly rich through a Croesus-like figure caught in the grip of a megalomaniac building folly.

229 Rousseau, *Discours sur les Sciences et les Arts*, and *Discours sur l'Origine de L'Inégalité parmi les Hommes*. I will refer to the English translation in *The First and Second Discourses*. For Rousseau's emphasis on the subjective losses as a symptom of a gradual shift occurring in the debate on luxury from the idea of social uses, to personal benefits, see Kwass, "Ordering the World," esp. 88–89.

230 Rousseau, "Second Discourse," in *The First and Second Discourses*, 147.

231 Ibid., 155–56.

232 Ibid., 179.

233 For Rousseau's critique in relation to Mandeville's views, see Hundert, "Mandeville, Rousseau"; and Hundert, *The Enlightenment's Fable: Bernard Mandeville and the Discovery of Society*.

234 While *Le Déjeuner* has sometimes been translated as *The Luncheon*—the arms of the wall clock could be seen to indicate two o'clock in the afternoon rather than ten past eight in the morning—I have opted for the more common translation as *Breakfast*, given the visible absence of any substantial meal. For the change in meal schedule during the Regency, including the appearance of breakfast (*petit déjeuner*), inspired by early morning meals in religious communities, and coffee replacing the more traditional milk soup, see Meyer, *La vie quotidienne en France au Temps de la Régence*, 133.

235 Although it has been sometimes seen as a hot chocolate pot, or a teapot (e.g., Hedley, *Seductive Visions*, 64), Laing has identified the wide-bottom, high-spouted silver serving pot as a typical *cafetière* (*Boucher* 1986, 181).

236 Voltaire, *Défense du Mondain*, 154. Bach's cantata is about a father trying to get his daughter off her serious addiction to coffee. For the eighteenth-century taste for coffee, tea, and chocolate, see Meyer, *La vie quotidienne*, 136–37; and Camporesi, *Exotic Brew: The Art of Living in the Age of Enlightenment*.

237 For Liotard's *Le Déjeuner Lavergne*, see Roethlisberger and Loche, *Liotard: Catalogue, Sources et Correspondence*, 1: 464–67, no. 299.

238 For the painting, see Leribault, *Jean-François de Troy*, 72–73 and 322–23 (P.203).

239 *De la distribution des maisons de plaisance et de la décoration des édifices en général* (1737–38). Boucher represents a typical "private apartment." For Blondel, see Braham, *Architecture of the French Enlightenment*, chap. 2; and Picon, *Architectes et Ingénieurs*, 53–94.

240 See Sargentson, *Merchants and Luxury Markets: The Marchand Merciers of Eighteenth-Century Paris*, and Kisluk-Grosheide, "The Reign of Magots and Pagods."

241 *Lettre sur le Luxe*, 33.

242 81 × 65.5 cm versus de Troy's 74 × 93 cm.

243 See Pardailhé-Galabrun, *Birth of Intimacy*, and Roche, *History of Everyday Things*, esp. chap. 3. See also Maza, *Myth of the French Bourgeoisie / An Essay in the Social Imaginary, 1750–1850*, chap. 2.

244 See Maza, *Myth of the French Bourgeoisie*, 41–61. For the transformation of the aristocratic *hôtels* into emblematic sites of conspicuous consumption, see Coquery, *L'Hôtel Aristocratique*.

245 Pardailhé-Galbrun, *Birth of Intimacy*, 93. For the widespread vogue for porcelain in this period, see also Smentek, *Rococo Exotic: French Mounted Porcelains and the Allure of the East*.

246 Brooks, "Marianne in the World," in *The Novel of Wordliness*, 96–99. *La Vie de Marianne* was published in installments, between 1731 and 1742, right before and during Boucher's production of the group of his genre paintings discussed here.

247 "Il y avait une *douce sympathie* entre mon imagination et le objets que je voyais, et je devinais qu'on pouvait tirer de cette multitude de choses différentes je ne sais combien d'agréments que je connaissais pas encore; enfin il me semblait que le plaisirs habitaient au millieu de tout cela." *La Vie de Marianne*, 69, italics mine.

248 For a discussion of Chardin's painting in relation to fashion for tea, see Duleau, *Boucher and Chardin: Masters of Modern Manners*. For the Liotard, see Roethlisberger and Loche, *Liotard*, cat. 130.

249 See *Chardin* 2000, no. 46.

250 See *Inventaire après décès de Marguierite Saintaird, épouse Chardin* (Archives Nationales, Minutier Central, Étude CXVII, liasse 417), where the table featured in the painting is listed. The inventory was published in Pascal and Gaucheron, *Documents sur la Vie et l'Oeuvre de Chardin*. See Savina, "Biographie," in *Chardin* 1979, 384.

251 Baxandall, "Pictures and Ideas: Chardin's *Lady Drinking Tea*."

252 Albrecht Dürer's *The Four Apostles* panels (1526, Alte Pinakothek, Munich) come to mind.

253 See Camporesi, *Exotic Brew*, 108–14 and 140–44, and Mousseau, *Thé, Café, ou Chocolat? Le Boissons exotiques à Paris au XVIIIe Siècle*.

254 Although some scholars saw *Le Déjeuner* as an image of a family, even as a representation of Boucher's own household, this suggestion, due to lack of any corroborating evidence, has been dismissed in favor of a more widely accepted view of the aproned figure as a servant. See Laing, *Boucher* 1986, 181.

255 For the importance of Dutch and Flemish genre painting for Boucher, see Joulie, *Boucher et les Peintres du Nord*.

256 On the changing role of servants in the eighteenth century, see Maza, *Servants and Masters in Eighteenth-Century France: The Uses of Loyalty*, and Fairchilds, *Domestic Enemies: Servants and Their Masters in Old Regime France*.

257 For servants as liminal figures in a social sense, see Maza, *Servants and Masters*.

258 As Brunel aptly put it, "son corps fait parti du décor." "Boucher: Le Corps et le Decor," 91. One is also reminded of Fairchilds's comment on the effect of liveries on the status of servants in eighteenth-century households: "When they donned their gold-laced coats, lackeys became part of the decorative background of their masters' lives; a liveried domestic was all too often in the eyes of his employer just one more fancy *objet d'art* adorning the *antichambre*." *Domestic Enemies*, 103.

259 On the Chicago drawing, see Laing *Drawing*, 125, no. 41 (though the drawing is reproduced in reverse).

260 Wahrman, *Making of Modern Self: Identity and Culture in Eighteenth-Century England*, 182. See also Deidre Lynch on the market economy's impact on the definition of character in the English novel wherein "the individual specimen of character is meant to refer to an overarching standard of impersonal uniformity." *Economy of Character: Novels, Market Culture, and the Business of Inner Meaning*, 40.

261 Michael Fried, *Absorption and Theatricalit: Painting and Beholder in the Age of Diderot*.

262 For the analysis of the gaze as a new principle of the "post-sacred" world that emerged in the eighteenth century, see Copjec, "The Invention of Crying," in *Imagine There's No Woman*, esp. 110–18.

263 This is then a deliberate complication of the Rousseauian distinction, cited earlier ("Second Discourse," 179), between living within oneself and existing only in the gaze of others. I am adapting and altering the Lacanian notion of the gaze to conceptualize this new historically determined principle of social visibility.

264 For de Hooch's and others' paintings as exemples of the clear distinction between the inside and outside evident in Dutch culture, see Simon Schama, *The Embarassment of Riches: An Interpretation of Dutch Culture in the Golden Age*, 570–71.

265 An argument developed by Marx, see "Fetishism of Commodities and the Secret Thereof," in *Capital: A Critique of Political Economy*, 1: 76–87.

266 Rousseau, "Second Discourse," 155–56.

267 The etymology of the "trope" is linked to the Greek *tropos*: turn, way, manner style, akin to the Greek verb *trepein*: to turn (OED).

268 See Laing in *Boucher* 1986, no. 38, and Hedley, *Seductive Visions*, 71.

269 On the circumstances of this commission, see Laing in *Boucher* 1986, no. 51.

270 See Fairchilds, "The Production and Marketing of Populuxe Goods in Eighteenth-Century Paris"; and Berg, "New Commodities, Luxuries, and their Consumers in Eighteenth-Century England."

271 On these *marchandes*, also called *mercières* or *dentelières*, see Mercier, "Marchandes de Modes," in *Tableau de Paris*, vol. 1, DXXXVI, 1478; and Maza, *Myth of the French Bourgeoisie*, 49.

272 Roche, *Culture of Clothing*. See also Jones, *Sexing* La Mode*: Gender, Fashion, and Commercial Culture in Old Regime France*.

273 For perceptive remarks on the non-narrative dimension of Boucher's art, see Lipton, "Women, Pleasure, and Painting (e.g., Boucher)," 75. On the conceptual instability of eighteenth-century genre painting in general, see Susan L. Siegfried, "Femininity and the Hybridity of Genre Painting."

274 See Holmes, *Nicolas Lancret, 1690–1743*, no. 16. Rand suggests Boucher may have seen the Lancret at the Salon of 1739 (*Intimate Encounters*, 112).

275 Hedley, *Seductive Visions*, 71.

276 For the fashionable details, see ibid., 70–71.

277 As Bailey put it, "the mood created by so much fashionable bric-à-brac is faintly improper, even lascivious." (*The Age of Watteau*, 222.) Rand saw the myriad of details shown in disarray as a commentary on the lady's impetuous character. (*Intimate Encounters*, 112.)

278 Laing, *Boucher* 1986, 195–96.

279 This small gouache, tentatively identified as Dutch, ca. 1680–1700, and depicting an imagined interior of a Chinese merchant, was originally a fan leaf. See http://collections.vam.ac.uk/itemO96508interior-of-a-chinese-shop-fan-leaf-unknown/.

280 For the uses of metonymy vs. metaphor, see Barthes, *Elements of Semiology*, 58–88.

281 Béat-Louis Muralt, *Lettres sur les Anglois, les Francois, et sur les Voiages* (1728), quoted in Maza, *Masters and Servants*, 202.

282 Deslandes, *Lettre sur le luxe*, 33.

283 Ibid.

284 For the suggestion that the maid is a modiste presenting her wares to the lady, see Ribeiro, *Dress in Eighteenth-Century Europe, 1715–1789*, 38, 178.

285 For a shorter version of this kind of dress being worn by lower classes, see Delpierre, *Dress in France in the Eighteenth Century*, 14. For *robes volantes* in general, and the habit of tucking it especially among servants, see ibid., 10 and 16. Fairchilds has noted apropos Boucher's painting that the only sure indication of this servant's social status is her unpowdered hair. (*Domestic Enemies*, 28.)

286 See Roche, *Culture of Clothing*, and, succinctly, Maza, *Myth of the French Bourgeoisie*, 48–51.

287 Marquis de Mirabeau, *L'Ami des Hommes* (Paris, 1752), quoted in Delpierre, *Dress in France*, 112.

288 J. Berthelé, *Montpellier en 1768*, cited in Maza, *Masters and Servants*, 118.

289 On Marivaux's representation of servants, see Maza, *Masters and Servants*, 236.

290 Roche, *Culture of Clothing*, 111.

291 Maza, *Masters and Servants*.

292 See Laing *Drawings*, no. 72, Laing speculates that the drawing may have been a rehearsal for Tessin's toilette scene. This would make the painting's difference from the Stockholm drawing the more significant. For the elevated status and privileges accorded *femmes* and *valets de chambre* in eighteenth-century households, see Fairchilds, *Domestic Enemies*, 27–28.

293 "Quel fête! C'était la première fois que j'allais jouir en peu du mérite de ma petite figure. J'étais tout émue de plaisir de penser à ce qui aller en arriver, j'en perdais presque haleine; car j'étais sûre du succès, et ma vanité voyait venir d'avance les regards qu'on allait jeter sur moi." *La Vie de Marianne*, 114.

294 "en faveur d'une main nue qui se montrait en y retouchant, et qui amenait nécessairement avec elle un bras rond, qu'on voyait pour le moins à demi, dans l'attitude où je le tenais alors." Ibid., 116.

295 On the change of behavioral models and the emergence of commercial personality evident in the British literature and politeness manuals of the period, see Klein, "Politeness for Plebes: Consumption and Social Identity in Early Eighteenth-Century England."

296 *La Vie de Marianne*, 112. For the analysis of this aspect of the novel, and the new ethics it implied, see Russo, "The Self, Real and Imaginary."

297 On folding screens as a kind of clothing, see Pardhailhé-Galabrun, *Birth of Intimacy*, 122.

298 See Leribault, *Jean-François de Troy*, 335, nos. P22a and 22b. Leribault notes the similarity of the milliner's boxes in Boucher to those of de Troy. I am reproducing a studio copy of de Troy's painting, the original of which is in a private collection.

299 For an entirely different approach to the motif of an empty bed in Fragonard, see chap. 3 here.

300 As Laing has noted (*Boucher* 1986, 218), we have no record of the existence of this picture before the twentieth century, and thus no documentary or even anecdotal basis to think of the Frick painting as Mme Boucher's likeness. The considerable physiognomic difference between the Frick woman and Alexandre Roslin's portrait of Boucher's wife certainly doesn't encourage such identification.

301 Brooks ("Marianne in the World," 97) sees her as "a female predecessor of the Balzacian *arriviste*," though her quest is, I would say, not only for a social position but also for identity tout court.

302 On privacy as an emergent architectural concern, see Eleb-Vidal and Debarre-Blanchard, *Architectures de la vie privée: Maisons et mentalités, XVIIe–XIXe Siècles*; Gallet, *Paris Domestic Architecture of the 18th Century*; Mérot, *Retraites mondaines: Aspects de la décoration intérieure à Paris, au XVIIe siècle*; DeJean, *The Age of Comfort: When Paris Discovered Casual and the Modern Home Began*; and, as a broader cultural concern, Ranum, "The Refuges of Intimacy."

303 Cited in Fontanel, *Daily Life in Art*, 115. (I am altering slightly Fontanel's translation.)

304 Watteau's similar earlier drawing, *Jeune femme allongée sur un lit de répos*, was etched for *Figures des différents caractères* by Boucher's colleague J. Audran. (Prat and Rosenberg, *Antoine Watteau*, no. 274, and fig. 274a.) For the Lugt drawing and related examples, see Bailey in *De Watteau à Degas: Dessins français de la Collection Fritz Lugt*, 40–42, no. 6, and 194, fig. 6.1. Boucher may have been inspired by Watteau's drawing(s), both in his use of the motif of the woman reclining on a daybed and the daybed itself, a typical Regency *lit de répos* that was outmoded in Boucher's time and that is, as it has been noted, dissonant in the context of the Louis XV style furniture in the Frick painting. (See Verlet, *La maison du XVIIIème siècle*, 153, caption to ill. 105.)

305 Lilley, "The Name of the Boudoir."

306 Laing, *Boucher* 1986, 218; and Bailey, *Age of Watteau*, 224.

307 For this iconography, see Rand, *Intimate Encounters*, 154–56; Sheriff, *Moved by Love: Inspired Artists and Deviant Women in Eighteenth-Century France*, 94–96 and 118–19; and Faroult, "La Lecture Dangereuse," 178–81.

308 Freud, "Ego and the Id," in *The Standard Edition*, 19: 30. For the discussion of Freud's concept of narcissism, see Green, *Narcissisme de vie, naricssisme de mort*.

309 For the discussion of an alternative, negative kind of narcissistic relation, see chap. 2 below.

310 See Françoise Borin's brief but incisive discussion of this image in Davis and Farge, *A History of Women in the West*, vol. 3, *Renaissance and Enlightenment Paradoxes*, 230–33. See also Cohen, *Art, Dance, and the Body in French Culture of the Ancien Régime*, 163–65.

311 *Encyclopédie*, 1765, 12: 432–33.

312 E.g., La Font de Saint-Yenne in his *Réflexions*.

313 In the *Toilette*, the signature and the date appear, too, in the lower left, below the objects scattered on the floor. In *Breakfast*, the signature is in the bottom right, to the lower right of the doll.

314 See Kwass, "Ordering the World," 94.

315 Laing, citing Berch's letter to Tessin where the information about the price Boucher customarily charged for such paintings was included. (*Boucher* 1986, 224–45.)

316 It has been noted that overdoors were easier to execute and fetched higher prices, around 800 livres. See Hedley, *Seductive Visions*, 73.

317 In his letter to Tessin's envoy in Paris, Carl Fredrik Sheffer, Boucher excused himself for not finishing the commission, which included *The Miliner*, for the Crown Princess of Sweden, Louisa Ulrika, because of Pompadour's commissions, which, as he hinted at, he was not in a position to refuse. See "Lettre de François Boucher à Carl Fredrik Scheffer, le 29 avril 1750," in Scheffer, *Lettres particulières à Carl Gustaf Tessin, 1744–52*, 253–54.

318 The epigraph for this section is taken from [Pierre Rémy,] "Avant propos," *Catalogue raisonné des Tableaux, Desseins, Estampes, Bronzes, Terres cuites, Laques, Porcelaines de Différentes sortes montées & non montées; Meubles curieux, Bijoux, Minéraux, Cristallisations, Madrepores, Coquilles & autres Curiosités qui composent le Cabinet de Feu M. Boucher, Premier Peintre du Roi*, n.p. "Il desiroit avec la plus grande vivacité tout ce qui lui plaisoit, et . . . rarement il se refusoit au desir de posseder ce qui le flattoit." (Accents missing in the original.)

319 For the beginnings of Boucher's collecting habit, see Joulie, "François Boucher collectionneur de peinture nordique," 17.

320 "Les coquillages sur-tout attiroient les regards, soit par la rareté de l'espèce, soit par la grandeur, soit enfin par l'éclat et la variété de leurs couleurs, jointes à la plus belle conservation. Les minéraux y étoient d'un choix précieux, ainsi que les madrépores et les coraux; on remarquoit parmi ces derniers le rouge articulé, qui passoit deux pieds de hauteur." Desallier [*sic*] D'Argenville, *La Conchyliologie ou Histoire naturelle des Coquilles*, 1: 236. Already in the 1767 edition of Dezallier's pocket guide for the natural history collectors, Boucher's cabinet was described in some details. See [Dezallier d'Argenville], *Conchyliologie nouvelle et portative, ou Collections propres à orner les Cabinets curieux de cette partie de l'Histoire naturelle*, 312–13.

321 On the relation between the objects in Boucher's collection and his work, see Hedley, *Seductive Visions*, 76–77.

322 Joulie, "François Boucher Collectionneur de Peinture Nordique." For Boucher's purchases at the 1745 sale of La Roque's collection (a laquered case, a great number of shells, about three hundred Italian engravings), and for Boucher as Gersaint's client in the 1740s, see Glorieux, *À l'Enseigne*, 323. For his attendance of the sale of another Rémy client, Madame Dubois-Jourdain, see Dietz and Nutz, "Collections Curieuses: The Aesthetics of Curiosity and Elite Lifestyle in Eighteenth-Century Paris," 65, and for Rémy's annotated catalog from that sale, 74, n. 58.

323 For the detailed list of his collection, see [Rémy], *Catalogue Raisonné [du] Cabinet de Feu M. Boucher*.

324 For the attending figures, see Joulie, "François Boucher collectionneur de peinture nordique," and Wille, *Mémoires et Journal de J. G. Wille, Graveur du Roi*, 1: 470.

325 See Pomian, *Collectors and Curiosities*, 124; Stürmer, "An Economy of Delight," 505; Roland Michel, "Vallayer in Her Time," 21, and 35, n. 65. For shell collecting, see also Dance, *A History of Shell Collecting*.

326 See Stafford, *Artful Science: Enlightenment, Education, and the Eclipse of Visual Education*; Dietz and Nutz, "Collections Curieuses"; Lafont, *1740, Un Abrégé du Monde: Savoirs et Collections autour de Dezallier d'Argenville*; and, on natural and physical science collections, Augarde, "The Scientific Cabinet of Comte D'Ons-en-Bray and the Clock by Domenico Cucci," 80.

327 For Oudry's collection, see Bailey, "'A Long Working Life, Considerable Research, and Much Thought': An Introduction to the Art and Career of Jean-Baptiste Oudry (1686–1755)," 25.

328 See Dietz and Nutz, "Collections Curieuses"; Glorieux, *À l'Enseigne*, 430–48.

329 Brunel, *Boucher*, 35. On Boucher's collecting passion and the extent of his financial investment in it, see Jessica S. Priebe, whose important dissertation came to my attention too late to engage with in depth, "*Conchyliologie* to *Conchyliomanie*: The Cabinet of François Boucher, 1703–1770," and Priebe, "The Artist as Collector: François Boucher (1703– 1770)," esp. 29–31.

330 "Ce Peintre ingénieux a placé ses Coquilles sur des tables couvertes de glaces; elle présentent aux yeux du spectateur un

parterre émaillé qui semble le disputer à la nature. A gauche en entrant on trouve une armoire de glace richement remplie de Madrepores, Minéraux, Cailloux, &c. qui sont de toute beauté. [Dezallier d'Argenville], *Conchyliologie Nouvelle*, 312–13.

331 "Un coquillier plaqué en bois de violette, par Oebene, & garni en bronze doré par Philippe Caffieri," lot 1863; lot 1021 lists the 16 glazed-over tables ("Seize tables de différentes grandeurs avec des cases de verre servant de coquilliers"), and other small furniture which was presumably part of the cabinet. See [Rémy], *Catalogue Raisonné [du] Cabinet de Feu M. Boucher*, 262 and 147.

332 For this collection, see Augard, "The Scientific Cabinet," where the *coquillier* is reproduced on 82, fig. 1.

333 Vincent, *Wondertoonel der Natur*, 1706–15. For a sumptuous multidrawer *coquillier* that belonged to Joseph Bonnier de Mosson, see Dance, *A History of Shell Collecting*, 42.

334 Dietz and Nutz, "Collections Curieuses," 45–46; and Lafont, "Du Cabinet à l'*Encyclopédie*: Avoir l'Oeil et la Main à l'Esprit," 6–21; Pelletier, "Cabinet," 60–74; Lacour, "Histoire naturelle," 112–29, all in Lafont, ed., *1740, Un Abrégé du Monde*.

335 For Saint-Aubin's image, see Terpak, "Selling Natural History," 168–69. For the aesthetics of display, see also Guichard, "Parterre" in Lafont, ed., *1740, Un Abrégé du Monde*.

336 Dietz and Nutz, "Collections Curieuses," 48.

337 See Hill, "The Cabinet of Bonnier de la Mosson (1702–1744)"; Morelon, "Unique" in Lafont, ed., *1740, Un Abrégé du Monde*; and Pons, "Hôtel du Lude."

338 See Courtonne, *Recueil des Dessins des Cabinets de Curiosités de M. Bonnier de la Mosson*, Institut National d'Histoire de l'Art, Paris, collections Jacques Doucet. See Hill, "The Cabinet of Bonnier de la Mosson," 153–54, and Morelon, "Unique," 237–39.

339 Dietz and Nutz, "Collections Curieuses," 66.

340 Bonnier was one of those noble amateurs "for whom," as Scott has put it, "science was not yet something to be done or produced so much as taste to be claimed and displayed." *Rococo Interior*, 176. For the discussion of taste as means of both social position-ing and individuation, see Guichard, "Taste Communities."

341 On public access to Bonnier's cabinet, see Hill, "The Cabinet of Bonnier de la Mosson," 151 and 159. Boucher's frontispiece, engraved by Charles Duflos, was designed originally for Gersaint's *Catalogue Raisonné de Coquilles et Autres Curiosités Naturelle* (1736) and reused again in 1737, before reappearing in the Bonnier's collection catalog in 1744. See Glorieux, *À l'Enseigne*, 360–62 and 367–70.

342 "un immense magasin de curiosités de l'art et de la nature, rangés uniquement pour le coup d'oeil et n'offrant aucune suite, mais une multitude de pièces rares et bien conservés." Count Michał Mniszek, "Un gentilhomme polonaise à Paris en 1767," cited in Bailey, "Marie-Jeanne Buzeau, Madame Boucher (1716–1796)," 227.

343 "tout ce qui pouvoit plaire à la vue, devenoit un objet digne de ses recherches, & il ne vouloit point d'autres. La rareté sans agrément n'avoit nul attrait pour lui: aussi ne s'attachoit-il pas à faire des collections suivies; dans chaque genre il ne choisissoit que de choses qui pouvoient plaire, ou par la forme ou par le couleurs." [Rémy], "Avant propos," *Catalogue Raisonné [du] Cabinet de Feu M. Boucher*, n.p. For the identification of shells in Boucher's collection, see Priebe, "*Conchyliologie* to *Conchyliomanie*," chap. 4; on the content of the collection, see also Mulherron, "François Boucher and the Art of Conchology."

344 "CURIEUX signifie Celui qui prend plaisir à faire amas de choses curieuses & rares, ou celui qui a une grande connoissance de ces sortes de choses." (*Curieux* [. . .] designates someone who takes pleasure in gathering curious and rare objects, or someone who has a great knowledge about these kinds of objects.) *Dictionnaire de l'Académie*, 1762.

345 "Ce goût que la nature avoit donné à M. Boucher pour tout ce qui est agréable, faisoit qu'il desiroit avec plus grande vivacité tout ce qui lui plaisoit, & que rarement il se refusoit au desir de posseder ce qui le flattoit. De là cette collection riche; immense & sur tout agréable, qu'il a laissée après son décès." [Rémy], "Avant propos," n.p. (Accents missing in the original.)

346 Rémy's sale catalog lists works by Charles Le Brun, Guido Reni, Cortona, Andrea del Sarto, Van Goyen, Rembrandt, Le Suer, Charles de la Fosse, among others. For the Enlightenment critique of *curiosité*, see Pomian, "Philosophers versus dilettantes," in *Collectors and Curiosities*, 135–38, and Dietz and Nutz, "Collection Curieuses," 46–47.

347 "The case of minerals that I delivered to Monsieur Boucher, that Monsignor le Duc promised him the year before, gave him such pleasure, that weak and decrepit that he was, he could not wait to unpack it. At each rare and well-chosen piece, he cried and was happy as a child. Yet, of all the case he kept only seven pieces for his cabinet, putting the rest aside to barter with the collectors and dealers with whom he had spent his life doing business." Mannlich, *Histoire de ma Vie*, 1: 156.

348 Their attraction, to paraphrase Marx, had to do not with the work of nature or with science based on nature but with the quality of a magic object. See Marx, "Fetishism of Commodities and the Secret Thereof."

349 "L'ordre et l'arrangement pittoresque qu'il avait mis dans la disposition de chaque morceau, formaient un coup d'oeil ravissant, qui ne pouvait être l'ouvrage que d'une âme sensible à l'harmonie de couleurs." Bret, "Éloge." (The order and the picturesque arrangement in the presentation of each object created a ravishing sight, something that could not but be a creation of a mind sensible to the harmony of colors.)

350 "goût auquel peu de gens peuvent prétendre." [Rémy], "Avant propos," n.p.

351 "Il a été aimé de tous ceux qui l'on connu, parceque, naturellement doux, honnête, bienfaisant, il auroit été fâché de nuire à quelqu'un. La finesse de ces pensées, l'agrément de ses idées, et le sel de la plaisanterie qu'il savoit placer à propos, le rendoient très aimable dans la société." Ibid.

352 On the need for aesthetic "improvement" of the collected shells, see Dézallier, *Histoire naturelle éclairci dans deux de ses parties principales, la Lythologie et la Conchyliologie*, 186; and Dezallier, *Conchyliologie Nouvelle*, 86. See also Smentek, *Rococo Exotic*, 23–24. On the abstracting quality of Boucher's depictions of shell and marine forms, see Hedley, *Seductive Visions*, 52–53, and Smentek, *Rococo Exotic*, 29.

353 Guiffrey, "Logements d'artistes au Louvre," *brevet de logement*, 92, no. 139. On the lodgings see also the most useful summary in Bailey, "Marie-Jeanne Buzeau," 226–27.

354 On Boucher's houses and studios before 1752, see Bailey, "Marie-Jeanne Buzeau," 224–25.

355 Ibid., 226. For details of the renovation request, AN O1 1907/140, "Dévis de la dépense a faire a l'Atelier de Monsieur Boucher," October 16, 1752. On details of the reimbursement that Boucher eventually received in 1756, see Brunel, *Boucher*, 36.

356 In March 1752, following the death of J-F. de Troy, Boucher was granted his pension of 1,000 livres. See Laing, *Boucher* 1986, 28.

357 "Ce célèbre artiste s'est pratiqué un fort beau logement, contenant une infinité de curiosités qui méritent l'attention de connoisseurs," Blondel, *Architecture françoise*, 4: 36.

358 Boucher asked for funds to reposition the nonbearing walls in his original request for renovation. The plan of Boucher's studio is at the Archives nationales, Paris, O1 1907/139.

The plan of the first floor of the Louvre (with Boucher's apt. marked as I; fig. 1.78 here), was reproduced in Blondel's *Architecture françoise*, Paris, 1752–56, IV.

359 E.g., "une table de marqueterie de boule [*sic*], en cuivre & etain à quatre gains, avec double traverses, ornée de bronze doré; le dessous est de marbre gruotte d'Italie" (lot 1001), and "une commode de bois d'ébène à trois tiroirs, ornée de masques & trophées, ouvrage de Boule" (lots 143 & 145). [Rémy] *Catalogue raisonné [du] Cabinet de Feu M. Boucher*. For discussion of Boucher's possessions, see also Hedley, *Seductive Visions*, 53–55.

360 "Une boîte à couleur, en forme de cabinet, garni de onze tiroirs, le dessus est de marbre." [Rémy], *Catalogue raisonné [du] Cabinet de Feu M. Boucher*, lot 1077. For other studio utensils, including an *appuie-main* decorated in ivory, and a camera obscura, see ibid., lots 1077–82.

361 Bret asserted that Boucher kept his studio open to visitors, "Éloge," 136. See also Maanlich, *Histoire de ma Vie*, passim.

362 The Chinese house is listed as lot 942 in Boucher's collection sale catalog. In the annotated version I consulted, it was sold for 1,199 livres; for the *pagodes*, see [Rémy], *Catalogue raisonné [du] Cabinet de Feu M. Boucher*, lots 659–80ff. There was also numerous lacquered furniture, Chinese and Japanese porcelain, ancient and new, and other collector's items meticulously registered by Rémy.

363 See Sargentson, *Merchants and Luxury Markets*, 10, plate 4.

364 For the interior decor of the *Petit Dunquerque*, see ibid., 119–36.

365 Coquery, "The Language of Success," 79.

366 See ibid., 78. For Gersaint's novel promotional strategies, see Glorieux, *À l'Enseigne*, 292–93.

367 Sargentson, *Merchants and Luxury Markets*, 121–22.

368 Other artists who used their lodging for representational purposes—though not in a commercially determined way like Boucher—were, notably, Charles-Anotoine Coypel and Jean-Baptiste Oudry. For the latter, see Bailey, "A Long Working Life," 25; for the former, see Scott, "Parade's End: On Charles-Antoine Coypel's Bed and the Origins of Inwardness."

369 Voltaire's *mondain* was dedicated to spending for spending's sake, which is what distinguished his impulses from the desire to accumulate, which characterized other social classes. (As he put it: "Le riche est né pour beaucoup dépenser / Le pauvre est fait pour beaucoup ammasser." Voltaire, *Défénse du Mondain*, 155.)

370 For the relation between Mme de Pompadour and Boucher, see Goodman-Soellner, "Boucher's *Madame de Pompadour at Her Toilette*"; Hyde, "The 'Makeup' of the Marquise"; Lajer-Burcharth, "Pompadour's Touch"; and Lajer-Burcharth, "Pompadour's Dream."

371 For Pompadour's use of art, see Goodman, *The Portraits of Madame de Pompadour: Celebrating the Femme Savante*; Hyde, "The 'Makeup' of the Marquise"; Lajer-Burcharth, "Pompadour's Touch"; Salmon, *Madame Pompadour et les arts* (Paris: RMN, 2002).

372 For Bellevue decor, see *Pompadour et les Arts*, 99–109. See also my "Pompadour's Dream."

373 "[il] ressemble beaucoup à l'original, peu à moi," "Lettre à M. de Vandières," April 26, 1751, in Pompadour, *Correspondence de Madame de Pompadour avec son Père, M. Poisson et son Frère, M. de Vandières*, 50.

374 Lajer-Burcharth, "Pompadour's Touch" 68–70.

CHAPTER TWO

1 The epigraph for this chapter is taken from *Description Raisonné des Tableaux exposés au Louvre ou Lettre à Mme la Marquise de S.P.R.* (1738), in Wildenstein, 68. "Son goût de peinture est à lui seul."

2 "Les nuances les plus vrais des corps sont saisies par M. Chardin avec une justesse admirable." *Dialogues Sur les Arts entre un Artiste amériquain et un Amateur françois* (1756), 29. The work was first published in Amsterdam in 1755. On the text and its reception, see Delpierre, "Chardin péruvien: Les *Dialogues sur les Arts entre un Artiste américain et un Amateur français* de Pierre Estève."

3 "Ô Chardin, c'est n'est pas du blanc, du rouge, du noir que tu broies sur ta palette; c'est la substance même des objets, c'est l'air et la lumière que tu prends à la pointe de ton pinceau, et que tu attache sur la toile." *Salon de 1763*, in Versini, *Oeuvres*, 4: 265.

4 *Memorial Address on Chardin* (1780), cited in Rosenberg, *Chardin*, 98–99. *Éloge funèbre de J.B.S. [sic] Chardin*, in Wildenstein, 33.

5 Conservator report on file at the Museum of Fine Arts, Boston.

6 For the objects painted by the artist that were listed in the inventory of his household made after the death of his first wife, Marguerite Saintard, see Rochebrune, "Ceramics and Glass in Chardin's Paintings," 37–53. For the utensils in the Boston still lifes featured in other painting, see PR *Chardin* 1999, nos. 75, 87, 87A, and 88. For dating, now accepted as 1755, see Rosenberg, "Chardin: New Thoughts," 30–31.

7 We have only seven extant drawings by Chardin, some of which are his student essays. See PR *Chardin* 1999, nos. 1b, c and d; 2a and c; 4b. Another drawing, *Curiosity*, not included in the 1999 catalogue raisonné, is in the Bonna Collection (Rosenberg, "New Thoughts," 82–83, and, on Chardin's limited draftsmanship, ibid., 71–85). Two other drawings, now lost, are known to us from Goncourts' etchings (PR *Chardin* 1999, nos. 1 and 51b). As for the oil sketches, there are two extant (PR *Chardin* 1999, nos. 120 and 126a); their exact function and authenticity have been debated. See Rosenberg, "New Thoughts," 39. I will have more to say about Chardin's preparatory process below.

8 Zafran, *French Paintings in the Museum of Fine Arts in Boston*, no. 35.

9 "Il faut en convenir, les tableaux de M. Chardin sentent trop la fatigue et la peine. Sa touche est lourde et n'est point variée. Son pinceau n'a rien de facile; il exprime tout de la même manière, et avec une sorte d'indécision, qui rend son ouvrage trop froid. [. . .] Faute d'être assez foncé dans le dessein et de pouvoir faire ses études et ses préparations sur le papier, M. Chardin est obligé d'avoir continuellement sous les yeux l'objet qu'il se propose d'imiter, depuis la première ébauche jusqu'à ce qu'il ait donné les derniers coups de pinceau, ce qui est bien long et capable de rébuter tout autre que lui. Aussi, a-t-il toujours à la bouche que le travail *lui coûte infiniment*. Quand il voudroit le cacher, son ouvrage le déceleroit malgré lui." *Abecedario*, 359–60, italics mine. According to the author's own marginal notation, he wrote this commentary in 1749.

10 "la sévérite à le [son génie] châtier, suite naturelle de la manière de voir d'un homme instruit qui ne se permet aucune licence et ne se contente pas des à-peu-près." *Essai sur la Vie de M. Chardin* (1780), in Wildenstein, 38.

11 "un juge si sévère de lui même." *Salon de 1769*, in Versini, *Oeuvres*, 844. Diderot recounts the story of the rabbits that rotted while Chardin was taking time to paint them; as a result, he couldn't finish his painting.

12 For the classic formulation of the notion of the author constituted by his or her text, see Barthes, "The Death of the Author" and Foucault, "What Is an Author."

13 Notably Baxandall, "Pictures and Ideas: Chardin's *Lady Taking Tea*."

14 The term "inifinitely complex process" is Jacques Lacan's in his account of the subject/

object relations. See Lacan, *Le Seminaire: Livre IV*, esp. 27. For the psychic dimension of the object in Chardin's work, see also Démoris, *Chardin, le chair et l'objet*; Podro, *Depiction*; and my "The Object as Subject." On the existence of the epistemic space of psyche avant la lettre in this period that warrants such approaches, see my introduction to this book.

15 On flesh-like appearance of Chardin's paintings, see Diderot, *Notes on Painting*, in Goodman, *Diderot on Art*, 1: 201. For the version in French, see Diderot, *Essais sur la Peinture*, in Versini, *Oeuvres*, 476.

16 For the inaccuracies of execution, in *Lady Drinking Tea*, see Baxandall, "Pictures and Ideas"; for the anatomically incorrect rendition of the draftsman in the *Drawing Lesson*, noticed by the Salon critics, see my "Scenes of Instruction."

17 For the subjectivity implied by the notion of pictorial illusion and for the psychological dimension of the early modern theorization of painting, see Lichtenstein, *Eloquence of Color: Rhetoric and Painting in the French Classical Age*, esp. 167–95.

18 This suggestion is related to the recent reconceptualization of the medium as irreducible to its technical bases. See Krauss, "Reinventing the Medium," and her *Under the Blue Cup*.

19 For example, Baxandall, "Pictures and Ideas"; *Shadows and Enlightenment*, 119–42; and "Attention, Hand and Brush: Condillac and Chardin"; Cohen, "Chardin's Fur: Painting, Materialism, and the Question of Animal Soul"; Johnson, "Picturing Pedagogy: Education and the Child in the Paintings of Chardin"; Crow, "Chardin at the Edge of Belief: Overlooked Issues of Religion and Dissent in Eighteenth-Century Painting."

20 In addition to the conservators' reports in the museums' curatorial files, among important published reports are Faillant-Dumas, "Des données de laboratoire sur Chardin," Faillant-Dumas, "Étude de la technique picturale de Chardin"; and Fronek, "The Materials and Technique of the Los Angeles *Soap Bubbles*." See also the discussion of this issue in my "Object as Subject."

21 For the materiality of painting that resists discourse, see Démoris, "Chardin and the Far Side of Illusion," and my *Chardin Material*.

22 For the discussion of craft, see Ayres, *The Artist's Craft*; Greenhalgh, "The History of Craft"; Sennett, *The Craftsman*; and Adamson, *The Invention of Craft*.

23 *Chardin*, 2000, 288. "On entend rien à cette magie." *Salon de 1763*, in Versini, *Oeuvres*, 265.

24 "It is said of him that his technique is totally idiosyncratic and that he uses his thumb as much as his brush. I don't know if this is true, but I'm sure of one thing, namely that I've never known anyone who's seen him work." Diderot in Goodman, *Diderot on Art*, 2: 86 (Versini, *Oeuvres*, 593).

25 *Notes on Painting*, in Goodman, *Diderot on Art*, 1: 200.

26 Métier: Profession d'un art mécanique (Dictionnaire de l'Académie, 1762 ed.). For the academic practice as distinct from craft, see Crow, *Painters and Public Life*, esp. 23–44; Heinich, *Du Peintre à l'Artiste: Artisans et Académiciens à l'Âge classique*; Duro, *The Academy and the Limits of Painting in Seventeenth-Century France*; Schnapper, *Le métier de peintre au Grand Siècle*, esp. 114–53; and Michel, *L'Académie royale de Peinture et Sculpture*.

27 "esprit grossiers et malfaisants," "troupe abjecte," "broyeurs de couleurs," or "ignorants et vénaux." Cited by Heinich, *Du Peintre à l'Artiste*, 13. For the in reality fluid distinctions between the maîtres peintres and the academic artists, see Schnapper, *Le métier de peintre*, 74–153.

28 On Félibien's notion of execution in his *Conférences* (1668), see Démoris, "Le Comte de Caylus et la Peinture."

29 Defining painting as "the imitation of visible objects by means of forms and colors," de Piles drew attention to the importance of execution. See his *Cours de peinture*, 2. For the discussion of de Piles's theory, see Teyssèdre, *Roger de Piles et le Débat sur le Coloris au Siècle de Louis XIV*, and Puttfarken, *Roger de Piles' Theory of Art*.

30 For the fundamental change in art practice produced by the Salons, see Crow, *Painters and Public Life*.

31 For the emergence and the formation of art criticism, see ibid., esp. 1–22 and 79–103; Wrigley, *The Origins of French Art Criticism: From the Ancien Régime to the Restoration*; and Démoris and Ferran, *Le peinture en procès: L'invention de la critique d'art au siècle des Lumières*.

32 *Les Misotechnites aux Enfers, ou Examen des Observations sur les Arts*.

33 On the polemic, and its context, see Michel, *Charles-Nicolas Cochin et l'Art des Lumières*, esp. 245–47 and 343. On *Misotechnites*, see also Bernadette Fort, "An Academician in the Underground: Charles Nicolas Cochin and Art Criticism in Eighteenth-Century France"; and Peltier, "*Les Misotechnites aux Enfers* ou l'imposture de la critique selon Charles-Nicolas Cochin."

34 In his preface to the dialogue, Cochin speaks of the critics as "des aveugles volontaires." Cochin, *Les Misotechnites*, iv.

35 La Font is also featured in the *Misotechnites* under the derisive pseudonym of Ardélion—from the Greek *ardaloō* = to smear—but, as a reformer of his ignorant interlocutor, Phylakei, he is shown in a more positive light than in Watelet's image. Fort, "An Academician in the Underground," 15.

36 *Les Misotechnites*, 40–41. For this point, see Peltier, "*Les Misotechnites aux Enfers*," 113.

37 Peltier, "*Les Misotechnites aux Enfers*," 118.

38 Fort, "An Academician in the Underground." It was precisely to diminish the risk that he published the pamphlet anonymously. See Michel, *Charles-Nicolas Cochin*, 256–57.

39 On the art market and on the role of the new professional figures of mediators between the work of art and its consumers—dealers, public sales commissaries, and appraisers—see Michel, *Le Commerce du tableau*.

40 For the rising importance of art expertise, see Pomian, *Collectionneurs, amateurs, et curieux: Paris, Venice; XVIe–XVIIIe Siècle*; Michel, *Le Commerce du tableau*, 73–87; and Guichard, *Les amateurs d'art*.

41 "Je ne sais pourquoi on a attaché une idée vile à ce mot; c'est des *métiers* que nous tenons toutes les choses nécessaires à la vie. Celui qui se donnera la peine de parcourir des ateliers, y verra par-tout l'utilité jointe aux plus grandes preuves de la sagacité." *Encyclopédie*, 10: 463.

42 Picon, "Gestes ouvriers, opérations et processus techniques: la vision du travail des encyclopédistes."

43 "C'est celui-ci qui est un peintre, c'est celui-ci qui est un coloriste" (This is the one who is a painter, this is a colorist), asserted Diderot at the Salon of 1763. Versini, *Oeuvres*, 264.

44 For Chardin's lack of interest in developing a bond with the Salon audience, see Crow, *Painters and Public Life*, 134–38. For a possibility of a more complicated, dual address of Chardin's paintings, see Herbert, "A Picture of Chardin's Making." On Chardin's reliance on prints for the reproduction and wider circulation of his work, see Scott, "Chardin Multiplied."

45 For Chardin's collectors, see Rosenberg, "Principaux Collectionneurs de Chardin," in *Chardin*, 1979, 73–78.

46 For the professional milieu of Chardin's parents, Jean Chardin and Jeanne-Françoise David, see the painter's first marriage contract, in Savina, "Biographie," in *Chardin*, 1979, 382. For the account of Chardin's artistic beginnings and his career, see Cochin, *Essai*, in Wildenstein, 35–40, and Haillet de Couronne's

Éloge de M. Chardin, Wildenstein, 40–44. I base what follows on these two sources, and on the documents published by Savina, "Biographie," 381–408.

47 On the potentially humiliating dimension of the term *peintre à talents*, see Démoris, *Chardin*, 15–21.

48 See Guiffrey, *Histoire de l'Académie de Saint-Luc*; Benhamou, "Public and Private Art Education in France, 1648–1793"; and Schnapper, *Le métier de peintre*, esp. 19–113.

49 On artisanal households, see Roche, *The People of Paris: An Essay in Popular Culture in the 18th Century*, esp. 97–159; *A History of Private Life*, vol. 3, *Passions of the Renaissance*, 397–571; and Farr, *The Work in France: Labor and Culture in Early Modern Times, 1350–1800*, 79–110.

50 For Chardin's household, see Herbert, "Les demeures de Chardin," and Wildenstein, "Le décor de la vie de Chardin d'après ses tableaux."

51 In his *Essai*, 37, Cochin comments on Chardin's father's unfamiliarity with the domain of the arts ([il était] "nullement au fait des arts").

52 On this transformation, see Heinich, *Du Peintre à l'Artiste*.

53 Ibid., 202.

54 Démoris, "La nature morte chez Chardin," 369.

55 Démoris, *Chardin*, 54.

56 The small size of this painting, which may have been viewed as it is installed now at the Musée Jacquemart-André, that is, standing on an easel on top of a *commode*, would have increased the sense of mobility and reversibility of its motif. Another example of the inside/out trope is a pair of still lifes in the Norton Simon Museum, Pasadena, ca. 1728–30 (nos. 53b and 54b in PR *Chardin* 1999), both being versions of the pendants now in Bordeaux and Raleigh, respectively (nos. 53 and 54 in ibid.).

57 See ibid., nos. 54 a–f.

58 Incidentally, it is only in 1756 that the notion of death enters the French terminology for still life, and what had previously been designated as *vie coye*, or *nature reposé*, becomes *nature morte*. Sterling, *Still Life Painting: From Antiquity to the Twentieth Century*, 64.

59 Bryson, *Looking at the Overlooked: Four Essays on Still Life Painting*, 167.

60 For a similar rendition of raw flesh, see PR *Chardin*, 1999, nos. 52 and 68.

61 The painting is approximately one by one and a half meters large (114 × 146 cm).

62 On the self-reflexive dimension of the *Ray*, see Bois et al., "La Raie," and Démoris, *Chardin*, 28–48. For the extensive literature on the painting, see *Chardin*, 1979, 114 and 116 (for publications before 1979), and *Chardin*, 2000, 118.

63 For orality as a distinct stage of psychic development, see Abraham, "A Short Study of the Development of Libido, Viewed in the Light of Mental Disorders"; and Klein, "Some Theoretical Conclusions Regarding the Emotional Life of the Infant."

64 Diderot, among others, reported that Chardin painted with his fingers. See Goodman, *Diderot on Art*, 2: 86 (Versini, *Oeuvres*, 593). Another instance of fingertips being used may be the *Still Life with Herrings* (Cleveland Museum of Art; PR *Chardin* 1999, no. 84A), where the digital imprints are scattered on the outer side of the ledge around his signature—as if they were an alternative mode of signing his work.

65 Démoris makes this point citing the *Dictionnaire de Furetière*, "On appelle populairement la raye le cul, la séparation qui est entre les deux fesses" (in the edition of 1690, and the subsequent ones), in Démoris, *Chardin*, 32.

66 The Thyssen-Bornemisza canvas and a similar one, *Ray with a Basket of Onions*, in the Norton Simon Museum in Pasadena, exist in several versions. See PR *Chardin* 1999, nos. 30, 30a–b, and 54, 54a–f. For the late sixteenth- and seventeenth-century examples on which Chardin may have drawn, see Lüdke, "Chardin und die niederländische Malerei des 17. Jahrhunderts Dargestellt an sieben Stilleben," 43.

67 See Herbert, "Les demeures de Chardin," and Wildenstein, "Le décor de la vie."

68 Chardin's relocation must have occurred between 1744, when he remarried, and 1747, when he is formally registered at his new address. See Savina, "Biographie," 386 and 388.

69 See Wildenstein, "Le décor de la vie," 103, and for the layout of the third floor of Chardin's domicile reconstructed after cadastre records, 106.

70 For another account of the connection between Chardin's work and the domestic space, see Bryson, *Looking at the Overlooked*, 95 and 166–69.

71 Wildenstein mentions a shop and storage space ("une boutique avec un magasin") on the ground floor of Chardin's house listed in the cadastre, "Le décor de la vie," 101–2. On the location of workshop, and on the relation between work space and living space in an artisanal household, see Farge, "The Honor and Secrecy of Families," 575–76.

72 The long working hours of the Parisian artisans, generally from dawn to dusk, dictated the rhythm of other household activities, such as meals, etc. See Farr, *The Work in France*, 86.

73 On work relations in artisanal households, see ibid., and Sonenscher, *Work and Wages*, esp. chap. 4. For paternalism of French artisanship, see Blanc, *Les Corporations de Métiers: Leur Histoire, leur Esprit, leur Avenir*, 133–37; and Auslander, *Taste and Power: Furnishing Modern France*, 110–12 and 122–28. We have no information regarding Jean Chardin's workshop, but, given his professional status as the "cabinetmaker to the King," and his importance within the community reported in the documents from the period (see Cochin, *Essai*, 35 and 37), he must have employed a considerable number of people.

74 Blanc, *Les Corporations de Métiers*; Auslander, *Taste and Power*, 122–28.

75 Auslander, *Taste and Power*. On familial relations between masters and journeymen, see also Scott, *Rococo Interior*, 61–65.

76 See Flandrin, *Familles, parenté, maison, sexualité dans l'ancienne societé*, 128–38; Alain Collomp, "Families: Habitations and Cohabitations," 493–529; and Farge, "The Honor and Secrecy of Families," 571–607.

77 Ménétra, *Journal of My Life*. See also Roche, "Commentary: Jacques-Louis Ménétra; An Eighteenth-Century Way of Life," esp. 252–53.

78 For the discussion of the iconography of the artisanal interior, Hallé in particular, see Scott, *Rococo Interior*, 45–47.

79 Living with one's parents well into adulthood was not unusual in the bourgeois milieu in the eighteenth century, especially in artisanal families where skill was passed from father to son and cohabitation was one of the conditions of this transfer. See Flandrin, *Familles*, 79–81. Chardin's situation was, however, different insofar as his profession was not his father's.

80 *Premier contract du mariage entre Jean-Siméon Chardin et Marguerite Saintard*, 6 mai, 1723 (A.N. M.C., Étude CVI, liasse 215), repr. in Savina, "Biographie," 382). One presumes that the mentioned sum of 2,000 livres represented what his father was willing to put up to purchase Chardin's maîtrise.

81 For marriages being postponed due to the groom's insufficient income, see Collomp, "Families," 512.

82 The bride's dowry diminished by one-third while Chardin's financial situation had not significantly improved. See *Deuxième contrat de mariage entre Jean-Siméon Chardin et Marguerite Saintard*, 23 janvier, 1731 (A.N. M.C. Étude CXVII, liasse 377), repr. in Savina, "Biographie," 383.

83 In addition to his parents, and his brother Juste, the family living in the house

included Chardin's younger brother, Noël-Sébastien, and a sister Marie-Claude, as well as his stepsister, Marie-Agnès, from his father's first marriage. There may have been other members of the family inhabiting the house, as Chardin *père* had three surviving children from his first marriage, and Chardin's mother had one child from her first marriage. Later on, Juste's wife and their children also lived in the house (Savina, "Biographie," 382).

84 For Chardin's commission to paint six pictures for Rothenbourg, a Prussian aristocrat who served as the French ambassador to Madrid, see Roland Michel, *Chardin*, 20, and 35, n. 26. For the details of the commission, including payments, see Savina, "Biographie," 382–83.

85 On it being Chardin's first canvas, see Conisbee, *Chardin*, 57. Rosenberg is more cautious, listing it as one of the earliest works and dating it for "shortly after 1720" (PR *Chardin* 1999, 26, and no. 2). Roland Michel suggested that the painting may have been a shop sign for Chardin's father's business as a *menuisier de billard* (*Chardin*, 13).

86 See Jean-Siméon Chardin, *Study of Seated Man*, ca. 1720–25. Charcoal and white chalk. The J. Paul Getty Museum, Los Angeles.

87 The measured construction of visual space on Chardin's canvas, accentuated by the even-distanced balusters of the billiard table and echoed by both the checkered pattern of the floor below and the rhythmically distributed candelabra above it, resembles the modal construction of the billiard table as described and illustrated by Roubo, *L'Art du Menuisier*, 3: 703.

88 In eighteenth-century bourgeois households, mothers were in charge of the kitchen and presided over family meals. See Flandrin, *Familles*, 103; Collomp, "Families" 514–15. For the association between still life as a genre and femininity, see Bryson, *Looking at the Overlooked*, 136–78.

89 See Auslander, *Taste and Power*, 126.

90 For identity, see Locke, *An Essay Concerning Human Understanding*, 2: xxvii, 296–314.

91 Shylock's phrase from Shakespeare's *Merchant of Venice* was used by Lacan to conceptualize the costs of the subject's entry into the realm of the Symbolic, an exchange of flesh for sign: "that self-sacrifice, that pound of flesh, which is mortgaged in (the) relationship to the signifier." Lacan, "Desire and the Interpretation of Desire in Hamlet," 28.

92 PR *Chardin* 1999, 41. Rosenberg infers this dating from the period commentaries, notably Haillet de la Couronne's and Mariette's.

93 The masterpiece's required size was 3 and a half feet, i.e., 113.2 cm, which is almost exactly the length of Chardin's canvas (114 cm) (Guiffrey, *Histoire de l'Académie de Saint-Luc*, 9). For the guild regulations regarding the submission of chef-d'oeuvre, see also Savary des Bruslons, *Dictionnaire Universel du Commerce*, 830–32; and Kaplan, "The Luxury Guilds in Paris in the Eighteenth-Century," *Francia*, 285–86. What is puzzling is that, judging from the documentation published by Guiffrey, neither Chardin's name nor his masterpiece figure in the archives of the guild, unlike that of Oudry who also left the guild for the Academy. Is it possible that *The Ray* was indeed Chardin's chef-d'oeuvre but was withdrawn by him when he renounced his membership?

94 For the *Ray*'s exhibition at the Place Dauphine, see *Nécrologue*, 1779, in Wildenstein, 46. On the Place Dauphine exhibitions where Chardin showed his paintings in 1728, 1732, and 1734, see de la Chavignerie, "Notes pour Servir à l'histoire de l'Exposition de la Jeunesse"; and, on its cultural function as the site of "artistic communication and value-formation," Crow, *Painters and Public Life*, 82–88.

95 On the high expectations and standards of work maintained by the guilds in the eighteenth century, see Guiffrey, *Académie de Saint-Luc*, 8–9; Kaplan, "The Luxury Guilds"; Sonenscher, *Work and Wages*, 211–13; and Scott, *Rococo Interior*, 48–49.

96 In the discourse of the guild, the mastery of execution was inseparable from the social and gender identity of the master as a man and father. See Auslander, *Taste and Power*, 127–28.

97 *Nécrologue*, in Wildenstein, "Le décor de la vie," 46.

98 Traditionally, the process of admission to the Academy consisted of two steps, the provisional acceptation of the candidate as an associate (*agrée*), followed by admission to full membership upon submission of a significant work (*morceau de réception*). The anecdote about Chardin's admission was told by Cochin (*Essai*) and Hallet de la Couronne, among others. For the full account of all the sources, see *Chardin*, 1979, 116–17.

99 For the term "surprise invader," see Crow, *Painters and Public Life*, 134–38.

100 "A dog cranes its head but cannot reach up to them and makes them the more desirable for being truly desired. It samples them with its eye, surprising the blandness of their flavour in the moisture on their velvety skins." Proust, "Chardin and Rembrandt," 124. (Cited in French in *Chardin*, 1979, 128.)

101 In his reading of the painting, Proust discerns a lower social register of the *Buffet* when he describes the knife left behind by a servant in haste. "Chardin and Rembrandt," 124.

102 Cited by Farr, *The Work in France*, 93.

103 See Heinich, *Du Peintre à l'Artiste*, 13.

104 Still life occupied the lowest rank in the academic hierarchy of genres insofar as it was based on imitation of objects rather than representation of human actions. For the analysis of the notion of hierarchy, see Ledbury, "The Hierarchy of Genres in the Theory and Practice of Painting in Eighteenth-Century France."

105 "Monsieur Pierre, regardez bien ce morceau, quand vous irez à l'Académie, et apprenez, si vous pouvez, le secret de sauver par le talent le dégoût de certaines natures" (Monsieur Pierre, look carefully at this painting when you will go to the Academy and learn from it, if you can, the secret of redeeming by painting the disgusting aspects of nature). *Salon de 1763*, in Versini, *Oeuvres*, 265.

106 To echo Brunaubois-Montador's term cited earlier.

107 The epigraph for this section is taken from de Piles, *Cours de peinture*, 260. "Je ne vois rien, mes yeux sont au bout de mes doigts."

108 For the Dutch and Flemish examples, notably Jan Weenix and Pieter Boel, on which Chardin may have drawn, see *Jean Siméon Chardin, 1699–1779: Werk, Herkunft, Wirkung*, 286–94.

109 "Cet objec paroist bien peu important; mais la manière dont il désiroit le faire le rendoit une etude sérieuse. Il voulait le rendre avec la plus grande vérité à tous égards et cependant avec goust, sans aucune apparence de servitude qui en put rendre le faire sec et froid. Il n'avoit point encore tenté de traiter le poil. Il sentoit bien qu'il ne falloit pas penser à le compter ni à le rendre en détail. 'Voilà, se disoit-il à lui même, un objet qu'il est question de rendre. Pour n'être occupé que de le rendre vray, il faut que j'oublie tout ce que j'ay vu, et même jusqu'à la manière dont ces objets ont été traittés par d'autres. Il faut que je le pose à une distance telle que je n'en voye plus les détails. Je dois m'occuper surtout d'en bien imiter et avec la plus grande vérité les masses générales, ces tons de la couleur, la rondeur, les effets de la lumière et des ombres.' Il y parvint et y fit paroistre le prémices de ce goust et de ce faire magique, qui depuis a toujours caractérisé les talents qui l'ont distingué." *Essai*, in Wildenstein, 36.

110 See also Sarah R. Cohen's suggestive account of the insistent materiality of fur in her "Chardin Fur," 39–61.

111 On this effect, see also ibid.

112 We witness similar spatial inconsistencies in the Karlsruhe still life with rabbits, game bag, and orange, where Rosenberg discerns "un certain maladresse dans la mis en place des lapins" (PR *Chardin* 1999, no. 35). Another example is the *Dead Rabbit with Red Partridge and Seville Orange*, Musée de la Chasse et de la Nature Paris (PR *Chardin* 1999, no. 36), where the motif seems to be falling off from the uneven ledge.

113 Another, signed version of the Fogg painting, considered by Rosenberg to be the original, was in the Rothshild collection and was destroyed in World War II. Both versions were dated for around 1733, though Roland Michel suggested 1735–40 (PR *Chardin* 1999, nos. 90 and 90a; and Roland Michel, *Chardin*, 61). See also Rosenberg, "The *Blind Man of the Quinze-Vingts* by Chardin and the *Young Girls with a Marmot* by Fragonard at the Fogg," 211–15 and 391–93.

114 The only other known outdoor scene by Chardin is the *Genre Scene* (private collection, Sweden), which, though signed and dated (1730), is of such mediocre quality that it has been only hesitantly accepted as the painter's work (PR *Chardin* 1999 no. 51). Adult males were notably absent from Chardin's genre paintings featuring women and children.

115 Jacques Callot, *L'Aveugle et son Chien*, 1622–23. Etching. Bibliothèque national, Paris.

116 *Les Quinze-Vingts: Notes et Documents, Recueillis par Feu L'Abbé J.-H.-R. J.-L. Prompsault*, 25.

117 For the history of the Quinze-Vingts establishment, see *Les Quinze-Vingts*; and Guillaumat and Bailliart, *Les Quinze-Vingts de Paris: échos historiques du XIIe au XXe siècle*. For the social history of the blind in France, see also Weygand, *The Blind in French Society from the Middle Ages to the Century of Louis Braille*.

118 Later in the eighteenth century, beggars were detained in the *dépôts de mendicité* created for that purpose. See Kaplow, *The Names of Kings: The Parisian Laboring Poor in the Eighteenth Century*, 127–34.

119 Guillaumat and Baillart, *Les Quinze-Vingts de Paris*, 39. The location of Chardin's beggar was recognized by the critic Estève who referred to the painting shown at the Salon of 1753 as "le petit aveugle à la porte d'une église." *Lettre à un Ami sur l'Exposition des Tableaux dans le grand Salon du Louvre, le 25 Août 1753*, 5 (Collection Delyones, 89).

120 The caption under Bosse's image reads: "Faut-il pas avoüer que je suis bien à plaindre, / Et que dans les dangers qui m'obligent a creïdre, / Puis que j'ay ce malheur de vivre sans voir rien, / Ma conduite depend d'un baston et d'un chien" (orthography of the original). (You must admit that I have reasons to be pitied and that, with the dangers I have to fear, having the misfortune of living without sight, my movements depend on a stick and a dog.)

121 Guillaumat and Baillart, *Les Quinze-Vingts de Paris*, 40.

122 Published in 1737, Bouchardon's *Aveugle de Quinze-Vingts* was executed sometime between 1732 and 1737, i.e., contemporaneously with Chardin's painting. See Scott, "Edme Bouchardon's 'Cris de Paris': Crying Food in Early Modern Paris," 66.

123 Conisbee made a similar point in *Chardin*, 162.

124 When the painting was shown at the Salon of 1753, one critic saw the signs of blindness not in the eyes but in the beggar's body. See [Laugier], *Jugement d'un Amateur sur l'Exposition des Tableaux* (1753), in Wildenstein, 88. As for the blind man's mouth being shut in Chardin's rendition, it is worth knowing that, when begging for bread, the Quinze-Vingts blind would walk the streets emitting their cries: "Aux Quinze-Vingts, Pain-Dieu!" (Guillaumat and Baillart, *Les Quinze-Vingt de Paris*, 39).

125 "l'auteur en a sçu faire, à force d'ailleurs d'art et de magie, un petit tableau très piquant." *Sentiments d'un amateur . . .* (1753) (l'abbé Garrigues de Froment), in Wildenstein, 90. Fréron stated that it was painted "avec tout l'art imaginable." *L'Éloge du Salon*, in Wildenstein.

126 This mode of painting was compared by one contemporary, Abbé Raynal, to a mosaic or a tapestry technique called *point carré*. (Raynal, *Correspondance Litteraire* [1750], 464, cited in PR *Chardin* 1999, 169.) For a different account of Chardin's tactility, see Baxandall's "Attention, Hand and Brush," esp. 190.

127 As far as we know, the painter used neither preparatory sketches nor underdrawings for his paintings. Thus, while for us, his mode of painting may amount to, as Baxandall argued ("Attention, Hand, and Brush," 187), *visualization* of touch, for Chardin, it was the opposite, a tactile production of vision that the painter, his nose to the canvas, was not in a position to see.

128 "L'oeil trompé par tant de légèreté, et la facilité aparente qui y règne, voudrais en vain par son attention et ses recherches multipliées, en apprendre d'eux le secret; il s'abîme, il se perd dans ta touche," Baillet de Saint-Jullien, *Caractères des Peintres Français Actuellement Vivants*, 5, in Wildenstein, 91.

129 "Sentiment sur le Discours du Mérite de la Couleur par M. Blanchard," lecture delivered at the Academy on January 9, 1672, cited in Lichtenstein, *Eloquence of Color*, 153.

130 "Coloris," in *Cours de peinture*, 238–305. See also de Piles, *Dialogue sur le coloris*.

131 For this point, see Lichtenstein, *Eloquence of Color*, 158–59.

132 *Cours de peinture*, 260.

133 For a brief discussion of the "Guercino" drawing, see Derrida, *Memoirs of the Blind*, 42–43.

134 The size of the canvas is 140 × 215 cm (PR *Chardin* 1999, no. 58).

135 See Démoris, "Dessin et couleur chez Diderot (1749–66)."

136 Tunstall, *Blindness and Enlightenment: An Essay*, esp. 47–67. For the textual life of the blind man's figure before the Enlightenment, see also Weygand, *The Blind in French Society*, 11–35.

137 The question of how a blind person who regained sight would perceive the world was first posed by the Irish philosopher William Molyneux, and taken up by Locke in his *Essay Concerning Human Understanding* (1690, and in more expanded way, in the second edition of 1694). Having started in Britain, these inquiries were transmitted by, among others, Voltaire, to France where the debate on the senses intensified in the late 1730s and '40s and continued to reverberate throughout the eighteenth century, notably in and through the work of Étienne Bonnot de Condillac. The modern literature on this debate is too abundant to be cited in full here. For this discussion, the most important were: Paulson, *Enlightenment, Romanticism and the Blind in France*, 21–94; Degenaar, *Molyneux's Problem: Three Centuries of Discussion on the Perception of Forms*; Jay, *Downcast Eyes: The Denigration of Vision in Twentieth-Century French Thought*, 21–147; Clark, *Vanities of the Eye: Vision in Early Modern European Culture*; and Tunstall, *Blindness and Enlightenment*.

138 *Lettre sur les aveugles à l'usage de ceux qui voyent*. English ed. in new translation by Tunstall in *Blindness and Enlightenment*, 169–219.

139 See Montaigne, *Complete Essays*, 665–66; and Descartes, "La Dioptrique," in *Discours de la Méthode*, 117–32. For the importance of Montaigne and Descartes for Diderot, see Tunstall, *Blindness and Enlightenment*, 53–61.

140 "One of us decided to ask our blind man whether he would like to have eyes. He replied, 'If I wasn't so curious, I'd just as well have long arms, as it seems to me that my

hands can teach me more about what's happening on the moon than your eyes or telescopes can, and besides, eyes stop seeing well before hands stop touching. It would be just as good to improve the organ I already have, as to grant me the one I lack.'" *Letter on the Blind*, 176.

141 Diderot's figure of the blind man, lifted from an eighteenth-century edition of *La Dioptrique* (1724), is thus not the bearded old man with a dog that appeared in Descartes's original 1637 edition, but a clean-shaven and elegantly dressed youth (see fig. 2.36). For Diderot's commentary on Descartes, see *Letter on the Blind*, 174. For the discussion of the relation between Descartes and Diderot, see Tunstall, *Blindness and Enlightenment*, 59–61 and 72; and Lojkin, "Diderot, Le goût de l'art," 39–42.

142 The discussion of blindness in the *Encyclopédie*—the entries on *Aveugle* (Blind Man), written by Diderot's collaborator d'Alembert (*Encyclopédie*, 1: 870), and on *Aveugles* (Blind Men) penned by Diderot himself (ibid., 873), pointed to the need for reevaluation of the social status of the blind. See Tunstall, *Blindness and Enlightenment*, 25–26. On the gradual shift in attitude toward the blind resulting in the creation of the Institute of Blind Youth in Paris, which in 1801 briefly merged with the Quinze-Vingts establishment, see Weygand, *The Blind in French Society*, 121–35.

143 Condillac's *Treatise* was in fact written largely in response to the critique of his earlier work leveled by Diderot in his *Letter on the Blind*. See O'Neal, *The Authority of Experience: Sensationist Theory in the French Enlightenment*, 20–21.

144 See *Traité des Sensations*, 103–7 and 157–219. For the discussion of the *Traité*, see Knight, *The Geometric Spirit: The Abbé de Condillac and the French Enlightenment*, and O'Neal, *The Authority of Experience*, 13–59 and 107–10.

145 The connection between the *Blind Beggar* and this broader discursive context became salient when Chardin exhibited the painting at the Salon of 1753, his decision to do so twenty years after he produced it being possibly related to the intensification of the debate on blindness after the publication of Diderot's letter.

146 The Fogg painting's original size was 29 × 17 cm. It has been slightly expanded on the sides resulting in the current size, 30 × 23 cm, still very small. The other version was 28 × 18 cm (see PR *Chardin* 1999, nos. 90 and 90a).

147 Cohen, "Chardin's Fur."

148 For the notion of detail as a semiotic rupture, see Didi-Huberman, *Confronting Images: Questioning the Ends of a Certain History of Art*, 229–71.

149 The first epigraph in this section is taken from Estève, *Dialogues sur les Arts*, 10. "Je vois dans un beau tableau des figures qui ont du relief, qui ne sont point terminées par des lignes; mais qui en conservant leur rondeur, fuient pour ainsi dire en dessous de ce qui est visible."

150 "Un peintre doit connoître à quel genre de peinture il est propre, et se borner à ce genre." (The painter should know which type of painting is suitable for him and limit himself to this type.) Louis, chevalier de Jaucourt, "Peintre," in *Encyclopédie*, 252. For a historical account of the eighteenth-century terminology and meaning of "genre," see Bailey, "Surveying Genre."

151 Mariette, *Abecedario*, 356–58.

152 Roland Michel, *Chardin*, 38–55; Rosenberg adds the rising popularity of the Northern genre in Paris at the time to the reasons for Chardin's shift to genre painting. (PR *Chardin*, 1999, 75–76.) Conisbee, *Chardin*, 106–7, cites a combination of these reasons.

153 See Savina, "Biographie," 383–85.

154 "Il s'est créé un genre nouveau et qui est tout à lui" (He created a new type of painting entirely his own). Lacombe, *Le Salon* (1753), in Wildenstein, 89. Baillet de Saint-Jullien addressed the painter as "l'inventeur d'un genre rare et particulier" (inventor of a rare and particular type of painting). *Lettre a M. Ch [Chardin] sur les caractères en peinture* (1753), in Wildenstein, 90. After 1751, Chardin painted only replicas of his earlier pendants, the *Drawing Lesson* and the *Good Education*, exhibiting both at the Salon of 1753. (PR *Chardin* 1999, nos. 127 and 128.)

155 Chardin occasionally painted still lifes after his "conversion" to genre painting, but they were mostly repeats of earlier compositions. The first new still life composition, the Frankfurt *Dead Partridge and Pear*, dates from 1748. (PR *Chardin* 199, no. 129.)

156 See, for example, his 1730 *Still Life with Leg of Mutton* in Musée des Beaux-Arts, Bordeaux (PR *Chardin*, no. 53). The sizes of these paintings are similar: the Bordeaux still life measures 40 × 32 cm, the Glasgow *Kitchen Maid* is only slightly larger (45.5 × 37 cm).

157 Mercier, *Le Tableau de Paris*, 1: 255–57, cited in Roche, *The People of Paris*, 97.

158 On Flaubert, see Barthes, "The Reality Effect."

159 "On admire dans celui-ci le talent de rendre avec un vrai qui lui est propre, et singulièrement naïf, certain moments dans les actions de la vie nullement intéresants, qui ne méritent par eux-même aucune attention. [. . .]" La Font de Saint-Yenne, *Réflexions*, 79. For Chardin's distinct treatment of Northern subjects, see Conisbee, *Chardin*, 118–26.

160 Conisbee, *Chardin*, 22–23 and figs. 9 and 11. Edizel (*Jean-Siméon Chardin: Seeing, Playing, Forgetting, and the Practice of Modern Imitation*, 76–100) interpreted the oddly distracted figures as allegories of labor.

161 For the iconography of labor in the *Cris de Paris*, see Milliot, *Les "Cris de Paris" ou le Peuple travesti: Les représentation des pétits métiers parisiens (XVIe–XVIIIe siècles)*; and Scott, "Edmé Bouchardon's *Cris de Paris*."

162 Démoris, *Chardin*, esp. 134–42.

163 "The remarkable thing about Chardin's compositions is that they are virtually devoid of men." Snoep-Reitsma, "Chardin and the Bourgeois Ideals of His Time," 151. Démoris states that "man doesn't seem to have left any traces" in these spaces. *Chardin*, 135.

164 I am retaining the French title (*Pourvoyeuse* = literally, Provider, or Cateress) under which the painting was exhibited at the Salon of 1739 (see PR *Chardin* 1999, no. 16), because I find it more suitable in its ambiguity than the oft-used bland alternative, *The Return from the Market*.

165 See PR *Chardin* 1999, nos. 116, 116a–b.

166 "Chardin and Rembrandt," 126.

167 Silence was one of the defining tropes in the critical response to Chardin's work (e.g., Diderot). For the relationship between Chardin's art and language, see Démoris, "Chardin and the Far Side of Illusion."

168 "Vision takes place inside the subject and is predicated on nothing else than the action of imagination. Apparition addresses the subject from the outside and implies the external object. [. . .] Heated brains deprived of nutrition often believe to have visions. Timid and credulous minds sometimes take for apparitions what is nothing, or what amounts to a play [of appearances]." Entry on "Vision, Apparition [synonymous]" (Chevalier de Jaucourt), *Encyclopédie*, 17: 343.

169 As an earliest example of medical use, OED cites Sir T. Browne: "If vision be abolished it is called *cæcitas*, or blindnesse, if depraved and receive its object erroneously, Hallucination." *Pseudodoxia Epidemica*, 1646, 3: xviii. 153. According to the *Dictionnaire de l'Académie française*, 6ème ed. (1835), "Hallucination: Error, Illusion of a person who believes in perceiving something that does not exist. This is a subject of hallucinations." For its use in French medical discourse, see Brierre de Boismont, *Des hallucinations, ou Histoire raisonnée des apparitions, des visions, des songes, de l'extase, du magnétisme et du somnabulisme*.

170 Bryson, *Word and Image*, 103–4.

171 Green, *Narcissisme*, 88–147.

172 Green, *The Fabric of Affect in the Psychoanalytic Discourse*, 256.

173 The process described by Green precedes and is related to, but ultimately differs from, what Lacan described as the "mirror stage" in the child's subjective development, the difference having to do with Green's emphasis on the role of affect in the child's negotiation of the bodily self-image. Cf. Lacan, "The Mirror Stage as Formative of the Function of the I."

174 For the discussion of Green's preoccupation with negativity, see Philips, "André Green and the Pragmatics of Passion," 165.

175 The relation staged by Chardin may be related to the spatial operations of "double reversal" (*double retournement*) characteristic of the subject's relation to its imaginary frame in the early stages of psychic development described by Green: the subject's turning in upon itself, and becoming its opposite. See Green, *Narcissisme*, 63–65.

176 See Cochin, *Essai*, 35.

177 Mariette mentioned that, in the course of his study with Cazes, Chardin won "quelques médailles" (*Abécedario*, 355). Cochin, on the other hand, indicated that Chardin achieved only very ordinary results while training with Cazes ("il n'y eut que des succès très ordinaires," *Essai*, 35). For the archival evidence indicating that Chardin received two so-called small or quarterly prizes, a second-class drawing medal in December 1719, and a first-class drawing medal in September 1720, see Piotrowska, "Chardin, Van Loo, and the Académie Royale during the Regency: New Archival Information." For the quarterly prizes, see Cahen, "Le Prix de quartier à l'Académie royale de peinture et de sculpture."

178 As Chardin himself acknowledged in his speech to the Salon critics reported by Diderot, drawing instruction usually started at the age of seven or eight. (See *The Salon of 1765*, in Goodman, *Diderot on Art*, 1: 4.) However, this was not his case. According to Wildenstein, the painter entered Cazes's studio in 1718, that is, when he was nineteen years old (Wildenstein, 59). Consequently, he received drawing instruction relatively late, when he was in his early twenties, which is what the dates of his quarterly prizes confirm. For comparison, Charles-Antoine Coypel won prizes at the Academy's drawing school at the age of twelve. See Bell, "Charles Coypel and the Age of Eclecticism," 36.

179 For the instruction at the Academy, see Benhamou, "Public and Private Art Education," 46–89; and Brugerolles, *L'Academie mise à nu: L'école du modèle à l'Académie royale de peinture et de sculpture.*

180 The lower part of Chardin's *académie*, now at the Getty Museum (*Male nude*, ca. 1720–25), is equally tentative.

181 For the long-term aesthetic consequences of this mode of training on pictorial practice in eighteenth-century France, see Cahen, "L'École du modèle au XVIIIème siècle"; Brugerolles, *L'Académie mise à nu*; and Caviglia-Brunel, "Life Drawing and the Crisis of *Historia* in French Eighteenth-Century Painting." For the emergence of the artist as a new professional identity, see Heinich, *Du Peintre à l'Artiste*.

182 Through such exercises, Diderot asserted, "the truth of nature is forgotten, while the imagination is filled with gestures, postures, and figures that are false, forced, ridiculous, and cold. There they're stored away, re-emerging for application to the canvas. Whenever the artist takes up his chalk or brushes, these *limp phantoms* revive and present themselves to him." *Notes on Painting*, in Goodman, *Diderot on Art*, 1: 194, italics mine. For more on the subjective dimension of academic instruction, specifically in regard to Chardin, see my "Scenes of Instruction."

183 While Chardin's limitations as a draftsman have been acknowledged by scholars (e.g., Rosenberg, "New Thoughts," 71–90), the deeper implications of the lacunae in his training on the painter's practice have not been considered.

184 For the inhabitants of 21 rue du Four, see Savina, "Biographie," 382–86. For the suggestion that the members of Chardin's household posed for him, see, among others, Wildenstein, "Le décor de la vie," 104. It has been widely accepted that the painter's first wife, Marguerite Saintard, sat for the *Lady Taking Tea* and his second wife, Françoise-Marguerite Pouget, for the *Domestic Pleasures* and *La Serinette*.

185 Following Cochin, Rosenberg states that Marguerite Pouget helped Chardin to manage the Academy's accounts and to conduct his correspondence (PR *Chardin* 1999, 162). Savina established that Chardin's letter of July 27, 1770, to Marigny was written in his second wife's hand (Savina, "Biographie," 400).

186 See Ayres, *Artist's Craft*, 42–45; and Munro, *Silent Partners: Artist and Mannequin from Function to Fetish*.

187 Ayres, *Artist's Craft*, 42–43. Laing (*Boucher* 1986, 226) reports on Boucher's use of mannequins especially made for some of his paintings. Another Chardin contemporary who used a lay figure was Hubert-François Gravelot. See Munro, *Silent Partners*, 20.

188 Most of the single figure paintings are about 47 × 37 cm; the *Attentive Nurse* is 45 × 34.5 cm. This is smaller than Roubiliac's mannequin, which was 64 cm (25 ½ inches) high. (Ayres, *Artist's Craft*.)

189 This is to say that rather than following the typical roundabout ways of an academically trained history painter—or an ambitious genre painter, such as Greuze—who would rehearse the pose, bodily details, and facial expressions in preparatory drawings, Chardin painted the figure the way a still life painter paints a motif, by direct transcription of the observed reality (the live model, the lay figure, or, in the case of replicas, his own previous painting), onto the canvas or, in rare cases (e.g., the Stockholm *Embroiderer*), wood.

190 For Chardin's idiosyncratic use of chalk, see Faillant-Dumas, "Des données de laboratoire sur Chardin"; and Ross Merrill's conservation report in the *Attentive Nurse*'s curatorial files, National Gallery, Washington, DC, 123. We don't know if Chardin got any instruction at the guild school, and if so, of what kind, but his technique as well as his secrecy about it strongly suggests the habits of an artisanal studio. (After the painter's death, Cochin passed on some of the evidently coveted secrets of Chardin's chromatic technique to a younger artist. See "Billet de C.-N. Cochin à M. Belle le Fils," in Wildenstein, 51.) For the instruction at the Academy of Saint-Luc, see Guiffrey, *Histoire de l'Académie de Saint-Luc*, 27; and Benhamou, "Public and Private Art Education," 32.

191 Merrill, conservation report, 127.

192 On the physical vicissitudes of the painting, and its pendant, *Domestic Pleasures*, see Grate, *French Painting II: The Eighteenth Century*, nos. 108 and 109, 94–97, esp. 97.

193 On the *Dialogues* as a critique of academic training, see Delpierre, "Chardin péruvien," 294–305. On Estève as a theorist, see also Becq, *La Genèse de l'Esthétique française moderne, 1680–1814*, 523, 597, and 642.

194 "En étudiant la nature je n'y ai jamais observé que des rondeurs et jamais le trait distinct qui terminât séchement les chairs. Qu'entendez-vous donc, [. . .] par la science du dessein? Est-ce qu'on peut représenter les corps autrement que par des couleurs dégradées qui en arrondissent les parties? Je vois dans un beau tableau des figures qui ont du relief, qui ne sont point terminés par des lignes; mais qui en conservant leur rondeur, fuient, pour ainsi dire, *en dessous de ce qui est visible*." *Dialogues*, 9–10, italics mine.

195 Ibid., 97.

196 Ibid., 48. Delpierre ("Chardin péruvien," 294) links Estève's argument to Condillac's sensationism.

197 The slowness of Chardin's process was common knowledge. As one critic referred to the painter's singular handling, "cette pratique est séduisante, mais elle demande sûrement beaucoup de patience et de tems [*sic*]" (this practice is seductive but it surely requires a lot of patience and time). Lacombe, *Le Salon* [de 1753], 24, in Wildenstein, 87.

198 For pairing these paintings, see Démoris, "Inside/Interiors: Chardin's Images of the Family," 457; Conisbee, *French Painting of the Fifteenth through the Eighteenth Century*, 78.

199 "Ce ne sont pas des traits finis, ce n'est pas une touche fondue, c'est au contraire du brut, du raboteux. Il semble que ses coups de pinceau soient appuyés et néanmois ses figures sont d'une vérité frappante; et la singularité de sa façon ne leur donne que plus de naturel et d'âme." (It is not the case of finished outlines, or of a fluid touch; on the contrary, it is brutal and rugged. It seems as if the strokes of his brush were exaggerated, and yet his figures are of striking realism, and the singularity of his manner only makes them more natural and spirited.) *Lettre à Mme la Marquise*, in Wildenstein, 68. I am following Conisbee's translation of the passage in his *Chardin*, 21–22.

200 See Green, *Narcissisme*, 148–93.

201 For *La Serinette* as a meta-commentary on artistic practice, see Sheriff, "Reflecting on Chardin"; and Edizel, *Chardin*, 134–45. For the connection to academic pedagogy, see Démoris, *Chardin*, 114–18.

202 See my "Scenes of Instruction."

203 The notion of reproduction is referenced also by the presence of reproductive prints made after Charles-Antoine Coypel paintings on the wall behind the lady. They are discussed and reproduced in *Chardin*, 1979, 288–89.

204 These anatomical inaccuracies are discernible in both versions of this painting, the one reproduced here and the one at the Louvre, which Rosenberg takes to be the original one. See his arguments in *Chardin* 1979, no. 93, and reasserted in PR *Chardin* 1999, nos. 134 and 134a. However, if, as Rosenberg maintains, the New York painting was based on the Louvre version, it is puzzling that it still took the painter as much effort as it did to situate the figure on canvas.

205 The epigraph for this section is taken from [Turgot], entry on "Existence," *Encyclopédie*, 6: 261. "Mais qu'est-ce qu'exister?"

206 For this suggestion, see Rosenberg in *Chardin*, 1979, 237, and, more developed, Conisbee in *French Paintings*, 73.

207 For gravity as the distinguishing feature of Chardin's depictions of children, see Roland Michel, *Chardin*, 44.

208 On the relation of these paintings to the earlier eighteenth-century iconography of *jeu d'enfants*, and on Chardin's distinct view of play as a creative and culturally productive activity, see Scott, "Child's Play," and "Chardin: On the Art of Building Castles." On Chardin's distinct emphasis on the pedagogical value of play, see Johnson "Picturing Pedagogy," esp. 66–68.

209 In addition to Scott and Johnson, see Fried, *Absorption and Theatricality*, 11–17 and 44–53; Snoep-Reitsma, "Chardin," 198–219; Conisbee, *Masterpieces in Focus "Soap Bubbles"*; Démoris, *Chardin*, 84–90 and 99–110; Démoris, "Inside/Interiors"; and Herbert, "A Picture of Chardin's Making."

210 For this painting being the first in the series, see PR *Chardin* 1999, no. 103. For its rich contextualized discussion prompted by its acquisition by the Rothschild Foundation, Waddesdon Manor in 2007, see Carey, *Taking Time*. For the Louvre *House of Cards*, see PR *Chardin* 1999, no. 104.

211 "A man who lived only a private life, who like the slave was not permitted to enter a public realm, or like a barbarian, had chosen not to establish such a realm, was not fully human," states Arendt referring to the Greek context. *The Human Condition*, cited in Lukes, *Individualism*, 60.

212 This developmental stage was described in the discourse on children's education from Locke to Rousseau. See Johnson, "Picturing Pedagogy," 59–68. For the psychological dimension of this development, see also Démoris, *Chardin*, and Scott, "Child's Play," 98–102.

213 For an illuminating philosophical history of this notion, from Antiquity to the present, see Heller-Roazen, *The Inner Touch: An Archeology of Sensation*.

214 *An Essay concerning Human Understanding*, 547, italics mine. Locke discusses the role of "internal sense" as the source of ideas in Book 2, esp. 110–11.

215 On Locke's early reception in France, see Yolton, *Locke and French Materialism*. On the importance of Locke's legacy for French sensationist philosophy, particularly Condillac, see O'Neal, *The Authority of Experience*, esp. 13–59.

216 Rousseau, "Fourth Walk," 86–87. For the discussion of Rousseau and abbé Joseph-Adrien Lelarge de Lignac, *Élements de Métaphysique* (1753), and *Testimony of an Inner Sense and of Experience* (1760), see Heller-Roazen, *The Inner Touch*, 215–16. For broader discussion of the "inner sense" in the eighteenth century, see Heller-Roazen, *The Inner Touch*, chap. 22. For the interest of late seventeenth- and early eighteenth-century materialist thinkers in England and France, among them La Mettrie, in the notion of the inner sense, see also Thomson, *Bodies of Thought: Science, Religion, and the Soul in the Early Enlightenment*, esp. 198–203.

217 Although he was better known for his progressive social and economic theories, and his political career that included a meteorically short tenure as the de facto finance minister of the ancien régime from 1774–76, Turgot was also a contributor to the *Encyclopédie* for which, in 1756, he penned five articles, among them one on "Existence," published anonymously. See Dakin, *Turgot and the Ancien Régime in France*, 16; and Grimsley, "Turgot's Article on 'Existence' in the *Encyclopédie*."

218 "cette multitude de sensations confuses qui ne nous abandonnent jamais, qui nous circonscrivent en quelque sorte notre corps, qui nous rendent toujours présent, & que par cette raison quelques metaphysiciens ont apellées *sens de la coexistence de notre corps*." "Existence," in *Encyclopédie*, 6: 621. (Italics in the original.) In the last sentence, Turgot is no doubt referring to abbé de Lignac.

219 "nous bornons le sentiment du *moi* à ce petit espace circonscrit par le plaisir et par la douleur" (*Encyclopédie*, 6: 262). The "small space" is here our body, in relation to much bigger objects such as the moon or stars that produce in us similar sensations but that we nonetheless do not identify with "our own peculiar being." (Let us note the connection between Turgot's sense of bodily contours established by the psychological, sense-based experience and Green's notion of negative hallucination discussed earlier.)

220 *Encyclopédie*, 6: 231.

221 "la connexité qui enchaîne entr'eux les changement de tous les êtres et nos propres sensations comme causes et effets les uns des autres." Ibid., 6: 262.

222 Ibid., 6: 263; and Grimsley, "Turgot's Article," 114. Rousseau, too, has later offered a similar assessment of the importance of affect for children's sensory development. See his Rousseau, *Emile; or, On Education*, esp. 62–63.

223 To be clear, I do not wish to establish Turgot as a belated "source" for the painter, but rather to foreground their shared concern with internal experience. Much of what Turgot put into words in 1756, Chardin had already painted in the mid-1730s. The condition of possibility for their respective formulations was the French reception of British empiricism.

224 I am referring to Fried's argument in *Absorption and Theatricality*, 11–17 and 44–53.

225 Turgot, "Existence," 262.

226 Michel Foucault has been the most influential in making us aware of this phenomenon. See his *History of Sexuality: Volume 1, An Introduction*. See also Laquer, *Making Sex: Body and Gender from the Greeks to Freud*.

227 Démoris, *Chardin*, 85.

228 The title under which this painting was exhibited at the Salon of 1737, retained by Cochin when he engraved the image a year later, registers the pleasure being taken in lunch rather than the fact of lunching, as does the caption under the print (likely Cochin's own): "Simple are the pleasures I take in my meal, / I also know how to find diversion in it." See Wildenstein, 64; and PR *Chardin* 1999, no. 92.

229 For the erotic resonance of the cherry-picking iconography from the sixteenth to the eighteenth century, see Snoep-Reitsma, "Chardin," 212–17.

230 Chardin's choice of the subject may have had something to do with the fact that the maternal side of his family, the Davids, were artisans specializing in making rackets and instruments for racket games.

231 See Claretie, *Un enlèvement au XVIII*[e] *siècle, documents tirés des Archives nationales*. On the commentaries from the period, among them Barbier, *Chroniques de la Régence et du Règne de Louis XV (1718–1763)* and Duc de Luynes's *Mémoirs*, see Démoris, "Postface," in Mouhy, *Mémoirs d'Anne-Marie de Moras*.

232 *Mémoirs d'Anne-Marie de Moras*. Journalist and playwright, Mouhy was the author of five novels, including the most popular *La Mouche* (1736), *Le Masque de Fer* (1737), and *Lamedis* (1735–37).

233 For a nuanced analysis of Mouhy's heroine's psychological development, see Démoris's "Postface," esp. 226–29.

234 Although limited in her resources at the convent, Anne-Marie finds an ingenious way to simulate breasts by using rubber bands, and to produce fake proofs of menstruation in order to pass for a sexually mature young person.

235 Greuze's *Broken Jug* (Louvre), close in size and format to the *Girl with a Shuttlecock*, makes explicit the bodily and moral risks involved in an adolescent girl's entry into the social sphere of desire.

236 See *Salon of 1765*, in Goodman, *Diderot on Art*, 1: 97–99.

237 See Johnson, "Picturing Pedagogy."

238 *Good Education* was the title of Le Bas's print made after the painting and adopted since in Chardin's literature. The painting was exhibited at the Salon of 1753 under the title *Une jeune fille qui récite son Évangile* (*A Young Girl Reciting the New Testament*). While the meaning of the girl's expression is ambiguous, one critic saw her as "working with her memory" (*Jugement d'un Amateur*, in Wildenstein, 88.)

239 The other two versions of the painting are in the Metropolitan Museum, New York, and in the National Gallery, Washington, respectively. For the summary of the discussions regarding all the versions of the painting, see Conisbee, *French Painting*, 64–67, no. 12.

240 The connection between the two is the clearer if we remember that painters at the time mix their pigments themselves, the vials and sacs with substances needed for this purpose having been featured in Chardin's own early *Attributes of the Arts* (Princeton).

241 For an extensive discussion of Chardin's use of Dutch sources, see Snoep-Reitsma, "Chardin." For those relevant for the *Soap Bubbles*, see Roland Michel, *Chardin*, 122–26.

242 Fried, *Absorption and Theatricality*, 51.

243 *Cours de peinture*, 99–105. For the discussion of de Piles's "unity of the object," see Puttfarken, *Roger de Piles' Theory*, 80–105.

244 De Piles, *Principles of Painting*, 231.

245 See Puttfarken, *Roger de Piles' Theory*, 125–38.

246 "De l'Illusion dans la Peinture" (1765), in *Receuil de quelques pièces concernant les Arts*, 2: 44–75. The essay was reprinted in Watelet's *Dictionary of Art* (1788), a fact indicating its importance. For in-depth analysis of the text, see Michel, *Charles-Nicolas Cochin*, 267–78 and 603.

247 Michel, *Charles-Nicolas Cochin*, 270.

248 "L'une des plus grandes beautés de l'art, qui a encore moins de rapport avec illusion, puisqu'elle n'a pas même fondement dans la nature, et qu'elle est uniquement l'effet du *sentiment qui meut l'artiste en opérant*; c'est cet art dans le travail." "De l'Illusion," 69, italics mine.

249 For the earlier understanding of sentiment, including Dubos's, see Becq, *La Genèse de l'Ésthetique*, 243–73. For the tradition of connecting color and sentiment, see Démoris, "Dessin et couleur."

250 "De l'Illusion," 68.

251 For the anecdote, recounted also by Diderot (Salon of 1769), see *Essai*, 40.

252 Note the deliberate choreography of the boy's hands arranged in a way that emphasizes the connective role of touch as the means of transfer of his experience of the object onto his experience of his own body. For the conjunction of vision and sight in this image, see the short but suggestive reading offered by Crary (*Techniques of the Observer*, 64–66).

253 The epigraph for this section is taken from Diderot, *Salon de 1765*, in Versini, *Oeuvres*, 345. "Vous revoilà, donc, grand magicien, avec vos compositions muettes." I quote Goodman's translation in *Diderot on Art*, 1: 60.

254 At the Salon of 1748, abbé Gougenot calls for Chardin to exhibit more works and not to neglect still life painting in particular. (*Lettre sur la Peinture*, in Wildenstein, 83.) In 1751, after praising the painter, another critic states that "Nature, showering him with her favors, has worked for an ingrate, the public is angry at not seeing more than one painting by so knowing a hand." *Jugement sur les principaux ouvrages*, in Wildenstein, 85.

255 See *Explications des peintures*, 1753, nos. 59–65 (nos. 59 and 64 listing two paintings each).

256 According to Rosenberg, the painting, shown, unlisted, at the Salon of 1761, was painted around 1754. See PR *Chardin* 1999, 126, and nos. 140 and 140a, 263.

257 How unconventional this was may be gauged from Chardin's colleague Oudry's recommendation to the young painters to carefully remove all traces of their brushes, even when sketching. See his *Discours sur la Pratique de la Peinture et ces Procédés Principaux: ébaucher, peindre à fond et retoucher* [1752], 11, 13 and 17.

258 Bosschaert's vision, on the other hand, combines, to borrow Svetlana Alpers words, "absorption in what is seen with a *selflessness* or anonymity that is [. . .] characteristic of the Dutch artists." *The Art of Describing: Dutch Art in the Seventeenth Century*, 83, italics mine.

259 To be sure, some sense of difficulty especially in the disposition of objects persisted, as the 1755 *Kitchen Table* with which I began this chapter suggests, but overall these still lifes manifest a new approach to the object.

260 *Salon de 1763*, in Versini, *Oeuvres*, 265.

261 See "Partage de la succession de Jeanne-Françoise David mère de Chardin," A.N., M.C., Étude LXXXII, liasse 263, repr. in Wildenstein, 76–77. For documents regarding the financial situation of Chardin's family, see Savina, "Biographie," 386.

262 See Savina, "Biographie," 386 and 388.

263 Between 1759, when he started writing Salon criticism, and 1775, Diderot reviewed Chardin's work regularly. His most elaborate and significant commentaries on Chardin's paintings were offered in the period 1763–69. See Sahut and Volle, *Diderot et l'Art*, 146–59.

264 The two men knew each other, as Diderot's frequent mentions of his direct interactions with the painter in the *Salons* indicate. At the outset of the Salon of 1765, he reports Chardin's speech addressed to him and other critics

(Goodman, *Diderot on Art*, 1: 4–7; Versini, *Oeuvres*, 292–94). The critic also frequently evokes Chardin's knowledge about art and his ability to talk about it. (E.g., *Salon de 1759* and *Salon de 1761*, in Versini, *Oeuvres*, 197 and 218.) It is likely that the painter knew what Diderot wrote about him.

265 See Leblanc, *Observations sur les ouvrages de MM. de l'Académie*, 23–25; Baillet de Saint Jullien, *Caractères des Peintres*, 5, cited in PR *Chardin* 1999, 169; Lacombe, *Salon* [de 1753], 24. *Mercure de France* also offered consistently admiring reviews of Chardin's new work. (E.g., October 1765, 193–94.) For these and other commentaries on Chardin's new still lifes, see Wildenstein, 87ff.

266 Chardin indeed used this power, choosing to pair paintings judiciously, sometimes to other painters' discontent. See Roland Michel, "Chardin Tapissier," in *Chardin*, 77–91; Whyte, "Exhibiting Enlightenment: Chardin as Tapissier"; and Pichet, *Le Tapissier et les Dispositifs Discursifs au Salon (1750–1789): Expographie, Critique et Opinion.*

267 The connection between these two paintings has been first established by Rosenberg in *Chardin* 1979, no. 74, 237–39.

268 Bryson, *Looking at the Overlooked*, 93.

269 The smoker's case was listed in the inventory of Chardin's household made after the death of his first wife, in 1737: "une tabagie de bois de palisandre fermant à clef et main d'acier doublée en dedans de satin bleu." *Chardin* 1979, 238.

270 The motif of the porcelain bowl of berries, usually a flower stuck into them for contrast, was standard in Dutch and Flemish still life. One example is Jacob van Hulsdonck, *Wild Strawberries and Carnation in a Wan-li bowl*, 1620, at the National Gallery of Art, Washington, DC.

271 See the *Treatise on the Sensations* (1754), discussed above. For Jonathan Crary, the epistemic grid sustaining the composition, such as the *Basket of Wild Strawberries*, is Cartesian rather than sensationist. See his *Techniques of the Observer*, 62–66.

272 The connection between Condillac and Chardin has also been suggested by Baxandall in his nuanced discussion of the painter's textures ("Attention, Hand and Brush"). For Baxandall, while Chardin's execution speaks to both senses, it ultimately privileges vision over touch.

273 For these, see PR *Chardin* 1999, nos. 144, 146, and 190.

274 See PR *Chardin* 1999, nos. 148–48A.

275 The *Butler's Table* is about one-sixth of the *Buffet* (194 × 129 cm).

276 These are the terms in which Diderot described Chardin's still lifes in his *Salon de 1763*, on which more below. For *Grapes and Pomegranates* and *The Brioche*, both in the Louvre, see PR *Chardin*, nos. 167, 168.

277 Goodman, *Diderot on Art*, 1: 60 (Versini, *Oeuvres*, 345).

278 For the discussion of the individuated mode of contemplation of the work of art based in its direct sensory experience, see Griener, *La République de l'oeil.*

279 I follow the English translation in *Chardin*, 2000, 288. (Versini, *Oeuvres*, 265.)

280 "C'est la nature même; les objets sont hors de la toile et d'une verité à tromper les yeux." (It is nature itself; the objects come out of the painting and their truthful appearance deceives the eyes.) *Salon de 1763*, in Versini, *Oeuvres*, 264. Diderot makes a similar observation in *Salon de 1759*: "C'est toujours la nature et la vérité." (Versini, *Oeuvres*, 197.)

281 Diderot evokes Chardin's "*sublime du technique*" in the *Salon of 1765* (Goodman, *Diderot on Art*, 1: 56). For a discussion of this notion, see Démoris, "The Far Side of Illusion," 107–9.

282 Goodman, *Diderot on Art*, 1: 63; and *Salon 1763*, in Versini, *Oeuvres*, 264.

283 *Chardin*, 2000, 288. (I have slightly altered the translation.) "On entend rien à cette magie. Ce sont des couches épaisses de couleur appliquées les unes sur les autres et dont l'effet transpire de dessous en dessus. D'autres fois, on dirait que c'est une vapeur qu'on à soufflée sur la toile; ailleurs, une écume légère qu'on y a jetée. [. . .] Approchez-vous, tout se brouille, s'aplatit et disparât, éloignez-vous, tout se recrée et se reproduit." Versini, *Oeuvres*, 265.

284 *Chardin*, 2000, 288. (Versini, *Oeuvres*, 264.)

285 For the scopic dimension of Diderot's gaze, see Lojkin, "Diderot," 40–42.

286 *Notes on Painting*, in Goodman, *Diderot on Art*, 1: 201.

287 Ibid., 2: 86 (Versini, *Oeuvres*, 593). The passage directly precedes, and anticipates, Diderot's commentary on Vernet's landscapes, which the critic treats as a series of imaginary locations into which he transports himself.

288 *Diderot on Art*, 1: 60–61 (Versini, *Oeuvres*, 36). "Genre" was then a term that comprised all "lower" types of paintings, including still life. See Bailey, "Surveying Genre."

289 In the original manuscript of the review, Diderot exhorted the reader, "Réfléchissez à cette ressemblance des philosophes avec les peintres de genre" (Do reflect on this resemblance between philosophers and genre painters), a fragment of the sentence crossed out in the final version. *Oeuvres Complètes de Diderot*, 300.

290 Chardin was also portrayed by Joseph Ducreux, in 1767 (this work has now been lost; see Lyon, *Joseph Ducreux (1735–1802), Premier peintre de Marie Antoinette*, 165), and by Cochin, who drew medallion portrait busts of his friend and colleague in 1755 (Louvre) and ca. 1776 (British Museum).

291 On the infirmities that led Chardin to abandon oil painting and turn to pastel, see Cochin, *Essai*, 39. Rosenberg has suggested that it was the lead in the painter's favorite white pigment that contributed to the deterioration of his sight ("New Thoughts," 15).

292 Shown at the Salons of 1771 and 1775, respectively, the first two self-portraits, which are signed and dated, were listed as head studies (*têtes d'étude*) but were identified as the painter's likenesses by the commentators. (See the *livret* listings repr. in Wildenstein, 126 and 132.) The last self-portrait is neither signed nor dated, but Rosenberg has suggested it may have been one of the two "têtes de veillard" mentioned by a critic in his review of the Salon of 1779. (*Le Miracle de nos Jours* [1779], 40, cited in Wildenstein, 141.) See PR *Chardin* 1999, 288. For the discussion of all three self-portraits, see McCullagh and Rosenberg, "'The Supreme Triumph of the Old Painter': Chardin's Final Work in Pastel."

293 References to Chardin's first self-portrait can be found in *Lettre de Baron X*** à Milord X**** (1771); and *Plaintes de M. Badigeon, Marchand de Couleurs, ou les Critiques du Salon 1771* (1771), 10–11, both cited in *Chardin*, 1979, 364. The second self-portrait was mentioned in *Observations sur les Ouvrages exposés* (1775); and in Bachaumont, *Mémoirs secrets*, vol. 13 (1775), 211. (Both cited in Wildenstein, 132.) For the critical reception of the self-portraits, see McCullagh and Rosenberg, "The Supreme Triumph."

294 "Il y eût [au pastel] les plus grands succès par son savoir et par sa manière large et facile, du moins en apparence, car elle était le fruit de beaucoup de réflexions, et il se satisfait difficilement. Ces morceaux firent connaître combien il avait le sentiment du grand, et ce qu'il eût pu être dans le genre de l'histoire s'il s'y fut attaché." Cochin, *Essai*, 39. ("He succeeded in this extremely well through his ability and his bold, easy manner, easy at least in appearance, for it was the fruit of much reflection, and he was hard to satisfy. These pieces let it be known to what extent he had a feeling for what is great and what he might have accomplished in history genre if he had put his mind to it.") Conisbee's trans. in *Chardin*, 226, with slight alteration.

295 On this institutional formula of portrayal, see Williams, *Académie Royale*, 17–75. It was used in both portraits of artists and self-portraits, the latter having not yet been established in France as a separate category (self-portrait was then called "portrait de l'artiste par lui-même").

296 Roland Michel referred to the 1779 likeness as "a ruthless portrait of an old man with an absent look" (*Chardin*, 226).

297 "'Chardin n'est pas un peintre d'histoire, mais c'est un grand homme': Les autoportraits tardifs de Jean-Siméon Chardin," 279–97.

298 Vincent's presentation of his sitter without a wig, "en tenue d'intérieur presque agressivement affichée," has been judged as inconceivable outside the artistic milieu. See Cuzin, *Vincent 1746–1816: Entre Fragonard et David*, 44–46.

299 "Tien, régarde-moi, je suis [cet artisan fameux,] cet unique dans ma profession," *Cours de peinture*, 279.

300 "Chardin et ses oeuvres à Potsdam et à Stockholm," 395. I am citing the passage in McCullagh's translation. (McCullagh and Rosenberg, "The Supreme Triumph," 46.)

301 Unlike oils, the opaque and powdery pastels cannot be applied in glazes to modify the hues because they would produce only gray or muddled effects. See Shelley, "Painting in the Dry Manner: The Flourishing of Pastel in 18th-Century Europe," 12.

302 See *Traité des principes et de règles de la peinture, par M. J-É. Liotard*. For the discussion of Liotard's views in this matter, see my "Jean-Etienne Liotard's Envelopes of Self."

303 "Letter to Émile Bernard," June 27, 1904, cited in *Chardin* 1979, 370. Cézanne was so impressed by this particular effect of Chardin's craft that he reported it also in a letter to the mathematician Félix Klein. "Léttre de Paul Cézanne à Félix Klein," 319.

304 Denk, "Chardin n'est pas un peintre," 290–93.

305 The first term refers to the double lenses connected by a bridge with a spring mechanism that allowed them to attach directly to the nose (later called *pince-nez*), the second to spectacles with arms that ran along the temples and rested on the ear lobes. See Vitols, *Dictionnaire des lunettes: historique et symbolique d'un object culturel*.

306 Barral and Michel, *Oeuvres complètes*, 20.

307 Widely read, Montaigne's *Essays* had fourteen French editions in the eighteenth century, including an unexpurgated French edition published by Pierre Coste in London in 1724 that became a primary reference throughout the period. Among the avid readers of Montaigne were the *philosophes*, Diderot and Rousseau in particular. For the eighteenth-century reception of the *Essays*, see Dréano, *La Renommée de Montaigne en France au XVIIIe siècle*, 1677–1802.

308 Screech, "Introduction," in Montaigne, *The Complete Essays*, xiii–xlviii.

309 "To the reader," in Montaigne, *The Complete Essays*, n.p.

310 I am paraphrasing Stephen Greenblatt, *Renaissance Self-Fashioning: From More to Shakespeare*, 87. For self-performance in the *Essays*, see also Regosin, "Montaigne and His Readers," 248–53.

311 In 1774 Chardin, too, retired from his post as a treasurer and *tapisseur* at the Academy.

312 "To the reader."

313 From the evidence at hand, the pastels and their replicas belonged to Chardin's friends, most of them artists, and family members. The Louvre version of the 1771 *Self-Portrait* was owned by a draftsman, Jacques-Augustin de Sylvestre (1729– 1790), and later by the painter and pastelist Gounod (1758–1823). The autograph and dated copy of this work (1773, the Musée des Beaux-Arts, Orléans), was offered by the painter to his pupil, Mlle de la Marsaulaye, "par son maître." (Inscription on the back of the canvas.) Another version was listed in the sculptor Pigalle's inventory made after his death in 1785, though it is unclear which of the *Self-Portraits* it actually was. (PR *Chardin* 1999, nos. 194 and 194A, 284.) We have no information about the original owner of the *Self-Portrait with Visor* (Louvre), but an autographed replica of it (now in the Art Institute, Chicago) remained in Chardin's possession upon his death and was passed on to his wife, and, after her death, to Chardin's brother, Juste. (McCullagh and Rosenberg, "'The Supreme Triumph,'" 44.) The provenance of the last *Self-Portrait* is not clear. Rosenberg has proposed that it belonged to Pigalle. (PR *Chardin* 1999, nos. 204, 288.)

314 Chardin announced the gift in his letter of resignation addressed to the Academy and read at the session of July 30, 1774. See Wildenstein, 129.

315 *The Moment of Self-Portraiture in German Renaissance Art*.

316 I borrow the term from Louis Marin. See his "'C'est moi que je peins . . .': De la figurabilité du moi chez Montaigne," 114.

317 For eighteenth-century men's habit of wearing bonnets, turbans, or head wraps at home, due mainly to the badly heated interiors, see Ribeiro, *Dress in Eighteenth-Century Europe*, 27 and 175, and Ribeiro, *The Art of Dress: Fashion in England and France 1750 to 1820*, 50–52.

318 Only in 1757 was Chardin offered a studio and lodging in the Louvre. See "Brevet de don d'un logement aux Galleries du Louvre pour le Sieur Chardin," May 27, 1757, repr. in Savina, "Biographie," 391–92.

319 Chardin's first self-portrait was known through an engraving (1780) by Juste Chevillet.

320 The exception was besicles produced as a luxury object, such as those offered by duc de Luynes to Marie Leszczyńska as a New Year's gift in 1751. Corson, *Fashions in Eyeglasses*, 63.

321 See *Memoirs of the Blind*.

322 For the letters and other sources documenting Chardin's decline in the 1770s, see Wildenstein, 124–51, and Savina, "Biographie," 399–407.

323 See Conisbee, *Chardin*, 217–19.

324 *Procès-verbaux de l'Académie*, cited in Wildenstein, 129.

325 See Wildenstein, 130–40.

326 "Il est dur de molester un vieillard à qui le Roi a accordé les invalides." "Lettre de Chardin à M. Angiviller," March 21, 1777, in Wildenstein, 134.

327 Documents of this acrimonious exchange are reprinted in Wildenstein, 137–40. For the account of it, see also Conisbee, *Chardin*, 218–9.

328 When he was in power, Cochin made sure Chardin received appropriately high payments for royal commissions—e.g., his overdoors for the chateaux de Choisy (1764) and Bellevue (1766)—and he successfully lobbied for the painter's royal pension, granted in 1752, and for its augmentation later on. (See Savina, "Biographie," 398–401.) Moreover, it was no doubt thanks to Cochin's intercession that Chardin received his lodging at the Louvre. (Ibid., 391.)

329 See Wildenstein, 138.

330 The details of Chardin's financial situation were documented in Savina, "Biographie," 399. For a comparative account of French incomes at the time, see Jean Sgard, "L'Échelle de revenus," 427.

331 "M. Chardin me rapelle ces athlêtes qui, chancellant après un combat terrible, rappelont toutes leur forces pour aller expirer dans l'arène." *La Prêtresse, ou nouvelle Manière de prédire ce qui est arrivé* (1777), 13, cited in Wildenstein, 136.

CHAPTER THREE

1 The epigraph for this chapter is taken from Boyer d'Argens, *Thérèse philosophe*, 143. "Pour faire son bonheur, chacun doit saisir le genre de plaisir qui lui est propre."

2 In addition to Sheriff's groundbreaking attempt to define the erotics of Fragonard's art (*Fragonard*), the indispensable modern sources in Fragonard's vast literature are: Wildenstein, *The Paintings of Fragonard*; PR *Fragonard*; Cuzin *Fragonard*; Cuzin et al., *Jean-Honoré Fragonard*; Dupuy-Vachey, *Fragonard: Les Plaisirs d'un Siècle*; Reuter et al., *Fragonard: Poesie und Leidenschaft*; and Faroult, *Fragonard Amoureux*. Fragonard's vast bibliography can be found in those works.

3 The most extensive, historically contextualized analysis of Fragonard's handling has been offered by Sheriff, in her *Fragonard*, esp. 112–52. See also Bryson, *Word and Image*, esp. 99–109 and 195– 203. In the more recent scholarship, see especially Molotiu, *Fragonard's Allegories*; Padiyar, "Out of Time: Fragonard and David"; and Sheriff, "Aux Prises avec le désir."

4 For the account of Fragonard's training, see Rosenberg, "Fragonard's Early Years (1732–56)," in PR *Fragonard*, 31–33, and Dupuy-Vachey, *Fragonard*, chap. 1. For re-evaluation of his relation to the Academy, see Cuzin, "Fragonard en 2006," in Cuzin et al., *Jean-Honoré Fragonard*, 194–201.

5 As Natoire's letters to Marigny on his performance at the Rome Academy attest. See Montaiglon and Guiffrey, *Correspondence des Directeurs de l'Académie de France à Rome*, 11: 207–385.

6 On *Coresus and Callirhoë*, see Sheriff, *Fragonard*, 30–57; and Rabreau and Henry, *Corésus et Callirhoé de Fragonard*.

7 See Goodman, *Diderot on Art*, 1: 141–48.

8 Aside from the *Groups*, Fragonard exhibited only a small painting, *Head of an Old Man in Profile*, and several drawings (*Livret* listing cited in PR *Fragonard*, 227). For Diderot's comment, see *Salon of 1767*, in Goodman, *Diderot on Art*, 2: 256. From then on, Diderot gave up on Fragonard as a critic but he continued to value him as an artist, referring to him as the painter of importance in his *Jacques le Fataliste* (1778–80).

9 Fragonard was only residually present at the Salon through prints made after his work that were exhibited there. He also continued to exhibit in the unofficial public venues, such as the Salon de la Correspondance, but these displays did not generate the same amount or, because of their openly commercial status, the same *kind* of critical response as the Salon.

10 The work required of him to be accepted as a full member of the Academy, a decoration of one of the ceilings of the Galerie d'Apollon was assigned to him in May 1766. On his failure to complete this official commission, see Gallini in Bresc-Bautier, *The Apollo Gallery in the Louvre*.

11 "On prétend que l'appas du gain l'on détourné de la belle carrière où il étoit entré et qu'au lieu de travailler pour la gloire et pour la posterité, il se contente de briller aujourd'hui dans les boudoirs et dans les gardes-robes." (*Mémoirs secrets*, 8, 32–33.) "Année 1769, Lettre I," in *Les Salons des Mémoirs secrets*, 49.

12 "M. Fragonard? Il perd son temps et son talent: il gagne de l'argent." Madame d'Épinay to Galiani, October 5, 1771, in Galiani, *L'Abbé F. Galiani: Correspondence*, 441. For an early critical reassessment of Fragonard as an artist "painting for money," see Sheriff, "For Love or Money? Rethinking Fragonard." Fragonard's odd position within the artistic culture of his time has recently been nuanced. See Ledbury, "The Hierarchy of Genres," 198–202; Guichard, *Les amateurs d'art*, and "Fragonard et les jeux de la signature au XVIIIe siècle." For a less Academy-focused account of the painter's career, see also Dupuy-Vachey, *Fragonard*.

13 "Fragonard jouit de la plus grande réputation, ces bon dessins se payent au poids de l'or et ils le méritent." President Haudry in a letter to Desfriches, 1787, cited in PR *Fragonard*, 429. At the sale of the Randon de Boisset collection in 1777, Fragonard's painting of *Visitation* fetched a phenomenal prize of 7,000 livres, a fact that elicited many commentaries. For comparison, his own large-scale history painting of *Coresus*, purchased by the state for 2,300 livres, was not paid in full until 1773. See PR *Fragonard*, 212. On the high prices of Fragonard's work and its position on the art market, see Schieder, "Jean-Honoré Fragonard und der Pariser Kunstmarkt im ausgehenden Ancien Régime."

14 The phrase "la légèreté et l'esprit de sa touche" was used by one commentator à propos Fragonard's landscape exhibited in 1782 at the Salon de la Correspondance. Cited in PR *Fragonard*, 425. In 1786 Thiéry lauded his "magical execution [that] cannot be too highly praised" (ibid., 428).

15 See PR *Fragonard*, 226.

16 For the discussion of erotic terminology in seventeenth- and eighteenth-century literary and artistic culture, see Leoni, "Plaisir des mots"; Christian Michel, "Nature and Moeurs: Thoughts on the Reception of Genre Painting in France"; and Kristel Smentek, "Sex, Sentiment, and Speculation: The Market for Genre Prints on the Eve of the French Revolution." As Leoni has pointed out, what we now call "erotic art" was referred to in the eighteenth century through other terms, such as "voluptuous" or "licentious," the term *eros* (except for references to the god of love) having been introduced in common usage only a century later. Nonetheless, the term *erotic* has been customarily used in regard to Fragonard's art, and I too will use it interchangeably with the period's terms.

17 See La Font de Saint-Yenne's attack on private patrons, especially women (*Réflexions* [1746], in Jollet, *Oeuvre Critique*, 52–53); and Diderot attacking M. De La Borde for commissioning paintings by Vernet for his private abode and refusing to share them with the wider audience by sending them to the Salon exhibition (*Salon de 1769*, in Versini, *Oeuvres*, 4: 825–27). On this question more broadly, see Crow, *Painters and Public Life*. For a different appreciation of private collecting in this period, see Michel, *Peinture et Plaisir*.

18 "S'il y avait quelque homme pervers qui put s'offenser d'éloge que je fais de la plus auguste et de la plus générale des passions, j'evoquerais devant lui la nature, je la ferais parler." *Encyclopédie*, 8: 889. Diderot offered a similar attack on prudes who would criticize literary references to sexuality in his *Jacques le Fataliste*.

19 This is the term he uses in relation to Boucher. See Diderot, *Notes on Painting*, in Goodman, *Diderot on Art*, 1: 224. For Diderot's views on Boucher, see also chap. 1 here. We have also seen how careful Diderot was in divorcing his pleasure taken in Chardin's paintings from the libidinal register, calling it "philosophical" precisely for that reason (see chap. 2 here).

20 Foucault, *The History of Sexuality: Volume 1*.

21 Ibid., 78. See also Dubost, "Libertinage and Rationality: From the 'Will to Knowledge' to Libertine Textuality," 59.

22 Foucault, *History of Sexuality: Volume 1*, 59. See the helpful discussion of this issue in Rajchman, *Truth and Eros: Foucault, Lacan, and the Question of Ethics*.

23 It is in this respect that these new pursuits of sexual truth were, in Foucault's view, the harbingers of the nascent *scientia sexualis* distinct from *ars erotica* of the premodern period. They produced a certain form of "knowledge-power" through which the state could exercise control over the subject in the modern era. Foucault, *History of Sexuality: Volume 1*, 53–73.

24 For a critique of Foucault, see Giddens,

The Constitution of Society; *The Transformation of Intimacy*; and "Critique of Foucault." Among feminist critiques, see especially Judith Butler, *Gender Trouble: Feminism and the Subversion of Identity*; *Bodies That Matter: On the Discursive Limits of "Sex"*; *Excitable Speech: A Politics of the Performative*; and *Giving an Account of Oneself: A Critique of Ethical Violence*.

25 The construction of Fragonard as a belated rococo painter goes back to Edmond and Jules de Goncourt. See their "Fragonard," in *French Eighteenth-Century Painters*, 259–312. As for the view of him as proto-romantic, see Molotiu, *Fragonard's Allegories*. For a different account, see my "Fragonard in Detail" and "Genre and Sex." A provocative reassessment of the temporality of Fragonard's style has been offered by Padiyar, in his essay "Out of Time: Fragonard and David."

26 For the *Bolt*, see Faroult, *Jean-Honoré Fragonard: Le Verrou*.

27 Evocative analysis of the painting has been offered by Sheriff in "Aux Prises avec le désir," 41–47.

28 Marianne Roland Michel notes as much: "C'est ne sont ni des héros de romans, ni des divinités olympiennes, mai des êtres de chair et de sang, des filles fraiches, des garçon amoureux, tout le monde et n'importe qui." "Fragonard, Illustrateur de l'Amour," 30. She also noted that Fragonard depicts sex as a distinctly physical activity.

29 Boucher's protagonists are emphatically generic as well, but differently so: they are *actors*, manifestly fictional characters enacting pastoral scenarios. For a lucid account of Boucher's generic figures and gender, see Hyde, "Confounding Conventions: Gender Ambiguity and François Boucher's Painted Pastorals."

30 See Chartier, *A History of Private Life*. The status of sexual activity as distinct and separate from other activities finds parallel and articulation in the emergence of new structures of domestic architecture, with separate rooms for separate activities. There is rich literature on this, see, among others, Eleb-Vidal, *Architecture de la vie privée: Maisons et mentalités, XVIIe–XIXe siècles*; DeJean, *The Age of Comfort: When Paris Discovered Casual—and Modern Home Began*; and Hellman, "Staging Retreat: Designs for Bathing in Eighteenth-Century France."

31 See Desné, *Le Matérialistes français de 1750 à 1800*. For useful nuanced account of eighteenth-century materialism in its diverse manifestations, see Ann Thomson, "Materialism," in Kors, *Encyclopedia of the Enlightenment*.

32 "Un individu se présente-t-il à un individu de la même espece [*sic*] & d'un sexe différent, le sentiment de tout autre besoin est suspendu; le coeur palpite; les membres tressaillient; des images voluptueuses errent dans le cerveau; de torrens d'esprit coulent dans les nerfs, les irritent, & vont se rendre au siège d'un nouveau sens qui se déclare & qui tourmente. La vûe se trouble, le délire naît; la raison esclave de l'instinct se borne à le servir, & la nature est satisfaite." [Diderot], *Encyclopédie*, entry on "Jouissance."

33 See Jacob, "The Materialist World of Pornography." On the connection between pornography and Enlightenment philosophy, see also Darnton, "Philosophical Pornography," in *The Forbidden Best-Sellers of Pre-Revolutionary France*, 85–114; and Darnton, *The Literary Underground of the Old Regime*.

34 It is by now largely accepted that the author of this novel, published anonymously, is Jean-Baptiste de Boyer, comte d'Argens (1704–1771). See "Thérèse-philosophe de Boyer d'Argens," in Wald Lasowski, *Romanciers libertins du XVIIIe siècle*. The striking similarities between its arguments and the postulates advanced by La Mettrie have been stressed. See Jacob, "The Materialist World of Pornography," and Darnton, "Philosophical Pornography." See also Kavanagh, *Enlightened Pleasures: Eighteenth-Century France and the New Epicureanism*, 52–70, who sees *Thérèse* as an Epicurean allegory.

35 *Thérèse philosophe*, 143. Italics mine. This idea is close to La Mettrie's arguments. See his *De la Volupté*, 139–40.

36 For the different artists' illustrations for the editions of *Thérèse philosophe*, see *Thérèse-philosophe: Erotische Küpferstiche aus fünf berühmten Büchern*, and Darnton, "Philosophical Pornography."

37 Jean Barrin, *Venus dans le Cloître*, 1746. Fragonard himself had tried his hand in book illustration, some of it erotic (though not pornographic), as in some of La Fontaine's fables. For this unrealized project see Roland Michel, "Fragonard—Illustrator of the 'Contes' of la Fontaine"; Guillerm, "Les Illustration de Fragonard pour les 'Contes' de La Fontaine"; Los Llanos, *Fragonard et le dessin français au XVIIIe siècle dans les collections du Petit Palais*, nos. 128–84; Dupuy-Vachey, *Fragonard*, 54–65; and Schroder, "Fragonard's Later Career: The *Contes et Nouvelles* and the Progress of Love Revisited."

38 La Mettrie, *De la volupté*, 153.

39 The phrase "une manière uniquement à lui même" was used by the *Mercure* à propos his *Coresus* shown at the Salon of 1765. (Cited in Wrigley, *The Origins of French Art Criticism*, 318.)

40 See Bryson's discussion of rococo eros as a function of "the cultivated insufficiency" of the visual sign (*Word and Image*, 105). See also most extensively Sheriff, *Fragonard*, esp. chap. 4, and Sheriff, "Aux Prises avec le désir." For an illuminating discussion of *non-fini*, see also Démoris, "Le Comte de Caylus et la peinture."

41 Sheriff, *Fragonard*, 151–52 and 198–202.

42 On Natoire's promotion of drawing from nature at the Roman Academy, see Caviglia-Brunel, *Charles-Joseph Natoire, 1700–1777*, 132–37, and Benhamou, *Charles-Joseph Natoire and the Académie de France in Rome: A Re-Evaluation*, 89–99. On Robert's and Fragonard's joint practice in Rome, see Cuzin and Rosenberg, *J. H. Fragonard e H. Robert a Roma*.

43 The painting was likely done soon after Fragonard's return to Paris. The motif was repeated by him in several versions in drawing. See PR *Fragonard*, no. 66.

44 A version of the same motif painted in oil on wood is at the Metropolitan Museum in New York.

45 In Clark, *Mastery and Elegance: Two Centuries of French Drawings from the Collection of Jeffrey E. Horvitz*, 288, no. 88.

46 See Williams, *Drawings by Fragonard in North American Collections*, no. 4. Williams linked this composition to the sheet 28 r in Fragonard's Roman sketchbook at the Harvard Art Museums.

47 For the *Fête at Saint-Cloud*, see PR *Fragonard*, no. 161. It is generally assumed that it was executed in the mid- to late 1770s (Rosenberg dates it to either 1773 or 1775–80, the latter having been accepted by Vogtherr and Tavener Holmes, *De Watteau à Fragonard: Les Fêtes Galantes*, no. 58). We know little about the origins of *Fête de Rambouillet*, long assumed to depict an outdoor party scene taking place in the park of Rambouillet. The present title, based on the 1795 sale catalog where the painting was listed as *L'Isle d'Amour*, has been adopted following PR *Fragonard*, no. 168. Its dating, however, remains uncertain. While Cuzin situates it between 1768 and 1770 (Cuzin *Fragonard*, no. 193), Rosenberg (PR *Fragonard*, no.168) dates it to 1775. I am inclined to agree with Cuzin's earlier dating. The painting hardly looks like any of Fragonard's work produced in the wake of his second trip to Italy.

48 *View of the Park* has long been considered a preparatory study for the *Fête de Saint-Cloud* even if it differs considerably from the painting. See Williams, *Drawings by Fragonard*, no. 39, for perceptive comments on this and

another related, far more finished, study at the Rijksmuseum in Amsterdam. See also Mary Tavener Holmes's entry on it in Stein and Tavener Holmes, *Eighteenth-Century French Drawings in New York Collections*, 168–69.

49 As Rosenberg has observed about the gouache study for—or, as Williams has suggested, made *after*—the Lisbon painting, now in a private collection in New York: "He gave free rein to his imagination [. . .] so that Nature not the spectator, becomes the true subject of this work." PR *Fragonard*, 358.

50 For a recent comparison, see Faroult, *Fragonard Amoureux*, no. 67.

51 Richard Rand ("Fragonard dans le jardin d'amour") has suggested connections between this painting and the *jardin pitturesque*. In my view, Fragonard's mode of representation suggests, rather, how nature exceeds these garden constructions. For an earlier version of my arguments regarding this painting, see my "Fragonard in Detail."

52 "arbres insensés, aux cimes croulant comme des neiges." "Notes sur Hercule Seghers," *l'Improbable et autres essais* (1983), 211. Cited in PR *Fragonard*, 18.

53 PR *Fragonard*, 357.

54 For the classic account of this shift, see Gay, "The Uses of Nature," in *The Enlightenment: An Interpretation*, 2: 126–66. An argument about the pertinence of the law of gravity to Fragonard's art has been made by Jollet in his *Les Figures de la pesanteur: Newton, Fragonard, et les Hasards heureux de l'Escarpolette*.

55 Buffon, *Histoire naturelle, générale et particulière*. On Buffon, see Roger, *Buffon: A Life in Natural History*; Roger, *The Life Sciences in Eighteenth-Century French Thought*; and Cherni, *Buffon, la nature et son histoire*. On his involvement in the Jardin du Roi, see Laissus, "Le Jardin du Roi"; and Spary, *Utopia's Garden: French Natural History from Old Regime to Revolution*.

56 As Daniel Mornet's study of the most important private libraries in this period has established, *Histoire Naturelle* was third on the list of the eighteenth-century best sellers. See his "Les Enseignements des bibliothèques privées (1750–1780)."

57 Buffon, "Premier Discours: De la Manière d'Étudier et de Traiter l'Histoire Naturelle," in *Histoire naturelle*; English ed.: "Initial Discourse: On the Manner of Studying and Expounding Natural History," in Lyon and Sloan, *From Natural History to the History of Nature: Readings from Buffon and His Critics*, 97–127.

58 *Histoire naturelle*, in Piveteau et al., *Oeuvres philosophiques*, 7. I cite after the English translation in Gay, *The Enlightenment*, 2: 153.

59 "Creative energy from *within*, not a static design from *without*, was increasingly being perceived as a fundamental characteristic of the natural world." Charlton, *New Images of the Natural in France: A Study in European Cultural History, 1750–1800*, 78. Diderot's *Rêve d'Alembert* (1769) and *Principes philosophiques sur la matière et le mouvement* (1770) testify to this perception (Charlton, *New Images*, 77). On how in Diderot the materialist problematic of form gives way to the appreciation of force, see Ibrahim, *Diderot, un matérialisme écléctique*.

60 See Charlton, *New Images*, 71. It is precisely in this period that we witness the emergence of what in French is called "les sciences de la vie" (life sciences). See Roger, *Les sciences de la vie dans la pensée française de XVIIIe siècle*.

61 For theories of generation in the eighteenth century, see Roger, *The Life Sciences in Eighteenth-Century French Thought*, esp. 259–353 and 369–474; Gasking, *Investigations into Generation, 1651–1828*; Stafford, "Conceiving," in *Body Criticism: Imaging the Unseen in Enlightenment Art and Medicine*, 211–79; and Correia, *The Ovary of Eve: Egg and Sperm and Preformation*. See also Thomson, *Bodies of Thought: Science, Religion, and the Soul in the Early Enlightenment*, 189–98. For the broader cultural impact of these theories, see Müller-Sievers, *Self-Generation: Biology, Philosophy, and Literature around 1800*.

62 Müller-Sievers, *Self-Generation*, 28.

63 See Lyon and Sloan, *From Natural History to the History of Nature*, 233–34.

64 The second volume, *Histoire des Animaux*, was written in 1746. See Roger, *The Life Sciences*, 440. See "The Generation of Animals, Chapter II: Of Reproduction in General," excerpted in Lyon and Sloan, *From Natural History to the History of Nature*, 170–209.

65 "De la même façon que nous pouvons faire des moules par lesquels nous donnons à l'extérieur des corps telle figure qu'il nous plaît, supposons que la Nature puisse faire des moules par lesquels elle donne non-seulement la figure extérieure mais aussi la forme intérieure." *Histoire des Animaux*, 34 (cited by Cherni, *Buffon*, 71). For the interpretation of Buffon's concept of the interior mold, which differs among scholars, see Fellows and Milliken, *Buffon*; and Roger, *The Life Sciences*, 442.

66 For the function of these forces, see Buffon, *Histoire des Animaux*, in Piveteau et al., *Oeuvres Philosophiques*, 288. See also Thomson, *Bodies of Thought*, 196. As with the "interior mold," the views of the role of the penetrating forces widely differ among scholars. Thus while Sloan (*From Natural History to the History of Nature*, 165) sees the mold itself as a "micro-force analogous to Newton's microforces," Müller-Sievers (*Self-Generation*), does not even mention the forces, focusing only on the mold and the molecules.

67 Roger, *The Life Sciences*, 439. Some debate on the inconsistency of Buffon's concept, which included Diderot, is mentioned in Thomson, *Bodies of Thought*, 197–98.

68 "La matière organique toujours active, toujours prête à se mouler, à s'assimiler et à produire des êtres semblables à ceux qui la reçoivent." Buffon, "Récapitulation," *Histoire des Animaux*, 162 (Piveteau et al., *Oeuvres Philosophiques*, 287A–289B). I cite the passage in the translation offered in Roger, *The Life Sciences*, 450.

69 Ernst Cassirer summed up the major transformation in the Enlightenment conception of nature by stating that eighteenth-century natural science was "no longer seeking to derive and explain becoming from being, but being from becoming." *Philosophy of the Enlightenment*, 80.

70 For the vicissitudes of the notion of *ordonnance* and *distribution* in the French theory of painting, see Puttfarken, *The Discovery of Pictorial Composition: Theories of Visual Order in Painting, 1400–1800*, esp. chap. 10.

71 As Roger noted, *Les Sciences*, 549. See also Ibrahim, "La Pensée de Buffon: Système ou Anti- Système?," 184.

72 The effect of bodily interiority is even stronger in the bister drawing related to this composition, formerly in the Forsyth Wickes collection and now presumably lost. (See PR *Fragonard*, 357, fig. 1.)

73 Pineau, *Opusculum Physiologum et Anatomicum, Secunda Figura*, 145.

74 For the discussion of these plates, reproduced in color, see Rodari, *Anatomie de la couleur: L'invention de l'estampe en couleurs*, 133, fig. 121; and Petherbridge, "Art et anatomie: La rencontre du texte et de l'image," esp. 40–42. Jenty was French, trained in Paris, but settled in London in 1745, where he privately taught anatomy and published his work. Cazort, *The Ingenious Machine of Nature: Four Centuries of Art and Anatomy*.

75 See Jordanova, "Gender, Generation, and Science: William Hunter's Obstetrical Atlas"; Jordanova, *Sexual Visions: Images of Gender in Science and Medicine between the Eighteenth and Twentieth Centuries*; and Henderson, "Doll-Machines and Butcher-Shop Meat: Models of Childbirth in the Early Stages of Industrial Capitalism." On the visual

conventions of these anatomical illustrations and their meaning, see also Massey, "Pregnancy and Pathology: Picturing Childbirth in Eighteenth-Century Obstetric Atlases."

76 Petherbridge and Jordanova, *The Quick and the Dead: Artists and Anatomy*, 104. Jordanova also commented on the gratuitous violence of the eighteenth-century fragmenting corporeal displays, such as Hunter's, in "Gender, Generation, and Science."

77 "Anatomie," in *Encyclopédie*, pl. 22, nos. 1–2.

78 Newman, *Fetal Positions: Individualism, Science, and Visuality*, 88. See also Keller, "Embryonic Individuals: The Rhetoric of Seventeenth-Century Embryology and the Construction of Early Modern Identity."

79 For the technical aspects of these plates, see Rodari, *Anatomie de la couleur*, 133.

80 For the persistence of preformation, see Roger, *The Life Sciences*, 498–509, and for unresolved problems posed by epigenesis, see ibid., 514–29.

81 For Voltaire's belief, cited by Daston and Park, *Monsters*, 330, see the entry "Imagination, Imaginer," in *Encyclopédie*, 8: 561. For the discussion of Diderot, who believed the womb was "endowed with a special instinct" (*Eléments de Physiologie*, 167), see Steinbrügge, *The Moral Sex: Woman's Nature in the French Enlightenment*, 44–47. For the belief in the power of the mother's imagination that survived well into the nineteenth century, see Huet, *Monstrous Imagination*.

82 Diderot's *Bijoux Indiscrets*, a tale of the speaking womb's betraying women's sexual misdemeanours, is one example of this broader cultural fascination.

83 Cassirer, *Philosophy of the Enlightenment*, 37.

84 E. and J. de Goncourt, *French Eighteenth-Century Painters*, 289.

85 I owe to Eunice Williams the suggestion that the drawing was done while the artist was walking.

86 For the concept of the "enigmatic signifier" and its role in the process of subjective formation, see Laplanche, "The Drive and Its Object-Source: Its Fate in the Transference," in *Seduction, Translation, and the Drives: A Dossier*, esp. 188–95. While Laplanche's psychoanalytical discussion focuses on individual subjectivity, I am suggesting here a possibility of seeing the enigmatic signifier as a pictorial and (shared) cultural construct.

87 The title, *The Island of Love (L'Isle d'amour)*, was evidently a result of its association with Watteau's *Pilgrimage to the Island of Cythera*. For Alain Viala, though (*La France galante: essai historique sur une catégorie culturelle, de ses origines jusqu'à la Révolution*, 476), the idyllic *fête galante* of Watteau's time is menaced in Fragonard, indicating the twilight of this cultural ideal.

88 For Fragonard's painting, see Milam, "Fragonard's 'Le Furet,'" who identified the game played by the protagonists as *le furet*. For drawings related to the painting, where the predominance of nature as the frame of human activity is even more emphatic, see PR *Fragonard*, 76-77. For Boucher's *Les Charmes de la Vie Champêtre* (around 1735–40, Louvre), see Faroult, *Fragonard Amoureux*, no. 1.

89 McLaren, *Reproductive Rituals: The Perception of Fertility in England from the Sixteenth Century to the Nineteenth Century*, esp. 26–27, cites many examples of persisting confusion regarding women's reproductive functioning and their sexual pleasure in eighteenth-century France and Britain. On this issue, see also Corbin, *L'Harmonie de plaisirs. Les manières de jouir du siècle des Lumières à l'avènement de la sexologie*. That the audience of the eighteenth-century obstetric literature, as well as wax models of female anatomy, consisted not only of doctors and scientists but also amateurs of pornography, may be seen as another symptom of the persistent confusion regarding the female body and its image as a signifier of both sex and procreation. See Jordanova, "Gender, Generation, and Science," 401, and Newman, *Fetal Positions*, 88.

90 The epigraph for this section is a translation of: "Je peindrais avec mon cul." The origin of this phrase, much quoted in Fragonard's literature, is Renouvier, *Histoire de l'art pendant la Révolution considéré principalement dans les estampes: ouvrage posthume*, 167.

91 For an earlier version of my analysis of some of the works discussed in this section as well as other works, see my "Genre and Sex."

92 Rosenberg dates the *Bathers* sometime between 1761 and 1770 (PR *Fragonard*, no. 74), which situates the painting roughly in the same period as the *Island of Love*, if we assume, as does Cuzin, that *Island of Love* dates from ca. 1768–70. See slso Faroult, *Fragonard Amoureux*, no. 50.

93 See PR *Fragonard*, 165.

94 A painting, attributed to Fragonard, that may be related to the *Bathers*, being similar in size and mode of execution, though considerably more clumsy, makes even more compositionally explicit the idea of the figures' emergence from a natural source in the background. (Wildenstein, *L'Opera complete di Fragonard*, no. 250, pl. 19.)

95 For voyeurism in *The Spring*, see Bryson (*Word and Image*, 98–99). For a different, asexual account of the dynamics of this painting, see Jollet, *Les Figures de la pesanteur*.

96 See PR *Fragonard*, no. 237; Massengale, *Jean-Honoré Fragonard*, 114; and Faroult, *Jean-Honoré Fragonard: Le Verrou*, 10, and n. 12, 48.

97 *Le Sopha, Conte Moral* (1742). For the account of the novel's wide popularity and its importance, see Jean Sgard, "Introduction," in Crébillon, *Le Sopha*.

98 Despite its title, the protagonist of the Munich painting emphatically lacks the *gimblette* (the round biscuit) that women in other versions hold in their hands. For other extant variants of this composition, see PR *Fragonard*, no. 110.

99 See, for example, Jean-Baptiste Le Prince, *The Sultana*, 1772, Musée d'art et d'histoire, Metz; and Nicolas-Bernard Lépicié, *Fanchon Rising*, 1773, Musée de l'hôtel Sandelin, Saint-Omer.

100 This key element in the aesthetic theory of Roger de Piles continued to exert strong influence throughout the eighteenth century. In 1766 Charles Jombert published a new revised and expanded edition of de Piles's *Elémens de Peinture Pratique*. See Chatelus, *Peindre à Paris*, 85.

101 *The Principles of Painting*, 2–3. "La veritable Peinture est donc celle qui nous appelle (pour ainsi dire) en nous surprenant: et ce n'est que par la force de l'effet qu'elle produit, que nous ne pouvons nous empêcher d'en approcher, comme si elle avoit quelque chose a nous dire." De Piles, *Cours de peinture*, 3. Sheriff (*Fragonard*) drew attention to the relevance of de Piles's aesthetics of pleasure for the painter's practice.

102 See Hobson, *The Object of Art: The Theory of Illusion in Eighteenth-Century France*, chap. 1, esp. 47–48.

103 Renouvier, *Histoire de l'Art pendant la Révolution*, 167.

104 For an account of the connection between semiotic activity and the maternal body see the classic essays by Julia Kristeva, "Giotto's Joy," and "Motherhood According to Giovanni Bellini," in Kristeva, *Desire in Language: A Semiotic Approach to Literature and Art*, 210–70. See also Laplanche, "The Drive and Its Object-Source."

105 Girard, "From Mimetic Desire to the Monstrous Double," in *Violence and the Sacred*; Baudrillard, *De la Séduction*. See also Saint-Amand, *The Libertine's Progress: Seduction in the Eighteenth-Century French Novel*.

106 For the psychoanalytic notion of the

object-source, see Laplanche, "The Drive and Its Object-Source."

107 Duncan, "Happy Mothers and Other New Ideas in French Art." See also Sheriff, "Fragonard's Erotic Mothers and the Politics of Reproduction."

108 PR *Fragonard*, no. 159, and Massengale, *Jean-Honoré Fragonard*, 100–101. The MFA painting reproduced here is a version of another one, now in a private collection. Rosenberg has disputed the attribution of the Boston painting (PR *Fragonard*, no. 159), but Cuzin has not (*Fragonard*, no. 262). Fragonard's gouache of the same composition (Saint Petersburg, Florida), was shown at the Salon de la Correspondance in 1781. (PR *Fragonard*, no. 160.)

109 For the *Venus Refusing Cupid a Kiss*, see Cuzin *Fragonard*, no. 222, who dates it ca. 1772, and Massengale, *Jean-Honoré Fragonard*, 78, who dates it to the 1760s. Cuzin lists four different versions of *Sappho, or the Muse Inspired by Cupid*, all in private collections (Cuzin *Fragonard*, nos. 355–58; repr. in color, 216). For the pendants, see PR *Fragonard*, nos. 72–73. For *Useless Resistance*, a generic title given to many libertine paintings at the time, see Cuzin *Fragonard*, no. 305 and, briefly, PR *Fragonard*, 310. Dupuy-Vachey discusses Nicolas-François Regnault's print after Fragonard's painting in "Mauvais Genre ou la fabrique d'une réputation," 38.

110 Rousseau, *The Confessions of Jean-Jacques Rousseau*, 106–7.

111 In the drawn version of the same theme, the boy's look is directed more predictably, as is everyone else's, at the infant in the crib. Pen and brown wash. Private collection. See Cuzin *Fragonard*, 91, fig. 119. For other versions of the subject, see Dupuy-Vachey, *Fragonard*, nos. 46–47.

112 Sheriff, "Fragonard's Erotic Mothers," 21–24.

113 That the providing and sexual aspects were amalgamated in the body of the eighteenth-century "good mother" was part of Carol Duncan's argument ("Happy Mothers"). She saw this amalgamation as an aspect of the visual propaganda campaign to make motherhood appealing, even sexually rewarding to women, but also to circumscribe female sexuality within the boundaries required for reproduction. But if we look at such paintings as implying—if only potentially—an erotic liaison between mother and child, the propagandistic value of this iconography becomes problematic.

114 The point in noting this painting's similarity to Fragonard's Louvre *Adoration of the Magi* is thus not to imply—as did Massengale (*Jean-Honoré Fragonard*, 62)—that the *Italian Family* is suffused by religious overtones, but rather to suggest that both scenes share the ethos of infantile adoration of the mother.

115 Mariette, *Abecedario*, 263. With his usual ungenerousness, Mariette saw it as a habit that obstructed Fragonard's talent.

116 Cuzin (*Fragonard*, fig. 233, 191, and no. 276) dates the canvas tentatively to 1775. Among other canvases are the *Young Mother and Child* (1775–78, Besançon), and *Mother and Child* (1775) in a US private collection. For the former, see Cuzin *Fragonard*, no. 304, and Rosenberg and Lebrun Jouve, *Les Fragonard de Besançon*, no. 95; for the latter, see Cuzin *Fragonard*, no. 278. For the discussion of these and other related works, see my "Genre and Sex," 209–10.

117 It has often been said that the appearance of the portraits of children, as well as the proliferation of the happy household scenes, in Fragonard's oeuvre had to do with the major event in the painter's life that occurred in 1769 when, at the age of thirty-seven, he first became a father. Yet it seems that if the birth of the artist's first child, Rosalie, resonated aesthetically, it was not by "paternalizing" Fragonard's brush but, less expectedly, by reinforcing the identification of the painter with the infantile realm.

118 The epigraph for this section was taken from La Mettrie, *L'École de la volupté* (1747), in *De la volupté*, 139. "Le Plaisir est de l'Essence de l'Homme, et de l'Ordre de l'Universe."

119 The painting was listed in the Salon *livret* as belonging to Monsieur Bergeret ("tiré du cabinet de M. Bergeret"). (PR *Fragonard*, 227.) It has been accepted that the Louvre painting, which entered the museum collections with the Péreire bequest, is indeed the one shown at the Salon of 1767. (See Cuzin *Fragonard*, 92.) It has also been assumed that the Bergeret in question was indeed Jacques-Onésyme Bergeret de Grancourt, and not his uncle who owned a *Landscape* by Fragonard. On this, and on the relation of the painting to other commissions of this kind, see PR *Fragonard*, no. 109.

120 Produced in 1763, the decoration, comprised of five panels, one with Apollo and four with putti, was engraved in 1767 by J. Ch. François. Ananoff and Wildenstein, *L'Opera completa*, nos. 439–43.

121 Goodman, *Diderot on Art*, 2: 256. Other commentaries included the *Mercure de France*—"The public was expecting something more considerable from the author of Callirhoé" (cited in PR *Fragonard*, 230)—and the *Mémoirs secrets* (*Salon 1767* in *Mémoirs secrets*, 38) that offered a similar assessment.

122 See Gallini in Bresc-Bautier, *The Apollo Gallery in the Louvre*, 129–48.

123 See Ledbury, "The Hierarchy of Genres."

124 Ibid., 198–202. As my account of these two painters' practices in the preceding chapters indicates, my view accords with Ledbury's.

125 These included the painter's famous falling out with Mlle Guimard over the commission to decorate her house (1770–71) and his unsuccessful relation with Madame du Barry, who rejected his cycle of paintings, *The Pursuit of Love*, produced for her residence in Louveciennes (1771–72). For the documented summary account of both conflicts, see PR *Fragonard*, 295–99. The quarrel with Bergeret had to do with Bergeret's appropriation of the artist's drawings executed during their voyage to Italy, conducted at the patron's invitation. PR *Fragonard*, 361–64. I will have more to say on Bergeret and on the *Pursuit of Love* below.

126 E. and J. de Goncourt, *French Eighteenth-Century Painters*, 261–62. (The painter came from Grasse in Provence.)

127 "The painting of love in its most refined forms, that was his pleasure." Portalis, *Honoré Fragonard: Sa Vie et Son Oeuvre*, 1: 72.

128 "[I]l faut tâcher de faire pénétrer le plaisir par toutes les portes qui l'introduisent jusqu'à notre âme; nous n'avons pas d'autres affaires." Madame du Châtelet, *Discours sur le Bonheur*, 74. In her preface to this edition Elisabeth Badinter dates the *Discours* between 1746 and 1747 ("Préface," 16).

129 The classic, magisterial work on the subject, Mauzi, *L'Idée du bonheur dans la littérature et la pensée françaises au XVIII*[e] *siècle*, remains the most useful.

130 For the distinction between these terms, which were understood differently by different authors in this period, see ibid., esp. 417–31. See also Thomson, "L'Art de jouir de La Mettrie à Sade"; Benrekassa, "L'Article 'Jouissance' et l'idéologie érotique de Diderot"; and Corbin, *L'Harmonie de plaisirs*.

131 "Bonheur," in de Viguerie, *Histoire et Dictionnaire du Temps des Lumières, 1715–1789*, 770–72. For the extensive discussion of several eighteenth-century authors who considered *bonheur* as the most stable, shared, and defining aspect of the self, see Mauzi, *L'Idée du bonheur*, esp. chaps. 8–11. For the surge of concern with pleasure in French literature, see also Kavanagh, *Enlightened Pleasures*.

132 *La Nouvelle Héloïse*, Lettre VIII, cited in Viguerie, *Histoire et Dictionnaire*, 770.

133 La Mettrie, *Discours sur le bonheur*. This work was rewritten several times by the

author, its second edition having been published under the title *Anti-Senèque ou le Souverain bien*, in 1750 in Potsdam. (In English: *Anti-Seneca or the Sovereign Good*, in Thomson, *Machine Man and Other Writings*, 117–43.)

134 La Mettrie, *Anti-Seneca, or the Sovereign Good*, 121.

135 On this point, see Wellman, *La Mettrie: Medicine, Philosophy, and Enlightenment*, 215.

136 Casanova, *History of My Life*. For eros as a creative force behind Casanova's writing, see Thomas, *Casanova: Un voyage libertin*. Casanova visited Paris on several occasions between the 1750s and 1783.

137 Heinich, *Du Peintre à l'Artiste*, 34.

138 See PR *Fragonard*, 61–66. Fragonard's independence led the director, Natoire, to write reassuring letters to Marigny to excuse the young artist's irregularities and lack of responsibility. Natoire cited Fragonard's astonishing ease of execution. See Montaiglon and Guiffrey, *Correspondence des Directeurs*, 11: 232. For Fragonard's ways in Rome, see also Guimbaud, *Saint-Non et Fragonard d'après des documents inédits*.

139 See Guimbaud, *Saint-Non et Fragonard d'après des documents inédits*; Saint-Non, *Panopticon Italiano: Un Diario di Viaggio ritrovato, 1759–1761*; and Guichard, *Les amateurs*, 195–96, 208, 254–56.

140 Montaiglon and Guiffrey, *Correspondence des Directeurs*, 11: 164–378.

141 Guimbaud especially (*Saint-Non et Fragonard*, 99) emphasizes the formative role of Saint-Non for the young artist. See also Rosenberg, far more restrained in his assessment of the *amateur's* aesthetic impact, in his "Introduction" in Rosenberg and de Lavergnée, *Panopticon Italiano*, 54–57.

142 This is what the *amateurs* were criticized for by Diderot who objected to their neglect of the moral function of art in favor of sheer aesthetic pleasure. See Guichard, "Taste Communities," 526–27.

143 Guichard, *Les Amateurs*, and "Taste Communities."

144 See "*Journal* de Saint-Non," in Rosenberg and de Lavergnée, eds., *Panopticon Italiano*, 63–324. Rosenberg notes this surprising silence in his "Introduction," *Panopticon Italiano*, 45.

145 For Fragonard's relations with Bergeret, their trip to Italy in particular, see PR *Fragonard*, 361–67; Chappey, *Fragonard et le Voyage en Italie, 1773–1774: Les Bergeret, une Famille de Mécènes*; and Tornézy, *Bergeret et Fragonard, journal inédit d'un voyage en Italie*. See also Raux, "Le Voyage de Fragonard et Bergeret en Flandre et Hollande durant l'Été 1773." For Bergeret as *amateur*, see also Guichard, *Les amateurs*, esp. 33, 113–14, 195–201.

146 Although the full archival documentation of the case is lacking, we know that Fragonard received a sum of 3,000 livres, which is assumed to be his remuneration for the disputed drawings from Bergeret. On the dispute, see PR *Fragonard*, 362–64 and 370; Bailey, "*Toute seule*," 82, discussing the dispute in the broader context of the market for drawing and stressing its financial importance for Fragonard; and Guichard, *Les amateurs*, 341.

147 There are no extant painted self-portraits by Fragonard. He apparently painted one in Italy but this work has been lost. (PR *Fragonard*, 554.) However, in addition to the Lugt tondo, we have three drawn self-portraits, undated, but most likely executed in the early to mid-1780s, all now in the Louvre. See PR *Fragonard*, nos. 287–90; and Cuzin *Fragonard* (Louvre: Drawing Gallery), nos. 40–42.

148 "se ipsum delineabat frago / apud de Bergeret / anno 1789." See PR *Fragonard*, 557–58, no. 290; and Bailey, in Bailey, *De Watteau à Degas: Dessins français de la Collection Frits Lugt*, no. 23. The inscription was no doubt added later, either by Bergeret's son, who owned the drawing, or by someone else.

149 It was in Cassan that Fragonard's daughter, Rosalie, died in 1788. For relations between Fragonard and the Bergeret family, see Chappey, *Fragonard et le Voyage*.

150 Bailey has suggested Folie Beajon on the basis of the style of the *fauteil* on which Fragonard sits. Bailey, *De Watteau à Degas*, 84.

151 Cuzin *Fragonard*, 257, Conclusion, n. 1.

152 On Bergeret's amateur drawing practice, see Tornézy, in Tornézy, *Bergeret et Fragonard*; and Guichard, *Les amateurs*, 201. On Vincent's portrait, see Guichard, *Les amateurs*, 48.

153 According to Guichard, the relation between Bergeret and Fragonard exemplifies the typically personal nature of the interactions between the *amateurs* and artists. *Les Amateurs*, 199. While she emphasizes the camaraderie between the two men, Bergeret's *Journal* testifies also to the animosity and quarrels between them during their travels. On this aspect, see Rosenberg, in Chappey, *Fragonard et le Voyage*, 38.

154 The epigraph for this section comes from Tancock, *Rameau's Nephew, and D'Alembert's Dream*, 87. Wildenstein (*The Paintings of Fragonard*, 12–15) was the first to propose the paintings constitute a group. For the account of the group, with full bibliography, see Cuzin *Fragonard*, 102–34; PR *Fragonard*, 255–93; and Dupuy-Vachey (*Fragonard*, 111–17 and 153–57), who suggested a hypothetical connection between the paintings and a private literary society, *l'ordre du table ronde*.

155 Sheriff, *Fragonard*, 163, and her extensive analysis of the whole corpus, chap. 5.

156 See Percival, "Fragonard and Pastiche: The Case of the *Girl in Spanish Costume* in Dulwich," and Percival, *Fragonard and the Fantasy Figure: Painting the Imagination*.

157 Percival discusses the connection to the amateur circles, considered earlier by Sheriff (*Fragonard*, chap. 5) in terms of specific practices, such as the *amateurs'* habit of commissioning replicas of the old master paintings to be hung on the wall side by side with their originals (*Fragonard and the Fantasy Figure*, 42; and Guichard, "Fragonard et les jeux," 53–54).

158 Guichard, *Les amateurs*.

159 See Guimbaud, *Saint-Non et Fragonard*, esp. 123–38, and Guichard, "Fragonard et les jeux," 53, and 55, n. 29. For Saint-Non's etchings after Fragonard's work, see also Stein, in Stein et al., *Artists and Amateurs: Etching in Eighteenth-Century France*, 163–64, and nos. 12, 99, 100. Saint-Non's *Little Park*, etched after Fragonard, no. 12, is discussed by Hoisington, in Stein et al., *Artists and Amateurs*, 33–34.

160 Guichard, "Fragonard et les jeux," 52–53.

161 The sheet appeared on the auction sale at Druot in June 2012 and was purchased by a private collector. It has been published by Blumenfeld, *Une facétie de Fragonard: Les révélations d'un dessin retrouvé*. While the sheet contains eighteen sketches, it does not include two other known portraits traditionally associated with this group of works: the *Portrait of François-Henri duc d'Harcourt* (Rau collection for UNICEF, sold at Bonhams in 2013), and *Portrait of Anne-François d'Harcourt, duc de Beuvron* (Louvre). Blumenfeld, *Une facétie de Fragonard*, 10–11.

162 The painting is in a private collection (ibid., 38–39). For the identities of the sitters, see ibid., 15–53.

163 For suggestions regarding the display of the paintings, and for other interpretive possibilities opened up by the discovery of the *Sheet*, see ibid., 55–70, and Dupuy-Vachey, "Fragonard's 'Fantasy Figures': Prelude to a New Understanding." For the cultural functions of the *gravure de société*, see Guichard, "Gravures de société et identité d'amateur à Paris au XVIIIe."

164 In addition to the extraordinarily resourceful archival and interpretive work done by Blumenfeld (*Une facétie de Fragonard*) and Dupuy-Vachey ("Fragonard's 'Fantasy Figures'"), the discovery of the sheet prompted the Washington's *Reader* restoration project, the findings of which were published in Jackall,

Delaney, and Swicklik, "'Portrait of a Woman with a Book': A 'Newly Discovered Fantasy Figure' by Fragonard in the National Gallery of Art, Washington."

165 While the discovery of the *Sheet of Sketches* challenges Percival's assertion that the fantasy figures did not constitute a group, her overarching argument about their status as fictions made for amateur consumption still stands. The new identifications of figures as artists and elite members closely associated with the *amateur* circles (Blumenfeld, *Une facétie de Fragonard*, 15–53) further confirms this historical contextualization. The question of how profitable these pictures were remains open. The miniaturist Hall states that Fragonard was selling them for 1 luis and he got his for only 4 livres. Ibid., 44.

166 Guichard, "Taste Communities," 526.

167 For the seductive aspect, see Percival, *Fragonard and the Fantasy Figure*, 122.

168 Diderot's *Jacques, the Fatalist* and *D'Alembert's Dream* are based on the same principle. Although the precise date of *Le Neveu de Rameau*'s creation is uncertain, it is widely accepted that it was written between 1761 and 1774 (Undank, "Diderot at the Crossroad of Speech," 519). L. W. Tancock ("Introduction to *Rameau's Nephew*," in Tancock, *Rameau's Nephew, and D'Alembert's Dream*), dates it for 1761, with final touches made in 1777 to 1779. The text was first published only in 1805, in Goethe's German translation, and it did not appear in France until 1821. It thus shares with Fragonard's series a certain mystery of origins and function. On the work, see McDonald, "Notes on the *Neveu de Rameau*," and Hobson, "Introduction," in Diderot, *Satyre Seconde: Le Neveu de Rameau*, iii–xxxvii.

169 Tancock, "Introduction to *Rameau's Nephew*," 15.

170 Diderot, *Rameau's Nephew*, in Tancock, *Rameau's Nephew, and D'Alembert's Dream*, 34.

171 As Marian Hobson notes, this is what differentiates him from the actor, another performative character analyzed by Diderot in *Paradoxe sur le Comédien*, whose *métier*, however, is a source of income and greater social stability. Hobson, "Introduction," in Diderot, *Satyre Seconde: Le Neveu de Rameau*, xv.

172 Diderot, *Rameau's Nephew*, in Tancock, *Rameau's Nephew, and D'Alembert's Dream*, 87.

173 Ibid.

174 Undank, "Diderot at the Crossroad," 520.

175 Blumenfeld considered two possible candidates evoked by this name, scribbled by the painter on the *Sheet*, the miniaturist Pierre-Adolphe Halle (1739–1793) and the painter Noël Hallé (1711–1781), but ultimately rejected them on the grounds of lack of resemblance (*Une facétie*, 44).

176 Blumenfeld (*Une facétie*) makes a similar observation, noting the fragility and insecurity conveyed by the *Warrior's* features: "Paradoxalement, Fragonard insiste sur sa fragilité et son insécurité, son pincement de lèvres et le froissmement de sourcils montre le poids qui semble s'abbattre sur lui."

177 Diderot, *Rameau's Nephew*, in Tancock, *Rameau's Nephew, and D'Alembert's Dream*, 34.

178 One of Fragonard's fantasy figures, now at the Art Institute of Chicago, used to be identified as Cervantes's protagonist. See Dupuy-Vachey, *Fragonard*, 140–42, and Blumenfeld, *Une facétie*, 16–17.

179 Percival, *Fragonard and the Fantasy Figure*, 122; Guichard, "Fragonard et les jeux," 53.

180 Blumenfeld, *Une facétie*, 20.

181 Ibid., 34.

182 For the long tradition of fantasy portraits in France and elsewhere, see Hémery, *Figures de fantaisie du XVIe aux XVIIIe Siècle*.

183 The still uncertain provenance of many of these paintings—the uncertainty that raises the issue of whether the sitters actually ever owned them—makes it difficult to reject completely the hypothesis launched by Rosenberg, based on the testimony of Fragonard's grandson, Théophile, that most if not all of these paintings actually hung in the artist's studio, forming a kind of self-promoting gallery on display for the visitors (PR *Fragonard*, 255–58). The interpretation offered here—the fantasy figures as a relational self-representation (in relation to the clients)—would certainly be compatible with this hypothesis.

184 Guichard, "Fragonard et les jeux."

185 Ibid., 53.

186 Rosenberg (PR *Fragonard*, 279 and fig. 1) reads it as "frago"; it looks to me as "froogo." How unusual this mode of signing was for Fragonard is evident in comparison to his "normal," elegantly scripted signatures in the panels of the Frick's *Pursuit of Love*.

187 We are reminded of Boucher's inarticulate early signatures before he established one consistent way of signing (chapter 1 here.) Fragonard, however, doesn't rehearse signing but simulates inarticulateness deliberately.

188 As Dupuy-Vachey has demonstrated in her exhibition, Fragonard was more cultured—and certainly knew how to read and write—than some scholars, notably Rosenberg, had assumed. (See Dupuy-Vachey, *Fragonard*.) Here, though, he is deliberately playing a game with the learned in order to differentiate himself from them.

189 See PR *Fragonard*, 274, fig. 2 and 276, fig. 1.

190 As we know from the conservator's analysis of the Clark's *Warrior*. Percival, *Fragonard and the Fantasy Figure*, 20.

191 Hegel's idea developed in Undank, "Portrait of the Philosopher as a Tramp," 427.

192 La Mettrie, *Anti-Seneca or the Sovereign Good*, 121.

193 Cf. Sheriff's discussion of Fragonard's marks as "natural signs" in *Fragonard*, 144–48.

194 As was the case with Fragonard's Louveciennes paintings—on which more below—sent back to him by Mme du Barry, and with Mademoiselle Guimard's commission. On these conflicts in relation to the fantasy figures, see Percival, *Fragonard and the Fantasy Figure*, 183–84. My take on this is, though, slightly different from hers.

195 The epigraph for this section is taken from *Vénus physique*, 103. I cite it in Mary Terrall's translation in *The Man Who Flattened the Earth: Maupertuis and the Sciences in the Enlightenment*, 220. Scholars use both titles, *The Progress* and *The Pursuit of Love*, though neither of them came from Fragonard but was imposed later. I opted for *Pursuit* because, as Sheriff has demonstrated, there is no narrative progress in this cycle. See her *Fragonard*, 65.

196 See Gallet, *Claude-Nicolas Ledoux, 1736–1806*, 91–96; and Vidler, *Claude-Nicolas Ledoux: Architecture and Social Reform at the End of Ancien Régime*, 54–57.

197 See Cayeux, "Le Pavillon du Madame Du Barry à Louveciennes et son architecte, C. N. Ledoux"; Biebel, "Fragonard and Madame du Barry"; Sauerländer, "Uber der Urspüngliche Reinhenfolge von Fragonards 'Amours des Bergers'"; Posner, "The True Path of Fragonard's 'Progress of Love'"; Roland Michel, "Fragonard, Illustrateur de l'Amour," 25–32; Cuzin *Fragonard*, 142–55; PR *Fragonard*, 295–97; Sheriff, *Fragonard*, 58–94; and Bailey, *Fragonard's Progress of Love at the Frick Collection*.

198 A thoroughly documented and nuanced version of this argument has been offered by Colin Bailey, who puts the blame for the painter's dismissal on du Barry's architect, Ledoux, on the ground of stylistic incompatibility of Fragonard's panels with the architect's neoclassic decor (*Fragonard's Progress*, 87–102). Persuasive as Bailey's stylistic analysis is, it does not explain why Ledoux, knowing Fragonard well—they had worked together on La Guimard's residence—and thus being

aware of his style, would get him involved in the project in the first place.

199 "quatre grands tableaux du Sieur Fragonard qui roulent sur les amours de bergers et semblent allégoriques aux aventures de la maîtresse du lieux." Bauchomont, *Mémoirs secrets* (1772), cited in PR *Fragonard*, 301.

200 On *La Culbute*, see Faroult, in Faroult, *Fragonard Amoureux*, no. 16, and Sheriff, "Aux Prises avec le désir," 45–47.

201 E.g., PR *Fragonard*, 323; and Sheriff *Fragonard*, 65.

202 "Vous avez vous à Loussienne encore le *nec plus ultra* pour le heurté, le roullé, le bien fouetté, le tartouillis. Le voilà, le voilà le véritable Tartouillis." *Dialogues sur la Peinture*, 1773, cited extensively in PR *Fragonard*, 302. The *Dialogues*, attributed by Rosenberg to the painter Antoine Renou, features a Monsieur Remi (reference to the renowned art expert Pierre Rémy), an amateur, a certain Fabretti, and an unidentified Englishman, Milord Littleton.

203 "—*M. Fabretti*: The rolled, the well whipped, the Dauber, are these insults, Monsieur Remi, or praises?—*M. Remi*: What, you must be kidding, I am telling you about the divine Frago, the number one brush according to our leaders in painting." PR *Fragonard*, 302. According to the Littré: *Heurté* was a term referring to a mode of painting that left the colors unblended, the contours unsoftened. As such it was used negatively, e.g., "sa torche est lourde, sa manière est heurtée" (Diderot, *Salon 1767*), and positively, to refer to a bold manner, obtained with hard strokes, a free and vigorous composition, in both painting and sculpture. *Roullé*, or *roulé*, was not a pictorial term, but was used, among others, in mineralogy (Buffon). The term *fouetté* was also not a pictorial term. *Tartouillis* was a version of *tartouillade*, which referred to a very loose composition and one that neglected drawing in favor of color. In the nineteenth century, it became mostly negative. See also Watelet and Lévesque, *Dictionnaire des Arts de Peinture, Sculpture, et Gravure* (1788–91), for the opposition between the *heurté* and *fondu* (blended) manners (20). Eik Kahng offers a useful discussion of Anne Vallayer-Coster's uses of both manners in her "Vallayer-Coster/Chardin," 48–51.

204 Again, the uncertain dating of the *Island of Love*—either the late 1760s or mid-1770s—makes it impossible to know if the Buffonian vision of nature it articulated so suggestively preceded or postdated the Louveciennes panels.

205 *Serre Chaude*, 1785, sanguine drawing, Musée Carnavalet, Paris. (Repr. in Vezin, *Les Artistes au Jardin des Plantes*, 31.) We don't know if Fragonard drew in the Jardin du roi, but the park was a popular site for walks in the daytime and, despite the fact that it was locked for the night, also for nightly adventures. Rétif de la Bretonne was a regular visitor in the night. See his *Nuits de Paris*, 152–58.

206 The picturesque garden as such has been discussed as important for the aesthetic of the Louveciennes panels and Fragonard's work in general. See Sheriff, *Fragonard*, 82–92; and Rand, "Fragonard dans le jardin d'amour."

207 For the relation between the garden and Buffon's theories, see Spary, "The Place of *Histoire Naturelle* at the Jardin du Roi," in *Utopia's Garden*, esp. 24–27. (That Fragonard's mode of painting was referred to as roullé, a term used in natural history, by, among others, Buffon himself, may not be accidental. See Littré as referenced above.)

208 I am thinking of Rousseau's views on female sexuality and the ideological uses to which they were put at the time. See Schwartz, *The Sexual Politics of Jean-Jacques Rousseau*, and Duncan, "Happy Mothers."

209 For Maupertuis's theory of generation, see Terrall, *The Man Who Flattened the Earth*, chap. 7, esp., 218–21 and 328–34; and Roger, *The Life Sciences*, esp. 383–94. Ann Thomson discusses the friendship between Maupertuis and Buffon in *Bodies of Thought*, 196.

210 I am offering here a highly condensed summary of Maupertuis's views. For the discussion of how Maupertuis's views evolved, see Roger, *The Life Sciences*, esp. 390–91, and Terrall, *The Man Who Flattened the Earth*, 328–34.

211 Terrall, *The Man Who Flattened the Earth*, 209–12, and more generally on Maupertuis's work and sociability, ibid., 3–6.

212 Maupertuis's ideas were widely known. In his *Lettre sur les désirs*, published approximately at the time of execution of the Louveciennes panels (1770), Frans Hemsterhuis also made a passing connection between the force of attraction operating in nature and human desire. (See Meyboom, *Oeuvres Philosophiques*, 52–53.) Hemsterhuis's work was popularized in France by Diderot.

213 The term "erotic science" is Terrall's. (*The Man Who Flattened the Earth*, 218–21.)

214 PR *Fragonard*, nos. 154 and 155; Munhall, "Fragonard's Studies for 'The Progress of Love'"; and Bailey, *Fragonard's Progress*, 74–78.

215 The format of the sketches, as Munhall has suggested, may have stemmed from the fact that, at this stage, the artist had not yet been given the precise dimensions of the paneling by Ledoux. ("Fragonard's Studies," 403.)

216 See PR *Fragonard*, no. 151; Munhall, "Fragonard's Studies," 403, for the view that it was a sketch for the Louvecienne panel; and Williams, *Drawings by Fragonard*, no. 21, 70, who disagreed. The dating of the drawing remains uncertain—Williams proposed 1772—its appearance at a Ghent sale in 1779 providing a terminus ante quem.

217 See Bailey, *Fragonard's Progress*, 71–74.

218 *Le Réveil de la Nature, ou Hommage rendu à la Nature par les Éléments*, 1780. See Wildenstein, *The Paintings of Fragonard*, no. 490; and Cuzin *Fragonard*, 207, and no. 354. The painting is presumed to have been destroyed in World War II. A print by Marie Louveau-Rouveyre after Fragonard was reproduced in Portalis, *Honoré Fragonard*.

219 It was Diderot who called Maupertuis's theory "seductive materialism." See Thomson, *Bodies of Thought*, 197.

220 This distinct group of paintings includes also *The Oath of Love*, ca. 1780, National Trust, Waddesdon Manor (another version is in Musée d'Art et d'Histoire de la Provence, Grasse); *The Sacrifice of the Rose*, 1785–88, Coll. Lynda and Stewart Resnick (two other versions in Museo Nacional de Arte Decorativo, Buenos Aires, and in a private collection, Paris). In addition to the oil sketch for the *Vow* (Louvre), two drawings on the subject, likely done after the painting, are in the Cleveland Museum of Art and at Princeton University Art Museum, respectively. In addition to *The Fountain of Love* in the Getty Art Museum, which I am reproducing here and which is considered the earliest version of the subject, two other versions of the painting are in the Wallace Collection, London, and in a private collection in the United States. For the most extensive discussion of these paintings, richly commented upon in Fragonard's literature, see Molotiu, *Fragonard's Allegories*, and his dissertation, "Allegories of Love in the Late Work of Jean-Honoré Fragonard." See also, more recently, Faroult, "Les Allegories Amoureuses," in Faroult, *Fragonard Amoureux*, 246–47, and nos. 95–98.

221 See Molotiu, *Fragonard's Allegories*, chap. 2, and Faroult, *Fragonard Amoureux*. Fragonard owned a copy of *Anacréon, Sappho, Bion et Moscus*, an anthology of new translations from Greek poetry by the Hellenist Julien-Jacques Moutonnet-Clarifon. The book was a gift from Jean Massard, the author of the engravings after Charles Eisen illustrating the volume. (Faroult, *Fragonard Amoureux*, 248–49, no. 91.)

222 The subject was popular. In 1775 Louis-Jean Lagrenée painted *The Vow to Love* (private collection, Paris; 1777 version in Wadsworth) for the duc de la Rouchefoucauld-Liancourt, an amateur of Fragonard's work who owned his *Vow*. At the Salon of 1773 Vien exhibited his *Young Greek Women Taking a Vow Never to Fall in Love*, one of the four canvases that replaced Fragonard's *Pursuit of Love* cycle at Mme du Barry's pavillion at Louveciennes. On the relation between Fragonard's *Vows* and the work of other artists, see Cuzin *Fragonard*, no. 377 and n. 22; PR *Fragonard*, no. 280; Molotiu, *Fragonard's Allegories*, 29–37; and Faroult, *Fragonard Amoureux*, 256.

223 Thuillier, *Fragonard*, 137. Referring to the Louvre sketch, Thuillier talked about the woman as levitating.

224 de Nolhac, *J. H. Fragonard, 1732–1806*, 122.

225 For this concept in Freud, see his "Three Essays in Sexuality" (1905), in *The Standard Edition*, 7: 217; and, most completely, the article "Libido-theorie" (1923), translated as "Two Encyclopaedia Articles," in *The Standard Edition*, 18: 235; and chapter 26 of the *Introductory Lectures in Psycho-Analysis* (1916–17), in *The Standard Edition*, vols. 15–16. See also "Libido," in Laplanche and Pontalis, *The Language of Psycho-Analysis*, 239–40.

226 Maupertuis, *Système de la Nature*, in *Oeuvres*, 2: 155; La Mettrie, *Traité de l'âme*, 69. La Mettrie sought to demonstrate that matter had a motive power and thus sensitive faculty in order to reinforce belief in an essentially active matter. See Thomson, *Bodies of Thought*, 183. The stances of these two thinkers differed, of course. But the point I am making is that, notwithstanding their disparity, various strands of eighteenth-century materialist thought sought to recast or eliminate the notion of the soul, replacing it by different conceptions of an internal agent, a mechanism of arousal operating in living matter. See on this ibid., esp. 175–89.

227 For sources, which include the well-known pair of sculptures, *Atalanta* and *Hippomenes*, executed by, respectively, Le Pautre and Coustou for the park of the chateau of Marly, and the Antique figures of the bacchantes, see most extensively Molotiu (*Fragonard's Allegories*, 29–43), who summarizes the findings in the earlier literature. See also Faroult, *Fragonard Amoureux*, nos. 95–97.

228 For the discussion of the merits and problems of defining these allegories as "pre-romantic" see Molotiu, *Fragonard's Allegories*, 18–21. His own interpretation opts, nonetheless, for the pre-romantic framework. (See ibid., 67–82.)

229 Faroult (*Fragonard Amoureux*, 260) bases his suggestion on Corbin's analysis of sexual manuals from the period. On the simultaneity of *jouissance* see Corbin's *L'Harmonie des plaisirs*, esp. 12 and 54–67.

230 The X-ray of the Getty version revealed the male figure turning his head toward the woman, which led the conservator, Mark Leonard, to suggest it was the earliest canvas. (Molotiu, *Fragonard's Allegories*, 37, n. 68.) The male figure bears a similarly frightened expression in a preparatory oil sketch for this composition, now in an American private collection (Cuzin *Fragonard*, fig. 263; Molotiu, *Fragonard's Allegories*, fig. 30).

231 Later on Freud will develop his concept of libido precisely along these lines, defining it as the energy of the sexual instincts and aligning it with the force of life. For Freud's evolving thinking on the matter, see Laplanche and Pontalis, *The Language of Psycho-Analysis*, 239–40.

232 For such an argument about Antiquity as it emerged in the battle between the ancients and the moderns, see Norman, *The Shock of the Ancient: Literature and History in Early Modern France*.

233 This was not, however, the case of the late allegories the aesthetic of which didn't seem to have deterred the patrons. While we have no precise information about the first owner of the *Fountain*, we know that the final version of the *Vow* was in the collection of the duc François-Alexandre-Frédéric de la Rochefoucauld-Liancourt. See Faroult, *Fragonard amoureux*, 256.

234 Fragonard's vast production included many repetitions, works done by rote.

235 For the attempt to link Fragonard's painting to this aesthetic, see Sheriff, *Fragonard*, 135–37.

236 For the distinction between *scientia sexualis* and *ars erotica*, see Foucault, *The History of Sexuality: Volume 1*, 53–73.

Bibliography

COMMON ABBREVIATIONS

Ananoff, followed by volume and page number: Ananoff, Alexandre, and Daniel Wildenstein. *François Boucher*. 2 vols. Lausanne: La Bibliothèque des arts, 1976.

***Boucher* 1986:** Laing, Alistair, J., Patrice Marandel, and Pierre Rosenberg, eds. *François Boucher, 1703–1770*. New York: Metropolitan Museum of Art, 1986.

***Boucher* ÉNSBA 2003:** Brugerolles, Emmanuelle, ed. *François Boucher et l'art rocaille dans les collections de l'École des beaux-arts*. Paris: École nationale supérieure des Beaux-Arts, 2004.

***Boucher* Gammel Holtegaard:** Joulie, Françoise, ed. *François Boucher: Fragments of a World Picture*. Translated by Jon and Dave Michaelson. Paris: Somogy; Holte, Denmark: Gammel Holtegaard, 2013.

Boucher RMN 2003: Joulie, Françoise, and Jean-François Méjanès. *François Boucher: Hier et aujourd'hui*. Paris: Réunion des Musées nationaux, 2003.

***Chardin* 1979:** Rosenberg, Pierre, ed. *Chardin, 1699–1779*. Paris: Ministère de la Culture et de la Communication, Réunion des musées nationaux, 1979.

***Chardin* 2000:** *Chardin*. London and New York: Royal Academy of Arts and Metropolitan Museum of Art, 2000.

Cuzin *Fragonard*: Cuzin, Jean-Pierre. *Jean-Honoré Fragonard: Life and Work*. New York: Harry Abrams, 1988.

Laing *Drawings*: Laing, Alistair. *The Drawings of François Boucher*. New York: American Federation of Arts in association with Scala Publishers, London, 2003.

PR *Chardin* 1999: Rosenberg, Pierre, and Renaud Temperini. *Chardin, suivi du Catalogue des oeuvres*. Paris: Flammarion, 1999.

PR *Fragonard*: Rosenberg, Pierre. *Fragonard*. New York: Metropolitan Museum of Art, distributed by H. N. Abrams, 1988.

Wildenstein: Wildenstein, Georges. *Chardin: Biographie et Catalogue Critiques, Oeuvre Complète de l'Artiste*. Paris: Les Beaux-Arts, Édition d'Études et de Documents, 1933.

SOURCES

Abraham, Karl. "A Short Study of the Development of Libido, Viewed in the Light of Mental Disorders" [1924]. In *Selected Papers of Karl Abraham, M.D.*, 442–53. Translated by Douglas Bryan and Alix Strachey. London: Hogarth Press, 1927.

Adamson, Glenn. *The Invention of Craft*. London: Bloomsbury, 2013.

Alpers, Svetlana. *The Art of Describing: Dutch Art in the Seventeenth Century*. Chicago: University of Chicago Press, 1983.

———. *Rembrandt's Enterprise: The Studio and the Market*. Chicago: University of Chicago Press, 1988.

Alsten, Stijn, et al., eds. *Raphael to Renoir: Drawings from the Collection of Jean Bonna*. New Haven, CT: Yale University Press, 2009.

Ananoff, Alexandre, with Daniel Wildenstein. *L'Opera completa di Boucher*. Milan: Rizzoli, 1980.

Antoine Furetière. *Dictionnaire universel*, 1708.

Arendt, Hannah. *The Human Condition*. Chicago: University of Chicago Press, 1958.

Assézat, J., ed. *Oeuvres Complètes de Diderot: Revues sur les Éditions Originales*. Paris: Garnier Frères, 1876.

Augard, Jean-Dominique. "The Scientific Cabinet of Comte D'Ons-en-Bray and a Clock by Domenico Cucci." *Cleveland Studies in the History of Art* 8 (January 2003): 80–95.

Auslander, Leora. *Taste and Power: Furnishing Modern France*. Berkeley: University of California Press, 1996.

Ayres, James. *The Artist's Craft*. Oxford: Phaidon, 1985.

Bailey, Colin B. *Fragonard's Progress of Love at the Frick Collection*. New York: Frick Collection with D. Giles Limited, London, 2011.

———. "'A Long Working Life, Considerable Research, and Much Thought': An Introduction to the Art and Career of Jean-Baptiste Oudry (1686–1755)." In *Oudry's Painted Menagerie: Portraits of Exotic Animals in Eighteenth-Century Europe*, edited by Mary Morton, 1–28. Los Angeles: J. Paul Getty Museum, 2007.

———. *The Loves of the Gods: Mythological Painting from Watteau to David*. New York: Rizzoli; Fort Worth: Kimbell Art Museum, 1992.

———. "Marie-Jeanne Buzeau, Madame Boucher (1716–96)." *Burlington Magazine* 147, no. 1225 (2005): 224–34.

———. *Patriotic Taste: Collecting Modern Art in Pre-Revolutionary Paris*. New Haven, CT: Yale University Press, 2002.

———. "Surveying Genre in Eighteenth-Century French Painting." In *The Age of Watteau, Chardin, and Fragonard: Masterpieces of French Genre Painting*, edited by Colin B. Bailey, 2–39. New Haven, CT: Yale University Press with the National Gallery of Canada, Ottawa, 2003.

______. "'Toute seule elle peut remplir et satisfaire l'attention': The Early Appreciation and Marketing of Watteau's Drawings, with an Introduction to the Collecting of Modern French Drawings during the Reign of Louis XV." In *Watteau and His World: French Drawing from 1700–1750*, edited by Alan Wintermute, 68–92. London: Merrell Holberton; New York: American Federation of Arts, 1999.

______. "Was There Such a Thing as Rococo Painting in Eighteenth-Century France?" In *Rococo Echo: Art History and Historiography from Cochin to Coppola*, edited by Melissa Lee Hyde and Katie Scott. Oxford: Voltaire Foundation, 2014.

Bailey, Colin B., ed. *The Age of Watteau, Chardin, and Fragonard: Masterpieces of French Genre Painting*. New Haven, CT: Yale University Press with the National Gallery of Canada, Ottawa, 2003.

Bailey, Colin B., Susan Grace Galassi, and Mària van Berge-Gerbaud. *De Watteau à Degas: Dessins français de la Collection Frits Lugt*. Paris; New York: Fondation Custodia; Frick Collection, 2009.

Barbier, Edmond-Jean François. *Chroniques de la Régence et du Règne de Louis XV (1718–1763)*. 8 vols. Paris: Charpentier, 1857–85.

Barral, Robert, and Pierre Michel, eds. *Michel de Montaigne: Oeuvres complètes*. Paris: Seuil, 1967.

Barthes, Roland. "The Death of the Author." [1968]. In *Image-Music-Text*, 143–48. Translated by Stephen Heath. New York: Hill and Wang, 1977.

______. *Elements of Semiology*. Translated by Anette Lavers and Colin Smith. New York: Hill and Wang, 1985.

______. "The Reality Effect." In *The Rustle of Language*, 141–48. Translated by Richard Howard. Oxford: Blackwell Press, 1985.

Baudrillard, Jean. *De la Séduction*. Paris: Denoël/Gonthier, 1979.

Baxandall, Michael. "Attention, Hand and Brush: Condillac and Chardin." In *The Beholder: The Experience of Art in Early Modern Europe*, edited by Thomas Frangenberg and Robert Williams, 183–94. Burlington, VT: Ashgate, 2006.

______. *Painting and Experience in Fifteenth-Century Italy: A Primer in the Social History of Pictorial Style*. New York: Oxford University Press, 1974.

______. "Pictures and Ideas: Chardin's *Lady Taking Tea*." In *Patterns of Intention: On the Historical Explanation of Pictures*, 74–104. New Haven, CT: Yale University Press, 1985.

______. *Shadows and Enlightenment*. New Haven, CT: Yale University Press, 1995.

Becq, Annie. *La Genèse de l'esthétique française moderne, 1680–1814*. Paris: Albin Michel, 1994.

Bell, Esther. "Charles Coypel and the Age of Eclecticism." In *Genius and Grace: François Boucher and the Generation of 1700*, edited by Alvin L. Clark Jr. Boston: Horvitz Collection, 2014.

Benhamou, Reed. *Charles-Joseph Natoire and the Académie de France in Rome: A Re-Evaluation*. Oxford Studies in the Enlightenment. Oxford: Voltaire Foundation, 2015.

______. "Public and Private Art Education in France, 1648–1793." *Studies on Voltaire and the Eighteenth Century* 308 (1993): 3–183.

Benrekassa, Georges. "L'Article 'Jouissance' et l'idéologie érotique de Diderot." *Dixuitième Siècle* 12 (January 1, 1980): 9–34

______. *Fables de la personne: pour une histoire de la subjectivité*. Paris: Presses Universitaires de France, 1985.

Berg, Maxine. "New Commodities, Luxuries, and Their Consumers in Eighteenth-Century England." In *Consumers and Luxury: Consumer Culture in Europe, 1650–1850*, edited by Maxine Berg and Helen Clifford, 63–85. Manchester: Manchester University Press, 1999.

Berg, Maxine, and Helen Clifford, eds. *Consumers and Luxury: Consumer Culture in Europe, 1650–1850*. Manchester: Manchester University Press, 1999.

Berg, Maxine, and Elizabeth Eger. "The Rise and Fall of the Luxury Debates." In *Luxury in the Eighteenth Century: Debates, Desires, and Delectable Goods*, edited by Maxine Berg and Elizabeth Eger, 7–27. Basingstoke, Hampshire; New York: Palgrave, 2003.

Bermingham, Ann, and John Brewer, eds. *The Consumption of Culture, 1600–1800: Image, Object, Text*. London: Routledge, 1995.

Biebel, Franklin. "Fragonard and Madame du Barry." *Gazette des Beaux-Arts* 102, no. 56 (1960): 207–21.

Binkley, Susan Carpenter. *The Concept of the Individual in Eighteenth-Century French Thought from the Enlightenment to the French Revolution*. Lewiston, NY: Edwin Mellen Press, 2007.

Birn, Raymond. "The Profit of Ideas: 'Privilèges en librairie' in Eighteenth-Century France." *Eighteenth-Century Studies* 4, no. 2 (1970): 131–68.

Blanc, Hippolite. *Les corporations de métiers: leur histoire, leur esprit, leur avenir*. Paris: Letouzey et Ané, 1898.

Blondel, Jacques-François. *Architecture françoise*. Paris: Chez Charles-Antoine Jombert, Paris, 1752–56.

______. *De la distribution des maisons de plaisance et de la décoration des édifices en général*. 2 vols. Paris: Charles-Antoine Jombert, 1737–38.

Blumenfeld, Carole. *Une facétie de Fragonard: Les révélations d'un dessin retrouvé*. Montreuil: Gourcuff Gradenigo, 2013.

Bois, Yve-Alain. *Painting as Model*. Cambridge, MA: MIT Press, 1991.

Bois, Yve-Alain, Jean-Claude Bonne, Christian Bonnefoi, Hubert Damisch, and Jean-Claude Lebensztejn. "La Raie." *Critique* 315–16 (August–September 1973).

Bonfait, Olivier. "Les Collections des parlementaires parisiens du XVIIIe siècle." *Revue de l'Art* 73, no. 1 (1986): 28–42.

Bonnefoy, Yves. *I'Improbable et autres essais*. Paris: Gallimard, 1983.

Bordeaux, Jean-Luc. *François Le Moyne and His Generation, 1688–1737*. Neuilly-sur-Seine: Arthena, 1984.

Bosse, Abraham. *De la Manière de graver à l'Eau-forte et au Burin*. Paris: Chez Charles Antoine Jombert, 1758.

Boudhors, Charles H. *Oeuvres complètes du chevalier de Méré*. 3 vols. Paris: Fernand Roches, 1930.

Boulot, Catherine, Jean-Pierre Cuzin, and Pierre Rosenberg. *J. H. Fragonard e H. Robert a Roma*. Rome: Palombi, Edizioni Carte Segrete, 1990.

Bourdier, Frank. "Le fastueux Cabinet de Bonnier de La Mosson." *Connaissance des Arts* 90 (1959): 52–59.

Boyer d'Argens, Jean Baptiste de. *Thérèse philosophe* [1748]. Paris: Édition la Musardine, 1998.

Braham, Allan. *The Architecture of the French Enlightenment*. Berkeley: University of California Press, 1980.

Brême, Dominique. *François de Troy, 1645–1730*. Toulouse: Musée Paul-Dupuy; Paris: Somogy, 1997.

Bresc-Bautier, Geneviève, ed. *The Apollo Gallery in the Louvre*. Paris: Gallimard, Musée du Louvre, 2004.

Bretonne, Rétif de la. *Les Nuits de Paris*. Edited by Jean Varloot and Michel Delon. Paris: Gallimard, 1987.

Brewer, John. "'The Most Polite Age and the Most Vicious': Attitudes towards Culture as a Commodity, 1660–1800." In *The Consumption of Culture, 1600–1800: Image, Object, Text*, edited by Ann Bermingham and John Brewer, 341–61. London: Routledge, 1995.

Brierre de Boismont, Alexandre-Jacques-François. *Des hallucinations, ou Histoire raisonnée des apparitions, des visions, des songes, de l'extase, du magnétisme et du somnabulisme*. Paris: G. Baillère, 1845.

Brooks, Peter. *The Novel of Worldliness: Crébillon, Marivaux, Laclos, Stendhal*. Princeton, NJ: Princeton University Press, 1969.

Brugerolles, Emmanuelle, and David Guillet. ". . . Un de ces hommes qui signifient le goût d'un siècle, qui l'expriment, le personnifient et l'incarnent." In *Boucher* ÉNSBA 2003, 11–34.

Brugerolles, Emmanuelle, ed. *L'Académie mise à nu: L'école du modèle à l'Académie royale de peinture et de sculpture*. Paris: Beaux-arts de Paris, 2009.

Brunel, Georges. *Boucher*. New York: Vendome Press, 1986.

———. "Boucher: Le Corps et le Décor." In *Boucher* ÉNSBA 2003, 88–93.

Bryson, Norman. *Looking at the Overlooked: Four Essays on Still Life Painting*. Cambridge, MA: Harvard University Press, 1990.

———. *Word and Image: French Painting of the Ancien Régime*. Cambridge: Cambridge University Press, 1981.

Buffon, Georges Louis Leclerc, comte de. *Histoire naturelle, générale et particulière*. 15 vols. Paris: Imprimerie royale, 1749–67.

Butler, Judith. *Bodies That Matter: On the Discursive Limits of Sex*. New York: Routledge, 1993.

———. *Excitable Speech: A Politics of the Performative*. New York: Routledge, 1997.

———. *Gender Trouble: Feminism and the Subversion of Identity*. New York: Routledge, 1990.

———. *Giving an Account of Oneself: A Critique of Ethical Violence*. Assen: Van Gorcum, 2003.

Cahen, Antoine. "Le Prix de quartier à l'Académie royale de peinture et de sculpture." *Bulletin de la Société d'Histoire de l'Art français* (1993): 61–84.

———. "L'École du modèle au XVIIIe siècle: La pratique de l'enseignement à l'Académie royale de peinture et de sculpture." MA diss., Université de Paris IV–Sorbonne, 1991.

Camporesi, Piero. *Exotic Brew: The Art of Living in the Age of Enlightenment*. Translated by Christopher Woodall. Cambridge, MA: Polity Press, 1994.

Carey, Juliet, ed. *Taking Time: Chardin's Boy Building a House of Cards and Other Paintings*. Waddesdon Manor, Buckinghamshire: Rothschild's Foundation, 2012.

Casanova, Giacomo. *History of My Life*. 12 vols. Translated by William R. Trask. Baltimore: Johns Hopkins University Press, 1997.

Casini, Paolo. "Buffon et Newton." In *Buffon 88: Actes du Colloque international pour le Bicentenaire de la Morte de Buffon*, edited by Jean Gayon et al., 299–308. Paris: Vrin, 1992.

Cassirer, Ernst. *The Philosophy of the Enlightenment*. Translated by Fritz C. A. Koelln and James P. Pettegrove. Princeton, NJ: Princeton University Press, [1951] 2009.

Castex, Jéan-Gerald. "L'utilisation de l'estampe et la peinture par les artistes et les ateliers." In *La Manufacture des Lumières: La sculpture à Sèvres de Louis XV à la Révolution*, edited by Tamara Préaud and Guilhem Scherf, 59–66. Quétigny: Faton Éditions, 2015.

Caviglia-Brunel, Susanna. *Charles-Joseph Natoire, 1700–1777*. Paris: Arthena, 2012.

———. "Life Drawing and the Crisis of *Historia* in French Eighteenth-Century Painting." *Art History* 39, no. 1 (2016): 40–69.

Cayeux, Jean de. "Notes sur le Pavillon de Madame Du Barry à Louveciennes et son architecte N. Ledoux." *Revue de l'Art ancien et moderne* 67 (January–May 1935): 213–24; 68 (June 1935): 35–48.

Caylus, Ann-Claude-Philippe de Tubières, comte de, "De la légèreté de l'outil" [1755]. In *Vies 'Artistes du XVIIIe Siècle: Discours sur la Peinture et la Sculpture, Salons*, edited by André Fontaine, 149–59. Paris: Librairie Renouard, 1910.

Cazort, Mimi, ed. *The Ingenious Machine of Nature: Four Centuries of Art and Anatomy*. Ottawa: National Gallery of Canada, 1996.

Cézanne, Paul. "Léttre de Paul Cézanne à Félix Klein." *Le Cahier (Collège international de philosophie)* 8 (October 1989): 317–26.

Chappey, Fréderic, ed. *Fragonard et le voyage en Italie, 1773–1774: Les Bergeret, une famille de mécènes*. Paris: Somogy, 2001.

Charlton, D. G. *New Images of the Natural in France: A Study in European Cultural History, 1750–1800*. Cambridge: Cambridge University Press, 1984.

Chartier, Roger, ed. *A History of Private Life*. Vol. 3, *Passions of the Renaissance*. Translated by Arthur Goldhammer. Series edited by Phillippe Ariès and Georges Duby. Cambridge: Belknap Press of Harvard University Press, 1989.

Châtelet, Gabrielle Emilie Le Tonnelier de Breteuil, marquise de. *Discours sur le Bonheur*. Preface by Elisabeth Badinter. Paris: Payot and Rivages, 1997.

Chatelus, Jean. *Peindre à Paris au XVIIIe Siècle*. Nîmes: Editions J. Chambon, 1991.

Chavignerie, Emile Bellier de la. "Notes pour servir à l'histoire de l'Exposition de la Jeunesse." *Revue universelle des Arts* 19 (1864): 131–50.

Cherni, Amor. *Buffon, la nature et son histoire*. Paris: Presses Universitaires de France, 1998.

Claretie, Jules. *Un enlèvement au XVIIIe siècle, documents tirés des Archives nationales*. Paris: E. Denty, 1882.

Clark, Alvin L., Jr., ed. *Mastery and Elegance: Two Centuries of French Drawings from the Collection of Jeffrey E. Horvitz*. Cambridge, MA: Harvard University Art Museums, 1998.

Clark, Stuart. *Vanities of the Eye: Vision in Early Modern European Culture*. Oxford: Oxford University Press, 2007.

Clifford, Timothy, ed. *French Drawings and Paintings from the Hermitage: Poussin to Picasso*. London: State Hermitage Museum, Hermitage Development Trust, 2001.

Cochin, Charles-Nicolas. "Supplication aux Orfèvres, Ciseleurs, Sculpteurs en bois pour les Appartements et autres, par une Société des Artistes." *Mercure de France*, December 1754, 178–87.

———. *Les Misotechnites aux Enfers, ou examen des Observations sur les arts* [Amsterdam, 1763]. Geneva: Slatkine Reprints, 1970.

———. "De l'Illusion dans la Peinture" [1765]. In *Receuil de quelques pièces concernant les arts*, vol. 2, 44–75. 1771.

Cohen, Sarah. *Art, Dance, and the Body in French Culture of the Ancien Régime*. Cambridge: Cambridge University Press, 2000.

———. "Chardin's Fur: Painting, Materialism, and the Question of Animal Soul." *Eighteenth-Century Studies* 38, no 1 (2004): 39–61.

Collomp, Alain. "Families: Habitations and Cohabitations." In *A History of Private Life*. Vol. 3, *Passions of the Renaissance*, edited by Roger Chartier, 493–529. Cambridge, MA: Belknap Press of Harvard University Press, 1989.

Condillac, Etienne Bonnot de. *Traité des Sensations*. Paris: Fayard, 1984.

Conisbee, Philip. *Chardin*. Lewisburg, PA: Bucknell University Press.

———. *French Paintings of the Fifteenth through the Eighteenth Century*. Washington, DC: National Gallery of Art, 2009.

Conisbee, Philip, ed. *French Genre Painting in the Eighteenth Century*. Washington, DC, and New Haven, CT: National Gallery of Art, distributed by Yale University Press, 2007.

Copjec, Joan. *Imagine There's No Woman: Ethics and Sublimation*. Cambridge, MA: MIT Press, 2002.

Coquery, Natacha. *L'Hôtel Aristocratique: Le Marché du Luxe à Paris au XVIIIe Siècle*. Paris: Publications de la Sorbonne, 1998.

———. "The Language of Success: Marketing and Distributing Semi-Luxury Goods in Eighteenth-Century Paris." *Journal of Design History* 17, no. 1 (2004): 71–89.

Corbin, Alain. *L'Harmonie de plaisirs. Les manières de jouir du siècle des Lumières à l'avènement de la sexologie*. Paris: Perrin, 2008.

Correia, Clara Pinto. *The Ovary of Eve: Egg and Sperm and Preformation*. Chicago: University of Chicago Press, 1997.

Corson, Richard. *Fashions in Eyeglasses*. London: Peter Owen, 2011.

Courboin, François. *L'Estampe française: Graveurs et marchands; Essais*. Brussels: G. Van Oest, 1914.

Crampe-Casnabet, Michèle. "Condillac: On ne touche que soi; Réflexion autour d'une statue." *Representations du toucher* (September 1994): 51–59.

Crary, Jonathan. *Techniques of the Observer: On Vision and Modernity in the Nineteenth Century*. Cambridge, MA: MIT Press, 1990.

Crébillon, Claude Prosper Jolyot de. *Collection complète des Oeuvres de M. de Crébillon*. London [Paris], 1777.

———. *Le Sopha: Conte Moral*. Paris: Desjonquères, 1984.

Crow, Thomas. "Chardin at the Edge of Belief: Overlooked Issues of Religion and Dissent in Eighteenth-Century Painting." In *French Genre Painting in the Eighteenth Century*, edited by Philip Conisbee, 91–103. Washington, DC: National Gallery of Art, 2007.

———. "The Critique of Enlightenment in Eighteenth-Century Art." *Art Criticism* 3, no. 1 (1986): 17–31.

———. *Painters and Public Life in Eighteenth-Century Paris*. New Haven, CT: Yale University Press, 1985.

Crowley, John E. *The Invention of Comfort: Sensibilities and Design in Early Modern Britain and Early America*. Baltimore: Johns Hopkins University Press, 2001.

Cuzin, Jean-Pierre. *Fragonard*. Louvre: Drawing Gallery. Translated by Susan Wise. Milan: 5 Continents; Paris: Musée du Louvre, 2003.

———. *François-André Vincent, 1746–1816: Entre Fragonard et David*. Paris: Arthena, 2013.

Cuzin, Jean-Pierre, et al. *Jean-Honoré Fragonard (1732–1806): Orígenes e influencias; De Rembrandt al siglo XXI*. Barcelona: Caixa Forum, 2006.

Dacier, Émile, and Albert Vauflart. *Jean de Julienne et les Graveurs de Watteau au XVIIIe siècle*. 4 vols. Paris: Pour les Membres de la Société [etc.], 1921–29.

Dakin, Douglas. *Turgot and the Ancien Régime in France*. London: Methuen, 1939.

Dance, S. Peter. *A History of Shell Collecting*. Rev. ed. Leiden: Brill, 1986.

Darnton, Robert. *The Forbidden Best-Sellers of Pre-Revolutionary France*. New York: W. W. Norton, 1995.

———. *The Literary Underground of the Old Regime*. Cambridge, MA: Harvard University Press, 1982.

Daston, Lorraine, and Peter Gallison. *Objectivity*. New York: Zone Books; Cambridge, MA: MIT Press, 2007.

Davis, Natalie Zemon, and Arlette Farge, eds. *A History of Women in the West*. Vol. 3, *Renaissance and Enlightenment Paradoxes*. Translated by Arthur Goldhammer. Volume 3 of series edited by Georges Duby and Michelle Perrot. Cambridge, MA: Belknap Press of Harvard University Press, 1995.

Degenaar, Marjolein. *Molyneux's Problem: Three Centuries of Discussion on the Perception of Forms*. Dordrecht, Netherlands: Kluwer Academic, 1996.

DeJean, Joan. *The Age of Comfort: When Paris Discovered Casual and the Modern Home Began*. London: Bloomsbury, 2009.

———. *Ancients against the Moderns: Culture Wars and the Making of Fin-de-siècle*. Chicago: University of Chicago Press, 1997.

Delaplanche, Jérôme. *Un tableau n'est pas qu'une image: La reconnaissance de la matière de la peinture en France au XVIIIe siècle*. Rennes: Presses Universitaires de Rennes, 2016.

Delpierre, Gilles. "Chardin péruvien: Les *Dialogues sur les Arts entre un Artiste américain et un Amateur français* de Pierre Estève." *Revue d'Histoire littéraire de la France* 95, no. 2 (1995): 294–305.

Delpierre, Madeleine. *Dress in France in the Eighteenth Century*. Translated by Caroline Beamish. New Haven, CT: Yale University Press, 1997.

Démoris, René. "Boucher, Diderot, Rousseau." In *Rethinking Boucher*, edited by Melissa Hyde and Mark Ledbury, 201–28. Los Angeles: Getty Research Institute, 2006.

———. "Chardin and the Far Side of Illusion." In *Chardin*, 99–109. London; New York: Royal Academy of Arts; Metropolitan Museum of Art, 2000.

———. *Chardin, la chair et l'objet* [1991]. Paris: Éditions Olbia, 1999.

———. "Le Comte de Caylus et la peinture: pour une théorie de l'inachevé." *Revue de l'Art* 142 (December 2003): 31–43.

———. "Le coup d'état du connaisseur délicat et sévère: Les *Réflexions de 1747*." In René Démoris and Florence Ferran, *La Peinture en procès: L'invention de la critique d'art au siècle des Lumières*, 65–85. Paris: Presses de la Sorbonne Nouvelle, 2001.

———. "Dessin et couleur chez Diderot (1749–66)." In *Méthode!* No. 13. Bandol: Vallongues, 2007.

———. "Inside/Interiors: Chardin's Images of the Family." *Art History* 28, no. 4 (2005): 442–67.

———. "La nature morte chez Chardin." *Revue d'Esthétique* 4 (1969): 363–85.

Démoris, René, and Florence Ferran, eds. *La peinture en procès: L'invention de la critique d'art au siècle des Lumières*. Paris: Presses de la Sorbonne Nouvelle, 2001.

Denk, Claudia. "'Chardin n'est pas un peintre d'histoire, mais c'est un grand homme': Les autoportraits tardifs de Jean-Siméon Chardin." In *L'Art et les normes sociales au XVIIIe Siècle*, edited by Thomas W. Gaehtgens et al. Paris: Éd. de la Maison des Science de l'Homme, 2001.

Dennis, Michael. *Court and Garden: From the French Hôtel to the City of Modern Architecture*. Cambridge, MA: MIT Press, 1986.

Derrida, Jacques. *Memoirs of the Blind: The Self-Portrait and Other Ruins*. Translated by Pascale-Anne Brault and Michael Naas. Chicago: University of Chicago Press, 1993.

———. *Writing and Difference*. Translated, with an introduction and additional notes, by Alan Bass. Chicago: University of Chicago Press, 1978.

Desboulmiers, [Jean-Augustin Julien des Boulmiers]. "Éloge de M. Boucher, premier peintre du roi et directeur de l'académie royale de peinture et sculpture." *Mercure de France*, September 1770, 181–89.

Descartes, *Discours de la Méthode* [1637]. Paris: Fayard, 1987.

Deslandes, M. (André François). *Lettre sur le Luxe*. Frankfurt: Chez Joseph-André Vanebben, 1745.

Desné, Roland, ed. *Les Matérialistes français de 1750 à 1800*. Paris: Buchet-Chastel, 1965.

Dewald, Jonathan. *Aristocratic Experience and the Origins of Modern Culture: France 1570–1715*. Berkeley: University of California Press, 1993.

Dezallier d'Argenville, Antoine-Joseph. *La Conchyliologie, ou Histoire Naturelle des Coquilles*. 3rd ed. 2 vols. Paris: G. de Bure fils ainé, 1780.

———. *Conchyliologie nouvelle et portative*. Paris: Regnard, 1767.

———. *Histoire naturelle éclairci dans deux de ses parties principales, la Lythologie et la Conchyliologie*. Paris, 1742.

Dictionnaire de l'Académie française, 4th ed. Paris, 1762.

Diderot, Denis. *Lettre sur les aveugles à l'usage de ceux qui voyent*. London: 1749. English ed.: *Letter on the Blind for the Use of Those Who Can See*. Translated by Kate Tunstall. In *Blindness and Enlightenment: An Essay*, 169–219. New York: Continuum, 2011.

———. *Satyre Seconde: Le Neveu de Rameau*. Introduction by Marian Hobson. Geneva: Droz, 2013. English ed.: *Rameau's Nephew, and D'Alembert's Dream*. Translated with introductions by L. W. Tancock. Harmondsworth: Penguin, 1966.

Diderot, Denis, and Jean le Rond d'Alembert. *Encyclopédie, ou Dictionnaire raisonné des Sciences, des Arts et des Métiers*. Paris, 1751–72.

Dietz, Bettina, and Thomas Nutz. "Collections Curieuses: The Aesthetics of Curiosity and Elite Lifestyle in Eighteenth-Century Paris." *Eighteenth-Century Life* 29, no. 3 (2005): 44–75.

Dilke, Emilia F. S. "Chardin et ses Oeuvres à Potsdam et à Stockholm." *Gazette des Beaux-Arts* 22 (1899): 177–90, 333–42, 390–96.

Dréano, Mathurin. *La Renommée de Montaigne en France au XVIIIe siècle, 1677–1802*. Angers: Editions de l'Ouest, 1952.

Dubost, Jean-Pierre. "Libertinage and Rationality: From the 'Will to Knowledge' to Libertine Textuality." *Yale French Studies*, special issue, *Libertinage and Modernity*, edited by Catherine Cusset, 94 (1998): 52–78.

Duffy, Stephen, and Jo Hedley. *The Wallace Collection's Pictures: A Complete Catalogue*. London: Unicorn Press and Lindsay Fine Arts, 2004.

Dulau, Anne, ed. *Boucher and Chardin: Masters of Modern Manners*. Glasgow: Hunterian, University of Glasgow, in association with Paul Holberton, London, 2008.

Duncan, Carol. "Happy Mothers and Other New Ideas in French Art." *Art Bulletin* 55, no. 4 (1973): 570–83.

Dupuy-Vachey, Marie-Anne. *Fragonard: Les Plaisirs d'un Siècle*. Gand: Snoeck; Paris: Musée Jacquemart-André, 2007.

———. "Fragonard's 'Fantasy Figures': Prelude to a New Understanding." *Burlington Magazine* 157, no. 1345 (2015): 241–47.

———. "Mauvais Genre ou la fabrique d'une réputation." In *Fragonard Amoureux: Galant et Libertin*, edited by Guillaume Faroult. Paris: Réunion des musées nationaux, Musée du Luxembourg-Sénat, 2015.

Duro, Paul. *The Academy and the Limits of Painting in Seventeenth-Century France*. Cambridge: Cambridge University Press, 1997.

Eleb-Vidal, Monique, and Anne Debarre-Blanchard. *Architectures de la vie privée: Maisons et mentalités; XVIIe–XIXe siècles*. Brussels: Archives d'Architecture moderne, 1989.

[Estève, Pierre]. *Dialogues sur les arts entre un Artiste amériquain et un Amateur françois*. Amsterdam, 1756.

Etienne, Pascal. *Le Faubourg Poissonnière: Architecture, Élégance et Décor*. Paris: La Délégation, 1986.

Explications des Peintures, Sculptures et autres Ouvrages de Messieurs de l'Académie royale, dont l'Exposition a été ordonnée suivant l'Intention de Sa Majesté . . . dans le grand salon du Louvre. Paris, 1753.

Faillant-Dumas, Lola. "Des données de laboratoire sur Chardin." *L'estampille* 107 (March 1979): 34–41

———. "Étude de la technique picturale de Chardin." In *Diderot et l'Art de Boucher à David*, edited by Marie-Catherine Sahut and Nathalie Volle. Paris: Éditions de la Réunion des Musées nationaux, 1984.

Fairchilds, Cissie C. *Domestic Enemies: Servants and Their Masters in Old Regime France*. Baltimore: Johns Hopkins University Press, 1984.

———. "The Production and Marketing of Populuxe Goods in Eighteenth-Century Paris." In *Consumption and the World of Goods*, edited by John Brewer and Roy Porter, 228–48. London: Routledge, 1993.

Faret, Nicholas. *L'Honnête Homme ou l'Art de plaire à la Cour*, edited by M. Magendie. Paris: Presses Universitaires de France, 1925.

Farge, Arlette. "The Honor and Secrecy of Families." In *A History of Private Life*. Vol. 3, *Passions of the Renaissance*, edited by Roger Chartier, 571–607. Cambridge, MA: Belknap Press of Harvard University Press, 1989.

Faroult, Guillaume. *Jean-Honoré Fragonard: Le Verrou*. Paris: Réunion des musées nationaux, Musée du Louvre, 2007.

Faroult, Guillaume, ed. *Fragonard Amoureux: Galant et Libertin*. Paris: Réunion des musées nationaux, Musée du Luxembourg-Sénat, 2015.

Farr, James R. *The Work in France: Labor and Culture in Early Modern Times, 1350–1800*. Lanham, MD: Rowman and Littlefield, 2008.

Faÿ-Hallé, Antoinette. "The Influence of Boucher's Art on the Production of the Vincennes-Sèvres Porcelain Factory." In *Boucher* 1986, 345–50.

Fellows, Otis E., and Stephen F. Milliken. *Buffon*. New York: Twayne, 1972.

Flandrin, Jean-Louis. *Familles, Parenté, Maison, Sexualité dans l'ancienne Société*. Paris: Seuil, 1984.

Fontanel, Béatrice. *Daily Life in Art*. New York: Abrams, 2006.

Fontenay, Abbé de. *Dictionnaire des Artistes*. Paris: Vincent, 1776.

Fort, Bernadette. "An Academician in the Underground: Charles Nicolas Cochin and Art Criticism in Eighteenth-Century France." *Studies in Eighteenth-Century Culture* 23 (1994): 3–27.

Foucault, Michel. *The History of Sexuality: Volume 1, An Introduction*. New York: Pantheon Books, 1978.

———. *Language, Counter-Memory, Practice*. Edited by Donald F. Bouchard. Translated by Donald F. Bouchard and Sherry Simon. Ithaca, NY: Cornell University Press, 1977.

———. "What Is an Author" [1969]. In *Aesthetics, Method, and Epistemology*. Edited by James D. Faubion. Translated by Robert Hurley and others. Vol. 2, 205–22. New York: New Press, 1998.

Fraenkel, Béatrice. *La Signature: genèse d'un signe*. Paris: Gallimard, 1992.

France, Peter. *Politeness and Its Discontents: Problems in French Classical Culture*. Cambridge: Cambridge University Press, 1992.

Freud, Sigmund. *The Standard Edition of the Complete Psychological Works of Sigmund Freud*. 24 vols. Edited and translated by James Strachey with Anna Freud. London: Hogarth Press, 1957–74.

Fried, Michael. *Absorption and Theatricality: Painting and Beholder in the Age of Diderot*. Chicago: University of Chicago Press, [1980] 1988.

Fronek, Joseph. "The Materials and Technique of the Los Angeles *Soap Bubbles*." In *Masterpieces in Focus: "Soap Bubbles" by Jean Siméon Chardin*, by Philip Conisbee. Los Angeles: Los Angeles County Museum of Art, 1990.

Fuhring, Peter. "Boucher et les dessinateurs d'ornement." In *Boucher* ÉNSBA 2003.

———. "The Print Publishing Privilege in Eighteenth-Century France, Part I." *Print Quarterly* 2 (1985): 174–93.

Galiani, Fernando. *L'Abbé F. Galiani. Correspondence*. Edited by Lucien Perey and Maugras Gaston. Paris: C. Lévy, 1881.

Gallet, Michel. *Claude-Nicolas Ledoux, 1736–1806*. Paris: Picard, 1980.

———. *Paris Domestic Architecture of the 18th Century*. Translated by James C. Palmes. London: Barrie and Jenkins, 1972.

Garnier, Nicole. "Les portraits de Watteau." In *Watteau et son Cercle dans les Collections de l'Institut de France*. Chantilly: Musée Condé, 1996.

Gasking, Elizabeth B. *Investigations into Generation, 1651–1828*. Baltimore: Johns Hopkins University Press, 1967.

Gay, Peter. *The Enlightenment: An Interpretation* [1966]. 2 vols. New York: Norton, 1977.

Girard, René. *Violence and the Sacred*. 2nd ed. Baltimore: Johns Hopkins University Press, 1982.

Glorieux, Guillaume. *À l'Enseigne de Gersaint: Edme François Gersaint, Marchand d'Art sur le Pont Notre-Dame, 1694–1750*. Seyssel: Champ Vallon; Paris: Diffusion, Presses Universitaires de France, 2002.

Goncourt, Edmond de, and Jules de Goncourt. *French Eighteenth-Century Painters*. Translated by Robin Ironside. New York: Phaidon, 1981.

Goodman, Dena. "The Secrétaire and the Integration of the Eighteenth-Century Self." In *Furnishing the Eighteenth Century: What Furniture Can Tell Us about the European and American Past*, edited by Dena Goodman and Kathryn Norberg, 183–204. New York: Routledge, 2007.

Goodman, Dena, and Kathryn Norberg, eds. *Furnishing the Eighteenth Century: What Furniture Can Tell Us about the European and American Past*. New York: Routledge, 2007.

Goodman, John, ed. *Diderot on Art*. 2 vols. New Haven, CT: Yale University Press, 1995.

Goodman-Soellner, Elise. "Boucher's 'Madame de Pompadour at Her Toilette.'" *Simiolus: Netherlands Quarterly for the History of Art* 17, no. 1 (1987): 41–58.

———. *The Portraits of Madame de Pompadour: Celebrating the Femme Savante*. Berkeley: University of California Press, 2000.

Grasselli, Margaret Morgan. Review of *Antoine Watteau, 1684–1721*. Catalogue raisonné des dessins by Pierre Rosenberg and Louis-Antoine Prat. *Master Drawings* 39, no. 3 (2001): 310–34.

Grasselli, Margaret Morgan, and Pierre Rosenberg, eds. *Watteau, 1684–1721*. Washington, DC: National Gallery of Art, 1984.

Grate, Pontus. *French Painting II: The Eighteenth Century*. Stockholm: Nationalmuseum, 1994.

Green, André. *The Fabric of Affect in the Psychoanalytic Discourse*. Translated by Alan Sheridan. London: Routledge, 1999.

———. *Narcissisme de vie, narcissisme de mort*. Paris: Éditions de Minuit, [1983] 2007.

Greenblatt, Stephen. *Renaissance Self-Fashioning: From More to Shakespeare*. Chicago: University of Chicago Press, 1980.

Greenhalgh, Peter "The History of Craft." In *The Culture of Craft: Status and Future*, edited by Peter Dormer, 20–51. Manchester: Manchester University Press, 1997.

Griener, Pascal. *La République de l'oeil: L'expérience de l'art au siècle de Lumières*. Paris: Odile Jacob, 2010.

Griffiths, Antony. "The Search for Facsimile." In *Prints, A History of an Art*, by Michel Melot, Antony Griffiths, and Richard S. Field. New York: Rizzoli; Geneva: Skira, 1981.

Grimsley, Ronald. "Turgot's Article on 'Existence' in the *Encyclopédie*." In *From Montesquieu to Laclos: Studies in French Enlightenment*, 109–23. Geneva: Droz, 1974.

Guichard, Charlotte. *Les amateurs d'art à Paris au XVIIIe siècle*. Seyssel, France: Champ Vallon, 2008.

———. "Fragonard et les jeux de la signature au XVIIIe siècle." *Revue de l'Art* 177, no. 3 (2012): 47–55.

———. *Graffitis: Inscrire son nom à Rome XVIe- XIXe siècle*. Paris: Éditions du Seuil, 2014.

———. "Gravures de société et identité d'amateur à Paris . . ." In *La Gravure: Quelles problématiques pour les temps modernes?*, edited by Isabelle Michel-Évrard and Pierre Wachenheim, 133–44. Bordeaux: Wm. Blake/Art and Arts, 2009.

———. "Taste Communities: The Rise of the Amateur in Eighteenth-Century Paris." *Eighteenth-Century Studies* 45, no. 4 (2012): 519–47.

Guiffrey, Jules. *Histoire de l'Académie de Saint-Luc*. Paris: Champion, 1915.

———. "Logements d'Artistes au Louvre." *Nouvelles Archives de l'Art Français* 2 (1873): 276.

Guillaumat, Louis, and Jean-Pierre Bailliart. *Les Quinze-Vingts de Paris: échos historiques du XIIe au XXe siècle*. Paris: Société Francophone d'Histoire de l'Ophtalmologie, 1998.

Guillerm, Alain. "Les illustrations de Fragonard pour les 'Contes' de La Fontaine." *Gazette des Beaux-Arts* (March 1977): 99–105.

Guimbaud, Louis. *Saint-Non et Fragonard d'après des documents inédits*. Paris: Le Goupy, 1928.

Hedley, Jo. *François Boucher: Seductive Visions*. London: Wallace Collection, 2004.

Heinich, Nathalie. *Du Peintre à l'Artiste: Artisans et Académiciens à l'Âge classique*. Paris: Éditions de Minuit, 1993.

Heller-Roazen, Daniel. *The Inner Touch: An Archeology of Sensation*. New York: Zone Books, 2007.

Hellman, Mimi. "The Joy of Sets." In *Furnishing the Eighteenth Century: What Furniture Can Tell Us about the European and American Past*, edited by Dena Goodman and Kathryn Norberg, 129–54. New York: Routledge, 2007.

———. "Staging Retreat: Designs for Bathing in Eighteenth-Century France." In *Interiors and Interiority*, edited by Ewa Lajer-Burcharth and Beate Söntgen, 49–72. Berlin: De Gruyter, 2016.

Hémery, Axel, ed. *Figures de fantaisie du XVIe aux XVIIIe Siècle*. Paris: Somogy éditions d'art, 2015.

Henderson, Andrea. "Doll-Machines and Butcher-Shop Meat: Models of Childbirth in the Early Stages of Industrial Capitalism." *Genders* 12 (Winter 1991): 100–119.

Herbert, Félix. "Les demeures de Jean Siméon Chardin." *Bulletin de la Société historique du VIe Arrondissement de Paris* 2 (1899): 142–47.

Herbert, James. "A Picture of Chardin's Making." *Eighteenth-Century Studies* 34, no. 2 (2001): 251–74.

Hesse, Carla. "Enlightenment Epistemology and the Laws of Authorship in Revolutionary France, 1777–1793." *Representations* 30 (Spring 1990): 109–37.

Hill, C. R. "The Cabinet of Bonnier de la Mosson (1702–1744)." *Annals of Science* 43, no. 2 (1986): 147–74.

Hobson, Marian. *The Object of Art: The Theory of Illusion in Eighteenth-Century France*. Cambridge: Cambridge University Press, 1982.

Holbach, Paul Henri Thiry, baron d'. *Système de la Nature*. London, 1771.

Holmes, Mary Tavener. *Nicolas Lancret, 1690–1743*. New York: H. N Abrams with the Frick Collection, 1991.

Huet, Marie-Hélène. *Monstrous Imagination*. Cambridge, MA: Harvard University Press, 1993.

Hundert, Edward. *The Enlightenment's Fable: Bernard Mandeville and the Discovery of Society*. Cambridge: Cambridge University Press, 1994.

———. "Mandeville, Rousseau, and the Political Economy of Fantasy." In *Luxury in the Eighteenth Century: Debates, Desires, and Delectable Goods*, edited by Maxine Berg and Elizabeth Eger, 28–40. Basingstoke, Hampshire; New York: Palgrave, 2003.

Hyde, Melissa. "Confounding Conventions: Gender Ambiguity and François Boucher's Painted Pastorals." *Eighteenth-Century Studies* 30, no. 1 (1996): 25–57.

———. "Getting into the Picture: Boucher's Self-Portraits of Others." In *Rethinking Boucher*, edited by Melissa Hyde and Mark Ledbury, 13–38. Los Angeles: Getty Research Institute, 2006.

———. "The 'Make-up' of the Marquise: Boucher's Portrait of Pompadour at Her Toilette." *Art Bulletin* 82, no. 3 (2000), 453–75.

———. *Making Up Rococo: Boucher and His Critics*. Los Angeles: Getty Research Institute, 2006.

Hyde, Melissa, and Mark Ledbury. "The Pleasures of Rethinking François Boucher." In *Rethinking Boucher*, edited by Melissa Hyde and Mark Ledbury, 1–9. Los Angeles: Getty Research Institute, 2006.

Hyde, Melissa, and Katie Scott, eds. *Rococo Echo: Art, History, and Historiography from Cochin to Coppola*. Oxford University Studies in the Enlightenment. Oxford: Voltaire Foundation, 2014.

Ibrahim, Annie. *Diderot, un matérialisme écléctique*. Bibliothèque des philosophies. Paris: J. Vrin, 2010.

———. "La Pensée de Buffon: Système ou Anti- Système?" In *Buffon 88: Actes du colloque international pour le bicentenaire de la morte de Buffon*, edited by Jean Gayon et al. Paris: Vrin, 1992.

Jackall, Yuriko, John K. Delaney, and Michael Swicklik. "'Portrait of a Woman with a Book': A 'Newly Discovered Fantasy Figure' by Fragonard in the National Gallery of Art, Washington." *Burlington Magazine* 157 (April 2015): 248–54.

Jacob, Margaret C. *The Cultural Meaning of the Scientific Revolution*. New York: McGraw-Hill, 1988.

———. "The Materialist World of Pornography." In *The Invention of Pornography: Obscenity and the Origins of Modernity, 1500–1800*, edited by Lynn Hunt, 157–202. New York: Zone Books; Cambridge: MIT Press, 1993.

Jacoby, Beverly Schreiber. *François Boucher's Early Development as a Draughtsman, 1720–1734*. New York: Garland, 1986.

———. "François Boucher's Stylistic Development as a Draftsman: The Evolution of His Autonomous Drawings." In *Drawings Defined*, edited by Walter Strauss and Tracie Felker, 259–80. New York: Abris Books, 1987.

Jay, Martin. *Downcast Eyes: The Denigration of Vision in Twentieth-Century French Thought*. Berkeley: University of California Press, 1993.

Jean-Richard, Pierrette. *L'Oeuvre gravé de François Boucher dans la Collection Edmond de Rothschild*. Paris: Éditions des musées nationaux, 1978.

Johnson, Dorothy. "Picturing Pedagogy: Education and the Child in the Paintings of Chardin." *Eighteenth-Century Studies* 24, no. 1 (1990): 47–68.

Jollet, Étienne. *Les Figures de la pesanteur: Newton, Fragonard, et les Hasards heureux de l'Escarpolette*. Nîmes: J. Chambon, 1998.

Jollet, Étienne, ed. *La Font de Saint-Yenne: Oeuvre critique*. Paris: École nationale supérieure des Beaux-Arts, 2001.

Jones, Jennifer Michelle. *Sexing* La Mode*: Gender, Fashion, and Commercial Culture in Old Regime France*. Oxford: Berg, 2004.

Jordanova, Ludmilla. "Gender, Generation, and Science: William Hunter's Obstetrical Atlas." In *William Hunter and the Eighteenth-Century Medical World*, edited by W. F. Bynum and R. Porter, 385–412. Cambridge: Cambridge University Press, 1985.

———. *Sexual Visions: Images of Gender in Science and Medicine between the Eighteenth and Twentieth Centuries*. Madison: University of Wisconsin Press, 1989.

Joulie, Françoise. "Boucher, Bloemaert et Watteau: La création d'un monde." In *Boucher* RMN 2003, 52–65.

———. "Boucher décorateur: Dessins pour la Manufacture de Beauvais." *La Revue du Louvre et des Musées de France* 38, no. 4 (1988): 320–24.

———. "Boucher et les arts décoratifs." In *Boucher* RMN 2003, 84–99.

———. "The Decorative Arts: Illustration, Invention, and Dissemination." In *Boucher* Gammel Holtegaard, 22–65.

———. "Formation et culture de François Boucher." In *Boucher* ÉNSBA 2003, 76–87.

———. "François Boucher Collectionneur de Peinture nordique." In *Boucher et les Peintres du Nord*, edited by Françoise Joulie. Paris: Réunion des Musées nationaux, 2004.

Joulie, Françoise, ed. *Boucher et les peintres du Nord*. Paris: Réunion des musées nationaux, 2004.

———. *Esquisses, Pastels et Dessins de François Boucher dans les Collections privées*. Paris: Somogy; Versailles: Musée Lambinet, 2004.

Kahng, Eik, and Marianne Roland Michel, eds. *Anne Vallayer-Coster: Painter to the Court of Marie-Antoinette*. Dallas: Dallas Museum of Art; New Haven, CT: Yale University Press, 2002.

Kaplan, Steven L. "The Luxury Guilds in Paris in the Eighteenth-Century." *Francia* 9 (1981): 257–91.

Kaplow, Jeffry. *The Names of Kings: The Parisian Laboring Poor in the Eighteenth Century*. New York: Basic Books, 1972.

Kavanagh, Thomas M. *Enlightened Pleasures: Eighteenth-Century France and the New Epicureanism*. New Haven, CT: Yale University Press, 2010.

Keller, Eve. "Embryonic Individuals: The Rhetoric of Seventeenth-Century Embryology and the Construction of Early Modern Identity." *Eighteenth-Century Studies* 33, no. 3 (2000): 321–48.

Kisluk-Grosheide, Daniëlle. "The Reign of Magots and Pagods." *Metropolitan Museum Journal* 37 (January 2002): 177–97.

Klein, Lawrence D. "Politeness for Plebes: Consumption and Social Identity in Early Eighteenth-Century England." In *The Consumption of Culture, 1600–1800: Image, Object, Text*, edited by Ann Bermingham and John Brewer, 362–82. London: Routledge, 1995.

Klein, Melanie. "Some Theoretical Conclusions Regarding the Emotional Life of the Infant." In *Developments in Psycho-Analysis*, by Melanie Klein et al., edited by Joan Riviere, 198–236. London: Hogarth Press, 1952.

Knight, Isabel F. *The Geometric Spirit: The Abbé de Condillac and the French Enlightenment*. New Haven, CT: Yale University Press, 1968.

Koerner, Joseph. *The Moment of Self-Portraiture in German Renaissance Art*. Chicago: University of Chicago Press, 1993.

Kors, Alan Charles, ed. *Encyclopedia of the Enlightenment*. 4 vols. New York: Oxford University Press, 2003.

Krauss, Rosalind E. "Reinventing the Medium." *Critical Inquiry* 25, no. 2 (1999): 289–305.

———. *Under the Blue Cup*. Cambridge, MA: MIT Press, 2011.

Kristeva, Julia. *Desire in Language: A Semiotic Approach to Literature and Art*. Edited by Leon S. Roudiez. Translated by Thomas Gora, Alice Jardine, and Leon S. Roudiez. New York: Columbia University Press, 1980.

Kwass, Michael. "Ordering the World of Goods: Consumer Revolution and the Classification of Objects in Eighteenth-Century France." *Representations* 82 (Spring 2003): 87–116.

La Mettrie, Julien Offray de. *De la volupté: Anti- Sénèque ou le souverain bien; L'École de la volupté; Système d'Epicure*. Edited by Ann Thomson. Paris: Ed. Desjonquières, 1996.

———. *Discours sur le bonheur* [1748]. Paris: L'Arche, 2000.

———. *Machine Man and Other Writings*. Edited and translated by Ann Thomson. Cambridge: Cambridge University Press, 1996.

———. *Traité de l'âme*. Edited by Theo Verbeeck. 2 vols. Utrecht, 1988.

Lacan, Jacques. "Desire and the Interpretation of Desire in Hamlet." *Yale French Studies* 55, no. 56 (1977): 11–52.

———. "The Mirror Stage as Formative of the Function of the I." In *Écrits: A Selection*, translated by Alan Sheridan, 1–7. New York: W. W. Norton, 1977.

———. *Le Seminaire, Livre IV: La Relation d'Objet*. Paris: Le Seuil, 1994.

Lacombe, Jacques. *Dictionnaire portatif des Beaux-Arts*. Paris: Hérrisant et Estienne, 1754.

Lafont, Anne, ed. *1740, Un Abrégé du Monde: Savoirs et collections autour de Dezallier d'Argenville*. Lyon: Fage, 2012.

Laing, Alastair. "Boucher — A Painter or a Draftsman Born?" In Laing *Drawings*, 20–37.

———. "Boucher: The Search for an Idiom." In *Boucher* 1986.

———. "A Group of Boucher's Designs for Coach Panels." In *Design into Art: Drawings for Architecture and Ornament; The Lodewijk Houthakker Collection*, vol. 1, edited by Peter Fuhring, 117–21. London: P. Wilson; New York: Harper and Row, 1989.

———. "La Re-Naissance de Vénus: Une oeuvre des débuts de Boucher retrouvée à Paris." *Revue de l'Art* 103, no. 1 (1994): 77–81.

Laissus, Yves. "Le Jardin du Roi." In *Buffon 88: Actes du colloque international pour le bicentenaire de la morte de Buffon*, edited by Jean Gayon et al., 49–71. Paris: Vrin, 1992.

Lajer-Burcharth, Ewa. "Chardin Cruel." In *Violence du Rococo*, edited by René Démoris, Jacques Berchtold, and Christophe Martin. Bordeaux: Presses Universitaires, 2011.

———. *Chardin Material*. Berlin: Sternberg Press, 2011.

———. "Fragonard in Detail." *Differences: A Journal of Feminist Cultural Studies* 14, no. 3 (2003) (issue dedicated to Naomi Schor): 34–56.

———. "Genre and Sex." In *French Genre Painting in the Eighteenth Century*, edited by Philip Conisbee, 201–19. Washington, DC: National Gallery of Art; New Haven, CT: Yale University Press, 2007.

———. "Image Matters: The Case of Boucher." In *Dialogues in Art History, from Mesopotamian to Modern: Readings for a New Century*, edited by Elizabeth Cropper, 277–303. Washington, DC: Center for Advanced Study in the Visual Arts, 2009.

———. "Jean-Etienne Liotard's Envelopes of Self." In *Cultures of Forgery: Making Nations, Making Selves*, edited by Judith Ryan and Alfred Thomas, 127–44. London: Routledge, 2003.

———. "The Object as Subject." In *The Lure of the Object*, edited by Stephen Melville, 157–77. Williamstown, MA: Clark Art Institute Publications, 2005.

———. "Pompadour's Dream: Boucher, Diderot, and Modernity." In *Rethinking Boucher*, edited by Melissa Hyde and Mark Ledbury, 229–52. Los Angeles: Getty Research Institute, 2006.

———. "Pompadour's Touch: Difference in Representation." *Representations* 73 (Winter 2001): 54–88.

———. "Scenes of Instruction." In *Painting beyond Itself*, edited by Isabelle Graw and Ewa Lajer-Burcharth, 22–53. Berlin: Sternberg Press, 2016.

Laplanche, Jean. *Seduction, Translation, and the Drives: A Dossier*. Edited by John Fletcher and Martin Stanton. Translated by Martin Stanton. London: Institute of Contemporary Art, 1992.

Laplanche, Jean, and J.-B. Pontalis. *The Language of Psycho-Analysis*. Translated by Donald Nicholson-Smith. New York: W. W. Norton, 1973.

Laquer, Thomas. *Making Sex: Body and Gender from the Greeks to Freud*. Cambridge, MA: Harvard University Press, 1990.

Lavezzi, Elizabeth. "The Encyclopédie and the Idea of the Decorative Arts." In *Between Luxury and the Everyday. Decorative Arts in Eighteenth-Century France*, edited by Katie Scott and Deborah Cherry, 37–62. Malden, MA: Blackwell, 2005.

Leblanc, Abbé Jean-Bernard. *Observations sur les ouvrages de MM. de l'Académie*. Paris, 1753.

Le Brun, Charles. "Sentiment sur le discours du mérite de la couleur par M. Blanchard." Lecture delivered at the Academy on January 9, 1672.

Leca, Benedict. "An Art Book and Its Viewers: The 'Recueil Crozat' and the Uses of Reproductive Engraving." *Eighteenth-Century Studies* 38, no. 4 (2005): 623–49.

Ledbury, Mark. "Boucher and Theater." In *Rethinking Boucher*, edited by Melissa Hyde and Mark Ledbury, 133–60. Los Angeles: Getty Research Institute, 2006.

———. "The Hierarchy of Genres in the Theory and Practice of Painting in Eighteenth-Century France." In *Théories et Débats esthétiques au dixhuitième Siècle*, edited by Elisabeth Décultot and Mark Ledbury, 187–209. Paris: Honoré Champion Éd., 2001.

Léoni, Sylviane. "Plaisir des mots et plaisir des sens chez Nicole et Bossuet." In *Eros in Francia nel Seicento*, 279–98. Bari: Adriatica; Paris: Nizet, 1987.

Leribault, Christophe. *Jean-François de Troy (1679– 1752)*. Paris, Arthena, 2002.

Lichtenstein, Jacqueline. *The Eloquence of Color: Rhetoric and Painting in the French Classical Age*. Translated by Emily McVarish. Berkeley: University of California Press, 1993.

Lilley, Ed. "The Name of the Boudoir." *Journal of the Society of Architectural History* 53, no. 2 (1994): 193–98.

Liotard, Jean-Étienne. *Traité des principes et de règles de la peinture, par M. J-É. Liotard, peintre, citoyen de Genève* [1781]. Geneva: Pierre Cailler, 1954.

Lipton, Eunice. "Women, Pleasure, and Painting (e.g., Boucher)." *Genders* 7 (1990): 69–86.

Locke, John. *An Essay Concerning Human Understanding* [1690]. Edited by Roger Woodhouse. London: Penguin Books, 1997.

Lojkin, Stéphane. "Diderot, Le Goût de l'Art." In *Le Goût de Diderot: Greuze, Chardin, Falconet, David*. Paris: Hazan, 2013.

Los Llanos, José-Luis de, and Thérèse Burollet, eds. *Fragonard et le dessin français au XVIIIe siècle dans les collections du Petit Palais*. Paris: Diffusion Paris-Musées, 1992.

Lüdke, Dietmar. "Chardin und die niederländische Malerei des 17. Jahrhunderts Dargestellt an sieben Stillebe." In *Jean Siméon Chardin, 1699–1779: Werk, Herkunft, Wirkung*. Ostfildern-Ruit: Hatje Cantz Verlag, 1999.

Lukes, Steven. *Individualism*. Oxford: Blackwell, 1973.

Luynes, Charles-Philippe d'Albert, duc de. *Mémoirs du duc de Luynes sur la Cour de Louis XV (1735–58)*. 17 vols. Paris: 1860–65.

Lynch, Deidre. *The Economy of Character: Novels, Market Culture, and the Business of Inner Meaning*. Chicago: University of Chicago Press, 1998.

Lyon, Georgette. *Joseph Ducreux (1735–1802), Premier peintre de Marie Antoinette*. Paris: La Nef de Paris, 1958.

Lyon, John, and Phillip R. Sloan, eds. *From Natural History to the History of Nature: Readings from Buffon and His Critics*. Notre Dame, IN: University of Notre Dame Press, 1981.

MacGregor, William B. "The Authority of Prints: An Early Modern Perspective." *Art History* 22, no. 3 (1999): 389–420.

Malassis, A. P., ed. *Correspondence de Madame de Pompadour avec son père, M. Poisson et son frère, M. de Vandières*. Paris: J. Baur, 1878.

Mandeville, Bernard. *The Fable of the Bees*. In *The Portable Enlightenment Reader*, edited by Isaac Kramnick. New York: Penguin Books, 1995.

Mannlich, Johann Christian von. *Histoire de ma Vie: Mémoirs de Johann Christian von Mannlich (1741–1822)*. 2 vols. Edited by Karl-Heinz Bender and Hermann Kleber. Trier: Spree, 1989–93.

Mariette, Pierre-Jean. *Abecedario de P. J. Mariette*. 8 vols. Edited by Philippe de Chennevières and Anatole de Courde de Montaiglon. Paris: J.-B. Dumoulin, 1851–60.

Marin, Louis. "'C'est moi que je peins . . .': De la figurabilité du moi chez Montaigne." In *L'Écriture de soi*. Paris: PUF, 1999.

Marivaux, Pierre Carlet de Chamblain de. *La Vie de Marianne*. Paris: Gallimard, 1997.

———. *Le Paysan parvenu*. Paris: Flammarion, 1965. English ed.: *The Upstart Peasant, or the Memoirs of Monsieur****. Translated with an introduction by Benjamin Boyce. Durham, NC: Seeman Printery, 1974.

Marmontel, Jean-François. *Mémoires*. Edited by Jean-Pierre Guicciardi and Gilles Thierriat. Paris: Mercure de France, 1999.

Marx, Karl. *Capital: A Critique of Political Economy*. 3 vols. Edited by Friedrich Engels. New York: International Publishers, 1973.

Massengale, Jean Montague. *Jean-Honoré Fragonard*. New York: H. N. Abrams, 1993.

Massey, Lyle. "Pregnancy and Pathology: Picturing Childbirth in Eighteenth-Century Obstetric Atlases." *Art Bulletin* 87, no. 1 (2005): 73–91.

Maupertuis. *Oeuvres*. 2 vols. Berlin: Éditions de Bourdeaux, 1753.

———. *P. L. M. Vénus physique* [1745]. Paris: Aubier Montaigne, 1980.

Mauzi, Robert. *L'Idée du bonheur dans la littérature et la pensée françaises au XVIIIe siècle*. Paris: Arman Colin, 1960.

Maza, Sarah C. *The Myth of the French Bourgeoisie: An Essay on the Social Imaginary, 1750–1850*. Cambridge, MA: Harvard University Press, 2003.

———. *Servants and Masters in Eighteenth-Century France: The Uses of Loyalty*. Princeton, NJ: Princeton University Press, 1983.

McAllister Johnson, William. "Les Morceaux de réception: Protocole et Documentation." In *Les Peintres du Roi: 1648–1793*, edited by Philippe Le Leyzour and Alain Daguerre de Hureaux, 31–49. Paris: Réunion des Musées nationaux, 2000.

McClellan, Andrew. "Watteau's Dealer: Gersaint and the Marketing of Art in Eighteenth-Century Paris." *Art Bulletin* 78, no. 3 (1996): 439–53.

McCullagh, Suzanne Folds, and Pierre Rosenberg. "'The Supreme Triumph of the Old Painter': Chardin's Final Work in Pastel." *Museum Studies: The Art Institute of Chicago* 12, no. 1 (1985): 42–59.

McKendrick, Neil, John Brewer, and J. H. Plumb. *The Birth of Consumer Society: The Commercialization of Eighteenth-Century England*. London: Europa Publications, 1982.

McLaren, Angus. *Reproductive Rituals: The Perception of Fertility in England from the Sixteenth Century to the Nineteenth Century*. London: Methuen, 1984.

Méjanès, Jean-François. "Le Séjour de François Boucher en Italie (1728–1731)." In *Boucher* RMN 2003, 33–51.

Melon, Jean François. *Essai politique sur le commerce*. n.p., 1734.

Ménétra, Jacques-Louis. *Journal of My Life*. Translated by Arthur Goldhammer. New York: Columbia University Press, 1986.

Mercier, Louis-Sébastien. *Tableau de Paris*. 2 vols. Edited by Jean-Claude Bonnet. Paris: Mercure de France, 1994.

Méré, Antoine Gombaud, Chevalier de. *Lettres*. 2 vols. Paris: Au Palais, 1689.

Mérot, Alain. *Retraites mondaines: Aspects de la décoration intérieure à Paris, au XVIIe siècle*. Paris: Le Promeneur, 1990.

Meyboom, L.S.P. *Frans Hemsterhuis, Oeuvres Philosophiques*. New York: Hildesheim and Georg Olms, 1972.

Meyer, Jean. *La vie quotidienne en France au temps de la Régence*. Paris: Hachette, 1979.

Michel, Christian. *L'Académie royale de Peinture et Sculpture*. Geneva: Librairie Droz, 2012.

———. "Boucher Professeur à l'Académie royale de Peinture et de Sculpture." In *Boucher* ÉNSBA, 94–101.

———. *Charles-Nicolas Cochin et l'Art des Lumières*. Rome: École française de Rome, 1993.

———. "Manière, Goût, Faire, Style: Les Mutations du Vocabulaire de la Critique d'Art en France au XVIIIe siècle." In *Rhétorique et Discours critique: Échanges entre la Langue et Métalangues*, edited by Françoise Berlan and Françoise Douay-Soubline, 153–59. Paris: Presses de l'École normale supérieure, 1989.

———. "Nature and Moeurs: Thoughts on the Reception of Genre Painting in France." In *French Genre Painting in the Eighteenth Century*, edited by Philip Conisbee, 275–93. Washington, DC: National Gallery of Art; New Haven, CT: Yale University Press, 2007.

———. "Le Peintre magicien." In *Le Goût de Diderot: Greuze, Chardin, Falconet, David*, 235–56. Paris: Hazan, 2013.

Michel, Patrick. *Le Commerce du tableau à Paris dans la seconde moitié du XVIIIe siècle: Acteurs et Pratiques*. Villeneuve d'Ascq: Presses Universitaires du Septentrion, 2007.

———. *Peinture et Plaisir: Les Goûts Picturaux des Collectionneurs Parisiens au XVIIIe siècle*. Rennes: Presses Universitaires de Rennes, 2010.

Milam, Jennifer. "Fragonard's 'Le Furet.'" *Burlington Magazine* 141, no. 1158 (1999): 542–43.

Milliot, Vincent. *Les "Cris de Paris" ou le Peuple travesti: Les Représentation des pétits Métiers parisiens (XVIe–XVIIIe siècles)*. Paris: Publications de la Sorbonne, 1995.

Mme Geoffrin: Une Femme d'affaires et d'esprit. Milan: Silvana, 2011.

Molotiu, Andrei. "Allegories of Love in the Late Work of Jean-Honoré Fragonard." PhD diss., New York University, Institute of Fine Arts, 1999.

———. *Fragonard's Allegories of Love*. Los Angeles: J. Paul Getty Museum, 2007.

Montaiglon, Anatole de, and Jules Guiffrey. *Correspondence des Directeurs de l'Académie de France à Rome*. 17 vols. Paris: Charavay, 1887–1907.

Montaigne, Michel de. *The Complete Essays*. Edited by M. A. Screech. London: Penguin Books, 1987.

Morizé, André, ed. *L'Apologie du Luxe aux XVIIIe Siècle et "Le Mondain" de Voltaire: Étude critique sur "Le Mondain" et ses Sources*. Geneva: Slatkine reprints, 1970.

Mornet, Daniel. "Les Enseignements des bibliothèques privées (1750–1780)." *Revue d'Histoire littéraire de la France* 17 (1910): 449–96.

Mouhy, Charles de Fleux. *Mémoirs d'Anne-Marie de Moras, Comtesse de Courbon, écrites par elle-même* [first published 1739]. Edited and with Postface by René Démoris. Paris: Éd. Desjonquères, 2006 [based on 1769 edition].

Mousseaux, Rose-Marie, ed. *Thé, Café, ou Chocolat? Le boissons exotiques à Paris au XVIIIe siècle*. Paris: Paris-Musées, 2015.

Mulherron, Jamie. "François Boucher and the Art of Conchology." *Burlington Magazine* 158 (April 2016): 254–63.

Müller-Sievers, Helmut. *Self-Generation: Biology, Philosophy, and Literature around 1800*. Stanford, CA: Stanford University Press, 1997.

Munhall, Edgar. "Fragonard's Studies for the Progress of Love." *Apollo* 93 (May 1971): 400–407.

Munro, Jane. *Silent Partners: Artist and Mannequin from Function to Fetish*. New Haven, CT: Yale University Press, 2014.

Nesbit, Molly. "What Was an Author?" *Yale French Studies* 73 (1987): 229–57.

Newman, Karen. *Fetal Positions: Individualism, Science, and Visuality*. Stanford, CA: Stanford University Press, 1996.

Nolhac, Pierre de. *J. H. Fragonard, 1732–1806*. Paris: Goupil, 1918.

Norman, Larry F. *The Shock of the Ancient: Literature and History in Early Modern France*. Chicago: University of Chicago Press, 2011.

O'Neal, John C. *The Authority of Experience: Sensationist Theory in the French Enlightenment.* University Park: Pennsylvania State University Press, 1996.

Oudry, Jean-Baptiste. "Discours sur la Pratique de la Peinture et ces Procédés Principaux: ébaucher, peindre à fond et retoucher." Lecture delivered on December 2, 1752, at the Royal Academy. Los Angeles: J. Paul Getty Trust, 2008.

Ovid. *Metamorphoses.* Translated by Frank Justus Millier. Loeb Classical. Cambridge, MA: Harvard University Press, 1994.

Padiyar, Satish. "Out of Time: Fragonard and David." In *Rococo Echo: Art, History, and Historiography from Cochin to Coppola*, edited by Melissa Hyde and Katie Scott, 213–32. Oxford University Studies in the Enlightenment. Oxford: Voltaire Foundation, 2014.

Papillon de la Ferté, Denis Pierre Jean. *Extrait des différens ouvrages publiés sur la vie des peintres.* 7 vols. Paris chez Roualt, 1776.

Pardailhé-Galabrun, Annik. *The Birth of Intimacy: Privacy and Domestic Life in Early Modern Paris* [1988]. Translated by Jocelyn Phelps. Philadelphia: University of Pennsylvania Press, 1991.

Pascal, G., and Roger Gaucheron. *Documents sur la Vie et l'Oeuvre de Chardin.* Paris: Éditions de la Galerie Pigalle, 1931.

Paulson, William R. *Enlightenment, Romanticism, and the Blind in France.* Princeton, NJ: Princeton University Press, 1987.

Peltier, Stéphane. "*Les Misotechnites aux enfers* ou l'Imposture de la Critique selon Charles-Nicolas Cochin." In *L'Invention de la Critique de l'art: Actes du Colloque international tenu à l'Université Rennes 2 les 24 et 25 juin, 1999*, edited by Pierre-Henry Frangne and Jean-Marc Poinsot, 107–20. Rennes: Presses Universitaires de Rennes, 2002.

Percival, Melissa. "Fragonard and Pastiche: The Case of the *Girl in Spanish Costume* in Dulwich." In *Enlightenment and Tradition.* Studies on Voltaire and the Eighteenth Century (6), 47–64. Oxford: Voltaire Foundation, 2007.

———. *Fragonard and the Fantasy Figure: Painting the Imagination.* Farnham, UK; Burlington, VT: Ashgate, 2012.

Perkins, Jean. *The Concept of the Self in the French Enlightenment.* Geneva: Droz, 1969.

Perrot, Philippe. "De l'apparat au bien-être: Les avatars d'un superflu necessaire." In *Du Luxe au Confort*, edited by Jean-Pierre Goubert, 31–63. Paris: Éditions Belin, 1988.

Petherbridge, Deanna. "Art et anatomie: La rencontre du texte et de l'image." In *Corps à Vif: Art et Anatomie*, edited by Deanna Petherbridge, C. L. Ritschard, and A. Carlino, 15–48. Geneva: Musée d'Art et d'Histoire, 1998.

Petherbridge, Deanna, and Ludmilla Jordanova. *The Quick and the Dead: Artists and Anatomy.* Berkeley: University of California Press, 1997.

Philips, Adam. "André Green and the Pragmatics of Passion." In *The Dead Mother: The Work of André Green*, edited by Gregorio Kohon. London: Routledge, 1999.

Pichet, Isabelle. *Le Tapissier et les Dispositifs discursifs au Salon (1750–1789): Expographie, Critique et Opinion.* Paris: Hermann, 2012.

Picon, Antoine. *Architectes et Ingénieurs au Siècle des Lumières.* Marseille: Parenthèses, 1988.

———. "Gestes ouvriers, opérations et processus techniques: La Vision du Travail des Encyclopédistes." *Recherches sur Diderot et sur l'Encyclopèdie* 13 (October 1992): 131–47.

Piles, Roger de. *Cours de peinture par principes.* Paris: Jacques Estienne, 1708. English ed.: *The Principles of Painting.* London: Printed for J. Osborn, 1743.

———. *Dialogue sur le coloris* [1673]. Paris: Langlois, 1699.

———. *L'Idée du peintre parfait* [1699]. Paris: Gallimard, 1993.

Pineau, Séverin. *Opusculum physiologum et anatomicum* [1597]. Paris, 1607.

Piotrowska, Anna. "Chardin, Van Loo, and the Académie Royale during the Regency: New Archival Information." *Burlington Magazine* 90, no. 1262 (May 2008): 296–300.

Piveteau, Jean, Maurice Fréchet, and Charles Bruneau, eds. *Buffon, Oeuvres philosophiques.* Paris: Presses Universitaires de France, 1954

Podro, Michael. *Depiction.* New Haven, CT: Yale University Press, 1998.

Pomian, Krzysztof. *Collectionneurs, Amateurs, et Curieux: Paris, Venice, XVIe–XVIIIe siècle.* Paris: Éditions Gallimard, 1987. English ed.: *Collectors and Curiosities: Paris and Venice, 1500–1800.* Translated by Elizabeth Wiles-Portier. Cambridge: Polity Press; Cambridge, MA: Basil Blackwell, 1990.

Pons, Bruno. "Hôtel du Lude." In *Le Faubourg Saint Germain, la Rue Saint-Dominique, hôtels et amateurs*, edited by Bruno Pons with Brigitte Gournay, 150–63. Paris: Le Musée, 1984.

———. *De Paris à Versailles, 1699–1736: Les Sculpteurs ornemanistes parisiens et l'Art décoratif des Bâtiments du Roi.* Strasbourg: Association des Publications près les Universités de Strasbourg, 1986.

Portalis, Roger. *Honoré Fragonard: Sa Vie et Son Oeuvre.* 2 vols. Paris: J. Rothschild, 1889.

Posner, Donald. "Concerning the 'Mechanical' Parts of Painting and the Artistic Culture of Seventeenth- Century France." *Art Bulletin* 75, no. 4 (1993): 583–98.

———. "The True Path of Fragonard's 'Progress of Love.'" *Burlington Magazine* 114, no. 833 (1972): 526–34.

Préaud, Tamara, and Antoinette Faÿ-Hallé, eds. *Porcelaines de Vincennes: Les Origines de Sèvres.* Paris: Ministère de la Culture et de l'Environnement, Éditions des Musées nationaux, 1977.

Préaud, Tamara, and Guilhem Scherf, eds. *La Manufacture des Lumières: La Sculpture à Sevrès de Louis XV à la Révolution.* Quétigny: Faton Éditions, 2015.

Priebe, Jessica Susan Main. "The Artist as Collector: François Boucher (1703–1770)." *Journal of the History of Collections* 28, no. 1 (2015): 27–42.

———. "*Conchyliologie* to *Conchyliomanie*: The Cabinet of François Boucher, 1703–1770." PhD diss., University of Sydney, 2011.

Prompsault, J.-L., ed. *Les Quinze-Vingts: Notes et Documents, recueillis par Feu L'Abbé J.-H.-R. J.-L. Prompsault.* Carpentras: E. Rolland, 1863.

Proust, Marcel. "Chardin and Rembrandt." In *Against Saint-Beuve and Other Essays*, translated by John Sturrock. London: Penguin Books, 1988.

Puttfarken, Thomas. *The Discovery of Pictorial Composition: Theories of Visual Order in Painting, 1400– 1800.* New Haven, CT: Yale University Press, 2000.

———. *Roger de Piles' Theory of Art.* New Haven, CT: Yale University Press, 1985.

Rabreau, Daniel, and Christophe Henry. *Corésus et Callirhoé de Fragonard: Un Chef-d'Oeuvre d'Émotion.* Bourdeaux: William Blake, Art and Arts, 2007.

Rajchman, John. *Truth and Eros: Foucault, Lacan, and the Question of Ethics.* New York: Routledge, 1991.

Rand, Richard. "Fragonard dans le jardin d'amour." In *L'Art et les normes sociales au XVIIIe siècles*, edited by Thomas Gaehtgens, 493–508. Paris: Éditions de la Maison des sciences de l'Homme, 2001.

______. "Love, Domesticity, and the Evolution of Genre Painting in Eighteenth-Century France." In *Intimate Encounters: Love and Domesticity in Eighteenth-Century France*, edited by Richard Rand, 3–20. Hanover, NH: Hood Museum of Art, Dartmouth College; Princeton, NJ: Princeton University Press, 1997.

Rand, Richard, ed. *Intimate Encounters: Love and Domesticity in Eighteenth-Century France.* Hanover, NH: Hood Museum of Art, Dartmouth College; Princeton, NJ: Princeton University Press, 1997.

Ranum, Orest. "The Refuges of Intimacy." In *The History of Private Life*. Vol. 3, *Passions of the Renaissance*, edited by Roger Chartier, 207–63. Cambridge, MA: Belknap Press of Harvard University Press, 1989.

Raux, Sophie. "La Main invisible: Innovation et concurrence chez les créateurs des nouvelles techniques de fac-similés de dessins au XVIIIe siècle." In *Quand la Gravure fait Illusion: Autour de Watteau et Boucher, le Dessin grave au XVIIIe siècle*, edited by Emmanuelle Delapierre and Sophie Raux, 56–64. Valenciennes: Musée des beaux-arts; Éditions Gourcuff Gradenigo, 2006.

______. "Le Voyage de Fragonard et Bergeret en Flandre et Hollande durant l'été 1773." *Revue de l'Art* 156 (June 2007): 11–28.

Raynal, Abbé. *Correspondance litteraire* [1750]. 1877. Cited in PR 1999, 169.

Reddy, William M. *The Rise of Market Culture: The Textile Trade and French Society, 1750–1900.* Cambridge: Cambridge University Press; Paris: Éditions de la Maison des sciences de l'homme, 1984.

Regosin, Richard L. "Montaigne and His Readers." In *A New History of French Literature*, edited by Denis Hollier, 248–53. Cambridge, MA: Harvard University Press, 1994.

Rémy, Pierre. *Catalogue raisonné des Tableaux, Desseins, Estampes, Terres cuites, Lacques, Porcelaines de différentes sortes, montées, & non montées; Meubles curieux, Bijoux, Minéraux, Cristallisations, Madrepores, Coquilles & autres Curiosités qui composent le Cabinet de Feu M. Boucher, Premier Peintre du Roi.* Paris, 1771.

Renouvier, Jules. *Histoire de l'art pendant la Révolution considéré principalement dans les estampes: ouvrage posthume.* Paris: J. Renouard, 1863.

Rétat, Pierre. "Luxe." *Dix-Huitième Siècle* 26 (1994): 79–88.

Reuter, Astrid, et al. *Fragonard: Poesie und Leidenschaft*. Berlin, Karlsruhe: Deutscher Kunstverlag, Staatliche Kunsthalle Karlsruhe, 2013.

Ribeiro, Aileen. *The Art of Dress: Fashion in England and France, 1750 to 1820*. New Haven, CT: Yale University Press, 1995.

______. *Dress in Eighteenth-Century Europe, 1715–1789*. 2nd ed. New Haven, CT: Yale University Press, 2002.

Roberts, K. B., and J. D. W. Tomlinson. *The Fabric of the Body: European Traditions of Anatomical Illustrations*. New York: Clarendon Press, 1992.

Roche, Daniel. "Commentary: Jacques-Louis Ménétra; An Eighteenth-Century Way of Life." In Jacques-Louis Ménétra, *Journal of My Life*, translated by Arthur Goldhammer, 243–359. New York: Columbia University Press, 1986.

______. *La culture des apparences: une histoire du vêtement (XVIIe–XVIIIe siècle)*. Paris: Fayard, 1989. English ed.: *The Culture of Clothing: Dress and Fashion in the Ancien Régime*. Translated by Jean Birrell. Cambridge: Cambridge University Press, 1996.

______. *France in the Enlightenment*. Translated by Arthur Goldhammer. Cambridge, MA: Harvard University Press, 1998.

______. *Histoire des choses banales: Naissance de la consommation dans les sociétés traditionnelles (XVIIe–XIXe siècle)*. Paris: Fayard, 1997. English ed.: *History of Everyday Things: The Birth of Consumption in France, 1600–1800*. Translated by Brian Pearce. Cambridge: Cambridge University Press, 2000.

______. *The People of Paris: An Essay in Popular Culture in the 18th Century*. Translated by Mary Evans. Leamington Spa: Berg Publishers, 1987.

Rochebrune, Marie-Laure. "Ceramics and Glass in Chardin's Paintings." In *Chardin*, 37–53. London; New York: Royal Academy of Arts; Metropolitan Museum of Art, 2000.

Rodari, Florian, ed. *Anatomie de la couleur: L'invention de l'estampe en couleurs*. Paris; Lausanne: Bibliothèque nationale de France; Musée Olympique, 1996.

Roethlisberger, Marcel, and Renée Loche. *Liotard: Catalogue, Source et Correspondence.* 2 vols. Doornspijk: Davaco, 2008.

Roger, Charles. *A Collection of Prints in Imitation of Drawings*. 2 vols. London: J. Nichols, 1778.

Roger, Jacques. *Buffon: A Life in Natural History*. Ithaca, NY: Cornell University Press, 1997.

______. *Les sciences de la vie dans la pensée française de XVIIIe siècle: la génération des animaux de Descartes à l'Encyclopédie*. Paris: Armand Colin, 1963. English ed.: *The Life Sciences in Eighteenth-Century French Thought*. Edited by Keith R. Benson. Translated by Robert Ellrich. Stanford, CA: Stanford University Press, 1997.

Roland Michel, Marianne. *Chardin*. Translated by Eithne McCarthy. New York: Harry N. Abrams, 1996.

______. "Fragonard, Illustrateur de l'Amour." In *Aimer en France, 1760–1860: Actes du Colloque international de Clermont-Ferrand*, 25–32. Clermont-Ferrand, Association des Publications de la Faculté des lettres et sciences humaines, 1980.

______. "Fragonard — Illustrator of the 'Contes' of la Fontaine." *Burlington Magazine* 112, no. 811 (October 1970): i–vi.

______. "The Rosenberg-Prat Catalogue of Watteau's Drawings." *Burlington Magazine* 140, no. 1148 (1998): 749–54.

______. "Vallayer in Her Time." In *Anne Vallayer-Coster: Painter to the Court of Marie-Antoinette*, edited by Eik Kahng and Marianne Roland Michel. Dallas: Dallas Museum of Art; New Haven, CT: Yale University Press, 2002.

______. "De Watteau à Boucher: Formation d'une manière et d'un genre." In *Boucher* ÉNSBA 2003, 38–45.

______. "Watteau et les *Figures de différents caractères*." In *Antoine Watteau (1684–1721): Le Peintre, son Temps, et sa Légende*, edited by François Moreau and Margaret Morgan Grasselli, 117–27. Paris: Champion Slatkine; Geneva: Éditions Clairefontaine, 1987.

Rosenberg, Pierre. "The *Blind Man of the Quinze-Vingts* by Chardin and the *Young Girls with a Marmot* by Fragonard at the Fogg." In *Shop Talk: Studies in Honour of Seymour Slive*, edited by Cynthia P. Schneider, William W. Robinson, and Alice I. Davies, 211–15 and 391–93. Cambridge, MA: Harvard University Art Museums, 1995.

———. *Chardin: An Intimate Art*. New York: Harry N. Abrams, 2000.

———. "Chardin: New Thoughts." The Franklin D. Murphy Lectures, University of Kansas. Lawrence: Helen Foresman Spencer Museum of Art, University of Kansas, 1983.

———. "The Mysterious Beginnings of the Young Boucher." In *Boucher* 1986, 41–55.

———. "Principaux collectionneurs de Chardin." In *Chardin 1699–1779*, edited by Pierre Rosenberg, 73–78. Paris: Ministère de la culture et de la communication, Réunion des musées nationaux, 1979.

———. *Vies anciennes de Watteau*. Paris: Hermann, 1984.

Rosenberg, Pierre, and Claudine Lebrun Jouve, eds. *Les Fragonard de Besançon*. Milan: 5 Continents; Besançon: Musée des Beaux-Arts et d'archéologie de Besançon, 2006.

Rosenberg, Pierre, and Louis-Antoine Prat. *Antoine Watteau, 1684–1721: Catalogue raisonné des dessins*. 3 vols. Milan: Leonardo Arte, 1996.

Rosenthal, Angela. "She's Got the Look! Eighteenth-Century Female Portrait Painters and the Psychology of a Potentially 'Dangerous mployment.'" In *Portraiture: Facing the Subject*, edited by Joanna Woodall, 147–66. Manchester: Manchester University Press, 1997.

Ross, Ellen. "Mandeville, Melon, and Voltaire: The Origins of the Luxury Controversy in France." *Studies on Voltaire and the Eighteenth Century* 155 (1976): 1897–912. Edited by Theodor Besterman.

Roubo, André Jacob. *L'Art du menuisier*. Paris: 1769–75.

Rousseau, Jean-Jacques. *The Confessions of Jean-Jacques Rousseau*. Translated by J. M. Cohen. New York: Penguin Books, 1953.

———. *Discours sur les Sciences et les Arts* [1750]. *Discours sur l'Origine et Fondements de l'Inégalité parmi les Hommes* [1754]. Edited by Jacques Roger. Paris: Flammarion, 1995.

———. *Emile; or, On Education* [1762]. Translated by Allan Bloom. New York: Basic Books, 1979.

———. *The First and Second Discourses*. Translated by Roger D. and Judith R. Masters. New York: St. Martin's Press, 1964.

———. *Julie, ou, La Nouvelle Heloise*. [1761]. Edited by Henri Coulet. Paris: Gallimard, 1993.

———. *Reveries of the Solitary Walker*. Translated by Peter France, 63–81. London: Penguin Books, 1979.

Russo, Elena. "The Self, Real and Imaginary: Social Sentiment in Marivaux and Hume." *Yale French Studies*, no. 92 (1997): 126–48.

Sahut, Marie-Catherine, and Natalie Volle, eds. *Diderot et l'Art de Boucher à David*. Paris: Éditions de la Réunion des Musées nationaux, 1984.

Saint-Amand, Pierre. *The Libertine's Progress: Seduction in the Eighteenth-Century French Novel*. Translated by Jennifer Curtiss Gage. Hanover, NH: Published by University Press of New England for Brown University Press, 1994.

Saint-Non, Jean Claude Richard de. *Panopticon Italiano: Un diario di viaggio ritrovato, 1759–1761*. Edited by Pierre Rosenberg with the collaboration of Barbara Brejon de Lavergnée. Rome: Elefante, 1986.

Salmon, Xavier, ed. *Dansez, embrassez qui vous voudrez: Fêtes et Plaisirs d'Amour au Siècle de Pompadour*. Balsamo (Milan): Silvana, 2015.

———. *Madame Pompadour et les Arts*. Paris: Réunion des musées nationaux, 2002.

———. *Le voleur d'âmes: Maurice Quentin de La Tour*. Versailles: Artlys, 2004.

Les Salons des Mémoirs secrets. Edited by Bernadette Fort. Paris: École nationale supérieure des beaux-arts, 1999.

Sargentson, Carolyn. *Merchants and Luxury Markets: The Marchand Merciers of Eighteenth-Century Paris*. Malibu, CA: Victoria and Albert Museum with the J. Paul Getty Museum, 1996.

Sauerländer, Wilibald. "Uber der Urspüngliche Reinhenfolge von Fragonards 'Amours des Bergers.'" *Münchner Jahrbuch der bildenden Kunst* 19 (1968): 127–56.

Savary des Bruslons, Philémon-Louis. *Dictionnaire universel du Commerce*. Paris, 1744.

Savill, Rosalind. "Boucher: The Muse for Sèvres Porcelain and Gold Boxes in the Wallace Collection." In Hedley, *François Boucher: Seductive Visions*, 182–89. London: Wallace Collection, 2004.

———. "François Boucher and the Porcelains of Vincennes and Sèvres." *Apollo* 115, no. 241 (1982): 162–70.

Schama, Simon. *The Embarrassment of Riches: An Interpretation of Dutch Culture in the Golden Age*. New York: Knopf, Random House, 1987.

Scheffer, Carl Fredrik. *Lettres particulières à Carl Gustaf Tessin, 1744–1752*. Stockholm: Kungl, Samfundet för utgivande av handskrifter rörande Skandinaviens historia, 1982.

Schieder, Martin. "Between *Grâce* and *Volupté*: Boucher and Religious Painting." In *Rethinking Boucher*, edited by Melissa Hyde and Mark Ledbury, 61–87. Los Angeles: Getty Research Institute, 2006.

———. "Jean-Honoré Fragonard und der Pariser Kunstmarkt im ausgehenden Ancien Régime." *Kritische Berichte Mitteilungsorgan des Ulmer Verein Verband für Kunst- und Kulturwissenschaften* 21, no. 3 (1993): 10–20.

Schnapper, Antoine. *Le métier de peintre au Grand Siècle*. Paris: Gallimard, 2004.

Schroder, Anne L. "Fragonard's Later Career: The *Contes et Nouvelles* and the Progress of Love Revisited." *Art Bulletin* 93, no. 2 (2011): 150–77.

Schwartz, Joel. *The Sexual Politics of Jean-Jacques Rousseau*. Chicago: University of Chicago Press, 1984.

Scott, Katie. "Authorship, the Académie, and the Market in Early Modern France." *Oxford Art Journal* 21, no. 1 (1998): 29–41.

———. "Chardin Multiplied." In *Chardin*, 61–95. London; New York: Royal Academy of Arts; Metropolitan Museum of Art, 2000.

———. "Chardin: On the Art of Building Castles." In *Taking Time: Chardin's Boy Building a House of Cards and Other Paintings*, edited by Juliet Carey, 37–52. Waddesdon Manor, Buckinghamshire: Rothschild's Foundation, 2012.

———. "Child's Play." In *The Age of Watteau, Chardin, and Fragonard: Masterpieces of French Genre Painting*, edited by Colin B. Bailey, 89–105. New Haven, CT: Yale University Press, 2003.

———. "Edme Bouchardon's 'Cris de Paris': Crying Food in Early Modern Paris." *Word and Image* 29, no. 1 (2013): 69–89.

———. "Framing Ambition: The Interior Politics of Mme de Pompadour." In *Between Luxury and the Everyday: Decorative Arts in Eighteenth-Century France*, edited by Katie Scott and Deborah Cherry, 110–52. Malden, MA: Blackwell, 2005.

———. "Parade's End: On Charles-Antoine Coypel's Bed and the Origins of Inwardness." In *Interiors and Interiority*, edited by Ewa Lajer-Burcharth and Beate Söntgen, 17–48. Berlin: De Gruyter, 2016.

———. "Reproduction and Reputation: 'François Boucher' and the Formation of Artistic Identities." In *Rethinking Boucher*, edited by Melissa Hyde and Mark Ledbury, 91–132. Los Angeles: Getty Research Institute, 2006.

———. *The Rococo Interior: Decoration and Social Spaces in Early Eighteenth-Century Paris.* New Haven, CT: Yale University Press, 1995.

Scrutton, Robert. "Flesh from the Butcher." *Times Literary Supplement*, April 15, 2005, 11.

Seigel, Jerrold. *The Idea of the Self: Thought and Experience in Western Europe since the Seventeenth Century*. Cambridge: Cambridge University Press, 2005.

Sennett, Richard. *The Craftsman*. New Haven, CT: Yale University Press, 2008.

Sgard, Jean. "L'Échelle de revenus." *Dix-huitième siècle* 14, no. 1 (1982): 425–33.

Shelley, Marjorie. "Painting in the Dry Manner: The Flourishing of Pastel in 18th-Century Europe." In *Pastel Portrait: Images of 18th-Century Europe*, edited by Katharine Baetjer and M. Shelley, 5–60. New York: Metropolitan Museum of Art, 2011.

Sheriff, Mary D. "Aux prises avec le désir." In *Fragonard Amoureux: Galant et Libertin*, edited by Guillaume Faroult, 41–54. Paris: Réunion des musées nationaux, Musée du Luxembourg-Sénat, 2015.

———. "For Love or Money? Rethinking Fragonard." *Eighteenth-Century Studies* 19, no. 3 (1986): 333–54.

———. *Fragonard: Art and Eroticism*. Chicago: University of Chicago Press, 1990.

———. "Fragonard's Erotic Mothers and the Politics of Reproduction." In *Eroticism and the Body Politic*, edited by Lynn Hunt, 14–40. Baltimore: Johns Hopkins University Press, 1991.

———. *Moved by Love: Inspired Artists and Deviant Women in Eighteenth-Century France.* Chicago: University of Chicago Press, 2004.

———. "Reflecting on Chardin." *Eighteenth Century: Theory and Interpretation* 29, no. 1 (1988): 19–45.

Shovlin, John. "The Cultural Politics of Luxury in Eighteenth-Century France." *French Historical Studies* 23, no. 4 (2000): 577–606.

———. *The Political Economy of Virtue: Luxury, Patriotism, and the Origins of the French Revolution*. Ithaca, NY: Cornell University Press, 2006.

Siegfried, Susan L. "Femininity and the Hybridity of Genre Painting." In *French Genre Painting in the Eighteenth-Century*, edited by Philip Conisbee, 14–35. Washington, DC: National Gallery of Art, 2007.

Slatkin, Regina Shoolman. *François Boucher in North American Collections: 100 Drawings.* Washington, DC: National Gallery of Art, 1973.

Smentek, Kristel. "The Collector's Cut: Why Pierre-Jean Mariette Tore Up His Drawings and Put Them Back Together Again." *Master Drawings* 46, no. 1 (2008): 36–60.

———. "'An Exact Imitation Acquired at Little Expense': Marketing Color Prints in Eighteenth-Century France." In *Colorful Impressions: The Printmaking Revolution in Eighteenth-Century France*, edited by Margaret Morgan Grasselli, 9–33. Washington, DC: National Gallery of Art, 2003.

———. *Mariette and the Science of the Connoisseur in Eighteenth-Century Europe*. Farnham, UK, and Burlington, VT: Ashgate, 2014.

———. *Rococo Exotic: French Mounted Porcelains and the Allure of the East*. New York: Frick Collection, 2007.

———. "Sex, Sentiment, and Speculation: The Market for Genre Prints on the Eve of the French Revolution." In *French Genre Painting in the Eighteenth Century*, edited by Philip Conisbee, 221–43. Washington, DC: National Gallery of Art, distributed by Yale University Press, New Haven, CT, 2007.

Snoep-Reitsma, Ella. "Chardin and the Bourgeois Ideals of His Time." *Nederlands Kunsthistorisch Jaarboek* 24 (1973): 147–243.

Solkin, David. *Painting for Money: The Visual Arts and the Public Sphere in Eighteenth-Century England*. New Haven, CT: Yale University Press, 1993.

Sollers, Philippe. *Les Surprises de Fragonard*. Paris: Gallimard, 1987.

Sombart, Werner. *Luxury and Capitalism* [1913]. Translated by W. R. Dittmar. Ann Arbor: University of Michigan Press, 1967.

Sonenscher, Michael. *Work and Wages: Natural Law, Politics, and the Eighteenth-Century French Trades*. Cambridge: Cambridge University Press, 1989.

Spary, E. C. *Utopia's Garden: French Natural History from Old Regime to Revolution*. Chicago: University of Chicago Press, 2000.

Stafford, Barbara. *Artful Science: Enlightenment, Entertainment, and the Eclipse of Visual Education*. Cambridge, MA: MIT Press, 1994.

———. *Body Criticism: Imaging the Unseen in Enlightenment Art and Medicine*. Cambridge, MA: MIT Press, 1991.

Standen, Edith A. "Boucher as Tapestry Designer." In *Boucher* 1986, 325–33.

Stanton, Domna C. *The Aristocrat as Art: A Study of the* Honnête Homme *and the* Dandy *in Seventeenth- and Nineteenth-Century French Literature*. New York: Columbia University Press, 1980.

Stein, Perrin. "Les Chinoiseries de Boucher et leurs Sources: L'Art de l'Appropriation." In *Pagodes et Dragons: Exotisme et Fantaisie dans l'Europe rococo, 1720–1770*, edited by Georges Brunel, 86–100. Paris: Paris-Musées, 2007.

———. "Notes on the Boucher Exhibitions Marking the Tercentenary of the Artist's Birth." *Burlington Magazine* 146, no. 1212 (2004): 169–73.

Stein, Perrin, ed. *Artists and Amateurs: Etching in Eighteenth-Century France*. New York: Metropolitan Museum of Art; New Haven, CT: Yale University Press, 2013.

Stein, Perrin, and Mary Tavener Holmes. *Eighteenth-Century French Drawings in New York Collections*. New York: Metropolitan Museum of Art, 1999.

Steinbrügge, Lieselotte. *The Moral Sex: Woman's Nature in the French Enlightenment*. Translated by Pamela E. Selwyn. New York: Oxford University Press, 1995.

Sterling, Charles. *Still Life Painting from Antiquity to the Present Time*. 2nd rev. ed. New York: Harper and Row, 1981.

Stürmer, Michael. "An Economy of Delight: Court Artisans of the Eighteenth Century." *Business History Review* 53, no. 4 (1979): 496–528.

Terpak, Francis. "Selling Natural History." In *Devices of Wonder: From the World in a Box to Images on a Screen*, edited by Barbara Maria Stafford and Frances Terpak, 165–71. Los Angeles: Getty Research Institute, 2001.

Terrall, Mary. *The Man Who Flattened the Earth: Maupertuis and the Sciences in the Enlightenment*. Chicago: University of Chicago Press, 2002.

Teyssèdre, Bernard. *Roger de Piles et le débat sur le coloris au siècle de Louis XIV*. Paris: Bibliothèque des arts, 1957.

Thirsk, Joan. "Luxury Trades and Consumerism." In *Luxury Trades and Consumerism in Ancien Régime Paris: Studies in the History of the Skilled Workforce*, edited by Robert Fox and Anthony Turner. Aldershot, UK; Brookfield, VT: Ashgate, 1998.

Thomas, Chantal. *Casanova: Un voyage libertin*. Paris: Denoël, 1985.

Thomson, Ann. "L'art de jouir de La Mettrie à Sade." In *Aimer en France, 1760–1860: Actes du Colloque international de Clermont-Ferrand*. 2 vols., edited by Paul Viallaneix and Jean Ehrard, 315–22. Clermont-Ferrand, France: Association des Publications de la Faculté des lettres et sciences humaines, 1980.

———. *Bodies of Thought: Science, Religion, and the Soul in the Early Enlightenment*. Oxford: Oxford University Press, 2008.

Tillerot, Isabelle. "Engraving Watteau in the Eighteenth Century: Order and Display in the *Recueil Jullienne*." *Getty Research Journal* 3 (2011): 33–52.

———. "Graver les Dessins de Watteau au XVIIIe siècle." In *Quand la gravure fait illusion: Autour de Watteau et Boucher, le dessin gravé au XVIIIe siècle*, edited by Emmanuelle Delapierre and Sophie Raux, 27–55. Valenciennes: Musée des Beaux-Arts; Éditions Gourcuff Gradenigo, 2006.

———. *Jean de Jullienne et les Collectionneurs de son Temps: Un Regard singulier sur le Tableau*. Paris: Éditions de la Maison des Science d'Homme, 2010.

Tornézy, M. A., ed. *Bergeret et Fragonard, journal inédit d'un voyage en Italie*. Paris: May et Motteroz, 1895.

Tunstall, Kate. *Blindness and Enlightenment: An Essay*. New York: Continuum, 2011.

Undank, Jack. "Diderot at the Crossroad of Speech." In *A New History of French Literature*, edited by Dennis Hollier. Cambridge, MA: Harvard University Press, 1998.

———. "Portrait of the Philosopher as a Tramp." In *A New History of French Literature*, edited by Denis Hollier. Cambridge, MA: Harvard University Press, 1998.

Veblen, Thorstein. *The Theory of the Leisure Class: An Economic Study in the Evolution of Institutions*. New York: Macmillan, 1899.

Verlet, Pierre. *La maison du XVIIIe siècle en France: société, décoration, mobilier*. Paris: Baschet; Fribourg: Office du Livre, 1966.

Vernière, Paul. *Diderot, Oeuvres Esthétiques*. Paris: Garnier Frères, [1959] 1965.

Versini, Laurent. *Diderot, Oeuvres*. 5 vols. Paris: R. Laffont, 1994–97.

Vezin, Luc. *Les Artistes au Jardin des Plantes*. Paris: Herscher, 1990.

Viala, Alain. *La France galante: essai historique sur une catégorie culturelle, de ses origines jusqu'à la Révolution*. Paris: Presses Universitaires de France, 2008.

Vidal, Fernando. *The Sciences of the Soul: The Early Modern Origins of Psychology*. Translated by Saskia Brown. Chicago: University of Chicago Press, 2011.

Vidler, Anthony. *Claude-Nicolas Ledoux: Architecture and Social Reform at the End of Ancien Régime*. Cambridge, MA: MIT Press, 1990.

Vigarello, Georges. *Histoire des pratiques de santé. Le sain et le malsain depuis le Moyen Âge*. Paris: Éditions de Seuil, 1993.

Viguerie, Jean de. *Histoire et Dictionnaire du Temps des Lumières, 1715–1789*. Paris: R. Laffont, 1995.

Virgil. *The Aeneid*. Translated by H. Rushton Fairclough. Loeb Classical. Cambridge, MA: Harvard University Press, 2000.

Vitols, Astrid. *Dictionnaire des Lunettes: Historique et Symbolique d'un Object culturel*. Paris: Éditions Bonneton, 1994.

Vogtherr, Christoph Martin. *Watteau at the Wallace Collection*. London: Wallace Collection, 2011.

Vogtherr, Christoph Martin, and Jennifer Tonkovich. *Jean de Jullienne: Collector and Connoisseur*. London: Trustees of the Wallace Collection, 2011.

Vogtherr, Christoph Martin, and Mary Tavener Holmes. *De Watteau à Fragonard: Les Fêtes Galantes*. Brussels: Fonds Mercator, 2014.

Voltaire. *Le Temple du Goût*. Amsterdam: Etienne Ledet, 1733.

Wahrman, Dror. *The Making of the Modern Self: Identity and Culture in Eighteenth-Century England*. New Haven, CT: Yale University Press, 2004.

Wald Lasowski, Patrick. *Romanciers libertins du XVIIIe siècle*. 2 vols. Paris: Gallimard, 2000–2005.

Watelet, Claude-Henri. *L'Art de Peindre*. Amsterdam, 1761.

Watelet, Claude-Henri, and Pierre-Charles Lévesque. *Dictionnaire des Arts de Peinture, Sculpture, et Gravure*. 5 vols. Geneva: Minkoff Reprints, 1972.

Wellman, Kathleen. *La Mettrie: Medicine, Philosophy, and Enlightenment*. Durham, NC: Duke University Press, 1992.

Weygand, Zina. *The Blind in French Society from the Middle Ages to the Century of Louis Braille*. Translated by Emily-Jane Cohen. Stanford, CA: Stanford University Press, 2009.

Whyte, Ryan. "Exhibiting Enlightenment: Chardin as *tapissier*." *Eighteenth-Century Studies* 46, no. 4 (2013): 531–54.

Wildenstein, Daniel, and Gabriele Mandel. *L'Opera complete di Fragonard*. Milan: Rizzoli, 1972.

Wildenstein, Georges. "Le décor de la vie de Chardin d'après ses tableaux." *Gazette des Beaux-Arts* 53 (February 1959): 98–106.

———. *The Paintings of Fragonard*. Translated by C. W. Chilton and A. L. Kitson. London: Phaidon, 1960.

Wille, Johann Georg. *Mémoirs et Journal de J.-G. Wille, Graveur du Roi*. 2 vols. Edited by Georges Duplessis. Paris: Jules Renaud, 1857.

Williams, Eunice. *Drawings by Fragonard in North American Collections*. Washington, DC: National Gallery of Art, 1978.

Williams, Hannah. *Académie Royale: A History in Portraits*. Farnham, UK, and Burlington, VT: Ashgate, 2015.

Willk-Brocard, Nicole. *Une dynastie les Hallé: Daniel (1614–1675), Claude-Guy (1652–1736), Noël (1711–1781)*. Paris: Arthena, 1995.

Wintermute, Alan. "Pélerinage à Watteau: An Introduction to the Drawings of Watteau and His Circle." In *Watteau and His World: French Drawing from 1700 to 1750*, edited by Alan Wintermute, 8–49. London: Merrel Holberton; New York: American Federation of Arts, 1999.

Wintermute, Alan, ed. *Watteau and His World: French Drawing from 1700 to 1750*. London: Merrel Holberton; New York: American Federation of Arts, 1999.

Wittkower, Rudolf, and Margot Wittkower. *Born under Saturn: The Character and Conduct of Artists*. New York: Norton Paperbacks, 1969.

Wrigley, Richard. *The Origins of French Art Criticism: From the Ancien Régime to the Restoration*. Oxford: Clarendon Press; New York: Oxford University Press, 1993.

Yolton, John W. *Locke and French Materialism*. Oxford: Clarendon Press; New York: Oxford University Press, 1991.

———. *Thinking Matter: Materialism in Eighteenth-Century Britain*. London: Basil Blackwell, 1984.

Zafran, Eric M. *French Paintings in the Museum of Fine Arts in Boston*. Vol. 1. Boston: Museum of Fine Arts, Boston, 1998.

Index

absence, 44, 121, 128–31, 133, 138, 143, 144, 168, 188, 196, 199; as the core of painter's practice, 133, 136, 188; of interiority, 129, 132; maternal, 129; mental, 5; of representation, 129
absorption, 56, 144; in Chardin, 139, 144, 150. *See also* self, -absorption
abstraction, 31, 32, 63; and decoration, 77; of meaning, 63; of self, 19, 21, 32
Académie de Saint-Luc, 91, 93, 94, 105. *See also* guild; *maîtrise*
Académie royale de peinture et de sculpture (the Academy), 4, 9, 11, 14, 31, 33, 91–94, 105, 106, 108, 109, 118, 121, 132–34, 137–38, 170–71, 174–78, 186, 208, 210, 236
accommodation: agents of, 55; artistic, 14; habits of, 53; morphological, 18, 32; of self, 210–12
Alembert, Jean le Rond d', 13, 256n142
amateur, 12, 13, 19, 26, 44, 75, 77, 85, 91, 93, 134, 178, 210–13, 215–18, 221–22. *See also* Guichard
âme (mind or soul), 7, 235, 240n17, 270n226
amour-propre, 49, 66. *See also* self-esteem; vanity
Angiviller, Charles-Claude Flahaut de la Billarderie, comte de, 174
Arendt, Hannah, 142
Argens, Jean-Baptiste de Boyer, Marquis d', 184; *Thérèse philosophe*, 177, 183–84, 230, 236; art dealer, 12, 19, 22, 26, 74, 80, 91–93. *See also* Gersaint; Rémy
artisan, 4, 28, 31, 33, 74, 94, 105, 108; ethos of, 4, 102; family life of, 102–3; gender relations and, 103–5; households of, 102–3, 105, 253n49, 253n71, 253n73; paternalistic principle of, 102; visual constructions of, 103. See also *menuisier*
Aubert, Louis, 131
auction, 12, 73
author, 19–21, 26, 35, 51, 72, 102, 106, 170, 212, 221, 230; cultural invention of, 19; cultural meaning of, 20; as effect of trace, 21; as a material effect, 20, 90; as a morphological function, 20; persona of, 31, 73; personality of, 19. *See also* authorship
authorship, 19–20, 221, 242n83; as a legal and commercial mechanism, 20; as a sign, 21. *See also* copyright
Aved, Joseph, 93; 123
Aveline, Pierre, 32

Bach, Johann Sebastian, 50; *Coffee Cantata*, 50
Barry, Jeanne Bécu, Madame du, 223, 229
Baudouin, Pierre-Antoine, 14, 70, 71
Baudrillard, Jean, 202
Baxandall, Michael, 4, 53–54
Beauvais, tapestry manufactory, 27, 30
Bellevue, Château de, 80, 82. *See also* Pompadour
Berger, François, 38
Bergeret, Pierre-Jacques, 211
Bergeret de Grancourt, Pierre-Jacques-Onésyme, 167–69, 208–9, 211–12
Bernard, Emile, 168
blind man, 92, 116–18, 120, 121; as man born-blind of Puiseaux, 120
blindness, 92, 111–22, 116–18, 119–20, 121, 136–37, 165, 170, 173–74, 197, 202, 235, 255n117, 255n124; of Chardin, 165; in Diderot, 120; iconography of, 116, 117; and connection to subjectivity, 116; of touch, 118, 120, 121, 137, 149; trope of, 92, 118–20, 173. *See also* blind man
Blondel, Jean-François, 51; *Architecture Françoise*, 78
Blondel d'Azincourt, Barthélemy-Augustin, 24
body: academic conception of, 109, 132; accessories of, 6; as aesthetic invention, 45; as agent of sex, 186; appearance of, 79; and artistic individuation, 186; in artistic training, 132; autonomy of, 129, 221; awareness of, 149; body language, 39, 56, 66; Boucher's treatment of, 5, 38; as the locus of aesthetic invention in Boucher, 45; in Chardin, 104, 115, 127, 131, 136, 143–48, 152, 160, 171, 173; of Chardin, 171, 174–75; in relation to commodity and consumption, 51, 54, 60, 79; and eros, 5, 147, 182, 184, 198, 234; and fashion, 64, 70; female, 5, 40, 43–45, 60, 70, 101, 138, 145, 147–48 171, 184–85, 193–94, 198–200, 235; in Fragonard, 185, 186, 200, 202, 207, 209, 212, 217, 220, 223; and generation, 5, 203; in Greuze, 142; imaginary, 163; imago of, 132; of the infant, 202; and inner touch, 143–44, 153; as an insubordinate force, 223, 236; interior of, 106; libidinal relation to, 72; as *machine à jouir* (machine for enjoyment), 183–84; male, 101; materialist philosophy of, 6, 7, 13, 183; maternal, 5, 105, 129, 194–98, 200, 202, 205, 206–8, 223; mental absence of, 5; and narcissism, 70, 129, 153; in relation to the negative hallucination, 129; new knowledge of, 236; nude, 39, 185; as object, 39, 55, 57, 82; oral impulses of, 106; of the painter, 44, 99, 104, 123, 132, 135, 136, 156, 171–75, 185–86, 198, 202, 205, 208, 212, 215, 221, 223, 236; painting as process of, 202; performance of, 4, 66; physical, physiological, and physic process of, 127, 128, 136, 143, 182, 184, 202, 234; and pleasure, 54, 145, 162, 182, 212, 221, 235; reproductive, 198; and self, 13, 104, 120, 136, 144, 145, 148, 152, 212, 234; and senses, 143, 160; and soul, 240n17; in relation to the surface of the canvas, 206; and tools of painting, 155, 175; and touch, 4, 20, 115, 153. See also *écorché*; eros; self-portrait; touch
Boffrand, Germain, 34
bonheur (happiness, well-being), 54, 177, 183, 209, 210, 266n131; of the amateur, 221; of the artist, 209; domestic, 211, 212; materialist notion of, 209. *See also* pleasure
Bonnac, Jean-Louis, Marquis de, 75
Bonnefoy, Yves, 191
Bonnet, Louis-Marin, 26, 27, 125
Bosschaert, Ambrosius, 155, 259n258
Bosse, Abraham, 16, 116

Bouchardon, Edmé, 93, 117, 125, 243n111, 256n161; *Cris de Paris*, fig. 2.31, 117, fig. 2.42, 125, 256n161

Boucher, François: apartment in the Louvre of, 78–80, 243n106, 250n358; *bergeries*, 228, 229; body in, 5, 38, 45; body of, 167; circulation of motifs in, 30–31; as collector, 73–77; commercial imagination of, 13, 22–32; as consumer, 73–80; and culture of consumption in, 4, 28, 29, 31–32, 47, 50, 54, 57, 60, 66, 72, 80; drawings, 9, 14–16, 19, 22, 24, 26–28, 31, 32, 45, 63, 64, 68, 77; eros in, 38–42, 60–61, 70; etching and, 14–18; fashion and, 60–63, 67–68, 72–73; female body in, 5, 11, 40–45; and the market, 23–47; personal mythologies of, 33–46; personality of, 9–13; and Pompadour, 80–85; portrait of, 13–14; sexuality in, 41, 234; signature of, 19–21, 72, 73, 85; studio of, 79–80; and tact, 4, 13–21, 23, 32, 85; and touch, 13–14, 17, 19, 21, 27; trace of, 10, 15–21, 31, 85; as visual mythologist of the self, 6, 45; Venus in, 11, 35–45; and Watteau, 4, 14–19, 21, 23–24, 26, 32, 64–65, 68, 85; woman in, 40, 43–44, 50, 53, 57, 60–63. *See also* luxury; materiality; signature. Works: *Amours*, 35; *Aurora*, fig. 1.39, 39; *Aurora and Cephalus*, fig. 1.36, fig. 1.42 (detail), 35, 37, 39, 40, 41, 42, 44; *Autumn Pastoral*, fig. 1.28, 29; *Bacchus and Ariadne*, fig. 1.29, 28, 30; *The Birth of Venus*, 35, 39; *Black-haired Odalisque*, fig. 1.45, 44, 45; *Boy Holding a Parsnip*, fig. 1.16, 24; *Chinese Gallant*, fig. 1.31, 30, 31; *Chinese Garden*, fig. 1.22, 27; *Les delices de l'enfance*, 28; *Delights of Life in the Country*, fig. 3.36, 198; *Design for Theater Animated by Figures*, fig. 1.24, 28; *Designs for Cut-out Marionettes*, fig. 1.14, 22; *Flora*, 27; *The Four Seasons: Spring*, fig. 3.45, 208–9; *Girl on the Sofa (Blonde Odalisque)*, fig. 1.46, 45–46; *The Graces at the Tomb of Watteau*, 15; *Group of Children around a Drapery, Premier Livre de Groupes d'Enfants* fig. 1.32, 32; *Hercules and Omphale*, fig. 1.40, 39–41; *Le Jeune Suppliant*, 27; *Kitchen Maid and a Young Boy*, fig. 1.17, 24; *La Marchande de modes (The Milliner)*, fig. 1.57, fig. 1.73 (detail), 57–58, 72–73; *La Toilette, or A Lady Fastening her Garter*, fig. 1.56, fig. 1.61(detail), 47, 57–58, 64; *Lady and Maid*, fig. 1.64, 65; *A Lady on a Day Bed*, fig. 1.66, fig. 1.70 (detail), fig. 1.72 (detail) 47, 67, 68, 69, 70, 71, 72, 73, 148; *Le Déjeuner, or The Breakfast*, fig. 1.48, fig. 1.55 (detail), 47–49, 50, 52, 56; *Leda and the Swan*, fig. 1.44, 44–45; *Little Gardener*, 27; *Livre des Cartouches*, 32; *Madame de Pompadour* (Munich version), fig. 1.85, fig. 1.86 (detail), 83–85; *Madame de Pompadour* (Waddesdon version), fig. 1.84, 83; *Madame de Pompadour with her Hand Resting on a Harpsichord Keyboard*, fig. 1.83, 82–83; *Mercury Confiding Bacchus to the Nymphs*, fig. 1.33, 34–35, 39; *Naiads with a Triton*, fig. 1.18, 24–27; *Neptune's chariot, Livre de cartouches Inventés*, fig. 1.26, 28; *Project for a Trade Card for Gabriel Huquier*, fig. 1.15, 22–23; *The Rape of Europa*, fig. 1.34, 35; *Reclining Nude* (Harvard version), fig. 1.20, 24–25; *Reclining Nude* (MFA Boston version), fig. 1.19, 24–25; *Recueil de fontaines*, 28; *Rising of the Sun*, 24; *Rocaille*, fig. 1.25, 28, 39; *Standing Woman Seen from Behind*, fig. 1.62, 63, 64; *Study of a Foot*, fig. 1.47, 45–46; *Study of a Valet with Coffee Pot*, fig. 1.54, 55; *Suite de cinq sens*, 28; *Suite de quatre elements*, 28; *The Toilette of Venus*, fig. 1.81, 80–82; *Triton* (Hertford house), 26; *Venus Requesting Arms from Vulcan*, fig. 1.35, fig. 1.43 (detail), 35–36, 44–45; after Watteau: *Bust of a Woman under the Hood of her Mantle* (*Woman in Black*), fig. 1.11, 17–18; *Italian Troupe*, fig. 1.6, 15–16, 18; *Portrait of Antoine Watteau, Figures de différents caractères*, fig. 1.12, 20

boudoir, 67, 69–70, 178

Bréa, Charles-Paul-Jérôme, 215, 220, 221

Bret, Antoine, 11, 22, 26, 31, 77

Brooks, Peter, 53

Brunaubois-Montador, Jean Florent Joseph de Neufville, Chevalier de, 87, 137

Brunel, George, 31

Bryson, Norman, 41, 123, 129, 218

Buffon, George-Louis Leclerc, comte de, 191–93, 230; *Histoire naturelle*, 191–92, 230; conception of nature, 7, 191–93, 229–30; theory of generation, 192. See also *moule intérieure*

Caffieri, Philippe, 75

Callot, Jacques, 116, 117

Cars, Jean-François, 14, 27

Casanova, Giacomo, 209–10

Catherine the Great, 24, 93

Caylus, Anne Claude de Tubières de Grimoard de Pestels de Lévis, comte de, 13, 82, 125; after Boucher, *Trade Card of Edme Gersaint*, fig. 1.82, 82. See also *légèreté d'outil, la* (*lightness of touch*)

Cazes, Pierre-Jacques, 93, 132, 257n177

Cézanne, Paul, 168

Champaigne, Philippe de, 9, 10

Chardin, Jean-Siméon: abandonment of genre scenes by, 104, 123, 153; and absorption, 139, 144, 150; and blindness, 92, 111–22, 116–18, 119–20, 121, 136–37, 165, 170, 173–74; body of, 171, 174–75; chromatic method of, 3, 97, 111, 115, 119, 133–35, 137–38, 150–51, 157, 159, 162, 168, 171, 174–75; deep materiality in, 3, 6, 87–95, 118, 170; distinct tactile talent of, 94, 99, 111–12, 115, 120–21, 137, 144, 150, 153, 162–63, 173; domestic conditions of the studio of, 101, 133; and drawing, 89, 103, 115, 132–35, 175; and effect of unreality, 125; genre scenes of, 104, 123, 136–37, 153; and the guild, 93–94, 105–6, 108, 133; the logic of inside/out in, 95–110, 113, 136; magic of, 87–90, 93, 111, 152, 155, 162; first marriage of, 103, 123; second marriage of, 103, 157; negativity of his process, 91, 128–31, 136; object in, 87, 89, 95–111, 150–51, 155–65, 167, 170, 259n243; and Oudry, 111–12, 115, 150, 174; as the painter of interiors and interiority, 6; as *peintre à talents*, 94, 101; self-portraits of, 165–75, 260n292; sexuality in, 144–48; signature pigments of, 94, 137, 138, 150; still life, 95, 96, 105, 131, 136, 155–57; return to still life, 101, 104, 123, 153; and the subject, 139–54; as *tapissier*, 157, 174; technique of, 87, 96, 97, 99, 101, 115, 116, 118, 133–35, 137, 156, 163, 168, 258n199; touch of, 99, 111, 121, 138, 155–57, 159–60, 165, 168, 170–71, 173–75; training of, 93–94, 131–32; use of the lay figure in, 133, 140; women in, 5, 127–40, 142, 153, 171. *See also* blindness; genre painting, *le faire*, still life. Works: *Attentive Nurse*, fig. 2.38, fig. 2.54 (detail), 123–25, 128–29, 133–34, 136, 171; *Study for the Attentive Nurse*, fig. 2.39, 123–24, 137; *Attributes of the Arts*, fig. 2.35, 118–19; *Basket of Wild Strawberries*, fig. 2.81, 158–60; *Blind Beggar*, fig. 2.29, fig. 2.32 (detail), fig. 2.33 (detail), 116–21, 123, 128, 133; *Bouquet of Carnations*, fig. 2.78, 154–56, 159, 162; *Boy Building a House of Cards*, fig. 2.65, 142; *The Brioche*, 161–62; *Buffet*, fig. 2.16, 106–9, 113, 161; *Butler's Table*, fig. 2.82, 160–61; *Cat with Ray, Oysters, Pitcher and Loaf of Bread*, fig. 2.13, 100–101; *Child with a Top*, fig. 2.61, fig. 2.66 (detail), 139–40, 142–44; *Dead Hare with Powder Flask and Game-Bag*, fig. 2.24, fig. 2.23 (detail), 113–16; *Dead Hare with Rifle*, fig. 2.26, 115; *The Diligent Mother (La mère laborieuse)*, fig. 2.47, 128–29, 131, 171; *The Drawing Lesson*, fig. 2.59, 137–38, 155; *Game of Billiards*, fig. 2.15, 103–5; *Girl with a Shuttlecock*, fig. 2.69, fig. 2.70 (detail), 145–49; *The Good Education,* fig. 2.72, 149; *The Governess,* fig. 2.49, 130–31, 148; *Grapes and Pomegranates,* 161–62; *Hare with Game Bag and Powder Flask,* fig. 2.25, 114–15; *The House of Cards* (London version), fig. 2.60, 138–40, 142; *House of Cards,* (Washington version), fig. 2.63, 140–41; *Housekeeper,* fig. 2.55, 133–34; *The Jar of Apricots,* fig. 2.83, 161–62; *The Jar of Olives,* fig. 2.84, 161; *Kitchen Still Life with Loin of Mutton,* fig. 2.9, 96–97, 155; *Kitchen Table,* fig. 2.1, 87–88, 95, 160; radiograph of, fig. 2.2, 87–89; *La Pourvoyeuse,* fig. 2.46, 127–29, 171; *La Serinette (The Bird-Song Organ),* fig. 2.56, 134–38; *Lady Taking Her Tea,* fig. 1.51, 53; *Madame Chardin,* fig. 2.92, 169; *Male Nude,* fig. 2.51, 132; *Menu de gras (The Meat-day Meal),* fig. 2.5, 94–95; *Menu de maigre (The Fast-day Meal),* fig. 2.6, 94–95; *The Morning Toilette,* fig. 2.41, 124–25; *Rabbits and Partridge,* fig. 2.22, 112; *The Ray,* fig. 2.11 (detail), fig. 2.12, 97–99, 101, 104–6, 108–9, 113, 175; *Scullery Maid,* fig. 2.40, 124–25, 129; *The Sedan Chair* (recto of fig. 2.68), fig. 2.52, 132; *Self-Portrait (at His Easel),* fig. 2.88, fig. 2.97 (detail), 166–67, 174–75; *Self-Portrait Wearing an Eyeshade,* fig. 2.87, fig. 2.95 (detail), 165, 173; *Self-Portrait Wearing Spectacles,* fig. 2.85, 164–65; *The Sliced Melon,* 161; *Smoker's Case,* fig. 2.80, 157–59; *Soap Bubbles,* fig. 2.62, fig. 2.75 (detail), 140–43, 150–53, 173; *Turnip Scraper (La Ratisseuse),* fig. 2.43, fig. 2.58 (detail), 125–28, 136–37; *The Washerwoman,* fig. 2.44, 127; *Wild Rabbit with Game Bag and Powder Flask,* fig. 2.19, fig. 2.20 (detail), fig. 2.27 (detail), 110–11, 115; *Woman Drawing Water from A Fountain,* fig. 2.45, 127; *X-ray Radiograph of La Serinette (The Bird-Song Organ)* fig. 2.57, 134–35

Chardin, Juste, 94, 102, 156,

Charpentier, François-Philippe, 194, 228; after Fragonard, *The Tumble,* fig. 3.64, 228

Châtelet, Emilie Le Tonnelier de Breteuil du, 209; *Discours sur le bonheur,* 209

Chedel, Pierre-Quentin, 43, 74, 77; after Boucher, frontispiece to *La Conchyliologie,* fig. 1.75, 74, 77

chinoiserie, 62; *goût chinois,* 62, 79. *See also* taste

Claesz, Pieter, 95, 96

Cleve, Joos van, 69

Cochin, Charles-Nicolas, 10, 67, 89, 91–94, 111, 112, 121, 145, 151, 152, 165, 171, 174; after Chardin, *Little Girl Enjoying Her Lunch,* fig. 2.67, 145, 159; *Les Misotechnites aux Enfers,* 91–92

coffee, 49–54, 55, 125, 247n234; in Bach, 50; as a commodity, 50, 53; a new object of consumption, 50, 54; representation of, 125

collections, 12, 13, 15, 24, 33, 62, 73–80; *curieuses,* 75–77, 79; as a practice, 7, 24, 73–77, 117; as a form of self-representation, 77; *suivies* (systematic), 76. *See also* collector; conchology; Kunstkammer and Wunderkammer

collector, 12, 19, 24, 26, 32, 73–77, 82, 178, 240n25

color, 26, 40, 41, 67, 70, 73, 76, 87, 91, 111, 116, 118–19, 133–35, 152, 159, 162–63, 165, 168, 174–75, 195, 229, 231–32; and *boîte à couleurs,* 79; in the concept of *coloris,* 118, 162; and pigments, 69, 87, 96–99, 101, 115–19, 131–34, 139, 147, 150 155, 156, 165, 168–69, 172, 175, 182, 185, 205, 219–21, 229, 259n240

commerce, 21, 23, 31, 33, 49, 50, 54, 60; and Boucher, 22–32; of curiosities, 74–75; as *le doux commerce,* 23; meaning of, 23

commercial imagination, 13, 22–32, 80

commodity, 5, 29, 41, 43, 45, 47, 50–54, 57, 60, 61, 67, 70, 72, 76, 77, 80, 92; as accommodating object, 47; as attribute of private space, 52; as comfort, 51; as a commercial article, 52; culture of, 73; as a desirable material object, 60, 72; as effect on social and individual life, 50–57; in the era of goods, 67; as fetish, 246n189; as object of pleasure, 5, 44, 47 49, 52, 61, 72, 77; paintings as, 72, 80, 92; as possession, 28, 31, 47, 49, 50, 52, 53, 57, 61, 63, 67, 74, 75, 77, 80; subjective effects of, 53, 57. *See also* consumption; luxury

conchology, 73, 74. *See also* collections

Condillac, Étienne Bonnot de, 4, 120, 143, 160; *Treatise on the Sensations,* 4, 120

Conisbee, Philip, 125

connoisseur, 45, 91, 93, 206, 212, 220; and connoisseurship, 7

consumer, 28, 31, 32, 33, 34, 41, 43, 44, 47, 52, 53, 54, 58, 72–80; artist as, 33, 49, 73–80; benefits of, 49; in relation to the object, 53, 54

consumption, 4–6, 28, 29, 33, 34, 41, 42, 47, 49–57, 63, 64, 66, 70, 72, 73, 76, 79, 80, 82, 99, 159–60; of art, 28; benefits of, 49; conspicuous, 28, 49, 247n244; culture of, 4, 28, 29, 32, 47, 57, 66, 72, 80; ethics of, 63; habits of, 56, 67; and sensual pleasure, 41, 145; subjective register of, 41. *See also* consumer; luxury

copyright, 19–20, 242n87

corporeality, 4, 185, 223, 236

Courson, Marie-Émilie Coignet de, 218, 219, 222

Courtonne, Jean-Baptiste, 76

Coypel, Charles-Antoine, 78, 167

craft, 4, 32, 89–94, 103–6, 118, 152, 162, 175, 185, 252n22; and craftsman, 32, 168; as craftsmanship, 31; cognitive dimension of, 93; as an exercise of mechanical art, 91; as *métier,* 93–94, 103, 210, 252n26; as self-definition, 175; as technical skill, 10, 90, 94, 151, 162

crayon manner engraving, 26, 244n123

Crébillon, Claude Prosper Jolyot de, 200, 241n41, 265n97

critic, 10, 11–12, 29, 33, 77, 87, 90–93, 117, 118, 125, 155, 163, 165, 168, 171, 175, 177, 178, 180, 212; as the aesthetic arbiter, 12, 91; aesthetic autonomy of, 12, 91; as the enemy of the artist, 12, 77, 91; as *misotechnite,* 91–92, 171; visual tropes of, 91–92, 171. *See also* blindness; criticism

criticism, 7, 11, 91; of art, 7, 11; as critical discourse, 12, 91, 153; and expertise on painting as a material object, 92–93. *See also* critic

Crow, Thomas, 12

Crozat, Pierre, 19, 74, 242n79

culture of appearances, 29, 32, 42, 57; and dressing for another, 32

curiosity, 12, 73–79; and Boucher, 73–77; collection of, 73, 75–79; as *collections curieuses,* 79; as a conception (*curiosité*), 75, 77; culture of, 75–77; market for, 76, 77

Cuzin, Jean-Pierre, 211

d'Hondecoeter, Melchior, 108

De Troy, François, 5, 47, 50–51, 52, 60, 61, 62, 66–67, 182

décorateur, 23, 243n10

Delacroix, Eugène, 232

Demarteau, Gilles, 26, 244n126; after Boucher, *Naiads with a Triton,* fig. 1.21, 26–27

Démoris, René, 95, 125, 127

Denk, Claudia, 167, 168

Derbais, François, 33, 34–35, 39, 40, 41, 42, 43, 44, 45–46, 47, 60, 80, 82, 245n160

Derrida, Jacques, 173

Descartes, René, 120; *La Dioptrique,* 120

design, 9, 12, 16, 17, 18, 22–23, 26–34, 38–39, 43–44, 51–52; 74–77, 79–80, 82, 87, 92, 147, 170, 213, 223, 230. *See also* interior, decorations for

desire, 5, 31, 40, 41, 49, 62, 63, 73, 76, 109, 144, 182, 185, 200, 202, 231–36; of the amateur, 212, 221; of the artist, 208, 212, 215; of the critic, 163; as energy of attraction, 230; as *envie de posséder* (to possess), 28, 41, 62, 77, 108; and fantasy, 31; as *flambeaux de la volupté* (torches of sensual pleasure), 184, 234; literary theorist of, 202; materialist understanding of, 182, 234; in Maupertuis, 230, 234; in modern conception of self, 236; and nature, 231, 235; and object, 40, 76, 99, 144, 205; in painting, 40, 185, 200, 202,

desire (*continued*)
231–32; as psychic force, 184, 233–35; in relation to physiognomy, 182; as self-individuation, 236; in relation to sexuality, 180, 184; subject of, 182; woman as object of, 5, 41, 147, 148
Deslandes, André François, 47
Desportes, Alexandre-François, 106, 106, 108, 109, 121
Dezallier d'Argenville, Antoine-Joseph, 73–75; *History of Conchology*, 74
Diderot, Denis, 9, 10, 11, 13, 31, 47–49, 93, 96, 132–33, 148, 155–57, 168, 180, 182–83, 195, 212–13, 216–17, 222; *Bijoux indiscrets*, 265n82; *Letter on the Blind for the Use of Those Who Can See*, fig. 2.36, 120; *Rameau's Nephew*, 212, 216–17; *Salons*, 9, 10, 14, 87, 89, 90–91, 109, 148, 155, 157, 162, 163, 177, 178, 208, 238n15
Dietz, Bettina, 75
Dilke, Emilia, Lady, 168
domesticity: in architecture, 263n30; cultural notions of, 5, 54–55, 101, 103–5, 131, 138, 153, 157, 167–68, 211–12; in painting, 5, 51, 54, 64, 67–68, 94, 101, 103–5, 108, 112, 113, 123, 125, 128, 131, 137–38, 155, 167–68, 171, 175, 211–12, 253n70
Dou, Gerrit, 150
Doyen, Gabriel François, 178
drawing: in relation to artistic training, 89, 118, 132–35, 177, 186, 193, 210; as autonomous and marketable form, 24, 26; and blindness, 117–19; in Boucher, 9, 14–17, 19, 22, 24, 26–28, 31, 32, 45, 63, 64, 68, 77; in Chardin, 89, 103, 115, 132–35, 175; as collector's item, 24, 74, 77; in relation to color, 118, 134–35, 175; and crayon manner engraving, 26; and etching, 14–18, 19; in Fragonard, 177, 178, 186, 187, 188, 193, 196, 210, 211–13, 228, 231; framing of, 24, 26; as intellectual basis of painting, 118, 134, 193; and the market, 26; for another, 32; and Pompadour, 85; as a means of representation, 175; wall power of, 24
drives: as psychic forces, 202, 221, 223; subject of, 223
Dubos, Jean-Baptiste, abbé, 152
Duflos, Charles, 26, 74
Duflos, Claude-Augustine II: after Boucher, frontispiece to *Catalogue raisonné de coquilles et autres curiosités naturelles*, fig. 1.74, 74
Duncan, Carol, 203
Dürer, Albrecht, 171
Duveaux, Lazare, 80

École des Élèves Protégés, 177, 210
écorché, 98, 108
empiricism, 4, 90, 143; and epistemology, 90
Encyclopédie, 13, 17, 20, 21, 49, 72, 79, 93, 139, 143, 178, 182, 183, 192, 195, 200, 207
Enlightenment, 3, 4, 11, 90, 93, 120, 183, 184, 191, 195, 198, 203, 209, 236, 239n17, 250n346, 255n136, 263n33, 264n69
epigenesis, 191–93, 195–97, 199, 265n80; as fantasy, 191; of nature, 191–93, 195–97; in relation to painting, 193, 207. *See also* generation
Épinay, Louise Florence Pétronille Tardieu, Madame d', 178
eros, 4–6, 39–41, 60–61, 70, 128, 144–45, 180–81; as ars erotica, 236; as autoeroticism, 70, 182; body as the vehicle of, 5; in Boucher, 38–42, 60–61, 70; as desirability of the material object, 41, 60–61; of display, 39; economic process as, 41; and Enlightenment, 184; as erotic experience, 180–81; as a force of attraction, 232; Fragonard's aesthetics of, 4, 6, 177–91, 197–99, 200–212, 222–23, 228, 230, 234–36; and individuality, 177–91; as internal force, 184, 235; and life, 230, 232–34; as a literary subject, 147; materialist understanding of, 182–84, 236; maternal, 200, 203–12; and Maupertuis's *scientia sexualis* (erotic science), 230, 236, 262n23, 269n213, 270n236; of nature, 198; of painting as a token of desire, 40; woman's body as the locus of, 43, 198
Estève, Pierre, 134–35, 175; *Dialogues sur les Arts*, 87, 89, 134
etching, 4, 14–19, 26, 85, 212, 228; and Boucher, 14–16; dialogical quality of, 16, 18; as a memory-trace, 18; morphological intimacy of, 16; reproductive quality of, 4, 16, 18; subjective effects of, 18; technical procedure of, 16–18. *See also* drawing, and etching
existence, 6, 7, 47, 57, 63, 69, 105, 143, 144, 155, 156, 159, 174, 191, 193–94, 200, 205, 216, 221, 230; artistic, 23; as autonomy of the object, 155, 156, 162; as coexistence, 143, 144, 156, 159; corporeal, 129, 132, 149, 152, 153; interiorized, 68, 69, 72; material, 56; in relation to materialism, 7; in Rousseau, 50, 143, 153; subjective, 54, 65, 66, 71, 128, 136; in relation to tact, 14; Turgot's entry of in the *Encyclopédie*, 143–44
exoticism, 11. *See also* chinoiserie; taste
exteriority, 56, 57, 68, 192

fantasy, 31, 41, 43, 44, 77, 99, 101, 121; of the consumer, 77; economic sphere and the market as, 43; erotic, 205; epigenetic, 191; in relation to femininity, 101, 105; *figures de fantaisie* of Fragonard, 212–22; male, 61, 101; of the mother, 205; painting as, 44, 142, 198; personal, 44; psychic, 198
Faret, Nicolas, 14
fashion, 41, 42, 50, 52, 54, 57, 60–64, 67, 68, 72, 73, 79, 223; in Boucher, 60–63, 67–68, 72–73; commercialization of, 57, 58; as a cultural symptom, 58; as identity, 64; personal and personalizing dimension of, 61; and society, 47, 58, 60; as subject of social commentary, 63; subjective dimension of, 170–71, 175. *See also* coffee; exoticism; luxury
femininity, 5, 43–44, 72, 101, 105, 138, 171, 193, 194. *See also* gender
Ferté, Papillon de la, 33
fête galante, 197, 265n87. See also *Watteau*
fetishism, 45–46; of commodity, 246n189
fiction, 43, 67, 215, 216, 218; friendship as, 221; of the self, 43, 67, 72 170, 215
Flaubert, Gustave, 125
force pénétrante (penetrating force): in Buffon, 192, 193, 264n66
Foucault, Michel, 180, 259n226, 262n23
Fraenkel, Beatrice, 20
Fragonard, Jean-Honoré: body in, 185, 186, 200, 202, 207, 209, 212, 217, 220, 23; drawings, 177, 178, 186, 187, 188, 193, 196, 210, 211–13, 228, 231; embodied pictorial practice of, 185–86; epigenetic conception of painting of, 191–97, 203, 205, 229–30; and eros, 4, 6, 177–91, 197–99, 200–212, 222–23, 228, 230, 234–36; the erotic mother in, 203–7; and *figures de fantaisie*, 212–23; and individuality, 177–86; internal dynamism of, 185, 195, 223; painting techniques of, 184–85, 188, 205, 219–22, 229; and the pastiche, 212, 216–18, 220; pictorial seduction of, 199–202; as the promoter of modern eros, 6; relationship with Bergeret de Grancourt, 208–12; relationship with Saint-Non, 210–13, 215, 220, 222; relationships with *amateurs*, 178, 210–22; artistic self-accommodation of, 210–12; self-portrait of, 211; performance of signature in, 221–22; and touch, 178, 185, 202, 206, 212–23, 236; and trace, 188, 196, 202, 205; the unseen in, 186–90; and Watteau, 182, 191, 197, 232. Works: *Abbé de Saint-Non*, fig. 3.47, 212–13; *All Ablaze*, fig. 3.9, 183, 199, 203; *Amsterdam Sketchbook*, fig. 3.33, 196–97; *Anne-Pauline Le Breton (The Singer)*, fig. 3.56, fig. 3.58 (detail), 219–22; *The Avenue of Cypresses at Villa d'Este*, fig. 3.16, 187, 196; *The Awakening of Nature*, 232; *Bathers*, fig. 3.13, 199–200, 233; *Bed with Cupids*, fig. 3.37, 199; *Blindman's Bluff*, fig. 3.34, 196–97;

The Bolt, fig. 3.5, 181–82, 228; *Bust of an Old Man*, fig. 3.52, 216–17, 222; *Charles-Pau-Jérôme Bréa (Naigeon)*, fig. 3.49, 214–15, 220; *Coresus Sacrificing Himself to Save Callirhoë*, fig. 3.1, 177, 208; *The Draftsman*, fig. 3.68, 231; *Fête at Saint-Cloud*, fig. 3.22, 188–90; *The Fountain of Love*, fig. 3.72, 233–34, 236; *Garden of an Italian Villa, with a Gardener and Two Children*, fig. 3.18, 187–88; *Gardens of the Villa d'Este (The Little Park)*, fig. 3.15, 186–87, 196; *The Good Mother*, fig. 3.39, 203; *Groups of Children in the Sky*, fig. 3.2, 178, 208; *Happy Lovers*, fig. 3.6, 5, 181–82, 184, 228; *The Island of Love* (*Fête at Rambouillet*), fig. 3.23, fig. 3.27 (detail), 188–91, 193, 195–99, 205–6, 229, 235; *Italian Family*, fig. 3.43, 205–7; *Jeu de la palette*, fig. 3.35, 197–98; *The Kiss*, fig. 3.7, 182, 184; *La Gimblette*, fig. 3.38, 200–201; *La Poursuite*, fig. 3.67, 230; *La Surprise*, fig. 3.66, 230; *Landscape (from Sketchbook from the Italian Period)*, fig. 3.19, 188; *Louis Richard de la Brèteche*, fig. 3.48, fig. 3.57 (detail), 212, 221; *The Pursuit of Love: Love Letters*, fig. 3.62, 223, 227, 232; *The Lover Crowned*, fig. 3.61, 223, 226–29, 231; *Mari-Émilie Coignet de Courson* (Lady with the Dog), fig. 3.55, 218–19; *The Meeting*, fig. 3.59, fig. 3.69 (detail), 223, 229, 231–33; *The Pursuit*, fig. 3.60, 223, 225, 228–31, 235; *The Ruins of the Hadrian Villa*, fig. 3.14, 186–87; *Sappho Inspired by Love*, fig. 3.40, 203; *The Seesaw*, fig. 3.4, 180–81; *Self-Portrait*, fig. 3.46, 211; *Shaded Avenue*, fig. 3.17, 187, 196; *Sheet of Portrait Studies*, fig. 3.51, 213, 215; *The Stolen Shift*, fig. 3.8, 5, 183, 199, 203; *The Swing*, fig. 3.3, 178–79, 199–200; *Temple in the Garden*, fig. 3.20, in infrared, 3.21, 188; *The Useless Resistance*, fig. 3.41, 204–5; *View of the Park*, fig. 3.24, 190; *Visit to the Nursery*, fig. 3.42, 204–5; *The Vow to Love*, fig. 3.71, 233–34; *The Vow to Love* (Louvre version), fig. 3.74, 235; *The Warrior*, fig. 3.54, 217–18; *Young Child Standing on the Windowsill*, fig. 3.44, 206–7
French Academy in Rome, 14, 210
Freud, Sigmund, 70, 232, 234, 242n76, 249n308, 270n225, 270n231. *See also* sexuality
Fried, Michael, 56, 144. *See also* absorption

Gabriel, Ange-Jacques, 34
gaze, 32, 39, 40, 43, 69, 71, 75, 104, 111, 115, 117, 128, 147, 156, 159, 161, 162, 165, 168, 170, 182, 187, 205, 216, 218, 219, 221; of the amateur, 221; of the connoisseur, 212, 220; as a new principle of the "post-sacred," 248n262; of others, 65, 68, 248n263; as a principle of social visibility, 66; of the world (of *le monde*), 56, 57, 66, 68, 71
gender, 5, 61, 101, 103–5, 200, 228; within artisanal households, 103–5; as sexual difference, 101, 105; visual constructions of, 5. *See also* femininity; masculinity
generation, 192–93, 195, 196, 203, 205, 229, 230; Buffon's theory of, 192; as enigma of the womb, 195; and epigenetic theory of, 192, 195; of self, 192–93; theories of, 192; as a universal natural phenomenon, 230. *See also* epigenesis; preformation
genre painting (genre scenes), 5, 30, 47, 61, 67, 103, 123–25, 129, 131, 133, 135–36, 138, 140, 142, 148, 153, 156, 159, 171, 203, 205, 246n216; and *bergeries*, 228, 229; in Chardin, 104, 123, 136–7, 153; and gallant scenes, 182; *l'espace de moi* in, 127; Northern, 47, 56, 63, 106, 125; *tableau de modes*, 47, 58, 218n246; temporality of, 60
Geoffrin, Marie Thérèse Rodet, Madame, 11
Gersaint, Edmé, 19, 65, 73, 74, 77, 79, 80, 82, 93; *Catalogue raisonné de coquilles*, 74, 77, 250n341. *See also* art dealer
Ghendt, Emanuel de, 70
Giacometti, Alberto, 169, 171
Girard, René, 202
Glomy, Jean-Baptiste, 26
Gobelins, tapestry manufactory, 27
Godefroy, Auguste-Gabriel, 140, 213
Goncourt, Edmond and Jules de, 3, 196, 209, 238n1, 251n7, 263n25, 265n84, 266n126
goût moderne, 51
grace, 11, 20, 77, 240n17
Granchez, Charles-Raymond, 80
Green, André, 129, 131, 257n173, 257n175. *See also* hallucination
Greuze, Jean-Baptiste, 142, 148, 217, 233, 235
Grimou, Alexis, 220
Guérard, Nicolas, 71, 72
Guercino (Giovanni Francesco Barbieri), 118, 119
Guichard, Charlotte, 221
guild, 4, 91, 93–94, 105–6, 133, 254n93, 254n95, 254n96, 257n190; and Chardin, 93–94, 105–6, 108, 133; and Fragonard, 210. *See also* Académie de Saint-Luc; *maîtrise*

Hallé, Noël, 102, 105, 253n78, 268n175
Halle, Pierre-Adolphe, 268n175
hallucination, 123, 129, 131, 132, 134, 136; as apparition, 129; etymology of, 129; negative hallucination, 129, 131, 138. *See also* Green; imitation
Heinich, Nathalie, 210
hierarchy of genres, 109, 178, 254n104
histoire naturelle (natural history), 73, 75, 77, 191, 269n207; as new science of nature, 74. *See also* Buffon; nature
Holbach, Paul Thiry, Baron d', 6, 14; *Système de la Nature*, 6, 14, 238n14
honnêteté, 14, 21; of *honnête homme*, 14, 49; as insinuation, 14, 16; Mandevillian revision of, 49
Hulsdonck, Jacob van, 160
Huquier, Gabriel, 22, 23, 28, 32, 243n103

identity, 5–7, 20–22, 33, 40, 44, 55, 58, 60, 63, 64, 66, 67, 80, 82, 85, 102–5, 106, 121, 140, 148, 170, 175, 182, 192, 209, 213, 215–18, 220; artistic, 5, 11, 13, 22, 44, 73, 80, 103–5, 132, 171; as compound, 43, 175; imaginary model of, 19; of self, 19, 20, 70, 77, 104; relational definition of, 105; social, 42, 63, 182, 216, 218; work as a site of, 20, 47, 58, 64, 79, 82
illusion, 42, 43, 44, 57, 66, 87, 89, 90, 94, 115, 150–52, 202; in Cochin, 151–52; as distinct from imitation, 151–52; as hallucination, 129. *See also* imitation; hallucination; trompe-l'oeil
imitation, 26, 63, 90, 131, 134, 136, 137, 150–53, 220, 222; Cochin's theory of, 151. *See also* illusion
incorporation, 99. *See also* interiority, orality
individualism, 31, 210, 223; cultural logic of, 195; as self-accommodation, 210
individuality, 3, 5, 6, 7, 11, 20, 33, 55, 136, 177, 180, 183, 195, 207, 236; as artistic individuation, 168, 186; constraint on, 20; cultural notion of, 3, 142; and eros, 177–86; self-, 3, 76, 94, 123, 168, 170, 216, 236
inner touch (*le tact intérieur*), 143–44, 149, 151, 153, 156, 159, 174; definition of in Turgot, 143, 144, 151; as the inner sensation, the sixth sense, 143. *See also* touch
interior, 6, 33, 42, 47, 50–57, 60–63, 66–67, 69, 71–72, 79, 80, 102, 104, 119, 124, 125, 137, 142, 144, 151, 182, 191–94, 196, 199–200, 202, 235; in relation to anteriority, 199; of the artist's studio as a decorative ensemble, 79–80; 199; of the body, 99, 106, 119, 192–94, 199, 200; as a cultural location of desire, 182; decorations for, 28, 29, 33, 34, 41, 43, 44, 50, 51, 55–57, 78, 80; relationship to exterior, 56, 57; in relation to inner life, 57, 71, 173; in relation to morality, 62; of painting, 101, 117, 119; and privacy, 52, 69
interiority, 6, 47, 56–58, 67, 68, 72, 90, 106, 109, 117, 121, 132, 141, 145, 148–52, 173, 187, 188, 191, 264n72; absence of, 129, 132; and blindness, 118, 120, 121, 173; in relation to commodity, 47, 53; of craft, 106; cultural ideal of, 56, 57; as inner life, 57, 90; as inner space, 47, 56; inwardness, 121; of medium, 4; and pleasure, 145; of self, 56–57, 70–71, 132, 145, 148, 149,

interiority (*continued*)
153, 173; of touch, 17, 21, 144. *See also* incorporation; subject; touch
intimacy, 50, 51–54, 87, 94, 105, 113, 182, 186, 205, 207, 231; agonistic, 221; as consequence of consumption, 52, 53; morphological, 16

Jacoby, Beverly Schreiber, 24
Jansenism, 90
Jardin du Roi, 191, 264n55, 269n205
Jaucourt, Chevalier, Louis de, 13
je ne sais quoi: aesthetics of, 236
Jenty, Charles-Nicolas, 194, 195, 264n74
jouissance (enjoyment, particularly sexual), 178, 180, 209, 222, 223
Jullienne, Jean de, 14, 15, 19, 27, 68, 74, 79
Jully, Laurent La Live de, 93, 217

Kalf, Willem, 125
Koedyck, Issac, 54, 55
Koerner, Joseph, 171
Kunstkammer and Wunderkammer, 40, 75. *See also* collection, as a practice

La Bretèche, Louis Richard, Monsieur de, 212–13, 217, 221, 222
La Garde, abbé Nicolas Bridard de la, 91, 92
La Haye des Fosses, Catherine-Charlotte-Edmé de, 24
La Mettrie, Julien Offray de, 183–84, 208, 209, 210, 222, 234
La Rochefoucauld, François, Duc de, 49
La Tour, Maurice Quentin de, 165, 167, 168, 171
labor, 4, 9, 19, 28, 73, 102, 106, 108, 125; artisanal ethos of, 4; manual, 9, 13, 108, 112
Lajoüe, Jacques de, 23
Lancret, Nicolas, 60, 62
Largillière, Nicolas de, 9, 10, 106
Le Bas, Jacque Philippe: after Boucher, *Painting Mocked by Envy, Stupidity, and Drunkenness*, fig. 1.4, 12–13
Le Blanc, Jean-Bernard, abbé, 11, 12, 13
Le Breton, Anne-Pauline, 219, 221–22
Le Brun, Charles, 9, 10, 22, 118, 235, 236
le faire, 9, 10, 11, 13, 46, 93, 151, 157, 163, 185, 202, 216; Cochin's conception of, 151; as cynicism of execution, 222; as magic of execution, 10, 13, 90, 238n4
Le Prince, Jean-Baptiste, 200, 265n99
Ledoux, Claude-Nicolas, 223
légèreté d'outil, la (lightness of touch), 13, 178, 238n3, 240n34
Lemoyne, François, 38
Lépicié, François-Bernard, 128–29; after Chardin, *The Diligent Mother* (*La mère laborieuse*), fig. 2.48, 128–29
Lépicié, Nicolas-Bernard, 102, 105, 200, 265n99
libertinage: aristocratic ethos of, 180, 236; culture of, 177–86; literary context of, 236
Liotard, Jean-Étienne, 50, 52, 53, 54, 55, 56, 168,
Locke, John, 4, 105, 143–44, 258n212, 258n215; *An Essay Concerning Human Understanding*, 254n90, 255n137, 258n214
Louveciennes, 223, 228–29, 231, 232–34, 266n125, 268n194
Louvre: Boucher's studio and dwelling in, 78–80, 243n106, 250n358; and Chardin, 261n318, 261n328; Fragonard's commission for, 208
love, 4, 43, 106, 177, 191, 198, 228; allegories of, 233; of art, 211; of gods, 41; immanence of, 235; letters of, 203; and life, 223–36; mythical, 40–41, 231, 232; of refinement and pleasure, 49; in Rousseau, 209; of self, 43, 49, 70, 153; of things, 41. *See also* narcissism; self, -love
Lundberg, Gustaf, 9, 13, 14
luxury, 5, 28, 29, 31, 33, 34, 41, 42, 47, 49, 51, 52, 53, 62, 108; consumption of, 28, 33, 34, 49, 50, 52, 73, 74, 79, 80; debates on, 7, 47, 49; designs of luxury goods, 12, 29, 31; merchants of, 75, 79; as origins of capitalism, 41; painting as, 5, 40, 41, 45, 47, 50; populuxe, 29, 58, 63; Rousseau's critique of, 49, 50; semiluxury, 29, 31, 58, 61; sensual appeal of, 41, 47; as a source of personal well-being and bodily comfort, 51, 52; and Voltaire, 28–29, 49, 80

maîtrise, 93–94, 253n80. *See also* guild; Académie de Saint-Luc
man of the world, 42, 49. *See also* mondain; Voltaire
Mandeville, Bernard, 43, 49–50; *Fable of the Bees*, 49
Mannlich, Johann Christian von, 26, 41, 77, 79
marchand mercier, 40, 50, 52, 68, 73, 74, 79, 80; au petit Dunquerque, 79, 80
Mariette, Pierre-Jean, 17, 33, 89–90, 91, 105, 123, 124, 206
Marigny, Abel-François Poisson de Vandières, Marquis de, 210
Marivaux, Pierre Carlet de Chamblain de, 42 43, 53, 55, 63, 65–67; *L'Isle de la Raison,* 63; *L'Isle des Esclaves*, 63; *Le Paysan Parvenu*, 42–44, 55; *La Vie de Marianne*, 42, 47, 53, 65–68
market, 4, 12, 13, 23, 24, 26, 27, 29, 32, 43, 47, 77, 85, 212; as aesthetic opportunity, 13, 23; as anti-modernity, 12; of art, 12, 47, 91–93, 208, 213, 239n15, 252n39; and artistic identity, 13; as commercial opportunity, 13, 23; of curiosities, 76; as fantasy or imaginary construct, 43, 240n32; interpretive engagement with, 13; for luxury, 28; and marketing of self, 27
Marmontel, Jean-François, 11
Marx, Karl, 246n189, 248n265, 250n348
masculinity, 101, 105. *See also* gender
materialism, 5, 6, 7, 90, 233, 236; and materialist philosophy, 4, 6, 13, 182, 183, 184, 191, 192, 195, 209, 230, 234; philosophical, 183. *See also* La Mettrie
materiality, 3, 6, 7, 96, 106, 175, 192, 200, 221, 232, 238n15; deep materiality, 3, 6, 87–95, 118, 170; of eighteenth-century vision, 6; in logic of material organization, 6, 192; and materialization, 6, 62, 79; painting as thick, 96, 221; and personality, 9–13
matter, 6, 7, 96, 192, 193, 195, 220, 230, 234. *See also* molecular formation
Maupertuis, Pierre-Louis Moreau de, 223, 230, 233–35; *Système de la Nature*, 230; *Venus physique*, 230
Maza, Sarah, 64
medium, 4, 13, 27, 30, 31, 92, 168, 173, 175, 252n18; etching as, 18, 47; painting as, 4, 7, 11, 91, 118, 168; pastel as, 165, 175
Meissonier, Juste Aurèle, 23
Melon, Jean-François, 49
Mémoires secrets, 178
Ménétra, Jacques-Louis, 102, 103
menuisier (cabinet maker), 93, 102, 156. *See also* artisan
Mercier, Louis-Sébastien, 125
Méré, Antoine Gombaud, Chevalier de, 14, 49
Mieris, Willem van, 150
Mirabeau, Marquis de, 63
Mniszek, Michał Jerzy Wandalin, Count, 76
Möbius strip, 129, 131
modernity, 7, 11, 33, 71, 180, 181, 232, 238n2; anti-, 12; commercial, 12, 23, 29, 43, 49, 77, 80
molecular formation, 6, 90, 192, 193, 195, 196, 200, 230, 235; in Buffon, 192, 193; and *molécules organiques* (organic molecules)
Montaigne, Michel de, 49, 120, 170–71; *Essays*, 165, 120, 170–71
morceau de réception, 106, 109, 178, 254n98
morphology, 6, 11, 17–20, 21, 32, 50, 109, 115, 119, 136, 156, 157, 159, 185, 187, 195, 196, 199, 200, 202, 203, 205, 222, 229, 230, 232, 238n14; as morphological intimacy, 16; tactile, 6
Mosson, Joseph Bonnier de la, 75, 76
mother, 5, 127–29, 131, 147, 149, 194–98; absence of, 129; in artisanal workshop, 103; in relation to artistic process, 196; body of, 105, 129, 194, 195, 196, 198, 200, 202, 207, 208, 223; role of in Chardin's practice, 93, 133, 156, 157; cultural construction of, 195; eros of the, 200, 203–7; iconography of, 203; as maternal font of representation, 5, 199, 202; as maternal image, 129; in moral arguments of motherhood, 203, 254; as an unconscious object-source, 202

Mouhy, Charles de Fieux, chevalier de, 147; *Mémoirs d'Anne-Marie de Moras*, 147
moule intérieure (interior mold), 192, 196–97; Buffon's conception of, 192, 196–97
Muralt, Béat-Louis, 63
mythology: in paintings, 5; personal, 43

Naigeon, Jacques-André, 212, 214–15, 220
Naiveu, Mathijs, 150
narcissism, 57, 70, 72, 127, 130, 137 308n249; in the era of consumption, 70; iconography of, 153; and Narcissus, 153; space of, 127; as stage in psychic development, 130; as mechanism of subjective formation, 70. *See also* self; subjectivity
Natoire, Charles-Joseph, 186, 210
nature, 75, 76, 91, 134, 180, 182, 186, 193, 199, 231; and art, 232; body as a force of, 6, 186, 221, 231, 236; Buffonian conception of, 7, 191–93, 230; as a creative force, 193; energy of attraction in, 230; epigenetic fantasy of, 191, 197; in Fragonard, 191–200, 203, 210, 221–23, 229–35; laws of, 183; materialist conception of, 6, 230, 236; as mother, 195, 196, 198, 199; personification of, 232–33; and sexuality and desire, 230–35; shift in the understanding of, 191, 235; spectacle of, 228; in still life, 162, 163
Netscher, Casper, 125
Nolhac, Pierre de, 233–34
nude: erotic mission of, 39; female, 5, 38, 39, 185; male, 132
Nutz, Thomas, 75

object: aesthetics of, 161; autonomy of, 155, 157; and the body, 61, 70, 72, 82, 83, 144, 147, 152, 153; Chardin's return to, 155–63; child's relation to, 99, 144; and consumption, 53, 54, 70, 76; contingency of, 143; composition, deconstruction, and recomposition of, 87, 95, 96, 159, 161; cynical view of, 77; desirable, 31, 49, 70; disorder of, 62; engagement with, 47, 53, 55, 156, 159; experience of, 152, 156, 159, 173; fidelity to, 87, 90; gender of, 200; immersion in the field of, 57; internal impression of, 144; language of, 105; and logic of inside/out, 95–110, 113, 136, 159, 253n56; magical quality of, 77, 93, 162; material and imaginary world of, 131; material traces of, 175; materiality of, 87; and narcissism, 70; in relation to objecthood, 5; painting as, 5, 163; perception of, 156; phenomenological truth of, 111, 163; as pictorial challenge, 89–91, 99, 105, 111, 135; pigments as substance of, 87, 96, 97, 99, 101, 115, 116, 118, 156, 163; pleasure of, 72, 77, 145, 156, 159, 161, 162; proliferation and circulation of, 29; psychic dimension of, 251n14; rapport of the artist to, 5; and the self, 67, 70, 144, 149; sensory engagement with, 160; still life as reinvention of, 95, 96, 105, 131, 136, 155–57; and the subject, 5, 70, 98–99, 101, 106, 136, 137, 139, 142–45, 148–53, 155–57, 162, 173; and touch, 144, 259n252; truth of in Chardin, 87, 89, 111, 163, 165, 167, 170; unity of the, 150–51, 259n243; violence of, 96, 98–99; vision of, 156. *See also* subject
Oeben, Jean-François, 75
oeuvre, 14, 16, 19, 20, 21, 23, 27, 31, 32, 35, 45, 73, 93, 94, 124, 135, 137, 139, 181, 191, 200, 203, 229; as authorial manufacture, 31; erotic, 4, 181, 198; as the field of the other, 20, 66; and reproduction, 4, 14, 15–16, 19, 21, 94; technical aspect of, 20
Opéra, 27
Opéra comique, 27
operations of surface, 3, 6
Oppenord, Gilles-Marie, 23
orality, 63, 113, 253n63. *See also* incorporation
ornemaniste, 22, 243n102
Oudry, Jean-Baptiste, 74, 111–12, 115, 150, 174; and Chardin, 111–12, 115, 150, 174
Ovid, 38; *Metamorphoses*, 35

painting: academic notion of, 193; act of, 4, 5, 97, 150, 153; allegory of, 11–12; and culture of the amateur, 215; and artistic identity, 5; autonomy of, 91; behavior of, 90, 185, 223; bodily conception of, 202, 209; and color, 118; craft and practice of, 92–93; decorative, 34; as a desirable object, 35, 40; as effect of inwardness, 94, 119, 121, 151; as an element of interior décor, 41; as an encounter with the canvas, 5; as a material object, 91–93, 108, 124; epigenetic understanding of, 193, 207; as furniture, 41; as both an image and a thing, 163; inner life of, 136; liberal status of, 91; as a lustful surface, 41; as a material practice, 11, 13, 30–32, 35, 40, 41, 56; as a medium, 4, 7, 11, 91, 118, 168; as a mode of self-imagination, 103; as object, 5, 91, 92, 163; in *paragone*, 119; patronage of, 22; as a precious possession, 5; as a private act, 182; process of, 87, 89, 96, 142; and sculpture, 118–19; as a site of signification, 6; symbolic realm of, 103–5; techniques of, 133–35, 222, 229; value of, 92. *See also* genre painting; molecular formation; still life
Pajot, Louis-Léon, comte d'Ons-en-Bray, 75
Panard, Charles François, 13, 21
Paris, 14, 53, 57, 63, 74, 75 76, 116, 117, 147, 157, 187, 210; and luxury consumption in, 28, 33, 50, 52, 74; places in, 43, 52, 116, 117, 211; the poor of, 117, 125. *See also* Bouchardon, *Cris de Paris*
pastiche, 212, 216–18, 220; as a mode of self-representation, 216;
Pausanias: *Description of Greece*, 177
performance and performativity, 19, 29, 32, 49, 73, 76, 125, 138, 139, 142, 150, 151, 153, 212, 215–17, 220, 221, 223, 228, 236; autoerotic, 182; of the body, 3, 4, 66; as culture, 212; oral performance, 99; painterly, 99, 219; of touch, 111, 119
person: as actor, 50; of the artist, 11, 14, 31, 42, 73, 77, 80; autograph of, 20; definition of, 72; effect of, 7; embodied, 163; identity of, 7, 55, 60, 64, 67, 79, 104, 132; new kind of, 56, 67; as the origin of the work, 21, 216; as performance, 216; private, 67, 69, 73; promiscuous, 66, 73; sartorial, 42; as space, 56; in relation to the world's gaze, 56
personality, 3, 11, 45, 49, 55, 89, 90, 151, 170, 182; artistic, 3, 10, 13, 19; authorial, 19; the generic or typological nature of, 55–56; and materiality, 9–13
Pierre, Jean-Baptiste Marie, 109, 174
Pigalle, Jean-Baptiste, 93, 138, 261n313,
Piles, Roger de, 10, 91, 111, 118–20, 134, 150–52, 163, 168, 200, 202 240n17; and concept of pictorial unity, 151; *Cours de peinture par principes*, 118, 150, 168; *Dialogue sur le coloris*, 134
Pineau, Séverin, 194
Place Dauphine, 105, 106, 123, 254n94
pleasure: aesthetic, 77, 157; of the amateur, 210; of appearance, 217; of the artist, 198, 208–12, 221, 212; autoerotic, 70, 182; bodily, 54, 162, 182 183, 197, 198, 221, 235; as comfort, 51; of commodity and consumption, 5, 6, 41, 44, 47, 49, 50, 52, 55, 61, 63, 72, 76, 77, 145, 159; of the critic, 157, 162, 163, 180, 181; of display, 65; domestic, 5, 155; of the elite, 106; of inner touch, 144; and *jouissance*, 222; as a natural force, 223; of the object, 72, 77, 145, 156, 159, 161, 162; as onanism, 70; of the pastiche, 217; of the patron, 178, 212, 223; personal, 47, 51, 76, 159, 160, 208; as a psychic drive, 221, 223; purveyors of, 51, 54; of self, 70, 72, 145, 216; in self-accommodation, 212; of self-interest, 43, 49; as sensory gratification, 5, 11, 40, 41, 47, 52, 61, 63, 70, 159, 162, 163, 209, 223, 235–36; sexual, 11, 143, 144, 178, 180, 181–82, 185; in still life, 156; subversive aspects of, 236; in Turgot's concept of *frissonement intérieur*, 143, 145; as a universal right, 222; of the viewer, 184; visual, 75, 76, 79; as *volupté*,

pleasure (*continued*)
184, 209, 234; and the woman, 5, 61, 66–67. See also *bonheur*; eros; desire; drives; narcissism
Pompadour, Jeanne-Antoinette Poisson, Madame de, 11, 73, 80–85
porcelain manufactories, 27, 28. *See also* Vincennes; Sèvres
pornography: authors of, 184; and the Enlightenment, 263n33; in novel, 183, 230; as pornographic literature, 183; repertoire of, 184
Portalis, Roger, 209
possession, 5, 6, 28, 31, 40, 41, 47, 49, 50, 52, 53, 57, 61, 63, 67, 74, 75, 77, 80, 91, 105, 184, 185. *See also* commodity
Poussin, Nicolas, 41, 42, 92,
preformation, 192, 193, 265n80. *See also* generation
privacy, 7, 33, 52, 56, 66, 68, 69, 90, 142, 170, 182; as internal publicness, 69; in private life, 47, 51. *See also* intimacy
Prix de Rome, 14, 33, 177
promiscuity: as the logic of the subject in the era of consumption, 66; as a mode of signification, 63; promiscuous persona, 66, 69; of self, 63, 66, 67; as self-display, 65, 68; sexual, 62; as social comportment, 65; visual, 66
Proust, Marcel, 95, 101, 128
psyche: epistemic space of, 7, 251n14; individual, 70; operations of, 242n76
public sphere, 11, 12, 93, 143, 238n2
Puget, Marguerite, 156

Quinze-Vingts hospice for the blind, 116–17, 120–21

Rameau, Jean-François, 216–17, 221, 223
Rameau, Jean-Philippe, 216, 217
Raphael (Raffaello Sanzio da Urbino), 92
Raspal, Antoine, 60
Raux, Jean, 220
Recueil Jullienne, 15
Rembrandt van Rijn, 40, 212
Rémy, Pierre, 73, 74, 75, 76, 77
Reni, Guido, 92
Renou, Antoine, 87
representation, 4–7, 11, 19, 21, 22, 29–32, 33, 38, 43, 44, 51–58, 60–61, 63, 70, 77, 80, 85, 87, 89, 90, 98, 101, 105, 106, 109, 111, 112, 116, 120, 121, 131–34, 136, 138, 148, 152, 153, 156, 157, 160, 162, 170, 173–75, 187, 190, 197, 199, 200, 202, 205–8, 212, 215, 216, 218–19, 223; absence of, 129; artistic, 9, 132; process of, 105, 136, 185, 188, 198, 202, 220; of self, 32, 44, 71, 73, 77, 78, 79, 80, 105, 165–68, 170, 171, 173, 175, 208, 211, 216, 221, 222; subjective costs of, 89, 105, 254n91; trope of, 97. *See also* self,-representation; subject; violence
reproduction, 14, 15, 18, 19, 21, 22, 23, 26, 27, 29, 30, 31, 94, 138, 192, 198, 230; sexual, 7, 192. *See also* body; crayon manner engraving; etching; oeuvre; self,-reproduction; sexuality
Restout, Jean-Bernard, 15, 22, 23, 31
Reynolds, Joshua, 172, 173
Robert, Hubert, 186, 229
Roche, Daniel, 29, 63;
rococo, 4, 9, 28, 39, 50, 51, 52, 123, 129, 238n2, 245n148, 263n25, 263n40; as *goût rocaille*, 31, 39; as a modern taste, 29, 51; as a reaction against, 34. See also *goût moderne*
Roger, Jacques, 192
Roque, Antoine de la, 73, 93
Rosenberg, Pierre, 191
Rothenbourg, Conrad-Alexandre de, 103, 119
Roubiliac, Louis-François, 133
Rousseau, Jean-Jacques, 32, 43, 50, 57, 102, 143, 153, 203, 205, 209; *The Confessions*, 203, 205; *Discourse on the Arts and Sciences*, 49; *Discourse on the Origins of Inequality among Men*, 49; *Emile*, 205; *Reveries of the Solitary Walker*, 143
Rubens, Peter Paul, 92

Saint-Aubin, Augustin de, 75
Saint-Aubin, Gabriel de, 75, 145
Saint-Non, Jean-Claude Richard, abbé de, 210–13, 215, 220, 222; after Fragonard, *The Little Park*, fig. 3.50, 212, 215
Saint-Yenne, La Font de, 11, 41, 92, 125
Saintard, Marguerite, 53, 103
Salons, 4, 7, 10, 11, 14, 24, 31, 38, 53, 60, 87, 90–93, 105, 117, 118, 123, 145, 147, 148, 153, 155, 157, 161, 162, 163, 165, 168, 170, 175, 177, 178, 208, 233, 243n111. *See also* Diderot, Salons of
Santerre, Jean-Baptiste, 220
Sargentson, Carolyn, 80
Scott, Katie, 13, 26, 31
sculpture, 27, 74, 118, 119, 231, 234
seduction, 4, 5, 40, 41, 60, 185, 198–202, 216, 230; aesthetic of, 41; maternal, 205; social rituals of, 182; as a state of rapture, 233
self-esteem, 43, 44, 66. See also *amour-propre*; vanity
self-portrait, 15, 19, 21, 121, 165; and Chardin, 165–75, 260n292; and Fragonard, 211; as a separate category, 261n295
self: -absorption, 56, 121; -abstraction, 19, 21, 57, 63; -accommodation, 210–12; and appearance, 42; -articulation, 19, 202; -assertiveness, 212; authentic, 71; autonomy of, 5, 56, 72, 120, 140, 142, 148; auxiliary, 70; -awareness, 3, 10, 13, 65, 69, 70, 71, 106, 109, 143, 144, 149, 152, 210, 221, 222; -commodification, 45; -conception, 3, 7, 23, 44, 49, 121, 210, 236, 246n211; -confidence, 103, 206; -conscious strategies, 3, 4, 19, 28, 30–31, 57, 65, 66, 77, 94, 101, 121, 148, 157, 208, 212, 215, 216, 220, 221, 222, 230; -consistency, 20; -construction, 171; consuming, 45; -creation, 222; -definition, 3, 16, 28, 44, 49, 80, 101, 104, 105, 108, 143, 168, 171, 172, 175, 180, 209, 210; -depiction, 165, 212; -description, 104, 167, 170; -differentiation, 211, 215; -discovery, 19, 144, 145, 147, 149, 173, 210; -display, 39, 65, 66; -distinction, 93, 212; -embodiment, 171; -enclosure, 129; epicurean, 49; -estrangement, 221, 222; -examination, 168; -experience, 70, 94, 121, 136, 142, 144, 145, 152, 153; -exposure, 65, 69; -expression, 209; -fashioning, 170, 171; -fetishization, 45–46; fiction of, 43, 72, 170; -flattery, 167; -formation, 192; -fulfillment, 209; and gaze, 32; -identification, 20, 104; -identity, 19, 20, 70, 77, 104; -image, 9, 49, 66, 130, 132, 136, 168, 169, 175, 212; imaginary, 42; -imagination, 23; -immolation, 236; inauthenticity of, 71; -individuation, 3, 76, 94, 123, 147, 168, 170, 216, 223, 236; -inflation, 218; -interest, 43, 49; internalized, 70; -invention, 170; -involvement, 135, 145; -knowledge, 170; as *l'espace de moi*, 127; -love, 43, 49, 70, 153, 222; as mask, 71–72; mirage of, 5, 42, 43; -mockery, 222; modern, 7, 71; -pastiching practice, 24; -pleasure, 43, 70, 145; -presence, 140, 149; -presentation, 175, 212; -projection, 42; promiscuous, 63, 67, 181; -recognition, 156, 173, 212, 216; -reflection, 57, 145, 171; -reflexivity, 18, 106, 118, 121, 149, 150, 153, 159, 212, 216; -representation, 32, 44, 71, 78, 79, 80, 105, 165, 167, 168, 170, 171, 173, 175, 208, 211, 212, 216, 221, 222; -reproduction, 21, 27, 31; and sex, 180–81; space of the, 56; subjective evacuation of, 50; -understanding, 21, 66, 69, 80, 211. *See also* self-esteem; self-portrait; selfhood, 56, 41
sensationist philosophy, 4, 160; sensationism, 143; and subjectivity, 7. *See also* Condillac; Locke
senses, 5, 13, 41, 118, 120, 134, 143, 159, 160, 162, 255n137; in Condillac, 120, 160; in the constitution of the human subject, 120; in de Piles, 120; in Diderot, 120; in Locke, 143. *See also* touch; vision
servant, 5, 42, 50, 51, 57, 60, 64–66, 68, 78, 127, 128, 140, 147; as agent of accommodation, 55; cultural role of, 55; and fashion,

60, 61, 63, 171; as purveyor of daily pleasure, 54, 65
Sèvres, porcelain manufactory, 27, 29, 31
sex, 148, 170, 178, 180, 181–84, 186, 231, 235; and privacy, 182; relation between sex and self, 180–81
sexuality: adolescent, 144, 147, 148; and arousal, 184; as *ars erotica*, 236, 262n23; as attribute of the emergent subject, 148; and the body, 145, 147, 182; in Boucher, 41, 234; in Chardin, 144–48; as a cultural concern, 180, 235; cultural understanding of in the eighteenth century, 114–49; and Diderot, 178, 180, 262n18; as discourse, 180; emergence of, 180; and Enlightenment writers, 183; as erotic science (*scientia sexualis*) 230, 236, 262n23, 269n213, 270n236; as a form of conventional behavior, 230; in Foucault, 180; in Fragonard, 180, 183–84, 198, 230; as Freudian conception of libido, 234, 270n225, 270n231; as individuation, 147, 180; as internal negotiation, 147; as irreducible to anatomy, 147; materialist notions of, 184, 234; of the mother, 147, 266n113; and nature, 186, 230, 234; and onanism, 70; physical energy of, 182; and privacy, 182; and reproduction, 198, 266n113; and Rousseau, 269n208; and self, 180–81; revaluation of, 183; vision of, 234. *See also* desire; eros
Sheriff, Mary, 177, 184, 205, 212
signature, 31, 45, 72, 73, 85, 150, 221–22; as autograph, 20; as a bodily trace, 20, 44; of Boucher, 19–21, 72, 73, 85; as difference, 222; female body in Boucher as, 5, 44–45; of Fragonard, 221–22; as personalized sign, 20, 73; visual consistency of, 20, 31
Smentek, Kristel, 26
Snoep-Reitsma, Ella, 5
sociability, 32, 47, 51, 211, 217
Sombart, Werner, 33, 41, 61
souplesse, 14, 21
still life: in Boucher, 61, 77; in Chardin, 87, 89–90, 95–98, 101, 104, 106, 108–9, 111–13, 115–16, 119, 121, 123–25, 131, 136, 138, 153, 155–57, 159–63, 171; Chardin's return to, 101, 104, 123, 153; Diderot's commentary on, 87, 90, 109, 157, 162–63; and the figure, 124–25, 131, 136, 138; hunting trophy as subgenre of, 108, 111, 116, 121; interiorization of, 99, 101, 106, 109, 121; inviolability of the thing in, 162; of Largillière, 106; of Liotard, 52–53; morphology of, 109, 115, 156; Northern (Dutch and Flemish), 95, 96 101, 106, 108, 109, 111, 125, 155, 156, 254n108, 256n159, 256n152, 260n270; philosophical pleasures of, 157, 163; as a representational tradition, 108; spatial illusion in, 94; subjective appeal of, 109, 157; tropes of, 96
Stürmer, Michael, 33
subject: autonomy of, 156, 162; and blindness, 173; as a cipher, 82; and commercial modernity, 43; of consumption, 57, 66, 72; cultural construction of, 207; of desire, 5, 148, 182; of drives, 223; effect of, 90; and eros, 178, 202, 228; of the gaze, 69; gendered, 105; inner life of, 57, 173; interiorized, 152; and mask, 72; of love, 233; materialization of, 5; modern, 32; nascent, 129; and object, 5, 70, 98–99, 101, 136, 137, 139, 142–45, 148–53, 155–57, 162, 173; painter as, 5, 44, 45, 89, 90, 142, 207; of painting, 5, 106, 131, 136, 149, 163, 202; phantom/specter of, 105, 131; physical and psychic boundaries of, 90, 99, 136; of representation, 4, 5, 98, 190, 200; in Rousseau, 32; and senses, 41, 120, 160, 162; space of, 98, 101; subjective costs of, (as pound of flesh) 105; woman as, 195. *See also* self; subjectivity
subjectivity, 5, 7, 41–43, 57, 63, 83, 128–36; artistic, 5; effects of alienation and reification of, 53; and blindness, 116, 118, 121; of the child, 129, 148–49; and color, 119; of the culture of appearances, 42; in relation to the culture of consumption, 41, 67, 72; and Diderot, 163; as formation, 4; as a function of still life, 163; of the hero, 43; and imitation, 151; as a Möbius strip, 129; in narcissism, 70; and painting, 89; as self-sufficiency, 142; and senses, 159–60; sensationist understanding of, 7; and sentiment, 152, 153; space of, 127; as subjective autonomy, 72; as subjective evacuation, 50. *See also* subject
sympathy, 53; as *la douce symphathie* in Marivaux, 53, 77, 247n247; as subjective liaison, 53

tact, 4; and Boucher, 4, 13–21, 23, 32, 85; definitions of, 13–14, 240n36, 241n42, 242n70; as a mode of existence in the social arena, 14; moral, 14; as a principle of accommodation, 14, 21, 32, 85; taste as, 14; and touch, 13–21, 240n36, 242n7; and Turgot's notion of *tact intérieur*, 143–44. *See also* taste; touch
tapestry, 24, 27, 30, 32, 33, 244n130
Tardieu, Pierre François, 145
taste (*goût*), 14, 22, 23, 31, 34, 51, 52, 63, 76, 77, 79, 80, 223; as a category of social distinction, 29, 82; *goût Boucher*, 27, 31; *goût chinois*, 62, 79; for luxury, 28, 29, 79; as principle of self-individuation, 76; as tact, 14; woman of, 82. See also *goût modern*; luxury
technical skill, 10, 90, 94, 151, 162. *See also* craft
temporality: in representation, 60, 125, 187
Teniers, David, 125
Terborch, Gerard, 106, 108
Terrall, Mary, 230
Tessin, Count Carl Gustaf, 57, 58, 93
Théâtre de la Foire, 28
toilette, 58, 60, 61, 292n248
touch: as an alternative mode of cognition, perception, and experience, 4, 120; and anamnesis, 173; blindness of, 111–21, 137, 149; and the body, 236, 259n252; of Boucher, 13–21, 27; and Chardin, 121, 156–57, 159–60, 165, 168, 170, 173, 174; definition of, 13, 241n42; and Diderot, 120; inherent duality of, 5; and etching, 18; exteriorization of, 173; and Fragonard, 178, 185, 202, 206, 212–23, 236; hazards of, 216; as interiorization, 21, 144; and Liotard, 168; magic of, 87; materialization of, 7; mellifluous, 3, 41; and narcissism, 153; organ of, 14; of the painter, 87, 89, 113, 137, 153, 119, 207, 212–23; of the patroness, 85; performance of, 111, 119; as reciprocity, 5, 137, 144, 156; and Rousseau, 143; in sculpture, 119; as self-presentation, 168; and senses, 120, 159; and sight, 41; and the signature, 221–22; in still life, 96, 99, 111–15; and tact, 13–21, 240n36, 242n70; unseeing dimension of, 113; and vision, 112, 118, 120, 150, 156, 170, 255n127, 260n272. *See also* etching; inner touch; *légèreté d'outil, la* (lightness of touch); senses; signature; tact
trace, 10, 15–21, 155–56; artistic, 10; and the author, 21; bodily, 20, 99, 155, 196; of Boucher, 10, 15–21, 31, 85; in Chardin, 99, 111, 138, 155–56, 168, 171, 175; in crayon manner engraving, 26; in etching, 16–20; in Fragonard, 188, 196, 202, 205; memory-, 18, 242n76; of the object, 175; of the painter, 20, 85, 99, 155, 156, 168, 196, 205; and Rousseau, 32; as a signature, 20, 21, 44; as self-identification, 20, 175; as self-reflexivity, 18; sharing of, 26; tactile morphology of, 6; of use, 52. *See also* author; signature
trade card, 22, 23, 80, 82
trompe-l'oeil, 111, 115. *See also* illusion, imitation
Turgot, Anne-Robert-Jacques, 143–44, 145, 151, 156

Ulrika, Louisa, Crown Princess of Sweden, 58, 60

Vallayer-Coster, Anne, 74

Van der Ast, Balthasar, 96, 97
Van Loo, Carl, 22
vanity, 49, 57, 65, 246n200, 246n201, 247n228,
Veblen, Thorstein, 49, 247n221
Venus, 5, 11, 35, 38, 39, 40, 41,42, 44, 77, 80–81, 82, 203, 231–33, 236; in Boucher, 11, 35–45; as a figure for Pompadour, 80, 82
Veronese, Paolo, 92
Vien, Joseph-Marie, 223, 228
Vincennes, porcelain manufactory, 27
Vincent, François-André, 167, 168, 169, 212
Vincent, Levinus, 75
violence: oral dimension of, 98, 99, 108, 113; psychic dimension of, 98–101, 138; in representation, 96–98, 101, 105, 108, 109, 136, 138; in still life (of inside/out), 96, 98, 99, 101, 105, 108, 109, 113, 136; in subjective experience, 98, 101; as subliminal aggression in Chardin, 108, 136
Virgil, 35; *Aeneid*, 35
vision, 43, 46, 90, 97, 99, 101, 102, 109, 115, 117, 120, 129–31, 138, 150, 155, 156, 157, 162, 163, 165, 168,169, 170, 171, 172, 173, 175, 183, 185, 191, 192, 193, 195, 196, 198, 202, 203, 205, 207, 229, 230, 232, 234; epigenetic, 196, 197; erotic, 199; of femininity, 44, 101; materialization of, 6; of nature, 192, 196, 197, 232, 269n204; of sexuality, 234; of subjectivity, 42, 43, 109, 129, 142; and touch, 112, 150, 156
visuality, 238n2
Voltaire (François-Marie Arouet), 28–29, 43, 49, 63, 192, 195; *The Defense of the Man of the World*, 49, 50; *Man of the World*, 49; *Temple of Taste*, 34. *See also* man of the world; mondain; worldly man
voyeurism, 265n95; aspect of, 199; object of, 199; position of, 182; of the voyeur, 202

Watelet, Claude-Henri, 92, 238, 240n17
Watteau, Antoine, 4, 14–19, 21–24, 32, 64, 65, 68, 85, 182, 190–91, 197, 232; and Boucher, 4, 14–19, 21, 23–24, 26, 32, 64, 65, 68, 85; etching after, 4, 14–19, 21; and Fragonard, 182, 191, 197, 232
Williams, Eunice, 187
woman: as aesthetic ideal, 11; as apparition, 43; and autoeroticism, 70; autonomy of, 72, 147; body of, 5, 17, 39, 44, 45, 46, 61, 62, 70, 127, 184, 185, 194, 195, 198, 199, 200, 235; in Boucher, 40, 43–44, 50, 53, 57, 60–63; in Chardin, 5, 127–40, 142, 153; in relation to commodity and fashion, 43, 47, 50, 51, 53, 56, 57, 58, 60, 61, 62, 63, 64, 67, 68, 70, 72, 212, 231; cultural construction of, 195; in domestic realm, 54, 56, 124, 125, 127, 128, 131, 133, 137, 138, 140, 171; elite, 220; and eros, 11, 39, 40, 43, 57, 60, 61, 67, 198, 200, 205; as figure of corruption, 72; in Fragonard, 6, 197, 222; as framing structure, 136; gaze of, 128; as heroine, 147; and logic of promiscuity, 66; and man, 61, 182, 200, 231; as member of fashionable society, 47, 60, 63; as mother, 195, 203, 205; as nature, 199; as object of desire, 5, 41, 147, 148; as object of the gaze, 43, 71; in relation to the painter, 52, 142; as personification of the Academy, 138; as personification of painting, 11; and self, 5, 42, 57, 68, 69, 70, 159; sexuality of, 62, 70, 147, 182, 183, 198, 199, 203; as the subject of desire, 5; space of, 68, 71, 193; spectacle of, 44; of taste, 82; in relation to Venus, 5, 45, 233; in relation to the viewer, 61. *See also* femininity; mother; toilette; Venus
worldly man, 42, 49, 80. *See also* man of the world; mondain; Voltaire

Image Credits

Albertina, Vienna (fig. 1.26)

Alte Pinakothek, Munich, bpk Bildagentur/Alte Pinakothek, Bayerische Staatsgemaelde-sammlungen, Munich, Germany/Art Resource, NY (fig. 1.46)

Alte Pinakothek, Munich, bpk Bildagentur/Alte Pinakothek, Bayerische Staatsgemaelde-sammlungen, Munich, Germany, Collection HypoVereinsbank, Member of UniCredit/Art Resource, NY (figs. 1.85, 1.86, 3.38)

American Museum of Natural History Library (fig. 1.75)

Archives nationalies, photo: Sarah Grandin (fig. 1.79)

Art © Alberto Giacometti Estate/Licensed by VAGA and ARS, New York, NY (fig. 2.93)

Art Gallery of Ontario image © Art Gallery of Ontario (fig. 2.83)

The Art Institute of Chicago, IL, USA, Helen Regenstein Collection/Bridgeman Images (fig. 1.16)

The Art Institute of Chicago/Art Resource, NY (fig. 1.54)

Baltimore Museum of Art, photography by Mitro Hood (figs. 3.20, 3.50)

Baltimore Museum of Art, courtesy of Eunice Williams (fig. 3.21)

Banque de France, Paris, © RMN-Grand Palais/Art Resource, NY, photo: Gérard Blot (fig. 3.22)

Bibliothèque du Museum national d'histoire naturelle, Paris, © RMN-Grand Palais/Art Resource, NY (fig. 3.65)

Bibliothèque nationale de France (figs. 1.14, 1.71, 1.76, 1.78, 1.82, 2.3, 2.4, 2.30, 2.42, 2.48, 2.74, 2.76, 3.10, 3.11, 3.64)

Bridgeman Images (fig. 1.49)

British Library, London, by permission of the British Library (fig. 3.12)

British Museum, London, © The Trustees of the British Museum (figs. 2.31, 2.67, 2.68)

© Calouste Gulbenkian Foundation, Lisbon. Calouste Gulbenkian Museum, photo: Catarina Gomes Ferreira (figs. 3.23, 3.27)

Château de Fontainebleau, © RMN-Grand Palais/Art Resource, NY, photo: Gérard Blot (fig. 3.45)

Châteaux de Versailles et de Trianon, © RMN-Grand Palais/Art Resource, NY (fig. 3.26)

© Christie's Images/Bridgeman Images (fig. 3.40)

© The Cleveland Museum of Art (figs. 1.7, 2.21, 2.28)

Collection of Lynda and Stewart Resnick, Los Angeles (fig. 1.44)

David Collection, Copenhagen, photo: Pernille Klemp (fig. 1.31)

Courtesy of David Koetser (fig. 2.10)

École nationale supérieure des Beaux-Arts, Paris © Beaux-Arts de Paris, Dist. RMN-Grand Palais/Art Resource, NY (figs. 1.15, 1.25, 1.32)

Erich Lessing/Art Resource, NY (figs. 2.69, 2.70, 2.81)

Courtesy of the Fine Arts Library, Harvard University (fig. 1.74)

The Fine Arts Museums of San Francisco (figs. 2.17, 3.41)

Fondation Custodia, Collection Frits Lugt, Paris (figs. 1.62, 1.67, 3.14, 3.46)

Courtesy of the Francis A. Countway Library of Medicine, Harvard University (figs. 3.29, 3.30, 3.31)

François Doury (fig. 3.7)

Copyright the Frick Collection, New York (figs. 1.66, 1.70, 1.72, 2.56, 2.57, 3.59, 3.60, 3.61, 3.62, 3.69)

Gemäldegalerie Alte Meister, Dresden, Erich Lessing/Art Resource, NY (figs. 1.52, 3.70)

George Ortiz Collection, Geneva, Maurice Aeschimann, Geneva (fig. 3.6)

Harvard Art Museums, Cambridge, MA, Imaging Department © President and Fellows of Harvard College (figs. 1.19, 1.68, 2.29, 2.32, 2.33, 3.19)

© The Horvitz Collection, Wilmington (DE), inv. no. D-F-103, photo: Michael Gould (fig. 3.18)

Courtesy of Houghton Library, Harvard University (figs. 1.4, 1.8, 1.9, 1.13, 1.80, 3.32)

Hunterian Museum and Art Gallery, Glasgow © The Hunterian, University of Glasgow 2016 (figs. 1.51, 2.40)

Institut national d'histoire de l'art, Paris, Library, Jacques Doucet collection (fig. 1.77)

The J. Paul Getty Museum, Los Angeles (fig. 1.30)

The J. Paul Getty Museum, Los Angeles, digital image courtesy of the Getty's Open Content Program (figs. 1.50, 2.89, 3.72)

The John & Mable Ringling Museum of Art (fig. 2.77)

Los Angeles County Museum of Art (figs. 2.62, 2.75)

Metropolitan Museum of Art, New York (figs. 1.81, 2.18, 3.24, 3.43, 3.55, 3.68)

Middle Temple Library, London/Science Photo Library (fig. 3.28)

Minneapolis Institute of Art (fig. 1.21)

Museo Thyssen-Bornemisza/Scala/Art Resource, NY (figs. 1.56, 1.61, 2.13, 3.4)

© 2017 Museum of Fine Arts, Boston (figs. 1.20, 2.1, 2.2, 2.7, 2.73, 3.39)

The Museum of Fine Arts, Houston (fig. 2.72)

© Museum of London (fig. 2.53)

Musée Carnavalet, Paris © Roger-Viollet/The Image Works (figs. 1.47, 2.15)

Musée d'art et d'histoire de Narbonne, © Angélique Paitrault, Narbonne Museums, city of Narbonne (fig. 1.24)

© Musée de la Chasse et de la Nature, Paris—Sylvie Durand (fig. 2.26)

Musée de Picardie, Amiens, © RMN-Grand Palais/Art Resource, NY, photo: Bulloz (figs. 2.50, 2.90)

Musée des Arts décoratifs, Paris, © Photo Les Arts Décoratifs, Paris/Jean Tholance (fig. 1.69)

Musée des Beaux-Arts d'Angers, © RMN-Grand Palais/Art Resource, NY, photo: Benoît Touchard (figs. 3.66, 3.67)

Musée des Beaux-Arts de Chambéry, © RMN-Grand Palais/Art Resource, NY, photo: Gérard Blot (fig. 3.35)

Musée des Beaux-Arts de Nancy, photo: Pierre Mignot (figs. 1.36, 1.42)

Musée des Beaux-Arts et d'archéologie de Besançon, Bridgeman-Giraudon/Art Resource (fig. 1.22)

Musée des Beaux-Arts et d'archéologie de Besançon, © Besançon, Musée des beaux-arts et d'archéologie, photo: Charles Choffet (fig. 2.91)

Musée des Beaux-Arts et d'archéologie de Besançon, © Besançon, Musée des beaux-arts et d'archéologie, photo: Pierre Guenat (figs. 3.16, 3.37)

Musée du Louvre, Paris, photo: Hervé Lewandowski (fig. 2.47)

Musée du Louvre, Paris, Erich Lessing/Art Resource, NY (figs. 1.38, 1.45, 1.83, 2.5, 2.6, 2.16, 2.19, 2.20, 2.23, 2.24, 2.27, 2.37, 2.46, 2.61, 2.66, 2.85, 2.87, 2.88, 2.92, 2.95, 2.97, 3.1, 3.5, 3.8, 3.9, 3.13, 3.25, 3.36, 3.47, 3.48, 3.57, 3.63)

Musée du Louvre, Paris/France, Peter Willi/Bridgeman Images (figs. 1.35, 1.43)

Musée du Louvre, Paris, © Musée du Louvre, Dist. RMN-Grand Palais/Photo: Angèle Dequier/Art Resource, NY (figs. 1.6, 1.11)

Musée du Louvre, Paris, © RMN-Grand Palais/Art Resource, NY (fig. 1.1)

Musée du Louvre, Paris, © RMN-Grand Palais/Art Resource, NY, photo: Franck Raux (fig. 3.49)

Musée du Louvre, Paris, © RMN-Grand Palais/Art Resource, NY, photo: Gérard Blot (fig. 3.75)

Musée du Louvre, Paris, © RMN-Grand Palais/Art Resource, NY, photo: Jean-Gilles Berizzi (figs. 1.18, 3.2)

Musée du Louvre, Paris, © RMN-Grand Palais/Art Resource, NY, photo: Michèle Bellot (figs. 2.34, 2.86)

Musée du Louvre, Paris, © RMN-Grand Palais/Art Resource, NY, photo: René-Gabriel Ojéda (fig. 1.3)

Musée du Louvre, Paris, © RMN-Grand Palais/Art Resource, NY, photo: Stéphane Maréchalle (figs. 2.11, 2.12, 2.80, 2.82, 2.84, 3.74)

Musée du Louvre, Paris, © RMN-Grand Palais/Art Resource, NY, photo: Thierry Ollivier (fig. 1.2)

Musée du Louvre, Paris, Scala/Art Resource, NY (figs. 1.48, 1.55)

Musée Jacquemart-André—Institut de France © Studio Sébert Photographes (figs. 2.9, 2.35, 3.52)

Musée Reattu, Arles, Erich Lessing/Art Resource, NY (fig. 1.58)

National Gallery, London/Art Resource, NY (figs. 1.41, 2.60)

Courtesy National Gallery of Art, Washington, DC (figs. 1.12, 1.39, 2.38, 2.43, 2.54, 2.58, 2.63, 3.34, 3.42, 3.53)

National Gallery of Canada, Ottawa, photo: NGC (figs. 1.29, 2.49)

National Gallery of Ireland, Dublin, photo © National Gallery of Ireland (fig. 2.22)

© National Trust, Waddesdon Manor, Buckinghamshire (figs. 1.84, 2.65)

Nationalmuseum, Stockholm (figs. 1.57, 1.73, 2.41, 2.44, 2.45, 2.51, 2.52, 2.55)

Nelson-Atkins Museum of Art, Kansas City, photo: John Lamberton (fig. 1.65)

Palais des Beaux-Arts de Lille, Musée des Beaux-Arts, Lille, France/Bridgeman Images (fig. 1.53)

Palazzo Reale, Turin, © DeA Picture Library/Art Resource, NY (fig. 1.23)

Petit Palais, Paris, Snark/Art Resource, NY (fig. 3.17)

Philadelphia Museum of Art (fig. 2.25)

Pushkin State Museum of Fine Arts, Moscow (fig. 1.40)

Rijksmuseum, Amsterdam (figs. 2.79, 3.33)

The Royal Academy of Arts, Stockholm, photo by Thomas Wyreson (fig. 1.64)

Royal Collection Trust/© Her Majesty Queen Elizabeth II 2016 (figs. 2.94, 2.96)

Schloss Charlottenburg, Berlin, bpk Bildagenture/Charlottenburg Castle, Stiftung Preussische Schlösser & Gärten Berlin-Brandenburg, Berlin, Germany/Photo by Stiftung/Art Resource, NY (fig. 1.63)

Scottish National Gallery (figs. 2.64, 2.71, 2.78)

Sèvres, Cité de la céramique, © RMN-Grand Palais/Art Resource, NY, photo: Thierry Ollivier (fig. 1.27)

Staatliche Museen zu Berlin, bpk Bildagentur/Gemaeldegalerie, Staatliche Museen, Berlin, Germany/Photo: Jörg P. Anders/Art Resource, NY (fig. 2.8)

Staatliche Museen zu Berlin, bpk Bildagentur/Kupferstichkabinett, Staatliche Museen, Berlin, Germany/Photo: Jörg P. Anders/Art Resource, NY (fig. 1.5)

Sterling and Francine Clark Art Institute, Williamstown, Massachusetts, USA/Bridgeman Images (figs. 1.10, 3.54)

© Studio Sébert (fig. 3.51)

© Tokyo Fuji Art Museum, Tokyo, Japan/Bridgeman Images (fig. 2.59)

© Victoria and Albert Museum, London (fig. 1.60)

Wadsworth Atheneum Museum of Art, Hartford, Allen Phillips/Wadsworth Atheneum (fig. 2.14)

© The Wallace Collection, London (figs. 1.28, 1.33, 1.34, 1.37, 3.3, 3.15, 3.73)

Wellcome Library, London (fig. 2.36)

Williams College Museum of Art, Williamstown, MA (fig. 1.59)